An Introduction to Global Studies

AN INTRODUCTION TO
GL🌐BAL
STUDIES

Patricia J. Campbell,
Aran MacKinnon,
and Christy R. Stevens

WILEY-BLACKWELL

A John Wiley & Sons, Ltd., Publication

This edition first published 2010
© 2010 Patricia J. Campbell, Aran MacKinnon, and Christy R. Stevens

Blackwell Publishing was acquired by John Wiley & Sons in February 2007. Blackwell's publishing program has been merged with Wiley's global Scientific, Technical, and Medical business to form Wiley-Blackwell.

Registered Office
John Wiley & Sons Ltd, The Atrium, Southern Gate, Chichester, West Sussex, PO19 8SQ, United Kingdom

Editorial Offices
350 Main Street, Malden, MA 02148-5020, USA
9600 Garsington Road, Oxford, OX4 2DQ, UK
The Atrium, Southern Gate, Chichester, West Sussex, PO19 8SQ, UK

For details of our global editorial offices, for customer services, and for information about how to apply for permission to reuse the copyright material in this book please see our website at www.wiley.com/wiley-blackwell.

The right of Patricia J. Campbell, Aran MacKinnon, and Christy R. Stevens to be identified as the authors of this work has been asserted in accordance with the Copyright, Designs and Patents Act 1988.

Library of Congress Cataloging-in-Publication Data
Campbell, Patricia J.
   An introduction to global studies / Patricia J. Campbell, Aran MacKinnon, and Christy R. Stevens.
      p. cm.
   Includes bibliographical references and index.
   ISBN 978-1-4051-8737-4 (hardcover : alk. paper) – ISBN 978-1-4051-8736-7 (pbk. : alk. paper)
1. Globalization.   I. MacKinnon, Aran S.   II. Stevens, Christy.   III. Title.
   JZ1318.C356 2010
   303.48′2–dc22
                                                                              2009041790

A catalogue record for this book is available from the British Library.

Set in 10.5/13pt Minion by Graphicraft Limited, Hong Kong
Printed in the USA

6   2013

BRIEF CONTENTS

CONTENTS

4   Human Rights

TABLES

FIGURES

PREFACE

While the field of Global Studies is relatively new, its subject matter is old in the sense that humans around the world have always been connected through multiple layers of culture, trade, travel, migration, ecology, etc. It is only recently, however, that the academy has caught up with this reality. The academy's slowness in making the various globalization processes and effects the object of interdisciplinary analysis is due in part to organizational structures in higher education, many of which encourage disciplines to be protective of their boundaries. Despite such barriers, the interdisciplinary nature of so many of the major issues facing the world at the beginning of the twenty-first century has pushed against, and is increasingly breaking through, some of those long-standing disciplinary boundaries. The emergence of Global Studies as a distinct interdisciplinary field occurred at a time when globalization was increasingly and profoundly affecting multiple areas of people's everyday lives. Scholars and students have found that Global Studies enhances our understanding of global phenomena by bringing the methodologies and discourses from a variety of disciplines to bear on many of the most pressing issues of our day. Global Studies makes connections not only among various disciplines but also between the local and the global, and oneself and others. For example, while we might not make the immediate connection between what we think of as a personal action, such as reaching for our cell phones, and a conflict occurring on the other side of the world, like the conflict in Central Africa, Global Studies provides a framework that allows us to explore the ways in which the personal is global and the global is highly personal. To journey through this book is to explore these connections.

We start in chapter 1 by providing an overview of what constitutes Global Studies. The historical context for the evolution of the field is discussed in concert with competing conceptualizations of globalization. Various dimensions of globalization are addressed, including economic, political, and cultural processes. The chapter concludes with a discussion of the term "global citizenship" and its relationship to ideas like belonging, civic responsibility, and civic engagement.

Chapter 2 presents the historical background to the development of the nation-state as the primary social, political, and economic organizing structure of human society. The expansion of the nation-state from Europe via colonialism is traced. The chapter also outlines some of the internal and external threats facing the modern nation-state, including social cleavages like ethno-nationalism, cultural complexities posed by migration, as well as the dynamic nature of the roles played by international organizations, non-governmental organizations, and multinational corporations. The chapter concludes by exploring the increasing number of marginal and failed states and the dangers and opportunities these present.

Chapter 3 delves much deeper into the structure, roles, and relationships between international organizations and the nation-state. The historical background for the development of international organizations is presented, followed by a detailed examination of the major international organizations operating in the world today, including the UN, the WTO, and various regional organizations, such as the EU. The chapter ends with a discussion of the evolution of non-governmental organizations and the changing nature of the roles they play both within countries and within the international arena.

Human rights is the focus of chapter 4. The chapter begins with a discussion of the evolution of human rights, the various schools of thought that undergird human rights, and the key founding documents of the modern human rights movement. This is followed by an exploration of the debates over different interpretations of human rights, including, for example, disagreements about whether human rights are universal or must be tempered with respect to cultural norms. The monitoring and enforcement of human rights follows this discussion, with a particular focus on transnational justice mechanisms such as the International Criminal Court. Evolving notions of humanitarian intervention are also discussed, including the "right to protect" (R2P). Finally, newer human rights discourses are considered, including the right to water, sexual rights, and the right to one's own genetic material.

Perhaps more than the previous chapters, chapter 5 drives home the interconnectedness that characterizes our modern world. It begins with a detailed discussion of global climate change, including its causes and impacts. Other ongoing global environmental challenges are also discussed, such as the increasingly precarious situation facing the global water supply, the health impacts of air pollution, increasing plant and animal extinction rates, and the environmental impacts of waste production. The chapter concludes with a discussion of environmental discrimination. Woven throughout the chapter are discussions of various strategies being developed and deployed in an effort to improve the global environment.

Chapter 6 investigates the relationship between population and consumption patterns. The chapter begins by describing current population statistics and projections, including the demographic issues they will produce. The word's population is estimated to grow to 9 billion by 2040. This growth will bring with it serious challenges, particularly when it comes to issues of poverty, urbanization, and migration. Providing the basic necessities for so many people poses an equally serious challenge to the environment. Debates about and strategies for meeting these needs are the focus of the second half of the chapter, and it ends with an investigation of global consumption patterns.

From "swine flu" to SARS to AIDS, infectious diseases demonstrate how advances in technology and improved modes of travel and communication can help both to spread disease and to track, treat, and quarantine it. The first section of chapter 7 traces the history of infectious diseases, exploring the interactions between globalization and infectious diseases as well as the relationship between human interaction with the environment and the evolution and spread of disease. Disease in the context of migration, air travel, food production, and urbanization are discussed as examples of our global connectedness. The chapter concludes with a survey of the current challenges posed by infectious diseases, including treatment questions that arise over the availability of pharmaceuticals.

Chapter 8 explores the world through the lens of gender. It begins by defining its terms before launching into a detailed discussion of some of the ways in which globalization affects women and men differently. The intersection of gender, poverty, and development are then discussed, with a special focus on some of the labor and migration issues that have emerged in our globalized world. Human security and human rights issues that are particularly pressing for women are the chapter's next focus, including an overview of some of the UN's efforts to integrate gender analysis and gender equality into its mission and programs. The chapter concludes with a discussion of education and health issues that affect women, their families, and the communities in which they reside.

The fast pace of globalization is perhaps best illustrated in chapter 9, which focuses on information and communication technologies (ICTs). The chapter explores the relationship between ICTs and evolving conceptions of the Information Age and the Digital Age. It then looks at the emergence of networks and the communication changes that networks like the Internet and the World Wide Web have engendered. The web allows us instantly to connect with people around the world, breaking down traditional space/time barriers and opening up new avenues for both economic development and global citizenship. The chapter concludes by looking at the relationship between "new media" and globalization.

The final two chapters focus on war and peace. Chapter 10 traces the history of violent conflict and then looks at both its causes and attempts to prevent it. The chapter ends with an examination of some of the costs of war, including human casualties, environmental destruction, economic damage, and the diversion of resources from development to supporting the war machine. Chapter 11 moves us from war to peace, beginning with an exploration of the history of peace movements. It discusses peaceful forms of conflict resolution and ends with a focus on organizations that work to eradicate violent social conditions that are antithetical to peace.

Each chapter endeavors to provide readers with a thorough understanding of the competing approaches that scholars bring to bear on the topics presented. Instead of prescribing solutions, the book asks questions and presents multiple perspectives, encouraging readers to think critically about the issues presented and to come away with a better understanding of how connected we all are to one another. If our readers find themselves wondering about things like how their cell phones were made, who made them, and under what working conditions, how the materials were extracted that make up their parts, and where those materials are likely to go once they dispose of the phone, then we have succeeded in our mission.

The chapters also contain a number of special features. Each chapter begins with a series of thought-provoking quotations from notable people designed to get readers thinking about the complexities revolving around the chapter's main topic. These are followed by questions that frame the chapter. Students should be able to formulate thoughtful responses to each of these questions after having read the chapter. All the chapters also contain "Researching to Learn" sections that provide students with research ideas, sample search strategies, and authoritative academic resources, such as relevant websites and important primary and secondary sources on selected topics. Additionally, the chapters contain various graphs, charts, and tables designed to illustrate key points and to appeal to visual learners. Each chapter contains an "In Focus" section that provides a specific real-world example illustrating one of the chapter's themes. Each chapter ends with a conclusion that draws together the key themes.

ACKNOWLEDGMENTS

We would like to express our appreciation to editors and staff at Wiley-Blackwell who were instrumental in helping us complete this book.

Patricia J. Campbell: I would like to thank my family, especially my parents Barbara and Gerald, for their love and support (I promise not to worry about it Dad), and Christy for her endless patience and seemingly endless constructive feedback.

Aran MacKinnon: For my brother Gregor, for all his inspiration and because he so loves the world. Wonderful world, beautiful people. This book is also for Kieran, Alistair, and Duncan, brave new global citizens.

Christy R. Stevens: I would like to thank Patricia for bringing me in on this project and enduring my feedback and revisions with grace and good humor.

1

GOING GLOBAL

"As a society becomes more enlightened, it realizes that it is responsible not to transmit and conserve the whole of its existing achievements, but only such as make for a better future society. The school is the chief agency for the accomplishment of this end." (John Dewey, *Democracy and Education*, 1916)[1]

"The world is my country; to do good my religion." (Motto of American political theorist and writer Thomas Paine, 1737–1809)[2]

"Humanity is interwoven by many threads, and they grow stronger and longer each day. Professionals increasingly link their fortunes with those from afar, while significant challenges and problems transcend boundary lines. In an age of information overflow, though, it can be difficult to connect the dots and adapt to all that's new. To survive and succeed, individuals must increase their understanding of this interconnected world. And they must embrace global perspectives and viewpoints, for their own sake as much as for the benefit of humanity." (From J. Michael Adams and Angelo Carfagna, *Coming of Age in a Globalized World*)[3]

Learning to Question, Questioning to Learn

- How is global studies similar to/different from other fields?
- What are some of the various definitions of globalization?
- Is globalization a "good" or "bad" thing?
- Is globalization a new phenomenon or is it an extension and acceleration of processes that have been going on throughout human history?
- How does the concept of global citizenship differ from traditional definitions of citizenship?

Introduction

Global Studies. Globalization. Global Citizenship. This chapter explores these three terms in depth, beginning with a discussion of the emergence of global studies as a field of study in academic institutions around the world. Next, the chapter presents a working definition of globalization, describing some of its most prominent characteristics. It then looks at economic, political, and cultural globalization processes separately and in greater depth. The chapter ends with a discussion of global citizenship, comparing it with traditional definitions of citizenship and considering how it might function as a useful category in today's globalizing world.

Why Global Studies?

The word "global" is used a lot these days. From "the global war on terror" to "global climate change," we are growing more accustomed to viewing issues, activities, processes, ideas, problems, and solutions in global rather than in solely local or national terms. For example, today, more than ever before, communication is global. The Internet, email, blogs, RSS feeds, satellites, cell phones, webcams, and various electronic handheld devices allow human beings all over the world to connect with each other instantaneously, breaking down the barriers of time and space that have isolated (to varying degrees) individuals and communities from each other in the past. Today, more than ever before, business is also global. Take Subaru, the car company, as a fairly typical example. A small number of the Japanese cars were first imported into the US in 1968. Today, the company's "Subaru Global" website reveals that, though it is still headquartered in Japan, it now has many facilities all over the globe, including the United States, Canada, Europe, Singapore, and China.[4] And today, more than ever before, health and environmental problems are global. Human beings all over the world are contributing to problems (global climate change being an important example) that affect the entire globe and that can only be effectively responded to by coordinated global action.

The academic field of global studies emerged in this contemporary globalizing context, as scholars increasingly grappled with changes that were rapidly shrinking the globe and intensifying social, political, and economic connections. Initially, scholars seeking to understand these issues tended to do so within the framework of their specific *disciplines*. Even though global issues tend to go beyond the scope of any single discipline, the discipline-specific approach was used because of the way academic institutions are traditionally organized. Academic disciplines are among the most entrenched divisions in colleges and universities, serving as the basis for academic departments, professional associations, and scholarly journals. Scholars who earn a PhD in the discipline of philosophy, for example, have

disciplines   Most often used to refer to the division of fields of knowledge at the university or college level.

traditionally tended to apply for jobs in philosophy departments, write articles for publication in philosophy journals using the language and theoretical frameworks accepted by the field of philosophy, and join professional philosophy associations, such as the American Philosophical Association. As such, it makes sense that scholars tended initially to approach globalization solely through the frameworks of their specific disciplines. Over time, however, many began arguing persuasively that globalization involves too many different types of forces and issues for it to be understood adequately through the lens of any single discipline. This realization led scholars to begin reaching across disciplinary boundaries to study global issues in new ways and to develop global studies courses and programs in collaboration with colleagues from various academic departments.

Today, global studies is establishing itself as an academic field of study in its own right, with institutes,[5] associations,[6] academic conferences,[7] and degree-granting programs[8] emerging around the world with increasing frequency since the 1990s. Most academic pursuits that have adopted the "global studies" label are developed around the idea that this is a multidisciplinary and interdisciplinary enterprise.[9] That is, global studies attempts to understand the world by looking at it from multiple perspectives (*multidisciplinary*), drawing upon the insights and theoretical frameworks of various academic fields, such as history, political science, international relations, sociology, anthropology, philosophy, and economics. In addition, global studies also seeks to make connections between those different perspectives – to understand how they are related and how they might fit together as part of a larger whole (*interdisciplinary*).

> **multidisciplinary** Drawing upon different disciplinary perspectives without necessarily exploring the connections or blurring the boundaries among them.
>
> **interdisciplinary** Integrating the theories, methodologies, and insights of various disciplines and exploring the connections and blurring the boundaries among them.

Global studies students and scholars analyze the social, political, and economic processes and transformations that affect not only the world as a whole but also individual localities in particular, complex, and sometimes contradictory ways. Global studies also generally foregrounds an active ethical component that tends not to be as prominent in many other disciplines. In other words, global studies students and scholars often explicitly seek out ways to connect academics with action; their desire to understand global issues is inextricably linked to their desire to discover effective ways of improving the world.[10] Edward Kolodziej, Director of the Center for Global Studies at the University of Illinois at Urbana-Champaign, argues that exploring and devising new ways to meet the needs of the world's diverse populations is one of the central concerns of global studies programs. He points to the spread of weapons of mass destruction, viral infections, ecological disasters, and human rights as examples of global issues that are appropriate for both study and action within the global studies framework.[11] Similarly, David Jacobson and Ning Wang, Professor and Assistant Professor of Global Studies respectively at Arizona State University, observe that the questions and problems addressed in global studies classrooms are not simply academic in nature; rather, issues such as the environment and cultural conflict are "pressing global challenges" that demand

global citizens People who see their local actions as having global consequences and who have accepted that they have a responsibility to work to better the conditions of the world and its people.

"more effective policy."[12] In short, global studies is designed to educate people who are interested in finding solutions to these kinds of global problems, or, put another way, in making the world a better place. Many programs make this goal explicit through mission statements that profess a commitment to developing *global citizens*,[13] a term we will return to at the end of the chapter.

What We Talk About When We Talk About Globalization

globalization A complex web of social processes that intensify and expand worldwide economic, cultural, political, and technological exchanges and connections.

Westernization Process whereby non-Western countries and societies adopt social, legal, dietetic, religious, technological, linguistic, political, and economic ideals and norms of countries in the Western world – Western Europe and the US.

Global studies emerged in the context of and in response to *globalization*. But what exactly are we talking about when we talk about globalization? "Globalization" is a relatively new term. Although it made its dictionary debut in 1961,[14] it was rarely used until the 1980s, when it began appearing in academic literature with increasing frequency.[15] The term entered into common parlance in the 1990s, and today is "deployed across disciplines, across the world, across theoretical approaches, and across the political spectrum."[16] Despite the pervasiveness of the term today, it remains ambiguous and contested, perhaps because it is used in many different ways to support a variety of competing interests. Some believe globalization is intrinsically "good," others believe it is inherently "bad," and still others assert that while it is intrinsically neither good nor bad, it can have both positive and negative effects. Some conflate globalization with internationalization, while others equate it with *Westernization*. Some view globalization as a new phenomenon driven primarily by new technologies, such as satellites, cell phones, and the Internet, while others see it as an extension of ongoing processes that encompass all of human history. Scholars from a variety of disciplines have weighed in on the term, developing their own definitions of, and theories about, globalization. Manfred B. Steger, a Professor of Global Studies at the Royal Melbourne Institute of Technology, has developed a particularly useful definition that synthesizes the definitions of a number of prominent scholars.[17] According to Steger: "Globalization refers to a multidimensional set of social processes that create, multiply, stretch, and intensify worldwide social interdependencies and exchanges while at the same time fostering in people a growing awareness of deepening connections between the local and the distant."[18] Because Steger's definition is complex and multifaceted, it is useful to explore some its component parts in greater depth.

Globalization as series of social processes

The first important part of Steger's definition is that globalization is not an event, a singular process, or monolithic entity; rather, globalization consists of multiple, ongoing, interdependent actions and operations. It's also important to note that these processes are *social* (i.e., they relate to human society, its members, organizational patterns, and relationships). Additionally, these social processes are generative,

social   Refers to the way humans interact and organize.

meaning that they create and expand networks of connections. Steger points out that these networks "increasingly overcome traditional political, economic, cultural, and geographical boundaries."[19]

Deterritorialization

Other scholars use the term *deterritorialization* to refer to the ways that networks of connections are transcending traditional boundaries. The term foregrounds the idea that in a globalized world, many social activities and exchanges can take place with-

deterritorialization   Geographical territory, or place, becomes less of a constraint on social interactions.

out geography functioning as a constraint. In other words, territory, defined as a geographically identifiable space, is no longer the only locale in which social activity can occur.[20] Roland Robertson, for example, Professor of Sociology at the University of Pittsburgh, has described globalization as "the compression of the world,"[21] and Malcolm Waters, Professor Emeritus of Sociology at the University of Tasmania, Australia, has referred to it as "a social process in which the constraints of geography on social and cultural arrangements recede."[22] The Internet is a classic example of a deterritorializing technology, allowing people to communicate in real time with other individuals and groups around the world via text, audio, and video.

Deterritorialization also means that "people, services and goods are available to each other across the globe through a variety of means and in increasingly immediate ways."[23] For example, you might go online to purchase a laptop that was originally designed in Cupertino, California, but mass-produced in Changshu, China. A call to the company to learn more about the product might connect you with a customer service representative located in Bangalore, India. If you were to decide to purchase the laptop, your order would likely print out in a warehouse half a world away only minutes or even seconds after clicking the "Buy Now" button. Within two or three days, the laptop would arrive on your doorstep. From the consumer perspective, the process seems quick and easy, but that "simple" consumer experience is the product of a complex worldwide network of technologies, processes, and exchanges that are deterritorializing the globe.

Interconnectedness: the local and the global

Steger's definition of globalization also highlights connections between the local and the global. In an interconnected world, distant events and forces can have a profound impact on local endeavors.[24] Unexpected connections frequently emerge, some of which may be experienced positively by most who are affected by the connection, and others of which have devastating consequences for one or more affected groups. The link between consumer demand for electronic devices and a bloody civil war in the Democratic Republic of Congo (DRC) is one such tragic example. This connection between war and electronics emerged because the DRC holds 80 percent of the world's coltan reserves. Though not a household word, columbite-tantalite, or coltan for short, has become one of the world's most valued materials. Refined coltan produces tantalum, a metal powder used in the production of capacitors, which are critical components in electronic devices like cell phones and laptop computers. One might think that the abundance of such a valuable mineral would benefit the DRC, but, unfortunately, coltan has been mined by warring rebel groups and used to finance a devastating civil war. The conflict, which started in 1998, has claimed more than 4 million lives.[25] Although peace was proclaimed in 2003 with the establishment of a transitional government, much of the east of the country has remained insecure, contributing to the continuation of what researchers have called "the world's deadliest humanitarian crisis."[26]

In addition to shocking death rates, the pursuit of coltan has led to mass displacements, as rebels attacked villages and drove families from their homes in order to exploit their coltan-rich land. Coltan mining has also contributed to environmental destruction, including the massacre of endangered gorillas and the destruction of habitat in the DRC's national parks.[27] The chaos within the DRC has also allowed neighboring countries to violate the DRC's borders in order to mine the mineral for themselves. Rwanda, for example, has been strongly criticized for its role in plundering the DRC's valuable asset.[28] It is difficult to trace coltan mined by rebels and foreign militaries in the DRC on its convoluted route through coltan processing companies, capacitor manufacturers, and high-tech assembly factories. As a result, it is generally impossible to ascertain whether the electronic device you currently use everyday or the one you are thinking about purchasing is in any way related to the human rights abuses in the DRC. There can be no doubt, however, that consumer demand for these high-tech products has helped rebels to fund conflicts that have had many devastating consequences for the DRC's people, animals, and environment.

Researching to Learn   *The Conflict in the DRC*

Sample Keyword Searches

Broad search: war AND DRC

Narrower searches:
- coltan AND DRC AND environment
- "rebel groups" AND DRC AND electronics

Advanced search: ("Democratic Republic of Congo" OR DRC) AND (coltan OR columbite-tantalite) AND (electronics OR "cell phones")

Note:
- *Use quotation marks to search for terms as a phrase.*
- *Use AND to find documents with all terms listed.*
- *Use OR to find documents that contains at least one of the terms.*
- *Use parentheses to combine AND and OR statements in creative ways.*

Free Web Resources

Bureau of African Affairs, US Department of State. "Background Note: Democratic Republic of Congo." US Department of State. April 2008. www.state.gov/r/pa/ei/bgn/2823.htm

Cox, Stan. "War, Murder, Rape . . . All for Your Cell Phone." Global Policy Forum. www.alternet.org/story/41477/

"Gold Keeps War in the DRC on the Boil." Global Policy Forum. www.globalpolicy.org/security/issues/congo/2005/0307risevalue.htm

"NGOs Call for Embargo on Coltan from DRC War Zones." Global Policy Forum. www.globalpolicy.org/security/natres/generaldebate/2002/0114coltan.htm

"Population, Health, and Human Well-Being – Dem. Rep. of the Congo." EarthTrends Country Profiles. http://earthtrends.wri.org/pdf_library/country_profiles/pop_cou_180.pdf

Sanders, Jay O., Fred de Sam Lazaro, Kathryn Taverna, and Frank Keraudren, "Democracy in the Rough." Wide Angle: Human Stories. Global Issues. www.pbs.org/wnet/wideangle/shows/congo/video.html

Ware, Natalie D., "Congo War and the Role of Coltan." ICE Case Studies. The Inventory of Conflict and Environment (ICE), American University, The School of International Service. www.american.edu/ted/ice/congo-coltan.htm

The World Factbook, "Congo, Democratic Republic of the." CIA. https://www.cia.gov/library/publications/the-world-factbook/geos/cg.html

Books: Find Them @ Your Library

Arnson, Cynthia and William I. Zartman. *Rethinking the Economics of War: The Intersection of Need, Creed, and Greed*. Baltimore, MD: Johns Hopkins University Press, 2005.

de Torrente, Nicolas, Simon Robinson, and James Nachtwey. *Forgotten War: Democratic Republic of the Congo*. Millbrook, NY: de.Mo (Design Method of Operation), 2006.

Gourevitch, Philip. *We Wish to Inform You that Tomorrow We Will be Killed with our Families: Stories from Rwanda*. New York, NY: Farrar, Straus, and Giroux, 1998.

Lind, Jeremy and Kathryn Sturman. *Scarcity and Surfeit: The Ecology of Africa's Conflicts*. Pretoria, South Africa: Institute for Security Studies, 2002.

Nabudere, D. Wadada. *Africa's First World War: Mineral Wealth, Conflicts and War in the Great Lakes Region*. Pretoria, South Africa: African Association of Political Science, 2004.

Nest, Michael. *The Democratic Republic of Congo: Economic Dimensions of War and Peace*. Boulder, CO: Lynne Rienner, 2006.

Articles: Find Them @ Your Library

Draulans, Dirk and Ellen Van Krunkelsven. "The Impact of War on Forest Areas on the Democratic Republic of Congo." *Oryx* 36 (2002): 35–40.

Lalji, Nadira. "The Resource Curse Revised." *Harvard International Review* 29.3 (Fall 2007): 34–7.

Montague, Dena. "Stolen Goods: Coltan and Conflict in the Democratic Republic of Congo." *SAIS Review* 22.1 (Winter–Spring 2002): 103–18.

Naftalin, Mark. "The Congo Wars: Conflict, Myth and Reality." *Journal of Peace Research* 45.1 (January 2008): 125–6.

Tull, Dents M. "The Democratic Republic of Congo: Economic Dimensions of War and Peace." *Journal of Modern African Studies* 45.3 (September 2007): 474–6.

"Who Benefits from the Minerals?" *The Economist*. September 22, 2007: 62.

Compressing time

Moore's Law   Observation made by Gordon E. Moore, co-founder of Intel, that the number of transistors that can be placed on a circuit will double approximately every two years. It is also used more generally to refer to the rapid pace of technological change in the late 20th century.

Another common theme frequently discussed by globalization scholars is the compression of time. Globalization disrupts not only traditional spatial boundaries but also temporal ones, increasing the velocity of social activity. For example, high-speed communication and transportation technologies compress time, enabling "fast flows and movements of people, information, capital, and goods."[29] *Moore's Law* provides an example of this acceleration, illustrating how the compression of space and time are often linked. In 1965, Intel co-founder Gordon Moore predicted that the number of transistors that could be put on a chip would double every year. In 1975, he updated his prediction to every two years, and it has remained a guiding principle for the semiconductor industry.[30] The effort to put more transistors on a chip meant that the transistors themselves would have continually to get smaller, but it also meant that processing power would continually increase, making computers faster. Indeed, computers have continued to get smaller and faster at an astonishing rate, allowing information to circle the globe in seconds. News, personal communication, and the exchange of goods and services have all been speeding up as well.

New phenomena or old news?

Clearly, the accelerations discussed above were made possible by the development of new technologies. The Internet in particular has intensified and extended global connections and interdependencies since coming to prominence in the 1990s. Many scholars are quick to point out, however, that although the technologies that have accelerated globalization in recent years are new, the processes of globalization have a much longer history. How far back can we trace the processes of globalization? This remains an open question. The answer depends upon how far back one is interested in tracing the history of human migration, social networks, and technological innovation. One early globalization milestone was the settling of all five continents, a feat accomplished approximately 12,000 years ago when hunter-gatherers first reached the tip of South America, thus accomplishing "the truly global dispersion of our species."[31] The invention of writing between 3500 and 2000 BCE[32] and the invention of the wheel around 3000 BCE are also frequently cited as important moments in the history of globalization, as they were crucial developments that facilitated technological progress and social exchanges. Other significant globalization developments include the establishment of trading routes, such as the Silk Road, which linked the Chinese and Roman Empires, and the development of boats that could withstand long ocean voyages, establishing trade networks among some of the most populous regions of Europe, Asia, and Africa. These trade routes in turn triggered waves of migration, leading to population increases in urban centers.[33]

Other scholars point to the Early Modern Period, from 1500 to 1750, as particularly important in the history of globalization. During this period, European monarchs financed the exploration of "new worlds" and the development of trading posts, laying the groundwork for *colonialism*. The Early Modern Period also was marked by the development of the *nation-state system* and connections among these states.[34] Later, the European settling of the Americas paved the way for industry and expanded trade.

Nineteenth-century innovations in transportation and communication, such as the railroad and the telegraph, further extended and accelerated globalization. Eventually, twentieth-century forms of *mass media*, including newspapers, movies, radio, television, and magazines, developed the capacity to deliver information to millions of people, radically compressing time and space. In addition to dramatic technological advances, devastating world wars also marked the twentieth century and heightened our sense of connectedness, albeit in a much darker way. The *Cold War* that followed World War II further dramatized our interconnectedness through the introduction of the specter of planet-wide annihilation. Never before had political and ideological tensions between two countries, in this case the United States and the Soviet Union, posed such a threat to the future of humanity and the health of the planet.[35]

Clearly, globalization processes can be traced back as far as one is willing to follow the migratory flows and technological inventions that have played a role in enhancing, multiplying, and extending social connections and compressing space and time. The perspective adopted by some scholars, then, that globalization is as old as humanity, is important, because it acknowledges that globalization processes are gradual and that they have a long history. However, it is also important to note that an increasing social awareness of processes now associated with the term globalization began to emerge with the advent of industrial capitalism in the nineteenth and twentieth centuries. Writers as diverse as Karl Marx, Henry Adams, and John Dewey commented on the ways in which distance, space, time, and communication were being transformed by new technologies.[36] By the 1960s, this awareness had intensified, as evidenced in Marshall McLuhan's popularization of the term "global village." In his 1962 book *The Gutenberg Galaxy: The Making of Typographic Man*, McLuhan argued that the electronic mass media collapses space and time and engenders social interaction on a global scale, thus metaphorically shrinking the globe to the size of a village. Although many have since used the term "global village" positively, McLuhan took a darker view, warning that the interdependent nature of the technologically driven global village has the potential to lead to terror and totalitarianism.[37]

Awareness of and theorization about the processes of globalization clearly are not unique to this current historical moment. However, most scholars would agree that

colonialism   One territorial sovereign exerting control and sovereignty over another land by usurping control from local leaders, thereby destroying indigenous culture, economies, and political structures.

nation-state system   Refers to the division of the world into sovereign territories over which local rulers maintain the power to govern. Also known as the Westphalian model.

mass media   Media that is designed to reach a mass audience, such as the population of a nation-state. The term has traditionally referred to nationwide television and radio networks and mass-circulation newspapers and magazines.

Cold War   Refers to the ideological stand-off between two superpowers, the United States and the Soviet Union, from 1945 to 1989. While not directly fighting one another, each side sought to expand its influence by keeping the other from spreading its form of government and political system, resulting in many proxy wars throughout the world.

globalization processes have accelerated dramatically since the 1980s. Many scholars would also agree that this acceleration has led to a marked intensification of our awareness of the world as a whole and the connections between the distant and the local. Important dates in this more contemporary view of globalization include IBM's release of the first personal computer on August 12, 1981[38] and the invention of the World Wide Web in 1989 by Sir Tim Berners-Lee.[39]

Dimensions of Globalization

In order to extend our understanding of globalization, we'll now move away from general definitions to take a closer look at some of the different processes that the term encompasses. The following sections provide an overview of some of the theoretical frameworks, issues, and terms that are characteristic of economic, political, and cultural analyses of globalization. Although each facet of globalization is linked to the general components of globalization described above, isolating and examining the economic, political, and cultural dimensions of globalization will help us to understand better the ways in which these complex forces operate both autonomously and in concert with each other.[40]

Economics

On November 30, 1999, thousands of protesters descended upon the streets of Seattle, Washington near the Washington State Convention and Trade Center. Activists from around the world representing diverse causes, ideologies, and local, national, and international organizations (including labor, environmental, consumer protection, student, and religious groups) marched toward the convention center from various directions. Others took control of downtown intersections. The goal? To protest and disrupt the World Trade Organization (WTO) Ministerial Conference, preventing the approximately 5,000 delegates from more than 135 nations from getting from their hotels to the Convention Center.[41] The protest soon turned violent, as police fired pepper spray, tear gas, stun grenades, and eventually rubber bullets at protesters in an effort to reopen the streets and usher the WTO delegates through the blockades. The situation descended into chaos as black-clothed youths, reported to be anarchists, began smashing windows and vandalizing storefronts. Some protesters tried to stop the vandalism while other people joined in, pushing dumpsters into the middle of the street and lighting them on fire. Mayor Paul Schell imposed a curfew and a 50-block No-Protest Zone. Protests continued for days, however, culminating in 600 arrests and an estimated three million dollars in property damage.[42]

It was not only the size of the protests – more than 40,000 people – and the violence that ensued that came as a surprise to many people in the United States; it was also the object of protest, the WTO, that caused many to scratch their heads. As *Newsweek* magazine observed in the days following the riots, "until last week, not so many Americans had even heard of the WTO. Fewer still could have identified it as the small, Geneva-based bureaucracy that the United States and 134 other nations set up five years ago to referee global commerce."[43] Media coverage of the riots brought the economic aspects of globalization into the American popular consciousness for the first time, causing many to wonder, "What is globalization exactly, and why are the protesters so against it?" "What are those mysterious institutions – the WTO, the IMF, and the World Bank – that the media keep mentioning?" "And what could be so problematic about free trade?"

Historical roots of contemporary economic globalization
Although the activists in Seattle were a diverse group, many were protesting the forces of economic globalization, including multinational corporations, global economic institutions like the WTO, the IMF, and the World Bank, and the global economic policies, such as *free trade*, that these institutions promulgated, often at the expense, critics would argue, of developing nations, the environment, and the poor. Economic globalization as we know it today can be traced back to decisions made at a US- and British-led economic conference that took place during the final months of World War II. The United Nations Monetary and Financial Conference, which is now more commonly known as the *Bretton Woods Conference*, was held at a mountain resort in Bretton Woods, New Hampshire from July 1 to July 22, 1944. The economic conference, which welcomed more than 700 representatives from 44 Allied countries, was designed to create a system of rules, institutions, and procedures that would rebuild and regulate the international economy, preventing the monetary chaos of the interwar period (the period between the two world wars) from occurring again. Architects of the conference believed that interwar economic policies contributed to World War II. They argued that the privileging of national goals and the dismissal of international collaboration as a means of achieving those goals led to high *tariffs* and the devaluation of currencies in an effort to make goods more competitive on the international market. These policies in turn contributed not only to domestic economic and political instability but also to international war. According to American economist and senior US Treasury department official Harry Dexter White, who together with John Maynard Keynes dominated the Bretton Woods conference, the interwar period showed that "the absence of a high degree of economic collaboration among the leading nations will . . . inevitably result in economic warfare that will be but the prelude and instigator of military warfare on an even vaster scale."[44]

The countries participating in the conference agreed that a new "open" international economic system needed to be developed. This "open" system would be characterized by lower tariffs and the creation of an international monetary system that would reduce barriers to trade. However, they also agreed that the new system should not be a *laissez-faire* form of economic liberalism in

> **free trade**   The promotion of trade in goods and services by reducing tariffs and other trade barriers.
>
> **Bretton Woods Conference**
> An attempt to establish common rules for financial and commercial global transactions. By regulating the international monetary system, the industrial powers that met in 1944 in Bretton Woods sought to prevent the economic policies that led to the global depression of the 1920s–30s.
>
> **tariffs**   Taxes placed on imported goods.

> **laissez-faire**   An economic philosophy that suggests economies work best with limited government involvement.

which governments do not oversee/intervene in the market economy. Rather, Keynes's popular school of economic thought promoted a mixed economy, in which both the state and the private sector have roles to play. The new system thus included the establishment of rules regulating international economic activities. Conference members also agreed upon a more stable monetary exchange system that defined all currencies in relation to the US dollar.

Bretton Woods laid the foundation for three new international economic institutions that would exert tremendous influence over the international economy. The first, the International Bank for Reconstruction and Development (now one of five institutions in the World Bank Group), was initially designed to loan money to promote Europe's reconstruction after the war. Later, it took on the role of loaning money to developing countries to bolster economic development. The second, the International Monetary Fund (IMF), was created to take charge of the international monetary system, or, more specifically, to regulate and stabilize currency exchange rates. In the 1970s, the IMF expanded its role and began extending short-term loans to countries with *balance-of-payment* problems. The third, the General Agreement on Tariffs and Trade (GATT) (which evolved into the *World Trade Organization* in 1995), established and enforced the rules governing international trade agreements.

balance-of-payment Refers to the total exports and imports of a given country in a given time period.

World Trade Organization (WTO) An international organization designed to promote free and uniform trade and banking and finance rules and regulations.

Neoliberalism

The Bretton Woods system created a controlled form of capitalism that lasted until the early 1970s. In 1971, in an effort to counteract forces that were undermining the economic competitiveness of the US, President Nixon abandoned the *gold standard*, allowing the dollar to fluctuate in value. The 1970s were characterized by global instability, including inflation, low levels of economic growth, high unemployment, and energy crises. In the 1980s, the Bretton Woods system, which had been influenced by Keynesian interventionism, was further challenged in England and the US by British Prime Minister Margaret Thatcher and US President Ronald Reagan, both strong proponents of what is often described as *neoliberalism*. The term neoliberalism refers to a political movement, influenced by classical liberal economic theories, that pairs economic liberalism with economic development and political liberty. Neoliberalism portrays government control over the economy as inefficient and corrupt. Characteristic neoliberal policies include downsizing government, privatizing public or state-owned enterprises, deregulating the economy, cutting taxes, expanding international markets, and removing barriers to global trade.[45]

gold standard A monetary system that issues currency that is backed up by gold whereby the holder of the currency can redeem that note for an equivalent amount of gold.

neoliberalism A rejection of Keynesian economic theory, which posited that the state must play an active role in a capitalist economy in order to level out the inevitable boom and bust cycles. Neoliberals argue that deregulation and privatization of state-owned enterprises and limited government involvement in the economy as the best ways for countries' economies to grow and individual freedoms to flourish.

Free trade and multinational corporations

Neoliberal policies, with their emphasis on free trade, contributed to the globalization of trade and finance that we see today. Indeed, free trade has become one of the most common economic buzzwords associated with economic globalization. Regional and international trade-liberalization agreements, like *NAFTA* and *GATT*, reduced trade barriers among nations. Proponents of free trade argue that eliminating trade barriers increases global wealth, consumer choice, and international security and peace. However, while some economists maintain that free trade

> **NAFTA**   A free trade agreement between the US, Canada, and Mexico that sought to encourage trade between the three countries.
>
> **GATT**   The General Agreement on Tariffs and Trade was a treaty whose functions were taken over by the WTO.

increases the standard of living throughout the world, free trade critics point to studies that indicate that the gap between rich and poor countries is actually widening rather than shrinking. They claim that free trade allows developed nations to exploit developing countries, destroying local industry and undoing the "vital health, safety, and environmental protections won by citizen movements across the globe in recent decades."[46] Other critics maintain that free trade hurts developed nations as well, encouraging corporations to cut costs and increase profits by moving jobs to countries where they can pay workers less, avoid environmental and worker safety protections, and eliminate costly health and retirement benefits.

Central to the controversies revolving around free trade is the rise of multinational or transnational corporations (MNC/TNC). An MNC is a corporation that produces or delivers services in at least two countries. Their numbers have increased dramatically, from 7,000 in 1970s to approximately 50,000 in 2000.[47] Their economic power is extensive; some MNCs have budgets that are larger than those of many countries. As a result of the pervasive, international power of MNCs, some have referred to economic globalization as "corporate globalization."

Although MNCs are motivated by profit rather than altruism,[48] some studies suggest that multinationals generally pay an average wage that exceeds the average rate in the local area.[49] Other economists suggest that multinational companies help domestic companies learn how to be more effective and efficient, pushing all companies in an area where multinationals are operating to be more productive.[50] In contrast, critics of MNCs and free trade argue that MNCs have used international trade organizations and agreements to undermine the ability of local, state, and national governments to impose safety, environmental, and wage controls on business, thus limiting governments' abilities to protect their citizens and their environment from harm.[51] Specifically, MNCs are accused of crafting trade agreements in such a way that they pit countries against each other in "a race to the bottom." Poor countries want to attract corporations that will create jobs for their citizens, but the trade-off can be severe, as corporations are attracted to the countries that "set the lowest wage levels, the lowest environmental standards, [and] the lowest consumer safety standards."[52] As free trade critic Ralph Nader puts it, "it is a tragic 'incentives' lure . . . workers, consumers, and communities in all countries lose; short-term profits soar and big business 'wins.' "[53]

International economic institutions

The three economic institutions most commonly associated with economic globalization are the IMF, the World Bank, and the WTO, all of which emerged or evolved
from the Bretton Woods system. The IMF and the World Bank provided loans for
developing countries, but by the 1970s, they adopted a neoliberal agenda and started
integrating and deregulating markets around the globe. By the 1980s, they began
implementing structural adjustment programs (SAPs) in developing countries.
These programs were designed to make it more likely that debtor nations would
be able to repay their loans. In order to obtain a loan or restructure an existing
one, countries would have to reduce the amount of money they spent on public
services, including subsidies for basic food items, health care, and education.
Countries would also be required to promote foreign investment, privatize state
enterprises, devalue their currencies, promote export-led economic growth, and
deregulate their economies. In many countries, these new policies led to fewer social
programs for the poor. In some countries, the ending of subsidies for basic items,
such as bread, led to riots. For example, in Caracas, Venezuela in 1989, anti-IMF
riots were sparked as a result of a 200 percent increase in the price of bread. President
Carlos Andres Perez accused the IMF of practicing "an economic totalitarianism
which kills not with bullets but with famine," but in order to quell the riots,
he sent the military into the slums on the hills overlooking the capital, where they
fired upon people indiscriminately. According to unofficial estimates, more than
1,000 people were killed.[54]

Additionally, SAPs contributed to increases in pollution and the degradation of
the environment in many countries due to the removal of environmental regulations and the unbridled extraction of natural resources for foreign markets. In many
cases, SAPs not only failed to help develop debtor countries but also increased the
poverty of their people.[55] It was these kinds of IMF and World Bank policies and
programs that brought so many protesters together in Seattle in November of 1999
to raise awareness and rally for change.

Politics

Although the term "politics" is most commonly associated with government, it can
be used more generally to refer to the processes through which groups of people
make decisions. Politics consist of social relations, then, but because decision-
making is involved, politics are also about authority and power. How will a given
decision be made? Whose view of a situation and what should be done about it
will be adopted? How will the decision be applied and enforced? When viewed
in this way, it becomes evident that politics form a part of all group interactions,
from governments, to corporations, to clubs. However, at academic institutions,
political scientists tend to focus their analysis and research on politics at the larger
governmental level, examining political behavior and organization, systems of
governance, public policy, and the acquisition, allocation, application, and transfer
of power. When looking at globalization through a political science lens, the focus

Researching to Learn *Investigating the effects of Structural Adjustment Programs (SAPs) on developing nations*

Sample Keyword Searches

Broad searches:
- Debt AND developing nations
- Structural Adjustment Programs (SAPs)

Narrower searches:
- Debt AND development AND conditionalities
- Debt AND international aid AND developing nations

Advanced searches:
- ("Structural Adjustment Programs" OR SAPs) AND ("World Bank") AND ("developing nations")
- ("Structural Adjustment Programs" OR SAPs) AND (Argentina OR South America)

Note:
- *Use quotation marks to search for terms as a phrase.*
- *Use AND to find documents with all terms listed.*
- *Use OR to find documents that contain at least one of the terms.*
- *Use parentheses to combine AND and OR statements in creative ways.*

Free Web Resources

Dollar, David, and Jakob Svensson. "What Explains the Success or Failure of Structural Adjustment Programs?" *World Bank.*
www.worldbank.org/html/dec/Publications/Workpapers/WPS1900series/wps1938/wps1938-abstract.html

Imam, Patrick. "Effect of IMF Structural Adjustment Programs on Expectations: The Case of Transition."
www.imf.org/external/pubs/ft/wp/2007/wp07261.pdf

Structural Adjustment Participatory Review International Network.
www.saprin.org/
University of California, Santa Cruz.
"Does Structural Adjustment work?" *UC Atlas of Global Inequality.*
http://ucatlas.ucsc.edu/sap/does_it_work.php

Books: Find Them @ Your Library

Bello, Walden F., Bill Rau, and Shea Cunningham. *Dark Victory: The United States, Structural Adjustment and Global Poverty.* Oakland, CA: Institute for Food and Development Policy, 1994.

Danaher, Kevin. *50 Years is Enough: The Case Against the World Bank and the International Monetary Fund.* Boston, MA: South End Press, 1994.

Sahn, David E., Paul A. Dorosh, and Stephen D. Younger. *Structural Adjustment Reconsidered: Economic Policy and Poverty in Africa.* Cambridge, UK: Cambridge University Press, 1999.

SAPRIN. *Structural Adjustment: The Policy Roots of Economic Crisis, Poverty, and Inequality.* London, UK: Zed Books, 2004.

Articles: Find Them @ Your Library

Brawley, Mark R. and Nicole Baerg. "Structural Adjustment, Development, and Democracy," *International Studies Review* 9.4 (December 2007): 601–15.

Lele, Uma. "The Gendered Impacts of Structural Adjustment Programs in Africa: Discussion." *American Journal of Agricultural Economics* 73.5 (December 1991): 1452–5.

Prendergrast, John. "Blood Money for Sudan: World Bank and IMF to the 'Rescue.'" *Africa Today* 36 (Fall 1989): 43–53.

tends to be on issues revolving around the demarcation of the globe into nation-states, shifting territorial configurations, global governance, and other forms of supranational social and economic regulation.

> **nation**   Refers to a shared cultural or ethnic identity rather than to a legally recognized geographic territory.
>
> **state**   Refers to the actual governing apparatus of a geographically defined territory called a country.
>
> **sovereign/sovereignty**   The principle that emerged from the Peace of Westphalia (1648) which suggests that a political entity has the sole authority to make decisions about policy, procedure, and institutions within a given geographic territory.

The nation-state

Traditionally, political scientists have distinguished between the terms *nation* and *state*, using the former to describe an ethnic or cultural community and the latter to refer to a *sovereign* political entity. As such, some states may have many nations living within them, and, conversely, some nations are not sovereign states. For example, the Native American Iroquois are a nation but not a state, since they do not have sovereign authority over their internal and external affairs.[56] The term "nation-state" implies that the nation, the cultural/ethnic group, coincides with the state, the geopolitical entity. In theory, then, citizens of the nation-state share a common language, culture, and values, commonalities which historically often were not characteristic of the "state." For example, prior to our current nation-state system, Europe was divided into multiethnic empires, including the Austro-Hungarian, Russian, Ottoman, and British Empires.

In today's nation-state system, global migration and the presence of ethnic minorities disrupt the implied unity of the nation-state. In the absence of common descent, language, and ethnic identity, nation-states often try to create cultural uniformity via national language policies and compulsory education with a uniform curriculum. While some nation-states create state-enforced cultural assimilation policies, other reactions to the presence of ethnic minorities have historically included expulsion, persecution, and violence. Indeed, nation-states have been responsible for some of the worst examples of violence against people living within the nation-state's borders who were not considered part of the nation. However,

> **multiculturalism**   Belief that different cultures can coexist peacefully within a given territory.

many nation-states do accept some minorities, protecting and guaranteeing their rights. Some states have adopted *multiculturalism* as an official policy in an effort to establish peaceful relations between the multiple ethnic, cultural, and linguistic groups living within the state.

Whatever their responses to multiculturalism might be, nation-states are increasingly forced to address the issue, as the forces of globalization have led to a growth in human mobility, making it easier for people to migrate around the world. Some argue that increased migration has disrupted the coherency of the nation-state, eroding the commonalities of language, culture, and values upon which it depends. Others argue that the nation-state is in decline due to the general deterritorialization effects of globalization, which render bounded territory an increasingly less meaningful concept for understanding global power. Political power, they maintain, resides in global networks, eroding the ability of states to control social, political, and economic life within their borders. However, other scholars disagree, pointing out that it was the nation-states themselves that initiated the policies that unleashed the forces of globalization. Governments, they argue, remain important political entities on the global landscape, retaining various degrees of control over education, infrastructure, and migration.[57]

Global governance

Discussions of political globalization also often focus on *supranational* organizations and forms of regulation. These structures include local governments within nations, regional groups of nation-states, international organizations (IOs), and non-governmental organizations (NGOs). For example, "global cities," like Tokyo, New York, London, and Kuala Lumpur, sometimes have political interests that are more in common with other global cities than with cities within their nation-states. Additionally, regional groupings of nations, such as the European Union, have taken over some of the nation-state's traditional functions. Inter-

> **supranational**   A supranational organization is one that has been given the authority by its member nations to make decisions that take precedence over individual member nations' policies. The supranational organization relies on nations to carry out its decisions because it usually lacks any enforcement powers of its own.

national organizations, like the UN and the WTO, spread decision-making among member nation-states, and NGOs, such as Greenpeace, bring together millions of citizens from around the world to challenge decisions made by nation-states and IOs.[58] Political scientists are not in agreement about whether the expansion of supranational organizations is a positive development. Some believe that supranational organizations will evolve into more inclusive and advanced forms of self-government, while critics claim that local and national governments are being replaced by remote forms of government that are neither democratic nor responsive to people's needs.[59] Many of the Seattle protesters were also concerned about this issue; they attempted to make people aware that many economic policies that have a global impact are made by IOs that are neither democratic nor transparent in their decision-making.

Culture

Popular culture, youth culture, Chilean culture, academic culture, European culture, consumer culture, culture shock, cultural revolution, subcultures. *Culture* is a term that is used so often and in so many contexts that it sometimes seems to mean everything

> **culture**   Refers to the beliefs, values, norms, ideals, symbols, and lifestyles of a specified entity.

and nothing. Academic definitions of the term are also numerous and often quite broad as well. Influential anthropologist Edward B. Taylor, for example, wrote in 1871 that culture is "that complex whole which includes knowledge, belief, art, morals, law, custom, and any other capabilities and habits acquired by man as a member of society."[60] Clifford Geertz, another important anthropologist, takes a symbolic view of culture. Geertz states that "man is an animal suspended in webs of significance he himself has spun." He takes "culture to be those webs, and the analysis of it to be therefore not an experimental science in search of law but an interpretive one in search of meaning."[61] In Geertz's framework, culture provides unity and regularity to a society, allowing people to frame their thoughts and experiences in intelligible ways and to communicate with one another. The United Nations Educational, Scientific, and Cultural Organization (UNESCO) describes culture as "the set of distinctive spiritual, material, intellectual and emotional features of society or a social group. . . . [I]t encompasses, in addition to art and literature, lifestyles, ways of living together, value systems, traditions and beliefs."[62]

Manfred Steger's definition of culture brings some of the aforementioned definitions together. He claims that the "cultural" refers to "the symbolic construction, articulation, and dissemination of meaning." He goes on to explain, "given that language, music, and images constitute the major forms of symbolic expression, they assume special significance in the sphere of culture."[63] Although culture involves production, including the creation of things like music and art, it also involves constraint, in that it establishes "a set of limits within which social behavior must be contained, a repertoire of models to which individuals must conform."[64] Transgressing cultural norms may evoke disciplinary responses from a society, the most extreme of which include imprisonment and execution. However, social cues, such as glares, ridicule, or looks of pity, are a far more common way of encouraging adherence to cultural norms. Culture, then, is a set of beliefs, values, and practices that are learned through processes of *enculturation* and *socialization*.

enculturation   Process through which one becomes a member of a culture demonstrating an understanding of its rules, norms, and expectations.

socialization   The process through which one learns the accepted rules of behavior for a culture or society.

Many scholars (though certainly not all!) who study culture are professors of anthropology. Broadly speaking, anthropology is the study of humanity. It takes as its object of analysis both present and past human biological, linguistic, social, and cultural variations. Anthropology has four major subfields: archaeology, physical anthropology, cultural anthropology, and anthropological linguistics. Cultural anthropologists study cultural variations among humans, paying careful attention to the ways in which distinct peoples in different locales understand their own lives. Traditionally, they viewed culture as "something that differentiated one group from another, an identification of otherness."[65] Today, however, cultural anthropologists also study the ways that global economic and political forces affect local cultures, arguing that one cannot adequately understand a specific culture by looking at it solely through a local perspective. Rather, the local must be understood within a larger political, economic, and cultural framework, since these larger forces impact local realities.

Local and global cultures
Globalization processes, including the rise of transnational corporations, the ubiquity of Western popular culture, and the ease of long-distance, high-speed travel, have transformed societies, erasing some of the differences among them and creating similar environments in many places around the globe. As anthropologist Ted Lewellen observes, "On the surface, the life of a middle-class advertising executive working in midtown Sao Paulo or Singapore may not be that different from that of a similarly employed New Yorker."[66] Indeed, most major cities around the world share more similarities than ever before, and many of these similarities are

Western, such as the pervasiveness of American fast food, Western business suits, Hollywood movies, and the English language.

Many scholars point out that global cultural shifts toward *homogeneity*, or sameness, were hastened in the early 1990s after the collapse of the Soviet Union and the end of the Cold War. As the world's sole remaining superpower, the United States' ability to purvey its products, images, ideas, and values around the world increased. Also, as more governments became democratic, more countries became increasingly open to outside influences. Technological innovations, such as computer networks and fiber optic cables, also increased the speed at which products and ideologies spread around the world. The companies, values, and ideas that circle around the globe on these fast networks are largely Western and often American. Multinational corporations, such as Starbucks, McDonald's, Disney, the Gap, and Microsoft, spread not only their products, but also the values embedded within them, such as "speed and ease of use," an emphasis on leisure time, and "a desire for increasing material wealth and comfort."[67] Some critics describe this trend as American or Western *cultural imperialism*, a term that refers to "the control of cultural space and the imposition of a dominant culture – by either coercive or indirect means."[68] While some Westerners may view the spread of Western culture and values as natural, inevitable, and positive, other people see it as a threat to cultures around the world. Some critics of cultural globalization describe Western culture as a homogenizing force that is erasing local cultures, replacing cultural differences with a single world culture based on American values. For example, when Starbucks opened its first coffee shop in Zurich in 2003, critics warned that it was another example of the homogenization of global culture, which would culminate in a monoculture characterized by the replacement of local stores and restaurants with international chains.

Others argue that to position American or Western culture as an absolute, unstoppable force that erases local cultures is to miss the ways that local cultures negotiate Western products and values, incorporating some, rejecting others, and sometimes transforming them in new ways. Although it is true that elements of American culture can be found in almost every corner of the globe, those elements do not always have the same cultural meanings as they do in the United States, nor should the presence of American products in cultures around the world be confused with the adoption of an American cultural identity. As British economist Philippe Legrain points out, "You can choose to drink Coke and eat at McDonald's without becoming American in any meaningful sense."[69] Moreover, cultural flows don't just move in one direction, from the United States to the rest of the world, but rather "from the rest of the world to the rest of the world."[70] Writer Jackson Kuhl, for example, points out the complex cultural exchanges and transformations that ultimately led to the opening of the aforementioned Starbucks in Zurich. Tracing the history of coffee drinking though Africa, Islamic cultures, Europe, and the United States, Kuhl highlights the fact that the Starbucks phenomenon is not a one-way

> **homogeneity** Sameness, or lacking difference.
>
> **cultural imperialism** A form of domination that involves privileging one culture (usually that of a large, powerful nation) over less powerful ones or imposing/ injecting the cultural practices of a dominant culture into other cultures, often culminating in the adoption of the cultural practices of the imperial power.

cultural flow from the US to the rest of the world. Rather, Starbucks itself is a product of diverse global cultures: "Starbuck's customers, whether in Zurich or Beirut, are drinking an American version of an Italian evolution of a beverage invented by Arabs brewed from a bean discovered by Africans."[71]

Cultural cross-fertilizations have always occurred, and they do change cultures, sometimes in small ways and other times in larger ways. However, these exchanges do not necessarily turn less powerful cultures into replicas of a dominant culture. Legrain argues that "new hybrid cultures are emerging, and regional ones re-emerging" that are producing both greater singularity and diversity within societies.[72] The ubiquity of American food chains, for example, does not necessarily erase specific regional cuisines. In fact, the presence of American restaurants can actually incite a resurgence of interest in preserving local cuisines. These local and global food choices may coexist and/or contribute to the creation of culinary fusions that are neither one nor the other, but rather something altogether new. Likewise the explosion of Mexican, Indian, Thai, and other 'foreign' restaurants in the US suggests that US eating habits are also open to change and global influence. Most Americans who are over 40 years of age in the US can remember, for example, when the spice aisle of the local grocery store contained a dozen or so spices. Today, the average supermarket in the US may have an entire aisle devoted to spices.

While there are many cultures that take part in some of the facets of today's globalizing world without abandoning their own cultural practices and values, there are also those that attempt to isolate themselves from a global Western culture in order to protect their culture from outside forces that might change or "contaminate" it. Lewellen, for example, points out that consumerism is a dominant cultural force of globalization and, as such, people with money are the ones most likely to participate, to varying degrees, in global culture. Those without the financial ability to participate in the global consumer culture as well as those whose religious beliefs prevent such participation are more likely to see global culture as a threat. Indeed, the perceived threat of global culture can increase their sense of difference.[73]

American political theorist Benjamin Barber also discusses these different responses to global culture, arguing that two dominant forces are clashing on the world stage. He calls the first "McWorld," which he describes as the product of "the onrush of economic and ecological forces that demand integration and uniformity and that mesmerize the world with fast music, fast computers, and fast food – with MTV, Macintosh, and McDonald's, pressing nations into one commercially homogenous global network: one McWorld tied together by technology, ecology, communications, and commerce."[74] Barber argues that the forces of uniformity also produce cultural and political forces of resistance, which he calls "Jihad." In contrast to the homogenizing forces of McWorld, Jihad is a fragmenting force that pits culture against culture and rejects any kind of interdependence and cooperation. Barber sees both Jihad and McWorld as antidemocratic forces that undermine civil liberties. He advocates for a form of government that protects and accommodates local communities, while also helping them to become more tolerant and participatory.

Clearly, scholars take different positions regarding the effects and forces of cultural globalization. These disagreements are due in part to the fact that cultural flows are complex, and, as such, their results are often uneven and contradictory. As Steger points out, in some contexts, local cultures may largely be replaced by Western cultural products, practices, and values. In other cases, global pressures may lead to a resurgence of attention to and celebration of local cultures. In still others, cultural exchanges result in new forms of cultural hybridity.[75]

Although cultural, political, and economic globalizing forces can be discussed in isolation, they do not operate completely independently from one another. They are connected, though not in a uniform way. Together they affect and are affected by the actions of individuals, organizations, and governments, and these effects are distributed unevenly across the globe.

In Focus: Huntington's "Clash of Civilizations"

In 1993, prominent Harvard scholar Samuel Huntington published an article in *Foreign Affairs*, a leading scholarly journal, in which he argued that culture would be the cause of future global conflicts:

> It is my hypothesis that the fundamental source of conflict in this new world will not be primarily ideological or primarily economic. The great divisions among humankind and the dominating source of conflict will be cultural. Nation states will remain the most powerful actors in world affairs, but the principal conflicts of global politics will occur between nations and groups of different civilizations. The clash of civilizations will be the battle lines of the future.[76]

In 1996, Huntington expanded upon this argument with the publication of his book, *The Clash of Civilizations and the Remaking of World Order*. Huntington's worldview does not allow for productive forms of cultural hybridity nor the idea that cultural exchange can facilitate better relations among states. For Huntington, the more different civilizations interact with one another, the more they will clash. His ideas incited a vigorous debate within the academic community as well as among practitioners in the global policy arena that continues to run a decade and a half after the publication of his book.

In order to understand the debate that was triggered by Huntington's work, it is necessary to look at his arguments more closely. Huntington views civilizations as cultural entities that are defined "both by common objective elements, such as language, history, religion, customs, institutions, and by the subjective self-identification of people." He posits that there are seven or eight civilizations in the world: Confucian, Japanese, Islamic, Hindu, Slavi-orthodox, Latin American, Western, and perhaps African. Huntington argues that civilization is central to our sense of self, and that these identities are much more important and last longer than ideological or economic attachments. Because of the strength of our attachment to our respective civilizations, fault lines inevitably emerge. The more we trade and interact with other civilizations, the more aware we become of the differences between "us" and "them." For Huntington, these differences lead to conflict. Huntington then builds upon these assumptions by arguing that because the West is at the peak of its military, economic, and political power, it should adopt a "West vs. the Rest" approach to world politics. In other words, he maintains that the West should construct foreign policy aimed at nurturing Western relationships and promoting cooperation with other cultures that are similar to it. Western cultural dominance should be promoted, international institutions that undergird that dominance should be supported, and institutions that "that reflect and legitimate Western interests and values" should be strengthened.

Huntington is not without his critics.[77] Some have responded by positing a series of questions. Are identities ancient and unchanging? Do these identities motivate people to persecute and kill those of another civilization? Does ethnic diversity itself inevitably lead to violence? If Huntington is correct, then how do we explain Algeria, Afghanistan (both predominantly Muslim), and Northern Ireland (predominantly Christian), to name a few countries where civil wars erupted between peoples of the same religions? Why hasn't the US, with its multiplicity of civilizations, been torn apart? Are all cultures pure, or can we talk about subcultures within cultures? How do we explain mixed marriages and the resulting hybridization of their offspring? If we live in an interdependent world, what is the advantage of having conflict over concepts such as civilization? For example, nearly 90 percent of Saudi Arabia's export earnings come from oil,[78] the bulk of which is sold to Japan.[79] Were it to engage in conflict with Japan, or its allies, the entire Saudi economy would be ruined. Likewise, the US is becoming increasingly dependent upon China for trade, as well as for financial assistance. In 2008, 25 percent of the United States' debt ($8.5 trillion) was owned by foreign governments. Japan topped the list, owning $644 billion of US debt, and China owned $350 billion.[80] In short, *autarky*, or complete economic independence, is not possible in a world where global economic patterns are driving countries to interact with increased frequency. So while we may be attached to our cultures or "civilizations," such attachments tend not to override other concerns. Finally, Huntington's critics argue that he seems to be assuming that the more that countries trade and interact, the more likely they are to go to war. This idea conflicts with "liberal peace theory" research, which concludes that the more that nations trade with each other, the more interdependent they become, and the less likely they are to go to war.[81]

autarky Complete economic independence.

Global Citizenship: Rights, Responsibility, Inequalities, and Connections

Since the 1990s, there has been renewed interest in the concept of citizenship, generated at least in part by the pressures brought to bear on the concept by globalization.[82] What, after all, does it mean to be a citizen in a globalized world?

What exactly do academic programs in global studies mean when they say they want to facilitate the development of global citizens? What might global citizenship look like, and how might the concept disrupt traditional ideas about citizenship? Any coherent understanding of global citizenship must take into account the dominant discourses on citizenship that have influenced Western thought for centuries.

The term "citizenship," broadly defined, refers to membership in a political community and the attendant rights and responsibilities that this membership entails. The "rights and responsibilities" part of this general definition implicitly points to two competing conceptions of citizenship, both of which have long histories: (1) citizenship-as-activity and (2) citizenship-as-status.[83] The citizenship-as-activity model foregrounds the importance of political agency, defining the "citizen" as one who actively participates in a society's political institutions. This understanding of citizenship goes back to Aristotle and is inscribed in the writings of Cicero, Machiavelli, and Rousseau as well. Aristotle, for example, described the citizen as one capable of both ruling and being ruled. Similarly, Rousseau's notion of the *social contract* positions active participation in civic society as that which ensures that individuals are citizens and not *subjects*.[84]

Writers like Aristotle and Rousseau have contributed to the delineation of what has become known as the *republican model of citizenship* (or classical or civic humanist model). In the republican model, the best form of state is based on (1) a virtuous citizenry and (2) a constitutionally governed polity – a republic and not tyranny. These two preconditions for an ideal state are also viewed as interdependent; a free citizenry is impossible under tyranny and a republic is impossible without the active participation of a virtuous citizenry.[85] As a result, citizenship in the republican model is viewed as a desirable and valuable activity (rather than a state of being contingent upon one's legal status) that enriches both the self and the com-munity. Indeed, "the extent and quality of one's citizenship can shift and change, since it is a function of one's participation in that community."[86]

The second conception of citizenship, citizenship-as-status, focuses on legal rights, specifically the freedom both to act in accordance with the law and to claim the law's protection. Citizenship-as-legal-status is not so much about what you do, as it is in the republican model, but about who you are – specifically, your membership in a particular political community. Citizenship understood in terms of legal status rather than political participation is often referred to as the *liberal model of citizenship*. The liberal model focuses on the protection of individual freedoms from interference by both other individuals and the government. Although it emerged in the seventeenth century and grew stronger in the nineteenth and twentieth centuries, its origins are traceable back to the Roman Empire. As the empire expanded, it granted citizenship rights to conquered

social contract A political philosophy that suggests rulers and those they rule over have a contract whereby the ruled allow the rulers to reign as long as they act in the interests of the ruled. When a ruler no longer is seen to do so, the ruled reserve the right to replace the ruler.

subjects Historically, a term used in monarchical societies to refer to those whose lives were controlled by the king or queen. Modern usage refers to citizens of a monarchical society.

republican model of citizenship A model of rule that places the individual at the center suggesting he or she is capable of being ruled and of ruling. This view of citizenship focuses on the person as a political agent.

liberal model of citizenship Sees citizenship as a legal status, while stressing political liberty and freedom from interference by other citizens and political authority.

males, transforming in the process the definition of citizenship from participation in the formulation or execution of the law to protection by the law. While more passive than the republican model's "citizenship of virtue,"[87] the liberal legal model was also, at least potentially, more inclusive and expansive.[88]

By the twentieth century, citizenship, in the liberal model, came to be defined almost entirely in terms of the citizen's possession of rights. T. H. Marshall's influential *Citizenship and Social Class* (1949) argued that citizenship is primarily about ensuring that everyone is treated as an equal member of the society. The best way to do this is by granting an increasing number of citizenship rights, which Marshall identified as civil, political, and social. Marshall argued that in England, *civil rights* (equality before the law) arose in the eighteenth century, political rights (the vote) arose in the nineteenth century, and social rights (welfare state institutions, such as public education and health care) arose in the twentieth century.[89]

> **civil rights** Rights that individuals possess by virtue of their citizenship – for example, the right to free speech.

Expanded citizenship rights were accompanied by an expansion of the classes of people who were considered citizens. For example, civil and political rights had long been restricted to white, property-owning, Protestant men, but gradually they were extended to others as well, including women, the working class, Jews, and other previously excluded groups. Although this extension of rights is generally viewed positively today, the view of citizenship espoused by Marshall is sometimes criticized for "its emphasis on passive entitlements and the absence of any obligation."[90]

The framework for citizenship as both legal status and as an activity has long been the sovereign, territorial state. In other words, states have specific territorial boundaries, within which citizens may enjoy legal rights and may participate politically. The borders of the state also mark the boundaries of the political community and the rights and responsibilities extended by that community. Various globalizing forces, including new communication technologies, the mass media, transnational economic exchanges, and mass migrations, have highlighted how artificial and porous borders between states can be, calling into question whether there is a necessary relationship between citizenship and the territorially bounded political community.[91] Others point out that the nation-state's sovereignty can function as an impediment to global justice, arguing that it does not have the capacity to adequately address global economic, social, and environmental problems. As a result, they argue, we should explore possibilities beyond its boundaries.[92]

One proposed alternative to state-based citizenship is the notion of "global citizenship" or "world citizenship." The concept of world citizenship has a long history. For example, when Socrates was asked to what country he belonged, he reportedly responded: "I am a citizen of the universe."[93] The concept expressed in Socrates' statement can be traced back to a school of philosophy called *stoicism*, a Greek and Roman movement that enjoyed popularity and influence in waves roughly corresponding to 300 BCE, 100 BCE, and 100 CE.[94] The stoics taught that individuals should be loyal members of

> **stoicism** A philosophy, prevalent in ancient Greece and Rome, that maintains that freedom and universal understanding can be obtained by self-control and freeing oneself from mundane desires.

both the "polis," or state, and the "cosmopolis," or world city, which they understood as a universal moral community and not as a world government.[95] The notion
of world citizenship emerged again during both the Renaissance
and the Enlightenment. Over time, it evolved into the concept
of *cosmopolitanism*, which has been held up as an ideal and
described in a variety of different ways by moral and sociopo-
litical philosophers. An idea that most definitions of cosmopoli-

> **cosmopolitanism** Belief that all humans are connected and belong to one humanity.

tanism share is that all human beings, regardless of their state affiliations, belong
to a single community. However, some view this community as essentially a moral
one, while others view it in political, economic, or cultural terms.[96]

In her book *The Political Theory of Global Citizenship*, April Carter states that
today cosmopolitanism is generally understood in political and international relations theory as "a model of global politics in which relations between individuals
transcend state boundaries, and in which an order based on relations between states
is giving way to an order based at least partly on universal laws and institutions."[97]
According to Carter, cosmopolitanism is still associated with the moral position
advanced initially by the stoics that each individual should be valued as an auto-
nomous being. Carter points out that while cosmopolitanism is linked to humanitarianism by its active concern for others in need, it differs from humanitarianism
in that it stresses the dignity of those receiving aid. Cosmopolitanism is also linked
to the liberal belief in basic human rights, but it goes further to posit an ideal of a
world community that unites us all while simultaneously respecting the differences
among us.

Since the 1990s, the term "global citizenship" has been gaining popularity, and
it is used far more frequently in common parlance than is the term cosmopolitanism.
Current conceptions of "global citizenship" share many of the basic tenets of cosmopolitanism discussed above; however, the phrase also evokes the distinct history
of the term "citizenship." The concept of global citizenship can be viewed as
relying upon elements of both the republican and liberal models of citizenship.
For example, both global citizenship and the republican model of citizenship are
shaped by notions of active participation, responsibility, and civic virtue. Global
citizenship discourses often emphasize the importance of actively working to make
the world a better place, an idea that hearkens back to the republican notion of
citizenship as a desirable and valuable activity that enriches both the self and the
community. However, in the case of global citizenship, the community extends
far beyond the boundaries of the state. Self-identified global citizens who actively
participate in movements that address global issues clearly share some beliefs and
values that were important in the republican model. However, the notion of global
citizenship also retains the liberal model's emphasis on the protection of individual rights via its emphasis on protecting basic human rights. Historically, the
liberal model was often more inclusive and expansive than the republican model,
allowing, for example, for the extension of citizenship rights to conquered peoples,
as in the case of the Roman empire. Global citizenship takes inclusiveness and expan-
siveness beyond the empire to include all of humanity. So, on the one hand, one

could act as a global citizen by working to protect human rights. On the other, one could also be considered a global citizen in the liberal sense simply by virtue of being a human being whose human rights therefore deserve to be protected.

Despite points of similarity with both the republican and the liberal models of citizenship, critics of the term global citizenship argue that it is not a coherent category, since citizenship is generally understood as a legal relationship to a specific sovereign state.[98] In contrast, Carter argues that "the development of international law and the pressures of migration have challenged the exclusivity of the nation-state and therefore the old concept of citizenship."[99] The newer notion of global citizenship (1) recognizes emerging international laws and institutions and (2) broadens and extends the rights and responsibilities that have traditionally been a part of citizenship. As the planet shrinks under the forces of globalization, new institutions and media continue to emerge that foster the growth of a global civil society that transcends national boundaries. This book takes Carter's position that the term "global citizenship" is a useful category that makes connections among human rights, human duties, and cosmopolitan beliefs. The term also denotes the complex linkages among individuals, international laws, and political institutions that emerge in a globalizing world.[100]

Active global citizens, then, are those who seek to understand the links between human rights, human duties, and cosmopolitan beliefs. They are people who attempt to stay abreast of the complex connections between the local and the global and to understand the webs that link local actions (such as consumption patterns) to international outcomes (such as resource-based conflicts). They also attempt to transform their knowledge into responsible action, such as working for peace, human rights, environmental preservation, and economic equality.[101] In other words, global citizens seek out information about the world so that they can act in informed, ethical, and responsible ways.

Global studies courses and programs are often explicit in their goal of facilitating students' development into active global citizens. In addition to offering students the opportunity to learn about the world from a variety of academic perspectives and to make connections among them, global studies programs challenge them to learn about themselves, to question who they want to become, and to discover how they can actively participate in their world. Global studies, then, not only introduces students to the study of global issues but also encourages them to think about how to leverage that knowledge effectively and responsibly into meaningful action in a globalizing world.

Conclusion

Global studies takes as its object of analysis the global social, political, and economic processes and transformations that affect not only the world as a whole but also individual localities in particular, complex, and sometimes contradictory ways. It is an interdisciplinary field of study that emerged in response to the forces of globalization, which are multiplying and intensifying worldwide social "inter-dependencies and exchanges while at the same time fostering in people a growing awareness of deepening connections between the local and the distant."[102] Some of the dominant global forces that global studies scholars focus on include economic, political, and social forces and the complex connections and interplay among them. Globalization is also expanding traditional notions of citizenship, leading some to suggest that the concept of "global citizenship" may be a potentially productive way of responding to the growing reach and power of international organizations, corporations, and governmental bodies that are increasingly challenging the primacy of the nation-state as the primary player on the international stage.

What global political, cultural, economic, and environmental issues interest you? In what ways are you connected to larger global issues and forces? What kinds of organizations might you like to join or jobs might you like to pursue that would allow you to link your education and interests with active participation in movements to shape and improve life on this ever-shrinking planet?

Notes

1 John Dewey, *Democracy and Education* (New York: The Macmillan Company, 1955), 24.

2 Calvin Blanchard, *The Life of Thomas Paine* (New York, NY: Calvin Blanchard, 1860).

3 J. Michael Adams and Angelo Carfagna, *Coming of Age in a Globalized World: The Next Generation* (Bloomfield, CT: Kumarian Press, Inc., 2008), www.nextgenerationbook.com/.

4 Overseas Facilities, Corporate Information, Fuji Heavy Industries, www.fhi.co.jp/english/outline/inoutline/overseas/index.html.

5 Some examples include: The Global Studies Institute Indiana, www.gsiculver.org/; University of Minnesota, http://igs.cla.umn.edu/; Global Studies Institute-Massachusetts, www.gsinstitute.net/; Johns Hopkins University Institute for Global Studies in Culture, Power, and History, http://web.jhu.edu/igs; University of Wisconsin-Milwaukee, www.uwm.edu/Dept/IGS/; The Lawrence D. Starr Global Studies Institute, http://gsi.stmary.edu/; Global Studies Institute Australia, www.gsiaustralia.com/.

6 See, for example, The Global Studies Association (GSA), www.globalstudiesassociation.org/main/.

7 See, for example, the annual Global Studies Association Conference webpage at www.global-studiesassociation.org/main/conference.html.

8 Some examples of universities that offer global studies-related degrees in this category include: University of Wisconsin-Madison, University of California-Santa Barbara, University of New York, University of West Georgia, University of Pittsburgh, San Jose State University, University of California Riverside, Duke University, Meiji Gakuin University, University of Illinois, University of Windsor, York University, Tama University, California State University Monterey Bay, Hamline University, Penn State Berks College, St Lawrence University, University of Wisconsin-Milwaukee, University of Liverpool, University of Hawaii.

9 See, for example, Michael Bowler, "The Disciplined Undiscipline of Global Studies," *global-e* 1, no. 2 (September 21, 2007).

10 Ibid.

11 Edward Kolodziej, "What Should Be the Central Concerns of Global Studies?" *global-e* 1, no. 2 (September 21, 2007).

12 David Jacobson and Ning Wang, "The Intellectual Foundations of Global Studies," *global-e* 1, no. 1 (May 17, 2007).

13 For example, Mark Juergensmeyer, Director of the Orfalea Center for Global and International Studies at the University of California-Santa

Barbara claims that at the heart of the UC-Santa Barbara program is a "commitment to creating global citizens." See Mark Juergensmeyer, "Going Global the Santa Barbara Way," *global-e* 1, no. 2 (September 21, 2007).

14 *Webster's Third New International Dictionary of the English Language Unabridged* (Springfield, MA: Merriam, 1961).

15 Guy Lachapelle and Stéphane Paquin, *Mastering Globalization: New Sub-States' Governance and Strategies* (New York: Routledge 2005), 14; Roland Robertson, *Globalisation: Social Theory and Global Culture* (London: Sage, 1992), 8.

16 Lachapelle and Paquin, *Mastering Globalization*, 14.

17 Steger developed his definition of globalization by pulling out key themes in the following five influential definitions of globalization:

1 Globalization can thus be defined as the intensification of worldwide social relations which link distant localities in such a way that local happenings are shaped by events occurring many miles away and vice versa. (Anthony Giddens, ex-Director of the London School of Economics)

2 The concept of globalization reflects the sense of an immense enlargement of world communication, as well as of the horizon of a world market, both of which seem far more tangible and immediate than in earlier stages of modernity. (Fredric Jameson, Professor of Literature at Duke University)

3 Globalization may be thought of as a process (or set of processes) which embodies a transformation in the spatial organization of social relations and transactions – assessed in terms of their extensity, intensity, velocity and impact – generating transcontinental or interregional flows and networks of activity, interaction, and the exercise of power. (David Held, Professor of Political Science at the London School of Economics)

4 Globalization as a concept refers both to the compression of the world and the intensification of consciousness of the world as a whole. (Roland Robertson, Professor of Sociology at the University of Pittsburgh)

5 Globalization compresses the time and space aspects of social relations. (James Mittelman, Professor of International Relations at American University)

See Manfred B. Steger, *Globalization: A Very Short Introduction* (Oxford: Oxford University Press, 2003), 10.

18 Ibid., 13.

19 Ibid., 9.

20 William Scheuerman, "Globalization," *Stanford Encyclopedia of Philosophy* (June 16, 2006), http://plato.stanford.edu/entries/globalization.

21 Robertson, *Globalisation*, 8.

22 Malcolm Waters, *Globalization* (London: Routledge, 1995), 3.

23 Richard Edwards and Robin Usher, *Globalisation and Pedagogy* (New York: Routledge, 2000), 13.

24 Scheuerman, "Globalization."

25 Mvemba Phezo Dizolele, "Millions have Died for Our Cell Phones," *St Louis Post-Dispatch* (October 5, 2006), www.pulitzercenter.org/openitem.cfm?id=276.

26 Benjamin Coghlan, Richard J Brennan, Pascal Ngoy, David Dofara, Brad Otto, Mark Clements, and Tony Stewart, "Mortality in the Democratic Republic of Congo: A Nationwide Survey," *The Lancet* 367 (January 7, 2006), 44, www.thelancet.com.

27 Kristi Essick, "Guns, Money and Cell Phones." *The Industry Standard Magazine* (June 11, 2001), www.thestandard.com/article/0,1902,26784,00.html.

28 UN Security Council (UNSC), "Report of the Panel of Experts on the Illegal Exploitation of Natural Resources and Other Forms of Wealth of the Democratic Republic of Congo" (April 12, 2001), www.un.org/Docs/sc/letters/2001/357e.pdf.

29 Scheuerman, "Globalization."

30 "Gordon E. Moore." Intel Executive Biography, www.intel.com/pressroom/kits/bios/moore.htm.

31 Steger, *Globalization*, 20.

32 Throughout this book, the terms BCE and CE will be used in place of BC and AD. The notation BCE means Before the Common Era. BCE is an alternative notation for BC (before Christ), and CE is an alternative for AD (anno Domini, Latin for "In the year of Our Lord.") The Common Era (CE) is the period of measured time beginning with the

year 1 on the Gregorian calendar. The CE/BCE system of notation is chronologically equivalent to dates in the AD/BC system, but it is preferred by many because of the absence of religious references.

33 For a more in-depth discussion about whether globalization is old or new, see Steger, *Globalization*.

34 Ibid., 28–9.

35 Ibid., 33–5.

36 Scheuerman, "Globalization."

37 Marshall McLuhan, *The Gutenberg Galaxy: The Making of Typographic Man* (Toronto, Canada: University of Toronto Press, 1962), 23, 31.

38 "Press Release: Personal Computer Announced by IBM" (August 12, 1982), IBM Archives, www.03.ibm.com/ibm/history/exhibits/pc25/pc25_press.html.

39 "Welcome to info.cern.ch: The Website of the World's First-ever Web Server," CERN: European Organization for Nuclear Research, http://info.cern.ch/.

40 The discussion that follows on the economic, political, and cultural dimensions of globalization relies upon many of the categories identified by Steger in *Globalization*. For a more in-depth analysis of these topics, see chs. 3–5 in his book.

41 Susan Ariel Aaronson, *Taking Trade to the Streets: The Lost History of Public Efforts to Shape Globalization* (Ann Arbor, MI: The University of Michigan Press, 2001), 1.

42 Silja Talvi, "Seattle, One Year Later," *Mother Jones* (December 2, 2000), www.motherjones.com/news/feature/2000/12/seattle_anniversary.html.

43 Kenneth Klee, Patricia King, and Katrina Woznicki, "The Siege of Seattle," *Newsweek* (December 13, 1999), 6, 30; Jawara and Kwa maintain that "Until 1999, relatively few people outside the ranks of economists, diplomats and political analysts and commentators had heard of the WTO, or even knew that the initials stood for the World Trade Organization. That changed dramatically in November 1999, with the Third Ministerial Conference in Seattle – not because of the conference itself, but because of what went on outside it." Fatoumata Jawara and Aileen Kwa, *Behind the Scenes at the WTO: The Real World of International Trade Negotiation* (London: Zed Books, 2003), 1.

44 Quoted in Robert A. Pollard, *Economic Security and the Origins of the Cold War, 1945–1950* (New York: Columbia University Press, 1985), 8.

45 Steger, *Globalization*, 39–41.

46 Ralph Nader, "Introduction: Free Trade and the Decline of Democracy," in Ralph Nader et al., *The Case Against Free Trade: GATT, NAFTA, and the Globalization of Corporate Power* (San Francisco, CA: Earth Island Press, 1993), 1.

47 Steger, *Globalization*, 48.

48 "Postscript: Do International Financial Institutions and Multinational Corporations Exploit the Developing World?" in James E. Harf and Mark Owen Lombardi (eds.), *Taking Sides: Clashing Views on Controversial Global Issues*, 3rd edn. (Dubuque, IA: McGraw Hill, 2005), 265.

49 Jagdish Bhagwati, "Do Multinational Corporations Hurt Poor Countries?" in Harf and Owen (eds.), *Taking Sides*, 262.

50 Ibid., 263.

51 Nader, "Introduction: Free Trade and the Decline of Democracy," 2.

52 Ibid., 6.

53 Ibid., 6.

54 Michel Chossudovsky, "The Globalisation of Poverty," in Warwick Organizational Behavior Staff (eds.), *Organizational Studies: Critical Perspectives on Business and Management*, vol. IV (London and New York: Routledge, 2001), 1962–3.

55 Steger, *Globalization*, 52–3.

56 Nenad Miscevic, "Nationalism," *Stanford Encyclopedia of Philosophy* (September 24, 2005), http://plato.stanford.edu/entries/nationalism/.

57 Steger, *Globalization*, 61–3.

58 Ibid., 66–7.

59 Scheuerman, "Globalization."

60 Edward B. Tyler, *Primitive Culture: Researches into the Development of Mythology, Philosophy, Religion, Art, and Custom* (London: John Murray, 1871), 1.

61 Clifford Geertz, *The Interpretation of Cultures: Selected Essays* (New York: Basic Books, 2000; originally published 1973), 5.

62 "UNESCO Universal Declaration on Cultural Diversity" UNESCO (February 21, 2002), www.unesco.org/education/imld_2002/unversal_decla.shtml.

63 Steger, *Globalization*, 69.

64   Stephen Greenblatt, "Culture," in Frank Lentricchia and Thomas McLaughlin (eds.), *Critical Terms for Literary Study* (Chicago, IL: University of Chicago Press, 1995), 225.

65   Ted C. Lewellen, *The Anthropology of Globalization: Cultural Anthropology Enters the 21st Century* (Westport, CT: Bergin & Garvey, 2002), 50.

66   Ibid., 54.

67   James E. Harf and Mark Owen Lombardi, "Is the World a Victim of American Cultural Imperialism?" in Harf and Owen (eds.), *Taking Sides*, 237.

68   Richard E. Lee, *Globalization, Language, and Culture* (Philadelphia, PA: Chelsea House, 2006), 42.

69   Philippe Legrain, "In Defense of Globalization: Why Cultural Exchange Is Still an Overwhelming Force for Good," The International Economy (Summer 2003), http://findarticles-com/p/articles/mi_m2633/is_3_17/ai_106423909/.

70   Lee, *Globalization, Language, and Culture*, 43.

71   Jackson Kuhl, "Tempest in a Coffeepot: Starbucks Invades the World," *Reason* (January 2003), www.reason.com/news/show/28639.html.

72   Legrain, "In Defense of Globalization."

73   Lewellen, *Anthropology of Globalization*, 54.

74   Benjamin R. Barber, "Jihad vs. McWorld," *The Atlantic Monthly* (March 1992), www.theatlantic.com/doc/print/199203/barber.

75   Steger, *Globalization*, 76.

76   Samuel P. Huntington, "The Clash of Civilizations," *Foreign Affairs* 72, no. 3 (Summer 1993), 22–49.

77   For more complete discussion of the critiques offered by Huntington's critics, see Amartya Sen, *Identity and Violence: The Illusion of Destiny (Issues of Our Time)* (New York: W. W. Norton, 2006); Paul Breman, *Terror and Liberalism* (New York: W. W. Norton, 2004); Edward Said, "The Clash of Ignorance," *The Nation* (October 22, 2001), www.thenation.com/doc/20011022/said.

78   US Department of Energy, www.eia.doe.gov/cabs/Saudi_Arabia/Background.html.

79   "As OPEC Cutback Starts, Japan Gets Less Saudi Oil," *International Herald Tribune* (October 25, 2006), www.iht.com/articles/2006/10/23/business/oilcut.php.

80   John W. Schoen, "Just Who Owns the US National Debt? And is Growing Foreign Investment in the US Bad for America?" MSNBC (March 4, 2007), www.msnbc.msn.com/id/17424874/.

81   Solomon Polachek, Carols Seiglie, and Jun Xiang, "The Impact of Foreign Direct Investment on International Conflict," *Defence & Peace Economics* 18, no. 5 (October 2007), 415–29.

82   For a discussion of this resurgence of interest in citizenship, see Will Kymlicka and Norman Wayne, "Return of the Citizen: A Survey of Recent Work on Citizenship Theory," *Ethics* 104, no. 2, (January 1994), 352–381.

83   Ibid., 354.

84   Dominique Leydet, "Citizenship," *Stanford Encyclopedia of Philosophy* (October 13, 2006), http://plato.stanford.edu/entries/citizenship.

85   Derek Heater, *A Brief History of Citizenship* (New York: New York University Press, 2004), 4.

86   Kymlicka and Norman, "Return of the Citizen," 353.

87   Heater, *A Brief History of Citizenship*, 4.

88   Leydet, "Citizenship."

89   Heater, *A Brief History of Citizenship*, 3.

90   Kymlicka and Norman, "Return of the Citizen," 354.

91   Leydet, "Citizenship."

92   Ibid.

93   Heater, *A Brief History of Citizenship*, 106.

94   Ibid., 37.

95   Ibid., 105.

96   "Cosmopolitanism," *Stanford Encyclopedia of Philosophy* (November 28, 2006), http://plato.stanford.edu/entries/cosmopolitanism/.

97   April Carter, *The Political Theory of Global Citizenship* (New York: Routledge, 2001), 2.

98   Ibid., 5.

99   Ibid., 6–7.

100   Ibid., 10.

101   Ibid., 7.

102   Steger, *Globalization*, 13.

2

NATION-STATE SYSTEM

"In my view, the fact that the state, unlike all previous political constructs, was able to separate the ruler from the organization was the secret behind its outstanding success. What made the state unique was that it replaced the ruler with an abstract, anonymous, mechanism made up of laws, rules, and regulations." (Martin van Creveld, "The State: Its Rise and Decline")[1]

"When you see the earth from the moon, you don't see any divisions there of nations or states. This might be the symbol for the new mythology to come. That is the country that we are going to be celebrating." (Joseph Campbell, *The Power of Myth*)[2]

"Central to [our] future is the uncertain degree to which the sovereign state can adapt its behavior and role to a series of deterritorializing forces associated with markets, transnational social forces, cyberspace, demographic and environmental pressures and urbanization." (Richard Falk, "World Prisms")[3]

Learning to Question, Questioning to Learn

- How does the term "nation-state" differ from the terms "nation" and "state"?
- What factors contributed to the development of the nation-state system in Europe?
- How did the nation-state become the primary organizing structure of human societies?
- What factors pose a challenge to the dominance of the nation-state as the primary actor in the international arena?

Introduction

Although the terms "nation," "state," and "nation-state" are often used inter-changeably today, they also have distinct meanings and histories. This chapter will begin by exploring these terms in order to develop a more nuanced understanding of how our current international system has developed. The chapter will then trace the historical emergence of the nation-state as the primary organizing structure of human societies before going on to discuss the relationship between colonialism and today's struggling states. Finally, the chapter explores some of the internal and external challenges facing the nation-state.

Nations, States, and the Nation-state System

In academic discourses, the term *state* is used instead of the more commonly used "country" to refer to "an internationally recognized, politically organized, popu-lated, geographical area that possesses sovereignty."[4] States are geopolitical entities with the following characteristics:

- a fixed territory with boundaries;
- a population;
- a government;
- the capacity to enter into relations with other states.

state   Refers to a sovereign, internationally recognized, and geographically defined territory with a population and a government.

nation   Refers to a shared cultural or ethnic identity rather than to a legally recognized geographic territory.

nation-state   A type of state that provides sovereign territory for a particular culture or ethnic group. However, it is also frequently used interchangeably with the terms "state" and "country."

In contrast, the term *nation* refers to a shared cultural or ethnic identity rather than to a legally recognized geographic territory. The people of the Navajo nation, for example, share a cultural identity that does not depend upon fixed territory or outside legal recognition. Rather, their status as a nation is based upon shared historical and cultural experiences. The term *nation-state* liter-ally brings the two different definitions of "nation" and "state" together, as it refers to a specific kind of state, one that provides a sovereign territory for a particular nation. In other words, in a nation-state, the cultural/ethnic group coincides with the geopolitical entity. As such, citizens of the nation-state share a common language, culture, and values. The idea that Italy is a state where people speak Italian, identify themselves as Italian, partake in Italian culture, and behave according to Italian cul-tural norms may seem self-evident, and even the natural order of things, but the term nation-state reminds us that this connection between nation and state was not always the norm. In fact, the nation-state marks a shift away from other types of states that dominated the world-stage before it.

Emergence of the Nation-state System

The current nation-state system has its roots in seventeenth-century Europe. Prior to its emergence, the feudal system and the Catholic Church dominated European political life. Local barons ruled over inherited lands, or fiefdoms, and assumed the powers we typically associate with governments. Although there were monarchs who ruled over larger territories with frequently shifting boundaries, their power was generally weak, allowing barons to establish their own rule of law within their fiefdoms. However, many barons were also beholden to the Church, which sought to create a spiritually united Europe with religious and political power resting in the Papacy.[5] For more than 900 years, the Church wielded tremendous power over Europe, coronating and exerting control over kings, directly ruling over some territories, levying taxes, and amassing great wealth. In short, the Church established an empire, which has since been called the Holy Roman Empire, that included almost all of central Europe. It was ruled by the Holy Roman Emperor, a sovereign who was crowned by the Pope.

Despite its long rule and pervasive influence, the Church's power eventually began to decline. This decline was necessary to the emergence of the nation-state system, which is organized around

secular Not religious.

national, and generally *secular*, differences rather than spiritual unity. This decline was the result of many different complex factors. For example, Gutenberg's invention of the printing press (1430s) made the Bible more widely available. As more people read the Bible, more interpretations of its content began to circulate. These interpretations, sometimes conflicting, called into question the Church's role as the sole authority on the Bible. Once the Church's religious authority was called into question, its political authority became suspect as well.

The expansion of literacy was also a key component in the rise of the nation-state system, making possible written contracts, currency, the transference of ideals, norms of behavior, and laws that, once recorded, became easier to pass from one generation to another. Literacy also made the development and growth of universities, science, and educated bureaucrats possible, which in turn allowed for continuity of governments and organized scientific inquiry.

The Church's dominant position was also called into question when the *bubonic plague* (also known as the Black Death) spread though Europe, the Middle East, and Asia (1347–51). Between one-quarter to one-third of Europeans from every social class died, economies of vast regions came to a standstill, fields lay fallow, and millions of people fled their homes. The plague swept indis-

bubonic plague/Black Death
A pandemic caused by a bacterium that swept through Central Asia and Europe around the 1340s, killing millions.

criminately through Europe without regard for the religious piety of its victims, causing many to question their faith. These dramatic social and political upheavals left people feeling vulnerable and open to new ideas.

Several prominent theologians were also instrumental in challenging the Christian church's political and social authority. John Wycliffe (1330?–84) was one of the first to confront papal power by arguing against a strong role for the Church in political affairs, suggesting instead that the Church refrain from intervening in *temporal affairs*.[6] He further demanded that the Bible be translated from its original Latin in order to make it accessible to everyone in their local languages. Against the wishes of the Church, Wycliffe translated the Bible into English. Although the Church denounced him and his translation, others followed in his footsteps, including Martin Luther (1483–1546), who translated the Bible into German. Luther also challenged the authority of the Church, rising to prominence in 1517 when he posted his *95 Theses* on the Castle Church doors in Wittenberg, Germany. Luther wanted the Church to reform various doctrines and practices, most notably the sale of *indulgences* – spiritual pardons granted by religious authorities for profit. Additionally, he believed that people could have a personal relationship with God without the Church serving as an intermediary. His actions led to the fracturing of the Church and the emergence of the *Protestant Reformation* (sixteenth century). John Calvin (1509–64) also challenged the authority of the Church, but he went further, rejecting papal authority and founding a new church, the Protestant sect of Calvinism.

By the early 1600s, the religious and political tensions that had previously resulted in periodic episodes of violence erupted into one of Europe's bloodiest wars, the *Thirty Years War* (1618–48). The Thirty Years War, while fought mainly in what is modern-day Germany, devastated not only the areas where the conflict raged but also territories far beyond. With armies coming from as far away as Central Europe and Sweden, the impact of the war reached well beyond areas where the battles were fought. Disease spread as civilians fled, fields were destroyed or abandoned, and starvation took the lives of thousands. Prior to World War II, this was the bloodiest war in European history.[7]

The Thirty Years War ended with the *Peace of Westphalia* (1648). Many political scientists and scholars of international law point to this as being the beginning of the modern nation-state system, also known as the *Westphalian system*. This was the first time that many European leaders came together and recognized one another's territorial *sovereignty* – the ability of the state to make domestic and, to a lesser extent, international policy decisions free from outside control.

temporal affairs   Refers to secular, rather than sacred, matters.

indulgence   In the Catholic faith, after a sinner has confessed and received absolution, the guilt of sin is removed but temporal punishment is still required by Divine Justice, either in this life or in Purgatory. An indulgence removes the temporal punishment that the penitent had incurred in the sight of God.

Protestant Reformation   Martin Luther's attempt to reform the Catholic Church that led to a schism within the church and the development of the Protestant sect.

Thirty Years War   Beginning as a religious conflict, it spread across Europe and devastated the continent, lasting from 1618 to 1648.

Peace of Westphalia   Common term for two treaties signed in 1648 to end Europe's Thirty Years War.

Westphalian system   The current political structure of the sovereignty of the nation-state.

sovereign/sovereignty   The principle that emerged from the Peace of Westphalia (1648) which suggests that a political entity has the sole authority to make decisions about policy, procedure, and institutions within a given geographic territory.

From Europe to the rest of the world

In 1900 there were approximately 50 nation-states. By 2008, there were almost 200. What accounts for this dramatic increase and how did the nation-state system, which was initially unique to Europe, spread to the rest of the world? By the 1600s, extreme

Researching to Learn   *Investigating Nation-states Online*

Australian Department of Foreign Affairs and Trade

Australian Department of Foreign Affairs and Trade website, providing facts about the land, people, history, government, political conditions, economy, and foreign relations of almost 240 countries and economies.

www.dfat.gov.au/GEO/

Canadian Government Reports

The Canadian government provides this exhaustive site, which describes life in most of the countries on Earth. Included for each country is information on food, work, religion, education, and much more.

www.cp-pc.ca/english/index.html

The International Monetary Fund (IMF)

IMF Country Information Page contains IMF reports and publications arranged by country.

www.imf.org/external/country/index.htm

CIA – The World Factbook

An annual publication of the Central Intelligence Agency of the United States with almanac-style information about the countries of the world.

www.cia.gov/library/publications/the-world-factbook/

New Countries of the World

About.com website provides statistics and links to more information about the world's newest countries.

http://geography.about.com/cs/countries/a/newcountries.htm

Overseas Security Advisory Council (OSAC)

The OSAC provides reports and daily news by country and region for American businesses operating overseas.

www.osac.gov/

Population Reference Bureau

The Population Reference Bureau informs people around the world about population, health, and the environment, and empowers them to use that information to advance the well-being of current and future generations.

www.prb.org//?Section=PRB_Country_Profiles

United Nations Children's Fund

The United Nations Children's Fund website provides country information and statistics that are relevant to the health and well-being of children.

www.unicef.org/infobycountry/index.html

US Census Bureau

The International Data Base (IDB) offers a variety of demographic indicators for 226 countries and areas of the world. The IDB has provided access to demographic data for more than 25 years to governments, academics, other organizations, and the public.

www.census.gov/ipc/www/idb/

US Department of State Background Notes

The publications listed in this website include facts about the land, people, history, government, political conditions, economy, and foreign relations of independent states, some dependencies, and areas of special sovereignty.

www.state.gov/r/pa/ei/bgn

US Library of Congress Country Studies

The Country Studies Series presents a description and analysis of the historical setting and the social, economic, political, and national security systems and institutions of countries throughout the world.

http://lcweb2.loc.gov/frd/cs/cshome.html

World Gazetteer

The World Gazetteer provides a comprehensive set of population data and related statistics.

www.world-gazetteer.com/wg.php?x=&lng=fr&des=wg&srt=npan&col=abcdefghinoq&msz=1500&men=home&lng=en

World Health Organization (WHO)

Health and disease information by country provided by the WHO.

www.who.int/countries/en

World Statesmen

WorldStatesmen.org is an online encyclopedia of the leaders of nations and territories. This site provides detailed chronologies, flags, national anthems, maps and indexes for each country to give researchers an in-depth portrait of polities past and present.

www.worldstatesmen.org/

colonialism One territorial sovereign exerting control and sovereignty over another land by usurping control from local leaders, thereby destroying indigenous culture, economies, and political structures.

competition for markets and resources among European states led to exploration and *colonialism*. Modern colonialism refers to the dictatorial rule of Latin America, the Middle East, Africa, and Asia by major European powers that used their control to extract resources from these regions. It is worth observing that it was not long after European states embraced the concept of sovereignty that they launched into empire building in other parts of the world, where they refused to recognize the sovereignty of non-European political entities. European colonialism touched every part of the globe and lasted until the 1950s and 1960s (roughly 400 years). Europeans left behind states where once an amalgam of nations existed, expanding the nation-state system across the globe.

Struggling States

The colonial legacy

The majority of states that are struggling in the current global nation-state system are former European colonies. This is no coincidence, as many of their struggles are rooted in the history of colonialism. Invariably, contact with outsiders changes a society; the longer and broader the contact, the greater the impact. Europeans perceived the indigenous peoples who inhabited the areas they conquered as primitive, childlike, and in need of European guidance to become "civilized." From slavery, to the *encomienda system* of forced labor of indigenous Americans, to rape of indigenous women, colonialism was a brutal enterprise. Native Americans were enslaved, brutalized, and in some cases, annihilated. In some parts of Latin America, Native Americans were branded like cattle, while in the US they were slaughtered for their land. For example, Native Americans were given blankets infected with smallpox, a disease to which they were particularly susceptible.[8] Native women were often forced to become the sex slaves of the conquerors, and rape was not only common but often encouraged.[9] Indeed, access to native women was one of the tactics used to sell to European men the idea of migrating to these "new lands."[10]

encomienda system A forced labor system introduced by the Spanish during the conquest of the Americas that effectively transferred indigenous land to the Conquistadors and made the local populations landless slaves.

The practices and policies of King Leopold of Belgium provide a particularly shocking example of the brutality of the colonial enterprise. Leopold ran the Congo, located in central Africa, as his own fiefdom. The primary resource he was interested in extracting from the Congo was rubber, which was in great demand in Europe. Leopold's rubber plantations were notorious for their inhuman and brutal treatment of the workers. According to British foreign policy expert Martin Ewans:

> The local inhabitants were forced to collect rubber for minimal returns, and were subjected to a variety of compulsions if they failed to deliver the quotas demanded. Hostages were taken against deliveries, chiefs killed or intimidated, individuals slaughtered

and whole villages razed. A potentially lethal whip of dried hippopotamus hide, the *chicotte*, was widely used, and the regime's soldiers were ordered to produce severed hands, to prove that they had used their weapons effectively. The populations of the rubber producing areas were decimated, partly as a result of these practices, partly through flight, and partly as a result of the malnutrition and disease that followed.[11]

Although Leopold's abuses were considered extravagant even by European standards, the impacts of colonialism were similar, regardless of the specific colonizer: disease; destruction of indigenous social, political, and economic structures; repression; exploitation; land displacement; and land degradation.

In addition to the outrageous abuses of native peoples, colonialism's legacy included the creation of "artificial states" that have since had great difficulty becoming economically self-sufficient. Several factors have contributed to their struggles. Infrastructure within these states, such as roads, rail, and other communication lines, were designed with resource extraction in mind. For example, rail lines usually did not connect cities, but rather ran from a mine to a port, facilitating the exportation of resources out of the country rather than commerce within it. Additionally, many colonized lands were turned into mono-crop, export-driven economies. Farm land once used for food production was used to grow luxury items or non-edible items for export, including, for example, groundnuts, cocoa, cotton, coffee, and sugar. Other key exports included minerals, gold, and rubber. Upon independence, these new countries struggled to convert their economies to the production of more practical items, such as foodstuffs, with which they could feed their own people.

Politically, these states were also negatively impacted by their colonial experience. Under colonialism, native peoples were excluded from government and often from any position of authority, expected only to follow orders. As a result, upon independence, there were few, if any, native people with experience in administering the machinery of a nation-state. Ewans points out, for example, that in the Congo:

> There were no Africans in the senior judiciary and not a single army officer, while in the senior administrative ranks, out of a total of nearly 5,000, the numbers of Africans barely ran into double figures. There were no experienced political leaders, no educated citizenry, no indigenous administrators, no professional, commercial or military elite, no established middle class with a stake in the stability and well-being of the country.[12]

In addition to these problems, most newly independent countries faced cross-border conflicts, unstable governments, and heightened ethnic, religious, and social conflict as a result of illogical borders that dissected ethnic groups. These borders had been demarcated by Europeans in their struggles to establish their empires.

Neo-colonialism

Neo-colonialism is another factor contributing to the struggles of former colonies to establish themselves as successful independent states. Neo-colonialism refers to

Cold War Refers to the ideological stand-off between two superpowers, the United States and the Soviet Union, from 1945 to 1989. While not directly fighting one another, each side sought to expand its influence by keeping the other from spreading its form of government and political system, resulting in many proxy wars throughout the world.

the involvement of more powerful states in the domestic affairs of less powerful ones. For example, although ostensibly independent, former colonies were used as pawns in the *Cold War* between the West and the Soviet Union. During the Cold War, the US and its Western European allies and the Soviet Union and its allies intervened in many of these newly independent countries in an attempt to secure their allegiance. Corrupt leaders such as Mobutu Sese Seko of Zaire and Mengistu Haile Mariam of Ethiopia[13] were propped up with military assistance and international aid because each had pledged its allegiance to one side or the other. Weapons poured into these countries, with the vast majority being used internally to suppress civilian populations. Profits earned from the rich resources available in many of these countries were hidden in overseas bank accounts by corrupt indigenous leaders. These leaders used their positions in government to make themselves and their cronies rich rather than to appropriately manage their states. Many of these leaders also borrowed heavily from international financial institutions, creating a legacy of enormous debt that has further crippled these countries' ability to be truly independent.

The Nation-state's Challenges and Competitors

Internal challenges

migration Human movement from one location to another.

Although the term "nation-state" suggests a homogenous culture living within a geopolitical border, the reality is that both the presence of ethnic minorities and increasing global *migration* flows disrupt the implied unity of the nation-state. So while we may equate Russia, for example, with the Russian language and Russian culture, it is, like most states, home to people from various ethnic, cultural, and linguistic backgrounds. Religious, ethnic, linguistic, regional, and socioeconomic differences within a country are not always divisive, but they can sometimes lead to conflict. From Northern Ireland with its Catholic and Protestant split to India where Muslims and Hindus have struggled over control of the Indian province of Kashmir, to the Sudan where Muslims and Christians struggle to coexist, religious cleavages have led to violent clashes around the globe. In extreme circumstances, these conflicts can undermine the viability of the nation-state. Some of the most egregious examples of this occurred in the latter half of the twentieth century. In Rwanda, in 1994, a Hutu-led genocide left almost one million Rwandans, primarily Tutsis, dead. Similarly, Guatemala's native Mayan population has been the victim of ethnically motivated violence for centuries, but the late twentieth century saw a dramatic increase in the number of Mayans who died at the hands of the government, whose leaders are mainly of European descent.[14]

Another internal threat to the nation-state is *ethno-nationalism*. Ethno-nationalism is characterized by an extreme attachment to ethnicity, a belief that only ancestry gives one the right to belong to a particular group, and a desire to establish independent nation-states based solely on ethnicity. This was the driving factor in the Balkan conflict, where Serb nationalism conflicted with Croat and Bosnian nationalism. Violence between these groups led to the dissolution of Yugoslavia into six new nation-states: Bosnia-Herzegovina, Croatia, Macedonia, Montenegro, Serbia, and Slovenia. In 2008, Albanian-dominated Kosovo declared independence from Serbia, further fragmenting the territory that once was Yugoslavia. This impulse to secede from existing nation-states in order to form new ones based on ethnicity is not unique to the Balkans. Calls for secession are affecting areas as diverse as Russia, Canada, India, Iraq, Belgium, Rwanda, and the United Kingdom.[15]

> **ethno-nationalism** Characterized by an extreme attachment to ethnicity, a belief that only ancestry gives one the right to belong to a particular group, and a desire to establish independent nation-states based solely on ethnicity.

At the same time that many nation-states are fragmenting along ethnic and religious lines, global migration patterns are further complicating the implied unity of the nation-state. According to the United Nations: "It is estimated that the number of migrants crossing international borders has grown steadily over the past four decades to an estimated 175 million in 2000. One out of every 35 persons is an international migrant."[16] By 2005, the total number of international *migrants* had grown to 191 million. Migrants make up roughly 3 percent of the global population.[17] While migration is not a new phenomenon, increased access to information, expanded communication mechanisms, and well-developed transportation linkages have combined with changing demographics to dramatically increase the number of people migrating. The changing demographics that are affecting migration patterns include the developed world's slower population growth rate, which has resulted in a smaller and older population. In contrast, developing countries have seen a rapid increase in population growth – almost six times as fast as the developed world. According to the UN: "Rapid population growth combined with economic difficulties push people to move out of their habitat, and a declining and ageing population pressures countries to accept migrants."[18]

> **migrants** People who have left their homes in order to settle in another country or city.

Migrants often struggle to be accepted in their new homes as cultural differences and economic competition are perceived as a threat by local residents. For example, Europe has experienced a large growth in the number of migrants coming from Muslim countries in the past decade; roughly half a million migrants come to Europe each year from Muslim countries.[19] Religious and cultural differences between the Muslim migrants and Europeans have caused tensions and sometimes have led to violence. In France, for example, in 2005, and again in 2007, youths rioted in and around Paris, demanding better educational and job opportunities. Many of the protesters were Muslims who felt that French society was characterized by widespread anti-Muslim discrimination. In Denmark, the publication of cartoons depicting the Muslim prophet in a way that many people felt was derogatory sparked violence across the country, and the globe. These kinds of clashes are not limited

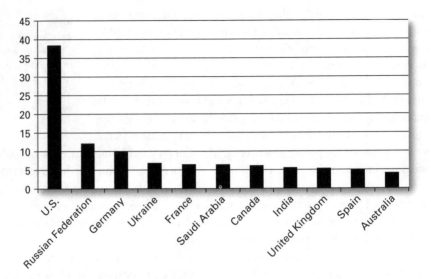

Figure 2.1   Countries that Received the Most Migrants in 2005.[20] Numbers are in millions.
Note: The top three countries sending migrants are: China (35 million), India (20 million), and the Philippines (7 million).

to Europe. In 2008, in South Africa, waves of anti-immigrant violence swept through the country leaving 50 dead and more than 40,000 displaced.[21] Many other countries have experienced clashes between migrants and residents and states are struggling to find ways to prevent these tensions from growing and potentially undermining the state's ability to maintain law and order.

External challenges

International governmental organizations

international governmental organization (IGO)   International organizations that nation-states join for specific purposes, such as promoting peace, enhancing trade, and encouraging cooperation.

In addition to internal challenges facing nation-states, their supremacy as actors in the international arena is being challenged by a variety of non-state actors, including *international governmental organizations* (IGO). IGOs are international organizations that nation-states join for specific purposes, such as promoting peace, enhancing trade, and encouraging cooperation. Although nation-states secure benefits from their membership in IGOs, these organizations can pose challenges to nation-states because members are required to modify their behavior in accordance with the IGOs' goals. Generally, nation-states accept this compromise because the perceived benefits of membership outweigh the loss of some degree of sovereignty. However, increasingly IGOs are gaining more power, punishing members that violate the organization's rules. This causes anxiety for the nation-states that find themselves the targets of such actions. For example, the World Trade Organization (WTO) has the power to declare a member's trade policy to be in violation of the terms of membership and to impose sanctions upon members that fail to comply with WTO decisions. When the US imposed tariffs on imported steel to protect the US steel industry, the WTO ruled in 2003 that this would violate global trade rules. As a result, the US removed the tariffs. Another IGO, established in 2002, that is challenging traditional notions of nation-state sovereignty is the International Criminal Court (ICC). The ICC was designed to adjudicate matters once thought to be the sole jurisdiction of the nation-state: the behavior of heads of states, their officials, and other individuals. Specifically, the ICC tries state officials for crimes such as genocide, crimes against humanity, and war crimes. This permanent court marks a significant shift, as nation-states have agreed to allow an outside court to render judgment on the actions of their officials. As nation-states continue to join IGOs, they have to confront the fact that these organizations, once begun, may acquire more duties, responsibilities, and powers. The history, structure, and purpose of various international organizations are discussed in more detail in chapter 3.

Non-governmental organizations

Even as IGOs expand their power and influence, another external non-state actor has moved in to fulfill duties once typically associated with the nation-state: the *non-governmental organization* (NGO). NGOs are organizations made up of private individuals from any number of nation-states. There are thousands of NGOs operating in the international arena, and increasingly, they

non-governmental organizations (NGOs) A legally constructed organization made up of individuals. These have a limited, if any, role for nation-states.

are taking on many of the services and functions once thought to be the exclusive purview of the nation-state. For example, NGOs are assisting people around the world with food aid, health care, infrastructure development, security, education, economic opportunities, shelter, legal services, and technical assistance for environmental and energy needs. In other words, when nation-states are unable or unwilling to provide important services, NGOs often respond or form to meet those needs. While these organizations may successfully meet people's needs, they may also inadvertently undermine existing governments. When citizens transfer their expectations for basic services from nation-states to NGOs, they also often begin to question the purpose and legitimacy of their governments, in some cases ceasing to support them altogether. One common way of registering dissatisfaction with an existing government is refusing to pay taxes. This lack of tax revenue compounds the problems facing poor governments, further impeding their ability to provide basic services and creating more of a perceived need for NGO assistance. In some countries, NGOs have become so powerful that their activities are seen as a new form of colonialism. Specifically, critics worry that unelected outsiders are exerting undue influence over the political, social, cultural, and/or economic affairs within various nation-states.[22]

Multinational corporations (MNCs)

Another external challenge to nation-states is the *multinational corporation* (MNC). MNCs are private companies that conduct

multinational corporations (MNCs) A corporation or enterprise that manages production or delivers services in more than one country.

business (or have business interests) in more than one country. Their growth has been significant – in 1969 there were roughly 7,000 and in 2003 there were more than 63,000 with more than 800,000 foreign affiliates.[23] MNCs are powerful because of the amount of money involved in their operations as well as their integral role in providing essential state services. Their financial power is demonstrated by the fact that MNCs account for 51 of the world's 100 largest economies, with the economies of countries making up the remaining 49 (see table 2.1). Additionally, governments are increasingly relying on MNCs to provide basic services to their citizens. Many governments have privatized such services as transportation, mining, resource extraction, access to water, and even security.

Table 2.1   The World's 100 Largest Economies (2000)[24]

Rank	Country/Corporation	GDP/Sales (US$million)
1	United States	8,708,870.00
2	Japan	4,395,083.00
3	Germany	2,081,202.00
4	France	1,410,262.00
5	United Kingdom	1,373,612.00
6	Italy	1,149,958.00
7	China	1,149,814.00
8	Brazil	760,345.00
9	Canada	612,049.00
10	Spain	562,245.00
23	*General Motors*	176,558.00
24	Denmark	174,363.00
25	*Wal-Mart*	166,809.00
26	*Exxon Mobil*	163,881.00
27	*Ford Motor*	162,558.00
28	*DaimlerChrysler*	159,985.70
37	*Mitsui*	118,555.20
38	*Mitsubishi*	117,765.60
39	*Toyota Motor*	115,670.90
40	*General Electric*	111,630.00
41	*Itochu*	109,068.90
43	*Royal Dutch/Shell*	105,366.00
47	*Sumitomo*	95,701.60
48	*Nippon Tel & Tel*	93,591.70
50	*Marubeni*	91,807.40
52	*AXA*	87,645.70
53	*IBM*	87,548.00
56	*BP Amoco*	83,556.00
57	*Citigroup*	82,005.00
58	*Volkswagen*	80,072.70
59	*Nippon Life Insurance*	78,515.10
61	*Siemens*	75,337.00
63	*Allianz*	74,178.20
64	*Hitachi*	71,858.50
66	*Matsushita Electric Ind.*	65,555.60

Table 2.1 *(cont'd)*

Rank	Country/Corporation	GDP/Sales (US$million)
67	*Nissho Iwai*	65,393.20
68	*ING Group*	62,492.40
69	*AT&T*	62,391.00
70	*Philip Morris*	61,751.00
71	*Sony*	60,052.70
73	*Deutsche Bank*	58,585.10
74	*Boeing*	57,993.00
77	*Dai-Ichi Mutual Life Ins.*	55,104.70
78	*Honda Motor*	54,773.50
79	*Assicurazioni Generali*	53,723.20
80	*Nissan Motor*	53,679.90
82	*E.On*	52,227.70
83	*Toshiba*	51,634.90
84	*Bank of America*	51,392.00
85	*Fiat*	51,331.70
86	*Nestle*	49,694.10
87	*SBC Communications*	49,489.00
88	*Credit Suisse*	49,362.00
90	*Hewlett-Packard*	48,253.00
91	*Fujitsu*	47,195.90
93	*Metro*	46,663.60
94	*Sumitomo Life Insur.*	46,445.10
96	*Tokyo Electric Power*	45,727.70
97	*Kroger*	45,351.60
98	*Total Fina Elf*	44,990.30
99	*NEC*	44,828.00
100	*State Farm Insurance*	44,637.20

Because of the wealth, reach, ability to move from country to country, and the role they often play in nation-state and global policy, MNCs can be very controversial. On the positive side, they bring jobs into a community, make products available for consumers, and bring investment opportunities for local people with capital. They can also be a catalyst for positive change by using their considerable power to put pressure on governments to improve their human rights record. For example, responding to demands of NGOs and citizen activists around the globe, many MNCs pulled their businesses out of South Africa in the 1980s because of its *apartheid* policies. However, this type of "activism" by MNCs is still rare and usually only occurs when outside pressure is applied to the MNC.

apartheid A system of racial segregation in South Africa. From 1948 to 1994, citizens were divided into the following groups: Blacks, Coloureds, Whites, and Indians. This distinction determined access to all services and accommodations. All groups except Whites were denied their civil and political rights. Whites who questioned the system also had their rights violated.

The power to influence governments can have a negative side as well. MNCs have used their considerable power to put pressure on governments not to enforce workers' rights or safety laws. By threatening to close down their operations and to move elsewhere, MNCs have successfully convinced countries to decrease their labor standards. Although each state sets up the rules for how companies will operate while in their country, developing countries are often desperate for the jobs and the money an MNC can potentially bring. MNCs thus have the upper hand in negotiating trade agreements, which often pit developing countries against each other in "a race to the bottom." Poor countries want to attract corporations that will create jobs for their citizens, while corporations want to lower costs and increase their profits. MNCs are therefore attracted to countries that "set the lowest wage levels, the lowest environmental standards, [and] the lowest consumer safety standards."[25]

Also, developing countries are often pressured by international financial institutions, such as the World Bank and the International Monetary Fund, to privatize their state-owned industries. When they do so, they frequently find that wealthy MNCs, rather than local businesses, purchase these industries. After the MNCs take over, it is not unusual for them to replace local middle managers with foreign managers. Some MNCs then treat the local population as solely a source of cheap labor, failing to provide them with the opportunity to advance up the corporate ladder. MNCs also demand tax breaks, which works to shrink the tax base of the developing country's government, thus putting a greater tax burden on the local population. Rather than developing the economies of these countries, then, the policies of MNCs can sometimes devastate them further.

Several examples serve to illustrate the power of MNCs. Shell Petroleum Development Company of Nigeria (SPDC) has wielded enormous influence over the notoriously corrupt Nigerian government.[26] Operating for more than 60 years in Nigeria, SPDC produces more than one half of all Nigeria's oil and, as such, is responsible for generating much of the wealth upon which the state depends. In short, this makes the Nigerian government vulnerable to SPDC's demands. SPDC, in turn, has been criticized by various human rights groups for its unwillingness to withdraw its support from Nigeria's various dictators. SPDC critics argue that SPDC supports corrupt regimes because it benefits from the relationship in a variety of unethical ways. For example, oil production in the impoverished Ogoni region of Nigeria has caused a great deal of environmental damage, which in turn has generated local protests. In the 1990s these protests, and the excessive military and police response to them, began to draw international attention. A 1998 UN report found that the government of Nigeria had "put at SPDC's disposal a mobile police force to suppress protests and demonstrations."[27] Prominent among the protesters was Ken Saro Wiwa who, along with several other human rights activists, was arrested and executed by the Nigerian government in 1995. Shell was not directly responsible for the executions, but Nigerian dependence upon oil revenue contributed to the government's decision to attempt to eliminate those whom they believed posed a threat to its relationship with Shell.

Perhaps one of the most interesting developments in the world of MNCs is the expanding role they are playing in defending nation-states. Increasingly, they are branching into areas that have traditionally been the purview of states, including security and military support. Some developing countries have already hired security firms to assist with military training or to act as a *mercenary* force. For example, in 1995 a private security company known as Executive Outcomes stepped into a brutal civil war in Sierra Leone and gained control of a large section of the

> **mercenary** A private citizen who is paid by a political entity to provide armed support.

country, including its diamond fields. The company then used its position to ensure access to the region for another company, Branch Energy, to begin extracting the diamonds. The US has also become reliant upon private security firms to carry out traditional military duties in its wars in both Iraq and Afghanistan as well as to assist with disaster relief. One of the problems with relying on private companies to carry out military and other duties that were once the purview of the state is that traditional government oversight is lacking. Critics of these organizations express concern that these private security companies are operating outside any state or international law. Thus, when accusations of abuse are made against these firms, it is unclear under what legal authority they can be held responsible.

In Focus: Terrorists

Since the 2001 9/11 terrorist attacks in the US, one of the organizations most commonly associated with terrorism is al-Qaeda. Al-Qaeda is a non-state actor led by Saudi-born Osama bin Laden. While the organization has targeted primarily Western interests, their attacks have occurred across the globe, including in Kenya, Tunisia, Indonesia, Tanzania, Saudi Arabia, Morocco, Turkey, Yemen, Iraq, and Spain. Osama bin Laden has provided different reasons why his organization has targeted Western interests, including the presence of US troops in Saudi Arabia, the home of Mecca, Islam's most sacred site. He has also publicly stated that his attacks on the US in particular are motivated by US support for the state of Israel, which he views as a Western creation in the heart of the Muslim world. For bin Laden, the victims of this Western creation were the Palestinians, whose lands were taken away or occupied by non-Muslims. However, his critics argue that his motivation is less about defending Islam or the Palestinians and more about a megalomaniacal desire for power. Regardless of the motives, al-Qaeda's actions have killed thousands and prompted the US to call for a global war on terrorism. But just what is "terrorism?"

Although definitions of the term "terrorism" are multiple and highly contested, there are some common elements in many of them. For example, most definitions refer to acts of political violence designed to threaten and terrorize civilian popu-lations. That being said, defining what constitutes a "civilian" can also be problematic. Giving aid or support to a military or guerilla organization, willingly or otherwise, is seen by some as having crossed over from civilian to combatant status. What we do know about terrorism is that it has been around for generations and it is often used by those who are fighting an enemy that is larger, more powerful, and has access to more resources. It is a tactic and not an ideology. Sometimes, a specific outcome is desired – hijacking planes to secure release of prisoners, for example – while at other times the actions serve no broader purpose then to instill fear or exact revenge.

One significant difference between the various definitions of the term is the role of the state. Because states dominate the international arena and are often the targets of terror attacks, it is in their best interest to define terrorists as non-state actors. However, there are times when states sponsor acts of terror via targeted transmissions of intelligence or more tangible financial and military resources. States often couch these actions in terms of self-defense. For example, many states choose to try to silence opposition to their governments by targeting dissidents, both at home and abroad, with violence. Argentina "disappeared" more than 9,000 of its citizens during its "dirty war"(1976–83), and Chile, under Augusto Pinochet, disappeared more than 3,000 people. In both Argentina and Chile, the states argued their actions were done to protect the state from "dangerous" elements. Critics of both governments referred to these tactics as terrorism. During the apartheid era in South Africa, anyone who opposed apartheid was by definition a "terrorist." The government, arguing self-defense, routinely rounded up citizens for arrest, detention, and torture, choosing middle-of-the-night raids by the police in order to exact the maximum amount of fear. At the same time, the South African government sponsored (with weapons and intelligence) members of one ethnic group, the Zulus, to incite black on black violence. The South African government also sent letter bombs to dissidents living abroad, killing and maiming dozens. Likewise, in actions many termed terrorist, the US, during the 1980s, financially and militarily supported a group of fighters called the Contras that was trying to overthrow the government of Nicaragua. The Contras routinely invaded Nicaragua from their bases along its border, blowing up government buildings and intimidating and killing the local population. The US Reagan administration called the Contras "freedom fighters" and claimed they were defending the hemisphere from the spread of Marxist Leninism. In contrast, many Nicaraguans called the Contras terrorists.

Other targets of state-sponsored terror include NGOs, particularly those contesting a government's policy. In 1985, French operatives, using scuba gear, entered Auckland, New Zealand's harbor, and planted a bomb on a Greenpeace ship. Greenpeace is an environmental NGO. Their ship, the *Rainbow Warrior*, had been used to try to prevent France from conducting nuclear tests in the South Pacific. When the bomb detonated, the ship sank and one person was killed.

Because of the dominant position of states in the international arena, most definitions of terrorism continue to refer to the actions of "non-state actors." Still, when a state supports acts of terror against another state, particularly if the targeted state is a powerful state in the international community, it may be seen as a "rogue" state and suffer the consequences. After the 1988 bombing of a Pan Am flight over Lockerbie in Scotland, US and British intelligence linked the bombing to Libya. Libya was labeled a "rogue" state and the United Nations imposed *sanctions* upon it. After years of refusing to turn over suspects to an international tribunal, Libya finally

sanctions Typically refers to economic restrictions, or embargos, placed on a nation-state.

gave in to the demands of the international community and turned over the two suspects. This action allowed Libya to "re-enter" the international community and sanctions were lifted. Controversy erupted again in 2009 when the Scottish Justice Minister, Kenny MacAskill, ordered the release of Ali al-Megrahi, one of the Lockerbie bombers. The release was granted on compassionate grounds because al-Megrahi was diagnosed with terminal prostate cancer. Despite assurances by the Libyan government that his return would be "low-key and sensitive," al-Megrahi received a hero's welcome in Libya.[28]

Non-state terrorism poses many threats to the nation-state. For example, many nation-states are concerned about the possibility of terrorists obtaining weapons of mass destruction and quite literally destroying their states. Other threats posed by terrorists include criminal activities that destabilize states. For example, al-Qaeda was involved in the illegal diamond trading that contributed to the destabilization of the Western African nations of Sierra Leone and Liberia. Al-Qaeda operatives sold weapons to local guerillas in exchange for diamonds. This proliferation of weapons led to lawlessness, mass violence, and the emergence of competing rebel groups that outnumbered and outgunned government forces. As a result, both the Sierra Leonean and Liberian governments fell. Terrorists also pose a particular threat to weak nation-states that have limited control over their territories. Terrorists target these nation-states as prime places to establish training camps. These nation-states then become the targets of more powerful nation-states that attack them for harboring terrorists.

Organized crime

Another external threat to the nation-state is organized crime. While most people associate organized crime with the Italian or Sicilian mafia, there are others, including the Colombian Medellín drug cartel and the Russian mafia, whose activities threaten nation-states. These organizations differ from terrorists in that their goal is attaining money and power; they are not typically motivated by politics or a cause. They are often involved in the drug trade, which generates roughly US$100–500 billion a year. The effect these wealthy organizations can have on a state is often similar to terrorism, however, because organized crime relies on violence to further its ends. The success of these organizations often depends upon their ability to infiltrate and undermine the power and legitimacy of the state. For example, in Colombia, which has been at the center of the drug war for more than two decades, drug lords undermined the political institutions of the state. The three different drug cartels operating in Colombia, the Medellín cartel, the Cali cartel, and the Atlantic Coast cartel, have assassinated attorney-generals, justice ministers, and media personalities and bribed or intimidated other government officials into silence.[29] As a result, according to Latin American experts Kline and Gray, "the drug economy corrupts every aspect of the nation's institutions, undermines government control over monetary policy, exerts inflationary pressures, and prevents the rational allocation of financial resources and entrepreneurial energies."[30] Guerrillas and paramilitary groups that depend upon the drug trade also operate in Colombia.

These guerrillas are seeking to overthrow the Colombian government and use the drugs to trade for weapons. The state has had a difficult time maintaining any control over its territory and many of the institutions of the state are completely ineffectual.

Organized crime is also involved in the exchange of a variety of other commodities, including small arms and weapons of mass destruction. Nation-states are particularly concerned about the trade in biological, chemical, and nuclear weapons. One well-known arms trafficker who has been linked to conflicts from Africa, to Iraq, to Indonesia is Victor Bout, nicknamed the "Merchant of Death." A former Russian military officer, Bout is linked to arms sales to various groups, including the Taliban and al-Qaeda. The weapons Bout supplied have fueled dozens of violent conflicts and led to the destabilization of several nation-states.

Failed/marginal states

When states are unable to deal successfully with the various internal and external threats they face, they sometimes become what international relations scholars refer to as "failed states." Failed states can in turn pose a threat to surrounding states. The journal *Foreign Policy* and the Fund for Peace's "2007 Failed State Index" defines a failed state as one that has lost "physical control of its territory or a monopoly on the legitimate use of force . . . [and has experienced] erosion of legitimate authority to make collective decisions, an inability to provide reasonable public services, and the inability to interact with other states as a full member of the international community."[31] Additionally, some nation-states can be classified as "marginal" because they are on the verge of failing. John McCormick, a scholar of comparative politics, describes marginal states as those that are "the most politically unstable, the poorest, the least successful at meeting the basic needs of their people, and the furthest from achieving workable state systems."[32] In assessing the viability of states, the Index of Failed States looks at a variety of risk elements, "such as extensive corruption and criminal behavior, inability to collect taxes or otherwise draw on citizen support, large-scale involuntary dislocation of the population, sharp economic decline, group-based inequality, institutionalized persecution or discrimination, severe demographic pressures, brain drain, and environmental decay."[33] The 2007 index lists 60 countries as being in danger of falling apart. This suggests that a staggering 30 percent of the countries in the world are struggling to function.

Marginal and failing states are a concern because their instability can spill over to other states. The inability of a state to control its own territory creates a vacuum in which terrorists and other criminal elements can thrive. The general lawlessness can lead to devastation for the citizens of that state. Often these citizens have little recourse but to flee to neighboring states in order to survive. The conflict these refugees are fleeing from then often follows them across the border, thereby spreading conflict to other areas. For example, in 1994 following the genocide, many Hutu Rwandans fled to Zaire (now the Democratic Republic of the Congo) as the Tutsi-led military began to take control of the country. These refugees went to the very same camps that housed the surviving Tutsis who had escaped the Hutu-led genocide. The Rwandan Tutsi-dominated armed forces crossed into Zaire in pursuit of Hutus, some of whom were continuing their genocidal rampage in the camps. Battles between the Hutus and the Tutsi military in Zaire drew Zairians into the conflict. The violence spread across the country and ultimately led to the overthrow of the Zairian president Mubuto Sese-Seko. As the violence escalated, various other African nations intervened, leading to what has been called "Africa's Great War."

Conclusion

The nation-state system emerged in seventeenth-century Europe with the Peace of Westphalia in 1648. The historic peace marked the first time that many European leaders came together and recognized one another's territorial sovereignty. Colonialism contributed to the spread of the nation-state system from Europe to the rest of the world. Today, the nation-state system is the dominant social, political, and economic system on the planet. However, the contemporary nation-state faces a variety of challenges that have begun to erode its primacy. These challenges present opportunities for states, NGOs, IOs, and various other groups to work together, but they also serve to highlight the limitations of the Westphalian system.

Notes

1 This is an excerpt from the keynote lecture given at the Mises Institute conference, posted on the institute's website (October 16, 2000), www.mises.org/story/527.

2 Joseph Campbell, *The Power of Myth* (New York: Doubleday, 1988).

3 Richard Falk, "World Prisms," *Harvard International Review* 21, no. 3 (Summer 1999), 30–6.

4 Richard J. Payne and Jamal R. Nassar, *Politics and Culture in the Developing World: The Impact of Globalization*, 2nd edn. (New York: Pearson Longman, 2006), 8.

5 Paul R. Viotti and Mark V. Kauppi, *International Relations and World Politics, Security, Economy, Identity* (Upper Saddle River, NJ: Prentice Hall, 1997), 62.

6 Stephen E. Lahey, *Philosophy and Politics in the Thought of John Wyclif* (Cambridge: Cambridge University Press, 2003).

7 Michael G. Roskin and Nicholas O. Berry, *IR The New World of International Relations*, 6th edn.

(Upper Saddle River, NJ: Pearson Prentice Hall, 2005), 7.

8 David Stannard, *American Holocaust: The Conquest of the New World* (Oxford: Oxford University Press, 1992).

9 Ibid.

10 Cynthia Enloe, *Bananas, Beaches and Bases: Making Feminist Sense of International Politics* (Berkeley, CA: University of California Press, 1990).

11 Martin Ewans, "Belgium and the Colonial Experience," *Journal of Contemporary European Studies* 11, no. 2 (November 2003), 168–9.

12 Ibid., 173.

13 Both Mobutu Sese Seko of Zaire and Mengistu Haile Mariam of Ethiopia are infamous for their brutal regimes and terrible human rights records. Sese Seko ruled Zaire from 1965 to 1997. His regime was notoriously corrupt and he is believed to have stolen more than $5 billion from the country. Mengistu Haile Mariam ruled Ethiopia from 1977 until 1991 when a coalition of rebel groups overthrew

his regime. He instituted policies that led to a massive famine and denied food aid to areas he felt supported the rebel groups. More than 7 million Ethiopians were on the verge of starvation during the 1984–5 famine. He instituted forced relocation programs designed to move people from areas sympathetic to rebels, to more remote areas.

14   Stannard, *American Holocaust*.

15   Walker Connor, *Ethnonationalism: The Quest for Understanding* (Princeton, NJ: Princeton University Press, 1993).

16   International Organization for Migration, "Migration," Office of the United Nations High Commissioner for Human Rights, www.iom.int/jahia/Jahia/pid/3.

17   Ibid.

18   Ibid.

19   "An Islamic Journey Inside Europe," National Public Radio (February 24–28, 2003), www.npr.org/programs/atc/features/2003/feb/europe_muslims/.

20   Source: www.un.org/esa/population/publications/migration/UN_Migrant_Stock_Documentation_2005.pdf.

21   "Rising Violence Pushes Immigrants to Flee South Africa," www.pbs.org/newshour/bb/africa/jan-june08/saviolence_05-29.html. Originally aired May 28, 2009.

22   See for example, Rotimi Sankore, "What are the NGOs Doing?" *New African* 443 (August/September 2005), 12–15. For a counter-argument, see Sat Obiyan, "A Critical Examination of the State versus Non-Governmental Organizations (NGOs) in the Policy Sphere in the Global South: Will the State Die as the NGOs Thrive in Sub-Saharan Africa and Asia?" *African & Asian Studies* 4, no. 3 (2005), 301–25.

23   Richard A. Love and Maryann Cusimano Love, "Multinational Corporations Power and Responsibility," in *Beyond Sovereignty Issues for a Global Agenda*, 2nd edn., ed. Maryann Cusimano Love (Belmont, CA: Thomson Wadsworth, 2003), 98–9.

24   Source: Sarah Anderson and John Cavanagh, "Report on the Top 200 Corporations," Institute for Policy Studies, www.corporations.org/system/top100.html.

25   Ralph Nader, "Introduction: Free Trade and the Decline of Democracy," in *The Case Against Free Trade: GATT, NAFTA, and the Globalization of Corporate Power* (San Francisco, CA: Earth Island Press, 1993), 6.

26   "Shell Admits Fuelling Corruption," BBC (June 11, 2004), http://news.bbc.co.uk/2/hi/business/3796375.stm.

27   United Nations High Commissioner for Human Rights, 1997, "Question of the Violation of Human Rights and Fundamental Freedoms in Any Part of the World, with Particular Reference to Colonial and Other Dependent Countries and Territories: Situation of Human Rights in Nigeria, Report submitted by the Special Rapporteur of the Commission on Human Rights, Mr Soli Jehangir Sorabjee, pursuant to Commission resolution 1997/53," www.unhchr.ch/Huridocda/Huridoca.nsf/0/a55c3d667425f3cfc125660f004afbcf?Opendocument.

28   "Minister Stands by Bomber Release" BBC, August 24, 2009, http://news.bbc.co.uk/2/hi/uk_news/scotland/8216897.stm.

29   Harvey F. Kline and Vanessa Gray, "Colombia: Drugs, Guerrillas, Death Squads, and U.S. Aid," in Howard J. Wiarda and Harvey F. Kline (eds.), *Latin American Politics and Development* (Boulder, CO: Westview Press, 2000), 198–227.

30   Ibid., 224.

31   Foreign Policy and the Fund for Peace, "The Failed State Index" (July/August 2007). For more information on the Index, go to: www.foreignpolicy.com/story/cms.php?story_id=3865.

32   John McCormick, *Comparative Politics in Transition*, 5th edn. (Belmont, CA: Thomson Wadsworth, 2007), 485.

33   Foreign Policy and the Fund for Peace, "The Failed State Index," July/August 2007.

3

INTERNATIONAL ORGANIZATIONS

"A general association of nations must be formed under specific covenants for the purpose of affording mutual guarantees of political independence and territorial integrity to great and small states alike." (Point 14 of US President Woodrow Wilson's 14 points speech delivered to the United States Congress on January 8, 1918)[1]

"More than ever before in human history, we share a common destiny. We can master it only if we face it together. And that, my friends, is why we have the United Nations." (Kofi Annan's UN Millennium Speech 1999)[2]

"I am also here today as a representative of the millions of people across the globe, the anti-apartheid movement, the governments and organisations that joined with us, not to fight against South Africa as a country or any of its peoples, but to oppose an inhuman system and sue for a speedy end to the apartheid crime against humanity.

"These countless human beings, both inside and outside our country, had the nobility of spirit to stand in the path of tyranny and injustice, without seeking selfish gain. They recognised that an injury to one is an injury to all and therefore acted together in defence of justice and a common human decency.

"Because of their courage and persistence for many years, we can, today, even set the dates when all humanity will join together to celebrate one of the outstanding human victories of our century." (Nelson Mandela accepting the Nobel Peace Prize in 1993)[3]

Learning to Question, Questioning to Learn

- How do intergovernmental organizations (IGOs) differ from non-governmental organizations (NGOs)?
- Why was the United Nations formed and what are some of its strengths and weaknesses?
- Why are nation-states sometimes willing to compromise their sovereignty in order to gain or maintain membership in international and/or regional organizations?
- Why are NGOs increasingly performing activities once thought to be the purview of nation-states?

Introduction

Since the end of World War II, international organizations (IOs) have grown in both number and influence, becoming an increasingly powerful force in the international arena. IOs can be divided into two broad categories: intergovernmental organizations (IGOs) and non-governmental organizations (NGOs). This chapter describes the historical development of various IGOs and the political, economic, social, and cultural roles they play. Specific attention is given to the development of the United Nations (UN), one of the most prominent IGOs. The chapter concludes with a discussion of NGOs, highlighting their types, roles, activities, and challenges.

Intergovernmental Organizations (IGOs)

intergovernmental organizations (IOs) Organizations made up of nation-states.

nation-state A type of state that provides sovereign territory for a particular culture or ethnic group. However, it is also frequently used interchangeably with the terms "state" and "country."

treaty A legally binding agreement between two or more states, sovereigns, or international organizations.

organs Agencies within organizations that perform specific functions.

adjudication Settling a dispute through a formal structure such as a court room.

An *intergovernmental organization*, sometimes also referred to as an international governmental organization and both abbreviated as IGO, consists of three or more *nation-states* that have signed a *treaty* legally establishing the organization and specifying its purposes. In addition to the founding treaty, most IGOs also have a variety of *organs* that are designed to help the organization achieve its purposes. Specifically, IGOs typically have a deliberative body, which discusses policy; an executive organ, which makes policy decisions; an administrative organ, which implements policy; and a variety of specialized agencies. In addition to these typical IGO organs, many IGOs have some mechanism for the *adjudication* of conflicts and disagreements that arise among members.

The development of IGOs

IGOs emerged relatively recently in the international area. In 1900, for example, there were only a few dozen; by 2008, that number had increased to more than 300 formal IGOs.[4] Like nation-states, IGOs have their roots in Europe. One of the first IGOs was the Commission for the Navigation of the Rhine (1831), whose purpose was to facilitate cooperation between the various countries that used the Rhine River for commerce. Because of the success of this Commission, the establishment of other IGOs quickly followed, including the Danube River Commission (1856), the International Telegraph Union (now the International Telecommunications Union, 1865), and the General Postal Union, (now called the Universal Postal Union [UPU], 1874). Each of these IGOs was designed to set standards and rules in order to facilitate communication and commerce as well as to decrease the chances of conflict. Because these organizations were effective at reducing conflicts, nation-states began to explore the

Researching to Learn *Investigating International Organizations Online*

United Nations(UN)

The UN website provides extensive statistics on economic, social, environmental, political, and demographic data. Information on the various organs of the UN can be found here as can a collection of international treaties.
www.un.org/

African Union (AU)

The AU website provides detailed information about the organization, its structure, and its recent activities. Additionally, it provides information on the latest news and events relevant to both the organization and the continent.
www.africa-union.org/

African Development Bank

The website for the African Development Bank provides information on the various projects supported by the bank as well as a database containing documents about economic activity and development projects in Africa.
www.afdb.org/

Asian Development Bank

Like its African counterpart, this website provides detailed economic information about Asia and the Pacific, including a list of publications relevant to Asian development.
www.adb.org/

The Commonwealth

A group of 53 independent nation-states, most of which were former colonies of Britain, that seek to promote democracy, human rights, and good governance. The website provides detailed information on the organization's activities.
www.thecommonwealth.org

European Union (EU)

The site provides detailed information on the purpose, structure, and agencies that comprise the EU. A database of information on member nations and organization activities can also be found here.
www.europa.eu.int/index-en.htm

G8 (Group of 8)

Made up of the wealthy nations of the world, the G8 seeks to set global economic policy. Its website contains information on the organization's history, purpose, initiatives, and structure.
www.g7.utoronto.ca/

International Criminal Police Organization (INTERPOL)

With 186 members, this is the world's largest police organization. The website provides information about the organization's structure, purpose, and initiatives.
www.interpol.int/

The International Monetary Fund (IMF)

IMF Country Information Page contains IMF reports and publications arranged by country.
www.imf.org/external/country/index.htm

International Organization for Migration (IOM)

Working with governments, NGOs, and IGOs, the IOM seeks to assist with humane and orderly migration. Migration statistic can also be found on its website.
www.iom.int/

Islamic Development Bank Group

Seeking to promote development among Islamic countries, the Islamic Development Bank tries to foster economic growth and social progress while keeping practices within the framework of Islamic Law. Membership, publications, and organization activities can be found on its website.
www.isdb.org/

International Telecommunication Union

Based in Geneva, Switzerland with 191 members, the organization seeks to help the world communicate by promoting standardization.
www.itu.int

International Trade Centre

A joint agency of the WTO and the UN, the organization's website contains information about development projects and trade issues.
www.intracen.org/

International Whaling Commission

The website contains information about various treaties as they pertain to whaling and conservation and management of whales.
www.iwcoffice.org

North American Development Bank

This binational organization's (the US and Mexico) website contains information about joint environmental initiatives.
www.nadbank.org/

North American Free Trade Agreement Secretariat (NAFTA)

Mexico, the US, and Canada make up this trinational free trade zone. The website contains information about dispute settlement and legal agreements as well as organization reports.
www.nafta-sec-alena.org/DefaultSite/index.html

Non-Aligned Movement (NAM)

Begun in 1961, NAM sought to distance itself from the arms race between the U.S. and the Soviet Union. Made up of roughly 80 developing countries, the organization has shifted its focus from the arms race to global economic issues.
www.nam.gov.za/index.html

North Atlantic Treaty Organization (NATO)

The website contains information about the organization, its actions vis-à-vis various conflicts, as well as an elibrary and multimedia link.
www.nato.int/home.htm

Organization for Security and Co-operation in Europe (OSCE)

The world's largest security organization, the OSCE has 56 member nations. Its website provides detailed information about the organization's institutions, operations, and activities.
www.osce.org/

Organization of American States (OAS)

Comprising the nations of the Western Hemisphere, except Cuba, the OAS seeks to promote dialogue within the region. The website provides information on the organization's institutions, activities, and programs.
www.oas.org/

Organization of the Petroleum Exporting Countries (OPEC)

Made up of many of the world's oil producing nation-states, OPEC seeks to regulate the production of oil, stabilize the oil market, and ensure investors a return on their capital. The website contains information on the member nation's oil production as well as various relevant publications and multimedia presentations.
www.opec.org/

World Trade Organization (WTO)

The organization's website contains information on the structure, legal documents, and members (153 of them) that make up the WTO. Detailed information on the various trading rounds can also be found here.
www.wto.org/

possibility of establishing broader, more complex IGOs that could help maintain peace and foster prosperity. In the aftermath of World War I's (1914–18) devastation of Europe, Western leaders and activists from across the globe sought new ways to prevent conflict between nation-states. Using the Rhine and Danube River Commissions and other IGOs as models, they began exploring the development of one IGO whose main purpose was to keep peace between nation-states.

League of Nations

The idea for a single global IGO designed to prevent conflicts was propagated by a variety of people and organizations, including peace groups. In the US, the League to Enforce Peace led this effort; in Britain, the idea was championed by a group of diplomats, lawyers, and historians led by Lord Phillimore; and in France, Leon Bourgeois led a ministerial commission that called for enforcement of peace through an elaborate system of sanctions.[5] In the US, President Woodrow Wilson was one of the leading proponents of an international conflict prevention organization. As World War I was ending in Europe, President Wilson gave a speech outlining what the postwar period should look like. His "*Fourteen Points*" speech, as it came to be known, called for the establishment of an international organization designed to promote peaceful conflict resolution. Many world leaders agreed that such an organization was necessary, and by the end of the war, an international conference was convened to draft a *charter* for a new international conflict-prevention organization. This new organization, the *League of Nations*, was established in 1920, and though it included nation-states around the globe, the US was not one of them. Despite Wilson's championing of the organization, the Senate rejected US membership. Many scholars point to the US absence from the League as one of the factors that contributed to its limited effectiveness and brief presence on the world stage.

One of the key goals of the League was the maintenance of peace. Of the 26 articles in the League's charter, 10 dealt directly with the promotion of peace. Nation-states that joined the League pledged to refrain from war as a foreign policy tool and to respect the territorial integrity of other nation-states. League members could vote to punish nation-states that threatened the peace and/or the territorial integrity of another by imposing political and economic *sanctions*; however, in reality, sanctions were rarely authorized or enforced.

Although the maintenance of peace was its primary purpose, the League failed to prevent another world war; World War II erupted just 19 years after the League's creation. Despite the enormity of this failure, it is important to remember that the League of Nations was no more than a compilation of its member nation-states, and, as such, it could only do what the members wanted it to do. Also, because the League constituted the world's first real attempt to work toward the maintenance of peace and the pursuit of world order through an IGO, it is not surprising that the organization had flaws that led to failures. What is perhaps more surprising is the number of successes the organization achieved. In its first decade, the League heard and resolved more than 30 disputes, most of which were among small nations that were not particularly powerful. For example, a Greek incursion into Bulgarian territory in 1925 was quickly resolved when the League, led by the major powers, condemned the action and sent observers to the border region between the two countries.

Fourteen Points A speech given by US President Woodrow Wilson to the US Congress on January 8, 1918. Given 10 months before the end of World War I, it became the framework for the peace treaty that ended the war. Included in it was a call for an association of nations that would protect nation-state sovereignty and keep the peace.

charter A document incorporating an institution and outlining its rights and duties.

League of Nations Established by the Treaty of Versailles which ended World War I, this organization was designed to provide a forum for conflict dispute resolution, thereby preventing war.

sanctions Typically refers to economic restrictions, or embargos, placed on a nation-state.

One of the primary reasons why the League was successful in dealing with less powerful states was that the more powerful nation-states stood behind the League's decisions. The League was often less successful when it attempted to resolve disputes between more powerful nation-states. Some notable failures of the League include its inability to prevent or adequately respond to Japan's incursions into Manchuria in 1931. Neither France nor Britain, both powerful members of the League, was willing to apply sanctions to Japan to punish it for violating China's territorial integrity. As a result, Japan's action went relatively unchallenged. One of the other major "test cases" for the League was Italy's brutal invasion of Ethiopia in 1935. In this case, the League condemned the action and placed sanctions on Italy, but it did not extend the sanctions to include vital materials, such as oil. Italy proceeded to further provoke the League by killing thousands of Ethiopians with mustard gas, thus violating the worldwide ban on chemical warfare. When it became apparent that Mussolini's forces had conquered all of Ethiopia, the more powerful nations of the League, led by Britain, called for an end to sanctions against Italy, effectively abandoning Ethiopia, one of the founding members of the League. Later, when Hitler violated the *Treaty of Versailles* (which had ended World War I) by moving into Austria and Czechoslovakia in 1938, League members had already established a pattern indicating that they lacked the political will to challenge powerful countries' acts of war.

Treaty of Versailles   Ended World War I and demanded that Germany take full responsibility for the war and make reparations to the states it had injured.

While the League's success at preventing conflict was mixed at best, many of its economic and social contributions have proven invaluable. The League began the important task of information collection and analysis of economic, social, and political data.[6] Despite suffering from a lack of funding, the League's work in this area laid the groundwork for the kind of comprehensive collection and dissemination of demographic statistical data that the United Nations Economic and Social Council (ECOSOC) would later undertake. Similarly, the League of Nations established the Permanent Court of International Justice (PCIJ), which was a precursor to the United Nations' International Court of Justice. The purpose of the PCIJ was to provide a forum for members to nonviolently resolve conflicts through judicial proceedings. Another example is the League's establishment of the *International Labour Organization* (ILO), which still exists today. The ILO's purpose is to promote better labor conditions worldwide. It seeks to do this by working with nation-states to construct labor legislation that eliminates inhumane working conditions. Toward this end, the ILO has helped to design international labor standards that have been codified in more than 150 labor treaties. One unique feature of the organization was that membership includes employers, employees, and government representatives. The concept of sending a "worker's delegate" was unique because no other agency of the League, nor the League itself, provided this opportunity for citizen participation. Today, nations are required periodically to provide the ILO with reports on labor conditions within their countries. As a result, the ILO produces the most comprehensive data

International Labour Organization (ILO)   Founded in 1919, this specialize agencies of the UN works to promote decent working conditions across the globe.

about labor issues. For its efforts, the ILO has won the esteem of the world community and was awarded the *Nobel Peace Prize* in 1969.

United Nations

After World War II, the international community again set up an IGO designed to prevent conflict. The *United Nations*, or UN, founded in 1945 and headquartered in New York City, became the successor to the League. Like its predecessor, it has struggled to prevent conflict between nation-states. Still, it continues to function and has proven an invaluable institution in many ways. In order to understand better how the world's largest and most comprehensive IGO functions, each of its six principal organs is discussed below.

United Nations International organization founded to prevent war and to promote peace and international cooperation. Total membership in 2009: 192 nation-states.

United Nations General Assembly (UNGA)

The United Nations Charter lays out the make-up and responsibilities of the *United Nations General Assembly*, or UNGA. Nation-states that join the UN are permitted to send one delegate, or ambassador, to the UNGA. In 2008, the Assembly consisted of representatives from 192 countries. The UNGA is the only organ of the UN that has representation from all member nation-states. Its main purpose is to provide a forum for debate and discussion among members. The real powers of the UNGA rest in its control of the UN budget and in its ability to make recommendations regarding any matter that is within the scope of the UN. Although the UNGA cannot make recommendations about a subject that is simultaneously being discussed by the United Nations Security Council (UNSC), it can and does make recommendations regarding a wide range of subjects. For example, in 1947, the UNGA recommended that Palestine be split into two territories, one for Palestinians and one for Jews, thereby creating the state of Israel. The UNGA also oversees the operations of all the agencies within the UN, analyzing their annual and periodic reports and making recommendations for actions by these agencies. In addition, the UNGA has the power to elect the non-permanent members to the UNSC, the representatives for ECOSOC, and various members of the Trusteeship Council. Finally, the UNGA is required to work closely with the UNSC. For example, the UNSC has the power to recommend judges for the International Court of Justice (ICJ) as well as to make nominations for the position of *Secretary-General*, the UN's chief spokesperson and diplomat. The UNGA votes to accept or reject those recommendations. Likewise, the UNGA votes to approve a country's application for admission to the UN or to expel a member, but only after consulting with the UNSC. While amending the Charter is the duty of the UNGA, any change requires a two-thirds vote within the Assembly and the

United Nations General Assembly The organ of the UN that acts as its legislative branch. All member nations can send delegates to the General Assembly. It is also a forum for international dialogue.

Secretary-General (UN) The official spokesperson for the UN. In charge of the administrative machinery of the organization. Ban Ki-moon from South Korea became the Secretary-General in 2007.

permanent members Refers to the five members of the UN Security Council who wield veto power: the US, France, Britain, China, and Russia.

approval of all the *permanent members* of the UNSC. The UNGA meets for a three-month period each year, beginning the third Tuesday of September and ending before Christmas. Special sessions can and have been called on more than 20 occasions to deal with various crises; these meet after Christmas.

Membership in the UNGA has been and continues to be very political. While not all nation-states have joined the UN (for example, until 2002, Switzerland had refused to join, preferring complete neutrality), other nations refuse to join because of domestic concerns, such as public opinion, for example. Still others are not members because of international complications. For example, in 1949, the island of Taiwan became the refuge of those who were on the losing side of the Chinese civil war. The UN chose to recognize Taiwan as the Republic of China rather than the Chinese mainland because many powerful members of the UN were strongly opposed to the communist government that had emerged as the victors of the civil war. The UN continued to recognize Taiwan as the "real China," as it were, until 1971, when it reversed its position. Not only was the People's Republic of China, which resides on mainland China, finally recognized as "China" but also Taiwan was expelled from the UN altogether. Taiwan has repeatedly lobbied the UN for membership, but it has been denied more than 15 times; it still remains outside the UN today.

Cold War Refers to the ideological stand-off between two superpowers, the United States and the Soviet Union, from 1945 to 1989. While not directly fighting one another, each side sought to expand its influence by keeping the other from spreading its form of government and political system, resulting in many proxy wars throughout the world.

Balkans Geographic and historic term for a peninsula in Southeastern Europe. Countries most commonly included in the Balkan region are Albania, Bosnia and Herzegovina, Bulgaria, Croatia, Greece, Kosovo, Montenegro, Macedonia, and Serbia.

The China case illustrates the deep international divisions that developed as a result of the *Cold War*. During that period, the Soviet Union and the United States took turns in blocking membership applications from nations that were not sympathetic to their respective countries and ideologies. However, blocking UN membership for political reasons has been used by other countries as well. In the late 1990s, for example, Greece attempted to block Macedonia's membership. Macedonia had been part of the former Yugoslavia, and upon its independence, it sought membership in the UN. Greece has an area within its nation-state that is also called Macedonia. Greece argued that the new nation-state of Macedonia had territorial designs on Greek Macedonia, even though no such indications were forthcoming from the Macedonian government. Given that similar ethnic groups straddled the border of the new state of Macedonia and the Macedonian area of Greece, and that ethnic violence had torn apart the *Balkans* for most of the 1990s, many other nation-states were sympathetic to Greece's concerns. In a strange compromise that took more than 18 months to sort out, Macedonia was allowed to join the UN, but only under the provisional title, "the Former Yugoslav Republic of Macedonia" (FYROM).

One complaint leveled against the UNGA over the years has been the slow pace at which it operates, particularly where speeches and debates are concerned. Given that membership continues to increase, and that this is the only forum most nations have for expressing their views to the rest of the world, it is unlikely that the process will speed up any time soon. Others, however, do not see this as a problem, arguing that because of the importance of the issues discussed by the UNGA, it would be unwise to push for a faster process that might not allow enough time for deliberation and debate.

United Nations Security Council (UNSC)

The *United Nations Security Council*, or UNSC, was designed by the founders of the UN to be the most important organ of the organization. The UNSC is responsible for making recommendations to the UNGA for the application of new members as well as for nominating the Secretary-General. Significantly, the UNSC also has the power to authorize the use of force by the organization.

> **United Nations Security Council (UNSC)** The 15-member organ of the UN that is responsible for maintaining peace and security. There are 10 rotating members who serve two-year terms and five permanent members who have veto power: US, Britain, China, Russia, and France.

Like the UNGA, UNSC members must be available at any time to deal with a crisis. Unlike the UNGA, however, not all nation-states are represented in the UNSC. In fact, the UNSC is made up of only fifteen nation-states: five members are permanent and ten others are chosen by the UNGA for a two-year term.[7] Half of the non-permanent members are elected each year and the seats are allocated as follows: five for Africa and Asia, two for Latin America, one for Eastern Europe, and two for Western Europe. The five permanent members are the victors of World War II: the US, Britain, France, Russia (or the Soviet Union from 1917/22 to 1991), and China. After the war, these five countries assumed that they would bear most of the responsibility for maintaining world order and peace in the postwar period and that they should therefore have more authority within the organization. Permanent membership gave them the greater authority they sought, including veto power. Any one of the permanent five can veto any action or decision under discussion or review in the UN. During the Cold War, the Soviet Union and the US often took turns vetoing actions that each perceived as favorable to the other. For many years, this worked to limit the effectiveness of the organization. Although the end of the Cold War has seen the US and Russia on the same side of many issues, veto power remains controversial. For example, in 1996, incumbent Secretary-General Boutros Boutros-Ghali was nominated by the UNGA for re-election. He had the support of almost every member, including 14 members of the UNSC. The US, however, did not believe that Boutros-Ghali was sufficiently sympathetic to its interests.[8] As a result, the US used its veto to prevent him from serving another term, thereby overriding the wishes of the majority. In another example, China has repeatedly threatened to use its veto to protect a key trading partner, Sudan, from UN sanctions designed to force Sudan to put an end to the ongoing genocide in its Darfur region. These kinds of scenarios have led to heated debates in the UN over the power of the veto. Many non-permanent UNSC members, for example, question whether any one nation-state should have the ability to exert its will over the consensus of the rest of the world.

United Nations Economic and Social Council The organ of the UN that promotes international cooperation and development. It performs the majority of the United Nations' work.

United Nations Statistical Yearbook Published each year by the UN, it catalogues a wide range of economic, social, and environmental data.

United Nations Economic and Social Council (ECOSOC)
The third organ of the UN, the *United Nations Economic and Social Council* (ECOSOC), consumes roughly 80 percent of the UN budget. Growing from only 18 members at the founding of the UN to 54 members in 2008, ECOSOC is responsible for:

- promoting higher standards of living, full employment, and economic and social progress;
- identifying solutions to international economic, social, and health problems;
- facilitating international cultural and educational cooperation; and
- encouraging universal respect for human rights and fundamental freedoms.[9]

ECOSOC also oversees a variety of agencies whose work is critical to the mission of the UN, many of which are listed in table 3.1. Another key function of ECOSOC is research. For example, the annually published *United Nations Statistical Yearbook*

Table 3.1   UN ECOSOC Agencies[10]

Functional Commissions	Specialized Agencies
Global Commissions: • Narcotic Drugs • Crime Prevention and Criminal Justice • Science and Technology for Development • Sustainable Development • Status of Women • Population and Development • Commission for Social Development Statistical Commission Regional Commissions • Economic Commission for Africa (ECA) • Economic Commission for Europe (ECE) • Economic Commission for Latin America and the Caribbean (ECLAC) • Economic and Social Commission for Asia and the Pacific (ESCAP) • Economic and Social Commission for Western Asia (ESCWA) Other Bodies Permanent Forum on Indigenous Issues United Nations Forum on Forests Sessional and standing committees Expert, ad hoc and related bodies	International Labour Organization (ILO) Food and Agriculture Organization of the United Nations (FAO) United Nations Educational, Scientific and Cultural Organization (UNESCO) World Health Organization (WHO) International Monetary Fund (IMF) International Civil Aviation Organization (ICAO) International Maritime Organization (IMO) World Meteorological Organization (WMO) United Nations Industrial Development Organization (UNIDO) World Tourism Organization (UNWTO) International Telecommunication Union (ITU) Universal Postal Union (UPU) International Fund for Agricultural Development (IFAD) World Intellectual Property Organization (WIPO) World Bank Group: International Bank for Reconstruction and Development (IBRD) International Development Association (IDA) International Finance Corporation (IFC) Multilateral Investment Guarantee Agency (MIGA) International Centre for Settlement of Investment Disputes (ICSID)

has become one of the most extensively used and broadly respected collections of data related to economic activity, population and social statistics, and international economic relations.

Trusteeship Council (TC)

The forth organ of the UN, the *Trusteeship Council* (TC), was designed to make itself obsolete – and it succeeded. The duty of the TC was to decolonize non-self-governing territories, overseeing and leading them to eventual self-government. A total of 11 territories, most of which were becoming independent after years of colonialism, were placed under "trusteeship," including seven in Africa and four in *Oceania*. With the 1994 independence of Palau, the last of the trust territories, the TC completed its work and became inactive. The UN is still trying to decide what role,

> **Trusteeship Council** The organ of the UN that was responsible for assisting with the transition of former colonies to independent countries. It went out of commission in 1994.
>
> **Oceania** Refers to a group of islands located in the Pacific Ocean.

if any, the TC should play. Former Secretary-General Kofi Annan recommended that the TC be completely eliminated,[11] which would require the revision of the UN Charter. Others have suggested that it could be charged with new duties, such as coordinating "the protection of environment, extraterritorial spaces and zones, the resources of the seas and sea bed, the climate, human rights, the rights of future generations, the rights of people in situations where there has been a complete breakdown of the states or of the institutions guaranteeing the rule of law."[12] Following this idea, another option might be for the TC to oversee and develop programs to respond to the growing number of "failed/failing" states – states that for one reason or another are unable to self-govern. Examples of such states in 2008 included Somalia, Sudan, and Zimbabwe.[13]

International Court of Justice (ICJ)

The fifth organ of the UN, the *International Court of Justice*, or ICJ, has its origins in the League of Nations' Permanent Court of International Justice (PCIJ). However, unlike the PCIJ, which was not technically an organ of the League of Nations, the ICJ is an organ of the UN. Therefore, when a state becomes a member of the UN, it also becomes a party to the ICJ. The court, which is headquar-

> **International Court of Justice (ICJ)** The judicial organ of the United Nations that has the power to hear cases involving nation-states.

tered in The Hague (the third largest city in the Netherlands), is made up of 15 judges from various geographical regions who are recommended by the UNSC and approved by the UNGA. Judges serve renewable, nine-year terms. Typically, six are from Europe, one is from the US, one is from Latin America, three are from Asia, three are from sub-Saharan Africa, and one is from the Middle East. The ICJ only adjudicates cases that involve nation-states. While many nation-states prefer not to turn over important issues to the ICJ, others do bring cases to the court and abide by its decisions. In addition to hearing cases, the court can issue advisory opinions regarding points of international law. Also, the UN General Assembly often seeks advisement on legal issues from the ICJ.

Table 3.2   Secretary-Generals of the United Nations

Name	Country of Origin	Years Served
Trygve Lie	Norway	1946–53
Dag Hammarskjöld	Sweden	1953–61
U Thant	Burma	1961–72
Kurt Waldheim	Austria	1972–82
Javier Pérez de Cuéllar	Peru	1982–92
Boutros Boutros-Ghali	Egypt	1992–7
Kofi Annan	Ghana	1997–2006
Ban Ki-moon	South Korea	2006–present

Secretariat   The administrative organ of the UN led by the Secretary-General.

Suez Crisis   A military attack on Egypt by Britain, France, and Israel after Egypt nationalized the Suez Canal.

Secretariat

The last organ, the *Secretariat*, is responsible for the day-to-day running of the UN's administrative machinery. Heading up the Secretariat is the Secretary-General. He or she is the chief administrator of the UN, the liaison between the various organs, and the spokesperson for the entire organization. The Secretary-General also often acts as peace initiator, attempting to ease tensions between countries and resolve crises. However, the duties taken on by the Secretary-General often depend upon the personality of the person serving in the position. Some Secretary-Generals have been seen as effective peacemakers and active agents of change. For example, Dag Hammarskjöld, the UN's second Secretary-General, worked to resolve many international disputes and conflicts, including the 1956 *Suez Crisis*. He was posthumously awarded the Nobel Peace Prize in 1961. In contrast, other Secretary-Generals have been viewed as weak and ineffective. Boutrous Boutrous-Ghali, for example, was criticized for the UN's failure to intervene in the 1994 Rwandan genocide, which left more than a million people dead. For some of his critics, he became the personification of the UN's ineffectiveness in the face of humanitarian crises.

UN budget

The UN has three budgets that it draws upon to run its various programs and agencies: the regular budget, the peacekeeping budget, and the voluntary contributions budget. The regular budget funds the General Assembly, the Secretariat, the Security Council, the Economic and Social Council, and the International Court of Justice. The regular budget also partially funds some UN agencies, including the United Nations High Commissioner for Refugees. The peacekeeping budget pays for UN military operations. International war crimes tribunals are financed by funds taken from the contributions to the regular budget and the peacekeeping budget. The voluntary contributions budget is supported through donations by member states, and it funds humanitarian and development programs, such as the World Food Program and the UN Children's Fund.[14]

The UN draws mandatory financial support for the general and peacekeeping budgets from its member states. Each country's *assessment* is based on factors such as national income, population, and level of debt. As a result, wealthier nations contribute significantly more to the budgets than poorer ones do. For example, in 2006, Japan was assessed 19.47 percent of the regular budget, while Liberia was assessed the minimum contribution level of 0.001 percent. The maximum rate a nation can be assessed is 22 percent of the regular budget. The US, the UN's largest contributor, is assessed at the ceiling rate of 22 percent.[15]

> **assessment** The amount of money each country is asked to contribute to the UN's regular budget.

The peacekeeping budget, which is developed after the regular budget assessments have been made, is based on a percentage of the budget a state pays. However, unlike the regular budget, which every member must contribute to, some developing nations, for whom an additional assessment would be a significant financial burden, are exempt. In contrast, the five permanent members of the Security Council pay extra fees.[16]

Although states that do not pay their mandatory dues risk the loss of their vote in the General Assembly, many states, including the US, are perpetually in *arrears*. In the 1980s, the US began withholding its UN dues in an effort to force the UN to comply with US wishes. After prolonged negotiations with the UN that included a reduction in the regular budget assessment rate ceiling from 25 to 22 percent, the US eventually repealed its policy of withholding funds. However, because the US had not paid its full dues from 1986 to 2001, it had fallen into arrears of more than $1 billion. Other nations have also failed to pay their dues, bringing the total owed to the UN in 2003 to more than $3 billion (see table 3.3). These budget shortfalls make running an effective and efficient organization exceedingly difficult.[17]

> **arrears** The portion of a state's assessment that remains unpaid after it is due.

Peacekeeping

According to the UN Charter, the UN Security Council is charged with keeping the peace. The second Secretary-General, the aforementioned Dag Hammarskjöld, is considered by many to be the "father" of modern UN peacekeeping because it was during his tenure that the use of peacekeeping forces became the primary means through which the UNSC sought to fulfill this charge. Hammarskjöld was a strong advocate of *preventive diplomacy*, a term that refers to efforts to prevent conflicts before they erupt into violent confrontations. He also argued for "quiet diplomacy," or the kind of behind-the-scenes negotiations that de-escalate tensions by allowing nations to "save face" to the rest of the world. As Secretary-General, Hammarskjöld initiated two of the UN's larger operations, the United Nations Emergency Force (UNEF in Egypt 1956–67) and the United Nations Congo Operation (ONCU 1960–4). Unfortunately, he did not see the latter operation to its conclusion, as he died in 1961 in a plane crash on his way to negotiate a ceasefire in Central Africa.

> **preventive diplomacy** Diplomatic efforts designed to reduce chances of impending conflict, or to prevent an imminent conflict.

Table 3.3   Payments Owed to the UN by the 15 Major Debtor
Countries: 2007 (in US$ millions)[18]

Country	Total Debt
United States	1,493
Japan	730
France	187
Spain	148
Ukraine	141
China	70
Argentina	47
Greece	45
Belgium	40
Belarus	39
Germany	39
Saudi Arabia	32
United Arab Emirates	29
Portugal	18
Republic of Korea	10
Total Owed by Top 15 Debtors	3,067
Total Owed by All UN Member States	3,183

The UN has since continued not only to deploy peacekeepers but also to expand
its interpretation of how these forces should be used. Generally, peacekeeping
has referred to the process whereby soldiers from nation-states not involved in a
conflict are introduced into a conflict area to act as a buffer between conflicting
forces, to maintain a ceasefire, or simply to maintain order so that humanitarian
aid can be delivered to those in need. Peacekeepers are not given authority to
assist any one side in a conflict; rather, they are generally deployed simply to keep
the peace while the warring sides are, ideally, working to resolve the conflict.
Peacekeepers are usually unarmed or lightly armed, and, if they do have weapons,
they can only use them in self-defense. This understanding of peacekeeping has
expanded to include military actions in some circumstances as well. Chapter VII
of the Charter states that the Security Council "may take such action by air, sea,
or land forces as may be necessary to maintain or restore international peace and
security. Such action may include demonstrations, blockade, and other operations
by air, sea, or land forces of Members of the United Nations."[19] This section has
been interpreted as allowing for troops to engage militarily with warring parties in
an effort to secure the peace.

Peacekeeping is not without its critics. Some charge that peacekeeping is ineffective and rife with problems. They argue, for example, that the UN is inconsistent in
its use of peacekeeping forces, failing to utilize them when they are most needed, as
was the case in Rwanda in 1994. Critics also charge that the same countries pushing
for the use of peacekeepers are often the ones making money from the sale of weapons

to the various sides in the conflicts. Additionally, they argue that peacekeeping missions are often ill-defined and, as a result, they can end in disaster for the soldiers. Still others complain that peacekeepers have harmed communities rather than helped them by engaging in a variety of illegal activities while on their missions, including rape, sexual exploitation, and illegal mineral and weapons sales.[20]

Supporters of peacekeeping point to successful missions and to the relatively low costs involved. For example, the UN asserts that "peacekeeping is far cheaper than war," noting that "the approved peacekeeping budget for the year from 1 July 2005 to 30 June 2006 . . . represented only 0.5% of global military spending" and that the UN "spends less per year on peacekeeping worldwide than the City of New York spends on the annual budget of its police department."[21] Nevertheless, peacekeeping operations are often hampered by debt. Although UN member states are legally obliged to pay their share of peacekeeping costs, in 2007 they owed approximately $2.7 billion in peacekeeping dues.[22] Even with these financial constraints, many UN peacekeeping operations have been successful, saving lives and providing safe passage for those bringing humanitarian assistance to conflict victims. (See table 3.4 for a list of all the UN peacekeeping operations.)

Table 3.4   List of UN Peacekeeping Operations 1948–2008

Name		Timeframe
UNTSO	United Nations Truce Supervision Organization	May 1948–present
UNMOGIP	United Nations Military Observer Group in India and Pakistan	January 1949–present
UNEF I	First United Nations Emergency Force	November 1956–June 1967
UNOGIL	United Nations Observation Group in Lebanon	June 1958–December 1958
ONUC	United Nations Operation in the Congo	July 1960–June 1964
UNSF	United Nations Security Force in West New Guinea	October 1962–April 1963
UNYOM	United Nations Yemen Observation Mission	July 1963–September 1964
UNFICYP	United Nations Peacekeeping Force in Cyprus	March 1964–present
DOMREP	Mission of the Representative of the SG in the Dominican Republic	May 1965–October 1966
UNIPOM	United Nations India–Pakistan Observation Mission	September 1965–March 1966
UNEF II	Second United Nations Emergency Force	October 1973–July 1979
UNDOF	United Nations Disengagement Force	June 1974–present
UNIFIL	United Nations Interim Force in Lebanon	March 1978–present
UNGOMAP	United Nations Good Offices Mission in Afghanistan and Pakistan	May 1988–March 1990
UNIIMOG	United Nations Iran–Iraq Military Observer Group	August 1988–February 1991
UNAVEM I	United Nations Angola Verification Mission I	January 1989–June 1991
UNTAG	United Nations Transition Assistance Group	April 1989–March 1990
ONUCA	United Nations Observer Group in Central America	November 1989–January 1992
UNIKOM	United Nations Iraq–Kuwait Observation Mission	April 1991–October 2003
MINURSO	United Nations Mission for the Referendum in Western Sahara	April 1991–present
UNAVEM II	United Nations Angola Verification Mission II	June 1991–February 1995
ONUSAL	United Nations Observer Mission in El Salvador	July 1991–April 1995

Table 3.4 *(cont'd)*

Name		Timeframe
UNAMIC	United Nations Advance Mission in Cambodia	October 1991–March 1992
UNPROFOR	United Nations Protection Force	February 1992–March 1995
UNTAC	United Nations Transitional Authority in Cambodia	March 1992–September 1993
UNOSOM I	United Nations Operation in Somalia I	April 1992–March 1993
ONUMOZ	United Nations Operation in Mozambique	December 1992–December 1994
UNOSOM II	United Nations Operation in Somalia II	March 1993–March 1995
UNOMUR	United Nations Observer Mission Uganda–Rwanda	June 1993–September 1994
UNOMIG	United Nations Observer Mission in Georgia	August 1993–present
UNOMIL	United Nations Observer Mission in Liberia	September 1993–September 1997
UNMIH	United Nations Mission in Haiti	September 1993–June 1996
UNAMIR	United Nations Assistance Mission for Rwanda	October 1993–March 1996
UNASOG	United Nations Aouzou Strip Observer Group	May 1994–June 1994
UNMOT	United Nations Mission of Observers in Tajikistan	December 1994–May 2000
UNAVEM III	United Nations Angola Verification Mission III	February 1995–June 1997
UNCRO	United Nations Confidence Restoration Operation in Croatia	May 1995–January 1996
UNPREDEP	United Nations Preventive Deployment Force	March 1995–February 1999
UNMIBH	United Nations Mission in Bosnia and Herzegovina	December 1995–December 2002
UNTAES	United Nations Transitional Administration for Eastern Slavonia, Baranja and Western Sirmium	January 1996–January 1998
UNMOP	United Nations Mission of Observers in Prevlaka	January 1996–December 2002
UNSMIH	United Nations Support Mission in Haiti	July 1996–July 1997
MINUGUA	United Nations Verification Mission in Guatemala	January 1997–May 1997
MONUA	United Nations Observer Mission in Angola	June 1997–February 1999
UNTMIH	United Nations Transition Mission in Haiti	August 1997–November 1997
MINOPUH	UN Civilian Police Mission in Haiti	December 1997–March 2000
UN Civilian	Police Support Group	January 1998–October 1998
UNOMSIL	United Nations Observer Mission in Sierra Leone	July 1998–October 1999
MINURCA	United Nations Mission in the Central African Republic	April 1998–February 2000
UNMIK	UN Interim Administration Mission in Kosovo	June 1999–present
UNAMSIL	United Nations Mission in Sierra Leone	October 1999–December 2005
UNTAET	United Nations Transitional Administration in East Timor	October 1999–May 2002
MONUC	UN Organization Mission in the Democratic Republic of the Congo	November 1999–present
UNMEE	United Nations Mission in Ethiopia and Eritrea	July 2000–present
UNMISET	United Nations Mission of Support in East Timor	May 2002–May 2005
UNMIL	United Nations Mission in Liberia	September 2003–present
UNOCI	United Nations Operation in Côte d'Ivoire	April 2004–present
MINUSTAH	United Nations Stabilization Mission in Haiti	June 2004–present
ONUB	United Nations Operation in Burundi	June 2004–December 2006
UNMIS	United Nations Mission in the Sudan	March 2005–present
UNMIT	United Nations Integrated Mission in Timor-Leste	August 2006–present
UNAMID	African Union/United Nations Hybrid operation in Darfur	July 2007–present
MINURCAT	United Nations Mission in the Central African Republic and Chad	September 2007–present

UN effectiveness

Assessing the UN's ability to prevent conflict depends in part upon how one defines success. If preventing war is the only criterion, then the UN, like its predecessor, the League, has not been very successful. If however, other criteria are used, such as assisting refugees and other vulnerable groups, working toward the eradication of diseases like smallpox, providing a forum for debate, and acting as a clearing-house for information, then the UN has proven to be a vital IGO. Assessments of the UN's success and value must also take into account that, as an IGO, its job is to carry out the will of the members that make it up.

World Trade Organization (WTO)

As the demand for more international cooperation increased after World War I, states began to see the need for a set of uniform international laws governing trade and commerce. The first step toward this kind of IGO was the UN's development of the International Trade Organization (ITO). As governments engaged in negotiations about the creation of the ITO, parallel discussions were occurring focusing on an expeditious way to reduce tariffs. The ITO effort ultimately failed, but the other talks focusing on ways to reduce barriers to international trade led to the creation of a series of documents collectively referred to as the General Agreement on Tariffs and Trade (GATT). Although GATT was a treaty and not an IGO, it helped standardize international economic transactions. Becoming a member of GATT meant observing certain rules of trade behavior as they related to commodities. Nations were free to grant preferable trade relations with some countries while denying it to others. GATT operated as the primary international trade agreement for almost 50 years. In 1995 it was replaced by a formalized international trade regime known as the *World Trade Organization* (WTO).

The WTO operates a system of trade rules, it attempts to *liberalize* trade, and it provides a forum for governments to negotiate trade agreements.[23] Although the WTO is based on GATT rules and principles, it is a formalized institution with the legal capacity to enforce its decisions and rules. By joining the WTO, nations agree to the same rules of trade for all members, eliminating GATT's preferential trading provisions. The WTO also differs from GATT in scope; like GATT, the WTO is concerned with trade in goods, but it also covers trade in services and trade in "products of innovation" (intellectual property).[24]

The WTO has also outlined a series of guiding principles for the trading system. In their view, the trading system should be free from discrimination. Countries should treat all trading partners equally, granting them all "*most-favored-nation*" (MFN) status. They should also treat foreign products and services the same as their own. The second principle is that the trading system should be freer, and that barriers to trade should be reduced

World Trade Organization (WTO)
An international organization designed to promote free and uniform trade and banking and finance rules and regulations.

liberalize   To reduce restrictions on trade.

most-favored-nation (MFN) status
Although most-favored-nation sounds like certain countries are granted special treatment, in the WTO the MFN principle means non-discrimination. Each member nation treats virtually every other member equally. So if a country improves the benefits it extends to one member nation, it must do so for all other WTO members so that they all remain "most-favored."

export subsidies A form of subsidy provided by a government to help companies or manufacturing sectors lower their export costs.

tariffs Taxes placed on imported goods.

quotas Limits on the amount of a product a country will allow into its market in an effort to protect domestic manufacturers.

or eliminated through negotiation. The third principle is that the trading system should be predictable. In other words, governments, companies, and investors should be able to feel confident that trade barriers will not be raised arbitrarily. The fourth principle is that the trading system should be more competitive. Practices considered by many to be unfair, such as *export subsidies* and "dumping" (selling products in another country at an artificially low price in an effort to gain market share) are discouraged. The final principle is that the trading system should be more beneficial for less developed countries, giving them greater flexibility and special privileges in an effort to facilitate development.[25]

These general principles guide the WTO's goals, which include:

- the reduction of *tariffs*, with the end goal of tariff elimination;
- the prevention of dumping;
- reductions in farm subsidies;
- the elimination of *quotas* on textiles from developing countries;
- the introduction of regulations on service sectors, including banking, insurance, and shipping, in order to standardize practices;
- the extension of protections for intellectual property such as copyrights on books, films, software, and similar items.[26]

Proponents of the WTO argue that the organization promotes global economic growth, raising living standards around the world and making it easier for people to access a wide variety of products. Many also applaud its liberal trade policies, arguing that they "sharpen competition, motivate innovation and breed success."[27] The WTO's efforts to discourage protectionism are lauded by those who believe the practice results in "bloated, inefficient producers supplying consumers with outdated, unattractive products" and ultimately in the reduction of economic activity.[28] WTO advocates also maintain that it is a democratic institution in which decisions are made by the consensus of its members.

WTO criticism comes from various positions on the political spectrum. Those on the political right argue that the organization takes away sovereignty from nation-states. Some also think that, like the UN, the WTO should grant more powerful nation-states with special veto power. Those on the political left, such as labor unions, have criticized the organization's promotion of free trade, arguing that it has encouraged companies to move to countries where unions that attempt to protect workers are either weak or absent. In short, critics see the WTO's championing of free trade as facilitating the exploitation of workers. Additionally, critics on both the right and the left complain that the organization has too much power and too little oversight. Much of the debate in the WTO takes place behind closed doors, and those making the decisions are not elected, which has contributed to charges that the organization lacks transparency and is undemocratic. Many developing countries are also critical of the organization, arguing that it protects the economic areas where wealthy nations have a competitive advantage while it implements restrictions that undermine poor countries' ability to compete. Environmental organizations have also criticized the WTO, arguing that the pursuit of free trade encourages countries to exploit their resources without paying adequate attention to the environmental impact of those decisions.

Regional organizations

In addition to global IGOs, such as the UN and the WTO, there are many regional IGOs that serve a variety of purposes. Some are designed for collective self-defense, such as the North Atlantic Treaty Organization (NATO), while others, such as the European Union, are designed primarily to promote economic integration. Still others, such as the Organization of American States, have multiple purposes.

European Union (EU)

With the exception of the UN, the *European Union* (EU) has become one of the world's most well-known IGOs. After World War II, the political climate in Europe favored a move away from the extreme forms of nationalism that had contributed to so much devastation on the continent and toward unification and centralization.

> **European Union (EU)** A regional organization for European states that seeks to create unified social, political, and economic policies.

The European Coal and Steel Community was an important step in the direction of European unity, centralizing control of the coal and steel industries. Belgium, France, Italy, Luxembourg, the Netherlands, and West Germany were the founding members of the Community. Six years later, two additional European communities were created: the European Economic Community and the European Atomic Energy Community. The 1967 Merger Treaty created a single set of institutions for the three communities, which together became known as the European Community (EC). In 1973, Denmark, Ireland, and the United Kingdom joined the EC, and, by 1979, democratic elections to the European Parliament were held. Greece, Spain, and Portugal joined in the 1980s. It wasn't until November 1, 1993, however, that the European Union was formally established with the creation of the *Maastricht Treaty*, or, formally, the Treaty on European Union (TEU). The TEU further formalized the integration of European member nations both economically, by working toward a common currency (the Euro, introduced in 2002) and removing all trade barriers, and socially, by providing free access across borders. By 2008, 27 European nations had joined the renamed European Union (EU). This *supranational* organization has moved far beyond simply promoting free trade between member nations; it has acquired a variety of complex functions, including establishing agricultural, commercial, foreign, defense, and human rights policies. Additionally, the organization has also created the European Court of Justice, an adjudicative body to settle disputes between member nations.

> **Maastricht Treaty** Signed in 1992, it formally created the EU.
>
> **supranational** A supranational organization is one that has been given the authority by its member nations to make decisions that take precedence over member nations' policies. The supranational organization relies on nations to carry out its decisions because it usually lacks any enforcement powers of its own.

While many have hailed the EU experiment in sovereignty transfer from the nation-state to a supranational organization as a success, the EU is not without its problems and critics. The organization has experienced internal strife over foreign policy toward Cuba, Israel, the former Yugoslavia, and the US, as well as serious disagreements over other policies and issues, including stem-cell research, abortion, human rights, and other environmental and economic policies.[29] Some critics also charge that the EU has become too involved in the day-to-day lives of its citizens. For example, the EU has a variety of rules and regulations that deal with the minutiae of daily life in Europe, including "the brands of ketchup to be used in US-owned fast-food restaurants in Paris, the angle of Ford headlights made in London, and the airing of 'I love Lucy' reruns in Amsterdam."[30] Finally, another area of contention within the organization involves its future growth, direction, and organization. In 2004, EU leaders drafted and signed a constitution designed to replace the various treaties and agreements that held the organization together with one governing document. Before going into effect, all EU members had to ratify the document. Some countries did ratify it, but France and the Netherlands voted it down, which in turn caused other countries to suspend their ratification votes. As a result, the European Constitution never came into force. Another plan, the Lisbon Treaty, designed to replace the failed European Constitution and to give the EU "a sitting president and foreign minister," was put to the test in 2008. Voters in one EU country, Ireland, turned it down,[31] only to accept it in 2009 when another referendum was held. The Czech Republic was left as the lone EU member to formally refuse to sign the Lisbon Treaty. However, by the end of 2009, the Czech government indicated that it would likely sign the treaty, paving the way for changes in how the organization is run.

North Atlantic Treaty Organization (NATO) A regional collective self-defense organization.

appease To be pacific, or to concede in order to avert or ameliorate conflict.

Warsaw Pact A collective self-defense organization made up of the Soviet Union and its allies. It was disbanded in 1991.

North Atlantic Treaty Organization (NATO)

The *North Atlantic Treaty Organization* (NATO) was established after World War II as a collective self-defense organization for Western Europe and the US. The establishment of NATO was based on the idea that aggression can be deterred via a system of mutual defense. The treaty was a formal statement that member countries would not *appease* aggressive states, as they had with Italy and Germany prior to the war, by allowing them to attack any state in the collective. Instead, an attack on one member nation by an external force would be considered an attack on them all, and all member nations would assist the attacked party militarily.[32] In 1955, six years after the signing of the North Atlantic Treaty, the *Warsaw Pact* was created. Like NATO, the Warsaw Pact was a collective self-defense organization, but it was designed for Eastern European states and the Soviet Union. With its creation, the two opposing sides of the Cold War were formally established.

With the break-up of the Soviet Union, the dissolution of the Warsaw Pact, and the end of the Cold War in the late 1980s and early 1990s, NATO's focus has shifted and new challenges have emerged, including disagreements regarding its purpose and policies. For example, controversy has surrounded the question of which countries should be allowed to become members. In 1999 and 2004, NATO opened up membership to all former Warsaw Pact members, except Albania, though it too was invited to begin accession talks in 2008. Russia opposes the expansion of NATO, which it views as an attempt to surround and isolate it. Several NATO members have also expressed concern about allowing more states to join, arguing that further expansion will result in loss of effectiveness.

In addition to internal and external questions about membership, the organization is also struggling to define its role in a post-Cold War world. Originally designed to be a collective self-defense organization that responded to aggression against its members, NATO has since expanded its role, responding to conflicts that do not involve member states. In 1993, for example, it conducted air raids on Bosnian Serbs who had been attacking civilians. The organization also used its troops to enforce an embargo on Yugoslavia that same year. Although NATO received approval for this action from the UN Security Council, it did not have Security Council approval for its bombing campaign during the Kosovo War in 1999. NATO argued it was upholding international law by intervening in Kosovo for humanitarian purposes;[33] however, some non-member nations saw it as a threatening attempt to circumvent the UN and ignore the rule of law.

Members of NATO are also at odds over the future direction of the organization. For example, the 2003 US-led invasion of Iraq divided NATO. Britain supported the action, while France and Germany issued their strong dissent.[34] Nevertheless, even though many maintain that the future of the organization is unknown and its purpose ill-defined, nations are still lining up to join it (see table 3.5 for a list of current members).

Organization of African Unity (OAU)/African Union (AU)
The first African attempt at regional IGO cooperation was the Organization of African Unity (OAU), which was formed in 1963. The idea for an African IGO, or a United States of Africa, emerged simultaneously with the end of colonialism in the late 1950s and early 1960s. Its major goals included promoting the sovereignty of African nations, human rights, and peaceful conflict resolution. Although there was a desire among some African leaders for a strong IGO, many others who had fought to secure freedom for their countries were not willing to give up their newly acquired power to a centralized structure. As a result, the OAU became a forum for African leaders to come together to discuss common goals, but it was plagued by poor financing and a founding charter that gave the organization very little power to enforce its decisions. Reluctance of members to interfere in the internal affairs of other states also prevented the organization from acting as a peace broker. Realizing the limitations of the OAU, various African leaders, led by Muammar al-Gaddafi of Libya, called for a new IGO, and in 1999, the *African Union* (AU) was born. The AU differs from its predecessor in several ways, one of the most important being its ability to intervene in members' internal affairs.

African Union An organization of African states that is designed to promote peace, human rights, democracy, and inter-continental cooperation.

Table 3.5 NATO Members

Name	Year Joined
Belgium	1949
Canada	1949
Denmark	1949
France	1949
Iceland	1949
Italy	1949
Luxembourg	1949
Netherlands	1949
Norway	1949
Portugal	1949
United Kingdom	1949
United States	1949
Greece	1952
Turkey	1952
Germany	1955
Spain	1982
Czech Republic	1999
Hungary	1999
Poland	1999
Bulgaria	2004
Estonia	2004
Latvia	2004
Lithuania	2004
Romania	2004
Slovakia	2004
Slovenia	2004
Albania	2009
Croatia	2009

In contrast with the OAU, the AU has both the legal power to respond to crises, such as genocide, war crimes, and crimes against humanity, as well as the military peacekeeping capabilities to carry out its missions. In May 2003, the AU conducted its first military intervention, deploying peacekeeping forces from South Africa, Ethiopia, and Mozambique to Burundi. AU troops were also deployed in Sudan for peacekeeping in the Darfur conflict.

Organization of American States (OAS)

Organization of American States (OAS) A regional organization for the states of the Americas, whose purpose is to promote social and economic development in the Western hemisphere.

The *Organization of American States* (OAS) is an IGO headquartered in Washington, DC that is designed to promote peace and cooperation among the 35 independent states of the Americas. The OAS's precursor, the International Union of American Republics, emerged in 1890 from the efforts of 18 nations at the First International Conference of American States.[35] In 1948, as

Table 3.6 OAS Member States

Antigua & Barbuda	Dominica	Panama
Argentina	Dominican Republic	Paraguay
Bahamas	Ecuador	Peru
Barbados	El Salvador	Saint Kitts & the Nevis
Belize	Grenada	Saint Lucia
Bolivia	Guatemala	Saint Vincent & the Grenadines
Brazil	Guyana	Suriname
Canada	Haiti	Trinidad & Tobago
Chile	Honduras	United States
Colombia	Jamaica	Uruguay
Costa Rica	Mexico	Venezuela
Cuba*	Nicaragua	

* Although Cuba is still technically a member state, the current government is denied representation and participation.

the Cold War lines between communist and democratic countries were being drawn across the globe, 21 American countries met at the Ninth International Conference of American States, where they signed a new charter for the creation of the OAS. During the Cold War, the US viewed the OAS as a mechanism for attempting to stop the spread of communism. In 1962, the OAS made its anticommunist mission explicit, suspending the Castro-led government of Cuba's membership three years after the island had been taken over by communist forces. The nation itself is still counted as a member, however, as a symbolic gesture indicating that Cuba will be welcomed back into the fold once a new regime is installed that meets the OAS's democratic standards (see table 3.6 for a full list of member states).[36]

While promoting democracy has been and continues to be an important focus of the OAS, the organization engages in a variety of activities, including cooperative economic and political development, peaceful dispute resolution, and human rights promotion. Increasingly, the OAS is focusing on economic integration, though there is wide disagreement regarding how to go about it. Some members have advocated for an expansion of the *North American Free Trade Agreement (NAFTA)*, an economic trade bloc that comprises the US, Canada, and Mexico, to include all of the Americas, while others are more cautious, fearing US economic dominance.[37]

> **NAFTA** A free trade agreement between the US, Canada, and Mexico that sought to encourage trade between the three countries.

Critics of the OAS argue that the organization is so dominated by the US that other member states have very little influence in the organization. They point out that the US provides the majority of the OAS's budget[38] and maintain that it uses this financial domination to control how the IGO functions. One frequently cited example of the US's influence over the organization is that even though every country in Latin and Central America has diplomatic relations with Cuba, Cuba is not allowed to participate in the OAS because of US opposition.[39] Others point to examples in which the US used its military in the region without OAS consultation, intervening in the internal affairs of sovereign nations and supporting dictators in direct opposition to its stated democratic agenda, as evidence of the OAS's impotence in the face of US unilateral action.[40] However, the end of the Cold War and the advent of the US "War on Terror" have shifted US attention to regions outside the American Hemisphere. Some welcome the US's lesser role in the region and in the OAS, while others see this as evidence that the OAS is no longer a relevant institution. While some may argue that the time has come to dissolve the organization, others maintain that, although it needs reform, it continues to function as an important forum where the United States, Canada, and the nations of Latin American can formally meet to discuss issues facing both the hemisphere and the individual countries within it.[41]

League of Arab States (LAS)

League of Arab States   A regional international organization of Arab states designed to promote cooperation among, and safeguard the sovereignty of, member states.

The Arab world also has an IGO – the *League of Arab States* (LAS), also referred to as the Arab League. The Arab League was founded in Cairo in 1945, just before the end of World War II, to promote cooperation among, to safeguard the sovereignty of, and to advance the political, economic, and social interests of its member states. The League began with seven member states: Egypt, Iraq, Lebanon, Saudi Arabia, Syria, Transjordan (Jordan from 1946), and Yemen. The primary issues of the day were freeing Arab countries under colonial rule and preventing the creation of a Jewish state in Palestine.[42] Currently, the League has 22 members including Palestine, which it regards as an independent state, and straddles two continents – Western Asia and Northern Africa (see table 3.7). It is an important forum where Arab leaders come together to advocate policy, to discuss regional issues and crises, and to mediate disputes.

Unlike the Organization of American States, membership in the Arab League is based on culture rather than geography. It also differs significantly from IGOs like the European Union, in that it has not achieved a significant degree of integration among member states. This has been due both to internal divisions among members as well as the League's own policies. There have been conflicts between traditional monarchies and new republics, for example, and members are often sharply divided about foreign policy decisions in regard to Israel, the US, Iran, and Iraq. Also, decisions made by the League are binding only for the members who vote for them, which severely limits its ability to coordinate and enforce foreign, defense, and economic policies.[43] The League has, however, achieved a variety of more modest albeit important successes, including the shaping of school curricula and the preservation of manuscripts.[44]

Organization of Petroleum Exporting Countries (OPEC)   Made up of oil-producing countries, this organization tries to stabilize the oil market by regulating the supply of the commodity.

Product-specific IGOs

In addition to cultural and regional IGOs, there are also a variety of product-specific international organizations. One such IGO is the *Organization of Petroleum Exporting Countries*

Table 3.7 Arab League Member States and Observers[45]

Member States	Admission Date
Egypt	March 22, 1945
Iraq	
Jordan	
Lebanon	
Saudi Arabia	
Syria	
Yemen	May 5, 1945
Libya	March 28, 1953
Sudan	January 19, 1956
Morocco	October 1, 1958
Tunisia	
Kuwait	July 20, 1961
Algeria	August 16, 1962
United Arab Emirates	December 6, 1971
Bahrain	September 11, 1971
Qatar	
Oman	September 29, 1971
Mauritania	November 26, 1973
Somalia	February 14, 1974
Palestine	September 9, 1976
Djibouti	September 4, 1977
Comoros	November 20, 1993

Observer States	Date
Eritrea	Observer since 2003
Venezuela	Observer since 2006
India	Observer since 2007

(OPEC), created in 1960 by Iran, Iraq, Kuwait, Saudi Arabia, and Venezuela, and then later joined by Qatar (1961), Indonesia (1962), Libya (1962), United Arab Emirates (1967), Algeria (1969), Nigeria (1971), Ecuador (1973), Angola (2007), and Gabon (1975–94).[46] The purpose of OPEC is to regulate the oil supply and help stabilize prices. Product-driven organizations like OPEC have had mixed results in achieving their goals, often because of the differences among the countries exporting the product. For example, OPEC is made up of both rich and poor states that have varying amounts of oil. Some nations depend upon oil for the majority of their revenues; for other countries, oil is just one among many products that they export. These differences lead to different ideas about policies and directions for the future. Another problem these types of organizations have is that they often lack enforcement mechanisms, which means they can create policies and make recommendations, but they lack the power to discipline members who fail to comply.

Non-Governmental Organizations (NGOs)

non-governmental organizations (NGOs) A legally constructed organization made up of individuals. These have a limited, if any, role for nation-states.

Non-governmental organizations, or NGOs, are private organizations without government participation or representation. Although there are many NGOs that operate at the national level, this chapter focuses on international organizations, and thus will concentrate on international NGOs, private organizations made of up individuals from a variety of countries. While they may be headquartered in one country, they are not a part of any one country or government. NGOs are funded in a variety of ways. Many receive funding from governments, retaining their non-governmental status by excluding government representatives from membership in the organization, while others rely solely on their members for support. Some are grassroots organizations with small budgets, while others have huge budgets and a large staff responsible for administering the organization's various programs.

Types of international NGO

Since the beginning of the 1900s, the growth of international NGOs has been dramatic. From roughly 175 in 1909, to more than 45,000 in 2002,[47] NGOs have grown not only in total numbers, but also in terms of their role in the international community. There are very few causes for which there is not an NGO, but there are three broad categories into which NGO work can generally be classified: human rights/humanitarian, development, and environmental.[48] Human rights NGOs monitor and report human rights abuses and advocate for better human rights standards and laws. Amnesty International, perhaps the most well-known international human rights NGO, undertakes research and action aimed at preventing and ending abuses of the rights enshrined in the *Universal Declaration of Human Rights*,[49] "demanding that all governments and other powerful entities respect the rule of law."[50] The organization engages in a variety of global and local campaigns designed to end violence against women, defend the rights of the poor, abolish the death penalty, end torture, free prisoners of conscience, protect the rights of refugees, and regulate the global arms trade.[51]

Universal Declaration of Human Rights Adopted by the United Nations in 1948, the declaration describes the rights to which all human beings are entitled.

Development NGOs provide aid to support the economic, social, and political development of developing countries. Although some NGOs may be classified as both humanitarian and development organizations, a common distinction made between the two is that humanitarian aid provides immediate relief to a problem, freeing a political prisoner, for example, or providing medical attention to a refugee, while development aid is focused on developing social and economic structures that will enrich communities and eliminate poverty in the long term. Development NGOs engage in activities such as establishing schools, providing microloans to help people start businesses, developing health-care facilities and programs in underserved communities, and educating farmers about sustainable agriculture. BRAC, formerly the Bangladesh Rural Advancement Committee, is the world's largest non-governmental organization, providing billions of dollars in microloans. It also provides health care to 80 million Bangladeshis. Working with the government's immunization program, BRAC instituted an anti-diarrhea drive that "cut child mortality for children under 5 from 25 to 7 percent over the past three decades." In addition to its healthcare initiatives, it has a network of "52,000 schools serving 1.5 million students." Although it began as a national NGO serving Bangladesh, it has extended its programs into sub-Saharan African and Afghanistan.[52]

Finally, environmental NGOs focus on improving the state of the natural environment. Areas of action include air, water, and land clean-up initiatives; the preservation of natural landscapes, animals, and resources; and sustainable use of land and resources. The World Wildlife Fund, for example, works to protect natural areas and wild plants and animals, to promote sustainable approaches to the use of natural resources, and to advocate for more efficient use of resources and energy and the reduction of pollution. Greenpeace, another international environmental NGO, has been more controversial in some of its approaches, sending its boats between whales and whalers as well as dispatching their vessels to nuclear test zones in an attempt to stop nuclear testing. (For more information on this, see the discussion of the *Rainbow Warrior* in chapter 2.)

NGO activities and effectiveness

Unlike governments, which have legal power, and *multinational corporations* (MNCs), which have financial power, NGOs rely on moral authority, information, and advocacy to be effective. So while some organizations, like Greenpeace, send people into the field in an effort to prevent specific actions, gathering and disseminating information are far more common NGO activities. The idea is that change

multinational corporations (MNCs)
A corporation or enterprise that manages production or delivers services in more than one country.

has a better chance of occurring if people know what's going on. If no one knows, for example, that a political dissident has been wrongfully imprisoned, or if no one knows that a company is polluting the town's water supply, then there is no impetus for change. However, once people are aware of the problem, they can engage in actions that pressure the offending parties to change their behavior. NGOs are often in the business, then, of making people aware of both problems and their potential solutions.

The Internet has made dramatic contributions to the growth and effectiveness of NGOs, transforming the way they communicate, coordinate, and advocate. The Internet allows citizens from all over the world to participate in global civil society, facilitating connections, communication, and the development of new kinds of communities. NGOs in the Internet age have also benefited from the speed at which information can be distributed worldwide. They can now draw immediate international attention to human rights abuses or environmental scandals simply by sending an email, posting a blog entry, or uploading a photograph or a video. As a result, it is increasingly difficult for nation-states to crackdown on their citizens without the eyes of the world upon them.[53]

The effectiveness of NGOs vary, but there are several factors that contribute to success. These include the number of members and their commitment and willingness to engage in organization activities, such as letter-writing and fundraising; the amount of money the NGO has to carry out its mission; the leadership of the organization; its access to policy-makers and the media; and its ability to maintain its autonomy from nation-states. Another way that some NGOs have sought to increase their effectiveness is by becoming accredited as a consultative body of the UN, a provision outlined in the original UN Charter. In 2008, the number of UN accredited NGOs had grown to more than 3,050.[54]

NGO relationships with states and multinational corporations

Relations between NGOs and states can be tense because NGOs often operate as watchdogs over government actions. For example, many demand government accountability, monitoring government compliance with treaties and other rules of international law. NGOs have increased their role in affecting state behavior by helping draft international conventions and treaties, by providing expert advice to states, and by performing functions that states cannot or would rather not perform. As a result, NGOs have mixed interactions with states. Some NGOs work closely with states, receiving funding from them and coordinating programs or relief efforts, while others go to great lengths to distance themselves from governments. Likewise, governments sometimes choose to work with NGOs, but some have also violently targeted organizations in an effort to silence them. During the late 1970s and 1980s, for example, the governments in El Salvador and Guatemala targeted a number of human rights-based NGOs that focused on issues such as justice for the poor and land reform. Many NGO members were arrested, others fled their country, and still others were killed.[55]

In addition to monitoring states, NGOs also monitor MNCs, reporting on their behavior and sometimes attempting to influence their actions via boycotts and other forms of pressure. For example, the Citizens' Clearinghouse for Hazardous Waste (CCHW) coordinated a three-year public relations and consumer awareness campaign focused on McDonald's use of Styrofoam, informing people about the ozone-depleting CFCs used to make the packaging material and its failure to degrade in landfills. CCHW also supplied ideas for and coordinated actions, such as having groups across the United States order food from McDonald's and then ask that they "hold the toxics" by not using the styrofoam packaging. In 1990, the worldwide fast food chain ended its use of Styrofoam packaging.[56]

While some MNCs have been accused of working closely with governments to suppress NGOs, other MNCs have worked successfully with NGOs to put pressure on governments to improve their human rights records.[57] One example of IGOs, MNCs, and NGOs coming together is the 1999 "Global Compact" (GC). Because of concerns raised by NGOs about human rights, workers rights, and environ-mental degradation, some MNCs signed the Global Compact, pledging to work with the United Nations to promote human rights and sustainable use of the environment. NGOs, corporate leaders, and UN Secretary General Kofi Annan held a press conference to launch the effort. While some NGOs believe that the GC constitutes an important step toward global corporate responsibility, critics argue that voluntary membership and the absence of policing mechanisms limit its effectiveness.[58]

NGO critics and supporters

NGOs are not without their problems and their critics. Because competition for resources is intense, NGOs do not always work well together, even when they share common causes. Also, broad-based, international memberships can lead to serious divisions within NGOs over which ideas and directions should be given priority. For example, some international human rights groups have experienced internal divisions: while Western human rights activists' have tended to push their organ-izations to focus on individual rights, such as freedom of speech, activists from developing countries have often been more interested in focusing on issues of poverty and barriers to development. The role of women has been a particularly divisive issue for international NGOs. Many NGO members from the developed world have decried the lack of human rights protections afforded to women, particularly in the developing world. Some human rights activists in the developing world, how-ever, have argued that women's roles in their society are dictated by religion and culture, which are as important, if not more important, than protecting the rights of women.

As the influence of NGOs has grown, so too has criticism against them and their role in national and international politics. Critics argue that NGOs have become too powerful and are wielding too much influence in the international community. Writer Michael Shaw-Bond summed up some of the criticisms against NGOs as follows: "Where once global politics were dictated exclusively by elected govern-ments, now elected governments must compete with 'civil society' – interest groups accountable only to themselves but often with significant financial resources, the management structure of a multinational company and a media image that governments can only envy."[59] According to international relations scholar Jessica Mathews, NGOs are stepping into roles that were once the purview of the nation-state: "Today NGOs deliver more official development assistance than the entire UN system (excluding the World Bank and the International Monetary Fund). In many countries they are delivering the services – in urban and rural community development, education, and health care – that faltering governments can no longer manage."[60] This increased role for NGOs has been criticized by governments in countries as diverse as Afghanistan, Russia, Australia, and the US. Concerns that NGOs are operating in the international system without oversight, transparency, and accountability are also driving some of this criticism. Finally, Mike Edwards,

Director of the Ford Foundation, suggests that the criticism of NGOs has reached such a peak that, "NGO bashing has become a favourite sport for government officials, business and the Press."[61] This criticism of NGOs led to the development of websites designed to monitor their activities and to provide a critique of their growing role.[62]

Supporters of NGOs point to a growing amount of evidence that their work is successful. For example, NGOs helped bring an end to apartheid in South Africa by informing people about its abusive and repressive policies and by organizing boycotts of both South African businesses and South African trading partners. NGOs drove the 1992 Earth Summit's focus on the reduction of greenhouse gas emissions, which in turn led to the *Kyoto Protocol*. NGOs have also successfully motivated nation-states to codify human rights and other humanitarian treaties and conventions. Additionally, they have provided much-needed aid and relief supplies when governments and IGOs were either unwilling or unable to do so. For example, after the devastating Indian Ocean tsunami hit Asia in 2004, NGOs were quickly on the ground providing relief to victims.[63] Supporters also maintain that NGOs are not a threat to national sovereignty; rather, they help and protect the interests of people within countries that have prioritized state security over "human security." In other words, when states focus resources on protecting themselves rather than on improving the conditions of daily life for their citizens, NGOs step in to focus on human security, "including food, shelter, employment, health, public safety."[64] NGO supporters maintain that the growth of NGOs focusing on these concerns in the international arena is a positive development because it gives individuals and communities a greater voice in a state-dominated international system.

> **Kyoto Protocol**   A UN Convention designed to lower greenhouse gas emissions that contribute to climate change.

In Focus: Amnesty International

> **Amnesty International**   An NGO dedicated to the protection of political and civil human rights.

Founded in 1961, *Amnesty International* (AI) now has more than 2.2 million members in more than 150 countries around the world. Its goal is to monitor and publish information about governments' human rights violations. In order to do this it;

- sends experts to talk with victims;
- observes trials;
- interviews local officials;
- liaises with human rights activists;
- monitors global and local media;
- publishes detailed reports;
- informs the news media;
- publicizes concerns in documents, leaflets, posters, advertisements, newsletters, and websites;

- helps stop human rights abuses by mobilizing the public to put pressure on governments, armed political groups, companies and intergovernmental bodies via public demonstrations, vigils, letter-writing campaigns, human rights education, awareness-raising concerts, direct lobbying, targeted appeals, email petitions and other online actions, partnerships with local campaigning groups, community activities, and cooperation with student groups.[65]

Each year, AI publishes a human rights report that details the abuses that people around the world suffer at the hands of governments. Many nations, well aware of the attention this report receives, try to cooperate with AI and their fact-finding missions, though this is not always the case. AI reports are also often used by governments to assess other countries' human rights records. For example, when answering reporters' questions about the US invasion of Iraq in 2003, then Secretary of Defense Donald Rumsfeld repeatedly referred to Amnesty International reports about human rights abuses by the Hussein regime as part of the rationale for the US invasion.[66]

Supporters of the organization claim that AI campaigns have saved the lives of thousands, promoted the acceptance of human rights, and forced governments to become more accountable. AI has brought the plight of prisoners of conscience and refugees to the world's attention, as well as focused attention on state-sponsored capital punishment and torture. It has also worked for the establishment of the International Criminal Court (2002) and the office of the United Nations High Commissioner for Human Rights (1993). In 1977, it won the Nobel Peace Prize for "having contributed to securing the ground for freedom, for justice, and thereby also for peace in the world." In 1978, it won the UN Human Rights Prize for "outstanding contributions in the field of human rights."[67] It also enjoys consultative status with the UN.

Detractors of AI's work claim that the organization is selective in the cases it highlights and that it is biased against certain governments and unduly influenced by others. Some claim that AI's actions have historically been aligned with US and British interests. For example, although AI was critical of the human rights record of the South African government, it refused to condemn apartheid, because, some critics argue, the British and US governments were the apartheid regime's biggest economic and political supporters. By 2005, however, the world had changed, and the US found itself featured prominently in AI's annual report as a top human rights offender. Among other issues, the report highlighted the US detention without trial of more than 500 men at Guantánamo Bay, Cuba. The Bush administration dismissed the allegations as "ridiculous and unsupported"[68] and "absurd." Vice President Dick Cheney went so far as to say that he did not take Amnesty International "seriously."[69] But as William F. Schultz, Executive Director of AI's US branch, pointed out in his *New York Times* letter to the editor, the Bush administration has taken the group seriously enough to cite its reports when they have served its purposes.[70] The US is not the first, nor will it be the last, to accuse Amnesty International of bias. And while each charge should be critically examined, it is also clear that being in the

Researching to Learn   *Investigating NGOs Online*

Global Policy Forum
"Paper on NGO Participation at the United Nations"
(March 28, 2006). This paper defines NGOs, discusses their relationship with states, businesses, and regional and international institutions.
www.globalpolicy.org/ngos/index.htm

NGO Global Network
A website designed to promote collaboration among NGOs.
www.globalpolicy.org/ngos/index.htm

World Association of Non-Governmental Organizations (WANGO)
A worldwide NGO directory that allows visitors to select geographic regions from which to conduct research on NGOs.
www.wango.org/resources.aspx?section=ngodir

Department of Public Information (DPI)
This site provides information on collaboration between the UN DPI and NGOs.
www.un.org/dpi/ngosection/index.asp

The Global Development Research Center: The NGO Café
This is a virtual library on NGOs. Contains general information on various NGOs.
www.gdrc.org/ngo/

Union of International Associations (UIA) – International Organizations and NGOs Project
This site provides a list of links to NGOs and IOs along with some information on each.
www.uia.org/organizations/home.php#

Global Governance Watch (Formerly NGOWatch.org)
A website dedicated to monitor actions by NGOs and IGOs and the impact these actions have on domestic policy, primarily in the US.
www.globalgovernancewatch.org/

Duke University Libraries' NGO Research Guide – Key Resources
Contains links to various NGOs and NGO directories.
http://library.duke.edu/research/subject/guides/ngo_guide/

United Nations Office at Geneva (UNOG) – Non-Government Organizations Database
A searchable database for NGOs with consultative states with the UN Economic and Social Council.
www.unog.ch/80256EE60057E07D/(httpPages)/3101491B86487F6D80256EFC0061DFD9?OpenDocument

business of publicly reporting on and chastising governments for their human rights abuses makes AI a target of criticism by governments that don't agree with or appreciate the picture that the organization is painting of them and distributing to the world.

Conclusion

While the nation-state continues to be the prominent actor in the international arena, international organizations such as IGOs and NGOs are playing an increasingly important role. In some cases these organizations are taking over duties that were once the purview of the nation-state, including providing education, health care, and infrastructure development. Although most states are generally willing to give up some degree of sovereignty in order to be part of an IGO, states are primarily motivated by self-interest, which causes them to resist giving IGOs too much power. This unwillingness to relinquish power also limits the effectiveness of

IGOs. As people call for more effective IGOs, states must grapple with the costs and benefits that come with surrendering varying degrees of power to IGOs.

While nation-states engage with each other via IGOs, individuals are able to both work with nation-states and challenge their power through NGOs. Like their IGO counterparts, NGOs often step in to address needs that are not being taken care of by governments, but they are also challenging states to expand their view of self-interest to include notions of global connectedness and human security. Although this push for global civil society engenders strong resistance in some quarters, it is likely to continue, facilitated by advances in technology and communication that are shrinking the globe and multiplying webs of connections. Technology not only facilitates the growth and proliferation of NGOs, but also makes it easier to monitor both NGO activities and how NGOs are treated in the countries in which they operate.

Notes

1 The Woodrow Wilson Presidential Library, "Wilson's Fourteen Points," www.woodrowwilson.org/learn_sub/learn_sub_show.htm?doc_id=377217.

2 "UN Millennium Message," BBC, http://news.bbc.co.uk/1/hi/special_report/millennium/584374.stm.

3 African National Congress, "Acceptance Speech of the President of the African National Congress, Nelson Mandela, at the Nobel Peace Prize Award Ceremony: Oslo, Norway. December 10, 1993," www.anc.org.za/ancdocs/speeches/nobelnrm.html.

4 Maryann Cusimano Love, "Intergovernmental Organization and Transsovereign Problems," in Maryann Cusimano Love (ed.), *Beyond Sovereignty Issues for a Global Agenda*, 2nd edn. (Belmont, CA: Thomson Wadsworth Publishing), 45.

5 A. LeRoy Bennett and James K. Oliver, *International Organizations Principles and Issues*, 7th edn. (Upper Saddle, NJ: Prentice Hall, 2002), 28.

6 Ibid., 42.

7 Ibid., 70.

8 Barbara Crossett, "US Still Alone in Opposition to New Term for Boutros-Ghali," *New York Times* (July 16, 1996), http://query.nytimes.com/gst/fullpage.html?res=9D04EFD71E39F935A25754C0A960958260.

9 "Background Information: Information about the Council," United Nations, www.un.org/ecosoc/about/.

10 Source: United Nations, www.un.org/aboutun/chart_en.pdf.

11 Kofi Annan, "'In Larger Freedom': Decision Time at the UN," *Foreign Affairs* (May/June 2005), www.foreignaffairs.org/20050501faessay84307/kofi-annan/in-larger-freedom-decision-time-at-the-un.html.

12 Kamil Idris and Michael Bartolo, *A Better United Nations for the New Millennium: The United Nations System: How It Is Now and How It Should Be in the Future* (The Hague, Netherlands: Martinus Nijhoff Publishers, 2000), 152.

13 The Fund for Peace and the Carnegie Endowment for International Peace, *Foreign Policy*, "Failed States Index 2008" (July/August 2008), www.foreignpolicy.com/story/cms.php?story_id=4350&page=1.

14 "All about the United Nations Budget," United Nations Association of the United States of America, June 2006, www.unausa.org/site/pp.asp?c=fvKRI8MPJpF&b=1813833.

15 Ibid.

16 Ibid.

17 Ibid.

18 Source: Global Policy Forum, www.globalpolicy.org/finance/tables/core/debt07.htm.

19 "Chapter VII," United Nations Charter, www.un.org/aboutun/charter/chapter7.htm.

20 For more on charges leveled against UN Peacekeepers, see Colum Lynch, "UN Faces More Accusations of Sexual Misconduct Officials Acknowledge 'Swamp' of Problems and Pledge Fixes Amid New Allegations in Africa, Haiti," *Washington*

Post (March 13, 2005), A22; "Peacekeepers Sell Arms to Somalis" BBC (May 23, 2008), http://news.bbc.co.uk/2/hi/africa/7417435.stm; and David Clarke, "Child Abuse By Aid Workers, Peacekeepers Rife – Study," Reuters-Africa (May 27, 2008), http://africa.reuters.com/top/news/usnBAN724534.html.

21   "United Nations Peacekeeping," United Nations, www.un.org/Depts/dpko/dpko/faq/q9.htm.

22   "Payments Owed to the UN by the 15 Major Debtor Countries: 2007," Global Policy Forum, www.globalpolicy.org/finance/tables/core/debt07.htm.

23   "What is the World Trade Organization?" Understanding the WTO: Basics, World Trade Organization, www.wto.org/english/thewto_e/whatis_e/tif_e/fact1_e.htm.

24   T. K. Bhaumik, *The WTO: A Discordant Orchestra* (Thousand Oaks, CA: Sage Publications, 2006), 35.

25   "Principles of the Trading System," Understanding the WTO: Basics, World Trade Organization, www.wto.org/english/thewto_e/whatis_e/tif_e/fact2_e.htm.

26   William R. Slomanson, *Fundamental Perspectives on International Law*, 2nd edn. (St Paul, MN: West Publishing), 581.

27   "The Case for Open Trade," Understanding the WTO: Basics, World Trade Organization, www.wto.org/english/thewto_e/whatis_e/tif_e/fact3_e.htm.

28   Ibid.

29   For further research into policy areas where EU member have disagreed, see: Gretchen Vogel, "At Odds Again Over Stem Cells," *Science* 301, no. 5631 (July 18, 2003), 289; Bernard E. Brown, "Europe Against America: A New Superpower Rivalry?" *American Foreign Policy Interests* 24, no. 4 (August 2003), 309; Mette Eilstrup Sangiovanni, "Why a Common Security and Defence Policy is Bad for Europe," *Survival* 45, no. 4 (Winter 2003/4), 193–206; *The Economist*, "Dissent and disagreement," 375, no. 8428 (May 28, 2005), 40–2.

30   Slomanson, *Fundamental Perspectives*, 136.

31   *Guardian*, "Ireland Delivers Stunning Blow to Europe's Leaders" (June 14, 2008), www.guardian.co.uk/world/2008/jun/14/eu.ireland1.

32   Article 5 of the North Atlantic Treaty reads as follows: "The Parties agree that an armed attack against one or more of them in Europe or North America shall be considered an attack against them all and consequently they agree that, if such an armed attack occurs, each of them, in exercise of the right of individual or collective self-defence recognised by Article 51 of the Charter of the United Nations, will assist the Party or Parties so attacked by taking forthwith, individually and in concert with the other Parties, such action as it deems necessary, including the use of armed force, to restore and maintain the security of the North Atlantic area." The North Atlantic Treaty, Washington DC, April 4, 1949, North Atlantic Treaty Organization On-line Library, www.nato.int/docu/basictxt/treaty.htm.

33   Kosovo became the scene of brutal battles between the primarily Albanian citizens of the region and the primarily Serb led government. Civilians were massacred, leading to charges that war crimes were being committed by Serb forces, led by Slobodan Milosevic.

34   "NATO Allies Clash Over Iraq Role Saturday," BBC (April 3, 2004), http://news.bbc.co.uk/2/hi/europe/3595501.stm.

35   "OAS History at a Glance," Organization of American States, www.oas.org/key_issues/eng/KeyIssue_Detail.asp?kis_sec=17.

36   Sean Bartlett, "The Organization of American States: On Its Deathbed?" Council on Hemispheric Affairs (October 19, 2007), www.coha.org/2007/10/the-organization-of-american-states-on-itsdeathbed/.

37   For more on the changing role of the OAS, see, Richard E. Feinberg, *Summitry in the Americas: A Progress Report* (Washington, DC: Institute for International Economics, 1997); Andrew F. Cooper, "The OAS Democratic Solidarity Paradigm: Questions of Collective and National Leadership," *Latin American Politics and Society* (Spring 2001); Dexter S. Boniface, "A Democratic Norm for the Western Hemisphere?," paper presented at the 2004 Latin American Studies Association (LASA) Conference, October 2004; T. A. Imobighe, *The OAU (AU) and the OAS in Regional Conflict Management: A Comparative Assessment* (Ibadan, Nigeria: Spectrum Books, 2003); Andrew F. Cooper and Thomas Legler, "The OAS in Peru: A Model for the Future?" *Journal of Democracy* 12, no. 4 (October 2001); Cynthia McClintock, "The OAS in Peru: Room for Improvement," *Journal of Democracy* 12, no. 4 (October 2001); and Arturo Valenzuela, "Paraguay: The Coup That Didn't Happen," *Journal of Democracy*, 8, no. 1 (January 1997).

38 For more on the US relationship to the OAS, see Clare Ribando, "Organization of American States: A Primer," Congressional Research Service, www.fas.org/sgp/crs/row/RS22095.pdf.

39 "Cuba remains a member, but its government has been excluded from participation in the OAS since 1962." "By resolution of the Eighth Meeting of Consultation of Ministers of Foreign Affairs (1962) the current Government of Cuba is excluded from participation in the OAS." "Member States and Permanent Missions," Organization of American States, www.oas.org/documents/eng/memberstates.asp.

40 For some discussion on the relations between the US and Latin America, see Andrew F. Cooper, "The Making of the Inter-American Democratic Charter: A Case of Complex Multilateralism," *International Studies Perspectives* 5 (2004), 92–113; and Gordon Mace and Louis Bélanger (eds.), *The Americas in Transition: The Contours of Regionalism* (Boulder, CO: Lynne Rienner, 1999).

41 Bartlett, "The Organization of American States: On Its Deathbed?"

42 "Profile: Arab League," BBC News, http://news.bbc.co.uk/2/hi/middle_east/country_profiles/1550797.stm.

43 "Profile: Arab League," BBC News.

44 Ibid.

45 Source: "About the Arab League: Member States," League of Arab States, www.arableagueonline.org/las/english/level2_en.jsp?level_id=11. Although the Arab League website lists March 22, 1945 as the date when Yemen joined the League, the "Pact of the League of Arab States, March 22, 1945," footnote 3, states that "The Pact was signed on Mar. 22, 1945, by the Contracting Parties, with the exception of Yemen, which signed on May 5, 1945." See "Pact of the League of Arab States, March 22, 1945," The Avalon Project at Yale Law School, www.yale.edu/lawweb/avalon/mideast/arableag.htm.

46 "Brief History: The Organization of the Petroleum Exporting Countries (OPEC)," Organization of the Petroleum Exporting Countries, www.opec.org/aboutus/history/history.htm.

47 Love Cusimano, "Nongovernmental Organizations," 75. However, this figure should be considered a rough estimate, as NGO numbers are notoriously hard to measure.

48 Bennett and Oliver, *International Organizations*, 283.

49 Commissioner for Human Rights, *Universal Declaration of Human Rights*, English Version, United Nations Department of Public Information, www.unhchr.ch/udhr/lang/eng.htm.

50 "About Amnesty International," Amnesty International, www.amnesty.org/en/who-we-are/about-amnesty-international.

51 Ibid.

52 Foreign Policy, "The List: The World's Most Powerful Development NGOs" (July 2008), www.foreignpolicy.com/story/cms.php?story_id=4364.

53 In 1994, in the state of Chiapas, a local rebellion against the government of Mexico was violently suppressed. As Jessica Mathews put it: "Within hours of the first gunshots of the Chiapas rebellion in southern Mexico in January 1994, for example, the Internet swarmed with messages from human rights activists. The worldwide media attention they and their groups focused on Chiapas, along with the influx of rights activists to die area, sharply limited the Mexican government's response. What in other times would have been a bloody insurgency turned out to be a largely nonviolent conflict. 'The shots lasted ten days,' Jose Angel Gurria, Mexico's foreign minister, later remarked, 'and ever since, the war has been . . . a war on the Internet.'" Jessica T. Mathews, "Power Shift: The Rise of Global Civil Society," *Foreign Affairs* (January/February 1997), 54.

In the case of the Chinese crackdown on pro-democracy demonstrators in Tiananmen Square (1989), fax machines were widely used to co-ordinate demonstrations as phone lines of known dissidents were routinely tapped.

54 United Nations Department of Economic and Social Affairs (August 5, 2008), www.un.org/esa/coordination/ngo/.

55 Love Cusimano, "Nongovernmental Organizations."

56 Penny Newman, "Killing Legally with Toxic Waste: Women and the Environment in the United States" in Vandana Shiva (ed.), *Close to Home: Women Reconnect Ecology, Health and Development* (London: Earthscan, 1993), 55.

57 Morton Winston, "NGO Strategies for Promoting Corporate Social Responsibility," *Ethics & International Affairs* 16, no. 1 (Spring 2002).

58 Ibid., 78. For more on the Global Compact, see United Nations, "Global Compact," www.unglobalcompact.org/.

59　Michael Shaw-Bond, "The Backlash Against NGOs," *Prospect Magazine* (April 2000).

60　Matthews, "Power Shift," 53.

61　Mike Edwards, "Time to put the NGO House in Order," *Financial Times* (June 6, 2000).

62　One such website was founded in 2003 by the politically conservative American Enterprise Institute and the Federalist Society for Law and Public Policy Studies and was called "ngowatch.org." It has since changed its name to globalgovernancewatch.org. According to its website, the goal of the site is to "to raise awareness of the growing global governance movement and to address issues of transparency and accountability at the United Nations, in NGOs, and related international organizations. In particular, the project monitors issues of national sovereignty and the ways in which the agendas of international organizations influence domestic politics." "About Global Governance Watch" www.globalgovernancewatch.org/about/.

63　P. K. Balachandran "Much maligned NGOs Fill a Gap in Tsunami-hit Lanka," *The Hindustan Times* (April 11, 2005).

64　Matthews, "Power Shift," 51.

65　"Frequently Asked Questions," Amnesty International, www.amnesty.org/en/who-we-are/faq#what-is-ai.

66　See for example the debriefings given by Rumsfeld: www.defenselink.mil/transcripts/transcript.aspx?transcriptid=2174; www.defenselink.mil/transcripts/transcript.aspx?transcriptid=2180; www.defenselink.mil/transcripts/transcript.aspx?transcriptid=2229.

67　"The history of Amnesty International," Amnesty International, www.amnesty.org/en/who-we-are/history.

68　Press Briefing by Scott McClellan, www.whitehouse.gov/news/releases/2005/05/20050525-3.html#l.

69　Lizette Alvarez, "Rights Group Defends Chastising of US," *New York Times* (June 4, 2005), www.nytimes.com/2005/06/04/international/europe/04amnesty.html?ex=1275&pagewanted=all.

70　William F. Schulz, "Rights Group Answers Bush," *New York Times* (June 4, 2005), www.nytimes.com/2005/06/04/opinion/l04amnesty.html?_r=1&oref=slogin.

4

HUMAN RIGHTS

"One part of mankind is set aside by nature to be slaves." (Juan Ginés de Sepúlveda [1494–1573] referring to Spanish treatment of Native Americans)[1]

"All the peoples of the world are men." (Bartolomé de Las Casas [1484–1566] referring to Spanish treatment of Native Americans)[2]

"It is never the people who complain of human rights as a Western or Northern imposition. It is too often their leaders who do so." (Kofi Annan, 1997, United Nations Secretary-General)[3]

Learning to Question, Questioning to Learn

- What are human rights and from where do they originate?
- What issues prevent universal agreement on what constitutes human rights?
- Are human rights culturally specific or universal?
- How are human rights monitored and how are human rights treaties enforced?

Introduction

This chapter begins by exploring the origins of human rights. This is followed by a discussion of how the protection of human rights became an obligation of nation-states. Next, the chapter focuses on various documents that underpin the human rights movement as well as the various debates that surround the conceptualization and implementation of human rights protections. The chapter then moves on to provide an overview of human rights monitoring and enforcement. Finally, the chapter concludes with a brief introduction to emerging human rights issues.

Where Do Human Rights Come From?

Schools of thought about the origins of human rights

schools of thought Groups of theorists who share common ideas.

natural law A set of universal and immutable moral laws that are inscribed in nature.

positivism In the context of human rights, this philosophy argues that consent is a fundamental precondition to the establishment of human rights norms.

There are two prominent *schools of thought* with regard to how one approaches the origins of human rights – *natural law* and *positivism*. The philosophical underpinnings of the natural law perspective can be traced back to the writings of Thomas Aquinas (1225–74), John Locke (1632–1704), Hugo Grotius (1583–1645), Francisco Suarez (1548–1617), and Thomas Hobbes (1588–1679). Though not derived from any one religion, natural law emphasizes duties imposed by God and suggests that a common human morality exists. In other words, all people have an inherent sense of right and wrong. Because natural law is considered part of nature, proponents argue that it has validity everywhere. More specifically natural law posits that

- good law must be in harmony with or reflect the essential nature of all peoples;
- good law incorporates only those principles of justice rooted in the natural reasoning process;
- laws that meet the above requirements are immutable.

This school of thought also posits the existence of human rights, arguing that they are inherent in the individual. As such, they are not dependent upon a state or a document to legitimize them. Rather, each individual is born with these rights. States can pass laws that deny peoples' rights, but that does not mean that people are not entitled to their rights. For example, natural law proponents point to the near universal condemnation of Nazi abuses during the Holocaust as evidence of the existence of natural law. Even though German law may have made legal much of the atrocities of the Holocaust, natural law suggests that there is a higher law than that of states, and that states should in fact abide by the natural law of respecting the life, liberty, and dignity of the individual.

Positivism, the second school of thought, has its roots in the *Protestant Reformation*. It permeates the writings of many prominent sixteenth- and seventeenth-century European philosophers such as John Austin (1790–1859) and Jeremy Bentham (1748–1832). Positivists argue that human rights laws should not be based on naturalist assumptions. Indeed, they question the

Protestant Reformation   Martin Luther's attempt to reform the Catholic Church that led to a schism within the church and the development of the Protestant sect.

very idea that anything can be "natural," since what might seem natural to some might not be considered natural by others. Rather, they argue that human rights exist because states consent to them.

Thus human rights are defined by states. States are also responsible for guaranteeing and protecting them. In other words, in the positivist framework, rights are always dependent upon the willingness of states to consent to protect them. Ironically, positivism itself rests on the naturalist assumption that governments *should* be bound by what they agreed to do.

Historical background

While both natural law and positivism have influenced the development of human rights, a few key events and documents can be identified as laying the groundwork for the modern human rights movement. Because of the dominance of the nation-state in the modern international system, human rights are often described as protections from state action or protection by the state from actions of others within the state. In order to have free speech, for example, a state must agree not to prohibit speech, but it must also establish rules and procedures for individuals to express themselves without interference from other citizens. Thus, it is not surprising that one of the first human rights related documents, the *Magna Carta*, was an attempt to contain the abuses of a government, in this case, the monarchy of Britain. The Magna Carta (1215), while very limited in its scope and breadth, addressed certain rights, including the writ of *habeas corpus*. The writ of habeas corpus prevents citizens from arbitrarily being detained by the government. Specifically, article 39 of the Magna Carta states: "No freemen shall be taken or imprisoned or disseised or exiled or in any way destroyed, nor will we go upon him nor send upon him, except by the lawful judgment of his peers or by the law of the land."[4] The Magna Carta also sought to subject the monarchy to the laws of Britain. Prior to this, monarchs positioned themselves above the laws of their country. The Magna Carta thus set a precedent that would later influence both political thought and action in Western world. It is widely believed to be one of the first modern "democratic" documents, as it sought to establish written rules to guide government action.

Magna Carta   Signed by King John of England in 1215, this document proclaimed certain rights inherent in individuals and declared the King himself was the subject of state laws.

habeas corpus   This Latin phrase refers to a legal action which provides relief from arbitrary detention and allows those held in detention to be informed of the charges against them.

French Revolution   Violent political upheaval in France beginning in 1789, which replaced the monarchy system of government.

It was not until several centuries later that the next significant human rights document emerged. Following the *French Revolution* (1789), the French national assembly passed the *Declaration*

Declaration of the Rights of Man and of the Citizen   Emerging in the aftermath of the French Revolution, this document espouses a series of both individual and collective rights to which all French men were entitled.

of the Rights of Man and of the Citizen, a document containing a list of rights to which all French citizens were entitled. Included among the delineated rights were the right to speak one's opinion, the right to have one's religious views respected, the right to be considered innocent until proven guilty, the right to liberty, and the right to protection of private property.[5] This set a precedent for nation-states to articulate, in some written form, the protections they were willing to offer their citizens. The Declaration of the Rights of Man and of the Citizen not only codified the state's responsibility to protect individuals but also solidified a shift that had begun earlier with the Protestant Reformation. This shift demanded that nation-states treat individuals as citizens with rights rather than as mere subjects of a monarchy.

While the French Revolution had profound consequences for Europe, across the Atlantic, another important human rights document was being formulated. The

constitutional government
A government that is ruled by a constitution which lays out the duties and functions of the government.

Bill of Rights   The first 10 changes, or amendments, to the US Constitution, laying out the rights of US citizens.

victory by the 13 colonies over Britain led to the formation of the United States as a *constitutional government*. The constitutional government established in the newly independent territories ensured that the US would be ruled by elected officials who were guided by a written document that spelled out what the government was entitled to do, how it should be done, and by whom. The constitution was designed to prevent the kinds of abuses that had been rampant in monarchical societies. However, many in the newly created United States believed that the document was not enough to ensure that individuals' rights would be protected. As a result, in 1791, the first 10 amendments to the US constitution were added. The *Bill of Rights* reflected a broader acceptance of the ideals of influential seventeenth- and eighteenth-century thinkers such as John Locke (1632–1794), Jean-Jacques Rousseau (1712–78), and Baron de la Brède et de Montesquieu (1689–1755), whose writings on liberty, freedom, and separation of political power greatly influenced the drafters of the US constitution and the first 10 amendments to it. Both the French Declaration of the Rights of Man and of the Citizen and the US's Bill of Rights broke with tradition, which had dictated that rights were entitlements of one's class. Both also declared that individuals, men specifically, were entitled to rights such as life, liberty, the ability to own property, and the right to due process in legal proceedings, regardless of class or social position. However, one half of the population, namely women, were absent from these documents. Additionally, the reality of discrimination ensured that white males with money would receive special protections. Nevertheless, these documents laid the groundwork for future human rights development.

Researching to Learn   *Genocide in the Twentieth Century*

Sample Keyword Searches

Broad search:
- Genocide
- Mass killings

Narrower searches:
- Genocide AND "20th Century" AND "Human rights"
- "Ethnic cleansing" AND Bosnia

Advanced search:
- (Genocide OR "ethnic cleansing") AND "20th Century" AND (Bosnia OR Serbia OR Yugoslavia OR Balkans)

Note:
- *Use quotation marks to search for terms as a phrase.*
- *Use AND to find documents with all terms listed.*
- *Use OR to find documents that contains at least one of the terms.*
- *Use parentheses to combine AND and OR statements in creative ways.*

Free Web Resources

Center for Excellence on the Study of the Holocaust, Genocide, Human Rights, and Tolerance
   www.csuchico.edu/mjs/center/affiliated_sites/index.html

Genocidewatch
This is a non-governmental organization dedicated to predicting, preventing, and punishing those responsible for genocide.
   www.genocidewatch.org/

PBS series: "The Triumph of Evil"
   www.pbs.org/wgbh/pages/frontline/shows/evil/

United State Holocaust Memorial Museum
This site provides a wealth of information about all genocides, not just the Holocaust.
   www.ushmm.org/

Books: Find Them @ Your Library

Fein, Helen. *Human Rights and Wrongs: Slavery, Terror, Genocide.* Boulder, CO: Paradigm Publishers, 2007.

Gourevitch, Philip. *We Wish to Inform You that Tomorrow We Will be Killed with our Families: Stories from Rwanda,* New York: Farrar, Straus, and Giroux, 1998.

Maimark, Norman M. *Fires of Hatred: Ethnic Cleansing in Twentieth-Century Europe.* Cambridge, MA: Harvard University Press, 2001.

Schabas, William A. *Genocide in International Law: The Crimes of Crimes.* Cambridge: Cambridge University Press, 2000.

Valentino, Benjamin A. *Final Solutions: Mass Killing and Genocide in the Twentieth Century.* Cornell, NY: Cornell University Press, 2004.

Articles: Find Them @ Your Library

Brunk, Darren. "Dissecting Darfur: Anatomy of a Genocide Debate." *International Relations* 22.1 (March 2008): 25–44.

Chung, Christine H. "The Punishment and Prevention of Genocide: The International Criminal Court as a Benchmark of Progress and Need." *Case Western Reserve Journal of International Law* 40.1/2 (2008): 227–42.

De Vito, Daniela. "Rape as Genocide: The Group/Individual Schism." *Human Rights Review* 9.3 (September 2008): 361–78.

Kreß, Claus. "The Crime of Genocide under International Law." *International Criminal Law Review* 6.4 (November 2006): 461–502.

Schabas, William A. "State Policy an Element of International Crimes." *Journal of Criminal Law & Criminology* 98.3 (Spring 2008): 953–82.

Human Rights in the Modern Era

The foregoing documents laid the groundwork for the modern human rights movement as they provided a legal framework from which to operate. The nineteenth century saw the rise of a variety of organizations that spoke to different human rights concerns. *Abolitionists, suffragists,* and peace activists all focused on a particular area of human rights. Though there was much overlap among them, they have often been treated as relatively discrete groups seeking specific aims. Analyzing their speeches and pamphlets, however, reveals that at the core, each was trying to ensure basic human rights protections. Abolitionists were appalled by the institution of slavery, which permitted ownership of one group by another, thereby denying the basic rights of freedom and dignity to the enslaved group. Suffragists rallied around promoting women's rights. Of particular interest was women's exclusion from public life, specifically being denied the full rights of citizenship, including the right to vote. Peace activists argued that war, with its devastating consequences, led to great suffering and many human rights abuses; thus human rights and dignity could be preserved through promoting peaceful alternatives to war. Peace activists believed that human beings had advanced to the point where problems between nation-states could be worked out through diplomacy, or arbitrated through a tribunal, thus eliminating the need for war. Though arguing for different causes, each group anchored their position in the inherent dignity and worth of the individual and questioned governments' abuses of their rights.

abolitionist Someone seeking the eradication of slavery.

suffragists Those who struggle for voting rights for women.

While various groups around the world were engaging in individual campaigns to eradicate certain human rights abuses, it was not until after World War I (1914–18) that the international community of nation-states began to address the topic of human rights via a newly created international organization, the *League of Nations* (see chapter 3). Specifically, negotiations for the organization's creation included lengthy discussions about the protection of minorities within nation-states. The creation of many nation-states in the eighteenth and nineteenth centuries in Europe left many ethnic groups as minority populations within the newly created nation-state. The League required nation-states seeking membership to pledge to protect their minority populations. In addition to this focus on minority rights, the League's Charter included specific human rights language. Article 23 states that members:

League of Nations Established by the Treaty of Versailles, which ended World War I, this organization was designed to provide a forum for conflict dispute resolution, thereby preventing war.

(a) will endeavour to secure and maintain fair and humane conditions of labour for men, women, and children, both in their own countries and in all countries to which their commercial and industrial relations extend, and for that purpose will establish and maintain the necessary international organisations;
(b) undertake to secure just treatment of the native inhabitants of territories under their control.[6]

Despite the language of the Charter, implementation of human rights protections proved difficult. The League's Charter contained no provision to punish nation-states that abused their citizens' rights. Debate over how to implement the human rights provisions of the Charter was permanently interrupted when war again began to spread across Europe, and eventually the rest of the world.

After World War II (1939–45) ended, the *United Nations* (UN) was established, which, unlike its predecessor the League of Nations, has focused more forcefully on human rights. The UN Charter itself contains aspirational provisions designed to internationalize human rights norms. The Preamble of the Charter states "We the Peoples of the United Nations Determined . . . to reaffirm faith in fundamental human rights, in the dignity and worth of the human person, in the equal rights of men and women . . . do hereby establish an international organization to be known as the United Nations."[7] Other articles require member nations to promote respect for human rights and fundamental freedoms. For example, Article 1 states that the purpose of the UN includes "promoting and encouraging respect for human rights and for fundamental freedoms for all without distinction as to race, sex, language, or religion."[8] This is repeated in Articles 55 and 56, which pledge all nations to work with the UN in order to protect human rights. The UN Charter also requires nations to work at both the regional and international level to develop treaties that articulate various human rights. Additionally, nation-states are expected to create the domestic legislation

> **United Nations** International organization founded to prevent war and to promote peace and international cooperation. Total membership in 2009: 192 nation-states.

Researching to Learn   *Finding Information on Human Rights*

Free Web Resources

American Civil Liberties Union
    www.aclu.org
Amnesty International
    www.aiusa.org
Anti-slavery organization
    www.antislavery.org
Business for Social Responsibility
    www.bsr.org
Center for World Indigenous Studies
    www.cwis.org
Council for Secular Humanism
    www.secularhumanism.org
Doctors Without Borders
    www.doctorswithoutborders.org
Equality Now
    www.equalitynow.org
Freedom House
    www.freedomhouse.org

Grassroots International
    www.grassrootsonline.org
Greenpeace
    www.greenpeace.org
Human Rights Campaign
    www.hrc.org
Human Rights Watch
    www.hrw.org
International Gay and Lesbian Human Rights Commission
    www.iglhrc.org
International Human Rights Law Group.
    www.hrlawgroup.org
Lawyers Committee for Human Rights
    www.lchr.org
The National Labor Committee
    www.nlcnet.org
National Organization of Women
    www.now.org

OXFAM America
  www.oxfamamerica.org
Physicians for Human Rights
  www.phrusa.org
Sierra Club
  www.sierraclub.org
Transparency International-USA
  www.transparency-usa.org
The UN High Commissioner for Refugees
  www.unhcr.ch
The UN High Commission for Human Rights
  www.unhcr.org
World Council of Churches.
  www.wcc-coe.org
World Wildlife Fund
  www.worldwildlife.org

Audio/Video on the Web:

Eleanor Roosevelt on the Universal Declaration of Human Rights.
  www.americanrhetoric.com/speeches/
  eleanorrooseveltdeclarationhumanrights.htm
"Torture Can Never Be Justified." Amnesty International video on Torture.
  http://jp.youtube.com/watch?v=tkz_FLxaKnI&
  feature=user
"Amnesty International Report 2008." video on the 60th Anniversary of the Universal Declaration of Human Rights.
  http://jp.youtube.com/watch?v=Fh8E1lx_
  TkM&feature=user
Global Voices.
  http://globalvoicesonline.org/

Books: Find Them @ Your Library

Alston, Philip, Ryan Goodman, Henry J. Steiner. *International Human Rights in Context: Law, Politics, Morals.* Oxford: Oxford University Press, 2007.

An-Naim, Abdullahi Ahmed, ed. *Human Rights in Cross-Cultural Perspectives: A Quest for Consensus.* Philadelphia, PA: University of Pennsylvania Press, 1992.

Anaya, S. James. *Indigenous Peoples in International Law.* Oxford: Oxford University Press, 1996.

Bell, Linda, Andrew Nathan, and Ilan Peleg, eds. *Negotiating Culture and Human Rights.* New York: Columbia University Press, 2001.

Brems, Eva. *Human Rights: Universality and Diversity.* The Hague, The Netherlands: Martinus Nijhoff Publishers, 2001.

Cook, Rebecca J. *Human Rights of Women: National and International Perspectives.* Philadelphia, PA: University of Pennsylvania Press, 1994.

Donnelly, Jack. *International Human Rights (Dilemmas in World Politics).* Boulder, CO: Westview Press, 2006.

Falk, Richard A. *Human Rights Horizons: The Pursuit of Justice in a Globalizing World.* New York and London: Routledge, 2000.

Forsythe, David P. *Human Rights and World Politics,* 2nd edn. Lincoln, NE: University of Nebraska Press, 1989.

Forsythe, David P. *The Internationalization of Human Rights.* Lexington, MA: Lexington Books, 1991.

Sen, Amartya. *Development as Freedom.* New York: Knopf, 1999.

Shepherd, George W. Jr. and Ved P. Nanda, eds. *Human Rights and Third World Development.* Westport, CT: Greenwood Press, 1985.

Welch, Claude E. Jr. and Virginia A. Leary, eds. *Asian Perspectives on Human Rights.* Boulder, CO: Westview Press, 1990.

Scholarly Journals: Find Them @ Your Library

Asia-Pacific Journal on Human Rights and the Law
African Human Rights Law Journal
Harvard Human Rights Journal
Health and Human Rights
Human Rights Brief
Human Rights Case Digest
Human Rights and Human Welfare
Human Rights Law Review
Human Rights Quarterly
Human Rights Review
International Journal of Human Rights
Journal of Human Rights
Muslim World Journal of Human Rights
Northwestern Journal of International Human Rights
Yale Human Rights and Development Law Journal

necessary to carry out the Charter's human rights provisions. Thus, the Charter sets the moral tone and principles for human rights discussion. In addition to the Charter, the UN has taken the lead, with assistance from NGOs, governments, and others, in promulgating dozens of human rights documents.

Some of the most significant human rights documents are collectively referred to as the "International Bill of Rights." The first document in the International Bill of Rights is the previously discussed UN Charter itself. The second is the *Universal Declaration of Human Rights* (UDHR). At the first UN meeting in 1945, a Panamanian delegation introduced a draft document that addressed human rights that was the work of NGOs, including the Inter-American Bar Association, the International League for the Rights of Man, and the American Law Institute, among others. The focus on human rights at that meeting led the *United Nations Economic and Social Council* to establish the Commission on Human Rights in June of 1946. Following this, the *United Nations Commission on Human Rights* selected 18 delegates to begin work on this first international human rights document. The chairperson, former First Lady of the US Eleanor Roosevelt, and representatives from various countries, including China, Lebanon, France, and Australia, all played key roles in promulgating the document and getting the UN *General Assembly* (GA) to pass it. On December 10, 1948, after much debate, the GA voted with little dissent to accept the document prepared by the committee. Only five nations of the *Soviet bloc*, South Africa, and Saudi Arabia abstained from the vote that affirmed the UDHR.[9] The UDHR (see figure 4.1) lays out the various rights to which all people are entitled, no matter where they live. However, the document was a "Declaration" and not a legally binding treaty. As a result, immediately following the GA's acceptance of the UDHR, work began on the promulgation of the legally binding treaties necessary to enshrine the aspirations the UDHR had laid out in international law.

Because the UDHR was not initially legally binding,[10] the next step was to codify the principles stated in the UDHR. The work began in the late 1940s to try to write legally binding treaties that addressed the principles of the UDHR. The end result was the promulgation in 1966 of two different human rights documents, the *International Covenant on Civil and Political Rights* (CPR) and the *International Covenant on Economic, Social and Cultural Rights* (ESCR). These two documents make up the remainder of the International Bill of Rights. The CPR stresses the rights that citizens in Western Europe and the US might find familiar. These rights are found in the beginning of the UDHR (Articles 1–21) and include, for example, the right to assemble, the right

Universal Declaration of Human Rights   Adopted by the United Nations in 1948, the declaration describes the rights to which all human beings are entitled.

United Nations Economic and Social Council   The organ of the UN that promotes international cooperation and development. It performs the majority of the United Nations' work.

United Nations Commission on Human Rights   Made up of 18 delegates chosen to begin work on the first international human rights document. The number was later expanded to 53.

General Assembly (UN)   The organ of the UN that acts as its legislative branch. All member nations can send delegates to the General Assembly. It is also a forum for international dialogue.

Soviet bloc   During the Cold War, this referred to the Soviet Union and its allies (East Germany, Bulgaria, Czechoslovakia, Hungary, Poland, and Romania). It is sometimes also referred to as the Eastern bloc.

International Covenant on Civil and Political Rights   This international human rights instrument codifies the rights found in the first section of the Universal Declaration of Human Rights. It came into force in 1976.

International Covenant on Economic, Social and Cultural Rights   This international human rights instrument codifies the rights found in the second part of the Universal Declaration of Human Rights. It came into force in 1976.

Figure 4.1   Universal Declaration of Human Rights

On December 10, 1948 the General Assembly of the United Nations adopted and proclaimed the Universal Declaration of Human Rights the full text of which appears in the following pages. Following this historic act the Assembly called upon all Member countries to publicize the text of the Declaration and "to cause it to be disseminated, displayed, read and expounded principally in schools and other educational institutions, without distinction based on the political status of countries or territories."

PREAMBLE
Whereas recognition of the inherent dignity and of the equal and inalienable rights of all members of the human family is the foundation of freedom, justice and peace in the world,

Whereas disregard and contempt for human rights have resulted in barbarous acts which have outraged the conscience of mankind, and the advent of a world in which human beings shall enjoy freedom of speech and belief and freedom from fear and want has been proclaimed as the highest aspiration of the common people,

Whereas it is essential, if man is not to be compelled to have recourse, as a last resort, to rebellion against tyranny and oppression, that human rights should be protected by the rule of law,

Whereas it is essential to promote the development of friendly relations between nations,

Whereas the peoples of the United Nations have in the Charter reaffirmed their faith in fundamental human rights, in the dignity and worth of the human person and in the equal rights of men and women and have determined to promote social progress and better standards of life in larger freedom,

Whereas Member States have pledged themselves to achieve, in co-operation with the United Nations, the promotion of universal respect for and observance of human rights and fundamental freedoms,

Whereas a common understanding of these rights and freedoms is of the greatest importance for the full realization of this pledge,

Now, Therefore THE GENERAL ASSEMBLY proclaims THIS UNIVERSAL DECLARATION OF HUMAN RIGHTS as a common standard of achievement for all peoples and all nations, to the end that every individual and every organ of society, keeping this Declaration constantly in mind, shall strive by teaching and education to promote respect for these rights and freedoms and by progressive measures, national and international, to secure their universal and effective recognition and observance, both among the peoples of Member States themselves and among the peoples of territories under their jurisdiction.

Article 1.
All human beings are born free and equal in dignity and rights. They are endowed with reason and conscience and should act towards one another in a spirit of brotherhood.

Article 2.
Everyone is entitled to all the rights and freedoms set forth in this Declaration, without distinction of any kind, such as race, colour, sex, language, religion, political or other opinion, national or social origin, property, birth or other status. Furthermore, no distinction shall be made on the basis of the political, jurisdictional or international status of the country or territory to which a person belongs, whether it be independent, trust, non-self-governing or under any other limitation of sovereignty.

Article 3.
Everyone has the right to life, liberty and security of person.

Article 4.
No one shall be held in slavery or servitude; slavery and the slave trade shall be prohibited in all their forms.

Article 5.
No one shall be subjected to torture or to cruel, inhuman or degrading treatment or punishment.

Article 6.
Everyone has the right to recognition everywhere as a person before the law.

Article 7.
All are equal before the law and are entitled without any discrimination to equal protection of the law. All are entitled to equal protection against any discrimination in violation of this Declaration and against any incitement to such discrimination.

Article 8.
Everyone has the right to an effective remedy by the competent national tribunals for acts violating the fundamental rights granted him by the constitution or by law.

Article 9.
No one shall be subjected to arbitrary arrest, detention or exile.

Article 10.
Everyone is entitled in full equality to a fair and public hearing by an independent and impartial tribunal, in the determination of his rights and obligations and of any criminal charge against him.

Article 11.
(1) Everyone charged with a penal offence has the right to be presumed innocent until proved guilty according to law in a public trial at which he has had all the guarantees necessary for his defence.
(2) No one shall be held guilty of any penal offence on account of any act or omission which did not constitute a penal offence, under national or international law, at the time when it was committed. Nor shall a heavier penalty be imposed than the one that was applicable at the time the penal offence was committed.

Article 12.
No one shall be subjected to arbitrary interference with his privacy, family, home or correspondence, nor to attacks upon his honour and reputation. Everyone has the right to the protection of the law against such interference or attacks.

Article 13.
(1) Everyone has the right to freedom of movement and residence within the borders of each state.
(2) Everyone has the right to leave any country, including his own, and to return to his country.

Article 14.
(1) Everyone has the right to seek and to enjoy in other countries asylum from persecution.
(2) This right may not be invoked in the case of prosecutions genuinely arising from non-political crimes or from acts contrary to the purposes and principles of the United Nations.

Article 15.
(1) Everyone has the right to a nationality.
(2) No one shall be arbitrarily deprived of his nationality nor denied the right to change his nationality.

Article 16.
(1) Men and women of full age, without any limitation due to race, nationality or religion, have the right to marry and to found a family. They are entitled to equal rights as to marriage, during marriage and at its dissolution.
(2) Marriage shall be entered into only with the free and full consent of the intending spouses.
(3) The family is the natural and fundamental group unit of society and is entitled to protection by society and the State.

Figure 4.1 (*cont'd*)

Article 17.
(1) Everyone has the right to own property alone as well as in association with others.
(2) No one shall be arbitrarily deprived of his property.

Article 18.
Everyone has the right to freedom of thought, conscience and religion; this right includes freedom to change his religion or belief, and freedom, either alone or in community with others and in public or private, to manifest his religion or belief in teaching, practice, worship and observance.

Article 19.
Everyone has the right to freedom of opinion and expression; this right includes freedom to hold opinions without interference and to seek, receive and impart information and ideas through any media and regardless of frontiers.

Article 20.
(1) Everyone has the right to freedom of peaceful assembly and association.
(2) No one may be compelled to belong to an association.

Article 21.
(1) Everyone has the right to take part in the government of his country, directly or through freely chosen representatives.
(2) Everyone has the right of equal access to public service in his country.
(3) The will of the people shall be the basis of the authority of government; this will shall be expressed in periodic and genuine elections which shall be by universal and equal suffrage and shall be held by secret vote or by equivalent free voting procedures.

Article 22.
Everyone, as a member of society, has the right to social security and is entitled to realization, through national effort and international co-operation and in accordance with the organization and resources of each State, of the economic, social and cultural rights indispensable for his dignity and the free development of his personality.

Article 23.
(1) Everyone has the right to work, to free choice of employment, to just and favourable conditions of work and to protection against unemployment.
(2) Everyone, without any discrimination, has the right to equal pay for equal work.
(3) Everyone who works has the right to just and favourable remuneration ensuring for himself and his family an existence worthy of human dignity, and supplemented, if necessary, by other means of social protection.
(4) Everyone has the right to form and to join trade unions for the protection of his interests.

Article 24.
Everyone has the right to rest and leisure, including reasonable limitation of working hours and periodic holidays with pay.

Article 25.
(1) Everyone has the right to a standard of living adequate for the health and well-being of himself and of his family, including food, clothing, housing and medical care and necessary social services, and the right to security in the event of unemployment, sickness, disability, widowhood, old age or other lack of livelihood in circumstances beyond his control.
(2) Motherhood and childhood are entitled to special care and assistance. All children, whether born in or out of wedlock, shall enjoy the same social protection.

Article 26.
(1) Everyone has the right to education. Education shall be free, at least in the elementary and fundamental stages. Elementary education shall be compulsory. Technical and professional education shall be made generally available and higher education shall be equally accessible to all on the basis of merit.
(2) Education shall be directed to the full development of the human personality and to the strengthening of respect for human rights and fundamental freedoms. It shall promote understanding, tolerance and friendship among all nations, racial or religious groups, and shall further the activities of the United Nations for the maintenance of peace.
(3) Parents have a prior right to choose the kind of education that shall be given to their children.

Article 27.
(1) Everyone has the right freely to participate in the cultural life of the community, to enjoy the arts and to share in scientific advancement and its benefits.
(2) Everyone has the right to the protection of the moral and material interests resulting from any scientific, literary or artistic production of which he is the author.

Article 28.
Everyone is entitled to a social and international order in which the rights and freedoms set forth in this Declaration can be fully realized.

Article 29.
(1) Everyone has duties to the community in which alone the free and full development of his personality is possible.
(2) In the exercise of his rights and freedoms, everyone shall be subject only to such limitations as are determined by law solely for the purpose of securing due recognition and respect for the rights and freedoms of others and of meeting the just requirements of morality, public order and the general welfare in a democratic society.
(3) These rights and freedoms may in no case be exercised contrary to the purposes and principles of the United Nations.

Article 30.
Nothing in this Declaration may be interpreted as implying for any State, group or person any right to engage in any activity or to perform any act aimed at the destruction of any of the rights and freedoms set forth herein.

to political dissent, the right to freedom from arbitrary arrest, and the right to an impartial trial. The fourth document, the ESCR, codified rights listed in the later section of the UDHR (Articles 22–30), such as the right to participate in one's culture, the right to work, and the right to leisure time. What is significant about the CPR and the ESCR when compared with both the Charter and the UDHR is that these new documents are legally binding treaties. Both the CPR and the ESCR include provisions that spell out how the rights will be monitored. The CPR, for example, established an 18-member *Committee on Human Rights* that monitors the compliance of participating states. Left unclear in the documents, however, is the issue of enforcement. Participating states must issue reports regarding their human rights record, but both the CPR and ESCR lack any enforcement provisions.

Committee on Human Rights The 18-member Committee monitors the compliance of participating states with the tenets of the Covenant on Civil and Political Rights.

The debate over rights

Cold War   Refers to the ideological stand-off between two superpowers, the United States and the Soviet Union, from 1945 to 1989. While not directly fighting one another, each side sought to expand its influence by keeping the other from spreading its form of government and political system, resulting in many proxy wars throughout the world.

The task of codifying the principles of the UDHR was difficult in part because the *Cold War* had driven a wedge between two former allies, the US and the Soviet Union (SU). In addition, UN membership had doubled as colonialism crumbled around the globe. This created new nations with their own ideas and concerns about human rights. So while the end of World War II saw the emergence of a human rights movement and the promulgation of many human rights documents, it also ushered in a period of deep disagreements over what constituted human rights and whether some rights were more important than others.

The issue of which rights would take primacy deeply divided the international community. One result was that the CPR and the ESCR became tools that the US and the SU used to assert their moral authority around the world. Because Western countries, including the US, were more focused on individual rights, such as the right to free speech or to practice one's religion, the West argued it was better at protecting human rights than was the Soviet Union and its allies. For example, the West was very critical of Soviet repression of religious and political freedoms. However, the SU had argued for a greater emphasis on economic, cultural, and social rights. Their different focus allowed the Soviets to argue that the West, particularly the US, regularly committed human rights violations by not ensuring its citizens had jobs, places to live, and health care. In contrast, the developing world argued that neither side in this debate was right. Many in the developing world argued that human rights should focus more on the human condition overall and not simply on the individual. For example, through the *African Charter of Human and Peoples' Rights*, many African countries articulated rights which they argued were even more fundamental to the human condition then those found in the CPR or ESCR. The rights covered by the African Charter include the right to develop, the right to peace, the right to a clean environment, and the right to the common heritage of humankind.

African Charter of Human and Peoples' Rights   Adopted by African nations in 1982, this international human rights document covers a wide range of human rights including the right to develop, the right to peace, the right to a clean environment, and the right to the common heritage of humankind.

colonialism   One territorial sovereign exerting control and sovereignty over another land by usurping control from local leaders, thereby destroying indigenous culture, economies, and political structures.

The right to develop refers to both the political and the economic development of the nation-state, with emphasis on the economic side. Many developing countries argued that they had a right to develop without outside interference and that this right had been violated by *colonialism*. They also maintained that the international economic system had been set up by and for the advantage of the developed world and that developing countries had been inherently disadvantaged in the international economic system. For example, colonial policies ensured that the colonizing country could use their colonies either for growing cheap agricultural products or for exploiting their natural resources. As a result, the colonized countries were not allowed to industrialize or to modernize in a way that would allow them to participate in the global economy with any degree of clout. Even after colonialism, most were still produ-cing the crop(s) imposed upon them by the colonial powers. As long as this unjust system dominated the international market, they argued, their countries would always remain poor. Thus they called for a restructuring of the international economy that would address these discrepancies once and for all.

Peace and freedom from outside intervention became central to developing countries' interpretation of human rights. The right to peace became a particular concern as many developing countries willingly or unwillingly found themselves pawns in the Cold War. Developing countries argued that while the US and the SU did not directly fight one another, they used the land and peoples of the developing world to fight the global battle of capitalism versus communism. As evidence, they pointed to the vast number of weapons that poured into developing countries, the majority of which were headed by corrupt leaders or puppet governments propped up by the superpowers. In addition, the developing world expressed its concern over the nuclear build-up that increasingly dominated US–Soviet relations. The impact of any war that utilized such weapons would be felt far beyond the intended targets. Thus, these countries argued that they had a right to peace, but that this right was being violated by nuclear proliferation and other actions taken beyond their borders.

Proponents of the right to a clean environment argued that nuclear weapons manufacturing, along with air pollution, acid rain, heavy use of chemicals and pesticides, and water pollution, all the byproducts primarily of the developed world, were profoundly impacting the global environment. Because environmental destruction can be deadly, developing countries argued that there was an inherent right to a clean environment. For these countries, this meant more responsible prac-tices in the developed world as well as the transfer of appropriate technologies to developing countries so that they could begin to make advances without causing the environmental destruction that accompanied industrialization elsewhere.

Finally, the right to the common heritage of humankind follows from the right to a clean environment, but it also deals with the issue of common resources. This debate centers on areas of the globe that do not belong to any one nation, such as international waters, air, outer space, and Antarctica. Specifically, the right to the common heritage of humankind indicates that any wealth derived from "international spaces" should be shared equally. The issue was hotly debated in 1970s and 1980s when the international community was negotiating a new convention on the Law of the Sea. Part of the debate centered around the discovery of nodules rich in minerals on the ocean floor in international waters. Concerns were raised because it was clear that wealthier countries would develop the technology to harvest the nodules from the great depths much faster than countries in the devel-oping world. As a result, a debate ensued over who owned the nodules found in international waters. Developing countries argued they belong to the entire inter-national community, not just to those countries that can harvest them. From their point of view, technology should not guarantee ownership, since poorer countries would then always be at a disadvantage.[11] Developed nations balked at the idea because they believed that the countries that developed the technology, explored the sea, and extracted the nodules should be entitled to the proceeds.

Negative and positive rights

The ongoing debate between the developed and developing world over what constitutes human rights is fueled in part by a philosophical divide regarding the role of government in our daily lives. Civil and political rights are often called negative rights because they involve the right *not* to be subjected to an action of another human being or group, such as the state. In other words, negative rights exist so long as individuals or governments don't do anything to take those rights away. For example, people can practice their right to free speech so long as their governments don't make and enforce laws restricting speech. Other negative rights include freedom of worship, the right to a fair trial, freedom from slavery, and the right to bear arms. In contrast, positive rights involve the provision of something through the actions of one or more individuals or the state. A right to food, for example, might require government action if its citizens are starving. Positive rights may include certain civil and political rights, such as police protection and the right to counsel, as well as economic and social rights, such as public education, health care, and social security. Because many people in the West, particularly in the US, are cautious about how active a role they want their government to play in their lives, they are often resistant to positive rights. However, the division between negative and positive rights is not as clear and distinct as many would like to believe. For example, in order for citizens to have the "right to a fair trial," a negative right, governments must take some action to set up a proper court system, thereby creating an obligation on government to take a positive action to insure that the negative right is protected.

Cultural relativists vs. universalists

Another human rights debate focuses on whether human rights are the same for everyone (universal) or whether they are different depending upon where a person lives or the culture to which they belong (culturally relative).[12] *Cultural relativists* argue that the human rights movement has been driven by rich and powerful Western nations that have defined human rights in terms of the cultural tenets of their own societies. More specifically, relativists argue that Western countries are very individualistic and that they put the individual, rather than the community, at the fore when creating human rights documents. Because cultural norms differ, they argue, Western standards should not be applied to non-Western cultures. The *universalist* perspective acknowledges that the promulgation of most human rights documents has been driven by Westerners who have indeed put the individual at the center. However, they

cultural relativist In the human rights context, this refers to those who argue that human rights must take into account the cultural values of a society.

universalist Someone who argues that human rights are universal and not dictated by culture. Thus, they argue that human rights are inherent in the individual – the same for everyone, everywhere.

argue that human beings' basic needs are universal, and that individual human beings have specific rights simply by virtue of being human. Human rights, they maintain, apply to everyone, regardless of their cultures or where they live. Universalists also argue that the cultural relativism argument is too often used as a cover to excuse the denial of basic human rights to a group or groups within a society. For example, feminist scholars point out that in many cultures, women lack power and the ability to define what counts as culture in their societies. Laws are passed and customs are established that infringe upon women's rights, but they are vigorously defended by their societies upon cultural grounds. So while it may be true, feminists argue, that preventing women from getting an education has historically been part of some cultures, that doesn't justify the continuation of that practice today. Finally, many proponents of universalism point to the growing acceptance of international tribunals, including the *International Criminal Court* (ICC), as evidence of universally accepted norms of behavior vis-à-vis human rights.[13]

International Criminal Court (ICC) Coming into force in 2002, this permanent international court is designed to hear cases of gross violations of human rights, genocide, crimes against humanity, and war crimes. It is a court of last resort and will only act when nation-states cannot or will not.

The universalism/cultural relativism debate heated up in the US in 1994 when an American teenager, Michael Fay, was arrested in Singapore for vandalism. He was found guilty and sentenced to what was a routine punishment for that crime in Singapore: caning. Caning is a form of corporal punishment in which the buttocks, back, shoulders, hands, or the soles of the feet are struck with a wooden cane. The process often results in lacerations, the severity of which depends upon the number of times a person is struck. Many Americans, noting the US Constitution's ban on cruel and unusual punishment, and various human rights organizations were very critical of Singapore's use of this practice, demanding that the US government intercede to prevent this particular caning as well as to take a stand against the practice in general. Singapore's government argued that harsh punishments like caning helped to prevent crime and to make their society safe. They also contended that the US and Singapore's disagreement over the caning of Michael Fay was ultimately the product of cultural differences. Singapore, they maintained, is community oriented, prioritizing the good of the community over individual rights. In contrast, Western culture, they contended, privileges the rights of the individual, regardless of whether the individual in question is a criminal, over the rights and safety of the community as a whole. The "*Asian values*" debate, as it became known, was a heated one that was actually more complex than most media coverage indicated. As some universalists pointed out, caning was introduced into Singapore by the British as a way to control the indigenous population. As such, Singapore's attempts to justify caning as both part of their cultural heritage and a reflection of Asian community values were undermined by the fact that caning is actually an artifact of colonial rule.

Asian values A political phrase used in the 1990s that suggested Asian institutions and political ideologies reflected the culture and history of the region. For human rights discourse, this referred to the primacy of group rights over individual rights.

International Conference on Human Rights Held in Austria in 1993, this global conference was designed to move forward a global human rights agenda.

The universalist position took a backseat, however, at the 1993 *International Conference on Human Rights* in Vienna,

Austria, where representatives from around the world gathered to discuss human rights. China and Indonesia strongly asserted the cultural relativist position, and, as a result, the final document included a clause stating that global human rights standards should be tempered with "regional peculiarities and various historical, cultural and religious backgrounds."[14] The debate, however, continues, manifesting itself in multiple ways. In 2005, for example, a Danish newspaper published cartoons depicting the Islamic Prophet Muhammad. Because Muslims consider the depiction of Muhammad to be offensive, this action was considered a deliberate attack by the "West" writ large on Muslims. Protests and violence followed, leaving more than 50 people dead.[15] Supporters of the cartoons argued on the side of freedom of expression, while Muslims argued that they constituted a deliberate attack on their religion and values. Because of the large number of Muslims living in Western countries, the controversy also raised questions about how to negotiate competing cultural norms within societies, such as freedom of speech and respect for religious practices and values.

In Focus: What Is Torture?

Although torture is an act that most people decry, defining the term can be problematic. Is it torture to shake a prisoner? If the prisoner is shaken so hard that his/her brain comes off its stem, then is it torture? What about the death penalty? The US argues that the death penalty is not a form of torture, but its European allies argue that it is. Are there circumstances where torture is allowable, or even desired? Would it be permissible to use torture, for example, if it resulted in the procurement of information that would save many lives?

Convention Against Torture and Other Cruel, Inhuman, or Degrading Treatment or Punishment
This international human rights instrument is designed to end torture. It came into force in 1987.

In 1984, in an effort to create an internationally accepted definition of torture and to outlaw its use, the international community produced the *Convention Against Torture and Other Cruel, Inhuman, or Degrading Treatment or Punishment*. This Convention defines torture as:

any act by which severe pain or suffering, whether physical or mental, is intentionally inflicted on a person for such purposes as obtaining from him or a third person information or a confession, punishing him for an act he or a third person has committed or is suspected of having committed, or intimidating or coercing him or a third person, or for any reason based on discrimination of any kind, when such pain or suffering is inflicted by or at the instigation of or with the consent or acquiescence of a public official or other person acting in an official capacity.[16]

Many countries have refused to sign up to the treaty. Additionally, among both the countries that have signed and those that have not, there are many that have their own definitions of torture that are not always in concert with the international treaty. Some states overtly argue that torture is acceptable in certain circumstances, while others engage in torture covertly. Indeed, despite the UN convention, torture continues to be a feature of the majority of nation-states. Amnesty International (AI) estimates that more than half the countries in the world commit acts of torture.[17] Millions of people have been tortured before being killed by state governments, paramilitary organizations, terrorist organizations, and other non-state actors, but there are also millions of people around the world who are survivors of torture. As a result, centers have emerged that are designed to help victims recover from the physical, emotional, and psychological traumas they've been through and to help them go on to live productive and healthy lives.[18]

In addition to disagreement over an exact definition of torture, there are also differences regarding to whom the Convention Against Torture applies. Since most treaties impose obligations on states, it has been generally assumed that states are to be considered the main perpetrators of torture. With the growth of non-state actors, including paramilitary groups and private military contractors (groups often funded by the state, though not always under its direct control), a debate has arisen over whether the torture treaty can be applied to these groups. Moreover, many *feminist theorists* have critiqued definitions of torture that are contingent upon the state occupying the role of the perpetrator. They argue that such definitions inappropriately exclude perpetrators of domestic violence who torture their spouses and partners. The torture inflicted in domestic relationships can be particularly severe in countries where state law either allows or does little to punish domestic violence.[19]

> **feminist theorists** Scholars who explore the nature of gendered politics, power relations, and sexuality by examining existing societal constructs.

How Are Human Rights Monitored and Enforced?

The UN and other human rights actors

The first UN body designed to protect and promote human rights was the *United Nations Commission on Human Rights*. The Commission, which consisted of 53 representatives from UN member states, monitored human rights around the world and set human rights standards. However, it primarily served a political purpose, providing a forum for member nations to draft international human rights treaties, investigate rights violations, and advise states on the implementation of rights agreements. In 1993, the UN created the *Office of the United Nations High Commissioner for Human Rights* (OHCHR), which was designed to take an "active role in removing the current obstacles to the global enjoyment of human rights."[20] They have attempted to be more active than the Commission on Human Rights in several ways. First, the OHCHR is administered by high-profile political figures, such as Mary Robinson, former president of Ireland, who use their status to draw attention to specific human rights violations. They also have

> **United Nations Commission on Human Rights** Made up of 18 delegates chosen to begin work on the first international human rights document. The number was later expanded to 53.
>
> **Office of the United Nations High Commissioner for Human Rights (UNHCHR)** The principal office for human rights at the UN.

Table 4.1   UN High Commissioners for the Office of the United Nations High
Commissioner for Human Rights

Name	Country	Term
José Ayala-Lasso	Ecuador	1994–7
Mary Robinson	Ireland	1997–2002
Sérgio Vieira de Mello	Brazil	2002–3 (killed in an attack on a UN building in Iraq on August 19, 2003)
Bertrand Ramcharan	Guyana	August 2003–4
Louise Arbour	Canada	2004–8
Navanethem Pillay	South Africa	2008–

been more aggressive in putting pressure on abusive governments to adhere to their human rights obligations. For example, they condemn abusive governments in media releases and lobby other governments to apply diplomatic, economic, and/or political pressure on offending states.

The OHCHR worked with the Commission by providing advisory services, holding workshops and training seminars, and helping nations strengthen their human rights protection systems.[21] The Commission, however, became very controversial in 2005 when nation-states with abysmal human rights records, including Sudan, Zimbabwe, China, Russia, and Saudi Arabia, were elected to serve on the Commission. Kofi Annan, then Secretary-General, suggested that a new Human Rights Council should be established that would be held to the highest of human rights standards.[22] In 2006, the UN General Assembly voted to replace the highly criticized Human Rights Commission with the Human Rights Council, which was equipped with a Universal Periodic Review mechanism to assess human rights situations in all 192 UN member states. The Council also differs from the Commission in that it has an advisory committee, which serves as the Council's "think-tank," and a revised complaints procedure mechanism, which allows individuals and organizations, rather than just nation-states, to complain to the Council about human rights violations.[23]

Complimenting the UN-led efforts to protect human rights are various regional organizations with human rights agendas of their own. Each of these efforts builds on UN human rights initiatives, but in several cases the regional organizations have more viable and useful enforcement mechanisms. For example, Europeans have put together their own human rights conventions: the *European Convention on Human Rights* (EHR), which is very similar to the CPR, and the *European Social Charter*, which is very similar to the ESCR. In order to be sure the provisions in the EHR are

European Convention on Human Rights Adopted in 1950, this Convention is designed to protect and promote human rights in the European context. It established the European Court of Human Rights.

European Social Charter Adopted in 1961 by EU, it establishes the social and economic rights of the member nations.

European Court of Human Rights Hears human rights-related cases for parties to the EU.

enforced, the European Union established the *European Court of Human Rights* in Strasbourg, France to hear pertinent cases. The European Court allows nation-states, groups, and individuals to bring cases against nation-states. One case brought to the European Court that received a great deal of publicity was *Dudgeon v. United Kingdom* (1981). In this case, the Court found that Northern Ireland's criminalization of homosexual acts between consenting adults was a violation of Article 8 of the European Convention on Human Rights. Because the European Conventions are legally binding and Britain is a signatory, it was obligated to accept the decision. This led to the decriminalization of consensual sexual relations between males in Britain (consensual sexual relations between females was never criminalized in Britain). The case had global ramifications, as similar cases were soon filed in other countries as a result.[24]

Various non-state actors also play a role in researching and promoting human rights as well as promulgating human rights documents. *Non-governmental organizations* (NGOs) have historically played a very important role in the promotion of human rights, as evidenced by their involvement in the creation of the UDHR. Many countries have internal organizations that

> **non-governmental organizations (NGOs)**   A legally constructed organization made up of individuals. These have a limited, if any, role for nation-states.

monitor how their state is abiding by its international human rights obligations. For example, in Israel there is B'Tselem, which monitors human rights in Israeli occupied territories,[25] while in Lebanon, the Palestinian Human Rights Organization monitors the rights of Palestinian refugees in Lebanon.[26] There are also human rights NGOs that work globally. Amnesty International[27] and Human Rights Watch[28] are two such organizations. AI works on behalf of those who are illegally detained, tortured, or harassed by their governments, issuing both urgent calls for actions and press releases. They also urge members to write letters to abusive governments calling for their compliance with international human rights law. Additionally, AI produces an annual report that reviews countries' human rights records. Countries pay close attention to this report and it is often cited by policy-makers.

Many individuals also play a role in defending human rights, such as jurists and publicists who write, publish, and rule on human rights situations and cases; individuals who courageously report human rights violations; and celebrities, who use their popularity to highlight human rights concerns. For example, the late Princess Diana used her status to lobby on behalf of the landmine treaty. Landmines are widely used, cheap, deadly devices that are easy to deploy. They kill indiscriminately, claiming the lives of combatants and non-combatants alike. Once the landmines are laid, they are very difficult and expensive to remove and many governments and rebels choose simply to leave them in the ground. As a result, they terrorize innocent civilians many years after a conflict has ended. One example where landmines were widely used was Angola. It is impossible to know exactly how many were deployed during its civil war (1975–2002), but experts put the figure at roughly 10 million landmines throughout the country.[29] As a result of this widespread use,

Angola has one of the world's largest per capita populations of amputees.[30] The attention that Princess Diana and many others were able to bring to victims of landmines helped create pressure necessary for the promulgation of the Convention on the Prohibition of the Use, Stockpiling, Production and Transfer of Anti-Personnel Mines and on their Destruction. By 2008, more than 150 countries had signed the treaty.

Enforcement mechanisms

Human rights proponents have achieved more success with the crafting of human rights documents than they have with securing nation-state compliance with them. The only way to measure nation-state compliance is through monitoring. Roger Clark, former Secretary-General of Amnesty International Canada, suggests that monitoring involves several components, including gathering information, providing the documentation necessary to authenticate the information, reporting the information, and using reports to promote education and advocacy.[31] State and non-state actors are involved in this monitoring process. Many human rights treaties require that participating nations prepare periodic reports detailing their compliance with their treaty obligations. These reports are then submitted to the monitoring body that was set up as part of the treaty. Reports are then issued that detail the nation-state's level of compliance with the treaty. Nation-states are rarely very self-critical in these reports. Thus, a good deal of the actual monitoring is done by NGOs such as AI. Monitoring human rights can be problematic for NGOs because they do not always get the access necessary within a state to evaluate fully how well a nation-state is living up to its treaty obligations. Nation-states with poor human rights records often try to thwart any investigation into their behavior, harassing human rights activists, denying visas to representatives of international human rights organizations, or, in some cases, covering up their crimes. However, human rights advocates are not without tools at their disposal to uncover abuses. Technological advances, such as cell phones, digital video cameras, and the Internet have provided human rights defenders with additional tools to monitor abuses.

Human rights proponents and activists have had difficulty in both monitoring and enforcing the treaties already in existence because the current international system relies on sovereignty, or non-interference in the domestic affairs of nation-states. Remedies for violations of human rights are thus limited, as nation-states are reluctant to interfere in one another's affairs. Nevertheless, they try to persuade each another to follow human rights treaties through the application of diplomatic, political, and/or economic pressure. This can take the form of quiet diplomacy or public statements condemning a country's actions. Nation-states may even cut aid or trade relations with a country over its human rights record. In particularly egregious cases, the international community, via the UN, has established international tribunals to try to bring to justice the perpetrators of the abuses and to act as a deterrent.

Using international tribunals to punish perpetrators of war crimes and other human rights abuses was first done after World War II with the *Nuremberg Trials* and the *Tokyo Tribunals*. The use of these types of tribunals was revised in the 1990s with the establishment by the UN Security Council of the International Tribunal for the Prosecution of Persons Responsible for Serious Violations of International Humanitarian Law Committed in the Former Yugoslavia Since 1991 (ICTY). The ICTY was given the mandate to hear cases relating to the massive human rights violations that occurred in the former Yugoslavia. Slobodan Milosevic, a Serb national who invoked ethnic superiority arguments to induce his troops to carry out genocide, had overseen the incarceration, torture, rape, and murder of members of the primarily Muslim Bosnian population. The ICTY applied various principles of international human rights law in their prosecutions, including, for example, the 1948 Geneva Convention for the Protection of War Victims and the 1948 Genocide Convention. Systematic rape had been one of the tools used against the population, and camps were established for this purpose. When news of the rape camps became public, human rights activists and others began to demand that rape be included as a war crime, marking the first time in history that rape was acknowledged as a crime in war and not as a "right" of soldiers during war. Shortly after this, another tribunal was established to punish those responsible for genocide in Rwanda – the International Tribunal for the Persons Responsible for Genocide and Other Serious Violations of International Humanitarian Law Committed in the Territory of Rwanda and Rwandan Citizens Responsible for Genocide and Other Such Violations Committed in the Territory of Neighbouring States between 1 January 1994 and 31 December 1994 (ICTR). Following on the heels of these two tribunals, similar ones were also established for Sierra Leone, Lebanon, Cambodia, and East Timor. However, scholars and human rights activists argued that the ad hoc system of tribunals was not adequate to deal with those accused of the most severe forms of abuse. As a result, a proposal was put forth to create a permanent court that would have the power to try heads of state and their representatives for massive and gross human rights violations including, genocide, war crimes, crimes against humanity, and aggression. The treaty that established the *International Criminal Court* was adopted in Rome in 1998 and came into force in 2002. (Table 4.2 provides a list of nations that have signed and ratified the treaty.) The ICC is designed to be a permanent court of last resort, acting only when states will not, or cannot, act against alleged human rights abusers.[32] In 2009, the ICC indicted its first head of state: Omar al-Bashir of Sudan was indicted over his country's support of paramilitary organizations that had been raping and murdering thousands in the Western region of the country known as Darfur.[33]

Nuremberg Trials Post-World War II (1945–9) trials of dozens of officials of Nazi Germany who were charged with war crimes, more specifically with the crime of waging an aggressive war.

Tokyo Tribunals War crimes trials for 25 Japanese defendants, seven of whom were sentenced to death. Thousands of other Japanese were charged with lesser crimes.

International Criminal Court (ICC) Coming into force in 2002, this permanent international court is designed to hear cases of gross violations of human rights, genocide, crimes against humanity, and war crimes. It is a court of last resort and will only act when nation-states cannot or will not.

Table 4.2 International Criminal Court

Participant	Signature	Ratification
Albania	Jul 18, 1998	
Algeria	Dec 28, 2000	
Andorra	Jul, 18, 1998	Apr 30, 2001
Angola	Oct 7, 1998	
Antigua and Barbuda	Oct 23, 1998	Jun 18, 2001
Argentina	Jan 8, 1999	Feb 8, 2001
Armenia	Oct 1, 1999	
Australia	Dec 9, 1998	Jul 1, 2002
Austria	Oct 7, 1998	Dec 28, 2000
Bahamas	Dec 29, 2000	
Bahrain	Dec 11, 2000	
Bangladesh	Sep 16, 1999	
Barbados	Sep 8, 2000	
Belgium	Sep 10, 1998	Jun 28, 2000
Belize	Apr 5, 2000	Apr 5, 2000
Benin	Sep 24, 1999	Jan 22, 2002
Bolivia	Jul 17, 1998	Jun 27, 2002
Bosnia and Herzegovina	Jul 17, 2000	Apr 11, 2002
Botswana	Sep 8, 2000	Sep 8, 2000
Brazil	Feb 7, 2000	Jun 20, 2002
Bulgaria	Feb 11, 1999	Apr 11, 2002
Burkina Faso	Nov 30, 1998	
Burundi	Jan 13, 1999	
Cambodia	Oct 23, 2000	Apr 11, 2002
Cameroon	Jul 17, 1998	
Canada	Dec 18, 1998	7 Jul 7, 2000
Cape Verde	Dec 28, 2000	
Central African Republic	Oct 3, 2001	
Chad	Oct 20, 1999	
Chile	Sep 11, 1998	
Colombia	Dec 10, 1998	Aug 5, 2002
Comoros	Sep 22, 2000	
Congo	Jul 17, 1998	
Costa Rica	Oct 7, 1998	Jun 7, 2001
Côte d'Ivoire	Nov 30, 1998	
Croatia	Oct 12, 1998	May 21, 2001
Cyprus	Oct 15, 1998	Mar 7, 2002
Czech Republic	Apr 13, 1999	
Democratic Republic of the Congo	Sep 8, 2000	Apr 11, 2002
Denmark	Sep 25, 1998	Jun 21, 2001
Djibouti	Oct 7, 1998	
Dominica	Feb 12, 2001	
Dominican Republic	Sep 8, 2000	
Ecuador	Oct 7, 1998	Feb 5, 2002
Egypt	Dec 26, 2000	
Eritrea	Oct 7, 1998	
Estonia	Dec 27, 1999	Jan 30, 2002

Table 4.2 *(cont'd)*

Participant	Signature	Ratification
Fiji	Nov 29, 1999	Nov 29, 1999
Finland	Oct 7, 1998	Dec 29, 2000
France	Jul 18, 1998	Jun 9, 2000
Gabon	Dec 22, 1998	Sep 20, 2000
Gambia	Dec 4, 1998	Jun 28, 2002
Georgia	Jul 18, 1998	
Germany	Dec 10, 1998	Dec 11, 2000
Ghana	Jul 18, 1998	Dec 20, 1999
Greece	Jul 18, 1998	May 15, 2002
Guinea	Sep 7, 2000	
Guinea-Bissau	Sep 12, 2000	
Guyana	Dec 28, 2000	
Haiti	Feb 28, 1999	
Honduras	Oct 7, 1998	Jul 1, 2002
Hungary	Jan 15, 1999	Nov 30, 2001
Iceland	Aug 26, 1998	May 25, 2000
Iran (Islamic Republic of)	Dec 31, 2000	
Ireland	Oct 7, 1998	Apr 11, 2002
Israel	Dec 31, 2000	
Italy	Jul 18, 1998	Jul 26, 1999
Jamaica	Sep 8, 2000	
Jordan	Oct 7, 1998	Apr 11, 2002
Kenya	Aug 11, 1999	
Kuwait	Sep 8, 2000	
Kyrgyzstan	Dec 8, 1998	
Latvia	Apr 22, 1999	Jun 28, 2002
Lesotho	Nov 30, 1998	Sep 6, 2000
Liberia	Jul 17, 1998	
Liechtenstein	Jul 18, 1998	Oct 2, 2001
Lithuania	Dec 10, 1998	
Luxembourg	Oct 13, 1998	Sep 8, 2000
Madagascar	Jul 18, 1998	
Malawi	Mar 2, 1999	
Mali	Jul 17, 1998	Aug 16, 2000
Malta	Jul 17, 1998	
Marshall Islands	Sep 6, 2000	Dec 7, 2000
Mauritius	Nov 11, 1998	Mar 5, 2002
Mexico	Sep 7, 2000	
Monaco	Jul 18, 1998	
Mongolia	Dec 29, 2000	Apr 11, 2002
Morocco	Sep 8, 2000	
Mozambique	Dec 28, 2000	
Namibia	Oct 27, 1998	Jun 25, 2002
Nauru	Dec 13, 2000	Nov 15, 2001
Netherlands	Jul 18, 1998	Jul 17, 2001
New Zealand	Oct 7, 1998	Sep 7, 2000
Niger	Jul 17, 1998	Apr 11, 2002
Nigeria	Jun 1, 2000	Sep 27, 2001

Table 4.2   *(cont'd)*

Participant	Signature	Ratification
Norway	Aug 28, 1998	Feb 16, 2000
Oman	Dec 20, 2000	
Panama	Jul 18, 1998	Mar 21, 2002
Paraguay	Oct 7, 1998	May 14, 2001
Peru	Dec 7, 2000	Nov 10, 2001
Philippines	Dec 28, 2000	
Poland	Apr 9, 1999	Nov 12, 2001
Portugal	Oct 7, 1998	Feb 5, 2002
Republic of Korea	Mar 8, 2000	
Republic of Moldova	Sep 8, 2000	
Romania	Jul 7, 1999	Apr 11, 2002
Russian Federation	Sep 13, 2000	
Saint Lucia	Aug 27, 1999	
Samoa	Jul 17, 1998	
San Marino	Jul 18, 1998	May 13, 1999
Sao Tome and Principe	Dec 28, 2000	
Senegal	Jul 18, 1998	Feb 2, 1999
Seychelles	Dec 28, 2000	
Sierra Leone	Oct 17, 1998	Sep 15, 2000
Slovakia	Dec 23, 1998	Apr 11, 2002
Slovenia	Oct 7, 1998	Dec 31, 2001
Solomon Islands	Dec 3, 1998	
South Africa	Jul 17, 1998	Nov 27, 2000
Spain	Jul 18, 1998	Oct 24, 2000
Sudan	Sep 8, 2000	
Sweden	Oct 7, 1998	Jun 28, 2001
Switzerland	Jul 28, 1998	Oct 12, 2001
Syrian Arab Republic	Nov 29, 2000	
Tajikistan	Nov 30, 1998	May 5, 2000
Thailand	Oct 2, 2000	
The Former Yugoslav Republic of Macedonia	Oct 7, 1998	Mar 6, 2002
Trinidad and Tobago	Mar 23, 1999	Apr 6, 1999
Uganda	Mar 17, 1999	Jun 14, 2002
Ukraine	Jan 20, 2000	
United Arab Emirates	Nov 27, 2000	
United Kingdom of Great Britain and Northern Ireland	Nov 30, 1998	Oct 4, 2001
United Republic of Tanzania	Dec 29, 2000	
United States of America	Dec 31, 2000	
Uruguay	Dec 19, 2000	Jun 28, 2002
Uzbekistan	Dec 29, 2000	
Venezuela	Oct 14, 1998	Jun 7, 2000
Yemen	Dec 28, 2000	
Yugoslavia	Dec 19, 2000	Sep 6, 2001
Zambia	Jul 17, 1998	
Zimbabwe	Jul 17, 1998	

Occasionally, a nation-state argues that a human rights or humanitarian situation in another country is so grave that outside intervention is the only way to end the abuse. In international relations, this is referred to as the "doctrine of humanitarian intervention." Since the creation of the UN, there have been many humanitarian interventions that have occurred without UN approval, despite the fact that the UN General Assembly has historically rejected the idea that nation-states posses a "right" to intervene in another nation-state without UN authorization.[34] Such interventions include the US invasion of the Dominican Republic in 1965, India's invasion of East Pakistan (now known as Bangladesh) in 1971, Vietnam's invasion of Kampuchea (now known as Cambodia) in 1978, Tanzania's invasion of Uganda in 1979, the Economic Community of West African States' (ECOWAS) intervention in Liberia in 1990 and Sierra Leone in 1998, NATO's use of force in Kosovo in 1999, and the 2003 US invasion of Iraq. Although unauthorized interventions have frequently occurred, many scholars and activists question the efficacy of such an approach to human rights enforcement.

By 2005, however, the UN appeared to be shifting away from its rejection of unauthorized humanitarian intervention. That year, the UN held a World Summit designed to celebrate the 60th anniversary of the organization, but also to promote international security, advance human rights, and reform the United Nations. At this meeting, the delegates agreed on the doctrine of a "*responsibility to protect*" (R2P). This argues that when nation-states cannot or will not protect their citizens from gross violations of human rights, including genocide, massive killings, and war crimes, the international community, led by the UN preferably, must act to end the abuse. According to the UN press sheet for the 2005 World Summit, responsibility to protect means:

> **responsibility to protect**
> Responsibility of the international community to protect people from gross human rights violations when individual nation-states cannot or will not.

> Clear and unambiguous acceptance by all governments of the collective international responsibility to protect populations from genocide, war crimes, ethnic cleansing and crimes against humanity. Willingness to take timely and decisive collective action for this purpose, through the Security Council, when peaceful means prove inadequate and national authorities are manifestly failing to do it.[35]

Nobel laureate Desmond Tutu, a noted supporter of R2P, argues:

> It is not a justification of military intervention. It simply requires states to protect their own people and help other states to build the capacity to do the same. It means that international organizations like the UN have a responsibility to warn, to generate effective preventive strategies, and when necessary, to mobilize effective responses.[36]

Other scholars of international relations have argued that state sovereignty does not trump the obligations states have to protect their citizens.[37] Thus, when states engage in widespread and massive human rights violations, unauthorized intervention by other nation-states is a reasonable and desired outcome. Fernando Tesón argues that in appropriate cases, humanitarian intervention is morally justified. Thus, he suggests that "tyranny and anarchy cause the moral collapse of sovereignty."[38] However, many developing countries, still dealing with the consequences of colonialism, remain very skeptical about the loss of sovereignty involved in any R2P norm.

Emerging Human Rights

The right to water

In addition to the rights that have been discussed throughout this chapter, human rights advocates suggest there are further emerging rights issues facing the international community. One such issue has developed in response to a growing trend by nation-states to privatize essential human services like water.

World Health Organization (WHO)
The UN agency that monitors health-related issues around the world.

In response, there has been a growing call for the right to clean water. In 2003, the UN endorsed this right when the *World Health Organization* (WHO) published the "The Right to Water." This endorsement was based upon enshrined rights, including the right to health found in the Universal Declaration of Human Rights (1948), Article 25, which states that "Everyone has the right to a standard of living adequate for the health and well-being of himself and of his family," as well as other treaties, including the Rights of the Child and the International Covenant on Economic, Social and Cultural Rights. In "The Right to Water," WHO connects water and health, observing that "in the past 10 years, diarrhoea has killed more children than all those lost to armed conflict in almost 60 years since the Second World War" and that "a child dies every 15 seconds from diarrhoea, caused largely by poor sanitation and water supply."[39] However, while WHO explains that access to clean water is critical to human health and, indeed, to human existence, critics argue that a "right to water" is problematic on many levels. For example, it is unclear who would be responsible for and capable of insuring and protecting this right. Additionally, assertions of a "right to water" could cause conflict over transboundary waters. There are also concerns about abuse; some people worry that governments might "over-allocate water to privileged groups, at the expense of both people and the environment."[40]

Sexual rights

The right to one's sexuality has also emerged as a new battleground for human rights. "Sexuality" is a broad term that is used in a variety of contexts, including a woman's right to choose/refuse sexual partner(s) (rather than having them chosen for or forced upon her), the right to choose whether or not to procreate, the right to choose a partner of the same or different sex, and the right to alter one's own sex. Sexuality, then, not only covers a wide variety of issues, but also engenders deep emotions and poses interesting challenges for human rights advocates. For example, many countries that outlaw homosexuality cite religious doctrine as the rationale behind such legislation. By doing so, they position religious freedom as the right that needs to be protected. However, others argue that imposing religious doctrines that limit citizens' sexual rights amounts to an abuse of freedom of religion.

In December 2008, the UN held its first vote on gay rights, with 66 nations calling upon states to decriminalize homosexuality. The declaration was sponsored by France and garnered support from many European and Latin American delegates. It condemned human rights abuses based on homophobia, maintaining that they are a violation of the Universal Declaration of Human Rights.[41] While this was the first official vote on homosexuality, it was not the first time that lesbian, gay, bisexual, and transgender (LGBT) issues had been addressed by UN agencies. In 1993, for example, following the World Conference on Human Rights in Vienna, the United Nations High Commissioner for Refugees (UNHCR) repeatedly recognized gays and lesbians as a type of social group that could be granted refugee status when facing persecution.[42] An increasing number of countries have since granted refugee status to LGBT people. Homosexuality is banned in more than 80 countries and is punishable by death in at least six. In other countries, however, LGBT debates center around various legal issues, such as partnerships, marriage, and the adoption of children.[43] Numerous Western European countries have recognized same-sex marriage and partnerships, as have several US states.

DNA rights

One other area of concern for human rights advocates is the right to one's human genetic data. Specifically, scientific advances have made possible the use of *Deoxyribonucleic acid (DNA)* as an identifier. DNA is widely used in criminal cases around the world, and many nations now have huge databases of DNA files.

> **deoxyribonucleic acid (DNA)** The building block of all living organisms. It contains the genetic blueprint for the cell.

While DNA is a powerful tool that can help law enforcement to not only identify and punish criminals but also vindicate individuals who have been falsely accused or convicted of crimes, there is also the potential for abuse, as Britain discovered. In December 2008, the European Court of Human Rights ruled that Britain had violated its citizens' rights by retaining the DNA of people who were arrested for a crime but who later were either acquitted or had the charges against them dropped. In the ruling, the Court argued that, "given the nature and the amount of personal information contained in cellular samples, their retention per se had to be regarded as interfering with the right to respect for the private lives of the individuals concerned."[44] Britain will have to respond to the Court's ruling, explaining how it will comport itself in concert with the Court's interpretation of the relationship between human rights and DNA.

As genetic testing becomes more widely available, the possibility of discrimination based on genetic profiles increases. *Civil libertarians* are particularly concerned about insurance companies accessing the genetic profiles of their clients or potential clients.

> **civil libertarians** Refers to people who place individual human rights over state authority.

They worry that genetic information, such as certain disease markers, might be used to deny people coverage. Others warn that employers who have access to their employees' genetic profiles might decide to fire people who are genetically predisposed to diseases that might interfere with productivity or cost the company money.[45] In contrast, supporters of genetic testing argue that genetic information is more likely to empower individuals than put them at the mercy of insurance companies and employers. They point out that only by knowing what diseases they might have can people take effective action to prevent, delay, or mitigate their manifestation and effects.

United Nations Educational, Scientific and Cultural Organization (UNESCO) Serves as a clearinghouse of information and promotes international cooperation in the areas of education, science, and culture.

International Declaration on Human Genetic Data Adopted unanimously in 2003 by the United Nations Education, Scientific, and Cultural Organization (UNESCO), this document sought to establish guidelines for the collection, use, and distribution of human genetic data.

Cognizant of the potential of DNA to be used to both protect and abuse human rights, the *United Nations Educational, Scientific and Cultural Organization* (UNESCO) issued the *International Declaration on Human Genetic Data* (2003), which demands the "protection of human rights and fundamental freedoms in the collection, processing, use, and storage of human genetic data and the biological samples from which they are derived."[46] This explicit linkage between genetic data and human rights suggests that while genetic data has positive uses, caution is nevertheless required to insure that this information is not used to violate human rights.

Human Rights and Non-State Actors

Human rights law was originally conceived of as a means of protecting people from abuses perpetrated or permitted by nation-states. In other words, the assumption was that the biggest threat to the enjoyment of human rights was generally the nation-state itself or citizens within the state. As such, treaties and laws required states not only to refrain from violating the human rights of their citizens but also to protect citizens from the abuses of other citizens. However, increasingly, non-state actors, such as NGOs, *multinational corporations* (MNCs), and criminal enterprises have been responsible for both violating human rights as well as taking on some of the roles originally assumed to be the purview of nation-states, including providing education, food, and health care. When states are no longer able or willing to fulfill these traditional functions, it becomes increasingly unlikely that they will be able or willing to protect their citizens' human rights as well. Indeed, in many countries, criminal enterprises are wreaking havoc on local populations, arbitrarily detaining, torturing, and executing citizens. In some cases these enterprises are working in coordination with states, while in others, the state is simply helpless to stop them. In some areas of Mexico, for example, drug wars are responsible for high levels of violence, but the police and even the military are often hesitant to confront the powerful and heavily armed criminal groups responsible.[47] MNCs with their money, power, and ability to easily move from country to

multinational corporation A corporation or enterprise that manages production or delivers services in more than one country.

country, have also been accused of serious human rights abuses, including forced labor, dangerous working conditions, child labor, and even murder.[48] In countries where governments are unable or unwilling to provide services and/or to stop the human rights violations perpetrated by criminal organizations, MNCs, and others, NGOs sometimes step in to provide services. Many faith-based NGOs are providing basic essentials to people when their governments fail to do so, including health care, education, food, and water, but they also often make assistance contingent upon listening to their religious messages or participating in a religious program.[49] Given the increased role these various types of actors are playing in both violating human rights and providing aid in the void left by weak governments, human rights advocates and policy-makers may need to broaden their focus from the ways governments interact with their citizens to the various roles that other types of organizations play in both protecting and abusing human rights.

Human Rights Abuses: Why They Affect Us All

While there are many moral and ethical arguments that can be made about why it is important to care about human rights and, by extension, human beings, the reality is that these arguments aren't always particularly effective. Indeed, it is not unusual for people to find that the faraway plights of people they've never seen before and know nothing about do little to stir their sympathies or move them to action. However, as William Schultz, Director of Amnesty International, points out, there are several compelling reasons why human rights abuses concern everyone. First, governments with bad human rights records tend to have more conflicts with other nations than do those with better human rights records. Second, nations that fail to observe the rule of law as it pertains to human rights are likely to ignore it in other spheres as well, including their economic and political relations with other countries. For example, the Taliban's blatant violations of human rights law proved to be a harbinger of the government's willingness to violate the rule of law in a variety of other ways, including providing terrorists with a safe haven in Afghan territory. Third, those violating the rule of law at home will be more likely to violate it elsewhere, thus spreading chaos throughout a region or regions. Fourth, nations that abuse one type of human right, discriminating against a minority group, for example, are likely to violate others.[50] Ultimately, self-interest is one of the most motivating reasons for caring about human rights and advocating human rights protections. If left unchecked, the abuses carried out against someone you don't know today might well be aimed at you or someone you care about tomorrow.

Conclusion

Although human rights have a long history, with relevant documents dating back as far as the thirteenth century, it was only in the post-World War II era that they assumed a central place in both international relations and relations between states and their citizens. The atrocities of World War II helped to propel the movement forward, but it was the advent of international organizations like the UN that made possible the codification of many human rights principles. While scholars, activists, and others continue to debate issues such as the universal applicability of rights and governments' responsibilities to protect them, one clear pattern has emerged: human rights are increasingly taken seriously by states, organizations, and individuals. This is evident not only in the number of human rights treaties that have been promulgated and acceded to by states, but also in the prevalence of human rights discourses around the world. It is clear that abuses such as torture still occur and that states remain reluctant to surrender too much sovereignty in the service of meeting human rights obligations. However, it is equally clear that human rights will continue to be one yardstick by which states, non-state actors, and international organizations are measured. New technologies, changing societal mores, and new roles for various international actors will require adaptations and revised interpretations of what constitutes human rights. Regardless of the future direction that human rights discourses take, their importance in our lives and in the world has been firmly established.

Notes

1 Sepúlveda appears to have taken this idea from Aristotle's doctrine of natural slavery. For more on this see, David Keane, *Caste-based Discrimination in International Human Rights Law* (Surrey, UK: Ashgate Publishing, Ltd., 2007), 80.

2 Gillian M. Bediako, *Primal Religion and the Bible: William Robertson Smith and His Heritage* (London: Continuum International Publishing Group, 1997), 42.

3 Lynne M. Healy, *International Social Work: Professional Action in an Interdependent World* (Oxford: Oxford University Press, 2001), 151.

4 Paul Finkelman, *Encyclopedia of American Civil Liberties* (Boca Raton, FL: CRC Press, 2006), 456.

5 "Declaration of the Rights of Man – 1789," http://avalon.law.yale.edu/18th_century/rightsof.asp.

6 Charter of the League of Nations, Article 23, www.geocities.com/Heartland/Valley/8920/European/leachart.html.

7 "Preamble," Charter of the United Nations, www.un.org/aboutun/charter/preamble.shtml.

8 "Chapter I: Purposes and Principles," Charter of the United Nations, www.un.org/aboutun/charter/chapter1.shtml.

9 For a detailed discussion of all the key players in the creation and eventual acceptance of the UDHR, see Mary Ann Glendon, *A World Made New: Eleanor Roosevelt and the Universal Declaration of Human Rights* (New York: Random House, 2002).

10 Many international legal scholars agree that the UDHR has almost universal acceptance and that it has passed into customary international law, thus it is binding on all nations, even those that did not sign the original document.

11 William R. Slomanson, *Fundamental Perspectives on International Law*, 3rd edn. (St Paul, MN: West Publishing, 2002).

12 For more on this topic, see, Theodore Downing and Gilbert Kushner (eds.), *Human Rights and Anthropology* (Boston, MA: Cultural Survival Report 24, 1988); Clifford Geertz, "Anti Anti-Relativism" in Michael Krausz (ed.), *Relativism: Interpretation and Confrontation* (Notre Dame, IN: University of Notre Dame Press, 1989); Melville Herskovits, *Cultural Relativism* (New York: Random House, 1973); Ronald Cohen, "Human Rights and Cultural Relativism: The Need for a New Approach," *American Anthropologist* 91 (1989), 1014.

13 For a discussion of how globalization is changing the nature of the human rights debate in this area, see Adamantia Pollis and Peter Schwab (eds.), *Human Rights: New Perspectives, New Realities* (Boulder, CO: Lynne Rienner, 2000).

14 Louis Henkin, Gerald L. Neuman, Diane F. Orentlicher, and David W. Leebron, *Human Rights* (New York: Foundation Press, 1999), 112.

15 Julien Spencer, "Republished Danish Cartoon of Prophet Muhammad Ignites Tensions," *Christian Science Monitor* (February 19, 2008), www. csmonitor.com/2008/0219/p99s01-duts.html.

16 Convention against Torture and other Cruel, Inhuman, or Degrading Treatment or Punishment, www1.umn.edu/humanrts/instree/h2catoc.htm.

17 Slomanson, *Fundamental Perspectives on International Law.*

18 Centers for victims of torture include: www.cvt. org/main.php/InsideCVT; www.ccvt.org/; www. cvict.org.np/; www.trc-pal.org/; and http://ncttp. dataweb.com/wsContent/default.view?_pagename= CO-Rocky+Mountain+Survivor+Center.

19 See, for example, www.cceia.org/resources/ publications/dialogue/2_10/articles/1048.html; www.unicef-irc.org/publications/pdf/digest6e.pdf. Amnesty International has also expanded its understanding of torture to include domestic violence; for more information on this, see: www.amnestyusa. org/violence-against-women/stop-violence-against-women-svaw/domestic-violence/page.do?id= 1108220.

20 Slomanson, *Fundamental Perspectives on International Law*, 508.

21 United Nations Human Rights Commission, www.unhchr.ch/html/menu2/2/chrintro.htm.

22 "Annan says rights body harming UN," BBC (April 7, 2005), http://news.bbc.co.uk/2/hi/europe/ 4419333.stm.

23 The Human Rights Council, www2.ohchr.org/ english/bodies/hrcouncil/.

24 Michael D. Goldhaber, *A People's History of the European Court of Human Rights* (Piscataway, NJ: Rutgers University Press 2007).

25 For more on this organization, see: www.btselem. org/English/About_BTselem/Index.asp.

26 For more on this organization, see: www. palhumanrights.org/.

27 For more on this organization, see: www.amnesty. org/.

28 For more on this organization, see: www.hrw.org/.

29 John Prendergast, "Angola's Deadly War: Dealing with Savimbi's Hell on Earth," *United States Institute of Peace Special Report* (October 12, 1999), www. usip.org/pubs/specialreports/sr991012.html.

30 Norimitsu Onishi, "Sierra Leone Measures Terror in Severed Limbs," *New York Times* (August 22, 1999), http://query.nytimes.com/gst/fullpage.html?res= 9B00EED91338F931A1575BC0A96F958260.

31 Roger Clark, "Principles of Human Rights Monitoring," presented at the International Centre for Human Rights Education, 24th Annual Session of the International Human Rights Training Program, June 2003, www.equitas.org/english/programs/ downloads/ihrtp-proceedings/24th/Monitoring. pdf.

32 There are 18 independent judges who hear cases at the court's headquarters in The Hague, Netherlands. Nations that sign onto the treaty will have a vote in selecting both judges and prosecutors. Those nations, along with the UN, shoulder the cost of the court. Any nation that is part of the treaty can bring a case, as can the Security Council of the UN and the ICC prosecutor. Defendants are given the presumption of innocence and there is an appeal process. No death penalty option exists for sentencing, and sentences will be served in the prisons of states that have agreed to incarcerate those found guilty. Although the US signed it under President Clinton, the Bush administration withdrew the US signature and has instituted a policy of denying US military aid to countries that are parties to the treaty if they do not ensure that Americans serving in their countries will be exempt from the ICC's reach.

33 Human Rights Watch, "ICC: Bashir Warrant Is Warning to Abusive Leaders" (March 4, 2009), www. hrw.org/en/news/2009/03/04/icc-bashir-warrant-warning-abusive-leaders.

34 For a detailed discussion and debate of the legality and legitimacy of humanitarian intervention, see J. L. Holzgrefe and Robert Owen Keohane (eds.), *Humanitarian Intervention: Ethical, Legal and Political Dilemmas* (Cambridge: Cambridge University Press, 2003).

35   "Fact Sheet 2005 World Summit High-Level Plenary Meeting," United Nations (September 2005), www.un.org/summit2005/presskit/fact_sheet.pdf. Further, the UN document argues:

> The UN The September 2005 World Summit outcome document endorsed the responsibility to protect:
>
> 138. Each individual State has the responsibility to protect its populations from genocide, war crimes, ethnic cleansing and crimes against humanity. This responsibility entails the prevention of such crimes, including their incitement, through appropriate and necessary means. We accept that responsibility and will act in accordance with it. The international community should, as appropriate, encourage and help States to exercise this responsibility and support the United Nations in establishing an early warning capability.
>
> 139. The international community, through the United Nations, also has the responsibility to use appropriate diplomatic, humanitarian and other peaceful means, in accordance with Chapters VI and VIII of the Charter, to help protect populations from genocide, war crimes, ethnic cleansing and crimes against humanity. In this context, we are prepared to take collective action, in a timely and decisive manner, through the Security Council, in accordance with the Charter, including Chapter VII, on a case-by-case basis and in cooperation with relevant regional organizations as appropriate, should peaceful means be inadequate and national authorities manifestly fail to protect their populations from genocide, war crimes, ethnic cleansing and crimes against humanity. We stress the need for the General Assembly to continue consideration of the responsibility to protect populations from genocide, war crimes, ethnic cleansing and crimes against humanity and its implications, bearing in mind the principles of the Charter and international law. We also intend to commit ourselves, as necessary and appropriate, to helping States build capacity to protect their populations from genocide, war crimes, ethnic cleansing and crimes against humanity and to assisting those which are under stress before crises and conflicts break out.

From the 2005 World Summit Outcome Document, World Health Organization (September 15, 2005), http://daccessdds.un.org/doc/UNDOC/GEN/N05/510/94/PDF/N0551094.pdf?OpenElement.

36   Desmond Tutu, "Taking the Responsibility to Protect," *International Herald Tribune* (February 19, 2008), www.iht.com/articles/2008/02/19/opinion/edtutu.php.

37   For a detailed discussion of several different approaches to the ethnical, legal and political dimensions of humanitarian intervention, see Holzgrefe and Keohane *Humanitarian Intervention*.

38   Fernando R. Tesón, "The liberal case for Humanitarian Intervention," in ibid., 93.

39   "The Right to Water" World Health Organization, Geneva, Switzerland (2003), www.who.int/water_sanitation_health/rightowater/en/.

40   Karen Bakker, "The 'Commons' Versus the 'Commodity': Alter-globalization, Anti-privatization and the Human Right to Water in the Global South," *Antipode* 39, no. 3 (June 2007), 430–55.

41   Neil MacFarquhar, "In a First, Gay Rights Are Pressed At the UN," *New York Times* (December 19, 2008), 22.

42   Julie Mertus, "The Rejection of Human Rights Framings: The Case of LGBT Advocacy in the US," *Human Rights Quarterly* 29, no. 4 (November 2007), 1036–64, as quoted from: Human Rights Education Association, Sexual Orientation and Human Rights, Study Guides, available at www.hrea.org/learn/guides/lgbt.html.

43   In 2008, the European Court of Human rights ruled that lesbian, gay, and bisexual individuals were eligible to adopt children. This effectively overruled a member nation's domestic laws prohibiting lesbians, gays, and bisexuals from adopting. See www.ilga-europe.org/Europe/News/European-Court-of-Human-Rights-says-lesbian-gay-and-bisexual-individuals-are-eligible-to-adopt-children.

44   Peter Aldhous, "British DNA Database 'Breached Human Rights'," *New Scientist* (December 2008), www.newscientist.com/article/dn16226-british-dna-database-breached-human-rights.html.

45   One organization that is very concerned about such possibilities is Genewatch, www.genewatch.org/sub-396421. Another London-based organization that has expressed similar concerns is Liberty, www.liberty-human-rights.org.uk/news-and-events/1-press-releases/2007/universal-dna-database.shtml. The US-based American Civil Liberties Union has

also expressed its concern about DNA databases – see Barry Steinhardt and Tania Simoncelli, "DNA Fingerprinting and Civil Liberties: Second in a Series of Articles," *Journal of Law, Medicine & Ethics* 33, no. 2 (Summer 2005), 279–93.

46 Xavier Bosch, "UN Agency Sets out Global Rules for Protecting Genetic Data," *The Lancet* 362, no. 9377 (July 5, 2003), 45. For the full text of the UN Declaration, see www.unhcr.org/refworld/publisher,UNESCO,,,4042241f4,0.html.

47 *Christian Science Monitor*, "Mexico Drug Violence Intensifies'" (June 2, 2008), www.csmonitor.com/World/terrorism-security/2008/0602/p99s01-duts.html.

48 For more on the discuss of the limitations of human rights law as it pertains to the behavior of MNCs, see Surya Deva, "Human Rights Violations by Multinational Corporations and International Law: Where from Here?" *Connecticut Journal of International Law* 19 (2003), 1–57.

49 Saroj Jayasinghe, "Faith-based NGOs and Healthcare in Poor Countries: A Preliminary Exploration of Ethical Issues," *Journal of Medical Ethics* 33, no. 11 (November 2007), 623–6.

50 William F. Schulz, *In Our Own Best Interest: How Defending Human Rights Benefits Us All* (Boston, MA: Beacon Press, 2001).

5

THE NATURAL ENVIRONMENT

"So today, we dumped another 70 million tons of global-warming pollution into the thin shell of atmosphere surrounding our planet, as if it were an open sewer. And tomorrow, we will dump a slightly larger amount, with the cumulative concentrations now trapping more and more heat from the sun.

"As a result, the earth has a fever. And the fever is rising. The experts have told us it is not a passing affliction that will heal by itself. We asked for a second opinion. And a third. And a fourth. And the consistent conclusion, restated with increasing alarm, is that something basic is wrong.

"We are what is wrong, and we must make it right."
(Al Gore, Nobel Lecture, Oslo, December 10, 2007)[1]

"All across the world, in every kind of environment and region known to man, increasingly dangerous weather patterns and devastating storms are abruptly putting an end to the long-running debate over whether or not climate change is real. Not only is it real, it's here, and its effects are giving rise to a frighteningly new global phenomenon: the man-made natural disaster." (Barack Obama, The Associated Press's Annual Luncheon, April 3, 2006)[2]

"I think the environment should be put in the category of our national security. Defense of our resources is just as important as defense abroad. Otherwise what is there to defend?" (Robert Redford, dedication of Mount Ansel Adams, Yosemite National Park, 1985)[3]

Learning to Question, Questioning to Learn

- In what ways will global climate change impact the environment?
- What are the biggest environmental concerns facing the international community?
- What steps have been taken to try to address global climate change and other pressing environmental issues?
- What groups are most affected by global environmental challenges?

Introduction

From *tsunamis* in Asia to hurricanes on the American coast to *water wars* in the Middle East, environmental issues are frequently the top global news stories. Although the international community has been wrestling with environmental issues for several decades, it wasn't until the turn of the last century that environmental concerns were catapulted to the forefront of many states' policy agendas. This chapter focuses on several complex and often interrelated environmental issues, beginning with a discussion of global climate change. It then looks at the role of greenhouse gases in other environmental problems, including deforestation, ozone depletion, and the health of the world's oceans. The chapter then examines a series of other global environmental issues and the challenges they pose to the international community, including clean water, air pollution, desertification, disappearing habitats and species, and pesticides. Next, the chapter focuses on waste production, including e-waste, military waste, and other miscellaneous human waste products. It then moves to a discussion of environmental discrimination and its effects on indigenous peoples and minority cultures. The chapter concludes with a discussion of international efforts that have been undertaken to address global environmental problems.

> **tsunamis** A series of huge waves.
>
> **water wars** Conflicts with controlling water as a central feature.

Global Climate Change

A strong scientific consensus supports the fact that global climate change, also known as "global warming," is underway. While the scope and pace of this change is uncertain, scientists have identified several key contributors to it, including carbon dioxide (CO_2) emissions and other *greenhouse gases.* Increases in greenhouse gases are the result of human activities, such as industrial processes, fossil fuel (coal, oil, and gas) combustion, and changes in land use (e.g., factory farming and deforestation).[4] In addition to CO_2, there exists a variety of other greenhouse gases, including sulfur dioxide, nitrous oxide, methane, aerosols, chlorofluorocarbons (CFCs), perfluorocarbons (PFCs), and hydrofluorocarbons (HCFCs). These gases get trapped in the Earth's atmosphere, with adverse effects. Heat that comes from the sun is both absorbed by the Earth and radiated back toward the atmosphere. Greenhouse gases act like a buffer, preventing the heat that once penetrated the Earth's atmosphere from escaping it. The effect is the gradual warming of the Earth.

> **greenhouse gases** Gases, such as carbon dioxide, methane, ozone, and nitrous oxide, that warm the earth's atmosphere by absorbing infrared radiation.

While the gradual warming of the Earth might not initially seem like such a bad thing, it is likely to have many profound effects that will be felt around the globe. According to a 2008 UN report, communities are likely to face a variety of challenges, including increased water stress and food insecurity. Additionally, climate change is likely to lead to an acceleration of human displacement resulting in increased competition for land, resources and housing with attendant unrest in both urban and rural settings, within and between countries. Africa, Small Island Developing States and Asian and African mega deltas are likely to be particularly affected. People living in poorly constructed settlements in high risk areas will increasingly be at the mercy of extreme weather events.[5]

Scientists also predict that an increase in global temperatures will result in rising sea levels, as ice caps and sheets melt. According to the US National Aeronautics and Space Administration (NASA), "New satellite measurements reveal that the Greenland and West Antarctic ice sheets are shedding about 125 billion tons of ice per year – enough to raise sea levels by 0.35 millimeters (0.01 inches) per year."[6] Rising sea levels will in turn flood river and coastal deltas, displacing the millions of people who now live in low-lying delta regions. Many of the approximately 10 percent of the world's population who live in coastal areas[7] will also be particularly vulnerable. In addition, the temperature of the oceans will rise, causing disruptions in storm patterns, such as the increased frequency and intensity of hurricanes.

Rising temperatures will have several other effects as well. The hydration cycle will be affected, as warmer temperatures mean more water evaporation. Atmospheric absorption will alter precipitation levels and the availability of fresh water supplies. While some areas will see a decrease in precipitation, others will see an increase. Another result of altered weather patterns will be changing disease patterns. For example, mosquitoes and other water-related disease-carrying organisms will migrate to areas with increased precipitation. This will introduce *malaria* and other diseases to new areas. Areas that flood will run the risk of endemic morbidity and mortality due to diarrheal disease. Rising temperatures will also affect entire *ecosystems*. According to the UN, roughly 20–30 percent of the world's species may face extinction as ecosystems dramatically change.[8]

malaria   A vector-born disease that is carried by mosquitoes and kills millions each year.

ecosystems   A community of plants, animals, and smaller organisms that live, feed, reproduce and interact in the same area or environment.

fossil fuels   Non-renewable sources of energy such as oil, gas, and coal.

One of the leading contributors to climate change is CO_2, which enters the atmosphere primarily as the result of the use of *fossil fuels*. Sources of CO_2 include power plants, especially those burning coal, commercial and residential buildings, and gasoline-powered vehicles. Although efforts to explore alternative sources of energy are underway, changing long-held patterns of fossil fuel usage has proven difficult. In fact, each year, we have seen an overall trend of increasing CO_2 emissions. Understanding the level of dependence that countries have on fossil fuels helps explain why moving away from fossil fuels such as petroleum has turned out to be so difficult. The US, for example, relies on fossil fuels for 97 percent of its transportation.[9] The US was also the largest producer of CO_2 gases in the world until it was surpassed by China in 2008.[10] (See table 5.1.) Because roughly one-third of China's emissions result from manufacturing products for overseas markets, primarily for developed countries, China is reluctant to accept responsibility for those emissions. This has led to sometimes

Table 5.1   The Top 20 Carbon Dioxide Emitters (2004)[11]

Country	Total Emissions (1,000 tons of C)	Per Capita Emissions (tons/capita)	Per Capita Emissions (rank)
1. United States	1,650,020	5.61	(9)
2. China (mainland)	1,366,554	1.05	(92)
3. Russian Federation	415,951	2.89	(28)
4. India	366,301	0.34	(129)
5. Japan	343,117	2.69	(33)
6. Germany	220596	2.67	(36)
7. Canada	174,401	5.46	(10)
8. United Kingdom	160,179	2.67	(37)
9. Republic of Korea	127,007	2.64	(39)
10. Italy (including San Marino)	122,726	2.12	(50)
11. Mexico	119,473	1.14	(84)
12. South Africa	119,203	2.68	(34)
13. Iran	118,259	1.76	(63)
14. Indonesia	103,170	0.47	(121)
15. France (including Monaco)	101,927	1.64	(66)
16. Brazil	90,499	0.50	(118)
17. Spain	90,145	2.08	(52)
18. Ukraine	90,020	1.90	(56)
19. Australia	89,125	4.41	(13)
20. Saudi Arabia	84,116	3.71	(18)

contentious discussions about whether a country's emissions should be measured by how much it produces or by the patterns of consumer demand and consumption that result in the production of emissions. In other words, a country may reduce its overall greenhouse gas emissions by reducing its manufacturing and by importing the goods it once made. The overall amount of emissions do not decrease, however, as the location of the emissions is simply transferred to another country. As a result, some suggest that we must take into consideration the consumption patterns driving the production and manufacturing that lead to greenhouse gas emissions.[12]

While CO_2 receives a good deal of attention as a leading greenhouse gas, other more potent gases are also contributing to the greenhouse effect. For example, "methane has 23 times the global warming potential (GWP) of CO_2 and nitrous oxide has 296 times the warming potential of carbon dioxide."[13] Methane (CH_4) is produced by a variety of sources, but one of the biggest single sources is livestock. According to a Food and Agriculture Organization (FAO) report:

> Livestock are responsible for 18 percent of greenhouse-gas emissions as measured in carbon dioxide equivalent.... This includes 9 percent of all CO_2 emissions, 37 percent of methane, and 65 percent of nitrous oxide. "Altogether, that's more than the emissions caused by transportation."[14]

anthropogenic Effects, processes, or materials that are the result of human activities.

Estimates are that the growing population together with a growing demand for meat will lead to an increase in annual global meat production from 229 million tons in 2000 to 465 million tons in 2050.[15] There are natural sources of CH_4 as well, but most are *anthropogenic*. As with CH_4, nitrous oxide (N_2O) is produced by both natural and human-related sources. According to the US Environmental Protection Agency:

> Primary human-related sources of N_2O are agricultural soil management, animal manure management, sewage treatment, adipic acid production, nitric acid production, mobile and stationary combustion of fossil fuel. Nitrous oxide is also produced naturally from a wide variety of biological sources in soil and water, particularly microbial action in wet tropical forests.[16]

The vast majority of N_2O is produced via agricultural soil management, otherwise known as farming (see figure 5.1).

deforestation The clearing of forests, usually by logging or burning, which not only releases carbon into the atmosphere but also often results in soil erosion, desertification, and the loss of habitats and biodiversity.

Deforestation

One of the biggest anthropogenic culprits for releasing CO_2 into the atmosphere is *deforestation*. Trees store carbon and, when they are cut down, that carbon is released into the atmosphere. The carbon then mixes with oxygen to create CO_2. According to the Nature Conservancy, "[e]very year, 20 million hectares of rainforest – an area the size of England, Wales and Scotland combined – are cut down, releasing millions of tons of carbon emissions into the atmosphere."[18] Michigan State University's Tropical Rainforest Information Center estimates:

> The plants and soil of tropical forests hold 460–575 billion metric tons of carbon worldwide with each acre of tropical forest storing about 180 metric tons of carbon.... From 1850 to 1990, deforestation worldwide (including the United States) released 122 billion metric tons of carbon into the atmosphere, with the current rate being approximately 1.6 billion metric tons per year. In comparison, the burning of fossil fuels releases about six billion metric tons per year.[19]

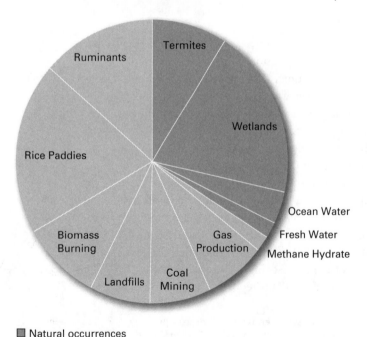

☐ Natural occurrences
☐ Anthropogenic influence

Figure 5.1   Sources of Methane Gas (CH_4)[17]

Thus, the removal of tropical forests dramatically increases the overall amount of CO_2 in the atmosphere, making deforestation the second largest contributor of carbon emissions.[20]

In 2005, the UN Food and Agriculture Organization (FAO) produced one of the most comprehensive reports on deforestation. The study looked at forest resources from 1990 to 2005 and found that global deforestation had slowed somewhat between the years 2000 and 2005; but the study also found that deforestation was nevertheless progressing at an alarming rate.[21] Areas are deforested for a variety of purposes, including commercial logging, clearing land for agriculture, and creating space for housing and commercial developments. Although the rate of deforestation varies from year to year and from region to region, tropical forests are particularly under threat. The FAO estimates that "53,000 square miles of tropical forests (rainforest and other) were destroyed each year during the 1980s."[22] Fifty-three thousand square miles is roughly the size of the US state of North Carolina. Most of this deforestation was in the Amazon Basin.

While the link between CO_2 emissions and climate change has received a lot of attention, one of the ancillary affects of deforestation that also contributes to climate change has not garnered as much coverage in popular media. Forests, particularly in tropical areas, also help to reduce evaporative cooling. With no cover from the sun, ground plants and the soil quickly dry out. Rain that reaches the ground is not held in place by trees, foliage, or root systems. This water either runs off too quickly, creating a series of problems, including loss of topsoil and general erosion, or disappears too quickly from the surface into the water table. The result is that less moisture is available to evaporate and return back to the ground in the form of rain.[23] Less rain increases the chances of fire. Forest fires then release even more carbon into the atmosphere. Because of the interconnectedness of ecosystems, the impact of the degeneration of the evaporative cycle is experienced far beyond the point of origin.[24] The impact of deforestation is felt for thousands of miles around the targeted region.

The removal of trees also results in the destruction of the habitats of thousands of animals and plants. The surviving animals that once lived in deforested zones move into new areas, putting a greater strain on those ecosystems. Additionally, deforestation can lead to outbreaks of infectious disease. Scientists now believe that logging roads often act as disease corridors. For example, in a series of studies done on the increase in malaria in Peru, a country which went from virtually no cases each year to 64,000 in 2007 alone, researchers found that logging roads leave deep ditches where pools of water form, providing fertile ground for mosquitoes to lay their eggs.[25] In addition, extensive logging in tropical areas allows workers to hunt for *bush meat*, which often carries disease. Scientists have traced several types of *human immunodeficiency viruses* to areas that have experienced extensive logging.[26]

Deforestation is also creating situations where humans are making themselves more vulnerable to "natural disasters." For

bush meat Meat from wild animals. It is also often used to refer to the unsustainable and sometimes illegal killing of wildlife, particularly in tropical areas.

human immunodeficiency viruses Types of viruses that break down the body's ability to fight opportunistic infections.

example, in 1997, hurricane Mitch came ashore in Central America and dropped more than 75 inches of rain in a very short time period. This was the most devastating Atlantic hurricane in more than 200 years.[27] Because of the amount of rain, devastation and floods were to be expected. However, the mud slides that left more than 10,000 dead were also a direct result of human activity.[28] Major urban areas had become migration magnets for rural people seeking employment. In the case of Tegucigalpa, in Honduras, migrants had settled in squatter camps on the outskirts of the city. Hillsides were denuded as the timber was used for shelters, warmth, and cooking fuel. When the rains came, the ground had nothing to hold it in place, and so it began to slide. Thousands of people were crushed by tons of mud and rocks. Millions of homes were destroyed and billions of dollars in damages were reported. This was not an isolated disaster, however. It also occurred in Venezuela in 1999, when heavy rains dislodged more than 15 cubic meters of mud, rocks, and trees. Between 5,000 and 30,000 people were buried by the ensuing mudslides.[29] In 2006, Indonesia and the Philippines were hit by mudslides that had resulted, in large part, from deforestation.

In addition to serving as "carbon sinks," helping to regulate climate, supplying wood products, and functioning as places of recreation, the Earth's forests also play a crucial role in conserving biological diversity, playing host to millions of plant and animal species. According to the FAO, more than half of the world's known plant and animal species are found in tropical rainforests.[30] A typical hectare (2.471 acres) in Brazil, home of much of the Amazon, contains more than 500 different species.[31] Deforestation may lead to the extinction of many of these species. Environmental activists and government agencies, as well as other state and non-state actors, have suggested that allowing species to become extinct may prove financially short-sighted and even dangerous for humans. Many plants serve as the basis for pharmaceuticals, for example. Roughly "25 percent of drugs prescribed in the US include chemical compounds derived from wild (plant) species." The value of these pharmaceuticals is $40 billion annually.[32] Species that go extinct may take possible cures to various diseases with them.

The importance of forests and the grave impacts of deforestation are also captured in the following UN statistics:

- global forest cover was just under 4 billion hectares in 2005, 36% of which were classified as primary forests (old growth forests);
- forests provide approximately 1.6 billion people with food, medicines, fuel and other basic necessities;
- over two thirds of known land-based species live in forests;
- approximately 8,000 tree species, or 9% of the total number of tree species worldwide, are currently under threat of extinction;
- the latest deforestation rates are estimated around 13 million hectares per year: a net loss of about 7.3 million hectares per year for 2000–5;
- deforestation is estimated to have been the cause of 20% of annual greenhouse gas emissions in the 1990s.[33]

In Focus: Chico Mendes and Brazil's Rubber-tappers

While humans cause deforestation, many people, including *indigenous peoples*, still make their homes and livelihoods in forests. However, because many indigenous forest-dwellers are minorities within their states, their concerns are often ignored. Additionally, they lack the financial resources that logging companies and big business firms have to influence the political

> **indigenous peoples** A particular group of inhabitants of a geographic space whose connections to that space are the earliest known human connections to that land.

process via campaign contributions. In short, they lack the political clout to stop deforestation. Groups that have chosen to remain somewhat isolated from society also tend to garner little attention and sympathy for their causes from the larger population. In an attempt to break that pattern, Francisco Mendes Filho (Chico) Mendes took his people's cause to the international community. Mendes represented a group of rubber-tappers whose families lived and worked in the Amazon. They depended upon the forests for items used in daily living, but they also worked the rubber trees, extracting latex from them without harming the trees. When logging, both legal and illegal, threatened the livelihood of the rubber-tappers, Mendes formed a group to try to protect the forest. Using protests, including sitting in front of bulldozers, and publicity, he tried to stop the logging. He also criticized local officials for working with the logger barons and for failing to protect the rubber-tappers. After receiving limited assistance from Brazilian government officials, he took his case to the international community and, in doing so, he became a hero to marginalized peoples around the world. The worldwide attention also allowed him to be more effective at home. According to a report in the *New York Times*, "As the movement grew under Mr Mendes, rubber tappers and their families became the only group in Brazil that physically prevented deforestation."[34] However, his fame and his success angered people with logging and agricultural interests, making him a target. He requested government protection for his people and himself, but was provided with only limited assistance. In 1988, he was assassinated at his home. His killers were arrested in 1990, but in 1993, they "escaped" with the apparent complicity of the local police.

Ozone depletion

Greenhouse gases are not only causing global climate change, they are also contributing to *ozone depletion*. The ozone layer in the upper atmosphere filters out ultraviolet rays from the sun, which are harmful in large doses to most life forms. Ozone depletion refers to both the slow decline of the total volume of ozone making up the ozone layer since the late 1970s and a

> **ozone depletion** Refers to the deterioration of the ozone layer, which serves to protect the earth from the dangerous ultraviolet light of the sun.

seasonal decrease in the ozone layer over the globe's polar regions during the same period. Of the greenhouse gases, chlorofluorocarbons (CFCs) are the biggest contributors to ozone depletion. CFCs are used in solvents and cleaners, refrigerants, and aerosols. When they are released into the air, they rise up to the stratosphere (the highest layer of the Earth's atmosphere) and their molecules begin destroying ozone molecules. The result has been a thinning of the ozone generally and a hole in the ozone roughly the size of the US over part of Antarctica and New Zealand.[35] Without the ozone, the sun's unfiltered rays penetrate the atmosphere, killing marine plankton and leading to a host of other problems, including skin cancer in humans. For example, increases in skin cancer in New Zealand have been linked to ozone depletion.[36]

International efforts to reduce CFCs have been successful. The Montreal Protocol, which was signed in 1987 and came into force in 1989, was designed to phase out the production of CFCs and other ozone depleting agents. According to the US National Ocean and Atmospheric Administration (NOAA):

> The Montreal Protocol, along with its subsequent amendments, is considered by many to be the most successful multilateral environmental agreement to date. Since being enacted in 1987, it has resulted in a significant reduction in global emissions of ozone depleting substances and there are signs that ozone depletion is slowly recovering.[37]

However, because the holes in the ozone layer are still there and because of the connection between the gases that contribute to global climate change and ozone depletion, scientists continue to monitor CFC emissions very closely.

Oceans

pH balance   The measure of a solution's acidity.

Climate change is also affecting the world's oceans in a variety of ways. Oceans play a critical role in CO_2 absorption. In fact, roughly half of all CO_2 produced by humans has been absorbed by the oceans. Because CO_2 is acidic, it is changing the *pH balance* of the oceans. Scientists are only at the beginning stages of measuring the long-term effects of increased acidity levels; however, some studies are already indicating that it will have a serious negative impact on marine life.[38] Additionally, climate change is causing ocean sea surface temperatures (SST) to increase. As the temperature of the ocean increases, scientists are concerned about the ability of the oceans to store oxygen. Warmer water holds less oxygen than cooler water. According to scientists, this may lead to "dead zones" – areas where there is not enough oxygen for marine life to survive. Currently, dead zones "make up less than 2 percent of the world's ocean volume." However, recent research indicates that climate change could cause "dead zones to grow by a factor of ten or more by the year 2100."[39]

coral reefs   Large marine formations created from the calcium carbonate skeletons of coral animals that support living corals and various forms of plant and animal life.

Of particular concern is the fate of *coral reefs*. Reefs play a critical role in local economies, both for what can be harvested from them and for tourism. They also help to control storm surge, the water pushed toward the shore by the force of winds. The wide variety of species that exist within a reef ecosystem has led some to refer to reefs as the "tropical rainforests of the sea." The deterioration of coral reefs around the world, but most acutely in the South Pacific, is reaching crisis proportions according to researchers at the University of North Carolina. They found that between 1968 and 2004, coral coverage in the Pacific had dropped by 20 percent, with roughly 1,500 square kilometers of reefs disappearing.[40] The UN estimates that approximately 27 percent of the world's reefs have already been lost. This loss results from a variety of factors, including overfishing and increased sedimentation, which is often associated with topsoil run-off from deforested areas. Increased sedimentation in the water prevents sunlight from reaching the reef. The absence of sunlight prevents *photosynthesis* from occurring, which is a necessary part of the reef building process. Natural events that damage reefs include flooding, violent storms, disease, and dramatic temperature changes. However, warming waters and increased exposure to UV rays as a result of a thinning ozone layer are two main causes of damage to coral reefs. They also cause a phenomenon called *coral bleaching*. Coral reefs exist in a *symbiotic* relationship with algae called *zooxanthellae*. These live within the corals' tissue and give the corals their color. Under stress, corals often expel their zooxanthellae, which causes the coral to whiten. Corals can be recolonized by zooxanthellae, but once bleaching begins, corals generally tend to continue to bleach, and ultimately to die even when the stressor is removed. The loss of the coral leads to the migration and/or death of other creatures, ultimately resulting in the death of the entire reef. The UN's Earthwatch found that in a nine-month period in 1998, 16 percent of the coral reefs of the world were destroyed. The cause was two of the largest climate change events in recent history – *El Niño and La Niña*.[41] El Niño brought increased SST, which killed the coral. Because climate change is predicted to increase both SSTs and the number of El Niño events, scientists are worried about the ability of reefs to survive.[42]

photosynthesis   Process by which plants, and some other species, use the energy of sunlight to create the sugars necessary for respiration.

coral bleaching   The whitening of corals resulting from the stress-induced expulsion of the algae zooxanthellae.

symbiotic   Refers to a relationship in which two dissimilar organisms rely upon each other for mutual gain.

zooxanthellae   Single-celled algae that live symbiotically with corals.

El Niño and La Niña   El Niño refers to a warming of Pacific water that creates changes in climatic weather patterns, such as increased rain in some areas. La Niña refers to unusually cold water in the Pacific that likewise causes weather disruptions.

Researching to Learn   *Investigating Global Climate Change Online*

Organizations

Centre for Atmospheric Science
This Cambridge University site promotes research on global climate change.
www.atm.ch.cam.ac.uk/cas/

Climate Institute
This organization is designed to bring together scientists, policy-makers, and activists in order to nurture dialogue, but also to provide information

about climate change and to encourage various sectors to work together.
www.climate.org/

Intergovernmental Panel on Climate Change
A scientific intergovernmental organization charged with evaluating the risk of climate change caused by human activity. It publishes special reports based on its analysis of the scientific literature that focus on topics relevant to the implementation

of the UN Framework Convention on Climate Change.
www.ipcc.ch/

The Pew Center on Global Climate Change
The Pew Center brings together business leaders, policy-makers, scientists, and other experts to develop strategies for combating global climate change, while sustaining economic growth.
www.pewclimate.org/

Union of Concerned Scientists
Begun in 1969 at MIT, this is a group of scientists and non-scientists who promote scientific understanding and civic engagement.
www.ucsusa.org/

United Nations World Meteorological Organization
A comprehensive site for data on the Earth's atmosphere and its interactions with oceans and the resulting weather events.
www.wmo.int/pages/index_en.html

Welcome to the Climate Action Network
This site represents a network of more than 450 non-governmental environmental organizations.
www.climatenetwork.org/

Woods Hole Research Center
A science, education, research, and public policy organization that provides a comprehensive overview of climate change.
http://whrc.org/resources/online_publications/warming_earth/index.htm

Worldwatch Institute
The Worldwatch Institute's climate change page has detailed reports and analysis on climate change.
www.worldwatch.org/taxonomy/term/110

Online Research Portals

California Climate Change Portal
This site provides visitors with information on climate change and the measures that the state of California has put in place to try to combat this. It also has links to research on climate change.
www.climatechange.ca.gov/

Gateway to the UN Mission's Work on Climate Change
This UN site provides links to all the various agencies within the UN that are dealing with climate change issues.
www.un.org/climatechange/

National Aeronautics and Space Administration (NASA)
Links to various research and policy websites can be found here. There are also links to various international environmental agreements.
http://globalchange.nasa.gov/Resources/pointers/glob_warm.html

National Oceanic and Atmospheric Administration (NOAA)
This site provides information on climate observations and monitoring, climate research and modeling, and climate information services.
www.noaa.gov/climate.html

The Potsdam Institute for Climate Impact Research
Provides access interdisciplinary research from various sources on climate change. Links to news and climate change related events are also housed here.
www.pik-potsdam.de/

The World Environmental Organization
The World Environmental Origination's site has links to 100 climate change organizations along with a brief description of each site.
www.world.org/weo/climate

Statistical Sources

Global Climate Research Explorer
This site provides statistics in a variety of categories, including how climate change is effecting the atmosphere, hydrosphere, cryosphere, and biosphere, along with other general statistics about the effects of global climate change.
www.exploratorium.edu/climate/index.html

NOAA Data Center
NOAA has a thorough list of resources related to climate change.
www.lib.noaa.gov/climatechangeresources.html

Ongoing Global Environmental Challenges

Water

As significant as global climate change is, it does not represent the only environmental issue facing the world community. Gaining access to clean water is increasingly difficult for many people around the world, leading scholars and activists to suggest that the political economy of water is one of the most pressing issues of our day. Given the following statistics, it is easy to see why water consumption and availability have emerged as potential flashpoints for conflict:

- only 2.5 percent of the Earth's water is fresh water, and, of that, two-thirds is locked in ice caps and glaciers;
- roughly 97 percent of all freshwater potentially available for human use is in underground basins;[43]
- from 1950 to 1990, water usage has tripled;
- the world's population is expected to grow to over 9 billion by 2054;[44]
- and roughly one-third of the world's population lives in countries that are experiencing *water scarcity*; by 2025 that number is expected to increase to two-thirds.[45]

Overuse and pollution are cutting into the limited supply of fresh water. According to the Global Policy Forum, "[m]ore than 50 countries on five continents might soon be caught up in water disputes unless they move quickly to establish agreements on how to share reservoirs, rivers, and underground water acquifers."[46] One example of water as a flashpoint between nations is the debate over who should control the two *West Bank* aquifers. Under a plan submitted as part of a broader Middle East peace agreement, Israel proposed that it retain control over the aquifers. Palestinians have protested this arrangement, arguing

> **water scarcity** Lacking enough water to meet basic daily needs.
>
> **West Bank** Refers to land on the West Bank of the Jordan river that has been central to the conflicts in the Middle East. Although made up primarily of Palestinians, much of the area has been controlled by Israel since 1967.

that Israel has subjected them to discriminatory water regulations that give more water to Israelis at the expense of Palestinian farmers.[47] Settling the political tensions in the Middle East may hinge, at least in part, on deciding who will control water in this semi-arid region. Water is also a source of conflict within nation-states. For example, in the US, the states of California, Nevada, Arizona, and Colorado fight over use of the Colorado River; Georgia, Alabama, and Florida also fight over various rivers that run through their respective states. Even within these states, urban and rural demands for water have sparked conflict. Farmers argue they should have a larger share of water because they produce the foods necessary for urban dwellers. Urban dwellers in turn argue that more water should be available for urban centers, which are the economic hubs of the states.

Fresh water supplies are under pressure and in some cases are disappearing. One of the sectors that uses the most water is agriculture, using roughly 65 percent of all the water that is removed from rivers, lakes, and aquifers. Another 22 percent is used for industry, and 7 percent is used for households and municipalities. For each ton of grain produced, more than 1,000 tons of water is used. A great deal of the grain produced globally is used for livestock. For example, for each kilo of pork produced, 6.9 kilos of grain are used.[48] Thus consumer demand for meat is also indirectly linked to water issues.

The Ogallala aquifer (also known as the High Plains aquifer) is the largest single water-bearing unit in North America, covering 174,000 square miles and stretching from the Texas Panhandle northward to South Dakota (see figure 5.2).[49] Despite its size, the aquifer is being drawn upon so heavily that water levels drop each year. According to a special report published by the BBC, the aquifer is "being depleted at a rate of 12 billion cubic metres a year – amounting to a total depletion to date of a volume equal to the annual flow of 18 Colorado Rivers. Some estimates say it will dry up in as little as 25 years."[50] Across the country from the Ogallala is another area that is being squeezed dry. Florida's Everglades have been directly affected by population increases along Florida's Atlantic coast as well as by increased water use by agribusinesses in the region. According to Melanie Schimek of the Delaware Geographic Alliance, "Today less than half the volume of water flows through the region's main fresh-water channel than a century ago. Once covering the southern Florida peninsula, the Everglades have become a jumbled series of disconnected pools."[51]

In addition to overuse, pollution poses an additional serious threat to the world's water supply. Sources of water pollution include the overuse of pesticides, leaking "*lagoons*" from factory farming, *tailings* and other byproducts from mining, and industrial and human waste that seeps into ground water, contaminating it. Globally, one of the better-known examples of pollution and poor water management resulting in the devastation of a water supply is the Aral Sea, once the fourth largest inland sea in the world. The Aral Sea is located in Central Asia between Kazakhstan in the north and Uzbekistan in the south. Intense irrigation use of the two main rivers that empty into the Sea has not only shrunk it significantly but also contributed to ecological devastation in the entire region. At several points, the shoreline has moved 70 miles inward (see figure 5.3). Declining sea levels deposited salt around the water's edge. This salt has been carried by the winds to surrounding areas creating

lagoons   Places where factory farms store animal waste.

tailings   Waste materials produced from the process of extracting minerals from ore. Tailings often contain toxic chemicals that can harm both humans and wildlife.

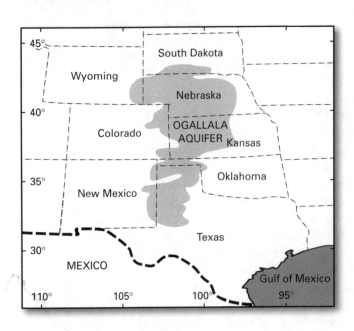

Figure 5.2 Ogallala Aquifer[52]

oversalinization, which has devastated the area's *flora* and *fauna*. In addition, the decreasing water level has increased the salinity of the remaining water and this, coupled with increased use of pesticides upriver from the Sea, has killed the marine life. The hundreds of thousands of people who once depended upon the Sea for their livelihoods have been devastated by its demise.

oversalinization The accumulation of too much salt in water or soil.

flora Refers to plant life.

fauna Refers to animal life.

According to 1999 Nobel Peace Prize-winning organization Médecins Sans Frontières (Doctors Without Borders), "the environmental impact resulting from the desiccation of the Aral Sea, coupled with worsening poverty and a general deterioration of health services, has exposed the population living in and around the Aral Sea area to an unprecedented humanitarian and health crisis."[53] So many studies have been conducted on the Sea and its surrounding areas that many of the locals joke that, "if everyone who'd come to study the Aral had brought a bucket of water, the sea would be full by now."[54]

In addition to access to clean water and water pollution, another pressing issue facing many countries in the world is the role of dams as sources of water for irrigation, as sources of energy, and for flood control. Many countries dammed their rivers in order to provide farmers and local communities with access to fresh water. Others have used dams to create hydroelectricity, and still others have used them as effective flood control mechanisms or to increase a river's navigability. However, the extensive use of dams has been called into question by recent research. Dams can cause environmental damage not only to the rivers themselves, but also to the species that exist within the rivers and to the surrounding river basins. For example, damming rivers prevents nutrient-rich silt from reaching delta regions. Without the influx of silt, deterioration of the delta can set in, as has occurred in

THE SHRINKING SEA

The changed shape of the Aral Sea since 1960

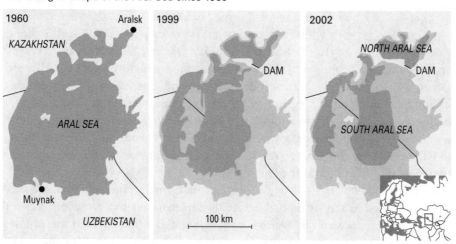

Figure 5.3 The Aral Sea, 1960–2004[55]

wetlands Land areas, such as swamps and marshes, in which the soil is either permanently or seasonally saturated with moisture.

the US's Mississippi river delta. Dams have dramatically reduced the amount of sediment pouring into the delta, and as a result, the delta area is sinking into the Gulf of Mexico. As the delta sinks, ocean levels rise and salt water moves in, replacing the freshwater that once flowed more freely into the freshwater parts of the coastal *wetlands*. The coastal wetlands of the Mississippi are rapidly disappearing; each year, 25 square miles of Gulf coast wetlands are lost.[56] Some scientists have linked the loss of wetlands that once served as a buffer from the Gulf to the ability of hurricanes, such as Katrina, to cause extensive damage to the region.[57]

Dams and increased demands for water have dramatically impacted wetlands areas in other places as well. According to the US Environmental Protection Agency, "[b]etween 1986 and 1997, an estimated 58,500 acres of wetlands were lost each year in the conterminous United States. . . . In addition to these losses, many other wetlands have suffered degradation of functions."[58] For example, California has lost roughly 95 percent of its wetlands. As a result, wetland bird and wildlife species decreased from 60 million in 1950 to 3 million in 1996.[59] The US is not alone in witnessing the disappearance of its wetlands. According to Wetlands International, a group dedicated to protecting global wetlands, "[w]orldwide around 50% of wetlands are estimated to have disappeared since 1900."[60] In response to growing concern about dams' effects on ecosystems, dam-removal has begun in many parts of the world. For example, in the US, more than 200 dams have been removed since 1999 in an effort to allow rivers to flow freely.[61]

Air pollution

Many urban areas are also wrestling with the problem of deteriorating air quality. Rapid urbanization, car exhaust, and industry emissions have all contributed to declining air quality in major urban centers. *Ex-urban* and rural areas are also feeling the effects of worsening air quality. The issue of air quality sparked some heated debate in 2008 when Beijing, a city whose air quality ranks among the worst in the world, played host to the summer Olympic Games. Fears revolving around athletes' health and ability to perform dominated much of the pre-Olympic discussion.[62] China instituted a variety of measures to protect athletes' health, including limiting the number of cars allowed into the city and relocating coal-intensive plants and heavy industry out of Beijing. Many of these industries were moved to neighboring provinces, but the pollution continued to make its way to Beijing. As a result, China even shut down some power plants in neighboring provinces in the lead up to the Olympics.[63]

ex-urban Areas beyond suburbs that serve as commuter towns to nearby urban areas.

China is not alone in its struggle for clean air. In many cities, children are periodically warned to stay at home because the air quality is too dangerous. Several studies that have focused on Mexico City have found that children who are "exposed to high levels of air pollution experience chronic respiratory tract inflammation, changes in inflammatory mediators in blood and changes in brain tissue" and that ambient air pollution causes "cognitive deficiencies in healthy children."[64] Children's lung growth is also negatively affected by exposure to high levels of air pollution.[65] But it is not just children who are negatively affected by air pollution. A Cornell study suggests that "[a]ir pollution from smoke and various chemicals kills 3 million people a year."[66] Some countries are making progress in their efforts to clean up their air. A 2009 study found that air pollution control measures instituted in the US added, on average, 5 months to its citizens' lives.[67]

Desertification

Global climate change is projected to alter some climates from wetter to drier while others will move in the opposite direction. Already existing dry climates may get even drier, and one contributor to this change is desertification. *Desertification* is the process whereby a desert expands and claims hectares of previously arable land, rendering that land useless for agriculture and human habitation. Once a desert starts expanding, it is near impossible to stop it. The Sahara in northern Africa is a good example of this. The Sahara has been spreading south at a rate of 5–6 kilometers per year. Settlements once on the edge of the desert have been swallowed up by it. Several factors contribute to this. Deforestation is one component of desertification. Without trees to hold topsoil in place, nutrient-rich soil is blown away and the desert sweeps in. In addition to deforestation, land overcultivation, *slash and burn farming*, overgrazing, and climate change all contribute to desertification. While the Sahara offers a stark example of desertification, it is not the only area threatened by expanding deserts. According to the UN Environment Programme: "One quarter of the earth's land is threatened by desertification. . . . The livelihoods of over 1 billion people in more than 100 countries are also jeopardized by desertification, as farming and grazing land becomes less productive."[68]

desertification The gradual transformation of habitable land into desert.

slash and burn farming A process whereby existing organic material is cut down and burned to clear land for farming.

As early as 1977, the international community recognized the need for a concerted effort to combat desertification. However, small local efforts proved ineffective, so state leaders ultimately addressed the issue at a 1992 world environmental summit in Rio. This led to the 1994 promulgation of the UN Convention to Combat Desertification (UNCCD), which came into force in 1996. The Convention establishes processes and procedures for monitoring both desertification and the various efforts made at combating it. The Convention commits countries to helping to secure funding for developing countries facing desertification. The funding is targeted at local groups and individuals who are directly affected. A number of programs in dozens of countries are currently underway.[69]

Disappearing habitat and species

Global climate change has also been linked to disappearing habitats and species extinction. In the 1990s, scientists became aware of an unusual phenomenon.

amphibians Cold-blooded vertebrates, such as frogs or salamanders, that can live in the water and on land.

chytrid fungus Transferred through water, this fungus attaches itself to amphibians' skin making it hard for them to breath. It also affects their nervous system and eventually leads to their death.

sentinel species A species whose presence, absence, or condition in an area indicates certain environmental conditions. They are often among the most sensitive species living in an area and can thus provide advanced warning of environmental degradation to monitoring biologists.

Amphibians around the world were dying, and at a fast rate. Between 1980 and 2006, roughly 112 species of amphibians had gone extinct.[70] As of 2009, roughly 40 percent of all known species of amphibians are threatened with some level of extinction, according to Vance Vredenburg, Professor of Biology at San Francisco State.[71] Researchers are busy trying to understand the cause of the mass extinctions, but evidence seems to suggest that they are the result of a combination of factors, including global climate change, use of pesticides, invasive species, overexposure to UV rays (resulting from a thinning ozone), loss of habitat, and disease. Among the diseases affecting amphibian populations, the *chytrid fungus* has been particularly damaging. In 1999, a new species of the chytrid fungus, *Batrachochytrium dendrobatidis* (Bd), was discovered to be infecting amphibians and causing chytridiomycosis, which is often a fatal disease. *Bd* has since been identified in association with declines in amphibian populations on every amphibian inhabited continent.[72] Scientists also suggest that frogs and other amphibians are *sentinel species* because they are very sensitive to changes in their environment. During their life-span, they exist in both water and on land. Their skin is a semi-permeable layer through which they breathe while in the water. Thus, any changes in either the land or in the water will affect them.[73]

Amphibians are not the only endangered or threatened species. According to the World Conservation Union's (IUCN) 1996 report, one in four vertebrate species is in decline and 25 percent of mammals are threatened with extinction. Each year, 1,000 species of marine invertebrates are lost.[74] Two out of three species of birds are in decline, while 10 percent of all birds are threatened with extinction. Some areas have been hit particularly hard.[75] For example, in the US state of Hawaii, of the more than 90 bird species that could once be found on the islands, only a third still exist, though they too are threatened with extinction.[76] Many other species are threatened as well. One half of all primates, 37 percent of all hoofed animals, 36 percent of all insectivores, 33 percent of marsupials, 33 percent of all cetaceans, 26 percent of all carnivores, and 17 percent of rodents are threatened. The 2008 IUCN follow up report indicated an increase in the numbers of threatened species for all species categories. The Sierra Club warns that:

[W]e are currently faced with the greatest rate of species extinction worldwide since the disappearance of the dinosaurs 65 million years ago. . . . In the United States, 526 species are listed in the Natural Heritage Central Database (the best single source of information on the status of species in the US) as extinct or missing, never to be seen again. Birds are the group that has suffered the most extinctions (21 extinct bird species). Following close behind, however, are freshwater mussels (19 extinctions), freshwater fishes (17 extinctions), and flowering plants (13 extinctions).[77]

One of the biggest threats to these species is habitat loss. This occurs through pollution, deforestation, desertification, corporate farming, urban development, introduction of nonnative species, mining, grazing, water development (damming rivers and redirecting channels, for example), and recreation. Attempts to protect various species sometimes fail because they do not take into account the connection between the ecosystem and the species. Scientists once thought that species could be protected or saved from extinction through breeding programs that placed species in protected environments, such as government protected lands or reserves. However, the complicated nature of ecosystems have forced scientists to re-evaluate some programs. For example, in Yellowstone (established in 1872), one of the oldest US National Parks, experts estimate that wildlife will be devastated within 10–20 years because of habitat loss in the areas surrounding the park. Roughly 10 percent of the greater Yellowstone area is a suitable winter habitat, and none of that is within the park proper. Thus animals are forced, especially during long, cold winters, to roam outside the park seeking lower elevations where food might be found. However, according to Paul Hansen, director of the Greater Yellowstone Program for the Nature Conservancy, a third of the greater Yellowstone area has been developed, and an additional third is scheduled to be developed. As a result, even though the park has done much to preserve wildlife within its confines, threats to the larger ecosystem are nevertheless leading to species loss within the park.[78] This example demonstrates the ecological complexities inherent in creating environs designed to protect species.

Protecting species and setting aside protected areas for scientific research have led to the creation of a variety of types of reserves. These often go by different names, including preserves, national parks, wildlife sanctuaries, marine parks, and game parks. The level of protection afforded the flora and fauna existing within the reserve differs from country to country. The more than 30,000 protected areas around the world have had successes in preserving some species from extinction. According to the IUCN:

> [Protected areas] are essential for conserving biodiversity, and for delivering vital ecosystem services, such as protecting watersheds and soils and shielding human communities from natural disasters. Many protected areas are important to local communities, especially indigenous peoples who depend for their survival on a sustainable supply of resources from them. They are places for people to get a sense of peace in a busy world – places that invigorate human spirits and challenge the senses. Protected landscapes embody important cultural values; some of them reflect sustainable land use practices. They are important also for research and education, and contribute significantly to local and regional economies, most obviously from tourism.[79]

Still, these reserves are under threat from a variety of sources, including climate change, pollution, poorly planned tourism, development, and poverty. There are hundreds of wildlife refuges scattered across Africa, for example. Wars, droughts, and population pressures all create conditions that threaten reserves. During the

Mozambican civil war (1977–94), almost all of the country's wildlife was slaughtered for food or killed as a consequence of the violence.[80] The neighboring country of South Africa built a 250-mile (402-kilometer) fence along its border with Mozambique as part of an effort to protect its largest national wildlife reserve, Kruger National Park, from the violence in Mozambique. While this did protect animals within Kruger, it cut across game trails and artificially divided ecosystems. In 2002, a novel approach was tried in an effort to repopulate Mozambique with wildlife and to open up the area to allow freer movement of wildlife. Large parts of the fence were removed and areas of Mozambique, Zimbabwe, and South Africa were joined together to form a new transborder park, the Great Limpopo Transfrontier Park (GLTP).[81] This is part of a broader trend to create what have been called "peace parks" or transfrontier conservation areas (TFCA). The goal is to create parks that are more logical and comprehensive from an ecological standpoint. These parks cross country borders and require states to work together to manage them.[82] Such parks are receiving a lot of support from states and international organizations, including the World Bank, which has provided some of the needed funding. It is too early to tell whether the parks will be successful. Their ability to succeed will depend upon a variety of factors, including the absence of violent conflict in the region, the establishment of cooperative relationships between the countries that house the TFCAs as well as between the governments and the local populations in the areas adjacent to the parks, the absence of weather-related events that could negatively affect the flora and fauna of the parks, and poaching prevention.

Poaching and the sale of endangered species has been so widespread that, despite the best efforts of states and NGOs, many endangered and threatened species continue to see a decline in their overall numbers. According to the World Wildlife Fund, the second biggest threat to species after habitat loss is the illegal wildlife trade. The most obvious problem associated with wildlife trade is that it can cause overexploitation to the point where the survival of a species hangs in the balance.[83] According to the Convention on International Trade in Endangered Species of Wild Fauna and Flora (CITES), illegal trade in wildlife is extensive: "From 1995 to 1999, CITES recorded an annual average of more than 1.5 million live birds, 640,000 live reptiles, 300,000 crocodilian skins, 1.6 million lizard skins, 1.1 million snake skins, 150,000 furs, almost 300 tonnes of caviar, more than 1 million coral pieces and 21,000 hunting trophies."[84] CITES is an international agreement that was conceived in 1963 and came into force in 1975. It is designed to ensure that the trade in plants and wild animals does not threaten their survival. Nations that volunteer to be parties to the Convention establish licensing agencies that monitor wildlife trade. More than 30,000 species are monitored as part of CITES program.[85]

Efforts to protect threatened species by reintroducing them into an environment they once inhabited have proven successful in some cases. Protection of species within a reserve can be problematic, as the boundaries are meaningless to wildlife, but purposefully introducing a species long extinct from an ecosystem can also prove complicated. One controversial example has been the reintroduction of the wolf. From Europe to the US, various countries have experimented with introducing wolves

Table 5.2 International Union for Conservation of Nature Red List of Threatened Species, 2008[86]

Species	1996	2008	Percent Endangered
Mammals	1,096	1,141	21
Birds	1,107	1,222	12
Reptiles	253	423	31
Amphibians	124	1,905	30
Fishes	734	1,275	37

into areas where they had once roamed, but where they had been hunted to near extinction. In the US, estimates of the *pre-Columbian* wolf population indicate that there were approximately one million; by 1990, there were only a few handfuls left. Wolves were once an integral part of ecosystems in many countries, controlling the populations of other species. Without a natural predator, species such as elk and deer have overproduced and, consequently, overgrazed areas, thus further damaging fragile ecosystems. Some areas where wolves once roamed have seen an explosion in the deer population. The deer compete with sheep for grazing opportunities and they eat young tree plants, thereby hindering efforts at reforestation. Although the reintroduction of wolves could help solve some of these problems, many ranchers and landowners have objected to reintroduction plans, fearing that wolves would attack their livestock. As a result, programs to reimburse ranchers for loss of livestock have accompanied many of the reintroduction programs, which has helped quell some objections. Still, many remain vigorously opposed to the wolves' reintroduction, and hundreds of wolves have been poached in the US alone.[87] Overall, however, the programs in the US and in various European countries appear to be successful.[88]

> **pre-Columbian** Refers to North and South America before Columbus landed.

Pesticides

Although pesticides have proven to be effective in aiding with agriculture and preventing the spread of *vector-borne diseases*, they are also associated with species decline and human health problems. Pesticides come in a variety of forms, including herbicides, fungicides, and insecticides, and they are used daily to kill insects, control parasites, kill unwanted plants, and rid an area of rodents. Manufacturers and consumers argue that the benefits are multiple and in some cases lifesaving. Given that a large percentage of the workforce in developing countries works in agriculture, the ability to use pesticides to protect crops from infestation is important to many people's livelihoods. Moreover, when pesticides became widely used in the 1950s, crop yields were dramatically increased. Additionally, the ability to spray pesticides in areas riddled with malaria and other vector-borne

> **vector-borne diseases** Pathogenic microorganisms that are transferred from host to host by blood-sucking arthropods like mosquitoes and ticks.

diseases increases the chances that people in those areas will not fall victim to deadly diseases.

On the other hand, the use of pesticides has become an international concern as it increases and as adverse, unintended consequences are revealed. Roughly 5 billion pounds (2.27 billion kilograms) of pesticides are being used around the world annually.[89] Critics point to the fact that insects become resistant to the pesticides, resulting in the need for stronger and/or more frequent application of pesticides. In addition, there are health concerns associated with pesticide use. According to the Worldwatch Institute, pesticides can impair the body's immune and reproductive systems. In their 2004 Report, they found that the prevalence of pesticides had caused breast milk to become one of the most contaminated foods, containing pesticides, PCBs, lead, and other toxins.[90] Critics also point out that each year, hundreds of thousands of people are poisoned by pesticides, with thousands losing their lives as a result.[91]

While the link between pesticide use and adverse health effects is sometimes clear, this is not always the case. There are more than 80,000 chemical compounds on the market today, with another 1,000 new chemicals introduced each year by manufacturers. The majority of these chemical compounds have little or no information available regarding their long-term health effects or their environmental impact. Of particular concern are *persistent organic pollutants* (POPs). According to the United Nations Environment Programme (UNEP), POPs "are chemical substances that persist in the environment, *bioaccumulate* through the food web, and pose a risk of causing adverse effects to human health and the environment." Thus the UNEP argues that "the evidence of long-range transport of these substances to regions where they have never been used or produced and the consequent threats they pose to the environment of the whole globe" demands urgent action "to reduce and eliminate releases of these chemicals."[92] There are 12 particularly dangerous POPs (see table 5.3): these are "long-lived chemicals that cause biological havoc as they bioaccumulate – collect and concentrate – in the food chain."[93] Because these 12 POPs were considered so dangerous, the international community came together in 2001 to promulgate the Convention on Persistent Organic Pollutants. This treaty provides for the gradual phasing out of most of the POPs and the strict limited use of the others. The treaty also allows for more compounds to be added if they qualify as a POP and pose a serious transboundary threat.[94]

persistent organic pollutants
Chemical substances that do not break down in the environment.

bioaccumulate To accumulate in a biological or ecological system over time. Usually refers to the accumulation of toxins.

Waste Production

Waste production refers to "the production of unwanted materials as a by-product of economic processes."[95] While this is a very general term, we will apply it here to several very specific areas where environmental concerns have arisen over the production and management of waste products. Specifically, we will explore the

Table 5.3 Persistent Organic Pollutants[96]

POP Name	Use	Effects
Aldrin	Pesticide used for soil insects such as termites.	It is toxic to humans.
Chlordane	Insecticide used on agricultural crops such as vegetables.	It is associated with cancer and immune system damage.
Dieldrin	A soil insecticide used on termites as well.	It is associated with cancer.
Dioxins and Furans	These are both byproducts of the production of other chemicals and get into the environment through pesticides and incineration of waste products.	These are associated with cancer and other diseases.
DDT	Used for malaria control.	It is associated with cancer and immune system suppression.
Enfrin	An insecticide used on cotton, grains and as a rodenticide against mice.	It is associated with cancer.
Heptachlor	An insecticide used on soil insects such as termites.	It can cause tremors and convulsions and compromise the immune system.
Hexachlorobenzen	A fungicide used on wheat.	It is associated with a variety of illnesses including skin lesions, hirsutism, hyperpigmentation, and other diseases.
Mirex	An insecticide used on fire ants that accumulates in the soil.	It is associated with cancer.
Polycholorinated Biphenyis, aka PCBs	Used in a variety of industries including as a paint additive.	It is associated with alterations of liver enzymes and dermatological abnormalities.
Toxaphene	An insecticide used on cotton, grains, vegetables, and fruit.	Is associated with chromosome aberrations.

impact of technology, arms production, and other human generated waste on the environment.

Technology

Technology offers us a paradox. The technology behind the industrial economy has wrought extensive damage to the planet, but technology also offers some of the most comprehensive solutions to addressing this damage. New technologies are developed to address a particular set of circumstances arising at a specific point in time. The consequences of this development cannot always be predicted and thus we may end up with unintended results that prove hazardous to our health or to the health of the planet. For example, the *green revolution* allowed countries like India to produce enough food to feed their growing

Green Revolution An effort by scientists (1940s–60s) to engineer fewer improved strains of wheat and corn in order to increase food supplies in developing countries.

populations. However, the intensive use of pesticides and fertilizers that are needed for such high-yield crops is now wreaking havoc on land and water. Fossil fuel combustion has also dramatically changed our lives, allowing for cars, transportation, and protection from the elements. It has also led to pollution and climate change, which will dramatically alter our lives in negative ways.

Yet another example is the paradox offered by computers. Computers have changed the way many societies are run. The benefits have been far beyond what anyone might have predicted. Yet the production of computers has proven environmentally problematic. Roughly 500–1,000 different toxic chemicals, including arsenic, mercury, lead, and cadmium, go into computer production, making it one of the more toxic industries.[97] Dealing with what has been termed *e-waste* has become an international concern. According to the UNEP, roughly 50 million tons of waste from electronic goods is generated each year. Burning is a common way to dispose of e-waste, but it is a practice that releases toxins into the air and into the soil. Rather than dealing with it themselves, many developed countries ship their waste to developing countries. A study conducted by the Basel Action Network reports that "a minimum of 100,000 computers a month are entering the Nigerian port of Lagos alone," most of which are useless.[98] In 1992, the Basel Convention on the Control of Transboundary Movements of Hazardous Wastes and Their Disposal came into force. This treaty is designed to stop the transfer of hazardous waste, particularly from the developed to the developing world.[99] Because the export of e-waste continues, however, many NGOs and nation-states are seeking to strengthen the convention by adding language that would put in place an immediate ban on all waste transfers from developed to developing countries.[100]

e-waste Surplus electronics that are not recycled – old computers, for example.

The fast pace of technology development has insured that new issues will arise, the consequences of which may not be felt in the near term. New products and chemical compounds are developing quickly. One fairly recent development has been the increased use of coltan, short for columbite-tantalite, a metallic ore.

> [When refined,] coltan becomes metallic tantalum, a heat-resistant powder that can hold a high electrical charge. These properties make it a vital element in creating capacitors, the electronic elements that control current flow inside miniature circuit boards. Tantalum capacitors are used in almost all cell phones, laptops, pagers and many other electronics. The recent technology boom caused the price of coltan to skyrocket to as much as $400 a kilogram at one point, as companies such as Nokia and Sony struggled to meet demand.[101]

Clearly coltan has benefits, but it also has led to some unintended consequences. While currently most coltan is mined in Australia, the world's biggest reserves are in the Democratic Republic of the Congo. Mining here has helped fuel a civil war where various militias use the sale of coltan to finance their military activities. The illegal mining has led to massive environmental damage, as hillsides have been denuded of trees, and gorilla, elephant, and other species' habitats have been destroyed. Gorillas and other species are also being gunned down to make areas safe for resource extraction and for food for the miners.

Environmental concerns have led many countries to consider different approaches to technology. For example, in 2004, the European community came together to draw up plans to create *environmental technologies* (ET). ETs, which include recycling systems for waste water in industrial processes, energy-efficient car engines, and soil remediation techniques, are technologies that do the same things as other technologies but with less environmental impact. Many can potentially both improve the environment and contribute to economic growth and employment. The Environmental Technologies Action Plan (ETAP) created by the EU brings together member nations and industry in an effort to create ETs.[102] Conferences where eco-innovations are unveiled occur regularly, and EU members are encouraged to work with ETAP to share ideas and to set performance targets for members. Types of ETs currently being explored include wave, solar, tidal, and wind energy technologies; *biofuels*; and *geothermal energy*.

> **environmental technologies** Technologies that cause limited to no harm to the environment or that use the environment in a sustainable way – solar power, for example.
>
> **biofuels** A fuel made from recently dead biological materials.
>
> **geothermal energy** A renewable energy source that uses heat from the Earth for energy – hot springs, for example.

Arms production and use

Arms production has had a catastrophic impact on the environment. From nuclear testing above ground, underground, and under the sea, to chemical and biological weapons manufacturing and destruction, the production and use of arms have left behind disastrous ecological consequences. Crafting strategies for the safe disposal of waste from arms production has proven challenging for many nation-states. For example, in the US there has been a great debate over what to do with nuclear waste. Because nuclear waste is highly radioactive and will remain so for many thousands of years, spent nuclear fuel is inherently dangerous to human health and to future generations. Additionally, spent fuel contains materials used to make nuclear weapons, which means it poses proliferation risks as well. Most countries' preferred option for isolating spent fuel from humans and the environment is to bury it underground in a deep geological repository.[103]

The site chosen for nuclear waste disposal in the US was Yucca Mountain, Nevada. Proponents argued Yucca was a safe storage facility because of the mountain's special physical, chemical, and thermal characteristics. They argued that waste from nuclear reactors all across the country could be stored there safely and easily monitored. However, critics pointed out that the site is roughly 80 miles from Las Vegas, and thus any accident would have a profound impact on a large urban center. Additionally, shipping the waste across country in trucks and on railroads would put many people at risk beyond those living close to the Yucca site. Critics also pointed to the US government's spotty history when it comes to properly storing dangerous waste. In one infamous case at Rocky Flats, 16 miles outside Denver, Colorado, workers at a plant that made plutonium triggers for nuclear weapons were exposed to plutonium that had been stored improperly. Plutonium had also leaked out into the surrounding air and water supply. Eventually, the site was shut down and cleaned up, and it now serves as a wildlife refuge. However, workers have sued the government, claiming to have health problems as a result of their exposure to dangerous toxins.[104] Other US Department of Energy storage facilities have had similar problems with the handling of toxic waste.

The US is not alone in experiencing difficulties in handling waste from nuclear weapons production. After the collapse of the Soviet Union, the world was able to learn more about Soviet nuclear activities. Russian President Boris Yeltsin appointed Dr Aleksel Yablokov as the top environmental advisor. His 1993 report on Soviet nuclear dumping revealed that the Soviet Union dumped 2.5 million *curies* of radioactive waste into the oceans, including 18 nuclear reactors from submarines and an icebreaker: "2.5 million curies is almost exactly twice what was previously thought to have been dumped at sea during the whole of the nuclear era." Of these reactors, 16 were cast into the shallow waters of the Kara Sea – 6 of them containing radioactive fuel – "turning this Arctic site near major northern fisheries into the world's largest known nuclear dump." The report also indicated that 2 of the 18 reactors (which are unfueled and less dangerous) went into the Sea of Japan. Japan was never told about this and was understandably shocked and dismayed over the report. The Yablokov report also indicated that the Russian navy was still "dumping minor amounts of radioactive waste because it lacks processing and storage plants on land."[105]

> **curie**   A unit of measurement that describes the amount of radioactivity in a sample. It measures the amount of atoms that decay each second. One curie equals 37 billion decays per second.

Environmental threats also come from the disposal of other dangerous chemical and biological weapons. In 2003, citizens surrounding Anniston, Alabama were informed that a chemical weapons incinerator located in their community was chosen to incinerate thousands of pounds of sarin, VX nerve gas, and mustard gas. Some citizens were outraged because they felt that they would be exposed to potentially hazardous chemicals, while others argued that it was their duty to aid the US military in its mission to rid itself of the illegal weapons. After citizens complained, the US Army issued citizens living close to the incineration site duct tape, plastic sheeting, and a pair of scissors. After some negotiations, the military agreed to create special rooms in local schools where students could safely stay in case of an accident.[106] Hundreds of thousands of pounds of deadly chemicals will be incinerated at the Anniston site with a projected completion date of 2013.

Miscellaneous human waste

One of the growing areas of concern for environmentalists and governments is garbage. Human refuse, household garbage, and industrial waste are growing yearly and will continue to increase as the population grows. Currently, floating in the Pacific is what scientists refer to as "*plastic soup*." This is an area about twice the size of the US that is covered with garbage. This floating flotsam

> **plastic soup**   Refers to the floating pile of garbage in the Pacific Ocean that is generally trapped in a fixed location due to wind and water patterns.

remains generally fixed in its location by currents and wind patterns. According to a report in the *Independent* newspaper in the UK, the drifting soup consists of two linked areas on either side of the Hawaiian islands, which are known as the Western and Eastern Pacific Garbage Patches. They stretch across the northern Pacific, starting about 500 nautical miles off the coast of California and nearly reaching Japan. The junk includes "everything from footballs and kayaks to Lego blocks and carrier bags." Roughly one-fifth of it is dumped off ships or oil platforms, while the rest comes from land.[107] Because plastics are not biodegradable, they remain a permanent part of the ocean, endangering the lives of marine animals. Scientists estimate that approximately one million seabirds and 100,000 marine mammals and sea turtles die annually by ingesting or becoming entangled in debris. Plastic also absorbs toxins such as POPs, and they in turn leach toxins into the water that are ingested by marine life.[108]

In addition to the waste floating in our oceans and washing up on our shores, each year humans produce millions of tons of household, commercial, and industrial waste. Landfills and incinerators are the two main strategies used to dispose of this waste. Each of these methods raises environmental concerns. Incineration leads to air pollution and the release of toxins, while landfills also leach toxins into surrounding soil and water. Communities near proposed incinerators and landfills often react strongly to having these "in their backyards," but government officials have limited options when trying to figure out what to do with solid waste. The best solution is to recycle where possible, but also to encourage less production of such waste.

A final waste issue that has serious environmental consequences is human waste. Each year, the average human produces roughly 13 gallons of feces and 130 gallons of urine. It takes approximately 4,000 gallons of water to flush this amount of waste.[109] According to Rose George, whose book *The Big Necessity: The Unmentionable World of Human Waste and Why It Matters* chronicles the health and environmental issues associated with human waste, "90 percent of the world's sewage ends up untreated in oceans, rivers and lakes, some of that filth burbling out of our supposedly sophisticated sewage systems." She notes that while sanitation is critical to human life, it gets very little attention, in part because people prefer not to talk about it. She points out that diarrhea, which is often caused by poor sanitation, is the "second biggest killer of children in the world after respiratory diseases." But despite the clear link between poor sanitation and health risks, people remain uncomfortable discussing human waste, and, as a result, the issue is often simply ignored.[110]

However, as the human population continues to grow, dealing with human waste in a way that is sustainable is vital. New technologies that turn waste into useful byproducts are one important approach to the problem. For example, one company in India has designed *biogas*, where human waste is contained with bacteria that digest it. As the bacteria digest the waste, methane is produced. The methane is then captured and sold to be used for cooking.[111] Additionally, once the bacteria have

biogas Gas produced when bacteria digest organic material.

finished digesting the waste, the remaining substance is suitable to be used as fertilizer. Norway is planning on making city buses run off the methane produced at their waste treatment plants. Previously, this methane was simply released into the atmosphere, contributing to greenhouse gas emissions. Using the gas for the buses instead will reduce Norway's total greenhouse gas emissions both by capturing and using the methane they were once releasing as well as by eliminating the use of fossil fuels in the bus system.[112]

Environmental Discrimination

The poor and minorities within countries often feel the adverse effects of environmental degradation the most. It tends to be their land that is selected by governments and corporations as easy targets for waste sites because the poor and minorities within countries wield less political clout than wealthy members of the dominant culture. This is particularly true for *indigenous peoples*, many of whom are intimately connected to their physical environment. For example, almost all global nuclear testing has been done on indigenous lands. This is true in the US, where the Western Shoshone of Nevada witnessed the majority of US nuclear testings.[113] It is also true of both the Soviet Union and China, where nuclear testing was conducted in areas dominated by ethnic minorities. France has done all of its recent testing on a Pacific atoll thousands of miles away from France, but very close to Pacific Islanders, despite their objections. Nuclear testing represents only one area where indigenous and ethnic minorities disproportionally endure the brunt of environmental damage caused by dominant states.

indigenous peoples A particular group of inhabitants of a geographic space whose connections to that space are the earliest known human connections to that land.

According to the ILO, "There are more than 5,000 different indigenous peoples living in some 70 countries in the world. About 70 per cent of them are in Asia and the Pacific, mostly in rural areas. They often lack control over land and resources and face high levels of discrimination and poverty."[114] In some cases indigenous peoples are not given citizenship in the nation-state that exerts its authority over them, making it almost impossible for them to seek redress for harm. Further, a 1995 study funded by the United Church of Christ Committee for Racial Justice determined "that people of color were twice as likely as white people to live near hazardous waste facilities."[115] Because indigenous peoples have historically lacked political clout, their concerns are often ignored. In some cases, special laws that are designed to help indigenous peoples can prove problematic when it comes to the environment. For example, in the US, Native American lands are governed by special rules that grant them some degree of autonomy. However, the federal government still retains the right to make decisions that affect native lands. For example, it allowed extensive mining, especially uranium mines, on Navajo lands. Because the mining took place on native lands, state and federal environmental laws were not applicable, yet Native Americans were not granted the authority to make their own environmental laws to regulate the mining industry.

For many indigenous peoples, the land is also central to their spiritual life, and many of their belief systems are tied to the physical world. For example, Ayers Rock or Uluru in Australia has great spiritual significance for several groups of aboriginal peoples. Over the years, hundreds of thousands of visitors have come to see the rock and many have climbed it. The aboriginal peoples do not climb the rock, nor do they want tourists who visit climbing it. Negotiations between the government and the local aboriginal communities have only recently allowed the indigenous peoples to control the site that is central to their belief system.

According to the UN, "indigenous peoples account for most of the world's cultural diversity." They estimate that there are approximately 6,000 cultures in the world, 4–5,000 of which are indigenous. Additionally, indigenous peoples speak about three-quarters of the world's 6,000 languages. The areas of highest biological diversity on the planet are also those that are inhabited by indigenous peoples. There are 17 nations that are home to more than two-thirds of the Earth's biological resources, and these areas are also the traditional territories of most of the world's indigenous peoples. The "Biological 17," as they are called, are made up of Australia, Brazil, China, Colombia, the Democratic Republic of the Congo, Ecuador, India, Indonesia, Madagascar, Malaysia, Mexico, Peru, the Philippines, South Africa, Papua New Guinea, the United States of America, and Venezuela. In addition to appreciating these cultures because of their intrinsic value, many scientists are concerned about the loss of knowledge about flora and fauna that will occur if these cultures are not protected. A 1991 workshop convened by the National Cancer Institute of the US National Institutes of Health concluded that "[t]raditional knowledge is as threatened and is as valuable as biological diversity. Both resources deserve respect and must be conserved."[116]

Indigenous peoples have been struggling to gain recognition from governments for the right to have some voice in the use of their lands. One of the most well-known cases that has come to represent the struggle of indigenous peoples to protect their lands and livelihoods is Chico Mendes's fight to save the Amazon from logging and development (see p. 129).[117] In part because of Mendes' work, the international community put the struggle for indigenous peoples' rights on the international agenda. The 1992 United Nations Conference on Environment and Development, also called the Earth Summit, "represented a turning point in the promotion of indigenous people's rights relating to the environment." International legal standards recognizing the unique relationship between indigenous peoples and their lands and protecting indigenous people's rights and practices were established.[118] Additionally, in 2007 the UN General Assembly adopted the United Nations Declaration on the Rights of Indigenous Peoples. While not legally binding, it is intended to function as an important tool for both "eliminating human rights violations against the over 370 million indigenous people worldwide" and assisting indigenous peoples in their struggles against "discrimination and marginalization."[119]

Article 29 of the resolution commits nations to the following:

1   Indigenous peoples have the right to the conservation and protection of the environment and the productive capacity of their lands or territories and

Researching to Learn *Is Ecotourism an Answer?*

Free Web Resources and Organizations

Center for Ecotourism and Sustainable Development
Conducts and produces research on ecotourism.
http://ecotourismcesd.org/home/index.html

The Global Partnership for Sustainable Tourism Criteria
A partnership of 27 organizations working to encourage sustainable travel.
www.sustainabletourismcriteria.org/

The International Ecotourism Society
An international organization that promotes ecotourism.
www.ecotourism.org/webmodules/webarticlesnet/templates/eco_template.aspx?a=12&z=25 www.nationalgeographic.com/travel/sustainable/about_geotourism.html

Nature Conservancy
A global conservation agency that promotes ecotourism as a way to benefit local communities while promoting conservation.
www.nature.org/aboutus/travel/ecotourism/

Sierra Club Policy: Ecotourism
The Sierra Club is one of the oldest environmental organizations in the US. Its goal is to protect wild places in the US.
www.sierraclub.org/policy/conservation/ecotourism.aspx

Sustainable Travel International
Since 2002 this organization has provided education and outreach services to travelers and provides information on how to promote and engage in travel that embraces cultural heritages while also bringing sustainable economic development.
www.sustainabletravelinternational.org/

Ecotourism Portals

The Ecotourism Portal
This site provides an interactive map with links to various countries around the world and their ecotourism efforts.
www.ecotourism.cc/

Planeta.com
A portal with links to resources, wikis, forums, and conferences on ecotourism.
www.planeta.com

Sustainable Tourism Gateway
Provides links to Charters, Declarations and Codes related to ecotourism.
www.gdrc.org/uem/eco-tour/st-codes.html

United Nations
This site provides links to sustainable development resources as they pertain to travel and tourism.
www.un.org/esa/sustdev/sdissues/tourism/tourism_decisions.htm

Books: Find Them @ Your Library

Buckley, Ralf. *Ecotourism.* Oxfordshire, UK: CABI Publishing, 2009.

Cater, Erlet and Gwen Lowman. *Ecotourism: A Sustainable Option?* Toronto, Canada: John Wiley & Sons, 1994.

Coccossis, Harry and Peter Nijkamp. *Sustainable Tourism Development.* Surrey: Ashgate, 1995.

Harrison, Lynn C. and Winston Husbands. *Practicing Responsible Tourism: International Case Studies in Tourism Planning, Policy and Development.* Toronto, Canada: John Wiley & Sons, 1996.

Honey, Martha. *Ecotourism and Sustainable Development: Who Owns Paradise?* Washington, DC: Island Press, 1998.

Page, Stephen and Ross Dowling. *Ecotourism.* Upper Saddle River, NJ: Pearson 2001.

Scholarly Journals: Find Them @ Your Library

Journal of Ecotourism
Journal of Sustainable Tourism

Articles: Find Them @ Your Library

Beck, Peter. J. "Regulating One of the Last Tourism Frontiers: Antarctica." *Applied Geography* 10 (1990): 343–56.

Boo, Elizabeth. "The Ecotourism Boom: Planning for Development and Management." *Wildlands and Human Needs Technical Paper Series (Paper #2)*. Washington DC: World Wildlife Fund, 1994.

Bottrill, Chris G. and D. G. Pearce. "Ecotourism: Towards a Key Elements Approach to Operationalising the Concept." *Journal of Sustainable Tourism* 3.1 (1995): 45–54.

D'Amore, Louis J. "A Code Of Ethics and Guidelines for Socially and Environmentally Responsible Tourism." *Journal Of Travel Research* 31, (1993): 64–6.

Driml, Sally and Mick Common. "Ecological Economics Criteria for Sustainable Tourism: Application to the Great Barrier Reef and Wet Tropics World Heritage Areas, Australia" *Journal of Sustainable Tourism* 4.1 (1996): 3–16.

Okazaki, Etsuko. "A Community-Based Tourism Model: Its Conception and Use." *Journal of Sustainable Tourism*, 16.5 (2008): 511–29.

resources. States shall establish and implement assistance programmes for indigenous peoples for such conservation and protection, without discrimination.

2   States shall take effective measures to ensure that no storage or disposal of hazardous materials shall take place in the lands or territories of indigenous peoples without their free, prior and informed consent.

3   States shall also take effective measures to ensure, as needed, that programmes for monitoring, maintaining and restoring the health of indigenous peoples, as developed and implemented by the peoples affected by such materials, are duly implemented.[120]

International Environmental Protection Efforts

The list of environmental disasters around the globe in the past 50 years reads like a frightening science fiction tale:

- in Bhopal, India, a gas leak caused thousands of deaths and hundreds of thousands of injuries;
- in Chernobyl, Soviet Union, an explosion at a nuclear plant killed hundreds and sent radiation as far away as the US;
- at Three Mile Island, in the US state of Pennsylvania, a reactor meltdown released radiation into the air;
- in Switzerland, a chemical leak into the Rhine caused one of Europe's most serious environmental disasters;
- in Kuwait, Iraqi forces set fire to hundreds of oil wells during their retreat, sending millions of tons of pollutants into the air;
- oil tanker leaks off the coasts of Spain and Alaska each sent thousands of tons of crude oil onto beaches, killing thousands of animals, ruining fishing habitats, and polluting hundreds of miles of coastline.

These are just a sampling of major disasters that caught the public's attention. However, environmental damage is more often the result of slow, continuous action over time (such as the release of CFCs into the atmosphere, for example) than of sudden disasters. In an effort to deal with these transnational issues, the international community has come together for a series of conferences designed to address environmental degradation in its varied forms. One result has been the promulgation of a series of environmental laws.

In Stockholm, Sweden (1972), representatives from around the world gathered at one of the first ever global conferences focusing solely on the environment. The conference produced a list of 26 principles outlining a global commitment to protect the environment. After the conference, many nations codified these principles into domestic legislation. Stockholm is thus recognized as the beginning of a concerted international effort to work toward global environmental protections.

One issue that emerged as a point of contention at Stockholm, and which continues to cause serious debate, was the relationship between development and environmental costs. Recognizing the costs often associated with development, particularly when following the Western industrialization model, many representatives wanted to focus on making sure future development would occur in a way that limited the impact on the environment. This kind of "green development" would require large capital inputs and advanced technologies. For example, building factories to produce widgets is easier and less costly if the amount of pollution emitted from it is not an issue. In Western countries, it has cost millions of dollars to retrofit some factories to limit their pollution emissions. Developing countries often lack both the sophisticated technology and the resources to ensure their development is "green." Additionally, some representatives from developing countries argued that their countries should not have to invest more to ensure that they did not contribute to global environmental damage when it was not they who had damaged the planet in the first place. These countries argued that the developed world produced more pollution and more garbage and that developed countries had a larger capacity to cause environmental destruction than did developing countries. Developed countries countered that while the industrial economies have produced enormous pollution, the technology being developed in their countries held the key to *sustainable development*. Consensus was eventually achieved around this concept, which balances economic development, social cohesion, and environmental protection. The idea was that the developed world would use its technology to help the developing world develop in a way that did not negatively impact the environment and that could be sustainable. The rate at which the developed world uses resources and contributes to environmental problems was not one the developing world could replicate because the environment simply could not sustain it. As a result, sustainable development became an imperative.

sustainable development The use of resources in such a way that human needs are met while environmental damage is minimized.

The debate continued over how to facilitate development of the world's poorer countries while preserving the environment at a second United Nations Conference on the Environment and Development (UNCED) in 1992 in Rio de Janeiro, Brazil. In all, 180 nations participated in the Rio Conference. The environmental agenda that emerged from it was spelled out in the following five documents: (1) Agenda

21; (2) Rio Declaration; (3) Climate Change Convention; (4) Biological Diversity Convention; (5) the Forest Principles. There were many interesting and controversial debates over these five documents. For example, Agenda 21 is a blueprint that lays out the environmental concerns facing the global community in the twenty-first century. Participating nations pledged to work toward various environmental goals. There are, however, no mandatory rules, and exactly how thorough the follow-up will be is uncertain. Nations argued over financing and none of the developed states committed any significant amount of money to assist developing nations with sustainable development. As a result, the document is aspirational at best and, at worst, provided a way for nations to pay lip service to environmental issues without having actually to do anything. In addition, oil-producing states such as Saudi Arabia were not happy with provisions in the Agenda that called for more development and use of renewable resources.

The Rio Declaration contained a relatively new principle, which stated that warfare was inherently destructive to the environment and that states should conduct warfare in such a way as to minimize its environmental impact. The historical context of this is important as it was written only one year after Iraq left Kuwait and set fire to hundreds of oil wells as their parting shot. It took months to get the fires under control, and, during that time, dangerous gases wafted over Kuwait. States were cautious about this principle, as they feared that a logical expansion of this idea would be to try to punish states for transborder pollution. At what point, many began to ask, does polluting one's neighbor's water, air, or ground become a crime?

Another area of controversy, one which left the US at odds with the rest of the Rio participants, was the Biodiversity Treaty. The treaty required nations to protect *biodiversity* and the ecosystems upon which various species depend. It also required the technology transfer of *biotechnologies* from developed states to developing states in order to aid the latter in their efforts to protect biodiversity. The US did not want to donate its biotechnology and was worried that any financial contributions toward the development of biotech capabilities it made in accordance with the treaty would lead to the development of competition from developing countries. The first Bush administration's decision not to participate in this treaty was reversed by the Clinton administration.[121] However, the second Bush administration moved away from the Biodiversity Treaty, citing some of the same objections as the previous Bush administration. It is too early to tell how the Obama administration will deal with this treaty.

The Forest Principles articulated the need for countries to conserve their forests and to use them in sustainable ways. Nations were also required to keep in mind both the wider ecosystem as well as the special needs of those dependent upon forests. Included among ways to conserve and protect forests were active replanting strategies and decreasing pollution that contributes to *acid rain.* According to the principles, "forests should be

biodiversity   The number and variety of different living organisms within an ecosystem as well as the genetic variation within each species.

biotechnologies   Use of microorganisms for industrial and commercial enterprise.

acid rain   Process through which sulfur dioxide (SO_2) and nitrogen oxides (NOx) that are emitted into the air mix with atmospheric water and oxygen and then fall back to the land in the form of acid.

managed to meet the social, economic, ecological, cultural and spiritual needs of present and future generations." Profits from genetic materials coming from forests should be shared with the countries where the forests are located. Likewise, international financial support should come from developed countries to help developing countries protect and manage their forests. Finally, the Forest Principles indicated that stronger international measures were needed to prevent discriminatory trade practices with regard to forest products.[122] These principles were aspirational rather than legally binding.

The climate change convention established a reporting system requiring governments to disclose their greenhouse gas emissions. Participants also agreed to meet five years later to design a strategy for reducing greenhouse gases. The Kyoto Protocol emerged from the subsequent 1997 summit. Designed to implement some of the goals of the Climate Change Convention, the Kyoto Protocol set goals for nations to reduce their emissions of gases that contribute to climate change. Kyoto was signed by the Clinton administration, but rejected by the George W. Bush administration, despite the fact that the US was the world's largest producer of greenhouse gases at the time. In December 2009, the world met in Copenhagen to construct new goals for reducing greenhouse gases that could be implemented after the expiration of the Kyoto Protocols in 2012. Disagreements again emerged regarding emission cuts for developed and developing countries, with particular concern revolving around the question of how much money wealthy countries should pledge to help developing countries adapt to climate change. Subsequent meetings will need to find new ways to bridge these divisions.

In 2002, Johannesburg, South Africa, the UN held the World Summit on Sustainable Development (WSSD) as a follow-up to the work done in Rio in 1992. More than 100 heads of state participated. One major exception was US President George W. Bush, who did not participate; nor did he send a delegation. Nevertheless, there were major commitments made by the attendees to "expand access to safe water, proper sanitation and modern, clean energy services, as well as to reverse the decline of ecosystems by restoring fisheries, curtailing illegal logging and limiting the harm caused by toxic chemicals."[123] A Plan of Implementation emerged from the summit containing targets and timetables designed to incite action on a variety of issues. For example, one goal was to cut in half the proportion of people who don't have access to clean water and sanitation by 2015. Others included restoring depleted fisheries by 2015, reducing biodiversity loss by 2010, and fostering the use and production of chemicals in ways that are not harmful to humans or the environment by 2020. In addition, countries committed to increasing the use of renewable energy, though a target was not adopted.[124]

Environmental issues are the concern not only of states, the UN, and activists, but also increasingly of international financial institutions. In recognition of the value and importance of environmental concerns in development, both the World Bank and the International Monetary Fund have linked loans to sustainable practices. For example, the World Bank recognizes that sustainable development is critical to its core objective of alleviating poverty. As a result, the World Bank Board of Directors endorsed an Environment Strategy in 2001 that was designed to guide the Bank's actions in the environmental arena. The strategy emphasized the following objectives: (1) improving the quality of life, (2) improving the quality of growth, and (3) protecting the quality of the regional and global commons.[125]

Conclusion

Nation-states, intergovernmental organizations, international financial institutions, and non-governmental organizations have all been active in seeking ways to address pressing global environmental concerns. While the international community has made great strides in collaborating to create global environmental goals and regulations, the changes facing the world will require much greater collective action to ensure that issues such as global climate change are addressed in a thorough and expeditious manner. The scientific consensus on the threats posed to the world from climate change represents a rare agreement among scientists that concerted collective action is required to head off one of the greatest challenges facing the human community. However, global climate change is not the only environmental challenge facing the international community. Population growth and consumption patterns will continue to threaten the habitats of many of the world's plants and animals as well as the homelands, values, and practices of the world's indigenous populations. We will also need to find ways to deal with the proliferation of waste, cleaning up contaminated sites and finding creative ways to recycle and repurpose waste products. Green or environmental technologies represent one way in which the developed world can work with the developing world to ensure that sustainable development becomes the norm. It is only through creative collective action and collaboration that we will be able to confront the various global environmental issues that affect us all.

Notes

1   Al Gore, Nobel Lecture, Oslo (December 10, 2007), http://nobelprize.org/nobel_prizes/peace/laureates/2007/gore-lecture_en.html.

2   Barack Obama, "Energy Independence and the Safety of Our Planet," The Associated Press Annual Luncheon, Chicago, IL (April 3, 2006), Obama News and Speeches, www.barackobama.com/2006/04/03/energy_independence_and_the_sa.php.

3   M. P. Singh, Quote Unquote: A Handbook of Quotations (New Delhi: Lotus Press, 2006), 129.

4   Pew Center on Global Climate Change, "Global Warming Basics Introduction," www.pewclimate.org/global-warming-basics/about.

5   United Nations System Chief Executives Board for Coordination, Acting on Climate Change: The UN System Delivering as One (New York: United Nations, 2008), 7.

6   "Potential Effects of Global Warming," NASA, Earth Observatory, http://earthobservatory.nasa.gov/Features/GlobalWarming/global_warming_update6.php.

7   Ibid.

8   Pachauri, R. K and Reisinger, A. (eds.), Climate Change 2007: Synthesis Report. Contribution of Working Groups I, II and III to the Fourth Assessment Report of the Intergovernmental Panel on

Climate Change (Geneva: IPCC, 2007), 26–8, www.ipcc.ch/ipccreports/ar4-syr.htm.

9   Institute for Energy Research, "Fossil Fuels," www.instituteforenergyresearch.org/pdf/2008/Fossil%20Fuels/Fossil%20Fuels%202%20-%20Percent%20of%20US%20Transportation%20Sector.jpg.

10 "China Tries to Clean Up Air," *All Things Considered*, National Public Radio (March 6, 2008), www.npr.org/templates/story/story.php?storyId=87961816.

11 Source: Gregg Marland, T. A. Boden, and Robert J. Andres, "Global, Regional, and National CO_2 Emissions," in *Trends: A Compendium of Data on Global Change* (Oak Ridge, TN: Carbon Dioxide Information Analysis Center, Oak Ridge National Laboratory, US Department of Energy, 2004), http://cdiac.esd.ornl.gov/trends/emis/tre_coun.htm.

12 Duncan Clark, "China's Increasing Carbon Emissions Blamed on Manufacturing for West," *Guardian* (February 23, 2009), www.guardian.co.uk/environment/2009/feb/23/china-carbon-emissions.

13 Brad Knickerbocker, "Humans' Beef with Livestock: A Warmer Planet," *Christian Science Monitor* (February 20, 2007), www.csmonitor.com/2007/0220/p03s01-ussc.html.

14 Ibid.

15 Ibid.

16 "Nitrous Oxide Sources and Emissions," Environmental Protection Agency, www.epa.gov/nitrousoxide/sources.html.

17 Source: www.giss.nasa.gov/research/features/methane/sources.gif.

18 "Saving Forests to Fight Climate Change The Critical Link between Trees and Carbon Emissions," Nature Conservancy (2009), www.nature.org/initiatives/climatechange/features/art19363.html.

19 "The Rain Forest Report Card, Deforestation of Tropical Rain Forests," Tropical Rainforest Information Center at Michigan State University, www.trfic.msu.edu/rfrc/status.html.

20 "Saving Forests to Fight Climate Change," Nature Conservancy.

21 "Deforestation Continues at an Alarming Rate," UN Food and Agricultural Organization (2005), www.fao.org/newsroom/en/news/2005/1000127/index.html.

22 "The Rain Forest Report Card, 1998," Tropical Rainforest Information Center at Michigan State University, www.trfic.msu.edu/rfrc/status.html.

23 "Background Information: Deforestation," Atmospheric Radiation Measurement, US Department of Energy and Office of Biological and Environmental Research (2006), http://education.arm.gov/teacherslounge/background/deforestation.stm.

24 Rebecca Lindsey, "Tropical Deforestation," NASA, Earth Observatory (March 30, 2007), http://earthobservatory.nasa.gov/Features/Deforestation/deforestation_update2.php.

25 Andrés Schipani and John Vidal, "Malaria Moves in Behind the Loggers," *Guardian* (October 30, 2007), www.guardian.co.uk/world/2007/oct/30/environment.climatechange.

26 Jonathan A. Patz, Peter Daszak, Gary M. Tabor, A. Alonso Aguirre, Mary Pearl, Jon Epstein, Nathan D. Wolfe, A. Marm Kilpatrick, Johannes Foufopoulos, David Molyneux, David J. Bradley, and Members of the Working Group on Land Use Change Disease Emergence, "Unhealthy Landscapes: Policy Recommendations on Land Use Change and Infectious Disease Emergence," *Environmental Health Perspectives* 112, no. 10 (July 2004), 1092–8.

27 "Mitch: The Deadliest Atlantic Hurricane Since 1780," National Ocean and Atmospheric Administration (1998), www.ncdc.noaa.gov/oa/reports/mitch/mitch.html.

28 Benjamin Wisner, Piers M. Blaikie, Terry Cannon, *At Risk: Natural Hazards, People's Vulnerability and Disasters*, 2nd edn. (New York: Routledge, 2004): this book provides a detailed account of natural disasters that were caused less by nature and more by human activity. They focus on those most vulnerable in society – those living on its margins.

29 Paul Hughes, "Venezuela Begins to Clear Rubble in Mudslide Zone," Reuters Foundation (December 22, 1999), www.reliefweb.int/rw/rwb.nsf/AllDocsByUNID/681f8f00be9e73b0c12568540034dbac.

30 "Millenium Ecosystem Assessment, 2005," IPPC, Fourth Assessment Report, 2007, UN Food and Agricultural Organization, www.unccd.int/publicinfo/factsheets/pdf/forest_eng.pdf.

31   Alan B. Durning and Holly B. Brough, *Taking Stock: Animal Farming and the Environment*, Worldwatch Paper #103 (Washington, DC: Worldwatch Institute, July 1991), 17–18.

32   John Tuxill, *Losing Strands in the Web of Life: Vertebrate Declines and the Conservation of Biological Diversity*, Worldwatch Paper #141 (Washington, DC: Worldwatch Institute, May 1998), 9.

33   UN Food and Agricultural Organization, "Millennium Ecosystem Assessment, 2005," IPPC, Fourth Assessment Report, 2007, www.unccd.int/publicinfo/factsheets/pdf/forest_eng.pdf.

34   Marlise Simon "Brazilian Who Fought to Protect Amazon Is Killed" (December 24, 1988), http://query.nytimes.com/gst/fullpage.html?res=940DE3DF173AF937A15751C1A96E948260&sec=&spon=&pagewanted=all.

35   Purdue University, "Chlorofluorocarbons," United State Environmental Protection Agency, Environmental Awareness Software Project, http://www.purdue.edu/envirosoft/housewaste/house/chlorofl.htm.

36   Aaron Sachs, *Eco-Justice: Linking Human Rights and the Environment*, Worldwatch Paper #127 (Washington, DC: Worldwatch Institute, December 1995), 25.

37   "NOAA Observes 20th Anniversary of the Montreal Protocol," National Ocean and Atmospheric Administration, www.noaanews.noaa.gov/stories2007/s2918.htm.

38   John Pickrell, "Oceans Found to Absorb Half of All Man-Made Carbon Dioxide," *National Geographic News* (July 15, 2004), http://news.nationalgeographic.com/news/2004/07/0715_04071 5_oceancarbon.html.

39   Ker Than, "Global Warming to Create 'Permanent' Ocean Dead Zones?" *National Geographic News* (January 28, 2009), http://news.nationalgeographic.com/news/2009/01/090128-ocean-dead-zones.html.

40   "Pacific Ocean Coral Reefs Dying Faster than Expected," Canadian Broadcasting Corporation (August 8, 2007), www.cbc.ca/technology/story/2007/08/08/coral-reefs.html.

41   United Nations System-wide Earthwatch, "Oceans and Coastal Areas Coral reefs under Pressure," www.un.org/earthwatch/oceans/coralreefs.html.

42   NOAA Coral Health and Monitoring Program, "Coral Literature, Education & Outreach (CLEO) Coral Bleaching, www.coral.noaa.gov/cleo/coral_bleaching.shtml.

43   UNWater, "Statistics: Graphs and Maps Water Resources," www.unwater.org/statistics_res.html.

44   Water usage statistics from Sandra Postel, *Dividing the Waters: Food Security, Ecosystem Health, and the New Politics of Scarcity*, Worldwatch Paper #132 (Washington, DC: World Watch, 1996) and population statistics from: Population Division Department of Economic and Social Affairs United Nations Secretariat, "The World at 6 Billion" (New York: United Nations, 1999), 3, www.un.org/esa/population/publications/sixbillion/sixbilpart1.pdf.

45   "Water 101 FAQ," United Nations Food and Agricultural Organization, www.fao.org/nr/water/art/2007/flash/101/2/gallery1.html.

46   Global Policy Forum, "Water in Conflict," www.globalpolicy.org/security/natres/waterindex.htm.

47   Fareed Taamallah, "Thirst for West Bank Water," *The Nation* (June 9, 2006), www.thenation.com/doc/20060626/taamallah. For more information, see Stephen Lendman, "Drought and Israeli Policy Threaten West Bank Water Security," *Countercurrents.org* (July 18, 2008), www.globalpolicy.org/security/natres/water/2008/0718westbank.htm; and "ICE Case Studies Case Number: Case Identifier: JORDAN1Case Name: JORDAN RIVER DISPUTE" www.american.edu/TED/ice/westbank.htm.

48   Postel, *Dividing the Waters*, 13.

49   "High Plains Regional Ground-Water Study," US Geological Survey, 2009, http://co.water.usgs.gov/nawqa/hpgw/factsheets/DENNEHYFS1.html.

50   "Water Hot Spots," *BBC*, http://news.bbc.co.uk/2/shared/spl/hi/world/03/world_forum/water/html/ogallala_aquifer.stm.

51   Melanie Schimek, "Humans Alter the Environment: Draining the Everglades," Delaware Geographic Alliance (October 2008), www.udel.edu/Geography/DGA/web/Draining%20the%20Everglades.pdf.

52   Source: www.meteor.iastate.edu/gccourse/issues/society/ogallala/ogallala.html.

53   Médecin Sans Frontières, "Aral Sea Area Programme" (October 2003), www.msf.org/aralsea.

54   Ali Okda, "The Aral Sea," 2001–2, http://nailaokda.8m.com/aral.html.

55   Source: Nicola Jones, "South Aral Sea 'gone in 15 years'," *New Scientist* (July 21, 2003), www.newscientist.com/article/dn3947-south-aral-sea-gone-in-15-years.html. Reproduced with permission of *New Scientist*.

56   "Mississippi Delta Controlling a River: The Mississippi River Deltaic Plain," Union of Concerned Scientists (2002), www.ucsusa.org/gulf/gcplacesmis.html.

57   John Tibbetts, "Louisiana's *Wetlands:* A Lesson in Nature Appreciation," *Environmental Health Perspectives* 114, no. 1 (January 2006), 40.

58   "Wetlands: Status and Trends," US Environmental Protection Agency, www.epa.gov/OWOW/wetlands/vital/status.html.

59   Postel, *Dividing the Waters*, 28–9.

60   "Wetlands for Water and Life," Wetlands International, http://wetlands.org/Aboutwetland-areas/Threatenedwetlandsites/tabid/1125/Default.aspx.

61   Brad Clark, "River Restoration through Dam Removal in the American West: An Examination into the Variation in Magnitude of Policy Change," paper presented at the annual meeting of the Western Political Science Association, Las Vegas, Nevada (March 8, 2007), www.allacademic.com/meta/p176515_index.html.

62   Juliet Macur, "Beijing Air Raises Questions for Olympics," *New York Times* (August 26, 2007), www.nytimes.com/2007/08/26/sports/othersports/26runners.html.

63   "China Tries to Clean Up Air," *All Things Considered*, National Public Radio, www.npr.org/templates/story/story.php?storyId=87961816.

64   Shweta Trivedi, "Air Pollution Linked to Cognitive Deficits and Brain Abnormalities," National Institute of Environmental Health Sciences" (November 2008), www.niehs.nih.gov/news/newsletter/2008/november/air-pollution.cfm.

65   "High Pollution Linked To Poor Lung Function Growth In Children In Mexico City," *Science Daily* (August 16, 2007), www.sciencedaily.com/releases/2007/08/070815085433.htm.

66   "Science News Pollution Causes 40 Percent Of Deaths Worldwide, Study Finds," *Science Daily* (August 14, 2007), www.sciencedaily.com/releases/2007/08/070813162438.htm.

67   "US Air Pollution Rules Gave Americans an Extra Five Months to Live, Report says," *Guardian* (January 22, 2009), www.guardian.co.uk/world/2009/jan/22/air-pollution-life-expectancy.

68   "UN Special Session of the General Assembly to Review and Appraise the Implementation of Agenda 21, New York, 23–27 June 1997, The United Nations Convention to Combat Desertification: A New Response to an Age-Old Problem," United Nations, www.un.org/ecosocdev/geninfo/sustdev/desert.htm.

69   Ibid.

70   Juliet Eilperin, "Warming Tied To Extinction Of Frog Species," *Washington Post* (January 12, 2006), www.washingtonpost.com/wp-dyn/content/article/2006/01/11/AR2006011102121.html.

71   KWED Television series, "Quest: Disappearing Frogs," A KQED Multimedia Series Exploring Northern California Science, Environment and Nature, www.kqed.org/quest/television/view/894.

72   "Chytrid Fungus," Amphibian Ark, http://www.amphibianark.org/chytrid.htm.

73   Ibid.

74   Tuxill, *Losing Strands in the Web of Life*, 9.

75   Ibid., 13.

76   Ibid.

77   "Habitat Report, 2004," Sierra Club, www.sierraclub.org/wildlife/species/habitat_report/speciesloss.asp.

78   "Yellowstone Preservation A Balancing Act," *Weekend Edition Sunday*, National Public Radio (September 21, 2008), www.npr.org/templates/story/story.php?storyId=94800481.

79   Rod East, *African Antelope Database 1998* (Gland, Switzerland: International Union for Conservation of Nature and Natural Resources Antelope Specialist Group, 1999).

80   Ibid.

81   "Fence Cutting Ceremony Opens African Super Park," *Environmental News Service* (December 12, 2002), www.ens-newswire.com/ens/dec2002/2002-12-12-03.asp.

82   Peter Godwin, "Without Borders: Uniting Africa's Wildlife Reserves," *National Geographic* (September 2001), http://ngm.nationalgeographic.

com/ngm/data/2001/09/01/html/ft_20010901.1. fulltext.html.

83 "Problems: Unsustainable and Illegal Wildlife Trade," World Wildlife Fund (February 28, 2008), www.panda.org/about_wwf/what_we_do/ species/problems/illegal_trade/.

84 "Wildlife Trafficking: What Is It?" TRAFFIC, the Wildlife and Monitor Network, A joint monitoring effort between the World Wildlife Fund and IUCN-The World Conservation Union, www.traffic.org/trade/.

85 Convention on International Trade in Endangered Species of Wild Fauna and Flora, www.cites.org/ eng/disc/what.shtml.

86 Source: The IUCN Red List of Threatened Species 2008, www.iucnredlist.org/documents/ 2008RL_stats_table_1_v1223294385.pdf.

87 Associated Press, "Resurgent Gray Wolves Killed, Despite Protection," *MSNBC* (December 14, 2008), www.msnbc.msn.com/id/28212074/.

88 For information on plans to reintroduce the wolf to one European country, see, "Wild Wolves 'Good for Ecosystems'," BBC (January 31, 2007), http://news.bbc.co.uk/2/hi/science/nature/6310211. stm.

89 Frederick M. Fished, "Pesticide Use Trends in the US: Global Comparison," Publication #PI-143, University of Florida Agricultural IFSA Extension, 2008, http://edis.ifas.ufl.edu/PI180.

90 Worldwatch Institute "Stepping Off the Toxic Treadmill" (2002), www.worldwatch.org/press/ news/2000/11/19/.

91 Michael Eddleston, Lakshman Karalliedde, Nick Buckley, Ravindra Fernando, et al., "Pesticide Poisoning in the Developing World: A Minimum Pesticides List," *The Lancet* 360, no. 9340 (October 12, 2002), 1163.

92 "Persistent Organic Pollutants," United Nations Environment Programme, www.chem.unep.ch/ pops.

93 Anne Platt McGinn, "From Rio to Johannesburg: Reducing the Use of Toxic Chemicals Advances Health and Sustainable Development," *Worldwatch Institute* (June 25, 2002), www.worldwatch.org/ press/news/2002/06/25/.

94 For more on the Stockholm Convention on Persistent Organic Pollutants, see http://chm. pops.int/.

95 "SDI Inventory, Economic Processes," Sustainable Development Indicator (SDI) Group (October 8, 1996), www.hq.nasa.gov/iwgsdi/FW_SDI_Econ_ Proc.html.

96 Source: United Nations Environment Programme, www.chem.unep.ch/pops/alts02.html.

97 Ibid.

98 "UN Warning on E-waste 'Mountain'," BBC (November 27, 2006), http://news.bbc.co.uk/2/ hi/technology/6187358.stm.

99 For more information, go to www.basel.int/.

100 For more information on what has been called the "Basel Convention Ban Amendment," go to www.basel.int/pub/baselban.html.

101 Imtiyaz Delawala, "What is Coltan?" ABC News, (September 7, 2001), www.globalpolicy. org/security/natres/generaldebate/2001/0907cobalt. htm.

102 "Environmental Technologies Action Plan," European Union, http://ec.europa.eu/research/ environment/policy/etap_en.htm.

103 "'If Not Yucca Mountain, Then What?' An Alternative Plan for Managing Highly Radioactive Waste in the United States," Institute for Energy and Environmental Research (2004), www.ieer. org/fctsheet/yuccaalt.html.

104 Ann Imse, "Rocky Flats Case Getting Closer to End," *Rocky Mountain News* (January 20, 2006), www.rockymountainnews.com/drmn/local/ article/0,1299,DRMN_15_4401749,00.html.

105 William J. Broad, "Russians Describe Extensive Dumping of Nuclear Waste," *New York Times* (April 27, 1993), http://query.nytimes.com/gst/ fullpage.html?res=9F0CE3D81238F934A15757C0A 965958260&sec=&spon=&pagewanted=all.

106 Amy Sieckmann, "Coldwater School Safety Equipment Demonstrated," *Anniston Star* (January 16, 2002), www.annistonstar.com/news/2002/as- calhoun-0116-asieckmann-2a15v4514.htm.

107 Kathy Marks and Daniel Howden, "The World's Rubbish Dump: A Garbage Tip that Stretches from Hawaii to Japan," *Independent* (February 5, 2008), www.independent.co.uk/environment/the- worlds-rubbish-dump-a-garbage-tip-that-stretches- from-hawaii-to-japan-778016.html.

108 Donovan Hohn, "Sea of Trash," *New York Times* (June 22, 2008), www.nytimes.com/2008/06/22/ magazine/22Plastics-t.html.

109 Rebecca Tuhus-Dubrow, "Waste? Not," *Boston Globe* (July 13, 2008), www.boston.com/bostonglobe/ideas/articles/2008/07/13/waste_not/?page=5.

110 Rose George interviewed by Katharine Mieszkowski, "Let's Talk Crap," *Salon.com* (October 16, 2008), www.salon.com/books/int/2008/10/16/big_necessity/.

111 Jeremy Kahn, "Waste Not, Want Not," *CNN Money* (February 27, 2008), http://money.cnn.com/2008/02/26/news/international/kahn_biogas.fortune/index.htm?postversion=2008022704.

112 "Human Waste Helps Oslo's Carbon Footprint," *Newser* (February 2, 2009), www.newser.com/story/49697/human-waste-helps-oslos-carbon-footprint.html.

113 Alan Durning and Ed Ayres, *Guardians of the Land* (Washington, DC: Worldwatch Institute, 1992), 18.

114 "Indigenous and Tribal Peoples," International Labour Organization, www.ilo.org/global/Themes/Equality_and_Discrimination/Indigenousandtribalpeoples/lang--en/index.htm.

115 Sachs, *Eco-Justice*, 18–21.

116 "Indigenous Peoples and the Environment, Leaflet No. 10," United Nations High Commissioner for Human Rights, www.unhchr.ch/html/racism/indileaflet10.doc.

117 Sachs, *Eco-Justice*, 5.

118 "Indigenous Peoples," UNHCHR.

119 "Frequently Asked Questions: Declaration of the Rights of Indigenous Peoples," United Nations, www.un.org/esa/socdev/unpfii/documents/FAQsindigenousdeclaration.pdf.

120 "United Nations Declaration on the Rights of Indigenous Peoples," adopted September 13, 2007, United Nations General Assembly, www.un.org/esa/socdev/unpfii/en/drip.html.

121 William R. Slomanson, *Fundamental Perspectives on International Law*, 2nd edn. (St Paul, MN: West Publishing, 1996), 543–4.

122 Michael Keating, "Agenda for Change: A Plain Language Version of Agenda 21 and Other Rio Agreements. Centre for Our Common Future, Geneva, Switzerland, 1993," International Institute for Sustainable Development, www.iisd.org/rio+5/agenda/principles.htm.

123 United Nations, Department of Economic and Social Affairs Division for Sustainable Development, March 24, 2003, Johannesburg Summit 2002, World Summit on Sustainable Development, www.johannesburgsummit.org/html/whats_new/feature_story40.html.

124 Ibid., www.johannesburgsummit.org/html/whats_new/feature_story39.htm.

125 "Environment Overview," The World Bank Group (2003), http://web.worldbank.org/WBSITE/EXTERNAL/TOPICS/ENVIRONMENT/0,,contentMDK:20270693~menuPK:242136~pagePK:210058~piPK:210062~theSitePK:244381,00.html.

6

POPULATION AND CONSUMPTION

"I have been assured by a very knowing American of my acquaintance in London, that a young healthy child, well nursed, is at a year old, a most delicious, nourishing, and wholesome food, whether stewed, roasted, baked, or boiled . . ." (Jonathan Swift, 1729)[1]

"No quantity of atomic bombs will stem the tide of billions . . . who will someday leave the poor southern part of the world to erupt into the relatively accessible spaces of the rich northern hemisphere looking for survival." (Houari Boumedienne, President of Algeria [1965–78] and Leader of the Group of 77 [less developed nations], in reference to the effect that insufficient aid from developed countries to developing countries would have)[2]

"Imagine a truck delivering to your house each morning all the materials you use in a day, except food and fuel. . . . If you are an average American, this daily delivery would be a burdensome load: at 101 kilos, it is roughly the weight of a large man. But your materials tally has only begun. By month's end, you have used three tons of material, and over the year, 37 tons. And your 270 million compatriots are doing the same thing, day in and day out. Together, you will consume nearly 10 billion tons of material in a year's time." (Worldwatch Institute)[3]

"Americans and other first worlders – that's to say Europeans and Japanese and Australians – consume 32 times more resources. That's to say we consume 32 times more gas, and 32 times more metals, but by the same token we put out 32 times more waste like plastics and greenhouse gases, than do citizens of third world countries, and that means that one American equals 32 Kenyans in his or her impact on the rest of the world." (Jared Diamond, UCLA Geography Professor)[4]

Learning to Question, Questioning to Learn

- What factors affect human population growth?
- What impact does growth have on the developed and developing worlds?
- Will the movements of large numbers of people into our ever-growing cities improve or worsen the problems posed by human population growth?
- How likely do you think it is that new technologies will emerge to provide answers to food and resource demands? What do you imagine such technologies might look like?
- Which do you think poses a bigger immediate threat to the health of the planet: population growth or consumption patterns?

Introduction

This chapter examines the global imperatives presented by population and consumption issues, beginning with a discussion of population statistics and projected population growth rates. It then delves into population pressures and issues, including poverty, aging populations, *migration*, and *urbanization*. The chapter ends with a discussion of consumption patterns and sustainable use of our planet's resources.

migration Human movement from one location to another.

urbanization The increase in the urban portion of the total population.

Global Population

Statistics and projections

In 1804, the world population reached one billion, a historic milestone for humanity, a species that the human fossil record tells us has lived on earth for nearly 200,000 years.[5] Remarkably, it took only an additional 123 years for that figure to double to two billion in 1927. We have since been adding billions to the population at an ever-increasing rate. From 1927 to 1960, a period of just 33 years, the population increased from two to three billion. It took an additional 14 years to reach four billion in 1974, 13 years to reach five billion in 1987, and 12 years to reach six billion in October of 1999 (see table 6.1).[6] While the annual percent of growth is now declining, population numbers will nevertheless continue to rise rapidly, reaching seven billion by 2012, eight billion by 2025, and nine billion by 2040.[7]

Although rapid population growth may be viewed as a fact of life or an unremarkable norm for many people today, it is actually a relatively new development in human history. Prior to the seventeenth century, population growth was slow and unsteady, with periods of growth followed by periods of decline due to war, famine, and disease epidemics. Outbreaks of the Bubonic Plague, also called the Black Death, for example, occurred periodically from the mid-1300s through the mid-1600s, killing anywhere from 30 to 50 percent of the population in Europe and the Middle East.[8] Some estimate that the Black Death may have killed 35 million people in Europe alone, a mortality rate that had a substantial impact on total

Table 6.1 World Population Milestones[9]

World population reached:	
1 billion in	1804
2 billion in	1927 (123 years later)
3 billion in	1960 (33 years later)
4 billion in	1974 (14 years later)
5 billion in	1987 (13 years later)
6 billion in	1999 (12 years later)

population size. By the middle of the seventeenth century, however, outbreaks of the plague were on the decline, death rates began to fall, people began living longer, and the rate of world population growth accelerated.[10]

The greatest human population growth occurred in the twentieth century, but particularly between 1965 and 1970, when growth rates soared to over 2 percent per year.[11] Prior to 1750, global population growth rates never exceeded 0.5 percent per year, and until 1930, they never surpassed 1 percent per year.[12]

In many developed countries, this dramatic growth, which included the post-World War II *baby boom*, was attributed to significantly improved health care and a concomitant reduction in death rates. Population growth rates did not begin to decline until other factors affecting birth rates emerged, such as the widespread availability and use of contraceptives and an overall shift in family planning patterns emphasizing fewer children. In less developed regions, such as Southeast Asia and parts of Latin America, we are only now seeing declining growth rates.

baby boom   Refers to a period of increased birth rates within a certain timeframe, and typically within a specific geographic region.

Declining birth rates in most of the world have led to decreases in the rate of population growth from 2 percent in 1971 to 1.3 percent in 1998, to 1.18 percent in 2008. By 2020, the growth rate is projected to reach below 1 percent per year (see figure 6.1). Some developed countries, such as Norway, are already approaching a *zero population growth rate*, while other countries, such as Japan, are experiencing *negative growth rates*.[13] But even at this reduced rate of growth, the annual population change, or the amount of people added to the planet each year, will continue to grow significantly. The annual population change is projected to reach its height in 2011, at 80,852,608, at which point the number of people added to the planet each year will slowly begin to decline.[14] One United Nations projection from 1999 indicates that the world will not achieve population stabilization until after the year 2200, when our numbers will have grown to over ten billion.[15]

zero population growth rate Population neither grows nor declines.

negative growth rates   Indicates that population figures are declining.

Although global population figures can give us a sense of the rapidity of population growth on the planet as a whole, it is also important to recognize that the world's population is not distributed evenly across the globe and that population growth rates vary by region. Asia, for example, has long had the highest population. In 1750, when the world population was estimated at 791 million, 65 percent of the population lived in Asia, 21 percent in Europe, and 13 percent in Africa. By 1900, 150 years later, major growth had occurred in Europe, which had

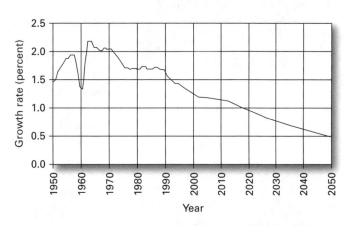

Figure 6.1 World Population Growth Rates: 1950–2050[16]
Note: U.S. Census Bureau, International Database, 2008 First Update.

jumped from 21 percent to 25 percent of the world population. Growth had also occurred in North America and Latin America, as each increased to 5 percent of the population. During the same period, both Asia's and Africa's percentages of the world population shrank to 57 and 8 percent respectively. UN population forecasters predict, however, that by 2050, Asia's share of the world population will increase back up to 60 percent, while Africa's will have more than doubled to 20 percent. In contrast, Europe's share of the total world population will have declined to 7 percent, less than one third its peak level in 1900. Put another way, more than 1.7 billion people will be living in Africa in 2050, while only 628 million people will reside in Europe.[17] What we're seeing, then, is a trend in which developed countries' populations are decreasing, while developing countries populations are still increasing.

Fertility and mortality

demographers Scholars and practitioners who study population and its impacts on society.

fertility Measure of reproduction; the number of children born per couple, person, or population.

mortality The relative frequency of deaths in a defined population during a specified interval of time.

natural increase The yearly difference in number of births and deaths in a population (birth rate minus death rate).

replacement levels The level that needs to be sustained over the long run to ensure that a population replaces itself. For most countries having low or moderate mortality levels, replacement level is close to 2.1 children per woman.

Demographers, people who study population, discuss population growth in terms of *fertility* and *mortality*, or birth and death rates. Population growth, which is sometimes referred to as the *natural increase*, occurs when fertility rates are higher than mortality rates. Fertility is influenced by both biological and social factors. Biological processes affecting fertility include the period of time between puberty and menopause when women are able to reproduce, while social factors include marriage patterns, the age at which it is considered culturally appropriate for people to become sexually active, and the availability and use of birth control devices.

Fertility rates are also linked to regions. Although the global average number of children per woman is estimated at 2.55 for the 2005–10 period, this average obscures the differences in fertility rates among regions (see table 6.2). Specifically, fertility rates in the developed world are often close to *replacement levels*, while fertility rates in much of the developing world are much higher. During the 2005–10 period, for example, 45 of the 73 countries with fertility levels below 2.1 children per woman are considered more developed. In contrast, all of the 122 countries with fertility rates above 2.1 children per woman are located in less developed regions. Finally, of the 27 countries with fertility levels that are at or above five children per woman, 25 are included among the world's least developed countries.[18]

Demographic transition

demographic transition
Theory/model that links industrial development with declining fertility.

The theory of *demographic transition* attempts to account for these regional population differences in economic terms, positing a link between population growth patterns and economic developmental

Table 6.2 Estimated Total Fertility for the World, the Major Development Groups, and the Major Areas[19]

Major Area	Total Fertility (children per woman)	
	1970–1975	2005–2010
World	4.47	2.55
More developed regions	2.13	1.60
Less developed regions	5.41	2.75
• Least developed countries	6.61	4.63
• Other less developed countries	5.25	2.45
Africa	6.72	4.67
Asia	5.04	2.34
Europe	2.16	1.45
Latin America and the Caribbean	5.04	2.37
Northern America	2.01	2.00
Oceania	3.23	2.30

stages. Specifically, it equates industrial development with declining fertility.[20] The "demographic transition," then, is the "movement of a nation from high population growth to low population growth, as it develops economically."[21] Most discussions of the demographic transition theory highlight four stages. Stage one is made up of pre-industrial countries with high birth rates and high death rates. Death rates are high due to factors such as famine and disease, while birth rates are high in order to increase the chances that children will survive into adulthood. Because the death rate almost completely offsets the birth rate, population growth is static or low. As countries begin to develop, they enter stage two. In stage two, living conditions, food availability, and health care improve, resulting in a decrease in the death rate; however, the birth rate remains high, since children are viewed as both sources of labor and caretakers for their aging parents. Declining death rates and high birth rates result in high population growth. In stage three, birth rates begin to fall due to many factors, including access to contraception, wage increases, better education, child employment legislation, and other urbanization factors that decrease the economic value of children. Finally, stage four is characterized by both low birth rates and low death rates, and thus by low rates of population growth as well.[22] Some countries, including a number of developed European countries, have achieved or are approaching population stabilization. In other words, the population is replacing itself but it is not getting larger. In other cases, stage four countries have seen their populations drop below replacement levels. Some demographers have suggested that population decline could be viewed as a fifth and separate demographic transition stage.[23]

The demographic transition model enjoyed widespread acceptance through the 1970s and 1980s, until studies emerged that began to undermine various aspects of it. For example, some studies suggest that fertility decline is not as closely linked to socioeconomic levels as the theory postulated; rather, patterns of fertility decline are more closely correlated with regions that share common languages and cultures.[24] Others point out that cultural values revolving around fertility change slowly and sometimes only partially in the wake of economic changes.[25] Additionally, some critics highlight the fact that the theory of demographic transition was based on observations of industrialized Western countries with primarily white populations. As a result, they argue that the theory is *ethnocentric* and thus flawed, since it assumes that all countries will go through similar transitions, regardless of cultural differences.

> **ethnocentric** Viewing the world primarily from the perspective of one's own culture.

Other critics argue that the theory fails to account for human agency and rational choice, reducing individuals to the pawns of a powerful theoretical principle over which they have no control.[26] Although critics of demographic transition theory remind us that socioeconomic changes are not the only source of demographic shifts, most scholars would agree that economic development is an important force that has influenced demographic changes in the past and that continues to influence them today. As such, despite its limitations, the theory remains useful as one among many ways of understanding demographic change.[27]

Population Pressures

Population and poverty

Many population analysts and social commentators insist that the best way to alleviate poverty in the developing world is to control population growth. In *The Population Bomb* (1968), for example, biologist and demographer Paul Ehrlich decried what he saw as the explosive problem of rapid population growth in developing countries. According to Ehrlich, masses of people and uncontrolled growth lead to poverty and chaos. In response to Ehrlich's expressed feelings of fear about population growth in developing countries like India, Columbia University professor Mahmood Mamdani pointed out, in *The Myth of Population Control* (1972), that Ehrlich might have been confronted with even larger crowds in Western cities such as New York and London than those that frightened him in Delhi. Mamdani suggested that what Ehrlich found problematic, and indeed feared, was the apparent "otherness" of the populations in places like India rather than the density of the population alone. A more recent study of the relationship between poverty and population growth indicates that high fertility increases poverty by slowing economic growth and "skewing the distribution of consumption against the poor."[28] The researchers estimate that, had the average country in the group of 45 studied lowered its birth rate by five births per 1,000 women during the 1980s, as had many Asian countries, poverty would have been reduced by a third.[29]

While population growth and poverty are often linked, it would be a mistake to think that population growth leads inevitably to poverty. In fact, historically, the reverse has frequently been true, as population growth has often been correlated with economic prosperity and population decline with economic decline.[30] For example, the Irish had comparatively stable population growth rates until the late eighteenth century, long before modern contraceptives were available. However, between 1780 and 1840, the Irish population doubled from four to eight million. Factors that contributed to the rising Irish fertility rates included the increase in the number of small farms made available by rent-seeking British landlords and the advent of wide-scale potato farming. Both of these factors increased economic opportunities for the Irish, which in turn allowed people to marry at a younger age, thereby increasing fertility. However, in 1846, when blight struck the potatoes – the principal food source for the Irish – calamity and famine resulted. More than 1.5 million people died, and hundreds of thousands emigrated. In the wake of the great famine and the economic devastation that accompanied it, the Irish population dropped from 8.2 million in 1841 to 4.5 million in 1901.[31]

Large populations also provide new markets and economic growth potential in ways that countries with small populations and/or stagnant population growth rates cannot. Consumer power, for example, is already shifting to growing economies with large populations, most notably China, which has a population of more than 1.3 billion people. While China has instituted a number of policies aimed at curbing population growth, it still has over a billion more people than the United States. However, its large population has not hindered its recent economic rise. China's economy, with its huge workforce and a large middle class, is now the second biggest in the world. It is predicted to surpass the US population by 2035 and to be nearly twice its size by 2050.[32] Clearly then, large populations cannot always be equated with poverty.

World population aging

Population aging, "the process by which older individuals become a proportionally larger share of the total population," began in the twentieth century in more developed countries and has now expanded to the developing world.[33] It is an unprecedented global demographic trend that will affect every country in the twenty-first century, though the pace of change will vary. Population aging is the result of declines in both fertility and mortality. In other words, we are both living longer and having fewer children (see figure 6.2). Today, global life expectancy is approximately 66 years, up a remarkable 20 years from 46.5 years in

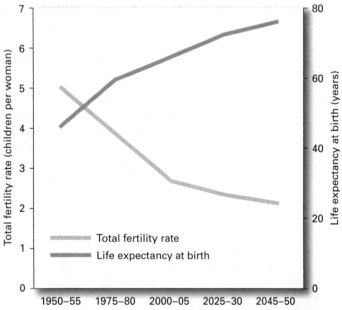

Figure 6.2 Total Fertility Rate and Life Expectancy at Birth: World, 1950–2050[34]

1950–5. By 2050, global life expectancy is projected to increase by another 10 years to reach 76 years.

The total number of older persons living on the planet tripled between 1950 and 2000 and is projected to triple again by 2050. To put these numbers in more concrete terms, in the year 2000, one in every ten people in the world was 60 years old or older; by the year 2050, more than one in every five people on earth is projected to be aged 60 or over.[35] In the more developed regions of the world, there are already more older people than children; about 19 percent of the population is 60 years or older, while children under 15 years make up 18 percent. By the year 2050, this slight difference between percentages of older people and children under 15 will have increased dramatically; the proportion of children is projected to shrink to 16 percent while the proportion of older adults will have grown to 34 percent. In developing countries, these trends have been slower, with people over 60 making up only 8 percent of the population. However, by 2050, the proportion of older people in developing regions is projected to reach 19 percent.[36]

Population aging will have many social and economic implications for societies around the globe. While some analysts argue that our economies can provide for the growing needs of the aged, such as health care and social security, others are not as certain. As people live longer, they will need social benefits for longer periods of time. If social security systems don't change to meet these increased needs, they will become increasingly ineffective, ultimately running out of resources altogether. Also, older people typically need more health services, which will lead to increased demands for long-term care and increased medical costs. Population aging also means that while more people will be drawing upon health and pension funds, these funds will be supported by a smaller number of contributors. This will place a heavier demand on the working age population to maintain benefits for the older population. Declines in fertility may also result in fewer family members for older people to turn to for help and support. However, an aging population may also push for reforms in pensions, social security, and health systems that will reduce the need for younger generations to support the older ones.[37] Moreover, some developing societies are actively trying to increase the younger working population that is supporting the growing older population by encouraging young people from developing countries to immigrate. This strategy has the potential both to increase the productive support base of workers in developed states and to reduce problems of unemployment in developing states.

Migration

migrants People who have left their homes in order to settle in another country or city.

push–pull factors Forces that drive people away from a place (push) and pull them to a new one.

Migrants are people who have left their homes for another. Some people migrate within their own country, while others leave their home country altogether. Various *push–pull factors* influence individuals' decisions to migrate. Pull factors, for example, include the promise of better living conditions in a new country, while push factors include the flight from violence, poverty, or oppression.

Historically, the movement of peoples from their places of origin to other regions around the globe has always affected patterns of population concentration and regional economic growth. However, there was a significant increase in international migration after World War II, and then again more recently, with the advent of the rapid globalization processes that began in the 1980s. Much of this recent international migration has been from the developing world to the developed world. Indeed, the number of migrants in developed countries more than doubled from 1980 to 2000 from 48 million to 110 million. During that same period, migration to developing countries grew at a slower pace, from 52 million to 65 million.[38] In 2005, there were 191 million international migrants, or, put another way, migrants made up approximately 3 percent of the world's population. Today, nearly one in every 10 persons living in more developed regions is a migrant, whereas in developing regions, only one of every 70 persons is a migrant. Most of the world's migrants live in Europe (64 million), followed by Asia (53 million) and North America (45 million).[39] As large as these numbers are, a great deal of migration still occurs within countries, or within regions. Many migrants move from the countryside into towns and cities, for example. This is particularly true of migration in the developing world, where over 81 percent of the world's population lives.[40]

Poverty is a primary push factor for migration. Many people realize that their only hope for escaping poverty is to migrate to another country. Africa, for example, which is projected to face a continued downward spiral of poverty coupled with increased population growth rates, will likely be a major source of migrants seeking work. Many Africans have already migrated to Europe in search of economic opportunities. Migrants from developing countries who find work in developed countries often send *remittances* home to their families. Total global remittances in 2004 amounted to $226 billion, $145 billion of which went to less developed regions. For some countries, remittances play a major role in the economy. For example, in 2004, remittances accounted for more than 20 percent of the *gross domestic product* (GDP) of Haiti, Jordan, the Republic of Moldova, and Tonga.[41]

remit/remittances Money sent home by workers employed in another country.

gross domestic product (GDP) A measure of a country's total output and national income in a year.

Table 6.3 International Migrants by Major Area, 1960–2000[42]

Major Area	Number of International Migrants (millions)					International Migrants as Percentage of Population		Distribution by Major Area (%)	
	1960	**1970**	**1980**	**1990**	**2000**	**1960**	**2000**	**1960**	**2000**
World	75.9	81.5	99.8	154.0	174.9	2.5	2.9	100.0	100.0
Developed countries	32.1	38.3	47.7	89.7	110.3	3.4	8.7	42.3	63.1
Developing countries	43.8	43.2	52.1	64.3	64.6	2.1	1.3	57.7	36.9

Researching to Learn *Investigating the Economic Impact of Recent Migration Patterns*

Sample Keyword Searches

Broad search: migration AND economics

Narrower searches:
- poverty AND "human migration"
- migration AND remittances

Complex search: "global migration patterns" AND (remittances OR poverty)

Note:
- *Use quotations to search for terms as a phrase.*
- *Use AND to find documents with all terms listed.*
- *Use OR to find documents with either one term or the other.*
- *Use parentheses to combine AND and OR statements in creative ways.*

Free Web Resources

Columbia Law School.
   www.law.columbia.edu/center_program/ migration
Inter-University Committee on International Migration
   http://web.mit.edu/cis/www/migration/
Migration Policy Institute
   www.migrationpolicy.org/
Population Council
   www.popcouncil.org
United Nations
   www.un.org
US Department of State
   www.state.gov/g/prm/mig/

Books: Find Them @ Your Library

Hatton, Timothy J. and Jeffrey G. Williamson. *The Age of Mass Migration: Causes and Economic Impact.* Oxford: Oxford University Press, 1998.

Lucas, Robert E. B. *International Migration and Economic Development: Lessons from Low-income Countries.* Cheltenham, UK: Edward Elgar Publishing, 2005.

McNeil, William H. and Ruth S. Adams, eds. *Human Migration: Patterns and Policies.* Bloomington and London: Indiana University Press, 1978.

Ozden, Caglar and Maurice Schiff, eds. *International Migration and Economic Development (World Bank Trade and Development Series).* Washington, DC: World Bank Publications, 2007.

Papademetriou, Demetrios G. and Philip L. Martin. *The Unsettled Relationship: Labor Migration and Economic Development.* Westport, CT: Greenwood Publishing Group, 1991.

Zarkovic Bookman, Milica. *Ethnic Groups in Motion: Economic Competition and Migration in Multiethnic States.* London, UK: Cass, 2002.

Zimmermann, Klaus F. *Migration and Economic Development.* New York, NY: Springer, 1992.

Articles: Find Them @ Your Library

Bauer, Thomas K., John P. Haisken-DeNew, and Christoph M. Schmidt. "International Labor Migration, Economic Growth and Labor Markets . . . The Current State of Affairs." RWI Discussion Paper No. 20 (August 2004). http://ssrn.com/abstract=784548

Borjas, George J. "The Economics of Immigration." *Journal of Economic Literature* 22 (December 1994): 1667–1717. http://ksghome.harvard.edu/ ~GBorjas/Papers/JEL94.pdf

Urbanization

Since the beginning of the twentieth century, the largest migration flows have been from rural to urban areas. This accelerating urbanization trend began with the *agricultural revolution*, which provided sufficient surplus food to sustain people in towns and cities. Then, in the late nineteenth century, the *Industrial Revolution* transformed working and living patterns. Millions of people flocked to urban industrial centers, putting increasing pressure on the environment through pollution and increased rates of consumption. The same patterns that emerged in Europe and the Americas have now hit Africa and Asia. In these regions, the urban population rose from 18 percent of the total population in 1950 to over 40 percent in 2000. This rapid growth is only going to continue in the coming decades; indeed, the urban population in Africa and Asia is expected to double between 2000 and 2030. To put these numbers into a broader context, "the accumulated urban growth of these two regions during the whole span of history will be duplicated in a single generation."[43]

> **agricultural revolution** A period of rapid change in agricultural production, including improved methods of farming and higher yields.
>
> **Industrial Revolution** Refers to changes in economic and social organization that began around 1760 in England and later in other countries as the result of the replacement of hand tools with power-driven machines.
>
> **megacities** Rapidly growing urban areas that have more than 10 million inhabitants.

The year 2008 marked the first time in human history that more than half of the world's population was living in urban areas.[44] By 2050, global urbanization levels are expected to rise to 70 percent.[45] Many people will live in so-called *megacities*, urban areas with more than 10 million residents. This dramatically increased trend toward urbanization has profound implications for patterns of population growth and consumption. In many urban environments, residents tend to be better educated and more affluent; they are often in better health and thus live longer than rural people. Additionally, they tend to have lower fertility rates, even to the point of negative growth. However, this is not the trend in many developing countries, where urban areas are growing at dramatic rates, and much of this growth is occurring in slums. Few, if any, of the benefits that have come to be associated with urban life in developed countries since the last half of the twentieth century can be found in the developing world's urban slums. There are also important consumption issues that have emerged because of this urbanization trend. Although urban residents live on less than 2 percent of the world's landmass, they consume a disproportionate amount of resources and contribute disproportionately to global pollution when compared with their rural counterparts. Continued rapid urbanization is likely to exacerbate these consumption and pollution disparities in the near future.

However, while cites currently are the locus for many of the world's major environmental problems, including pollution, resource degradation, and waste generation, urbanization itself need not necessarily lead to environmental problems. Rather, our current problems are due to unsustainable patterns of production and consumption as well as to inadequate urban management.[46] Experts point out that the concentration of the world's population in urban areas actually offers more opportunities for long-term sustainability than would the dispersion of that population across the globe. Also, the urbanization trend might ultimately help us approach population stability, since urbanization provides few incentives for large families. Nevertheless, the problems associated with urbanization will not magically take care of themselves; rather, they will require extensive research, careful planning, and strategic action by legislators, policy-makers, and activists.[47]

Consumption

Agricultural production and consumption

Famine, demographic pressures, and the unequal distribution of food are as old as the earliest human civilizations. As far back as 3500 BCE, the ancient Mesopotamians relied on agricultural surpluses to sustain settled urban populations. When drought struck, they suffered from hunger, *malnutrition*, and famine. In the Egyptian Old Kingdom (*c*.2800–2100 BCE), priests and pharaohs denied common people access to temple granaries during times of famine lest they deplete stores earmarked for royalty.[48] Historically, the victims of social and economic inequity have sometimes even been blamed for their own starvation. In the 1720s, for example, British observers condemned the people of Ireland for poverty, which they erroneously linked solely to overpopulation rather than to any of their own colonial policies. Rapid population growth continues today, and the accompanying consumption issues and questions are increasingly complicated and urgent. Though we still must face region-specific droughts, famines, and other crises, we must also confront the larger issue of the entire world's *carrying capacity*, or the ability of the Earth's natural environment to sustain the human population.

> **malnutrition** A medical condition in which the body receives too few of the nutrients it needs.
>
> **carrying capacity** The ability of the natural environment to sustain the human population.

In the late 1700s and early 1800s, English demographer and theorist Thomas Malthus was one of the first to highlight the potential problems of population growth and unbridled consumption. In his *Essay on the Principle of Population* (1798), Malthus argued that if population growth remained unrestricted, our numbers would increase geometrically (1, 2, 4, 8, 16 . . .) while our food supply could only ever be increased at an arithmetic rate (1, 2, 3, 4, 5 . . .), thus creating a widening gap between the number of people on the planet and the amount of food available to feed them.[49] In short, he argued that people were poor because there were too many of them and not enough resources. Although he warned that our inability to increase our food supply at the same rate as our population would lead to drastic levels of political and economic instability, he also suggested that population growth would generally be checked by factors such as famine, disease, and war.

Malthus's theories have had a significant influence on demographers ever since, and his ideas have contributed to growing concerns about the planet's carrying capacity. However, Malthus has his critics as well. Common criticisms include his failure to anticipate how advances in technology, transport, and agriculture would increase productivity, as well as how economic and medical advances would contribute to declining fertility.[50] Because of scientific and technological advances, massive geometric population growth in the twentieth century did not result in a *Malthusian Catastrophe*, as agricultural production outpaced population growth. From 1960 to 2000, the global production of cereals, such as corn, wheat, and rice, more than doubled, and meat production nearly tripled.[51] Per capita calorie consumption (all food available for consumption) also increased globally by 17 percent from 1970 to 2005. Daily per capita calorie consumption in 2005 was at 3,418 calories per day in developed countries and 2,733 calories in developing countries.[53] In short, due to increased agricultural production, there was enough food to feed everyone on the planet a nutritious and sustaining vegetarian diet, despite rapid population growth (see figure 6.3).

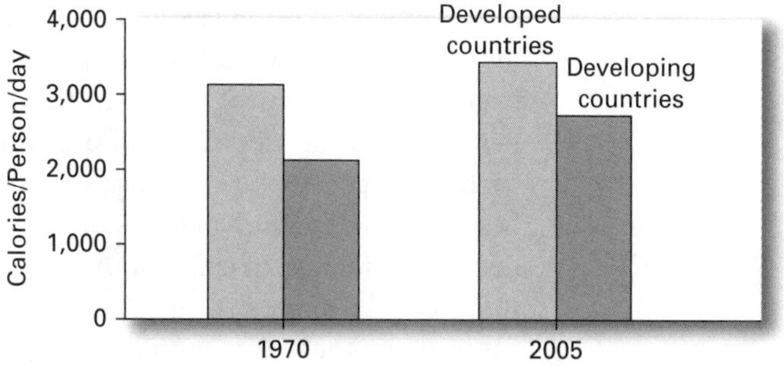

Figure 6.3 Calorie Availability: Developed vs. Developing Countries[52]
Note: UN, Food and Agriculture Organization.

Malthusian Catastrophe A society's return to a subsistence level of existence as a result of overtaxing its available agricultural resources.

Although some people believe that advances in science and technology will continue to meet the needs of the Earth's ever-growing population, most experts maintain that the planet's carrying capacity is finite, and that we are quickly depleting it. Many who subscribe to this perspective point to the millions of people for whom access to food is already a daily struggle and famine is a constant threat as evidence that the world cannot sustain such a large population. They argue for dramatic efforts to reduce population, targeting mostly the developing world where population growth rates are projected to remain high. Others argue that although it is true that many people around the world suffer from hunger, this situation is not always directly related to the planet's carrying capacity. Rather, these experts urge us to pay attention not only to the planet's carrying capacity but also to the fact that hunger, malnutrition, and famine are often products of human behavior and policies, including economic inequality and the lack of what Nobel Prize-winning economist Amartya Sen calls people's "entitlement" to food. Sen's studies have shown that modern famines and problems of hunger persist even when food is available. In many countries, famines have occurred when there was enough food to feed everyone, but the food was only accessible to those in power and/or it was exported to other countries for profit.[54]

In these kinds of scenarios, carrying capacity is not the issue. Rather, the issue is that people have been deprived of *food security*. According to the United Nations, food security is a "state of affairs where all people at all times have access to safe and nutritious food to maintain a healthy and active life."[55] Although the UN maintains that food security is a basic human right, millions of people throughout the world are hungry not because of a food shortage, but because of poverty.

food security State of affairs where all people at all times have access to safe and nutritious food to maintain a healthy and active life.

In other words, the food exists, but many people simply do not have enough money to purchase it. As a result, profound levels of poverty, undernourishment, and ill health affect billions of people in the developing world, while, at the same time, people in the developed world are increasingly suffering from the ill-effects of overconsumption. Obesity, diabetes, cardiovascular disease and a whole host of related health problems afflict millions of people who overconsume, including an alarmingly high number of children. Across the world, over 1.2 billion people consume more calories than they need, many of which have poor nutritional value. In contrast, another 1.2 million are hungry, experiencing a deficiency of calories and protein.[56] Millions more suffer from malnutrition, which results in ill health and compromised life expectancy. Women and children in the developing world are the hardest hit by malnutrition. More than five million children die of diseases related to hunger every year while thousands more are adversely affected physically and mentally by malnutrition.[57] Although hunger takes its greatest toll on children and women in South Asia and sub-Saharan Africa, increasing numbers of urban poor in Latin America suffer from hunger. Moreover, it is estimated that up to 10 percent of US households experience food insecurity.[58] In contrast, one in five (20 percent) of American children are considered overweight or obese.[59]

Costs of increased agricultural production

While improvements in food production have allowed us to feed our growing population, they have exacted many costs as well. The shift to intensive agricultural production to feed more people has increased our consumption of basic resources, such as energy, land, and water. Some of our strategies for producing larger amounts of food have been particularly problematic. For example, the so-called *Green Revolution* of the 1950s (which, despite its name, actually marked the advent of the large-scale use of chemically based agriculture) was an effort by scientists to engineer a limited number of improved strains of wheat and corn in order to increase food supplies in developing countries. Initially, this proved to be a great success because these strains yielded much larger crops than had previous grains. These new strains, however, required much more water and fertilizers than the earlier ones. As more farmers in the developing world switched to these varieties, they incurred greater and greater costs, as water grew scarce, and fertilizers, which are derived from declining petroleum oil reserves, became more expensive. The use of irrigation and fertilizers also created favorable conditions for the growth of weeds, which in turn caused farmers to seek out expensive and toxic herbicides. Overall, the Green Revolution proved a costly disaster for many poor farmers and it wreaked massive environmental damage.[60]

Green Revolution An effort by scientists (1940s–60s) to engineer fewer improved strains of wheat and corn in order to increase food supplies in developing countries.

Advocates of the Green Revolution and modern commercial agriculture point out that their techniques have led to dramatic increases in the world's food supply. Critics argue, however, that modern agriculture has achieved its goals through costly and inefficient practices, wasting resources and consuming more energy than it produces. Studies show that farmers in developing countries who use their own human power and basic tools, such as an ax, hoe, and machete, expend approximately 1 calorie to produce about 10 calories of food energy. In contrast, US farmers use about 2.8 calories of fuel per calorie of food grown.[61] Rice farming offers a startling example of the energy inefficiency of modern farming techniques. While modern rice farming produces a negative 1 to 10 energy return, traditional rice farmers in Bali are reported to produce up to 15 calories for every 1 calorie used.[62] It is also important to note that more energy is expended on food-processing, packaging, distributing, and marketing than on growing the actual food product.[63] The energy needed to produce, package, and transport the aluminum tray that a TV dinner sits in, for example, is more than the energy contained in the food itself.[64] The production and packaging of soft-drinks requires particularly high inputs that contrast sharply with the amount of food energy they contain. Energy is expended on both the pressurized systems that incorporate carbon dioxide into the liquid and the production of the aluminum can that holds it. A can of diet soda that contains one calorie, for example, requires about 2,200 calories of fossil energy to produce.[65]

As a result of these kinds of issues, new approaches to food production and consumption are emerging. One such approach is the *locavore* movement, which encourages people to eat foods produced locally, or within a short radius from their home. Locavores maintain that eating locally grown foods is an environmentally friendly practice because it reduces transportation distances and thus also reduces greenhouse gas emissions. They also argue that locally grown foods taste better and are more nutritious. Additionally, many view supporting small-scale, local producers as an added benefit of eating locally, contributing to the vitality of the community and encouraging responsibility. Local producers, for example, can be immediately identified and held accountable if they sell contaminated foods that make community members sick. In contrast, it can be much more difficult to ascertain the source of a food-related illness and to contain and limit its effects when, for example, contaminated spinach grown in Salinas, California is shipped all over the United States. Finally, some people favor supporting local over global food markets because of labor issues. The global coffee market has, for example, been condemned for favoring wealthy consumers in developed countries at the expense of poor and politically weak producers in Africa.[66] In some cases, however, as Peter Singer and others have shown, buying on the global market, but from small-scale producers who employ sustainable agricultural practices, can be an environmentally sound and ethical decision.[67]

> **locavore** The practice of eating only those foods produced within a short distance of where you live.

Consumer culture

Purchasing goods and consuming materials in excess of our basic needs is not a new phenomenon, but the rate and level of consumption shifted dramatically in the early years of the twentieth century. This period saw the invention of the category of the consumer – people who buy and accumulate goods – and with it the development of a consumer culture – a culture that is permeated by and encourages the production, sale, and purchase of commodities. Buying, selling, and accumulating are so integrated into people's lives in the developed world that consumer culture may seem to be the natural order of things or the logical way that societies should be organized. However, consumerism is not an innate human trait and many cultures around the world have discouraged the accumulation of wealth. Even in nineteenth-century America, moderation and self-denial were dominant cultural values, and people were expected to save money, purchasing only the necessities. During this period, more than half of the population lived on farms where they produced much of what they consumed.[68]

By the early twentieth century, however, American culture had changed. Merchants no longer waited passively for people to buy goods when they needed them; instead, increased attention began to be paid to marketing and presenting goods in a way that would make people want to buy them, whether they needed them or not. Business schools began to emerge at universities around the country, teaching people the fundamentals of marketing, sales, and accounting. Governmental agencies, such as the Commerce Department, were developed to promote consumption. The consumer economy was also advanced by the transformation of laborers into consumers as businesses began increasing workers' wages. Later, the expansion of credit introduced additional buying power into the economy. Mortgages, auto loans, and credit cards all became easier to acquire. With these changes came changes in values from frugality to fulfillment through spending. While these changes were not unique to the United States, as many occurred in Western European countries as well, they occurred with increased rapidity and intensity in America.[69] Today, financial institutions and manufacturers, such as automotive companies, have spread the pattern of debt-based consumption around the world.[70] Many argue that people's lives, particularly in the developed world, have been dramatically improved by consumer culture and the products it makes available – new machines, medicines, foods, transport, houses, and information and communication technologies. There are, however, important social and environmental costs involved in what and how we consume.

Global Consumption Patterns

The question "How many people can the earth sustain?" is inextricably linked to resource consumption issues. Although agricultural production and exploding population growth rates in the developing world are important concerns, so too are the high consumption and waste rates of the developed world. Resource consumption and waste production rates are about 32 times higher in North America, Western Europe, Japan, and Australia than they are in the developing world. According to UCLA geography professor Jared Diamond: "The estimated one billion people who live in developed countries have a relative per capita consumption rate of 32. Most of the world's other 5.5 billion people constitute the developing world, with relative per capita consumption rates below 32, mostly down toward 1."[71] What this means is that population booms in developing countries are not, at least initially, as big a threat to the world's resources as are current American consumption patterns. Each American consumes as many resources as 32 Kenyans, for example, and with a population 10 times the size of Kenya, the US consumes 320 times more resources.

The developed world's current consumption patterns are considered by many experts to be unsustainable, but the situation is exacerbated by the fact that many developing countries are slowly approaching the developed world's standard of living, which means that their consumption rates are at the same level as those in developed countries. If the populations of India and China were to consume like Americans, the world consumption rate would triple, and if the whole developing world were to do so, world consumption rates would increase 11 times. Should such a scenario come to pass, it would be as if the world population had expanded to 72 billion people, a figure which the planet could not support.[72]

Americans in particular consume more resources than any other nation in the world. The US not only has the world's largest *gross national product* (GNP) but also has the largest *ecological footprint*, impacting the planet's resources and ecosystems more than any other country.[73] Over the past 50 years, US consumption rates have dramatically increased. For example, in 1950, the average size of a new home was 983 square feet. By 2004, it had increased to 2,349 square feet, requiring more than twice as many resources to both build and maintain.[74] Suburban sprawl, characterized by low-density residential subdivisions, commercial strips, retail complexes, and large parking lots, has become the dominant land-use pattern in the US. Unfortunately, this pattern requires more of practically every resource, from energy to water. Since everything, from homes to jobs to malls, is so spread out, sprawl requires people to drive further distances, increasing fossil fuel combustion, which puts more greenhouse gasses into the atmosphere. Americans also love their cars, and many drive alone to work rather than carpooling or using public transportation. Additionally, Americans use 75 percent more water per capita than the average person in the developing world, lavishing it on lawns, water-intensive plants, and golf courses.[75] The US is also the world's largest consumer of forest products, using more than twice those of developing countries per capita and 10 times those of the world in 2000.[76] Americans also produce huge amounts of trash. Between 1960 and 2005, trash production doubled, from 83 million to 167 million tons.[77] Each American produces about five pounds of trash daily, which is five times the average amount produced by people in developing countries.[78] While recycling and composting efforts have also increased in recent years, they are far from keeping pace with patterns of consumption and waste production.

Among the costs of US consumption and waste-production trends has been severe environmental damage. Approximately 40 percent of the rivers, 46 percent of the lakes, and 50 percent of the estuaries in the US are too polluted to allow for fishing

> **gross national product (GNP)** A measure of the goods and services produced by a country in a given year, including gains on overseas investments.
>
> **ecological footprint** A measurement of human impact on the earth that compares human consumption of resources with the earth's capacity to renew them and to absorb waste.

and swimming. Additionally, 53 percent of America's wetlands have been lost to urban and suburban development and agricultural land-use changes.[79] Many fisheries are overfished or contaminated, and thousands of acres of prime farmland continue to be lost to development. More than 1,000 plant and animal species are listed by the US government as endangered, and more than 300 as threatened.[80] This is consistent with a worldwide biodiversity decline, which many scientists believe is actually the earth's sixth mass extinction.[81] Unlike previous mass extinctions, this one is due primarily to human activity.

Environmental challenges are not projected to get any better, in part because of climate change. Since the advent of the Industrial Revolution, concentrations of many greenhouse gases (natural and *anthropogenic* gases in the atmosphere that affect the earth's temperature – see chapter 5) have increased. For example, while the atmospheric concentration of the greenhouse gas carbon dioxide remained between 260 and 280 parts per million for the 10,000 years prior to the advent of the industrial era, CO_2 levels have since increased by about 100 parts per million (ppm). Also worth noting is the accelerated rate of CO_2 increases. During the 200 years marking the start of the Industrial Revolution to approximately 1973, CO_2 levels increased by 50 ppm. In just 33 more years, from 1973 to 2006, CO_2 levels increased by another 50 ppm. These rapid increases are the direct result of human activity, including the burning of fossil fuels, such as coal, gasoline, and natural gas. But CO_2 is not the only greenhouse gas that has been increasing in the atmosphere due to human activity. Increased concentrations of methane, for example, are due to food production practices. Livestock *enteric fermentation* and manure management, paddy rice farming, and the development of wetlands contribute to increased levels of methane in the atmosphere. Manmade chlorofluorocarbons (CFCs), which are used in refrigeration systems and fire suppression systems, are also contributing to the growing layer of greenhouse gases in our atmosphere. As the name suggests, greenhouse gases are contributing to an increase in global temperatures, a phenomenon which has been alternatively dubbed "global warming" and "global climate change." Climate change has the potential radically to alter our entire global ecosystem in potentially devastating ways. Rising sea levels and severe weather, for example, are predicted to severely impact coastal areas.[82]

Other population- and consumption-related environmental threats include the world's dwindling supply of renewable resources. For example, we have more than tripled our withdrawals of water from the planet since 1940, from 1,088 cubic kilometers per year in 1940 to 3,973 in 2000.[83] Freshwater reserves are finite, and, as we increase our use of them, we drain water tables and take ever more water out of circulation. As a result, many countries are experiencing *water stress*, where projected demand outstrips reserves. Some countries are currently in a state of depletion. They

greenhouse gases Gases, such as carbon dioxide, methane, ozone, and nitrous oxide, that warm the earth's atmosphere by absorbing infrared radiation.

anthropogenic Effects, processes, or materials that are the result of human activities.

enteric fermentation Fermentation that takes place in the digestive systems of ruminant animals, mammals that digest plant-based food by regurgitating semi-digested food and chewing it again.

water stress When demand for water outstrips availability.

have taken out more water than nature can replenish, leading to *desertification*. Many countries are already dependent upon external supplies of water. For example, 97 percent of Egypt's fresh water comes from external sources.[84] Humans have also depleted ocean fish stocks at a staggering pace, increasing our demand for the world fish catch fivefold since 1950, from 18 million tons to 90 million tons in 1990.[85] We have overfished some species, such as Atlantic cod, southern blue-fin tuna, and swordfish, to the point where they are no longer a commercially viable catch species.[86]

> **desertification**   The gradual transformation of habitable land into desert.
>
> **deforestation**   The clearing of forests, usually by logging or burning, which not only releases carbon into the atmosphere but also often results in soil erosion, desertification, and the loss of habitats and biodiversity.

Deforestation and the concomitant loss of biodiversity in rainforests and other sensitive ecological areas is another major challenge posed by population and consumption. Some argue that the global loss of forest areas is a product of population growth, which causes more people to cut down trees in an effort to eke out a living on the land. This problem is likely to continue, as grain production and available agricultural land have dropped on a per capita basis as our population grows. Others point out that forest losses are also driven by new and increasing consumer demands in the developed world for everything from paper products to old-growth tropical timber, such as mahogany. Problems posed by deforestation include the loss of our planet's biodiversity. Habitat loss has led to the endangerment and extinction of thousands of animal, insect, and plant species, threatening the livelihoods of many *indigenous peoples* in the process. The destruction of rainforests around the equator also contributes to global warming, accounting for up to 25 percent of global emissions of greenhouse gases.[87] And as the forests shrink, there are then fewer trees to absorb carbon dioxide, exacerbating global climate change. (For more on how deforestation and climate change are linked, see chapter 5.)

> **indigenous peoples**   A particular group of inhabitants of a geographic space whose connections to that space are the earliest known human connections to that land.

In Focus: Population Growth, Aging, and Consumption in the Land of the Lonely Hearts Club

China has long been recognized as one of the world's most important countries in terms of the global impact of its large population. China is about the same geographic size as the US, but its population, 1.3 billion strong, is nearly five times that of the US. Even though China's rate of population growth is slowing, its large population base has a momentum that will continue to add up to 200 million people over the next two decades. Thereafter, its population is projected to decline by nearly four million people during the years 2025–50. The reasons behind this dramatic population shift reside in China's recent history.

Following the *Communist Revolution*, China experienced unprecedented population growth and population fluctuations. Between 1949 and 1980, the population grew from 540 million to more than 800 million. Some have argued that this extremely

> **Communist Revolution**   A Marxist-inspired overthrow of a government in order to install a communist type of political and economic system.

Great Leap Forward   A political and social plan in China from 1958 to 1960 that was designed to transform China from an agrarian to an industrial society. Instead, it triggered a famine that left between 14 and 43 million dead.

rapid growth led to a severe Malthusian "check" in the form of a devastating famine. The famine hit during the *Great Leap Forward* (1958–61), a period when China's government sought to restructure its economy, building an industrial base by relocating rural farmers to industrial villages. It is estimated that more than 30 million people died during the famine, although the Chinese government attempted to conceal the figures. The causes of the famine are complex. While the shifting of farmers away from agricultural production may well have been a factor in reducing the harvest of crops, there were other factors as well. Severe weather, drought, and poor communication between regions contributed to localized shortages, but one of the main factors behind the long duration and extent of the famine was poor governmental planning. Although the government had long viewed population growth as a potential asset for economic growth, the disaster of the famine caused them to change their views.

In the 1960s, the Chinese government began encouraging families to have fewer children. By 1979, birth control clinics advocating family planning gave way to a much more concerted effort to reduce population growth via the "one-child policy" for urban families and a two-child rule for rural families. This policy employed a combination of propaganda, social pressure, and state coercion to limit Chinese families to just one child. Those who complied were given "one-child certificates," which brought significant rewards, including cash bonuses and highly desirable housing. In some cases, those who did not comply were pressured to have abortions or to undergo sterilization. There were also widespread occurrences of infanticide, particularly of female babies, since male children have traditionally been considered much more desirable in Chinese society. This patriarchal privileging of male children in conjunction with the one-child policy led to a significant gender imbalance. More recently, improvements in medical technologies that provide easy and inexpensive ways to determine the sex of the fetus, such as ultrasound scans and chromosomal testing, have helped to exacerbate the gender imbalance. Currently, between 117 and 120 boys are born in China for every 100 girls. The problem has become so severe that the government has outlawed doctors from revealing the sex of the fetus to the parents. Despite these efforts, there is a dramatic shortage of females in the population, and China has been dubbed the world's largest "lonely hearts club," as more than 23 million men are unable to find a female partner for marriage. State officials are now concerned that this imbalance could lead to social instability, higher rates of crime, and rampant prostitution, the latter of which also has the potential to contribute to a major AIDS epidemic.[88]

In addition to a gender imbalance, China will also have to confront the issues that accompany an aging population. A projected 397 million Chinese citizens will be 60 years of age and over by the year 2040. As the country continues to seek to reduce its population growth rates, and as the male–female imbalance continues to have the potential to undermine fertility, many are concerned that there will not be a sufficient support base to take care of the elderly. In the absence of familial support, the aged will have to turn to the state for financial help, significantly draining the country's resources. The pressing question will be whether China's surging economic growth can provide for this aging population.[89]

China's population growth and shifting demography are also connected to its dramatically increased role in the global economy. Along with the rest of Asia and the developing world, China is experiencing a dramatic rise in urbanization. Experts predict that Chinese cities will contain 800 million people by 2020.[90] These new urban dwellers will contribute to both economic growth and consumption, as city residents typically consume many more resources than rural people. Also, as China's population growth slows, it is shifting to policies that support *economic modernization*, and these policies are creating significant new demands on global resources. As its economy has grown, China has changed its patterns of consumption of global products. From a nation where virtually every household relied on a bicycle, it is now entering the auto-

> **economic modernization**   The transformation of an economy from one that focused on outmoded means of production to one that is able to keep pace with rapid technological and industrial changes.

mobile society, with car and light truck sales climbing yearly. This has had a major impact on gas prices the world over, as China's demand for oil rose by 11 percent in 2005. If China's 1.3 billion people start using the same amount of oil as Americans (who currently use about 26 barrels per person per year compared with 1.5 barrels per person in China), it would need some 80 million barrels of oil a day – 20 million more barrels than the entire world currently produces. Similar increases are likely for other products as well, from meat and fish to air travel. This increased production and consumption will, moreover, contribute to markedly increased rates of pollution and environmental degradation, including poor air quality and dried up or polluted rivers.

Still, there are some hopeful indicators for China's future. The Chinese government seems well aware of the potential pros and cons of economic liberalization and modernization. It retains a high degree of control, for the time being, over broader political policies and it can make choices about growth. It is acutely aware of rising costs for non-renewable energy sources, such as coal and oil, and it is grappling with mounting health costs from both pollution and potential epidemics. It has sought to use new renewable energy technologies and sources to offset the costs of other non-renewable energy sources. Solar and wind energy currently provide for some 35 million Chinese homes. China will, nevertheless, be a major player in the competition for global resources of all kinds in the near future.[91]

Conclusion

The world's population grew rapidly in the twentieth century, but particularly between 1965 and 1970, when growth rates soared to over 2 percent per year. Although the annual percent of growth is now declining, population numbers will nevertheless continue to rise rapidly, reaching nine billion by 2040. Population growth is often linked with poverty, but research shows that population growth itself does not lead

Researching to Learn   *China and Population*

Sample Keyword Searches

Broad search: China AND population

Narrower searches:
- China AND population AND projections
- "one child policy" AND China AND population

Complex search: "Chinese population" AND (aging OR elderly) AND "consumption patterns"

Note:
- *Use quotations to search for terms as a phrase.*
- *Use AND to find documents with all terms listed.*
- *Use OR to find documents with either one term or the other.*
- *Use parentheses to combine AND and OR statements in creative ways.*

Free Web Resources

China Population Information Center
   www.cpirc.org.cn/en/eindex.htm
International Human Dimensions Program on Global Environmental Change
   www.ihdp.unu.edu/
Population-Environment Research Network (PERN)
   www.populationenvironmentresearch.org/
United Nations
   www.un.org

Books: Find Them @ Your Library

Banister, Judith. *China's Changing Population.* Sanford, CA: Stanford University Press 1987.

Greenhalgh, Susan and Edwin Winckler. *Governing China's Population: From Leninist to Neoliberal Biopolitics.* Stanford, CA: Stanford University Press 2005.

Kane, Penny. *The Second Billion, Population and Family Planning in China.* Ringwood, Australia: Penguin Books, 1987.

Lee, James Z. *One Quarter of Humanity: Malthusian Mythology and Chinese Realities, 1700–20.* Harvard, MA: Harvard University Press, 1999.

Peng, Xizhe and Zhigang Guo, eds. *The Changing Population of China.* Oxford: Blackwell Publishing, 2008.

Scharping, Thomas. *Birth Control in China 1949–2000 Population Policy and Demographic Development.* New York: Routledge, 2003.

Articles: Find Them @ Your Library

Burdett, Richard. "Beyond City Limits." *Foreign Policy* 164 (Jan/Feb. 2008): 42–3.

Calvo, Esteban and John B. Williamson. "Old-age Pension Reform and Modernization Pathways: Lessons for China from Latin America." *Journal of Aging Studies* 22, no. 1 (January 2008): 74–87.

Flaherry, Joseph Henry, Mei Lin Liu, Lei Ding, Birong Dong, Qunfang Ding, Zia Li and Shifu Xiao. "China: The Aging Giant," *Journal of the American Geriatrics Society* 55, no. 8 (August 2007): 1295–300.

Nomile, Dennis. "China's Living Laboratory in Urbanization." *Science* 319, no. 5864 (2008): 740–3.

Nowak, Rachel. "China's Demographic Crunch." *New Scientist* 196, no. 2629 (November 2007): 62–3.

inevitably to poverty. However, as the population continues to grow, the world will have to confront a variety of issues emerging around aging populations, migration, and urbanization.

Although the populations of developed regions are slowly declining, they nevertheless are the biggest contributor to excessive consumption and the depletion of resources. In developed countries, smaller families have tended to be more affluent, and therefore more demanding of greater amounts of consumables. One child born today in the US will consume more and add more pollution to the world than 30 children born in many developing countries. However, rising levels of affluence in the developing world are leading to rising consumer demand and to an overall dramatic increase in global consumption. Current consumption patterns are already unsustainable, so we must find ways to reduce consumption and to rely upon renewable resources.

Notes

1   Jonathan Swift, "A Modest Proposal for Preventing the Children of the Poor People in Ireland From Being a Burden to their Parents or the Country and for Making them Beneficial to the Public" (Plain Label Books, 1729), 5.

2   Quoted in Philip Martin and Jonas Widgren, "International Migration: Facing the Challenge," *Population Bulletin* 57, no. 1 (March 2002), http://findarticles.com/p/articles/mi_qa3761/is_200203/ai_n9068737/pg_2. For the Group of 77, see www.g77.org.

3   Gary Gardner and Payal Sampat, *Mind Over Matter: Recasting the Role of Materials in Our Lives, 144* (Washington, DC: Worldwatch Institute December, 1998), 5.

4   Interview with Jared Diamond on the radio show "Living on Earth," *Public Radio International* (January 25, 2008), www.livingonearth.org/shows/segments.htm?programID=08-P13-00004&segmentID=3.

5   The oldest human fossils were discovered in Ethiopia on the banks of the Omo River by a team led by Richard Leakey in 1967. It wasn't until 2005, however, that new dating techniques revealed that the fossils were 195,000 years old, a figure that pushes back what had previously been believed to be the dawn of modern humans by 35,000 years. The 195,000-year-old date is consistent with findings from genetic research on human populations and it also adds further evidence to support the already widely accepted "Out of Africa" theory of human origins. This theory suggests that modern humans first appeared in Africa and then slowly spread across the entire globe. See Ian McDougall,

Francis Brown, and John G. Fleagle, "Stratigraphic Placement and Age of Modern Humans from Kibish, Ethiopia," *Nature* 433, no. 7027 (February 17, 2005), 733–6; Hillary Mayell, "Oldest Human Fossils Identified," *National Geographic News* (February 16, 2005), http://news.nationalgeographic.com/news/2005/02/0216_050216_omo.html.

6   "The World at Six Billion," United Nations Population Division (1999), 3, www.un.org/esa/population/publications/sixbillion/sixbilpart1.pdf.

7   "World Population Information," US Census Bureau, www.census.gov/ipc/www/idb/worldpopinfo.html.

8   Katherine Park, "VIII.16 Black Death," in Kenneth F. Kiple (ed.), *The Cambridge World History of Human Disease* (Cambridge: Cambridge University Press, 1993), 613.

9   Source: "The World at Six Billion," United Nations Population Division (1999), 8, www.un.org/esa/population/publications/sixbillion/sixbilpart1.pdf.

10   David Lucas, "World Population Growth and Theories," in David Lucas and Paul Meyer (eds.), *Beginning Population Studies* (National Centre for Development Studies, Australia: Asian Pacific Press, 1994), 13.

11   "World Population Information," US Census Bureau.

12   Joel E. Cohen, *Between Choices and Constraints* (New York: W. W. Norton & Company, 1995), 13.

13   Japan's Population Growth Rate: −0.139%. Norway's Population Growth Rate: 0.35%. Central Intelligence Agency (CIA), "Japan," "Norway," last updated May 15, 2008, *The World Factbook*, www.cia.gov/library/publications/the-world-factbook/index.html.

14 "World Population Information," US Census Bureau.

15 "The World at Six Billion," United Nations Population Division, 4.

16 Source: US Census Bureau, International Database, 2008 first update, www.census.gov/ipc/ www/ idb/worldgrgraph.php.

17 Ibid., 4, 6.

18 "World Population Prospects: The 2006 Revision," United Nations Department of Economic and Social Affairs, Population Division (2007), 9, www.un.org/esa/population/publications/wpp2006/WPP2006_Highlights_rev.pdf.

19 Source: "World Population Prospects: The 2006 Revision," United Nations Department of Economic and Social Affairs, Population Division (2007), 9, www.un.org/esa/population/publications/wpp2006/WPP2006_Highlights_rev.pdf.

20 Charles Hirschman, "Population and Society: Historical Trends and Future Prospects," in Craig Calhoun, Chris Rojek, and Bryan Turner (eds.), *The Sage Handbook of Sociology* (Thousand Oaks, CA: Sage Publications, 2005), 393.

21 Donald G. Kaufman and Cecilia M. Franz, *Biosphere 2000: Protecting Our Global Environment* (Dubuque, IO: Kendall/Hunt Publishing, 1993), 156.

22 Ibid.

23 David J. Campbell, "Assessing Human Processes in Society: Environment Interactions," in Mark E. Jensen and Patrick S. Bourgeron (eds.), *A Guidebook for Integrated Ecological Assessments* (New York: Springer, 2001), 424.

24 Hirschman, "Population and Society," 393.

25 Ibid., 394.

26 Margaret L. Anderson and Howard F. Taylor, *Sociology: Understanding a Diverse Society* (Belmont, CA: Thomson Wadsworth, 2006), 570.

27 Hirschman, "Population and Society," 394.

28 Nancy Birdsall and Steven W. Sinding, "How and Why Population Matters: New Findings, New Issues," in Nancy Birdsall, Allen C. Kelley, and Steven W. Sinding (eds.), *Population Matters* (Oxford: Oxford University Press, 2001), 14.

29 Ibid.

30 Richard H. Robbins, *Global Problems and the Culture of Capitalism* (Needham Heights, MA: Allyn & Bacon, 1999), 153.

31 Ibid., 167–9.

32 Albert Keidel, "China's Economic Rise: Fact and Fiction," Policy Brief No. 61, Carnegie Endowment for International Peace (July 2008), www.carnegieendowment.org/publications/index.cfm?fa=view&id=20279&prog=zch.

33 United Nations Population Division, "Introduction: The Dynamics and Consequences of Population Ageing," *World Population Ageing: 1950–2050*, 1, www.un.org/esa/population/publications/worldageing19502050/pdf/7introduction.pdf.

34 Source: United Nations Population Division, "Chapter I: Demographic Determinants of Population Ageing," *World Population Ageing: 1950–2050*, 5, www.un.org/esa/population/publications/worldageing19502050/pdf/8chapteri.pdf.

35 United Nations Population Division, "Chapter II: Magnitude and Speed of Population Ageing," *World Population Ageing: 1950–2050*, 11–12, www.un.org/esa/population/publications/worldageing19502050/pdf/80chapterii.pdf.

36 United Nations Population Division, "Chapter III: Changing Balance between Age Groups," *World Population Ageing: 1950–2050*, 15, www.un.org/esa/population/publications/worldageing19502050/pdf/81chapteriii.pdf.

37 United Nations Population Division, "Introduction: The Dynamics and Consequences of Population Ageing," 1.

38 "The State of the World's Refugees 2006," UNHCR, www.unhcr.org/publ/PUBL/4444d3c043.html.

39 United Nations Population Division, "International Migration 2006" (UN Wall Chart), www.un.org/esa/population/publications/2006Migration_Chart/Migration2006.pdf.

40 Ibid.

41 Ibid.

42 Source: United Nations Population Division, "International Migration 2006" (UN Wall Chart), http://www.un.org/esa/population/publications/2006Migration_Chart/Migration2006.pdf.

43 "State of World Population 2007: Unleashing the Potential of Urban Growth," United Nations Population Fund (UNFPA), 1, www.unfpa.org/swp/2007/presskit/pdf/sowp2007_eng.pdf.

44 Ibid.

45 "World Urbanization Prospects: The 2007 Revision," United Nations Population Division, 4, www.un.org/esa/population/publications/wup2007/2007WUP_ExecSum_web.pdf.

46 "State of World Population 2007," 55.

47 Ibid.

48 See John Iliffe, *Africans: The History of a Continent* (Cambridge: Cambridge University Press, 1995), 21, 27; John Iliffe, *The African Poor: A History* (Cambridge: Cambridge University Press, 1987).

49 Thomas R. Malthus, *Essay on the Principle of Population*, ed. Geoffrey Gilbert (New York: Oxford University Press, 1999).

50 David Lucas, "World Population Growth and Theories," in David Lucas and Paul Meyer (eds.), *Beginning Population Studies* (National Centre for Development Studies, Australia: Asian Pacific Press, 1994), 22.

51 Ron Nielsen, *The Little Green Handbook* (New York: Picador, 2006), 52.

52 Source: *Food Security Assessment, 2007* (Washington DC: United States Department of Agriculture, July 2008) 28, www.ers.usda.gov/Publications/GFA19/GFA19.pdf.

53 Shahla Shapouri and Stacey Rosen, "Global Diet Composition: Factors Behind the Changes and Implications of the New Trends," in *Food Security Assessment, 2007* (Washington DC: United States Department of Agriculture, July 2008) 28, www.ers.usda.gov/Publications/GFA19/GFA19.pdf.

54 Amartya Sen, *Poverty and Famines: An Essay on Entitlement and Deprivation* (Oxford: Oxford University Press, 1981).

55 Yaa Ntiamoa-Baidu, "Chapter One: Introduction," in *Wildlife and Food Security in Africa, Food and Agriculture Organization of the United Nations*, www.fao.org/docrep/w7540e/w7540e03.htm.

56 Gary Gardner and Brian Halweil, *Underfed and Overfed: The Global Epidemic of Malnutrition*, Worldwatch Paper No. 150 (Washington DC: Worldwatch Institute, March 2000), 7.

57 Ibid., 8.

58 Ibid., 13.

59 Ibid., 14.

60 Michael L. McKinney and Robert M. Schoch, *Environmental Science: Systems and Solutions* (Sudbury, MA: Jones and Bartlett Publishers, 2007), 315–17.

61 Audrey H. Ensminger and James E. Konlande, "Energy Required for Food Production," in *The Concise Encyclopedia of Foods and Nutrition* (Boca Raton, FL: CRC Press, 1995), 312.

62 Jack Manno, *Privileged Goods: Commoditization and Its Impact on Environment and Society* (Boca Raton, FL: Lewis Publishers, 2000), 89.

63 Ensminger and Konlande, "Energy Required for Food Production," 311.

64 David Pimentel and Marcia H. Pimentel, *Food, Energy, and Society* (Niwot, CO: University Press of Colorado, 1996), 252.

65 Ibid., 251.

66 See for example the American Public Broadcasting System documentary series Independent Lens film *Black Gold*. For similar negative impacts, see Herbert Sauper's documentary *Darwin's Nightmare* (2006) about the global Tilapia market and Tanzania.

67 Peter Singer and Jim Mason, *The Way We Eat* (New York: Rodale, 2006).

68 Robbins, *Global Problems and the Culture of Capitalism*, 14.

69 Ibid., 15–22.

70 Michael Renner, "Moving Toward a Less Consumptive Economy," in Erik Assadourian, Christopher Flavin, Hilary French, et al. (eds.), *State of the World 2004: The Consumer Society* (New York: W. W. Norton & Co., 2004), 112; and Gary Gardner, Erik Assadourian, and Radhika Sarin, "The State of Consumption Today," in *State of the World 2004: Special Focus: The Consumer Society* (New York: W. W. Norton & Co., 2004), 15.

71 Jared Diamond, "What's Your Consumption Factor," *New York Times* (January 2, 2008), www.nytimes.com/2008/01/02/opinion/02diamond.html?pagewanted=1.

72 Ibid.

73 Victoria D. Markham, *US National Report on Population and the Environment* (New Canaan, CT: Center for Environment and Population, 2006), 4.

74 Sandra Yin, "Lifestyle Choices Affect US Impact on the Environment," Population Reference Bureau, 2006, www.prb.org/Articles/2006/LifestyleChoicesAffectUSImpactontheEnvironment.aspx?p=1.

75 Ibid.

76 Markham, *US National Report on Population*, 7.

77   Yin, "Lifestyle Choices Affect US Impact on the Environment."

78   Markham, *US National Report on Population*, 8.

79   Ibid., 7.

80   "Summary of Listed Species," US fish and Wildlife Service, Threatened and Endangered Species System, October 19, 2008, http://ecos.fws.gov/tess_public/TESSBoxscore.

81   Alex Kirby, "Biodiversity: The Sixth Great Wave," BBC News (October 1, 2004), http://news.bbc.co.uk/2/hi/science/nature/3667300.stm.

82   Markham, *US National Report on Population*, 8.

83   Ron Nielsen, *The Little Green Handbook* (New York: Picador, 2006), 62.

84   Ibid., 78.

85   Lester Russell Brown and Linda Starke, *State of the World 1998* (New York: W. W. Norton, 1998), 5.

86   Joyhn D. Reynolds, Nicholas K. Dulvy, and Callum M. Roberts, "Exploitation and Other Threats to Fish Conservation," in *Handbook of Fish Biology and Fisheries* (Malden, MA: Blackwell, 2002), 319.

87   Daniel Howden, "Deforestation: The Hidden Cause of Global Warming," *Independent* (May 14, 2007), www.independent.co.uk/environment/climate-change/deforestation-the-hidden-cause-of-global-warming-448734.html.

88   *Economic and Social Commission for Asia and the Pacific Region Annual Report for 2005*, United Nations (2006), 8–12, www.unescap.org/61/English/E61/Annual%20Report/E_ESCAP_1359.pdf.

89   See Richard Jackson and Neil Howe, "The Graying of The Middle Kingdom: The Demographics and Economics of Retirement Policy in China," Center for Strategic and International Studies, Global Ageing Initiative, 2004, www.csis.org/media/csis/pubs/grayingkingdom.pdf; US Department of Commerce, "Bureau of the Census International Brief: Old Age and Security Reform in China" (November 1995), www.census.gov/ipc/prod/ib95-1.pdf.

90   W. John Hoffmann and Michael J. Enright, *China into the Future: Making Sense of the World's Most Dynamic Economy* (Hoboken, NJ: John Wiley & Sons, 2008), 143.

91   Gerhard Heilig, "Can China Feed Itself? A system for Evaluation of Policy Options," International Institute for Applied Systems Analysis Papers, Vienna, Austria (1999), www.iiasa.ac.at/Research/LUC/ChinaFood/index_m.htm.

7

INFECTIOUS DISEASE AND GLOBALIZATION

"Disease generally begins that equality which death completes." (Samuel Johnson [1709–84], *The Rambler*, London, September 1, 1750)

"Despair often breeds disease." (Sophocles (497–406 BCE), *Fragments*, 1. 585, *Tyro Shorn*)

"When there is disharmony in the world, death follows." (Navajo Medicine Man in reference to an outbreak of hantavirus infections in Arizona 1993)[1]

Learning to Question, Questioning to Learn

- What kinds of factors affect the transmission, manifestation, and treatment of disease?
- To what extent is disease a socially produced condition caused by human beings through our dynamic interactions with each other, the ecosystems we live and work in, and our local and global economic activity?
- In what ways might disease affect and be affected by an increasingly centralized and industrialized global food industry?
- What are some of the major challenges in the global fight against infectious disease?

Introduction

H1N1, Avian Influenza, SARS (Severe Acute Respiratory Syndrome). HIV/AIDS (Human Immunodeficiency Virus/Acquired Immune Deficiency Syndrome). TB (Tuberculosis). Polio. Malaria. West Nile Fever. Influenza. These and other infectious diseases are frequently headline news, reminding us that microscopic organisms can have a devastating impact on the quality of the lives of individuals and communities around the world. This chapter will consider the contexts, histories, and causes of infectious diseases – human illnesses caused by viruses, bacteria, parasites, fungi, and other microscopic organisms. It will also examine how disease functions in our global, interconnected world, and the ways in which diseases are caused and affected by social relations between people and societies. The chapter begins with a focus on the history of infectious disease. This section is followed by a discussion of the relationship between infectious disease and globalization that considers how local and global interactions with the environment relate to the ways that diseases emerge, re-emerge, and affect people. This section also looks at the impact of the food industry, urbanization, air travel, and migration on the nature of infection. The chapter then focuses on AIDS as an example of how disease is inextricably linked to patterns of poverty and inequality. The final section examines current challenges in the global fight against infectious disease.

Microbes and Infectious Diseases: A Brief Overview

From the earliest times, humans have affected and been affected by *microbes* – microscopic organisms, including viruses, bacteria, parasites, and fungi, that inhabit every imaginable niche in every ecosystem on the planet, including human communities and human bodies. For the most part, we have managed to live in a state of relative equilibrium with microbes, adapting to their needs and accommodating their adaptations to us. In some cases, we have even developed *symbiotic* relationships. Bacteria in our digestive systems, for example, help us break down foods. In other cases, however, microbes threaten humans, functioning as *pathogens*, or disease-causing agents that enter the host and begin to reproduce, weakening or killing the host in the process. Although this is how we often think of microbes – as potential killers – the most "successful" microbes, in terms of the larger struggle to survive and reproduce, are those that do not kill their hosts. Widespread death tends to occur primarily when a microbe infects a population that has had no prior exposure to it. In these cases, the microbe often kills all except those who are naturally the most resistant to it. Over time, the most susceptible hosts perish, while the survivors develop an enduring immunity. Eventually, the deadliest strains of the microbe die off, resulting in a relative balance or tolerance

microbes Microscopic organisms, including viruses, bacteria, parasites, and fungi.

symbiotic Refers to a relationship in which two dissimilar organisms rely upon each other for mutual gain.

pathogen A disease-causing organism, such as a bacteria, virus, parasite, or fungus.

between people and microbes. Although it may at first seem paradoxical, this process reveals that the more exposure a community has to disease, the less destructive are its *epidemics*.[2] Conversely, biologically naive populations with little exposure to disease, and thus no immunity, are more likely to be devastated by disease outbreaks.

> **epidemic** A disease outbreak affecting many individuals in a community or a population simultaneously.

History of infectious disease

Recent analyses of human DNA show the rich history of our biological interactions with a myriad of pathogens. The human genome includes genetic markers for a range of diseases that our ancient ancestors survived, some of which we still suffer from, including forms of tuberculosis. It also shows that we have genetic material that may make us more or less susceptible to some infectious diseases.[3] One example that scientists speculate may date back to our earliest origins in Africa is the gene trait for sickle-cell red blood cells, which can protect people from the malaria parasite.[4]

The earliest hunting and gathering societies – the foragers – probably lived with fairly constant levels of *endemic diseases.* Most of these societies were isolated enclaves, separate from other societies, which contributed to a state of equilibrium between people and microorganisms. Although diseases existed in these enclaves, hunting-gathering populations were too sparse and mobile to support acute diseases such as smallpox, measles, chickenpox, and other diseases that produce long-lasting immunities. Those kinds of diseases would have burnt themselves out by killing or *immunizing* all available hosts. So although living conditions may not have been ideal in these earliest of foraging societies, they also were not in a state of crisis brought about by disease epidemics.[5]

> **endemic disease** Diseases that persist in a specific place for a given population year-round at fairly constant rates.
>
> **immunize/immunization**
> The process/procedure of rendering a subject immune or resistant to a specific disease. Although the term is sometimes used interchangeably with vaccination and inoculation, the act of inoculation may not always successfully render a subject immune.

Disease and domestication

The emergence of agriculture and *domestication* had profound effects on human communities. First, they significantly increased food supplies, making them more consistent and predictable. Second, they allowed people to settle in one place and invest time and effort in building a community. Third, they provided for a larger and rapidly increasing population. However, the very strides humans made in terms of land settlement, food production, science and industry, and trade and travel also allowed for conditions to emerge that could potentially foster catastrophe.[6] A new reliance on a limited number of domesticated food sources, for example, increased the potential for famine. Domestication also dramatically altered human relationships with animals and the environment, bringing the population into closer contact with pathogens to which they had not previously been exposed.

> **domestication** The controlled selection and protected development of naturally occurring plant and animal species. Through the domestication process, wild animals become accustomed to living in the company of and/or laboring for human beings. As a result of human control for multiple generations, the behavior, life cycle, and/or physiology of domesticated animals are altered from their wild state.

As people settled down to undertake farming and as populations grew, humans intensified their interactions with potentially pathogenic microbes and parasites. Farming took people into new ecosystems – forests, river flood plains, and grasslands – where they encountered a range of disease-carrying organisms. Additionally, as farmers cleared the land for agriculture, they sometimes inadvertently exacerbated the impact of the disease vectors they encountered by creating breeding grounds for them to flourish. For example, irrigation systems created pools and canals of water, providing a welcome environment for mosquitoes – vectors of malaria, yellow fever, and filariasis (an infection of filarial worms, which can cause elephantiasis) – to rapidly reproduce. Even today, various farming techniques, such as the environmentally damaging slash and burn agriculture in the Amazon forest, create disease and vector breeding grounds in abundance. (For more on this topic, please see chapter 5.)

zoonotic/zoonosis   An animal disease that can be transmitted to humans.

social animals   Animals that live in close physical contact with other animals in large groups.

crowd diseases   Diseases, such as typhus, tuberculosis, and smallpox, that tend to develop in situations of overcrowding and poor sanitation.

Silk Road   Ancient trade route linking Rome and China. The 4,000-mile route started at Sian, followed the Great Wall of China to the northwest, bypassed the Takla Makan Desert, climbed the Pamirs, crossed Afghanistan, and went on to the Levant, where merchandise was then shipped across the Mediterranean Sea.

Success with farming also brought disease literally into the home. When storing surplus food in the structures where they lived, humans unwittingly invited in rodents and the potentially pathogenic parasites that these animals host. This more intimate living arrangement significantly increased the risk that infectious diseases affecting animals would evolve to become *zoonotic*, or transmissible to humans. So too did the domestication of *social animals*. Cattle, pigs, poultry, cats, dogs, sheep, goats, and horses were among the earliest social animals that humans brought into the domestic sphere, thus increasing the possibility that animal diseases would adapt and become ours as well. Many highly contagious *crowd diseases*, which tend to develop in situations of overcrowding and poor sanitation, likely made the jump from domesticated animals, including smallpox from cows, measles from sheep, cattle, and goats, influenza from poultry, and tuberculosis from cattle. Crowd diseases, which are among the oldest established infections that humans have endured, emerged in the Old World centers of Mesopotamian civilization (the region now occupied by modern Iraq, eastern Syria, and southeastern Turkey) and India, where settled agricultural and pastoral societies developed. Later, with the advent of long-distance commerce along the shipping and camel caravan routes of the ancient *Silk Road*, they exploded into the Roman world and China. These infections, which would also later take a ferocious toll on people in Africa and the Americas, have now become endemic on a global scale.

One of the primary factors fostering the increase in crowd diseases was the emergence of urban centers. Cities set the stage for major epidemics, becoming, in the words of British biochemist John Cairns, the "graveyards of mankind."[7] Beginning around 4000 BCE in places such as Mesopotamia and Egypt, people started to create concentrated urban centers. These cities were sustained by a constant influx of people, trade items, food surpluses, and animal products, which constantly replenished possible sources of infection. Moreover, specific developments in these urban centers provided ideal environments for disease to flourish. For example, people created public places where they could congregate, coming into close contact with each other socially and sexually; they butchered meat and prepared and sold food in common places; they defecated and urinated into the water sources they used for drinking and bathing; they generated vast amounts of garbage, which provided food sources and breeding grounds for parasites and disease carriers such as rats; and they created small pools and dark, sheltered havens where mosquitoes could hide and breed.

Epidemics and pandemics

As the expansion of human populations and urban centers accelerated, so too did the incidence and virulence of new epidemics. The principal means by which epidemics took hold of populations that had little or no tolerance for new diseases were war and long-distance trade. The people of Rome, the Middle East, India, and China all exchanged and suffered from a range of epidemic infectious diseases such as smallpox and measles, largely through trade connections. Then, between 1200 and 1500, it is likely that both the Mongol hordes and long-distance trade and travel across the *steppe* between China and Europe brought about devastating epidemics of *plague*, with major outbreaks occurring periodically from the mid-1300s until the mid-1600s. Bubonic plague, or the Black Death, was caused by the bacillus *Yersinia pestis*, a rodent disease transmitted to humans by fleas. As rats from the steppe (where plague is *enzootic* in various populations of rodents) joined humans in the more hospitable and food-rich farming and urban areas of China and Europe, they brought with them this devastating and terrifying disease. *Mortality* from the plague most commonly ranged from 30 to 50 percent in both Europe and the Middle East.[8] The massive demographic impact of the plague – with up to a third of the population of parts of Europe killed – helped limit the further spread of the disease, as too few people were left who could harbor and aid in its transmission. In some cases, such as in London in 1665, it took the combined effect of massive mortality and a raging fire to stifle the rampaging plague. Over time, there were increasing numbers of epidemics and infections, but the rates of mortality declined, suggesting that, overall, people in Europe were slowly developing their immunities.[9]

steppe   The belt of grassland extending over 5,000 miles, from Hungary in the west through Ukraine and Central Asia to Manchuria in the east.

plague   Infectious fever caused by the bacillus *Yersinia pestis*, a bacterium transmitted from rodents to humans by the bite of infected fleas. Plague was responsible for some of the most devastating epidemics in history, including the Black Death in the fourteenth century, which killed as many as one-third of Europe's population.

enzootic disease   Disease affecting or peculiar to animals of a specific geographic area.

mortality   The relative frequency of deaths in a defined population during a specified interval of time.

As European imperialists expanded their trade routes and territories into Africa from the early sixteenth century through the twentieth century, they encountered a completely new range of virulent infectious diseases. These included mosquito-borne diseases, such as malaria (one of the world's leading killers), dengue, and yellow fever, and parasitic diseases caused by various worms. While many Africans had developed immunities to these pathogens, Europeans died in alarming numbers. So high were the rates of mortality that terrified Europeans referred to Africa as the "white man's grave." In exchange, whites brought the equally devastating diseases of syphilis, tuberculosis, and smallpox. In the period of early contact and conquest, many indigenous peoples, such as the San of southern Africa, died in legions from smallpox, while other communicable infections, such as tuberculosis, spread and killed more slowly.

From the late 1500s on, the dramatically increased mobility of people and the infections they carried intensified the spread and severity of epidemics around the world. As Europeans ventured into the Caribbean and the Americas, they brought with them infections with which the local populations had no prior experience, and therefore no immunity. Although forms of tuberculosis, typhus, pneumonia, and various bacteria-based illnesses did afflict Native Americans prior to the arrival of Europeans, the new imports of crowd diseases, including influenza, smallpox, and measles, had a devastating and terrifying effect on them. Similarly, malaria and yellow fever were probably brought to the Americas by European travelers through the accidental importation of the mosquitoes that carry them.[10] These diseases overwhelmed the local peoples, some to the point of extinction. The population of Hispaniola upon Columbus's arrival in 1492, for example, was approximately eight million people. Twenty years later, the island natives had vanished, a casualty of both disease and violence.[11] Contact with Europeans was so devastating to the health and prosperity of native peoples that Europeans were sometimes explicitly paired with disease in native lore. The Kiowa Indians of North America, for example, tell a story about the arrival of a stranger dressed like a missionary in a black suit and tall hat. When asked who he is by Saynday, the tribe's mythic hero, the stranger responds:

> I'm smallpox. . . . I come from far away, across the Eastern Ocean. I am one with the white men – they are my people as the Kiowas are yours. Sometimes I travel ahead of them, and sometimes I lurk behind. But I am always their companion and you will find me in their camps and in their houses. . . . I bring death. My breath causes children to wither like young plants in the Spring snow. I bring destruction. No matter how beautiful a woman is, once she has looked at me, she becomes as ugly as death. And to men I bring not death alone but the destruction of their children and the blighting of their wives. The strongest warriors go down before me. No people who have looked at me will ever be the same.[12]

The Europeans did bring devastating diseases to native populations, but it is also important to remember that the epidemics that followed Western contact emerged in the context of broader social, political, economic, and environmental upheavals. The conquest and forcible implantation of the European political economy on the Americas had far-reaching and severely disruptive effects. Some local populations near the coast were struck by disease prior to the wars of conquest, while others further inland may have become infected after conquest. In both cases, the rates of mortality and people's responses to epidemics were affected by war and colonialization. Mounting deaths, social dislocation, loss of food stores, and the collapse of governments all increased the likelihood of infections spreading and prevented indigenous peoples from caring for the sick. As with later epidemics, especially in the developing world, social and economic vulnerability greatly exacerbated the impact of epidemics. Over time, however, survivors and their descendants developed resistance to the new diseases. Some indigenous peoples eventually were able to live through childhood infections with progressively fewer ill effects. In other communities, however, the importation of enslaved Africans contributed to the decimation of the remaining native populations. Confronted not only by European diseases but also those from Africa, some native populations did not emerge from this intensified pathogenic assault.[13]

Similar patterns of large-scale deaths of indigenous peoples from infectious disease occurred in other regions of the world where indigenous populations had no previous experience with Old World disease pools. Around the Pacific Ocean, European travelers and colonizers brought tuberculosis and venereal diseases to the Aborigines of Australia, the Maoris of New Zealand, and the Hawaiians. Many of these peoples saw their populations drop by 60–90 percent as a result of the new epidemics. The population of the Hawaiian islands upon Captain James Cook's arrival in 1778, for example, was likely around 800,000, a figure which was reduced to a mere 40,000 a century later due to the introduction of diseases such as syphilis, influenza, and tuberculosis.[14] As with indigenous people elsewhere, those who survived developed immunities, but their drastically reduced numbers and their marginalization by mainstream societies put them at greater risk for additional health problems.[15]

Other cultural practices and material developments have played major roles in the incidence of epidemics as well. The Industrial Revolution led to increases in both the availability of food and the size of the population, and better nutrition helped people develop antibodies to fight infection. Despite these advances, the Industrial Revolution also provided for two important disease catalysts. First, new inventions provided for more rapid and far-reaching transportation in the form of steamships and trains. Second, increased demands for agricultural commodities and potential new markets fueled new connections around the globe through imperial conquest. Europeans ventured into new ecological zones in their tropical colonies with greater frequency and so were exposed to additional new pathogens. They also transported these pathogens back to the metropolitan centers with greater ease.

As with later advances in transportation, shorter travel time with steamships and trains meant it was more likely that host humans and their pathogens would survive to transmit diseases to the urban centers of Europe. As more people crowded into cities around the world, congestion, urban squalor, poverty, and inadequate sanitation and public health measures all contributed to epidemics of smallpox and cholera. Although the preponderance of infectious diseases typically afflicted the poor, some epidemics threatened entire societies. Such was the case with a major cholera epidemic that emerged in the British colony of India in the early 1800s and then spread back to Britain. Cholera produces potentially lethal secretory diarrhea and is spread via water supplies contaminated with human waste. It causes severe dehydration and leads to death in approximately 50 percent of those infected (mortality rates are more than 75 percent for infants and the elderly). In 1824, it took hold in the bustling market cities of India and then spread, traveling along the lines of commerce through the Middle East and Europe to the major cities of Britain by 1834. The threat posed by that cholera epidemic around the world was so severe that it prompted the first major coordinated efforts at public health, including the provision of sanitation systems and cleaner drinking water in a number of cities in Europe and elsewhere.[16]

Napoleonic Wars   A series of global conflicts fought during Napoleon Bonaparte's rule over France from 1799 to 1815.

Crimean War   War fought from October 1853 to February 1856 mainly on the Crimean Peninsula between the Russians and the British, French, and Ottoman Turkish, with support, from January 1855, from the army of Sardinia-Piedmont.

South African War   Also called the Boer War, or the Anglo-Boer War (October 11, 1899–May 31, 1902). The war was fought between Great Britain and the two Boer (Afrikaner) republics: the South African Republic (Transvaal) and the Orange Free State.

pandemic   A disease outbreak affecting many people in many different regions around the world.

While industrialization and colonialism intensified the interactions between people and pathogens, warfare also created new paths along which infection could travel. During the *Napoleonic Wars* (1799–1815), more men died of diseases, especially typhus, than from battle. In the *Crimean War* (1853–6) as well as in the *South African War* (1899–1902), more soldiers and civilians died of diseases such as dysentery than from the fighting.[17] Noncombatants, moreover, faced markedly increased risks of infection as their societies were disrupted, their food supplies were destroyed, and their ability to care for each other was undermined.

The end of World War I in 1918 saw the emergence of a strain of influenza (flu), unprecedented in its virulence, that infected soldiers and civilians alike. The new global nature of warfare and the strains it placed on societies contributed to the creation of a worldwide *pandemic* of the so called "Spanish flu," as infected soldiers returned to their homes in the far reaches of the planet. Within months, millions of people who had no previous exposure to the flu succumbed to the particularly deadly strain. It was originally estimated that the pandemic claimed more than 20 million lives, but historians and demographers arrived at these figures in the 1920s before they had taken into account the records of Latin America, Africa, and Asia.[18] Recent estimates suggest that as many as 50 million people may have died of this deadly flu – about 2 percent of the global population.[19] More than 550,000 people died in the United States alone – 10 times the number of American deaths that occurred during battle in World War I. In places where the flu had rarely or never reached prior to the pandemic, the death tolls were even higher. In Western Samoa during the last two months of 1918, for example, 7,542 out of a population of 38,302 died of the flu. Worldwide, most of the deaths occurred within a six-month period and almost every human population in the world was affected, which has led some to argue that the 1918–19 pandemic was the greatest demographic shock humanity has ever experienced.[20]

The rapid spread and deadly toll of the Spanish flu clearly illustrated that the world was becoming increasingly interconnected, and, as a result, new epidemics could quickly explode into global pandemics. Thankfully, however, subsequent pandemics have thus far been less severe. The "Asian flu," for example, spread to the United States in June 1957, killing about 70,000 Americans.[21] Although the Asian flu and other subsequent flu epidemics have not been as virulent as the so-called Spanish variety, the medical profession has vigilantly watched for a resurgence of that extraordinarily lethal virus as well as struggled to eliminate its milder forms.

Combating disease

In the urban spaces of ancient civilizations, *quarantine* and the prompt disposal of the dead were the most widely used tactics to contain the spread of disease. However, because of the limits of knowledge about the origins and transmission of diseases, the

> **quarantine** Isolation imposed in order to prevent the spread of a disease.

success of these efforts was limited. More importantly, until recently, medical care was in short supply, available primarily to the wealthy. There was, of course, a variety of efficacious herbal remedies available to many people. Diviners and shamans also cared for patients using spiritual treatments. Nevertheless, prior to the mid-nineteenth century, there were few major public health measures in place to combat epidemics of infectious disease.

It was the devastating impact of disease on armies that first prompted organized efforts to contain infection. Initially, better food rations, clean clothing, fumigation for lice and fleas, and, most importantly, provision of clean water supplies and other sanitary measures helped reduce *morbidity* and *mortality* rates among soldiers. Later, the practice of *vaccination*, which had long been used in parts of Asia, started to be used in the West. English physician Edward Jenner developed the practice of vaccination with the cowpox virus in 1798, testing the claim of British dairy farmers that people who were infected with cowpox, a mild disease in humans, became immune to smallpox, a far more serious illness. Jenner collected pus from a cowpox-infected woman and injected it into a boy. Later he injected the boy with smallpox, and the boy did not get sick. Jenner called the procedure vaccination, after the Latin word for cow – *vacca*.[22]

> **morbidity** The incidence or prevalence rate of a disease. Morbidity rates refer to the number of people who have a disease, whereas mortality rates refer to the number of people who have died from it.
>
> **mortality** The relative frequency of deaths in a defined population during a specified interval of time.
>
> **vaccination** The introduction of a mild or "killed" form of a bacterium or virus, or pieces of the pathogen, into a person's body in order to train the immune system to resist infection by the agent.

Despite the success of Jenner's experiment, people were suspicious of the non-intuitive practice of purposefully infecting someone with a disease just in order to prevent further infection. As a result, the technique did not become widely accepted until the 1840s. This delay is illustrative of the types of difficulties that medical professionals face when trying to introduce treatments. Similarly, in London in 1849, another physician, John Snow, showed how a cholera epidemic could be stopped simply by cutting off access to the infected water supply. It would take time, however, before the wider society in Britain and Europe adopted safe water standards. Even today, millions of people still suffer from cholera and other diarrheal diseases because of a simple lack of clean water.

Robert Koch's landmark discoveries of the bacilli for tuberculosis, cholera, and anthrax in the late 1800s contributed to the development and acceptance of a more

germ theory The theory that certain diseases are caused by the invasion of the body by microorganisms. The French chemist and microbiologist Louis Pasteur, the English surgeon Joseph Lister, and the German physician Robert Koch are given much of the credit for the development and acceptance of the theory.

unified *germ theory* of contagion. Following these important medical discoveries, new public health and sanitation measures for combating contagious bacterial infections were rigorously applied in cities around the world. Improved urban housing, sanitation, and especially clean water dramatically curbed the spread of disease, as did the provision of basic health care to more people. Although these public health measures were effective and many millions were spared because of them, they were not able to eradicate infectious diseases altogether. One of the reasons for this is that pathogens continue to evolve, making it impossible for humans to wipe out disease once and for all. Moreover, social, economic, and political conditions continue to affect people's experience of disease, including diseases for which there may be cures. For example, although the incidence of tuberculosis (the most deadly disease of the nineteenth century) showed a remarkable decline in US cities by the end of the 1800s, tuberculosis raged on among the black population of South Africa despite the availability of newly discovered antibiotics. A cure existed, but the racist Apartheid regime relegated black South Africans to segregated urban townships where they were without access to proper treatment.[23]

By the turn of the twentieth century, many in the medical establishment realized that dealing with diseases would require coordinated global efforts. The International Office of Public Hygiene, established in Paris in 1909, helped pave the way for later international medical organizations such as the United Nations World Health Organization (WHO), the more recent Centers for Disease Control in the US (CDC), and a range of committed medical NGOs such as Doctors Without Borders (Médecins Sans Frontières). These organizations continue to monitor and combat disease, saving lives around the world. The twentieth century also saw the development of vaccines for a host of deadly infections, including smallpox, typhoid, diphtheria, polio, and cholera. Walter Reed, the US Army Medical Corps, and a legion of British doctors studying tropical diseases in colonial Africa and Asia made significant strides in combating malaria and yellow fever through mosquito control.

New drugs and chemicals were also developed in the twentieth century to attack pathogens in the environment and in the body. From the 1940s, antibiotics were used widely, perhaps even indiscriminately, to eradicate bacterial infections in people, and DDT (*dichlorodiphenyl trichloroethane*) was sprayed over vast stretches of the earth to eradicate mosquitoes. Both penicillin and DDT worked very effectively, for a time. In both cases, however, there were unforeseen consequences of their use. Misuses of antibiotics resulted in infecting organisms developing antibiotic resistance (see table 7.1). DDT was so toxic that it killed just about everything in its path. Because it did not break down, it remained in the water and the environment, ultimately making its way into the bodies of people and animals. The 1962 publication of *Silent Spring* by American biologist Rachel Carson, which alleged that DDT caused cancer and harmed bird reproduction by thinning egg shells, resulted in a large public outcry against DDT. By the 1970s, many countries, including the

Table 7.1 Examples of Drug-Resistant Infectious Agents and Percentage of Infections that are Drug-Resistant by Country or Region[24]

Pathogen	Drug	Country/Region	Percentage of Drug-Resistant Infections
Streptococcus pneumoniae	Penicillin	United States	10–35
		Asia, Chile, Spain,	20
		Hungary	58
Staphylococcus aureus	Methicillin multidrug	United States	32
		Japan	60
Mycobacterium tuberculosis	Any drug	United States	13
	Any drug	New York City	16
	Any drug	Eastern Europe	20
Plasmodium falciparum (malaria)	Chloroquine	Kenya	65
		Ghana	45
	Mephloquine	Zimbabwe	59
		Burkina Faso	17
		Thailand	45
Shigella dysenteride	Multidrug	Burundi, Rwanda	100

US, had banned its use. Controversy emerged, however, around the effects of this decision, since DDT is an effective way of killing disease vectors, such as mosquitoes. By 2006, the anti-DDT climate had begun to shift, as evidenced by WHO's advocacy for the careful, targeted use of DDT in malaria control programs.[25]

Researching to Learn *Investigating World Health and Disease Issues*

Organizations

American Society for Microbiology (ASM)

The ASM is the world's largest scientific society of individuals interested in the microbiological sciences. The Society's mission is to advance microbiological sciences through the pursuit of scientific knowledge and dissemination of the results of fundamental and applied research. Microbiology-related reports and publications are searchable on ASM's website.
www.asm.org/

Center for Biosecurity

The Center for Biosecurity is an independent, nonprofit organization of the University of Pittsburgh Medical Center. The Center works to affect policy and practice in ways that lessen the illness, death, and civil disruption that would follow large-scale epidemics, whether they occur

naturally or result from the use of a biological weapon.
www.upmc-biosecurity.org/

Centers for Disease Control and Prevention (CDC)

The CDC is one of the 13 major operating components of the Department of Health and Human Services (HHS), which is the principal agency in the US government for protecting the health and safety of Americans and for providing essential human services. The CDC website provides users with access to news, research publications, and statistics.
www.cdc.gov/

Infectious Diseases Society of America (IDSA)

IDSA represents physicians, scientists, and other health care professionals who specialize in infectious diseases. IDSA's purpose is to improve the health of individuals, communities, and society

by promoting excellence in patient care, education, research, public health, and prevention relating to infectious diseases. The IDSA website contains a variety of searchable resources and publications for researchers interested in health and disease related topics.
http://www.idsociety.org/

National Foundation for Infectious Diseases (NFID)
NFID is dedicated to educating the public and healthcare professionals about the causes, treatment, and prevention of infectious diseases.
www.nfid.org

The National Institute of Allergy and Infectious Diseases (NIAID)
NIAID conducts and supports basic and applied research to better understand, treat, and ultimately prevent infectious, immunologic, and allergic diseases. For more than 50 years, NIAID research has led to new therapies, vaccines, diagnostic tests, and other technologies that have improved the health of millions of people in the United States and around the world.
www3.niaid.nih.gov/

National Institutes of Health (NIH)
The NIH, a part of the US Department of Health and Human Services, is the primary Federal agency for conducting and supporting medical research. Helping to lead the way toward important medical discoveries that improve people's health and save lives, NIH scientists investigate ways to prevent disease as well as the causes, treatments, and cures for common and rare diseases.
www.nih.gov

Online Research Portals

Centers for Disease Control and Prevention
The CDC publishes the *Emerging Infectious Diseases Journal, Preventing Chronic Disease Journal,* Morbidity and Mortality Weekly Reports, and hundreds of reports and reference resources.
www.cdc.gov/

PubMed
Provides access to more than 12 million references from 4,600 biomedical journals. Many of these references link to abstracts and in some cases, the full text of articles.
www.pubmed.gov

MedlinePlus
MedlinePlus will direct you to information to help answer health questions. MedlinePlus brings together authoritative information from the National Library of Medicine (NLM), the National Institutes of Health (NIH), and other government agencies and health-related organizations. Preformulated MEDLINE searches are included in MedlinePlus and give easy access to medical journal articles. MedlinePlus also has extensive information about drugs, an illustrated medical encyclopedia, interactive patient tutorials, and latest health news.
http://medlineplus.gov/

National Institute of Allergy and Infectious Diseases (NIAID) Online Research
Click "Research by Topic" to find information about various global health issues and emerging and reemerging diseases.
www3.niaid.nih.gov/research/

National Library of Medicine (NLM) Gateway
Allows you to search across multiple resources and databases, including Medline, the NLM catalog, full text biomedical books, and others.
http://gateway.nlm.nih.gov/gw/Cmd

Statistical Sources

National Center for Health Statistics
This site provides statistics in a variety of categories, including Health Data for All Ages; Health Care in America: Trends in Utilization; Classification of Diseases and Functioning and Disability; Birth, Injury, and Death Statistics, surveys, reports, etc.
www.cdc.gov/nchs/

WHO Global Burden of Disease (GBD) Statistics
The WHO GBD project draws on a wide range of data sources to develop internally consistent estimates of incidence, health state prevalence, severity and duration, and mortality for more than 130 major causes, for WHO member states, and for sub-regions of the world, for the years 2000 and beyond. Find Death and Disability Adjusted Life Years (DALY) estimates, projections of mortality and burden of disease estimates, and health and life expectancy data.
www.who.int/healthinfo/bod/en/index.html

Infectious Disease and Globalization:
The Current Picture

In the years following World War II, advances in controlling and sometimes eradicating infectious diseases led many optimistically to predict that by the advent of the twenty-first century, infectious diseases would no longer pose a major threat to human health. This has not been the case, however, as at least 20 well-known infectious diseases have re-emerged since the 1970s, including tuberculosis, malaria, and cholera. Additionally, 30 previously unknown and currently incurable diseases have emerged, including HIV, Ebola, hepatitis C, and the Nipah virus (See table 7.2). Currently, diseases that account for the most deaths worldwide include acute lower respiratory tract infections, HIV/AIDS, diarrheal diseases, tuberculosis, and malaria.[26] Every year, about 8.8 million people develop TB and 1.7 million die of it. Unless efforts to control the disease become more successful, tuberculosis will claim more than 35 million lives between the years 2000 and 2020. Malaria takes approximately 3,000 lives a day, for a total of more than one million a year. In sub-Saharan Africa, AIDS is deadlier than war; while war killed 308,000 people in Africa in 1998, AIDS killed more than two million. Today, AIDS claims approximately three million lives a year (see table 7.3). It is estimated that in the absence of a cure, by 2020, AIDS will have caused more deaths than any other disease in history.[27]

Table 7.2 Emergent Diseases Identified Since 1973[28]

Year	Microbe	Disease
1973	Rotavirus virus	Infantile diarrhea
1977	Ebola virus	Acute hemorrhagic fever
1977	Legionella pneumophila bacterium	Legionnaires' disease
1980	Human T-lymphotrophic virus I (HTLV 1)	T-cell lymphoma/leukemia
1981	Toxin-producing Staphylococcus aureus bacterium	Toxic shock syndrome
1982	Escherichia coli bacterium	Hemorrhagic colitis
1982	Borrelia burgdorferi bacterium	Lyme disease
1983	Human Immuno-Deficiency virus (HIV)	Acquired Immuno-Deficiency Syndrome (AIDS)
1983	Helicobacter pylori bacterium	Peptic ulcer disease
1989	Hepatitis C virus	Parentally transmitted non-A, non-B liver infection
1993	Hantavirus virus	Adult respiratory distress syndrome
1994	Cryptosporidium protozoa	Enteric disease
1996	nvCJD prion	Creutzfeldt-Jakob disease
1997	HVN1 virus	Influenza
1999	Nipah virus	Severe encephalitis
2003	SARS-associated coronavirus (SARS-CoV).	Severe viral respiratory illness

Table 7.3   HIV/AIDS, Tuberculosis, and Malaria – The Basic Facts, 2000[29]

Disease	Deaths Per Year	New Cases Per Year	Percentage in Developing Countries
HIV/AIDS	3 million	5.3 million	92%
Tuberculosis	1.9 million	8.8 million	84%
Malaria	More than 1 million	300 million	Nearly 100%

Although the world has not experienced another flu pandemic like the deadly one that followed World War I, its milder forms remain pervasive and deadly. According to the CDC, every year in the United States, on average:

- 5–20 percent of the population gets the flu;
- more than 200,000 people are hospitalized from flu complications; and
- about 36,000 people die from flu.[30]

Historical patterns indicate that influenza pandemics with death tolls that dwarf these average yearly figures can be expected to occur approximately three to four times each century. Although the WHO warns that the occurrence of influenza pandemics is unpredictable, experts agree that another influenza pandemic is inevitable and possibly close at hand. Dr Samlee Plianbangchang, Regional Director for the WHO's Southeast Asia Region says: "The threat of a pandemic is very real. It is no longer a question of 'if' it will occur. It is now only a question of 'when?' When this happens, human casualties could be in the order of millions, and severe economic losses would result."[31]

In 2009, a new influenza strain emerged that was initially referred to as "swine flu" because early laboratory reports indicated that many of the virus's genes were similar to flu viruses that affect pig populations. Further analysis revealed, however, that the 2009 H1N1 virus contained genes from viruses that affect birds and people as well as pigs.[32] By June 2009, the WHO announced that a H1N1 pandemic was underway, and by October 2009, more than 440,000 confirmed cases and 5,700 deaths had been reported to WHO.[33] Although children and most adults under the age of 60 had no pre-existing immunity to the new strain, making it potentially very dangerous, the majority of infections in 2009 were mild. Experts warn, however, that the virulence of the virus could change as it mutates.

Scientists and public health experts have also been carefully monitoring Avian flu strains in an effort to prepare for and hopefully minimize the effects of another possible pandemic. Despite these efforts, flu viruses are constantly changing, frustrating scientists' attempts to create vaccines that can successfully combat them for more than a few years at a time. The process through which viruses change slightly from year to year is known as *antigenic drift*, while sudden and more substantial changes are called

antigenic drift   The process through which viruses change slightly from year to year.

antigenic shift   Sudden and substantial change, seen only with influenza A viruses, resulting from the recombination of the genomes of two viral strains.

antigenic shifts. When a virus undergoes the more dramatic antigenic shift, people are suddenly exposed to a strain to which they have no built-up immunological defenses. As a result, epidemics and pandemics are more likely to occur.[34] With regard to the threat of avian flu, the virus has already changed significantly. It now meets two of the three prerequisites that are necessary to incite an influenza pandemic. According to the WHO, these prerequisites are:

1   The emergence of a new virus to which all are susceptible.
2   The new virus is able to replicate and cause disease in humans.
3   The new virus can be transmitted efficiently from human-to-human.

Only the last prerequisite remains to be met in avian flu, and it is likely only a matter of time before the virus evolves to allow for efficient and sustained human-to-human transmission. The WHO reports that the virus continues to spread to poultry and wild birds in new areas, further broadening opportunities for human cases to occur. Every time a human catches the flu from an infected bird, the virus is given another opportunity to improve its transmissibility in humans, thereby increasing the possibility that a pandemic will occur.[35]

Despite advances in science and technology, infectious diseases clearly remain and will continue to be a major global health threat. In fact, in the first decade of the twenty-first century, the continual evolution of diseases and the acceleration of the HIV/AIDS pandemic in developing countries have heightened rather than lessened the global impact of infectious diseases. The strength of this impact has also been exacerbated by the widening gap between rich and poorer countries in the availability and quality of health care. The emergence and reemergence of infectious diseases, then, must be understood as a complex process that is influenced by many factors. Positioning microbes as the only cause of disease is inadequate and incomplete, as it ignores the fact that human activities are the most potent factors driving the emergence of disease (see table 7.4). Microbial adaptation and change are certainly important factors that shape disease patterns, influencing emergence, but so too are social, economic, political, climatic, technological, and environmental ones.[36]

Disease and the environment

The human population continues to grow at an astounding, exponential rate, doubling in the last half century to more than six billion people. (For more on population patterns, see chapter 6.) This dramatic expansion is placing increasing pressure on the natural environment and the resources we depend upon to survive. From air and water pollution to the explosive forces of urbanization, we have invaded ecosystems where previously unknown and potentially pathogenic microbes live, and we have created the conditions for infectious diseases to thrive and spread. Although there are many complex and interrelated environmental factors affecting the potential spread of pathogens, including temperature, rainfall, and extreme weather

Table 7.4   Basic Concepts in Disease Emergence[37]

Emergence of infectious diseases is complex.

Infectious diseases are dynamic.

Most new infections are not caused by genuinely new pathogens.

Agents involved in new and reemergent infections cross taxonomic lines to include viruses, bacteria, fungi, protozoa, and helminths.

The concept of the microbe as the cause of disease is inadequate and incomplete.

Human activities are the most potent factors driving disease emergence.

Social, economic, political, climatic, technologic, and environmental factors shape disease patterns and influence emergence.

Understanding and responding to disease emergence require a global perspective, conceptually and geographically.

The current global situation favors disease emergence.

events, human activity is often a key element. For example, air pollution has contributed to global warming, increasing temperatures in various regions where malaria and yellow fever carrying mosquitoes breed. Even this slight increase in average temperatures has significantly increased the geographic range and length of the breeding cycle for mosquitoes in some parts of Africa. In Rwanda, for example, mosquito numbers and incidences of malaria have increased between 300 and 500 percent during the 1980s, in large part because of an overall increase in average temperature.[38] Similarly, higher ocean water temperatures have led to an increase in various toxic algae growths, which can affect seafood and cause food illnesses.

> **schistosomiasis** An infection caused by small, parasitic flatworms and characterized by inflammation of the intestines, bladder, liver, and other organs. Annually affecting approximately 200 million people a year in Africa, Asia, South America, and the Caribbean, it is one of the world's most serious parasitic infections.
>
> **hemorrhagic fever** Any of a group of viral infections, such as Ebola and yellow fever, that occur primarily in tropical climates, are usually transmitted to humans by insects or rodents, and are characterized by high fever, small purple spots, internal bleeding, low blood pressure, and shock.

Direct expansions into and alterations of the natural environment have also increased the potential for pathogen-carrying parasites and viruses to thrive. For example, human engineering to dam rivers and to extend irrigation canals for agriculture has provided ideal new breeding sites for mosquitoes, leading to a dramatic increase in "human-made" malaria. Similarly, new road construction and dam building in tropical Africa and Asia have altered patterns of water flow and provided for an increase in the number of snails that harbor the parasite that causes *schistosomiasis* or bilharzia. In Argentina, the expansion of farming into grassland areas triggered the outbreak of a virus that causes *hemorrhagic fever*. As farmers introduced new plants, such as alfalfa and maize, the resident mouse population soared in response to the new food source and the reduction of natural predators. The mice left huge amounts of droppings containing the virus, and farmers and workers in the agricultural fields were infected in large numbers. A similar pattern developed in Arizona when suburban expansion in the "Four Corners" region of the US

Southwest (an area shared by Arizona, New Mexico, Colorado, and Utah) put people at risk of infection by a form of hantavirus, which are viruses spread primarily by rodents that cause respiratory illness, kidney failure, and other acute symptoms in humans. In May 1993, an unexplained pulmonary illness affected a number of previously healthy young adults. About half of them soon died. Researchers discovered that they had been infected by a form of hantavirus, and later they were able to isolate the principal carrier of the disease – deer mice. The sudden cluster of cases emerged because heavy rainfall in the area led to dramatic increases in plant and animal populations; in fact, there were 10 times more mice in the region in May 1993 than there had been in May 1992, thereby increasing the chances that mice carrying the hantavirus would come into contact with humans.[39]

Perhaps the best-known case of changing land-use patterns affecting the incidence of infectious disease in the US is that of Lyme disease. In Lyme, Connecticut, the expansion of suburban homes into forested zones contributed to the destruction of natural predators, such as wolves and bears. This led to a dramatic increase in the number of deer and mice (the usual hosts for Lyme disease-infected ticks), which in turn led to an increase in ticks. As more and more suburbanites entered the wooded areas, their risk of being bitten by Lyme disease-carrying ticks increased.[40]

The destruction of sensitive ecosystems like rainforests also jeopardizes the possibility of making new drug discoveries. Many drugs now used to prevent and cure infections are derived from discoveries made in nature, especially in rainforests, and often by indigenous people who have long used naturally occurring herbal medicines. An estimated one in four purchases from pharmacies in developed countries contains an active ingredient derived from a tropical forest species.[41] By destroying these fragile ecosystems through logging and land clearance, we risk losing the potential to develop a wide range of infectious disease-fighting agents.

Disease and the food industry

The food industry also affects the evolution and spread of infectious diseases. The world's food supplies have become increasingly industrialized and centralized in an effort to make farming and food-processing more efficient, but doing so has also led to new health threats. Conditions on factory farms are sometimes overcrowded, unsanitary, and thus unsafe for animals and the food products derived from them. For example, the beef supplies for Europe and North America have been threatened by Bovine Spongiform Encephalopathy (BSE or "Mad Cow Disease"). This infection is spread through the use of bad feeding practices – using ground-up cattle parts from infected animals (including the brain and spine) in the feed for other cattle. BSE has been linked to the human form of the disease, Creutzfeldt-Jakob disease, which has killed more than 100 people in Europe.[42] Factory farming has also led to increased use of antibiotics, which contributes to greater microbial resistance to these drugs. Additionally, manure has repeatedly contaminated meat and plant products, causing debilitating and sometimes deadly E.coli infections. In the Fall of 2006, for example, a strain of E.coli known as 0157:H7 caused sickness in 199 people in 26 states who had eaten contaminated spinach. This particularly lethal strain, unknown before 1982, is believed to have evolved into its current form as the result of industrial agricultural feeding practices. Instead of allowing the cattle to graze in the fields on grass, factory farms house cows in feedlots where they are fed grain. Unfortunately, grain-fed cows provide E.coli 0157:H7 with the ideal habitat in which to flourish. In contrast, the bacteria cannot survive long in cattle living on grass.[43]

The reach of the E.coli spinach outbreak also highlights another problem with the current farming and processing system: a centralized food system means that more people will be affected if the food supply is contaminated. The meat, milk, and salad that feed millions in the United States are processed by only a handful of companies, which makes them extremely vulnerable to both intentional and unintentional contamination. Rather than affecting only the local population where the food was grown or processed, food contamination today can have a national and sometimes international impact. According to the Centers for Disease Control and Prevention, The US's food supply yearly sickens 76 million, kills 5,000, and puts more than 300,000 people in the hospital.[44] An intentional contamination of the food supply by terrorists could have even far more widespread and devastating consequences.

Global connections: urbanization, air travel, and migration

In 2005, 3.17 billion people out of the total world population of 6.45 billion lived in urban centers. By the year 2007, half the world's population was living in cities, a historical first. Trend watchers predict that these figures will continue to rise, forecasting that by the year 2030, nearly 5 billion out of 8.1 billion people will live in urban centers. These figures indicate that the populations of cities will grow at almost twice the rate of the total global population. Most of this growth will be concentrated in the developing regions of Asia and Africa. While the developed world's cities in Europe, North America, and Latin America are currently growing at an average rate of .75 percent a year, annual urban growth rates are at 4.58 percent in sub-Saharan Africa and 3.82 percent in Southeast Asia.[45]

megacities Rapidly growing urban areas that have more than 10 million inhabitants.

metacities Agglomerations of several cities, towns, and suburbs that have expanded so that they coalesce into a single, sprawling urban mass of more than 20 million people.

Population growth in the twenty-first century has been and will continue to be accompanied by the increasing size and influence of *megacities* and *metacities*. Megacities are highdensity urban centers with populations of at least 10 million (see table 7.5). Although they are currently home to less than 10 percent of the world's urban population, megacities will likely be the primary locus of future urban growth in developing nations. Trend watchers predict that by the year 2020, there will be 12 megacities in Asia alone, and that all but four of the world's megacities will be in the developing world. Today, Lagos, Nigeria is the fastest growing megacity in the world, expanding at more than 5 percent a year. Like megacities, metacities are urban areas with huge populations, but metacities

Table 7.5 World Megacities 1975, 2000, and (projected) 2015: Population in Millions[46]

1975	2000	2015
Tokyo (19.8)	Tokyo (26.4)	Tokyo (26.4)
New York (15.9)	Mexico City (18.1)	Mumbai (26.1)
Shanghai (11.4)	Mumbai (18.1)	Lagos (23.2)
Mexico City (11.2)	São Paulo (17.8)	Dhaka (21.1)
São Paulo (10)	Shanghai (17)	São Paulo (20.4)
	New York (16.6)	Karachi (19.2)
	Lagos (13.4)	Mexico City (19.2)
	Los Angeles (13.1)	New York (17.4)
	Kolkata (12.9)	Jakarta (17.3)
	Buenos Aires (12.6)	Kolkata (17.3)
	Dhaka (12.3)	Delhi (16.8)
	Karachi (11.8)	Metro Manila (14.8)
	Delhi (11.7)	Shanghai (14.6)
	Jakarta (11)	Los Angeles (14.1)
	Osaka (11)	Buenos Aires (14.1)
	Metro Manila (10.9)	Cairo (13.8)
	Beijing (10.8)	Istanbul (12.5)
	Rio de Janeiro (10.6)	Beijing (12.3)
	Cairo (10.6)	Rio de Janeiro (11.9)
		Osaka (11.0)
		Tianjin (10.7)
		Hyderabad (10.5)
		Bangkok (10.1)

consist of several cities, towns, and suburbs that have expanded so that they coalesce into a single sprawling urban conglomeration of more than 20 million people. Today, Tokyo is the largest metacity in the world, with a population of more than 35 million, a figure that surpasses the population of Canada. Experts predict that by 2020, Mumbai, Delhi, Mexico City, Sao Paulo, New York, Dhaka, Jakarta, and Lagos will all have grown into metacities.[47]

Although cities are often assumed to be centers of wealth and culture that stand in sharp contrast to the difficult conditions characterizing rural life, poverty is increasingly shifting from rural areas to urban regions. Many people who migrate to cities in search of a better life instead find themselves among the nearly one billion residents of the world's slums – squalid and overcrowded urban areas populated by the poor. Approximately one out of every six people on the planet lives in an urban slum.[48] More than 90 percent of the world's slums are located in cities in the developing world. The slums of Mumbai alone are home to more than five million people.[49] Sub-Saharan Africa has the highest slum and urban growth rates, at 4.53 percent and 4.58 percent per year respectively, and in many of its cities, 70 percent of the population live in slums. Slums in sub-Saharan Africa are also the most deprived, with many residents lacking access to water, sanitation, and/or durable housing. Although countries such as Egypt, Thailand, and Tunisia have both reduced slum growth and improved existing slums, the slum problem is increasing so rapidly in other countries that forecasters predict that the global slum population will grow at the rate of 27 million per year between 2000 and 2020.[50]

Rapid urbanization in the form of slum growth creates sprawling venues where poverty and disease are pervasive and difficult to escape. According to UN-Habitat, the one billion people who live in slums around the world are more likely to suffer from hunger and disease and to die earlier than their urban counterparts who do not live in slums.[51] Poor living conditions, including contaminated water supplies and the absence of sewage systems, make slum residents vulnerable to a variety of diseases. In slums like those in Mumbai, 73 percent of the households only have access to public toilets, many of which are health hazards due to overuse and poor maintenance.[52] In Mbare, a neighborhood in Zimbabwe's Harare, up to 1,300 people share one communal toilet consisting of six squatting holes. Because of these types of unsanitary conditions, as many as 1.6 million people living in slums die annually.[53] The young are particularly vulnerable. In sub-Saharan African cities, for example, children living in slums are more likely to die of water-borne and respiratory illnesses than their rural counterparts.[54] Children under the age of 5 living in slums in Rio de Janeiro are three times more likely to die than those living in non-slum areas of the city, while the mortality rate for children under 5 in Cape Town is five times higher than the rate in high-income areas.[55] Pneumonia, diarrhea, malaria, measles, and HIV/AIDS – the five illnesses that cause more than half of childhood deaths – are all pervasive in slums. HIV/AIDS in particular is far more prevalent in slums than in rural areas. In sub-Saharan African countries such as Kenya, Tanzania, and Zambia, the number of city dwellers infected with HIV is nearly double that of rural populations. Women and girls living in slums are a particularly vulnerable population, as poverty forces them to engage in risky sexual behavior.[56]

Disease spreads swiftly in slums, which poses a danger both to the larger city of which the slum is a part as well as to the rest of the world. As a result of the prevalence of air travel, diseases can now rapidly and seemingly randomly criss-cross the globe. In 2005, Airports Council International (ACI) facilities handled 4.874 billion passengers, with Atlanta International Airport alone handling 90,039,280 travelers (see table 7.6).[57] The ease and prevalence of international air travel means that people who live in cities are more closely linked to the developing regions of any other major city around the globe than ever before. As Dr. Gro Harlem Brundtland, Director-General of WHO, has said, "In a globalized world, we all swim in a single microbial sea."[58]

People and the infections they carry tend to travel along the fault lines not only of poverty but also of displacement. In 2005, there were more than 190 million international migrants, comprising approximately 3 percent of the global population. Some of these migrants left home in search of work, while approximately 13,500,000 others were forced to flee their homes as refugees.[59] Because migrants are often poor and without access to health care, they are more likely to carry infections than many

Table 7.6 Passenger Traffic, 2008[60]

Rank	City (Airport)*	Total Passengers**
1	Atlanta GA (ATL)	90,039,280
2	Chicago IL (ORD)	69,353,876
3	London (LHR)	67,056,379
4	Tokyo (HND)	66,754,829
5	Paris (CDG)	60,874,681
6	Los Angeles CA (LAX)	59,497,539
7	Dallas/Fort Worth TX (DFW)	57,093,187
8	Beijing (PEK)	55,937,289
9	Frankfurt (FRA)	53,467,450
10	Denver CO (DEN)	51,245,334
11	Madrid (MAD)	50,824,435
12	Hong Kong (HKG)	47,857,746
13	New York NY (JFK)	47,807,816
14	Amsterdam (AMS)	47,430,019
15	Las Vegas NV (LAS)	43,208,724
16	Houston TX (IAH)	41,709,389
17	Phoenix AZ (PHX)	39,891,193
18	Bangkok (BKK)	38,603,490
19	Singapore (SIN)	37,694,824
20	Dubai (DXB)	37,441,440
21	San Francisco CA (SFO)	37,234,592
22	Orlando FL (MCO)	35,660,742
23	Newark NJ (EWR)	35,360,848
24	Detroit MI (DTW)	35,135,828
25	Rome (FCO)	35,132,224
26	Charlotte NC (CLT)	34,739,020
27	Munich (MUC)	34,530,593
28	London (LGW)	34,214,740
29	Miami FL (MIA)	34,063,531
30	Minneapolis MN (MSP)	34,056,443

* Airports participating in the ACI annual traffic statistics collection.
** Total passengers enplaned and deplaned, passengers in transit counted once.

other segments of the population. Moreover, many are forced to live in refugee camps, places that are notorious reservoirs of infection.

In Focus: AIDS and Globalization

The crisis of the current AIDS pandemic reflects the patterns of inequality and globalization that influence the spread of infectious diseases. AIDS, which develops from HIV (Human Immunodeficiency Virus), causes a debilitating and fatal suppression of the body's immune system, leaving the sufferer highly susceptible to a broad range of lethal illnesses, especially infectious diseases such as tuberculosis. It is transmitted primarily through unprotected penetrative sex with an infected partner, injections or transfusions of contaminated blood, and sharing needles with someone who is infected. It can also be transmitted from mother to child during pregnancy, at birth, or through breastfeeding.[61] Unless treated by an expensive and complicated regime of anti-retroviral drugs, it kills within a few short years. AIDS probably emerged from the central African rainforest, crossing from primates to humans sometime after World War II. Thereafter, it smoldered, slowly, until the intensification of trade, travel, and poverty ignited an explosive pandemic in the 1980s. As Paul Farmer has argued, AIDS followed the contours of the international socioeconomic order, and it traveled along the fault lines of poverty and inequality.[62]

In its early stages, the AIDS pandemic was stigmatized as a localized infection primarily afflicting gay men and Haitians. These were inaccurate views, however, often born of ignorance and fear. There are currently more than 39 million people infected with AIDS, the vast majority of whom are heterosexual. Although AIDS is a preventable disease, more than 30 million people have likely died of it. Of the 2.9 million people who died of AIDS in 2006, 2.1 million (or 72 percent) were from Africa.[63] The pandemic is particularly devastating for developing societies. It wipes out households, renders millions of children orphans, and reduces life expectancy by 20–30 years in some countries. Africa and Southeast Asia are currently the worst affected.

Increasingly, AIDS is also a disease of young women. In Africa, 59 percent of people infected are women, and young women between 15 and 25 years are three to five times more likely to become infected than their male counterparts.[64] This statistic is the result, in large part, of gender inequity, illustrating that AIDS, like many diseases, also strikes along the lines of inequality. Women are particularly susceptible because of their compromised social and economic status in many societies. For example, women are sometimes placed in financially and socially compromised positions where they cannot make independent decisions about their lifestyle, sexual practices, and work. Avoiding unprotected sex is critical, since it poses the greatest risk of infection, but it can be difficult for women to do so if they are expected or forced to have unprotected sex with, for example, promiscuous husbands upon whom they depend financially. Additionally, women withstand the worst of the stigma associated with AIDS, and many are accused of spreading the disease, even though the reality is that men tend to have more sexual partners than women, thereby increasing their risk of exposure and of infecting others.[65]

Although patterns of sexual behavior are an important and obvious component in the spread of AIDS, societal disruptions often set the context for the transmission of HIV/AIDS. In southern Africa, for example, civil wars have torn apart many communities, inciting men to leave their homes as soldiers or refugees, and subsequently to take new sexual partners. In other cases, particularly in conflict zones, rape is prevalent. The regional economy also has a profound impact on the spread of AIDS. Southern Africa has long been a place where people have been forced into migrant labor. From the early days of mining in South Africa to the recent explosion of trucking commerce throughout the region, African men and women have been driven out from their homes in search of work, often having to leave partners and family behind. This has disposed them to take up new partners or engage in the sex trade. Not surprisingly, the rates of HIV infection for sex workers, soldiers housed in same-sex barracks, and long-distance truckers and other migrants are very high. Similar patterns hold true for AIDS on the global dimension. The international search for work by migrant laborers, and the displacement of refugees by conflict has also increased the spread of AIDS and other infections. Although this disease has the potential to affect anyone, it is spreading most intensively among people in compromised situations who are least able to cope with it.

The Global Fight against Infectious Disease: Current Challenges

The AIDS crisis highlights some of the challenges involved in fighting infectious disease on a global scale. A patient's overall health status and level of nutrition, both of which are likely to be substandard for the poor in developing countries, are important for withstanding the effects of AIDS and AIDS-related secondary infections. Since AIDS makes people vulnerable to almost any type of infection, it also requires a broad range of treatments. But the poor cannot normally afford the high price of drug treatments for either AIDS or for the secondary infections associated with it. In South Africa, for example, which has one of the world's highest rates of HIV/AIDS, with more than 30 percent of the population likely infected, expensive drug treatments, some costing $10,000 or more a year, have been out of reach for most South Africans. In an unfortunate twist Thabo Mbeki, when President of South Africa, further discouraged the use of AIDS drugs by invoking fears that the West was using Africans as "guinea pigs" for drug regimens. The result has been a terrible delay on the part of both Western pharmaceutical companies and the South African government in making life-sustaining drugs available.

There is also a variety of other problems that prevent drugs from reaching the communities and people who need them. Although pharmaceutical companies are constantly developing new drugs, this process takes a long time and is very costly. As a result, companies guard their patents, arguing that the cost of developing the drugs requires that they recover their investment through high drug prices and bans on generic products. But because of these high prices and bans, the majority of the world's poor have no access to pharmaceuticals that could help them. For example, only after significant pressure from NGOs in South Africa and the West did drug companies relax their patents on AIDS drug treatments, allowing South African firms to produce and sell generic versions at a fraction of the cost.[66] There is also little financial incentive for pharmaceutical companies to develop drug treatments for the many diseases that predominantly affect the world's poor. Of 1,393 new drugs developed between 1975 and 1999, a mere 13 (less than 1 percent) were for treating tropical diseases that afflict the poorest countries.[67] Not only does this raise questions about the ethics of health care in the global community, it also allows infectious diseases to persist in vulnerable populations, which might in turn allow them to burst forth at a later date onto the world stage.

Global public health efforts have also been set back by violent conflicts. Armed conflict makes people more vulnerable to infectious diseases because it often leads to the breakdown of civil society, undermining a country's ability to provide sound health care or to mount public health initiatives. Such was the case in Nigeria, where local Islamic authorities in the north of the country foiled efforts to institute a polio vaccination program. Globally, polio was close to being eradicated, remaining in only six African countries. However, Nigerian Islamic leaders claimed that the vaccinations were intended to poison people and that they were part of an effort by Christians and the West to attack them. Underlying this posturing was a long-standing conflict between northern Nigeria and the rest of the country. Nevertheless, the full implementation of the vaccination program in Nigeria was delayed, which led to the emergence of new cases of polio in 17 African states.[68]

Another challenge in the global fight against infectious disease is that most developing countries do not have the funds to support broad public health initiatives. Unequal access to health care yields unequal health status. As such, people in countries without adequate health care are less healthy and less likely to survive infections than those who can afford it. In a vicious cycle, disease both creates and is a product of poverty. Overall, the clear pattern is that many millions of poor people in developed and developing countries alike suffer disproportionately from infectious disease, and as such, they pose a risk to the entire global community.

Conclusion

The history of infectious disease reveals that disease emergence is the product of complex contexts and processes and therefore cannot simply be understood as the result of microbial infections. Rather, human activities are among the most powerful factors driving disease emergence. Any thorough analysis of how disease functions in a global context must examine the social, economic, political, climatic, technologic, and environmental factors that shape disease patterns and influence the emergence and reemergence of diseases. Recent medical and technological advances have been instrumental in the fight against disease, but the risks and dangers have also increased, as contemporary urbanization, air travel, and migration trends, among others, make us more connected than ever before both to each other and to the diseases we carry. Although it is unlikely that we will ever completely win the fight against infectious disease, we probably can significantly reduce both the incidence of disease and its debilitating impacts. Even the most advanced medical and technological innovations will not make this goal a reality, however, if we fail to address the underlying problems of poverty and inequality that are at the core of this global problem.

Notes

1   Anne E. Platt, "Infecting Ourselves. How Environment and Social Disruptions Trigger Disease," *World Watch Paper 129* (Washington, DC: World Watch Institute, April 1996), 23.

2   William H. McNeil, *Plagues and Peoples* (Garden City, NY: Anchor Books, 1976).

3   For more information about the human genome, see the special issue of *Nature Magazine* (February 15, 2001). Also, detailed biomedical information is available at various US government websites, including the following: The Human Genome Project, www.ornl.gov/TechResources/Human_Genome/home.html; The US Department of Energy Office of Science Human Genome information: http://genomics.energy.gov/; and the US National Genome Research Institute: www.nhgri.nih.gov/.

4   Bertrand Lell, J. May, R. J. Schmidt-Ott, L. G. Lehman, D. Luckner, B. Greve, P. Matousek, D. Schmid, K. Herbich, F. P. Mockenhaupt, C. G. Meyer, U. Bienzle, P. G. Kremsner, "The Role of Red Blood Cell Polymorphisms in Resistance and Susceptibility to Malaria," *Clinical Infectious Diseases* 28, no. 2 (1999), 794–9.

5   David E. Stannard, "I.4 Disease, Human Migration, and History," in Kenneth F. Kiple (ed.), *The Cambridge World History of Human Disease* (Cambridge: Cambridge University Press, 1993), 37; David K. Patterson, "VII.1 Disease Ecologies of Sub-Saharan Africa," in Kiple (ed.), *The Cambridge World History of Human Disease*, 448.

6   See William H. McNeill's landmark work, *Plagues and Peoples* (Garden City, NY: Doubleday, 1976).

7   Quoted in Laurie Garrett, *The Coming Plague* (New York: The Penguin Group, 1995), 235.

8   Katherine Park, "VIII.16 Black Death," in Kiple (ed.), *The Cambridge World History of Human Disease*, 613.

9   Stannard, "Disease, Human Migration, and History," 38.

10 Suzanne Austin Alchon, *A Pest in the Land. New World Epidemics in a Global Perspective* (Albuquerque, NM: University of New Mexico Press, 2003), 39–59. For yellow fever in the Americas, see McNeill, *Plagues and Peoples*, 187. Yellow fever required the importation of the highly specialized mosquito *Aedes aegypti*.

11 David E. Stannard, *American Holocaust: Columbus and the Conquest of the New World* (New York: Oxford University Press, 1992), X.

12 From Alfred W. Crosby, *Ecological Imperialism: The Biological Expansion of Europe, 900–1900* (Cambridge: Cambridge University Press, 2004), 207–8.

13 Stannard, "Disease, Human Migration, and History," 39.

14 David E. Stannard, *Before the Horror: The Population of Hawai'i on the Eve of Western Contact* (Honolulu, HI: University of Hawaii Press, 1989).

15 See Fiona Bristow, *Utz' Wach'il: Health and Well Being among Indigenous Peoples* (London: Health Unlimited, London School of Hygiene and Tropical Medicine, 2003).

16 John Duffy, "History of Public Health and Sanitation in the West Since 1700," in Kiple (ed.), *The Cambridge World History of Human Disease*, 192–206.

17 McNeill, *Plagues and Peoples*, 251.

18 Alfred W. Crosby, "VIII.73 Influenza," in Kiple (ed.), *The Cambridge World History of Human Disease*, 809–10.

19 Robin A. Weiss and Anthony J. McMichael, "Social and Environmental Risk Factors in the Emergence of Infectious Diseases," *Nature Medicine* 10, (2004), S70–S76.

20 Crosby, "Influenza," 809–10.

21 Anne S. Harding, "Influenza," in *Milestones of Health and Medicine* (Phoenix, AZ: Oryx Press, 2000).

22 Anne S. Harding, "Vaccine," in *Milestones in Health and Medicine*.

23 For the case of tuberculosis in South Africa, see Randall M. Packard, *White Plague, Black Labour: Tuberculosis and the Political Economy of Health and Disease in South Africa* (Berkeley, CA: University of California Press, 1989); and Garrett, *The Coming Plague*, 245.

24 Source: National Intelligence Estimate (NIE), *The Global Infectious Disease Threat and Its Implications for the United States* (January 2000), 23, www.dni.gov/nic/PDF_GIF_otherprod/infectiousdisease/infectiousdiseases.pdf.

25   "World Health Organization (WHO) Announces New Policy Position On Indoor Residual Spraying For Malaria Control," *Medical News Today* (September 16, 2006), www.medicalnewstoday. com/medicalnews.php?newsid=52010.

26   Anthony S. Fauci, "Infectious Diseases: Considerations for the Twenty-First Century," *Clinical Infectious Diseases* 32 (2001), 675–85.

27   Mary Vallanjon (ed.), "Scaling up the Response to Infectious Diseases: A Way Out of Poverty," World Health Organization (2002), www.who.int/ infectious-disease-report/2002/pdfversion/indexpdf. html. For recent statistics on patterns of morbidity and mortality for infectious diseases, see the World Health Organization website, www. who.org.

28   Source: World Health Organization, "Combating Emerging Infectious Diseases in the Southeast Asia Region" (2005), 15, www.searo.who. int/LinkFiles/Avian_Flu_combating_emerging_ diseases.pdf.

29   Source: Mary Vallanjon (ed.), "Scaling up the Response to Infectious Diseases: A Way Out of Poverty," World Health Organization (2002), www. who.int/infectious-disease-report/2002/pdfversion/ indexpdf.html.

30   "Key Facts about Influenza and the Influenza Vaccine," *Centers for Disease Control and Prevention*, www.cdc.gov/flu/keyfacts.htm.

31   "WHO Warns Flu Pandemic Is Imminent; Millions May Perish," World Health Organization (October 6, 2005), www.searo.who.int/EN/ Section316/Section503/Section1861_10453.htm.

32   "2009 H1N1 Flu ('Swine Flu') and You," Centers for Disease Control and Prevention (October 20, 2009), www.cdc.gov/h1n1flu/qa.htm.

33   "Pandemic (H1N1) 2009 – update 72," World Health Organization, www.who.int/csr/don/2009_ 10_30/en/index.html.

34   Harding "Influenza," 124.

35   "Avian Influenza Frequently Asked Questions," World Health Organization (revised December 5, 2005), www.who.int/csr/disease/avian_influenza/ avian_faqs/en/index.html#areall.

36   Mary E. Wilson, "Travel and the Emergence of Infectious Diseases," *Emerging Infectious Diseases* 1, (April–June 1995), 39.

37   Source: Mary E. Wilson, "Travel and the Emergence of Infectious Diseases," *Emerging Infectious Diseases* 1 (April–June 1995), 39.

38   Platt, "Infecting Ourselves," 40.

39   National Center for Infectious Diseases: Special Pathogens Branch, "All About the Hantavirus Tracking a Mystery Disease: The Detailed Story of Hantavirus Pulmonary Syndrome," Center for Disease Control (April 2006), www.cdc.gov/ncidod/ diseases/hanta/hps/noframes/outbreak.htm#Outbreak.

40   Richard S. Ostfeld and Felicia Keesing, "Biodiversity and Infectious Disease Risk: The Case of Lyme Disease," *Conservation Biology* 14 (2000), 722–8.

41   See studies done by the Rain Forest Foundation at www.rainforestfoundationuk.org.

42   World Watch Institute, "Health Features," *Vital Signs 2002* (New York: Norton/World Watch, 2001), 139.

43   Michael Pollan, "The Vegetable-Industrial Complex," *New York Times Magazine* (October 15, 2006), www.nytimes.com/2006/10/15/magazine/15wwln_ lede.html?scp=1&sq=%22The%20Vegetable-Industrial%20Complex%22&st=cse.

44   Ibid.

45   UN-Habitat, "Urbanization: A Turning Point in History," *State of the World's Cities 2006/7* www. unhabitat.org/documents/media_centre/sowcr2006/ SOWCR%201.pdf.

46   Source: United Nations Population Fund (UNFPA) "Chapter 3: Development Levels and Environmental Impact," *The State of World Population 2001*, www.unfpa.org/swp/2001/english/ch03.html.

47   UN-Habitat, "Urbanization."

48   Jennifer Schmidt, "Cities of the Poor II: Housing Alone Cannot Cure Poverty (South Africa)," *The World*, www.theworld.org/?q=node/6709.

49   UN-Habitat, "Slums: Past, Present and Future," *State of the World's Cities 2006/7*, www.unhabitat. org/documents/media_centre/sowcr2006/SOWCR% 204.pdf.

50   UN-Habitat, "Slum Dwellers Suffer from an Urban Penalty: They Are as Badly if not Worse off than their Rural Relatives According to UN-HABITAT's State of the World's Cities 2006/7," *State of the World's Cities 2006/7*, www.unhabitat.org/documents/ media_centre/sowcr2006/SOWCR%20Press% 20release.pdf.

51 Ibid.

52 UN-Habitat, "Mumbai's Quest for 'World City' Status," *State of the World's Cities 2006/7*, www.unhabitat.org/documents/media_centre/sowcr2006/SOWCR%2012.pdf.

53 UN-Habitat, "Slums: Inadequate Sanitation & the Silent Tsunami," *State of the World's Cities 2006/7*, www.unhabitat.org/documents/media_centre/sowcr2006/SOWCR%207.pdf.

54 UN-Habitat, "Slum Dwellers Suffer from an Urban Penalty."

55 UN-Habitat, "The Urban Penalty: The Poor Die Young," *State of the World's Cities 2006/7*, www.unhabitat.org/documents/media_centre/sowcr2006/SOWCR%2022.pdf.

56 UN-Habitat, "Slum Dwellers Suffer from an Urban Penalty."

57 "Airports Report Flat Traffic Growth in 2008," Airports Council International, www.airports.org/cda/aci_common/display/main/aci_content07_c.jsp?zn=aci&cp=1-5-54_666_2__. Also Airports Council International, www.aci.aero/cda/aci_common/display/main/aci_content07_c.jsp?zn=aci&cp=1-5-54-55_666_2__.

58 WHO, "Globalization – How Healthy?" *Bulletin of the WHO* (Geneva: WHO Press, 2001), 9.

59 United Nations, "United Nations' Trends in Total Migrant Stock: The 2005 Revision," United Nations Population Division, http://esa.un.org/migration.

60 Source: Airports Council International, http://www.aci.aero/cda/aci_common/display/main/aci_content07_c.jsp?zn=aci&cp=1-5-54-55_666_2__.

61 "HIV and Its Transmission," Centers for Disease Control and Prevention (July 1999), www.cdc.gov/hiv/resources/factsheets/transmission.htm.

62 Paul Farmer, *Infections and Inequalities: The Modern Plagues* (Berkeley, CA: University of California Press, 2001), 50–1.

63 The World Bank, ActAfrica, AIDS Campaign Team For Africa, "HIV/AIDS in Africa: World AIDS Day 2006 Update," http://siteresources.worldbank.org/EXTAFRREGTOPHIVAIDS/Resources/AFR_World_AIDS_Day_Brief_NOV_2006.pdf.

64 Ibid.

65 Gary Barker and Christine Ricardo, "Young Men and the Construction of Masculinity in Sub-Saharan Africa: Implications for HIV/AIDS, Conflict, and Violence," *The World Bank Social Development Papers: Conflict Prevention and Reconstruction Paper No. 26* (June 2005), 38, www.hsrc.ac.za/fatherhood/laws/WorldBankSocDev26.pdf.

66 MSF Access to Essential Medicines Campaign and the Drugs for Neglected Diseases Working Group, "Fatal Imbalance. The Crisis in Research and Development for Drugs for Neglected Diseases," Médecins Sans Frontières, 2001, www.accessmed-msf.org/prod/publications.asp?scntid=30112001115034&contenttype=PARA.

67 Ibid.

68 See "Ethnic Strife Halts Polio War Nigerian State's Vaccination ban is Global Issue," *The Atlanta Journal-Constitution* (May 16, 2004), Sec. B, 1, and the Centers For Disease Control website: www.cdc.gov/.

8

THE GENDERED WORLD

"*Economic development, that magic formula, devised sincerely to move poor nations out of poverty, has become women's worst enemy.*" (Devaki Jain, development specialist)[1]

"*Gender shapes not only how we identify ourselves and view the world, but also how others identify and relate to us and how we are positioned within social structures.*" (V. Spike Peterson and Anne Sisson Runya, international relations and feminist scholars)[2]

"*Gender equality is more than a goal in itself. It is a precondition for meeting the challenge of reducing poverty, promoting sustainable development and building good governance.*" (Kofi Annan, former UN Security General)[3]

Learning to Question, Questioning to Learn

- What is gender and how does it differ from sex?
- How do gender roles and other assumptions about gender impact policy creation and policy implementation?
- How might gender affect labor and *migration* patterns?
- What strategies has the UN used to mainstream gender concerns into *development* initiatives?
- What are some of the ways that gender intersects with human rights concerns?

Introduction

Although globalization is often discussed as a neutral, *ungendered* concept, the reality is that globalization often affects men and women in very different ways. This chapter begins by defining its terms, revisiting the term "globalization," and then exploring

ungendered Lacking any recognition or acknowledgement of gender.

how the term "gender" is used in academic discourses. The chapter then moves to a discussion of the connections between gender, poverty, and development, exploring gendered manifestations of poverty and the ways that gendered assumptions impact development projects. Included here is a discussion of UN initiatives to infuse gender analysis into its planning and policy decisions. Next, the chapter looks at some of the gendered labor and migration issues that have emerged in our globalized world. This is followed by a discussion of human security and human rights issues that are particularly pressing for women, including an overview of some of the UN's efforts to integrate gender analysis and gender equality into its mission and programs. The chapter concludes with a discussion of education and health issues that affect women, their families, and the communities in which they reside.

Defining Our Terms

Because the intersection of globalization and gender is the focus of this chapter, it is useful to begin by briefly revisiting what we mean by the term "globalization" and then exploring how the term "gender" is used in academic discourses. As discussed in chapter 1, Manfred Steger, Professor of Global Studies at the Royal Melbourne Institute of Technology, developed a particularly useful definition of globalization that synthesizes the insights of a number of different globalization scholars. Steger describes globalization as "a multidimensional set of social processes that create, multiply, stretch, and intensify worldwide social interdependencies and exchanges while at the same time fostering in people a growing awareness of deepening connections between the local and the distant."[4] For a more thorough discussion of globalization definitions, please review chapter 1.

While definitions of globalization can be rather complex, the term "gender" initially seems more commonplace and transparent. After all, in common parlance, "gender" is often used interchangeably with the word "sex" to distinguish between males and females. However, in academic discourses, there are some important distinctions between the two terms. "Sex" is a biological distinction that is determined by anatomical characteristics and genetic material, while "gender" refers to the "socially learned behavior and expectations that distinguish between masculinity and femininity."[5] Characteristics and behaviors that are considered masculine and feminine vary across cultures and historical periods. They are also influenced by a variety of other socio-cultural factors, such as ethnicity, class, age, and race. So while biological sex remains constant regardless of culture, what sex means for people in terms of acceptable social roles, behaviors, and attitudes will vary from culture to culture.

However, across cultures, *masculinity* and *femininity* are defined in opposition to each other. Characteristics that are defined as masculine tend to be highly valued in societies, while characteristics deemed feminine are often denigrated. In many cultures, human characteristics like strength, courage, independence, stoicism, confidence, and leadership are associated with masculinity, while weakness, timidity, dependence, emotionalism, and insecurity are associated with femininity. While it is increasingly acceptable in many Western cultures for women to adopt characteristics that have traditionally been associated with masculinity, such as assertiveness and leadership, there are still many masculine behaviors, qualities, and perform-ances that women cannot easily assume without suffering real social consequences. For example, a woman in the US who dresses in men's clothes, cuts her hair short, and refuses to wear make-up is likely to be at a significant disadvantage when it comes to getting hired if she is competing against similarly qualified people whose appearance is consistent with traditional gender norms. Moreover, people whose outward performance of gender makes it hard to discern whether they are men or women also often encounter a variety of problems. Many cannot even enter a public restroom without fear of being harassed. Additionally, while it may be more acceptable for women in Western countries to adopt characteristics that have traditionally been considered masculine, qualities associated with femininity continue to be devalued, and men who exhibit them often face severe social consequences. Men who exhibit weakness or who perform an activity poorly are still ridiculed for behaving "like a girl." Moreover, men who choose to wear clothes associated with femininity, such as dresses, are likely to have difficulty not only finding employment but also, in certain areas, walking down the street without being verbally or even physically assaulted. Gender norms have such power over us, then, that the violation of them can evoke intense emotional responses, including revulsion and disgust. Indeed, hierarchical gendered distinctions are so thoroughly inscribed into our societies that they often appear to us as natural. They are, however, social constructs that are learned rather than etched into our DNA.

masculinity Socially constructed roles, behaviors, attitudes, and attributes that a given culture associates with men.

femininity Socially constructed roles, behaviors, attitudes, and attributes that a given culture associates with women.

These distinctions are important because this chapter does not simply discuss issues that affect women; rather, it explores the ways in which perceptions and expectations of gender affect our worldviews and the policies that result from them. The "lens" though which we view the world colors the questions we ask, the solutions we create, the actors we "see," and the valuations we impart.[6] Understanding the conscious and unconscious ways that power operates through gendered hierarchies allows us to create better policies and to develop a more nuanced understanding of the processes of globalization.

Gender, Poverty, and Development

Poverty

The *World Bank* defines poverty as existing on less than $1.25 per day. In 1981, there were 1.9 billion people, or 52 percent of the world's population, living in poverty. By 2005, the number had dropped to 1.4 billion or 26 percent of the world's population. However, in some countries and among some groups, the number of people living in *absolute poverty* has increased. For example, poverty in China has decreased overall, while the number of people living in absolute poverty in sub-Saharan Africa has increased.[7] Additionally, the gap between the world's poorest and wealthiest nations has also increased.

The UN has a more nuanced definition of poverty, describing it as a "multidimensional phenomenon" that involves not only low income and consumption but also "hunger and malnutrition, poor health, lack of education and skills, lack of access to water and sanitation, and vulnerability to economic and social shocks." The UN also points out that there is a cycle of poverty that is difficult to break. Poverty begets poverty, as "low income restricts access to basic goods and services, and lack of access to goods and services limits income-generating opportunities." Additionally, poverty is often connected to social factors like race, ethnicity, and gender and can be the result of discrimination against specific groups.[8]

Studies indicate that men and women often experience poverty differently. For example, World Bank and *International Monetary Fund structural adjustment programs* (SAPs), which imposed *neoliberal* economic policies on countries seeking to borrow money or to restructure their existing debt, led to increased rates of female poverty. This in turn led to an increase in poverty-related issues, including vulnerably to diseases and involvement in *survival sex*. Women were also affected differently by the fall of the Soviet Union. As Russia and many of its former allies struggled to restructure their economies, unemployment for women rose dramatically. The Gender Equality and Development Section of UNESCO reports that:

World Bank One of the international financial institutions created at Bretton Woods that sets global economic policy. It was designed to help countries with long-term development goals.

absolute poverty Poverty as defined in the same terms across cultures and countries (cf. relative poverty).

International Monetary Fund (IMF) One of the Bretton Woods international financial institutions that sets global economic policy. It was designed to help countries with short-term development goals.

structural adjustment programs (SAPs) World Bank and IMF programs that imposed neoliberal economic policies on countries seeking to borrow from these organizations or seeking to restructure their existing debt.

neoliberalism A rejection of Keynesian economic theory, which posited that the state must play an active role in a capitalist economy in order to level out the inevitable boom and bust cycles. Neoliberals argue that deregulation and privatization of state-owned enterprises and limited government involvement in the economy are the best ways for countries' economies to grow and individual freedoms to flourish.

survival sex Engaging in sex in order to survive a threat or to secure money for food or shelter.

> In the mid-1990s, some 66.3 percent of the unemployed in eastern Germany were women; in Poland it was 54–58 percent, in Romania 60 percent, and in Russia 68 percent (down from a high of 72–80 percent in the early 1990s). In the Czech Republic, 13.2 percent of women were unemployed, compared with 2.2 percent of men.[9]

In short, during this period of economic crisis, male privilege was asserted as women were the first to be let go. As a result, poverty rates for women soared.

Research indicates that gender-specific approaches to poverty eradication are often more effective than those that are ostensibly gender-neutral. For example, investments in rural women's education and leadership have been shown to increase agricultural yields by more than 20 percent. Other studies estimate that women's wages rise 21 percent for every year of school they attend beyond the fourth grade. Additionally, the UN reported in 2001 that "eliminating gender inequality in Latin America would increase national output by 5 percent."[10] Studies that examine the relationship between women and poverty, rather than assuming that men and women are affected in the same way, indicate that when female economic power is increased, families are the primary beneficiaries. As a result, many argue that the most effective way to combat poverty is to provide women with avenues for empowerment and education. An *International Labour Organization* (ILO) report on labor and women, for example, concludes: "At a basic level, women's employment, paid and unpaid, may be the single most important factor for keeping many households out of poverty."[11]

International Labour Organization (ILO) Founded in 1919, this specialized UN agency works to promote decent working conditions across the globe.

Development

The term "development" is generally used to describe efforts since the end of World War II to improve the economic status of the world's poorest nations. This focus on development was the product of a number of factors, including reconstruction needs in the aftermath of the war, as well as the end of *colonialism*, which led to the establishment of many new, and often very poor, states. Some point to Harry S. Truman's second inaugural address in 1949 as ushering in the development era. In his famous fourth point, Truman stated:

colonialism One territorial sovereign exerting control and sovereignty over another land by usurping control from local leaders, thereby destroying indigenous culture, economies, and political structures.

> We must embark on a bold new program for making the benefits of our scientific advances and industrial progress available for the improvement and growth of underdeveloped areas. . . . The old imperialism – exploitation for foreign profit – has no place in our plans. What we envisage is a program of development based on the concept of democratic fair dealing.[12]

Although Truman's ideas were not original, his words helped to galvanize a movement that was already coming together around the goal of combating world poverty.

economic liberalism Attributed to Adam Smith, this economic system has a very limited scope of government involvement in economic matters.

Economic models underlying development: two competing theories

Most development programs were modeled on the economic path taken by Western European countries and the US. This model was based on *economic liberalism*, the basic tenets of which were delineated by Adam Smith in *The Wealth of Nations* (1776). Smith argued that goods and services were best distributed through laws of supply and demand and that government's role in the economy should be kept to a minimum so as to allow the "invisible hand" of the market to function for the good of all society. According to Smith, this approach would lead to the maximization of global wealth and human welfare as well as to peace and cooperation among states. The basic unit of analysis for economic liberalism is "the rational man," who is by nature an economic animal driven by rational self-interest. He is highly individualistic and pursues his own economic goals in the market without any social obligation to the community of which he is a part. Benefits flow to all members of society because economic growth trickles down through the system. This free market capitalist approach to economic development was advanced by the developed nations of the world as the only path for economic success for developing countries.

Some critics of this approach to economic development argue that the individualistic "rational man" is a Western construct that is not universal across historical periods and cultures. Historically, in many African societies, for example, economic behavior had a communal rather than an individual orientation. Other critics point out that economic liberalism fails to account for gender.[13] The "rational man" approach suggests that rational individuals will pursue jobs that will maximize their income, but it does not acknowledge the social norms that limit or prevent some individuals from doing so. For example, some societies relegate women to positions of unpaid labor, which prevents them from making the same types of economic choices that are available to the "rational man." As a result, women spend much of their days performing non-income-generating tasks, such as fetching water, cooking, cleaning, and raising children. They participate in these types of activities not because they are rational decisions that are in their own economic best interests, but because of the values and expectations of their society and the limited opportunities available to them.

In many Western countries, women have played more of a role in the formal workforce, though they have historically been relegated to the "caring professions," such as teaching, nursing, and social work. These are generally lower-paying jobs, and thus they are not the most economically rational positions for individuals to pursue. Women have pursued them, however, because they were historically barred from many high-paying jobs. In the US, for example, women could not attend law school until 1869.[14] Columbia University did not allow women into its law school until 1927,[15] Harvard's law school waited until 1950 to grant women admission,[16] and Notre Dame's law school didn't graduate its first female until 1970.[17] Even after women broke down many of these barriers, they have continued to dominate lower-paying caring professions, in part because these jobs are consistent with societal constructs, expectations, and values ascribed to "females." In short, economic liberalism does not account for the ways in which societal constraints and assumptions about gender appropriate occupations can negate women's "rational choice."[18]

Marxists Followers of the economic and political theories of Karl Marx and Friedrich Engels who believe that capitalism exploits workers, that class struggle creates historical change, and that capitalism will ultimately be superseded by a classless society.

developing countries Usually refers to low-income countries with little industrialization compared to developed nations. These countries are also sometimes referred to as the "Third World," the "Global South," and the "less developed countries."

One alternative approach to liberalism is based on the writings of Karl Marx. According to *Marxists*, unbridled capitalism is responsible for the "under"-development of the world's poor countries. They also maintain that capitalism will continue to keep poor countries in a permanent state of underdevelopment. The current economic system, they argue, distorts *developing countries'* economies and exacerbates inequalities both within and among societies. The rich within developing societies will continue to get richer, but this wealth will not trickle down to the majority of people and development won't occur because capitalism is dependent upon a cheap labor force. As a result, the only way in which poor countries can develop is if the poor overthrow the system and take control of the means for generating wealth. Other Marxists argue that developing nations will only have chance to develop independently if they break away from the international capitalist system altogether.

Marxists use "class" as their unit of analysis as opposed to the "rational man." This focus on class leads many Marxists to argue that equality for women will come through a class-based struggle. In other words, class and class oppression will bind working men and women together in a common struggle against their oppression. The problem with a class-based Marxist approach to development is that it assumes that capitalism is the reason for the oppression of women, when, according to many feminist critics, the oppression of women is also a product of patriarchy. Feminists point out that when women are employed in the formal sector, they are often oppressed by their male colleagues rather than engaged in a common struggle against oppression. Many women find that they do not receive equal pay for equal work and many others are subjected to sexual harassment. Moreover, it is not unusual for their working husbands or partners to fail to share the burden of housework and childcare. As a result, women have very little time to organize around class-consciousness. Others have little desire to do so, believing that a focus on class will do little to address the patriarchal sources of their oppression.

Development failures and emerging gendered approaches

By the late 1960s and early 1970s, scholars and practitioners began calling into question the efficacy of the development programs that had been implemented over the previous 20 years in the world's poorest countries. The failure of many development initiatives to deliver on their promises provided an opportunity to revisit just what "development" meant, who it was supposed to help, how the programs themselves were structured, and the assumptions that undergirded them. *Feminist scholars*, whose voices were increasingly heard as a result of the political and social changes emerging from the women's rights movement of the late 1960s and early '70s, suggested that one of the reasons development projects had failed was because they were based on the assumption that development

feminist scholars Scholars who explore the nature of gendered politics, power relations, and sexuality by examining existing societal constructs.

is gender-neutral. For example, development specialists working in the agricultural sector assumed that men were the farmers who produced the cash crops and that women only farmed to produce extra or subsistence crops. These assumptions were incorrect and historically inaccurate. In Africa specifically, women produce more than 80 percent of the food.[19] In the developing world as a whole, women produce more than half of the cash crops.[20]

A Kenyan reforestation initiative provides another example of faulty gendered assumptions leading to the failure of a development project. Development officials had consulted with male village leaders about the project. They were told that it would be best to plant hardwood trees, since they produced the best wood for their furniture-making endeavors. Hardwood trees were planted, but the trees died shortly thereafter. A subsequent investigation revealed the cause. Both the local men and the development specialists had assumed that the women of the village would take care of the trees. However, the women preferred softwood trees because they grow much more quickly than hardwood trees and can be used for things like firewood for cooking. Because the women saw no value in the hardwood trees, they did not take care of them. Failure to take into account gender-specific roles and needs resulted in the project's failure.[21]

In response to these kinds of failures, Western feminists advocated the inclusion of women in both the creation and implementation phases of development projects. According to Sue Ellen Charlton, author of *Women in Third World Development*, feminist criticisms of the development policies of the 1950s and 1960s led to several positive changes, including an expansion of sex-disaggregated data on the role of women in economic and social systems, the establishment of "goals and plans for improving women's status around the globe," increased representation of women in official government positions, changes in many inequitable laws that discriminated against women, and the mobilization of women at the grassroots level around the world.[22] By the 1970s, women in development (WID) projects had become a central focus of development discourses, and including women in various aspects of development became a goal of many development agencies. Critics charged that WID projects merely included women in development projects.[23] This "add women and stir" approach did not account for the way gender roles and assumptions operate in specific societies. According to Razavi and Miller:

> WID identified women's lack of access to resources as the key to their subordination without raising questions about the role of gender relations in restricting women's access in the first place (and in subverting policy interventions, were they to direct resources to women). The work that was under way within various social science disciplines suggested the importance of power, conflict and gender relations in understanding women's subordination.[24]

However, by the late 1970s and early 1980s, development projects began to focus on gender and development issues (GAD). According to Charlton, GAD differed from WID in that its proponents argued the following:

1   Development processes in poor countries or less-developed countries (LDCs) were deeply influenced by the inequitable structures of the international economic system.

2   Women have always been integrated into development processes, but those processes [were] essentially flawed.

3   Men, as well as women, are hurt by development programs that do not alter repressive class, ethnic, and racial structures.

4   One cannot assume women's solidarity across class and racial lines, but patriarchal values and institutions may oppress women in every social-economic category.

5   Development policies should not isolate women's productive or reproductive roles: they are intertwined in women's lives.

6   Women are agents of change and must organize politically.

7   Successful development does not "target" women, it empowers them.[25]

international financial institutions
Financial institutions that are established in more than one state. The most notable are those established in Bretton Woods after World War II – the World Bank and the IMF.

Attempts to integrate GAD's principles into development projects were ultimately undermined in the 1980s and 1990s by the rise of neoliberal economic policies embodied in the SAPs imposed by *international financial institutions* (IFI) – primarily the World Bank and the IMF. SAPs required the privatization of state-owned enterprises, the reduction in the number of government workers, the devaluation of currency, and the reduction of government subsidies on items such as food, health care, and education. There is a general agreement among scholars, and now even among the IFIs, that SAPs were devastating for women. Loss of income, due to currency devaluation and increased unemployment, coupled with loss of public services, including access to subsidized health care, especially prenatal care,[26] made it more difficult for women to take care of the nutritional and health needs of their families. In short, SAPs required women to figure out how to get by on less. They allowed the state to save money by cutting services that women were then compelled to attempt to provide without pay. According to Pamela Sparr, author of *Mortgaging Women's Lives: Feminist Critiques of Structural Adjustment*:

> What is regarded by economists as "increased efficiency" may instead be a shifting of costs from the paid economy to the unpaid economy. . . . In cutting back on public services, for example, governments have implicitly relied on a quiet army of wives, co-wives, mothers, daughters, aunts, grandmothers, sisters, female friends and neighbours to pick up the slack.[27]

The World Bank has since reversed its position on SAPs, admitting that they had not been particularly successful. In a 1994 report, the Bank indicated that gender bias, or the assumption of gender neutrality, had made women's economic and non-economic work invisible, leading to an incomplete understanding of countries' total economic activities. As a result of this incomplete understanding, the Bank admitted that what conventional economic analyses pointed to as "efficiency improvements" might actually have constituted a "shift in costs from the visible (predominantly male) economy to the invisible (predominantly female) economy."[28] Today, the Bank asserts that:

> Gender equality is now a core element of the Bank's strategy to reduce poverty. There is a clear understanding that until women and men have equal capacities, opportunities and voice, the ambitious poverty-reduction agenda set out in the Millennium Declaration, and the specific goals attached to it, will not be achieved.[29]

It remains to be seen whether the Bank will be successful in creating better programs that incorporate gender analysis into development strategies.

United Nations

Like the World Bank, the United Nations has sought to infuse gender analysis into its planning and policy decisions, including women in decision-making processes and focusing on the unique challenges they face. The UN declared 1975 International Women's Year and held the first ever UN Conference on Women in Mexico City. This ushered in a new era for the UN in which it committed itself to seeking and promoting gender equality, the elimination of discrimination against women, the full participation and integration of women into the development process, and a commitment to women's active role in peace-building activities.[30] Several months after the conference, and at the urging of many of the attendees, the UN declared the UN Decade for Women (1976–85). During this time, a number of programs and agencies were created that were designed to address gender issues. For example, the United Nations Fund for Women (UNIFEM) was created in 1976. Today, UNIFEM works in more than 100 countries, primarily in the developing world, providing:

> financial and technical assistance to innovative programmes and strategies to foster women's empowerment and gender equality. Placing the advancement of women's human rights at the centre of all of its efforts, UNIFEM focuses its activities on four strategic areas: (1) reducing feminized poverty, (2) ending violence against women, (3) reversing the spread of HIV/AIDS among women and girls, and (4) achieving gender equality in democratic governance in times of peace as well as war.[31]

In addition to UNIFEM, a variety of other agencies and programs emerged to address women's concerns (see table 8.1 for a list of these organizations).

During the UN Decade for Women, two international conferences were held, in Copenhagen in 1980 and in Nairobi in 1985, to continue the work begun in Mexico City. These conferences brought together policy-makers, heads of states and their representatives, and officials from both NGOs and grassroots organizations, and

Table 8.1   Organizations with a Focus on Women

Name	Purpose
UN Division for the Advancement of Women (DAW)	Promotes women's empowerment, equality, and human rights through the support and monitoring of international agreements on gender equality, participation in the formulation of policy and global norms and standards as they relate to gender equity. The organization also promotes the mainstreaming of gender perspectives throughout the UN and with the various agents and agencies with which it works.
The Food and Agriculture Organization (FAO)	Works to end global hunger by acting as a clearinghouse for information and research on hunger related issues, sharing its expertise on agricultural policy with member nations, and by working with various humanitarian organizations in country to devise sustainable agricultural policies. Given women's extensive role in agriculture as the main producers of food, the organization has designed special programs for women that address the gender specific concerns women farmers encounter.
The International Fund for Agricultural Development (IFAD)	The goal of IFAD is to empower rural women and men to achieve food security and higher incomes. Working primarily in developing countries, the organization acts as an international financial institution and dedicates a good deal of its resources to agriculture in Africa, where the vast majority of farmers are women.
International Labour Organization (ILO)	Seeks to ensure that women and men have decent working conditions. Conducts specialized research into women's labor issues.
International Research and Training Institute for the Advancement of Women (INSTRAW)	Created as a result of the 1975 conference on women, this organization is a research and training institute that focuses on the advancement of women.
International Telecommunication Union (ITU)	One of the world's oldest international organizations, it seeks to promote international cooperation on information and communication technologies (ICT). Believing that ICT is one of the fields that has the potential to promote gender equality through emerging ICT jobs, the ITU has established specialized programs providing technology access and training for women in developing countries.
United Nations Development Programme (UNDP)	Promotes sustainable development in the world's poorest countries. Many specialized programs have been established to promote gender equity in development planning. The UNDP has established the Gender in Development Programme (GIDP) to carry out its gender-based initiatives, which include working to empower women politically, economically, and environmentally. GIDP also carries out health-related research and training sessions around issues pertinent to women, such as HIV/AIDS.
UN Educational, Scientific and Cultural Organization (UNESCO)	Promotes cooperation among members in the areas of science, culture, education, communication, and information. UNESCO has specialized programs for women and girls, including literacy training and the promotion of education for girls. It also promotes women's human rights and the participation of women in public life.

Table 8.1   *(cont'd)*

Name	Purpose
United Nations Population Fund (UNFPA)	Collects data on population trends as well as population policies and programs. Assists nations with programs that highlight the links between sustainable development, reproductive health, and gender equality. Promotes universal access to reproductive health services.
United Nations High Commissioner for Refugees (UNHCR)	The UN agency responsible for the protection of refuges, the majority of whom are female. It provides services such as food, shelter, education, health care, legal services, resettlement services, and skills training.
United Nations Children's Fund (UNICEF)	The organization works to eradicate the conditions that adversely affect children's development, including poverty, violence, disease, and discrimination. Its specialized programs for female children promote education and an end to discrimination faced by female children.
United Nations Industrial Development Organization (UNIDO)	Works with developing countries to provide the skills, technology, and information necessary to enable their economies to become more productive, increasing their trade capacity and improving their energy and environmental sectors. Mainstreaming gender into all of their activities has been a key priority of the organization.
United Nations Development Fund for Women (UNIFEM)	It is designed to reduce violence against women, reduce the incidents of female poverty, prevent the spread of HIV/AIDs among women and girls, and promote gender equity through democratic governance. It does these things by providing financial and technical assistance designed to foster female empowerment and equality.
United Nations Research Institute for Social Development (UNRISD)	Conducts research on social development, including a specialized research program on gender and development issues.
World Food Programme (WFP)	Provides emergency food aid to conflict and famine areas and works to reduce chronic hunger and malnutrition around the globe. Has specific programs that teach mothers about keeping malnutrition at bay.
World Health Organization (WHO)	The UN's main organization that deals with health-related issues. Specific health initiatives for women include programs focusing on reproductive health, disease prevention, and basic health care training.
The World Bank	International financial institution that provides development assistance, mainly in the form of loans to poor countries. Targeting women for development programs has become a key objective of the bank.

produced governmental action plans, providing women around the world with a framework for demanding action from their governments.[32] Although it was important that policy-makers, activists, and development planners were at least taking into consideration the issues raised at these conferences, progress on the overall conditions for women around the world had not improved by the end of the decade.

Platform for Action   An agenda for women's empowerment that emerged from the Fourth World Conference on Women in Beijing in 1995.

In 1995, more than 40,000 participants from 189 countries gathered in Beijing, China to assess progress on the plans of actions from the previous conferences as well as to chart a course for a new agenda.[33] This was the largest international gathering ever to focus solely on women. The *Platform for Action* that emerged from Beijing listed 12 areas of concern for women: poverty; education and training; health; violence; armed conflict; the economy; power and decision-making; institutional mechanism for advancement; human rights; the media; the environment; and the girl-child. For each area, problems were diagnosed and objectives for addressing them created. In addition, concrete actions for meeting these objectives were spelled out for various actors, and countries were required to submit reports on their progress in the 12 areas at the next meeting in 2000.[34]

The reports were presented to the UN in 2000 at "Beijing +5." Held at UN Headquarters in New York, Beijing +5 was a special session of the General Assembly entitled "Women 2000: Gender Equality, Development and Peace for the Twenty-First Century." Its purpose was to assess how well the Nairobi Forward-looking Strategies for the Advancement of Women (adopted in 1985 at the Nairobi conference) and the Beijing Platform for Action (adopted in 1995 in Beijing) had been implemented.[35] The UN assessed the country reports and found that profound changes on the status of women in the social, political, and economic spheres had occurred since the start of the UN Decade for Women in 1976. They found that NGOs in particular had played a significant role in "putting the concerns of women and gender equality on the national and international agenda."[36] Despite successes, however, there were many areas where improvement had not occurred and where much more work was needed. Specifically, the report found that violence and poverty remained major obstacles to gender equality and that globalization had "added new dimensions to both areas, creating new challenges for the implementation of the Platform." Examples of these challenges include the global trafficking of women and girls and the changing nature of armed conflict, which increasingly victimizes civilians, including women and children.[37]

The same year that Beijing +5 was held, the UN also held a summit on its own role in the twenty-first century. World leaders gathered and adopted the United Nations *Millennium Declaration*, which committed nations to a new global partnership to reduce extreme poverty by 2015. The Millennium Development Goals (MDGs) that emerged from the conference include the following:

Millennium Declaration   United Nations declaration signed in September 2000 consisting of eight goals and 21 targets that 192 United Nations member states and at least 23 international organizations have agreed to achieve by the year 2015. The 8 Millennium Development Goals (MDGs) are

1 eradicating extreme poverty and hunger
2 achieving universal primary education
3 promoting gender equality and empowering women
4 reducing child mortality
5 improving maternal health
6 combating HIV/AIDS, malaria, and other diseases
7 ensuring environmental sustainability
8 developing a global partnership for development

1 Eradicate extreme poverty and hunger.
2 Achieve universal primary education.
3 Promote gender equality and empower women.
4 Reduce child mortality.
5 Improve maternal health.
6 Combat HIV/AIDS, malaria, and other diseases.

Researching to Learn   *Gender and Development*

Free Web Resources

Australian Government: *Gender Equity and Development*
  www.ausaid.gov.au/keyaid/gender.cfm

EC/UN Partnership for Equality and Development: *Gendermatters.eu*
  www.gendermatters.eu/

Gender and Development Action
  www.gadanigeria.org/

Inter-American Development Bank: *Gender Equality in Development*
  www.iadb.org/sds/WID/index_wid_e.htm.

Organisation for Economic Co-Operation and Development: *Gender Equality and Development*
  www.oecd.org/department/0,3355,en_2649_34541_1_1_1_1_1,00.html.

UK Gender and Development Network
  www.gadnetwork.org.uk/

United Nations Development Programme: Women's Empowerment
  www.undp.org/women/

United Nations Economic Commission for Africa: *African Centre for Gender and Development*
  www.uneca.org/fr/acgd/en/1024x768/acgd.htm

The World Bank: Gender and Development
  http://web.worldbank.org/WBSITE/EXTERNAL/TOPICS/EXTGENDER/0,,menuPK:336874~pagePK:149018~piPK:149093~theSitePK:336868,00.html

Online Research Portals

Eldis.
  www.eldis.org/go/display/?id=17140&type=Document

Gender Responsible Budgeting
  www.gender-budgets.org/

Michigan State University's Women & International Development Program (WID) WorkingPapers
  www.wid.msu.edu/resources/publications.htm

World Bank Gender Statistics Database.
  http://genderstats.worldbank.org/

Zunia Knowledge Exchange, Development Gateway
  http://zunia.org/cat/gender

Scholarly Journals: Find Them @ Your Library

Development
Gender & Development
Journal of Development Economics
Journal of Development Studies
Journal of International Development
Peace, Conflict and Development
Yale Human Rights and Development Law Journal

Books: Find Them @ Your Library

Bouta, Tsjeard, Georg Frerks, and Ian Bannon. *Gender, Conflict, and Development.* Washington, DC: World Bank Publications, 2004.

Momsen, Janet Henshall. *Gender and Development.* New York: Routledge, 2004.

Østergaard, Lise. Commission of the European Communities. Directorate-General Development. *Gender and Development: A Practical Guide.* New York: Routledge, 1992.

Parpart, Jane L., M. Patricia Connelly, and V. Eudine Barriteau, eds. *Theoretical Perspectives on Gender and Development.* Ottawa. Canada: IDRC 2000.

World Bank. *Engendering Development: Through Gender Equality in Rights, Resources, and Voice.* Washington, DC: World Bank, 2001.

7   Ensure environmental sustainability.
8   Develop a global partnership for development.[38]

By including gender equality as a MDG, the UN highlighted the connections among gender equality, poverty reduction, and sustainable development.[39]

In Focus: Microcredit

The Grameen Bank of Bangladesh has become well known for its innovative approach to development. Muhammad Yunas founded the bank because he believed that, although poor women had skills that they could use to generate income, they lacked the necessary capital to get started. In response to this problem, he developed a lending system that has come to be referred to as "*microcredit.*" The organizing principle of microcredit is that smaller amounts of money given directly to the right people is more likely to be successful than multimillion-dollar state-run development projects, many of which historically had failed due to problems like poor design and corruption. The Grameen Bank began by loaning money only to poor women, a population that had typically been unable to borrow money from traditional banks because they lacked collateral and were thus considered high-risk borrowers. However, rather than loaning to individuals, the bank decided to loan money to groups of four or five women who together would be held responsible for each other's debt. Forming networks of women helped to build a sense of community and accountability, since if one member failed to make a payment, the others would have to pay her share of the loan. Reluctance to let the other members of the group down might explain why the repayment rate for the Grameen Bank is better than that of conventional banks.

microcredit   The extension of small loans to poor people who are typically ineligible for traditional lines of credit, facilitating their pursuit of income generating self-employment projects with the potential to help them escape from poverty.

Many of the women who have participated in the bank's microcredit program have started businesses that have enabled them to provide for their families. Some report that financial independence has improved their sense of self-worth, while others claim that the loans ultimately helped them to become literate and to pursue education for both themselves and their children. One of the reasons this program was successful is that it accurately analyzed and addressed a gendered problem: women are often the poorest of the poor because their societies do not offer them any viable opportunities to emerge from poverty. When they are provided with economic opportunities, they are often successful in their entrepreneurial endeavors, which ultimately benefit their families and the larger communities in which they reside. Because of the bank's success, various versions of this microcredit system have emerged in dozens of countries, including low-income areas in *developed countries*. In 2006, Yunas was awarded the Nobel Peace Prize for his work.

developed countries   Countries with high levels of economic development, protection of political rights, and high scores on the UN human development index. Developed countries typically have either industrial or post-industrial-based economies.

The bank is not without its critics, however, many of whom have argued that loaning money to poor women traps them in an endless cycle of debt. Additionally, some research suggests that many women are being manipulated by male relatives to take out loans on their behalf. Others report that some women have experienced increased incidents of physical violence by their male spouses and relatives who resent the women in their family taking a more active role in public life.[40] Despite such reports, several economic analyses of the overall impact of microcredit indicate that these programs have resulted in poverty reduction for the participants.[41]

Labor and Migration

Globalization and neoliberal economic policies have changed labor patterns, integrating economies around the world and allowing for more foreign-owned industries to emerge in developing countries. These industries often provide low-wage, precarious jobs, primarily hiring women because they can be paid less. Liberalization policies often lead to increased unemployment for men, which in turn forces women to seek employment in the formal economy. The ILO reports that women's participation in the labor force has been increasing "almost everywhere around the world, a process described as 'the feminization of labour.'" The ILO claims that "women's employment, paid and unpaid, may be the single most important factor for keeping many households out of poverty." However, while economic opportunities for women have grown, this has not translated into equal access to high-quality jobs, as women continue to be relegated to "lower quality, irregular and *informal employment*."[42] Additionally, a significant wage gap persists between men and women.

informal employment Economic activity that takes place outside the formal, measureable market of an economy.

migrants People who have left their homes in order to settle in another country or city.

The past two decades have seen a dramatic rise in the number of women leaving their homes in search of employment. Of the world's 95 million *migrant* workers[43] who have left their home countries for employment in another, roughly 50 percent are women.[44] Most regions of the world have seen an increase in the total percentage of women migrants, with sub-Saharan Africa experiencing a more than 7 percent increase in the past few decades.[45] Historically, women have migrated primarily in order to reconnect with their husbands who had previously migrated. Today, however, "women are on the move in all parts of the world," pursuing economic opportunities both for themselves and their families. According to a 2006 UN report on migration, "migrant women and men are both in demand," but men "are more likely to occupy highly skilled and better-paid jobs." Women are often limited to "traditionally 'female' occupations, such as domestic work, work in the service sectors (waitressing, etc.), and sex work." These jobs are often unstable, low-wage positions characterized by poor working conditions and the absence of any employment related benefits.[46]

One of the largest sectors for female migrant employment is domestic work. As more women in developed countries enter the workforce, more women from developing countries are being hired to care for the homes and families of working men and women in wealthier countries. One result has been the creation of a "chain of care," which refers to the phenomenon of women from developing countries leaving their families to migrate to a wealthier country where they care for their employers' families. In some cases, these women use the higher wages they are receiving to hire lower-income women in their home countries to care for their own children who had to be left behind when they migrated.[47]

remit/remittances Money sent home by workers employed in another country.

Many of these migrant women also *remit* money back home to their families. Women remit a higher percentage of their wages than do men, but because men make more money, the total amount of *remittances* might be more for males. One reason women remit more of their earnings is because they tend to invest their money in their children, while men tend to invest more in consumer goods.[48] Tracking the exact amount of money remitted each year can be difficult, as not all of it travels through official channels. However, the IMF estimates that roughly $100 billion is remitted each year. Because this has become the largest source of foreign currency for a large number of developing nations,[49] many countries have come to depend upon that income. According to the IMF, remittances to many developing countries exceed "export revenues, foreign direct investment (FDI), and other private capital inflows." In addition to providing a stable flow of income during economic downturns, remittances can help countries improve "development prospects, maintain macroeconomic stability, mitigate the impact of adverse shocks, and reduce poverty." They allow families to spend more on things like housing, education, and entrepreneurial endeavors, which in turn promotes "financial development in cash-based developing economies."[50]

In addition to the millions of women who migrate to other countries seeking employment, millions of women also migrate internally. Migration flows are usually from rural to urban centers, which serve as manufacturing hubs. For example, women constitute almost half of all rural to urban migration in China. Many of these women are finding employment in booming industries like manufacturing, where employers pay low wages and consider females to be "easier to manage than men."[51] Figure 8.1 provides a snapshot of global employment trends by gender and by sector. Although female participation in the industry sector has decreased in Europe and the Middle East, it has increased significantly in Asia, where we see significant rural to urban migration.

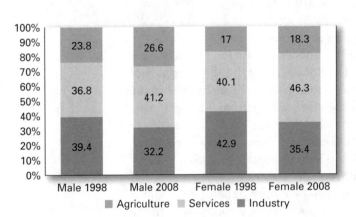

Figure 8.1 Employment by Sector by Gender, 1998 and 2008[52]

Human Security and Human Rights

What is human security?

In international relations and political science discourses, the term "security" has historically been used in the context of the nation-state. The job of the state was to keep its citizens safe by preventing outside attacks and invasions. Increasingly, however, the term is being used to describe the safety and well-being of the individual. Proponents of this shift have argued that both individual and community security are essential for the security of the state and for global stability.[53] The UN describes *human security* as including economic security, food security, health security, environmental security, personal security, community security, and political security.[54] According to Kofi Annan, former Secretary General of the UN:

> **human security** Rather than viewing security from a state-centered approach, human security is a people-, or person-, centered understanding of security that takes into account the multitude of variables that impinge upon a person's or community's ability to be safe and/or secure.

> Human security, in its broadest sense, embraces far more than the absence of violent conflict. It encompasses human rights, good governance, access to education and health care and ensuring that each individual has opportunities and choices to fulfill his or her potential. Every step in this direction is also a step towards reducing poverty, achieving economic growth and preventing conflict. Freedom from want, freedom from fear, and the freedom of future generations to inherit a healthy natural environment – these are the interrelated building blocks of human – and therefore national – security.[55]

Human trafficking

A pressing human security concern is the illegal trafficking of women and girls. It is one of the fastest growing areas of international criminal activity, ranked third behind drugs and guns. Although exact figures are hard to come by, the US government estimates that more than 800,000 people are trafficked each year. Typically, women and children from poor countries are trafficked to wealthier countries and placed in cities, tourist towns, or around military bases where demand for prostitution is high. Most of the victims are under the age of 25 and have been abducted or acquired through deception. False employment promises comprise one common approach.[56] The most common form of human trafficking (79 percent) involves sexual exploitation. It is also the most frequently reported. The second most common (18 percent) involves forced labor. Trafficking for exploitation in the following areas tends to be under-reported: domestic servitude, forced marriage, and organ removal.[57] Women kidnapped for sexual slavery often have their passports and/or identity papers stolen. They are then transferred to another country and forced to work as prostitutes. Many women are regularly beaten and abused, and HIV/AIDS contraction rates are high.[58] Research has also found that more women participate in human trafficking than in other forms of crime. In some cases, former victims become the perpetrators of these crimes.[59]

Researching to Learn   *Investigating Human Trafficking*

Free Web Resources

Organizations:

Anti-Slavery International.
For full text documents see "Resources" at:
www.antislavery.org/#.

Criminal Justice Resources. Human Trafficking
Maintained by the Michigan State University
Libraries.
http://staff.lib.msu.edu/harris23/crimjust/
human.htm#c

GlobalRights.org: Partners for Justice Online. Human Trafficking
www.globalrights.org/site/PageServer?pagename=
wwd_index_49

Human Rights Watch. Women's Rights
www.hrw.org/en/home

HumanTrafficking.Com
http://actioncenter.polarisproject.org/

Initiative Against Sexual Trafficking
www.iast.net/.

International Labour Organization. Project to Combat Trafficking in Children and Women
www.ilo.org/public/english/region/asro/bangkok/
child/trafficking/

International Organization for Migration
www.iom.int/

Interpol. Children and Human Trafficking
www.interpol.int/Public/THB/default.asp

Office to Monitor and Combat Trafficking in Persons
www.state.gov/g/tip/

Polaris Project
www.polarisproject.org/polarisproject/

Resources and Contacts on Human Trafficking
www.globalrights.org/site/DocServer?docID=643

United Nations Office on Drugs and Crime: Trafficking in Human Beings
www.unodc.org/unodc/en/human-trafficking/
index.html

US Department of Health & Human Services: The Campaign to Rescue & Restore Victims of Human Trafficking
www.acf.hhs.gov/trafficking/

US Department of Justice. Trafficking in Persons Information
www.usdoj.gov/whatwedo/whatwedo_ctip.html

US State Dept. Victims of Trafficking and Violence Protection Act of 2000: Trafficking in Persons Report 2007
www.state.gov/g/tip/rls/tiprpt/2007/

Women's International League for Peace and Freedom
www.peacewomen.org/resources/Trafficking/
traffickingindex.html

Reports:

2005 Country Reports on Human Rights Practices
www.state.gov/g/drl/rls/hrrpt/2005/index.htm
2005 Trafficking in Persons Report
www.state.gov/g/tip/rls/tiprpt/2005/
Bales, Kevin and Stephen Lize. *Trafficking in Persons in the United States.* Oxford, MS: University of Mississippi, 2005.
www.ncjrs.gov/pdffiles1/nij/grants/211980.pdf
Clawson, Heather J., Mary Layne and Kevonne Small. *Estimating Human Trafficking into the United States: Development of a Methodology.* Fairfax, VA: Caliber, 2006.
www.ncjrs.gov/pdffiles1/nij/grants/215475.pdf
Gest, Ted. *How Law Enforcement is Combating the Human Trafficking Problem.* Washington, DC: Forum on Crime and Justice, n.d.
www.sas.upenn.edu/jerrylee/programs/fjc/paper_
may5.pdf
Hughes, Donna M. "The 'Natasha' Trade: Transnational Sex Trafficking." *The National Institute of Justice Journal.* January 2001: 8–15.
www.uri.edu/artsci/wms/hughes/natasha_nij.pdf
Human Rights Center. University of California Berkeley. *Hidden Slaves: Forced Labor in the United States.* Berkeley, CA: 2004.
http://digitalcommons.ilr.cornell.edu/cgi/
viewcontent.cgi?article=1007&context=forcedlabor

The Human Smuggling and Trafficking Center. *Fact Sheet: Distinctions Between Human Smuggling and Human Trafficking*. Washington, DC: 2005. www.usdoj.gov/crt/crim/smuggling_trafficking_facts.pdf

International Association of Chiefs of Police. *The Crime of Human Trafficking: A Law Enforcement Guide to Identification and Investigation*. Alexandria, VA. http://new.vawnet.org/category/Documents.php?docid=1024&category_id=683

Laczko, Frank and Marco A. Gramegna. "Unbearable to the Human Heart: Trafficking in Children and Action to Combat it." *Browne Journal of World Affairs* X, no. 1 (2003): 179–94. www.watsoninstitute.org/bjwa/archive/10.1/SexTrafficking/Laczko.pdf

Office of Crime Victims Advocacy. *Human Trafficking: Present Day Slavery. The Report of the Washington State Task Force Against Trafficking of Persons*. Washington, DC: 2004. www.wcsap.org/advocacy/PDF/trafficking%20taskforce.pdf

Raymond, Janice G., Donna M. Hughes, and Carol J. Gomez, C. J. *Sex Trafficking of Women in the United States: International and Domestic Trends*. Coalition Against Trafficking in Women. 2001. www.uri.edu/artsci/wms/hughes/sex_traff_us.pdf

US Department of Justice. *Report on Activities to Combat Human Trafficking*. Washington, DC: 2006. www.justice.gov/crt/crim/trafficking_report_2006.pdf

United States Government Accountability Office. *Human Trafficking: Better Data, Strategy, and Reporting Needed to Enhance US Anti-Trafficking Efforts Abroad*. Washington, DC: 2006. www.gao.gov/new.items/d06825.pdf

Books: Find Them @ Your Library

Albanese, Jay. *Transnational Crime*. Whitby, ON: de Sitter Publications, 2005.

Archavanitkul, Kritaya and Philip Guest. *Managing the Flow of Migration: Regional Approaches*. Nakhon Pathom, Thailand: Institute for Population and Social Research, 1999.

Bales, Kevin. *Disposable People: New Slavery in the Global Economy*. Berkeley, CA: University of California Press, 2004.

Bales, Kevin. *Understanding Global Slavery: A Reader*. Berkeley and Los Angeles, CA: University of California Press, 2005.

Beeks, Karen and Delila Amir. *Trafficking and the Global Sex Industry*. Lanham, MD: Lexington Books, 2006.

Berdal, Mats and Monica Serrano. *Transnational Organized Crime and International Security: Business as Usual?* Boulder, CO: Lynne Rienner, 2002.

Carpenter, Charli R. *Innocent Women and Children: Gender, Norms and the Protection of Civilians*. Aldershot, UK and Burlington, VT: Ashgate, 2006.

Dupont, Alan. *East Asia Imperiled: Transnational Challenges to Security*. Cambridge: Cambridge University Press, 2001.

Emmers, Ralf. *Globalization and Non-Traditional Security Issues: A Study of Human and Drug Trafficking in East Asia*. IDSS working paper, No. 62. Singapore: Institute of Defence and Strategic Studies, Nanyang Technological University, March 2004.

Hazlewood, Nick. *The Queen's Slave Trade: John Hawkyns, Elizabeth I, and the Trafficking in Human Souls*. New York: William Morrow, 2004.

Hernandez, Carolina G. and Gina R. Pattugalan. *Transnational Crime and Regional Security in the Asia Pacific*. Quezon City, Philippines: ISDS, 1999.

Kelly, Robert J. et al. *Illicit Trafficking: A Reference Handbook*. Santa Barbara, CA: ABC-CLIO, 2005.

King, Gilbert. *Woman, Child for Sale: The New Slave Trade in the 21st Century*. New York: Chamberlain Bros., 2004.

Kumar Rupesinghe and Marcial Rubio C., *The Culture of Violence* (Tokyo/New York: United Nations University Press, 1994).

Kyle, David and Rey Koslowski. *Global Human Smuggling: Comparative Perspectives*. Baltimore,

MD: The Johns Hopkins University Press, 2001.

Malarek, Victor. *The Natashas: Inside the New Global Sex Trade.* New York: Arcade Time Warner Book Group, 2004.

McGill, Craig. *Human Traffic: Sex, Slaves and Immigration.* London: Vision, 2003.

Naim, Moises. *Illicit: How Smugglers, Traffickers and Copycats are Hijacking the Global Economy.* New York: Doubleday, 2005.

Newman, Edward and Joanne van Selm. *Refugees and Forced Displacement: International Security, Human Vulnerability, and the State.* New York: United Nations University Press, 2003.

Smith, Paul J. *Human Smuggling: Chinese Migrant Trafficking and the Challenge to America's Immigration Tradition.* Washington, DC: Center for Strategic & International Studies, 1997.

Stoecker, Sally and Louise Shelley. *Human Traffic and Transnational Crime: Eurasian and American Perspectives.* Lanham, MD: Rowman & Littlefield, 2005.

van Schendel, Willem and Itty Abraham. *Illicit Flows and Criminal Things: States, Borders and the Other Side of Globalization.* Bloomington, IN: Indiana University Press, 2005.

Williams, Phil and Dimitri Vlassis. *Combating Transnational Crime: Concepts, Activities and Responses.* Portland, OR: Frank Cass, 2001.

In 2003, the Protocol to Prevent, Suppress and Punish Trafficking in Persons, especially Women and Children, came into force. It is the first treaty that defines illegal trafficking. It also requires nations to take domestic and international actions to combat it. According to the UN Office on Drugs and Crime, the protocol was designed to facilitate "efficient international cooperation in investigating and prosecuting trafficking in persons cases." Another important objective was the protection and assistance of trafficking victims.[60]

Human rights

One key component of human security is the protection of human rights. According to renowned human rights scholar Louis Henkin:

> Human rights are universal: they belong to every human being in every human society. They do not differ with geography or history, culture or ideology, political or economic system, or stage of societal development. To call them "human" implies that all human beings have them, equally and in equal measure, by virtue of their humanity, regardless of sex, race, age; regardless of high or low "birth," social class, national origin, ethnic or tribal affiliation; regardless of wealth or poverty, occupation, talent, merit, religion, ideology, or other commitment. Implied in one's humanity, human rights are inalienable and imprescriptible: they cannot be transferred, forfeited, or waived; they cannot be lost by having been usurped, or by one's failure to exercise or assert them . . . human rights are claims we have upon society.[61]

However, nowhere in the world do women and girls enjoy the same level of rights protections as their male counterparts. In some cases, the differing levels are inscribed in state law, while in others they are a matter of custom or practice. For example, many countries, including Iran, Saudi Arabia, and Afghanistan, have state laws that restrict women's educational and occupational opportunities, as well as their ability to move about freely. In other countries, customary practices denying women access to land (Ethiopia), forcing young girls into marriages (India), and harassing women who seek non-traditional forms of employment (the US) are culturally inscribed ways in which women's rights are violated.

Sexual violence

One of the more persistent human rights violations endured by women is sexual violence. Sexual violence is common in almost every country in the world, but in some countries the problem has reached epidemic proportions. South Africa, for example, is now referred to as the "rape capital" of the world because it has the highest reported incidence of rape, with more than one-third of all women having been subject to violent rape. Rape has become so endemic in South Africa that a 2002 BBC report refers to its prevalence as a "war against women and children."[62] A 2009 study revealed that more than a quarter of South African men "admitted to having raped, and 46% of those said they had raped more than once."[63] Minority groups such as lesbians have also been deliberately targeted. A report in 2009 found there to be an increase in "corrective rapes," a term that refers to the gang-rape of lesbians by men who claim that they are attempting to "cure them" of being gay.[64] South Africa's constitution is one of the only ones in the world that explicitly includes protections for gays and lesbians, and it also contains very progressive statements on gender equality. However, there is a widening divide between the ideals espoused in its constitution and the reality of continued violence against women.

South Africa is not alone in seeing many of its female citizens subjected to sexual assault. According to *Médecins Sans Frontières* (Doctors Without Borders), Liberia, Burundi, the Democratic Republic of Congo, South Africa, and Colombia all experience some of the highest incidence of rape, with an average of 35 women and girls being attacked each day.[65] Rape and sexual violence have also become endemic in the US. According to the US *Centers for Disease Control and Prevention* (CDC), one in six women in the United States has experienced an attempted or completed rape. In 2000, the US Justice Department estimated that a woman was raped every 90 seconds in the US.[66] In Cambodia a dangerous new trend of gang-raping women has emerged. Known as *bauk*, groups of young men, often middle-class teenagers and college students, rape women and girls, many of whom, though not all, are prostitutes. Typically, one or two men either lure a girl away from a gathering or agree to pay a prostitute for her services, generally at a rate of $15 for the whole night. Once the woman is isolated, a group of the man's friends join him to victimize the girl or woman. As of mid-2009, no prosecutions of *bauk* cases had occurred, leading many to criticize the government for its failure to address this war on women.[67]

Médecins Sans Frontières An NGO that delivers medical and humanitarian assistance to underserved areas of the world.

Centers for Disease Control and Prevention US government agency that conducts research and disseminates information on health and safety issues.

Even in countries where rape is illegal, customary practices or ill-formed ideas about sexual violence lead to serious consequences for females. In some countries, victims of rape are killed for having "dishonored" their families. For example, in 2008, a 13-year-old Somali girl was stoned to death for "adultery" after having been raped by three militia men.[68] Although usually illegal in countries where it occurs, this type of human rights abuse against women is the product of long-standing cultural practices. Honor killings have occurred in Bangladesh, Great Britain, Brazil, Ecuador, Egypt, India, Israel, Italy, Jordan, Pakistan, Morocco, Sweden, Turkey, and Uganda. In some cases, an underage male relative is chosen to commit the crime because any penalty imposed would be reduced because of age.[69] In other countries, rape and/or sexual violence are something that women are accused of bringing upon themselves either by their clothing (wearing revealing clothes) or their actions (drinking).[70]

Prostitution

Another form of sexual violence that affects women disproportionately is prostitution. Globally, women make up an overwhelming percentage of those in dire poverty. Some women enter into prostitution in response to dire poverty and lack of economic opportunities, while others are forced into sexual slavery. As the economy of Zimbabwe collapsed in the late 1990s, for example, young college women turned to prostitution in order to pay tuition fees as well as to provide for basic items, such as food. In many countries, children are forced into prostitution, because of economic hardship. In the US, for example, there are approximately 300,000 child prostitutes.[71] In some countries, the sex industry has emerged as an economic engine. In a 1998 study, the ILO found that in Indonesia, Malaysia, Philippines, and Thailand, the sex industry generated between 2 and 14 percent of the countries' total *gross domestic product* (GDP).[72] Tourist companies cater to men, mainly from the United States, Western Europe, and Japan, who travel to developing countries, primarily the Caribbean, Latin America, and Southeast Asia, to participate in the sex industry. Trip prices include visits to prostitutes and sex industry-related bars, clubs, and teahouses. Because of a common but incorrect belief that young girls are less likely to have HIV/AIDS, there has been a drop in the age of girls in the brothels. It is not uncommon for Western men to pay for sex with girls as young as 9.[73] However, concern about the extent of sex tourism involving children has led UNICEF, *UNWTO*, and representatives from the tourist industry to create an ethical code of conduct for the industry.[74]

In South Africa, along the truck routes where prostitution flourishes, a form of high-risk sex called "dry sex" is practiced. Men will pay prostitutes more for "dry sex" because they find it more enjoyable. "Dry sex" involves making the vagina as dry as possible. This is accomplished through a variety of methods, including soaking the vagina in bleach or inserting herbs into it. For women, this type of sex is painful and even potentially deadly because, without lubrication, the tissue in

gross domestic product (GDP)   A measure of a country's total output and national income in a year.

United Nations World Tourism Organization (UNWTO)   The UNWTO promotes sustainable and responsible global tourism.

and around the vagina tears. As a result, disease-carrying viruses, such as HIV, can enter the body more easily.[75] Despite the risks, women engage in dry sex either because they have little choice but to do as the client instructs, or because they can earn twice as much money by doing so.

Armed conflict

Everyone's security and human rights are at risk during armed conflicts. Specifically, escalations of sexual violence are quite common during wars. However, as noted international relations scholar Cynthia Enloe has argued, the raping of conquered soldiers' women has often been configured as the victor's just reward, or excused as "just what soldiers do."[76] This view was challenged following the Balkans conflict in the 1990s, which saw the establishment of dozens of rape camps where tens of thousands of women and girls were sexually assaulted and tortured. The blatant and systematic use of rape as a tool of war was so extreme that the international community responded by elevating rape to the status of a war crime. The adoption of the *Crime Statute of the International Criminal Court* provides that "rape, sexual slavery, enforced prostitution, forced pregnancy, enforced sterilization and other forms of sexual violence are war crimes when committed in the context of armed conflict and also under defined circumstances, crimes against humanity."[77] Labeling this type of violence as a "*crime against humanity*" may help remove the stigma of sexual violence from the victim and help place the blame where it belongs, on the perpetrator.

Crime Statute of the International Criminal Court Establishes the International Criminal Court (ICC) and outlines the structure, types of crimes which can come before the court, and the rules under which the court will operate.

crime against humanity Widespread, systematic, gross violations of human rights by governments, their agents, or other ruling authorities.

Although women are usually the primary targets of sexual violence, men too are sometimes sexually violated during war, though the numbers are far fewer. More typically, males become the victims of physical violence, murder, and forced conscription, with boys as young as 7 being forced to participate in various conflicts. In 2009, more than 300,000 children, both male and female, were forced to serve as soldiers for various military and non-government militia groups.[78] Additionally, because males are perceived as a physical threat in conflicts, militaries and militias often target them when entering a village. For example, during the Bosnian war, there were many cases of Muslim men being rounded up by Serb militias and forced into concentration camps. In one notorious camp, Omarska, the men were starved, abused, and killed. The scene was so gruesome it drew comparisons to Auschwitz during World War II.[79]

Refugees are another product of armed conflicts. By the end of 2007, there were at least 11.4 million refugees, of whom at least half were female.[80] Refugees are people who have had to flee their home countries in other to stay alive or to avoid unjust persecution by their governments. People can only be classified as refugees if they have crossed an international border, have a well-founded fear of persecution, and are unable to seek assistance from their own government. According to international law, that fear

refugees People who have fled their home from persecution, crossed an international border, and cannot avail themselves of the protection of their home government.

Taliban   The ruling party/group in Afghanistan from 1996 to 2001. Their Sunni Islamic fundamentalist interpretation of the Koran resulted in a repressive state that violated its citizens' human rights, and particularly those of women. Resurgent again in 2004, but operating out of Pakistan and parts of Afghanistan.

asylum   Protection granted to individuals who have fled their home country typically due to political reasons. The protection is usually granted by a foreign sovereign authority.

of persecution must be based on "reasons of race, religion, nationality, membership of a particular social group or political opinion."[81] Because the definition does not include gender, women who fled from the *Taliban*, for example, because of its gender-based persecution practices, are not technically considered refugees. This distinction is important, because there are benefits accorded to those with refugee status, such as material things like food and shelter, but also the ability to apply for and receive *asylum* in another country. Asylum is the granting of protection by one government to a citizen of another country. For example, an Iraqi dissident who fled from Saddam Hussein's regime could have applied to the US for asylum. If the request was granted, that person would be allowed to stay in the US and become a US citizen. Because gender-based persecution is not recognized under international law, victims have traditionally been unable to apply for asylum. However, beginning in the 1990s, Canada paved the way for change when it began using the "social group" membership status referred to in the 1951 Refugee Convention as a way to classify women who fled gender-based persecution. The US and the EU followed suit. There have been several high-profile cases in the US of women who were allowed to stay after proving that they would be persecuted based on their gender if they were forced to return home. However, international law remains unchanged in this regard.

Most refugees are not granted asylum by any countries. For the millions of people around the world fleeing their homes or sitting in refugee camps, life can be exceedingly difficult. Women are often sexually and physically abused during their flights. In some cases, border guards demand sex for access into their countries. During the 1980s, the types of brutal violence that female refugees were subjected to could be summed up with the phrase "Thai pirate." Refugees fleeing the conflicts in Southeast Asia boarded rickety boats and headed for Thailand. On the seas, their boats were boarded by Thai pirates who stole the refugees' belongings and raped the women and girls who were on board. After several women came forward and accused the pirates of rape, the pirates quickly changed tactics. Rather than simply raping the refugee women, they began to kill them as well.[82]

Women and girls who manage to make it across an international border and find a refugee camp are still at risk of physical and sexual abuse. In some camps, sexual slavery is demanded in exchange for food and other necessary items. In other cases, women are in danger simply because their communities do not consult with them about their needs, allow them to make decisions that affect their own health and well-being, or provide them with access to important documentation. In cultures in which women's fates are decided by their nearest male relatives, women have to get their consent in order even to travel abroad. In some cases, travel documents are issued to the family but not to its individual female members. Should their male relatives desert them, the document-less refugee women could face arrest for being in a country illegally.

Table 8.2 UN Treaties Specific to Women

Treaty	Year
Convention for the Suppression of the Traffic in Persons and of the Exploitation of the Prostitution of Others	1949
Equal Remuneration Convention	1951
The Convention on the Political Rights of Women	1952
The Convention on the Nationality of Married Women	1957
The Convention on Recovery Abroad of Maintenance	1956
Discrimination (Employment and Occupation) Convention	1958
Convention against Discrimination in Education	1960
The Convention on the Consent to Marriage	1962
The Convention on the Elimination of all forms of Discrimination against Women	1979
Protocol to Prevent, Suppress and Punish Trafficking in Persons, Especially Women and Children, supplementing the United Nations Convention against Transnational Organized Crime	2003

UN human rights efforts

Addressing women's human rights has been a concern of the United Nations since its founding. It has promulgated a variety of treaties that include protections for women (see table 8.2). For example, the UN Charter, the Universal Declaration of Human Rights, the International Covenant on Civil and Political Rights, and the International Covenant on Economic, Social and Cultural Rights all state that the rights delineated in each apply to everyone, regardless of gender (though most often the word used by the UN is "sex"). For example, Article 55 of the Charter of the United Nations states that "the UN shall promote . . . universal respect for, and observance of human rights and fundamental freedoms for all without distinction as to race, sex, language or religion." Nations pledged themselves to achieve these objectives by taking both "joint and separate action in co-operation with the Organization."[83]

Although the Charter and the aforementioned human rights documents are significant, many human rights activists and feminists have argued that they did not do enough to stop discrimination against women. As a result, they called for the promulgation of several other international agreements designed to address gender specific concerns. For example, participants in the Mexico City (1975) conference suggested that a treaty specifically designed to end all forms of discrimination against women be promulgated. In 1979, just before the 1980 convention in Copenhagen, the General Assembly adopted the Convention on the Elimination of All Forms of Discrimination Against Women (CEDAW).[84] The CEDAW not only condemns discrimination against women but also confers upon nations that sign it a responsibility "to pursue by all appropriate means and without delay a policy of eliminating discrimination against women."[85] The Convention specifically demands that states refrain from actions that abuse women's rights and it also requires that states ensure that women are protected from abuse that may occur at the hands of non-state actors, such as individuals, organizations, or enterprises. The Convention describes discrimination against women as:

> any distinction, exclusion or restriction made on the basis of sex which has the effect or purpose of impairing or nullifying the recognition, enjoyment or exercise by women, irrespective of their marital status, on a basis of equality of men and women, of human rights and fundamental freedoms in the political, economic, social, cultural, civil or any other field.[86]

While 185 nations are parties to the CEDAW, the US did not ratify it because of senatorial reservations over provisions that mandated equal pay for equal work and that guaranteed reproductive rights for women. The Convention represented a step forward for women's rights, but the reservations (conditions states attach to treaties) were actually longer than the text of the treaty itself. For example, the reservation from Kuwait states: "The government of Kuwait enters a reservation regarding article 7 (a), inasmuch as the provision contained in that paragraph conflicts with the Kuwaiti Electoral Act, under which the right to be eligible for election and to vote is restricted to men." Egypt's reservation reads: "The Arab Republic of Egypt is willing to comply with the content of [Article 2], provided that such compliance does not run counter to Islamic Sharia."[87]

Education and Health

Education and training

A 2000 UN report found that there had been an increased awareness among member nations of the need to educate women and girls; however, the report also noted that there is often a lack of political will, insufficient resources, and/or cultural practices that work to prevent women and girls from having access to education.[88] This is particularly true of rural families, which are often reluctant to send girls to school because their labor is needed at home. They also often view educating women as a waste of money. For example, societies in which married women move in with their husbands' families tend not to be interested in spending money to educate a female child because that expenditure will not ultimately translate into benefits for the family paying for the education. In contrast, in communities in which male offspring are responsible for providing for their parents, it is considered a good use of money to spend it on the education of boys, since they can use that education to earn more money to support them. Rural areas are also often at an educational disadvantage, lacking adequate schools and requiring students to travel great distances to attend. This poses problems for the education of girls, who are often not allowed to travel without supervision. Fears about sending girls to school without familial supervision are not unfounded. Amnesty International (AI) reported that females in many countries suffer sexual harassment and sexual violence in schools. For example, AI found that 50 percent of girls in Zimbabwean junior secondary schools experienced unsolicited sexual contact by strangers as they went to and from their schools, with 92 percent of these reporting that the contact came from older men.[89] Similar situations were found in other countries as well.

In addition to these obstacles, other factors also negatively impact female education levels. In some countries, religion is used to prevent females from pursuing an education. For example, in Afghanistan under the Taliban, Islam was used to justify the state policy of not educating girls.[90] Schools for girls have been targeted for violence in Pakistan, Algeria, and Afghanistan. In one area of Pakistan, where Taliban insurgents organized after they were overthrown in 2003 by NATO led forces, the UN estimates that between 170 and 200 girls' schools have been torched, leaving more than 80,000 girls without a school to go to, or too afraid to attend school.[91] (See figure 8.2 for an overview, by region, of the numbers of boys and girls who are kept out of school.) In some countries, gender dictates the type of education a female may receive. For example, after the 1979 revolution in Iran, women were denied access to certain types of education, such as engineering for example, because, it was argued, these subject were inappropriate for women. Stereotyping labor by gender continues in many societies as well. The often higher-paying technology, industry, or heavy labor jobs are typically the domain of males, while females are relegated to menial labor, including textile- and domestic-related work. As a result, in many areas, vocational training, where available, is reserved for males. Because women's labor is assumed to be centered around the home, very few resources are dedicated to establishing formal training programs for females to learn vocational or technical skills. Finally, women who get married very young and begin to have children have no time for education and most schools do not have childcare facilities.

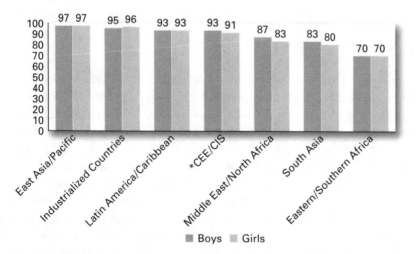

Figure 8.2 Percentage of Primary School Age Boys and Girls Out of School[92]
Primary School Net Enrollment/Attendance Ratio of Boys and Girls, by Region (2000–6)
* CEE/CIS refer to Russia and former Soviet allied countries.

Health

World Health Organization (WHO)
The UN agency that monitors health-related issues around the world.

Health care is another area in which biological differences and sociological factors affect women's needs and access to appropriate care. According to the *World Health Organization* (WHO), health is defined as "a state of complete physical, mental, and social well-being and not merely the absence of disease and infirmity."[93] Women's health is of particular concern because when they are sick and can't function, the whole family suffers. According to the WHO, the health of women and girls is at risk because of a variety of socio-cultural factors, including:

* unequal power relationships between men and women;
* social norms that decrease education and paid employment opportunities;
* an exclusive focus on women's reproductive roles; and
* potential or actual experience of physical, sexual and emotional violence.[94]

As discussed earlier, sexual violence and prostitution leave women vulnerable to various forms of sexually transmitted disease, and while women make up approximately 50 percent of AIDS victims, in several countries their numbers outpace men. For example, according to the UN, 75 percent of all Africans (15–24 years of age) with HIV are women.[95] This is often attributable not only to sexual violence, but also to women's lack of decision-making authority. Women the world over are in no position to abstain from sex or to demand that their partners wear condoms. UNAIDS Deputy Director Kathleen Cravero explains:

> A woman who is a victim of violence or the fear of violence is not going to negotiate anything, let alone fidelity or condom use. . . . Her main objective is to get through the day without being beaten up. Real-life prevention strategies for women include reducing the levels of violence against women, protecting their property and inheritance rights and ensuring their access to education.[96]

This reality for many women, particularly those living in poverty, partially explains the international outrage over comments made in the spring of 2009 by Pope Benedict XVI during a visit to several African countries. He claimed that condoms only serve to increase the spread of AIDS: "You can't resolve it with the distribution of condoms," the pope told reporters. "On the contrary, it increases the problem."[97] Critics of the Pontiff argued that his comments could provide an excuse for men who did not want to wear condoms, thereby making women even more vulnerable to contracting the disease.[98] Women's health is also jeopardized by extreme levels of poverty, which sometimes lead them to engage in risky sexual behavior. A study on women in Botswana and Swaziland indicated that women who lacked adequate access to nutrition were 80 percent more likely to engage in survival sex and 70 percent more likely to engage in unprotected sex than women with adequate nutrition.[99]

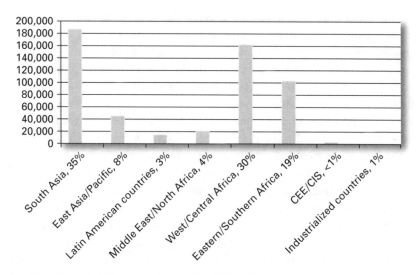

Figure 8.3   Maternal Mortality by Region, 2005[100]

Maternal mortality rates are also affected by poverty levels. Women in developing countries are much more likely to die in childbirth than women in developed countries. (See figure 8.3 for an overview of maternal mortality by region). While pregnancy can be dangerous in developed countries, health care systems in those countries are much better equipped to deal with the complications that can arise. In many developing countries, maternal mortality rate are high simply because of a lack of trained health professionals. Common causes of preventable maternal deaths include infections, bleeding, obstructed labor, and pre-eclampsia. Sierra Leone has the highest rate of maternal mortality, with 1 in 8 women dying, while Ireland has the lowest, at 1 in 48,000. According to a 2008 report in the *Washington Post*, somewhere in the world a woman dies every minute as a result of childbirth.[101] In addition, many women die because they have too many children, too often, too early, or too late.

Another issue that poses serious health consequences for women is female genital mutilation/cutting (FGM/C). There are several types of cutting/mutilation performed on female genitalia around the world, but the three most common are clitoridectomy, excision, and infibulation. Clitoridectomy, which is the removal of all or part of the clitoris, is generally considered the mildest form of FGM/C. Excision removes or partially removes not only the clitoris but also the labia minora and may include excision of the labia majora. Infibulation, the most extreme form of FGM/C, narrows the vaginal opening, creating a seal that is formed by "cutting and repositioning the inner, and sometimes outer, labia, with or without removal of the clitoris."[102] UNICEF reports that FGM/C is "normally performed by traditional practitioners with crude instruments, such as knives, razor blades and broken glass, usually without anesthetics."[103]

Both FGM/C and the terminology used to describe it are very controversial. Rationales for the procedure often revolve around religious and/or cultural beliefs and practices. Some scholars argue that outsiders should not impose their cultural standards and values on the cultures where FGM/C is performed. Others maintain that advocates for its elimination get so carried away by the emotion of the issue that they lose sight of the cultural significances of the practice.[104] Many critics of FGM/C claim, however, that the practice poses serious risks to women's health that outweigh any cultural value it might be perceived to have.[105] Critics also note that the cultural argument is problematic because culture is not static; it can and does change. Additionally, many cultures around the world have engaged in practices that are considered problematic if not heinous by today's standards, such as slavery. The fact that slavery has been part of many cultures does not justify its practice nor negate the harm it has done to countless individuals and communities. Critics of FGM/C employ the same argument, maintaining that the harm it causes to women cannot be justified or negated simply because the practice has existed in certain cultures. While the rationale behind the procedure can be debated, its effects cannot. Women and girls who undergo FGM/C are at increased risk for infection, disease, and death. Sex and childbirth are excruciatingly painful, and childbirth can lead to the mother's death. Of the 100–130 million women currently living with the consequences of this procedure, almost all were children when the procedure was performed, and almost all were given no choice in the matter. In communities that ostensibly allow girls or young women to choose, those who opt out are so stigmatized that the "choice" isn't a real one.

While proponents of the procedure sometimes dismiss criticisms as "Western feminist imperialism," much of the work currently being done to put an end to FGM/C is being carried out by local women (and some men), most of whom have undergone the procedure and do not want their daughters to have to go through it as well. For example, many women in the country of Eritrea have faced this dilemma. Eritrea achieved its independence in 1991 after a 30-year war with Ethiopia. Roughly 30 percent of the fighters were women. Many of these women were rural peasant women who found a sense of pride, self-worth, and confidence through their experiences fighting for their country's independence. Some of them have refused to have their daughters undergo FGM/C. However, these women have found that other family members, including women, want the practice to continue. In some cases, women who have steadfastly refused to subject their daughters to the procedure have returned home from work only to find that their children's grandmother, aunt, or a male relative took it upon themselves to have the child undergo the procedure.[106]

Conclusion

While globalization is frequently discussed in gender-neutral terms, its processes often affect men and women in different ways. The decisions of international economic institutions like the World Bank and International Monetary Fund, for example, affect women and men around the world, but in some cases, programs have led to increased rates of female poverty in developing countries. Development efforts designed to improve the well-being of people in developing countries have also sometimes failed because they did not include women in the development process and/or because plans and programs were based on inaccurate assumptions about gender. While the UN has demonstrated its commitment to formulating treaties and programs that attempt to achieve gender equality for people around the world, it is clear that there is still much work to be done. International organizations and policy-makers have found that just "adding women in" without addressing the gender norms, roles, and power structures underpinning societies is not likely to bring about dramatic change. Instead, policy-makers are working on "mainstreaming" gender issues and increasing their understanding of the conscious and unconscious operations of power relations within societies. Understating how globalization and gender intersect in the context of a variety of issues, such as labor, migration, human security, human rights, education, training, and health, can provide a solid foundation for both state and non-state actors to formulate policies that have the potential to benefit all members of society.

Notes

1 J. Ann Tickner, *Gender in International Relations: Feminist Perspectives on Achieving Global Security* (New York: Columbia University Press, 1992).

2 V. Spike Peterson and Anne Sisson Runyan, *Global Gender Issues* (Boulder, CO: Westview Press, 1993), 9.

3 "UN-Government Joint Programme Aims to Strengthen Gender Equality in Viet Nam" (March 19, 2009), www.un.org.vn/index.php?option=com_content&task=view&id=840&Itemid=260.

4 Manfred B. Steger, *Globalization: A Very Short Introduction* (Oxford: Oxford University Press, 2003), 13.

5 Peterson and Runyan, *Global Gender Issues*, 5.

6 Ibid., 1–5.

7 Lesley Wroughton, "World Bank Reports more People Living below Poverty Line," Reuters (August 27, 2008), http://uk.mobile.reuters.com/mobile/m/FullArticle/p.dskads/eUK/CWORUK/nworldNews_uUKN2638426620080827?kw=qa?keyWords=jpm%20jpmorgan%20chase%20and.

8 United Nations Economic and Social Council, Commission on Sustainable Development acting as the preparatory committee for the World Summit on Sustainable Development Organizational

session (April 30–May 2, 2001); "Combating Poverty Report of the Secretary-General" (March 14, 2001), http://daccessdds.un.org/doc/UNDOC/GEN/N01/290/82/PDF/N0129082.pdf?OpenElement.

9 Valentine M. Moghadam, "The 'Feminization of Poverty' and Women's Human Rights," UNESCO (Paris, France: Gender Equality and Development Section Division of Human Rights Social and Human Sciences Sector UNESCO, July 1995).

10 Christine Grumm, "Help Eliminate Poverty – Invest in Women," *Christian Science Monitor* (October 17, 2008), www.csmonitor.com/2008/1017/p09s01-coop.html.

11 James Heintz, "Globalization, Economic Policy and Employment: Poverty and Gender Implications," International Labour Organization (Geneva, Switzerland: International Labour Office, 2006), 9, www.ilo.org/public/english/employment/strat/download/esp2006-3.pdf.

12 Jacques Gelinas, *Freedom from Debt: The Reappropriation of Development through Financial Self-Reliance* (New York: St Martin's Press, 1998), 7.

13 Adam Smith, *An Inquiry into the Nature and Causes of the Wealth of Nations* (Chicago, IL: University of Chicago Press, 1977 [1776]).

14 Susan Ehrlich Martin and Nancy C. Jurik, *Doing Justice, Doing Gender: Women in Legal and Criminal Justice Occupations* (Thousand Oaks, CA: SAGE, 2006), 109.

15 Columbia Law School, www.law.columbia.edu/focusareas/legacy_portal.

16 Judith Hope and Justice Stephen Breyer, *Pinstripes & Pearls: The Women of the Harvard Law School Class of '64 Who Forged an Old-Girl Network and Paved the Way for Future Generations* (New York: Simon and Schuster, 2003), 26.

17 "Graciela Gil Olivarez (b. 1928, d. 1987)," Arizona Women's Heritage Trail, www.womensheritagetrail.org/women/GracielaGilOlivarez.php.

18 For a detailed analysis of several economic approaches and a feminist critique of each, see, Tickner, *Gender in International Relations.*

19 Megan Rowling, "Women Farmers Toil to Expand Africa's Food Supply," Reuters India (December 26, 2008), http://in.reuters.com/article/worldNews/idINIndia-37187320081226.

20 "Agricultural Gender and Food Security," FAO, www.fao.org/gender/en/agri-e.htm.

21 Fiona Flintan, *"Engendering" Eden.* Vol. II: *Women, Gender and ICDPs in Africa: Lessons Learnt and Experiences Shared,* IIED Wildlife and Development Series, no. 17 (June 2003), www.sarpn.org.za/documents/d0000512/P473_IIED2_June2003.pdf.

22 Sue Ellen M. Charlton, "Gender and Development" lecture, www.pitt.edu/~super1/lecture/lec1141/021.htm.

23 Shahrashoub Razavi and Carol Miller, "From WID to GAD: Conceptual Shifts in the Women and Development Discourse," United Nations Research Institute for Social Development, Occasional Paper 1, United Nations Development Programme (February 1995), www.unrisd.org/unrisd/website/document.nsf/0/d9c3fca78d3db32e80256b67005b6ab5/$FILE/opb1.pdf.

24 Ibid., 18.

25 Charlton, "Gender and Development" lecture.

26 For some examples of how SAPs affected women, see, Giovanni A. Cornia, Richard Jolly, and Frances Stewart, *Adjustment with a Human Face: Country Case Studies,* vols. 1 and 2 (Oxford: Oxford University Press, 2001), Charles Fonchingong, "Structural Adjustment, Women, and Agriculture in Cameroon," *Gender & Development* 7, no. 3 (November 1999), 73–9; Ailie Cleghorn and Rosemary Gordon, "The Effects of Structural Adjustment on the Educational Status of African Women: Zimbabwe," *Education & Society* 17, no. 2 (1999), 19–31; Saliwe M. Kawewe and Robert Dime, "The Impact of Economic Structural Adjustment Programs [ESAPs] on Women and Children: Implications for Social Welfare in Zimbabwe," *Journal of Sociology & Social Welfare* 27, no. 4 (December 2000), 79; Dooly Arora, "Structural Adjustment Program and Gender Concerns in India," *Journal of Contemporary Asia* 29, no. 3 (1999), 328.

27 Pamela Sparr, *Mortgaging Women's Lives: Feminist Critiques of Structural Adjustment* (London: Zed Books, 1994).

28 World Bank, "Gender and Economic Adjustment in Sub-Saharan Africa," no. 19 (June 1994), www.worldbank.org/afr/findings/english/find19.htm.

29 World Bank, "Gender and the Bank," http://web.worldbank.org/WBSITE/EXTERNAL/TOPICS/EXTGENDER/0,,contentMDK:20260262~menuPK:489120~pagePK:210058~piPK:210062~theSitePK:336868,00.html. For more on the Millennium Goals, see the section below, "United Nations."

30 United Nations World Conference of the International Women's Year, "Declaration of Mexico on the Equality of Women and Their Contribution to Development and Peace," Adopted at the World Conference of the International Women's Year Mexico City, Mexico (June 19–July 2, 1975), www.un-documents.net/mex-dec.htm.

31 UNIFEM, "About us," www.unifem.org/about/.

32 Judith P. Zinsser, "From Mexico to Copenhagen to Nairobi: The United Nations Decade for Women, 1975–1985," *Journal of World History* 13, no. 1 (Spring 2002), 139.

33 "Women 2000: Equity, Development and Peace," United Nations, www.unicef.org/beijing5/main.htm.

34 For more on the Beijing Platform for Action as well as the Fourth World Conference on Women, go to: www.un.org/womenwatch/daw/beijing/platform/.

35 "Beijing +5 Women 2000 Equality Development, and Peace, for the 21st Century," United Nations, www.un.org/womenwatch/confer/beijing5/about.htm.

36 "Beijing+5 Process and Beyond," United Nations, www.un.org/womenwatch/daw/followup/beijing+5.htm.

37 Ibid.

38 For more information on the MDGs and news about their progress, go to: http://endpoverty2015.org/goals.

39 Martha Chen, Joann Vanek, Francie Lund, James Heintz, Renana Jhabvala, and Christine Bonner, *Progress of the World's Women 2005 Women, Work, Poverty* (New York: United Nations Development Fund for Women, 2005), www.un-ngls.org/orf/women-2005.pdf.

40 Jennifer Pepall, "Bangladeshi Women and the Grameen Bank" (August 4, 1998), www.idrc.ca/en/ev-5066-201-1-DO_TOPIC.html.

41 See, for example, M. Jahangir Alam Chowdhury, Dipak Ghosh, and Robert E. Wright, "The Impact of Micro-credit on Poverty: Evidence from Bangladesh," *Progress in Development Studies* 5, no. 4 (October 2005), 298–309; Shahidur R. Khandker, Hussain A. Samad, "Income and Employment Effects of Micro-credit Programmes: Village-level Evidence from Bangladesh," *Journal of Development Studies* 35, no. 2 (December 1998), 96.

42 "Global Employment Trends for Women March 2009," International Labour Organization, 2009, www.ilo.org/wcmsp5/groups/public/---dgreports/---dcomm/documents/publication/wcms_103456.pdf.

43 "State of World Population 2006: A Passage to Hope Women and International Migration," United Nations Population Fund, www.unfpa.org/swp/2006/english/print/introduction.html.

44 Ibid., www.unfpa.org/swp/2006/english/chapter_2/index.html.

45 Susan Forbes Martin, "Women and Migration," Consultative Meeting on Migration and Mobility and How This Movement Affects Women United Nations Division for the Advancement of Women (December 2–4, 2003), www.un.org/womenwatch/daw/meetings/consult/CM-Dec03-WP1.pdf.

46 "State of World Population 2006: A Passage to Hope Women and International Migration."

47 United Nations Population Fund, www.unfpa.org/swp/2006/english/chapter_2/millions_of_faces.html.

48 Forbes Martin, "Women and Migration," 7.

49 "Migrant Remittances 'top $100bn,'" BBC (April 8, 2005), http://news.bbc.co.uk/2/hi/business/4423383.stm.

50 IMF, *World Economic Outlook Globalization and External Imbalances* (April 2005), 69, www.imf.org/external/pubs/ft/weo/2005/01/index.htm.

51 Max Tuñón, "Internal Labour Migration in China: Features and Responses," ILO (April 2006), 7, www.ilo.org/public/english/region/asro/beijing/download/training/lab_migra.pdf.

52 Source: "Global Employment Trends for Women, March 2009," ILO, www.ilo.org/wcmsp5/groups/public/---dgreports/---dcomm/documents/publication/wcms_103456.pdf.

53 For example, Yuen Foong Khong, "Human Security: A Shotgun Approach to Alleviating Human Misery?" *Global Governance* 7, no. 3 (July–September 2001); Astri Suhrke, "Human Security and the Interests of States," *Security Dialogue* 30, no. 3 (September 1999), 265–76; Peter Stoett, *Human and Global Security: An Exploration of Terms* (Toronto, Canada: University of Toronto Press, 1999); Caroline Thomas and Peter Wilkin, eds., *Globalization, Human Security, and the African Experience* (Boulder, CO: Lynne Rienner, 1999); Majid Tehranian, ed., *Worlds Apart: Human Security and Global Governance* (London: I. B. Tauris, 1999); Judith Large, Timothy D. Sisk, Vidar Helgesen, and Jan Eliasson, eds., *Democracy, Conflict and Human Security* (Concord, MA: Paul & Co Pub Consortium, 2007); and Thanh Dam Truong, Saskia Wieringa, and Amrita Chhachhi, *Engendering Human Security: Feminist Perspectives* (Hampshire, UK: Palgrave Macmillan 2007).

54 For more information on human security and the UN, see: http://ochaonline.un.org/Home/tabid/2097/Default.aspx.

55 Kofi Annan, "Secretary-General Salutes International Workshop on Human Security in Mongolia," Two-Day Session in Ulaanbaatar (May 8–10, 2000). Press Release SG/SM/7382

(August 27, 2001), www.un.org/News/Press/docs/2000/20000508.sgsm7382.doc.html.

56   Forbes Martin, "Women and Migration," 25–6.

57   UNODC, "Global Report on Trafficking in Persons Executive Summary" (February 2009), 2, www.unodc.org/documents/human-trafficking/Executive_summary_english.pdf.

58   Public Broadcasting Service, "Sex Slaves," *Frontline* (2006), www.pbs.org/wgbh/pages/frontline/slaves/.

59   UNODC, "Global Report on Trafficking In Persons Executive Summary."

60   "The United Nations Convention against Transnational Organized Crime and its Protocols," United Nations, www.unodc.org/unodc/en/treaties/CTOC/index.html.

61   Louis Henkin, et al., *Human Rights* (New York: Foundation Press, 1999), 3–4.

62   Carolyn Dempster, "Rape – Silent War on SA Women," BBC (April 9, 2002), http://news.bbc.co.uk/2/hi/africa/1909220.stm.

63   Megan Lindow "South Africa's Rape Crisis: 1 in 4 Men Say They've Done It," *Time* (June 20, 2009), www.time.com/time/world/article/0,8599,1906000,00.html.

64   Annie Kelly, "Raped and Killed for being a Lesbian: South Africa ignores 'corrective' attacks," *Guardian* (March 12, 2009), www.guardian.co.uk/world/2009/mar/12/eudy-simelane-corrective-rape-south-africa.

65   "Rape has become normal – MSF" News24 (May 3, 2009), www.news24.com/News24/South_Africa/News/0,,2-7-1442_2480780,00.html.

66   Resolution before the 108th Congress of the US, 1st Session, H. CON. RES. 57, "Supporting the Goals of International Women's Day," in the House of Representatives (February 27, 2003), http://thomas.loc.gov/cgi-bin/query/z?c108:H.+Con.+Res.+57.

67   Rachel Louise Snyder, "Gang Rape Pervasive across Cambodia," *All Things Considered*, National Public Radio (February 16, 2009), www.npr.org/templates/story/story.php?storyId=97550640.

68   Chris McGreal, "Somalian Rape Victim, 13, Stoned to Death," *Guardian* (November 3, 2008), www.guardian.co.uk/world/2008/nov/03/somalia-rape-amnesty.

69   Hillary Mayell, "Thousands of Women Killed for Family 'Honor'," *National Geographic News* (February 12, 2002), http://news.nationalgeographic.com/news/2002/02/0212_020212_honorkilling.html.

70   Colleen Ward, "The Attitudes toward Rape Victims Scale," *Psychology of Women Quarterly* 12, no. 2 (June 1988), 127; Mark Whatley, "The Effect of Participant Sex, Victim Dress, and Traditional Attitudes on Causal Judgments for Marital Rape Victims," *Journal of Family Violence* 20, no. 3 (June 2005), 191–200.

71   National Public Radio, "Keeping Young Girls Off the Streets," *All Things Considered* (August 12, 2003), www.npr.org/templates/story/story.php?storyId=1393770; Beth E. Richie, Kay Tsenin, and Cathy Spatz Widom "Research on Women and Girls in the Justice System: Plenary Papers of the 1999 Conference on Criminal Justice Research and Evaluation – Enhancing Policy and Practice Through Research, Volume 3," National Institute of Justice (September 2000), www.ncjrs.gov/pdffiles1/nij/180973.pdf.

72   International Labour Office, *The Sex Sector: The Economic and Social Bases of Prostitution in Southeast Asia*, ed. Lin Lean Lim (Geneva, Switzerland, 1998), www.ilo.org/global/About_the_ILO/Media_and_public_information/Press_releases/lang--en/WCMS_007994/index.htm.

73   Kimberly Bender and Rich Furman, "The Implications of Sex Tourism on Men's Social, Psychological, and Physical Health," *The Qualitative Report* 9, no. 2 (June 2004), 176–91, www.nova.edu/ssss/QR/QR9-2/bender.pdf.

74   Led by tourism industry representatives, nongovernmental organizations, and UN agencies, the code of conduct asks those working in the field of tourism to commit themselves to the following:

1   To establish an ethical policy regarding commercial sexual exploitation of children.
2   To train the personnel in the country of origin and travel destinations.
3   To introduce a clause in contracts with suppliers, stating a common repudiation of commercial sexual exploitation of children.
4   To provide information to travelers by means of catalogues, brochures, in-flight films, ticket-slips, home pages, etc.

5   To provide information to local "key persons" at the destinations.

6   To report annually.

For more information, see: www.thecode.org/.

75   Hank Hyena, "'Dry Sex' Worsens AIDS Numbers in Southern Africa," Salon.com (December 10, 1999), www.salon.com/health/sex/urge/world/1999/12/10/drysex/; "Concern Voiced over 'Dry Sex' Practices in South Africa," *The Lancet* 352 (October 17, 1998), 1292, www.cirp.org/library/disease/HIV/baleta1/.

76   Cynthia Enloe, *Does Khaki Become You? The Militarization of Women's Lives* (London: Pandora Press, 1983); *Bananas, Beaches and Bases: Making Feminist Sense of International Politics* (Berkeley, CA: University of California Press, 1989); *The Morning After: Sexual Politics at the End of the Cold War* (Berkeley, CA: University of California Press, 1993); and *Maneuvers: The International Politics of Militarizing Women's Lives* (Berkeley, CA: University of California Press, 2000).

77   "Gender Mainstreaming Mandates: Crime Prevention Beijing Platform for Action 1995)," Office of the Special Adviser on Gender Issues and Advancement of women, www.un.org/womenwatch/osagi/gmcrimeprev.htm.

78   United Nations, "Child Soldiers," www.un.org/cyberschoolbus/briefing/soldiers/soldiers.pdf.

79   Peter W. Van Arsdale, *Forced to Flee: Human Rights and Human Wrongs in Refugee Homelands* (Lanham, MD: Lexington Books, 2006), 79.

80   UNHCR Statistical Yearbook 2007, *Tends in Displacement, Protection and Solutions* (Geneva, Switzerland: UNHCR, December 2008), 12, www.unhcr.org/cgi-bin/texis/vtx/home/opendoc.pdf?id=4981c3252&tbl=STATISTICS.

81   "The 1951 Refugee Convention," United Nations, www.unhcr.org/cgi-bin/texis/vtx/protect?id=3c0762ea4.

82   Barbara Crossette, "Thai Fishermen Again Brutalizing Vietnam Refugees, Survivors Say," *New York Times* (May 2, 1988), www.nytimes.com/1988/05/02/world/thai-fishermen-again-brutalizing-vietnam-refugees-survivors-say.html.

83   UN Charter, 1945, www.un.org/aboutun/charter/chapter9.shtml.

84   UN, "Short History of CEDAW Convention," www.un.org/womenwatch/daw/cedaw/history.htm.

85   Convention on the Elimination of All Forms of Discrimination against Women, www.unhchr.ch/html/menu3/b/e1cedaw.htm.

86   Ibid.

87   Henkin, *Human Rights*, 363.

88   "Report of the Ad Hoc Committee of the Whole of the Twenty-third Special Session of the General Assembly, General Assembly Official Records Twenty-third Special Session Supplement No. 3 (A/S-23/10/Rev.1)," United Nations (New York: United Nations, 2000), http://www.un.org/womenwatch/daw/followup/as2310rev1.pdf.

89   "Violence against Girls in Schools: Key Facts," Amnesty International, www.amnesty.org/en/key-facts/violence-against-girls.

90   Rosemarie Skaine, *The Women of Afghanistan under the Taliban* (Jefferson, NC: McFarland, 2002), 65.

91   UN IRIN, "Pakistan: Origins of the Violence in Swat Valley" (March 30, 2009), www.irinnews.org/Report.aspx?ReportId=83105.

92   Source: UNICEF, "Progress for Children: A World Fit for Children Statistical Review," http://images.google.com/imgres?imgurl=http://www.unicef.org/progressforchildren/2007n6/images/pfc6_mdg3_primary_school_net_enrolment-attendance_ratio_of_boys_and_girls_by_region.gif&imgrefurl=http://www.unicef.org/progressforchildren/2007n6/index_41798.htm&usg=__w6hSv-oQF1iaMHuRbOAl5LgS4a0=&h=422&w=400&sz=14&hl=en&start=1&sig2=1dzTL2ZVzRgw2JC4i_vpXQ&um=1&tbnid=z4dnjCNJxVNPEM:&tbnh=126&tbnw=119&prev=/images%3Fq%3DPercentage%2Bof%2BPrimary%2BSchool%2BAge%2BBoys%2Band%2BGirls%2Bout%2Bof%2BSchool%26hl%3Den%26client%3Dfirefox-a%26rls%3Dcom.google:en-US:official%26sa%3DN%26um%3D1&ei=scLWSYyCJKbstQOnxf2tCg.

93   "Constitution of the World Health Organization," World Health Organization, www.who.int/governance/eb/who_constitution_en.pdf.

94   "Women's Health," World Health Organization, www.who.int/topics/womens_health/en/.

95   Michael Fleshman, "Women: The Face of AIDS in Africa," *Africa Renewal* 18, no. 3 (October 2004), 6, www.un.org/ecosocdev/geninfo/afrec/vol18no3/183women_aids.htm.

96   Ibid.

97   Associated Press, "Pope: Condoms not the answer in AIDS fight," MSNBC (March 17, 2009), www.msnbc.msn.com/id/29734328/.

98   Mario de Queiroz "Africa: Pope on Condoms – Out in the Cold," Inter Press Service News Agency (March 23, 2009), http://ipsnews.net/africa/nota.asp?idnews=46239.

99   UNAIDS, "2008 Report on the Global AIDS Epidemic" Executive Summary, http://data.unaids.org/pub/GlobalReport/2008/JC1511_GR08_ExecutiveSummary_en.pdf.

100   Source: UNICEF, World Health Organization, United Nations Children's Fund and the World Bank, "Maternal Mortality in 2005: Estimates developed by WHO, UNICEF, UNFPA and the World Bank," (Geneva: WHO, 2007), 35, www.unicef.org/sowc09/docs/SOWC09-Figure-1.2-EN.pdf.

101   Kevin Sullivan, "A Mother's Final Look at Life," *The Washington Post* (October 12, 2008), A01, www.washingtonpost.com/wp-dyn/content/story/2008/10/11/ST2008101102636.html?sid=ST2008101102636.

102   "Female Genital Mutilation," WHO, Fact sheet no. 241 (May 2008), www.who.int/mediacentre/factsheets/fs241/en/.

103   "Agencies Call for End to Female Genital Mutilation" (April 9, 1997), www.unicef.org/newsline/fgm2.htm.

104   Ahmed Abdel Magied, "Sloganeering and Over Simplification Approach to the Complex Issue of Female Genital Mutilation (FGM) in the Sudan," *Ahfad Journal* 24, no. 1 (June 2007), 3–15; Ellen Gruenbaum, "Socio-cultural Dynamics of Female Genital Cutting: Research Findings, Gaps, and Directions," *Culture, Health & Sexuality* 7, no. 5 (September/October 2005), 429–41; Norma Claire Moruzzi, "Cutting Through Culture: The Feminist Discourse on Female Circumcision," *Critique: Critical Middle Eastern Studies* 14, no. 2 (Summer 2005), 203–20.

105   UNFPA, "Gender Equality Calling for an End to Female Genital Mutilation/Cutting," www.unfpa.org/gender/practices1.htm; Neil Ford, "Communication for Abandonment of Female Genital Cutting: An Approach Based on Human Rights Principles," *International Journal of Children's Rights* 13, no. 1/2 (January 2005), 183–99; James Whitehorn, Oyedeji Ayonrinde, and Samantha Maingay, "Female Genital Mutilation: Cultural and Psychological Implications," *Sexual & Relationship Therapy* 17, no. 2 (May 2002), 161–70.

106   Patricia J. Campbell, "Gender and Post-conflict Civil Society," *International Feminist Journal of Politics* 7, no. 3 (September 2005), 377–99.

9

INFORMATION AND COMMUNICATION TECHNOLOGIES

"When we change the way we communicate, we change society." (Clay Shirky, *Here Comes Everybody: The Power of Organizing without Organizations*, 2008)[1]

"See, we're gonna take the news and put it on the satellite and then we're gonna beam it down into Russia, and we're gonna bring world peace, and we're gonna get rich in the process! Thank you very much!" (Ted Turner, CNN launch speech, 1980)[2]

"The explosion of information has changed everyone's life, nowhere more than on the Internet. Now, think about the Internet, how rapidly it's become part of our lives. In 1969 the government invested in a small computer network that eventually became the Internet. When I took office, only high energy physicists had ever heard of what is called the World Wide Web. . . . Now even my cat has its own Web page." (Bill Clinton, Knoxville Auditorium Coliseum, Tennessee, October 10, 1996)[3]

"Fifteen years ago, what is now a common every day sentence like 'I Googled his blog on my Blackberry' would seem positively screwy." (Mike Pesca, NPR Reporter, *All Things Considered*, April 9, 2008)[4]

Learning to Question, Questioning to Learn

- What are some of the ways that information and communication technologies have facilitated globalization processes?
- What kinds of information skills are needed to be personally, professionally, and academically successful in the Information Age?
- What factors contribute to the existence of digital divides both within specific countries and between developed and developing countries?
- How might information and communication technologies facilitate development?
- What are some of the potentially positive and potentially negative consequences of the globalization of media?

Introduction

This chapter begins with a general discussion of information and communication technologies (ICTs). It then explores the relationship between ICTs and conceptions of the Information Age and the Digital Age. Next, the chapter shifts to the topic of networks and networking, with a particular focus on the Internet. It provides a brief history of the Internet and the World Wide Web, followed by a discussion of online social networks. The chapter then discusses the digital divide and the role of information and communication technologies in international development efforts. The final section examines "new media," concluding with an analysis of common arguments about the relationship between the media and globalization processes.

Information and Communication Technologies

We live in a period of unprecedented technological change. The speed and extent of these changes are a direct result of a set of interrelated and converging technologies that are often referred to as information and communication technologies (ICTs). ICT is a broad umbrella term encompassing the technological infrastructure and products that facilitate the acquisition, storage, analysis, manipulation, and distribution of information. The past 20 years have seen the widespread adoption of the three dominant ICT technologies: the personal computer, the cell phone/mobile device, and the Internet. However, the term ICT also includes a variety of other technologies that enable the collection, processing, transmission, and presentation of information in a number of ways, including voice, data, text, images, video, and animation. As such, ICTs include things like webcams, email, DVDs, flash memory, hard drives, servers, and networks, as well as the software and infrastructure that support them.

It should be noted that pre-digital means of generating, transmitting, and archiving information can also be described as information and/or communication technologies, since the term "*technology*," broadly defined, refers to the development and use of tools, crafts, and techniques to solve problems and control/adapt to specific environments. In this framework, a tool as simple as a pencil is a technology. This might seem like an odd claim, since we are accustomed to equating "technology" with new technological products – inventions that are unfamiliar and often cutting-edge. What counts as technology in common usage, then, is always shifting; technology isn't so much a practical tool, craft, or technique, as it is the newest tools and inventions. As a result, when a technology becomes so pervasive that it is thoroughly integrated into our lives, it ceases to be considered a "technology" at all. For example, many of us don't consider things like writing and print or even film and

technology The development and use of tools, crafts, and techniques to solve problems and to control/adapt to specific environments.

television to be information technologies, because they have been thoroughly integrated into our societies for a long time. Instead, we tend to equate "technology" with computers and electronic gadgets. However, as these devices become more thoroughly integrated into our lives, they too are likely to cease to appear to us as "technologies" at all.

Today, the term ICT is generally used to refer to the *digital* technologies that have rapidly changed the world since the advent of the first personal computer, the Altair 8800, released in 1975 by the New Mexico-based company Micro Instrumentation and Telemetry.[5] Indeed, ICTs are the primary instruments facilitating globalization processes, as international communication flows, including the "transnational circulation of cultural commodities" such as texts, images, and videos,[6] are delivered through ICT services and platforms. ICTs penetrate "all areas of economic and social activity";[7] without them, the global economy and the networked information society would not have been possible. ICTs eroded the constraints of space and time on social interaction, and this erosion was a necessary prerequisite to the formation of a global economy "with the capacity to work as a unit in real time, or chosen time, on a planetary scale."[8]

> **digital**   Process whereby real-world information is converted into binary numeric form (0s and 1s).

ICT also encompasses terms like information technology (IT) and media. As a broader term, it is particularly useful because it reflects the *convergence* of communications, computer, and media technologies. Scholars who study ICTs use the term convergence to refer to the blurring of boundaries between these categories, which have traditionally been considered distinct. MIT political scientist Ithiel de Sola Pool was likely the first to outline the concept of convergence in his 1983 book entitled *Technologies of Freedom*. Pool claims that:

> **convergence**   Describes the blurring of boundaries between, or the coming together of, media, information technology, and telecommunications sectors.

> A process called the "convergence of modes" is blurring the lines between media, even between point-to-point communications, such as the post, telephone and telegraph, and mass communications, such as the press, radio, and television. A single physical means – be it wires, cables or airwaves – may carry services that in the past were provided in separate ways. Conversely, a service that was provided in the past by any one medium – be it broadcasting, the press, or telephony – can now be provided in several physical ways. So the one-to-one relationship that used to exist between a medium and its use is eroding.[9]

Today, much of what Pool foresaw has come to pass. Computers, the Internet, and mobile phones are delivering a variety of media and communication services that previously had been provided in separate ways. News articles, for example, are not confined to print newspapers, sitcoms are not confined to televisions, and radio programming is not confined to the AM and FM dials. Rather, the content traditionally associated with separate media can be accessed online. Sometimes we even see all three – a news article, an audio clip, and a video clip – on a single webpage that also includes communication options, such as discussion boards and chat forums.

Mobile phones in particular are increasingly emblematic of convergence. As Henry Jenkins, author of *Convergence Culture* (2006) points out:

> Our cell phones are not simply telecommunications devices; they also allow us to play games, download information from the Internet, and take and send photographs or text messages. Increasingly they allow us to watch previews of new films, download installments of serialized novels, or attend concerts from remote locations.[10]

However, the changes ICTs have engendered go beyond convergence. ICTs have created "new forms of action and interaction and new kinds of social relationships – forms that are different from the kind of face-to-face interaction which has prevailed for most of human history."[11] They allow people to share information and to communicate with each other at any time and in any place, effectively separating human interaction from spatial-temporal contexts. As such, ICTs extend human interaction, allowing people who are dispersed in space and time to act in response "to events taking place in distant locales."[12] Because of the important social and economic transformations brought about by ICTs, this chapter will look not only at ICT technologies but also at the political, social, and economic practices and social arrangements that emerge as the result of the development and diffusion of ICTs.

The Information Age

The period in which we are living today is sometimes referred to as "The Information Age," a time characterized by the proliferation of information and the ability to transfer, share, and instantly access information that previously would have been difficult, if not impossible, to find. Many consider this period to have begun in the last 20 years of the twentieth century and to have been expedited in the mid-1990s by the development and widespread use of the Internet. However, the Information Age and its related concepts – the Information Society, the Knowledge Society, and the Information Revolution – have a longer history. In 1962, Austrian-American economist Fritz Machlup examined knowledge as an economic resource and introduced the concept of the "knowledge industry," a term designed to distinguish information-based jobs from industrial ones. He divided the knowledge industry into five sectors with 52 branches, including jobs like publishing, broadcasting, research and development, information machines, and even religion.[13] In his book *The Production and Distribution of Knowledge in the United States* (1962), Machlup claimed that in 1958, approximately 29 percent of America's GNP came from "knowledge industries."[14] A few years later, Peter Drucker, building on Machlup's work, coined the term "knowledge work" and argued that "the base of our economy shifted from manual to knowledge work, and the centre of gravity of our social expenditure from goods to knowledge."[15] In *The Age of Discontinuity*, he argued that the "impact of cheap, reliable, fast and universally available information will easily be as great as was the impact of electricity."[16] In 1977, Marc Porat expanded upon these ideas in *The Information Economy*, an influential nine-volume report for the US government. The report claimed that information sectors accounted for over half of all economic activity in the US, a significant increase over Machlup's estimate. As such, Porat concluded that the US was quickly becoming an information society.[17] Writing around the same time as Porat, American sociologist Daniel Bell argued that the US was transitioning from an industrial society into a service-oriented information society, which he called "the post-industrial society." In his book *The Coming of Post-Industrial Society* (1976), Bell maintained that in post-industrial, service-based societies, "what counts is not raw muscle power, or energy, but information."[18] What unites researchers like Machlup, Drucker, Porat, and Bell is the idea that the Industrial Age was ending and a new economic order was emerging, "characterized by the central importance of information and theoretical knowledge, and by a shift from a goods-producing to a service society."[19]

These early writers helped popularize the idea that we are living in an Information Age, but they also had their critics. Some critics argued, for example, that their writings about post-industrialism actually helped to create the changes that they purported to describe.[20] Others maintained that the much heralded "information society" is better understood as a continuation and extension of former historical periods and processes rather than as a radical break with the past. In this framework, the current Information Age is not something new; it is simply the product of the ongoing relationship between technological development and the proliferation of information. From Johannes Gutenberg's development of the printing press around 1440, which allowed news and knowledge to spread across Europe much faster than ever before, to Larry Page and Sergey Brin's co-founding of Google in 1998,[21] increases in the availability of information have long been linked to the development of new technologies.

Information overload

Other writers have accepted the idea that we are living in an Information Age that is markedly different from previous historical periods, while taking issue with descriptions of this shift as inherently progressive and positive. Noted sociologist and futurologist Alvin Toffler is one such example. Toffler viewed the changes being wrought by the Information Age as constituting a revolutionary shift that is, "in all likelihood, bigger, deeper, and more important than the industrial revolution."[22] He coined the phrase "future shock" in 1970 to describe the inability to keep up with "the greatly accelerated rate of change in society"[23] and identified "information overload," or the inability to "absorb, manipulate, evaluate and retain information" due to cognitive overstimulation, as one of its causes.[24] In other words, information overload occurs when there is too much information to be able to access and use it effectively and efficiently. Toffler notes that as the speed of change accelerates, people are forced to "adapt to a new life pace, to confront novel situations and master them in ever shorter intervals . . . to choose among fast-multiplying options. . . . We are, in other words, forcing them to process information at a far more rapid pace than was necessary in slowly-evolving societies."[25] The negative side of the Information Age, then, is that people find themselves increasingly unable to adapt to the speed of change and to effectively access and use information in meaningful ways.

In his book *Data Smog* (1997), David Shenk too refers to the idea that human beings are now being asked to process information at much faster rates than has heretofore been required of them. He explains that for most of human history, people have been able to process information about as quickly as it could be created and circulated. Information and information technologies usually contributed positively to culture, facilitating the development of strategies to address life's challenges, from food production to building construction.[26] However, by the mid-twentieth century, technologies like computers, television, and satellites produced and distributed information much faster than people could process it,[27] creating a high-input "Babel of signals," in which information is more noisy than meaningful.[28] In his 1989 book *Information Anxiety*, Richard Saul Wurman recorded some startling claims that illustrate the extent of this change. For example, he reported that "more new information has been produced in the last 30 years than in the previous 5,000,"[29] and that "A weekday edition of the *New York Times* contains more information than the average person was likely to come across in a lifetime in seventeenth-century England."[30] He goes on to observe: "We are bombarded with material from the media, from colleagues, from cocktail party conversation. . . . The sheer volume of available information and the manner in which it is often delivered render much of it useless to us."[31] As such, some people see a paradox at the heart of the problem of information overload; there is a surfeit of information and yet there is also a paucity of useful information.[32]

Toffler, Wurman, and Shenk all point to information overload as one of the perils of the Information Age. Though we are surrounded, and in some cases even assaulted, by information, there is simply too much of it for it to penetrate our consciousness and be assimilated into our knowledge base. Moreover, even when we are consciously trying to uncover and access discrete units of information, it can be decidedly difficult to sift through all the available, but not particularly relevant, information to identify and access the information we need. As Shenk puts it, we have "vaulted from a state of information scarcity to one of information surplus – from drought to flood in the geological blink of an eye."[33] New information and communication technologies can thus exacerbate "information overload," since they "increase the number of people whose thoughts we encounter. Each successive development in communication technology – whether it's a cellular phone or an email account – brings a corresponding leap in the number of ideas we're forced to process."[34]

The web in particular is a technology that heightens and extends the attendant problems related to information overload. On the one hand, the web has dramatically increased the availability of information. On the other, there is so much information that it can be difficult to wade through all the inaccurate, outdated, and disreputable information in order to find the credible information that you need. In his 2004 book, *Surviving Information Overload*, Kevin A. Miller notes that when he was writing the book, a Google search for the phrase "information over-load" retrieved 725,000 results. In March of 2009, the same Google search (using quotation marks to search for the term as a phrase) retrieved just under two million results. It would take years to click through all the links, without even taking the time to read and evaluate the quality of the content.[35] To complicate the problem, the web just keeps expanding at a startling pace. Google reports that its first index in 1998 contained 26 million pages. Two years later, that number had increased to 1 billion. By 2008, Google's system for processing links found 1 trillion unique URLs on the web. Every day, several billion new pages are created and many are also deleted, making it impossible ever to know for sure how many unique pages exist.[36] What we do know is that the sheer volume of pages can actually make it more difficult to find the information we need.

In addition to texts focusing generally on information overload in society, the concept has also made its way into the academic literature of many disciplines, including medicine, business, computer and information science, and the social sciences, and many researchers have argued that it is a problem that has significant costs. Overall, researchers have found that "information overload negatively impacts the decision-making process, leading to low quality in decision-making and low complexity of output."[37] Information rates that are too high for the receiver of the information to process it efficiently lead to distraction, stress, and increasing errors.[38] Although information overload can be a problem for anyone, being information literate can reduce the possibility of being overwhelmed by information.

Information literacy – sometimes referred to as information competency, information fluency, and information and communication technology (ICT) literacy – has emerged as an important set of lifelong learning skills and values that can help people overcome information overload and successfully navigate the information society.

> **information literacy** The ability to define an information need and to effectively and efficiently find, evaluate, and use information ethically and responsibly.

Information literacy

The term "information literacy" was first used by Information Industry Association president Paul Zurkowski in a 1974 report to the National Commission on Libraries and Information Science. Zurkowski argued that new methods of information organization and storage would require new types of training to teach people how to sift through and use information effectively.[39] The term was used infrequently thereafter in the 1970s, but it gained popularity among library and information professionals in the 1980s, a time at which increasingly powerful information technologies were making it ever more apparent that people would need to learn new skills in order to retrieve and use information effectively and efficiently. In the late 1980s, for example, the American Library Association (ALA) formed a Presidential Committee on Information Literacy. The committee, which consisted of seven national leaders from the education field and six from the field of librarianship, issued their final report in January 1989. The report explicitly outlined a relationship between information overload and information literacy, arguing:

> Information literacy is a survival skill in the Information Age. Instead of drowning in the abundance of information that floods their lives, information literate people know how to find, evaluate, and use information effectively to solve a particular problem or make a decision – whether the information they select comes from a computer, a book, a government agency, a film, or any number of other possible resources.[40]

According to the report, information literate people are able to find specific information from the "super-abundance of available information" in order "to meet a wide range of personal and business needs."[41] The report also suggested that in order for the US to maintain a democratic way of life and to compete internationally in the Information Age, citizens must be trained to be information literate. The information literate person was defined as being able to "recognize when information is needed and have the ability to locate, evaluate, and use effectively the needed information." Information literate people are prepared to deal with fast rates of change because they "have learned how to learn. . . . They are people prepared for lifelong learning, because they can always find the information needed for any task or decision at hand."[42]

In 2000, the Association of College and Research Libraries (ACRL) refined its understanding of information literacy in the Information Literacy Competency Standards for Higher Education. The document consists of a series of five standards and corresponding performance indicators and outcomes for college-level educators seeking to integrate information literacy instruction into their classes. It also reaffirms librarians' commitment to an educational reform movement designed to equip students with the skills they need to succeed in the Information Age. Indeed, most academic librarians consider information literacy instruction to be one of their most important professional duties, so don't hesitate to ask them for research help and training when you need it!

Information literacy is an important discourse not only in academic institutions but also for some international organizations. For example, the United Nations Educational, Scientific and Cultural Organization (UNESCO) is committed to "fostering information and media literate societies by encouraging the development of national information and media literacy policies, including in education."[43] In November 2005, UNESCO, The National Forum on Information Literacy,[44] and the International Federation of Library Associations and Institutions (IFLA)[45] sponsored an international leadership colloquium on information literacy, which was held in Alexandria, Egypt. The meeting culminated in the Alexandria Proclamation of 2005, which recognized information literacy both as lying "at the core of lifelong learning" and as "a basic human right in the digital world" that "empowers people in all walks of life to seek, evaluate, use and create information effectively to achieve their personal, social, occupational and educational goals."[46] In addition to recognizing the importance of information literacy, UNESCO has also developed programs to equip disadvantaged people with information literacy skills. In September 2007, UNESCO's Information for All Program (IFAP) funded a global project on information literacy consisting of a series of regional Training-the-Trainers workshops at several institutions of higher education around the world. Participants are taught not only information literacy skills, but also how to teach their communities about how information literacy can help them "cope more efficiently and effectively with their personal, family and community challenges – whether social, economic or political."[47] Groups targeted to go through the training include "women; youth, including those out-of-school; unemployed and under-employed adults; migrant and refugee populations; disabled persons; rural and isolated populations; minorities living in majority cultures; and other disadvantaged groups."[48]

The Digital Age

Although conceptualizations of the Information Age and the Information Society have been around for a long time, today, they tend to trigger thoughts of contemporary digital technologies like the web, email, cell phones, high-definition television, digital cameras, rss feeds, instant messaging, texting, computer games, and other relatively new products and services. That's because the Information Age, as it manifests itself today, is linked to the Digital Age, a term that refers to the period from approximately 1980 to the present day and is characterized by the shift from *analog* electronic technology to digital technology. The term analog refers to the process of storing a set of physical properties in "another 'analogous' physical form."[49] In other words, there is an analogous relationship between input data, such as the sound of someone singing or the marks of someone's handwriting, and the media product, such as the "grooves on a vinyl disc or the distribution of magnetic particles on a tape."[50] The analogous physical form can then be decoded by some other device (e.g., a record player) so that the original properties can be replayed for the audience.[51] In contrast, the digital media process converts all input data into numbers. The smallest unit of digital information is the bit, which is either a 0 or a 1. When 0s and 1s are combined into a sequence that carries information, they are called bytes.[52]

> **analog**   Analog systems translate a signal into continuously variable, measurable, physical quantities, such as length, width, voltage, or pressure.

One way of thinking about the differences between analog and digital is to use the metaphor of communication. In the analog world, there are various media for delivering content, none of which can talk to each other. An LP record doesn't speak the same language as a video tape or a microfiche, so different devices are needed to access the content embedded in each medium. In the digital world, there is a similar language (coded as 1s and 0s) for all formats "that can be quickly read and exchanged by computers, and then decoded again by computers, and presented in a form that people can understand."[53] Digitization is the process of translating information recorded in analog forms into the language of 1, and 0s. Practically speaking, digitization and native digital production allow people to access text, music, images, video, etc. on a single computer rather than on a variety of devices. Also, because music, images, text, video, and games are no longer limited to physical media, they can all be transferred around the world on the Internet in seconds. In *Being Digital* (1995), Nicholas Negroponte describes this as a shift from "atoms to bits."[54]

Networked: The Impact of the Internet

Today's information-saturated society is not only a digital society but also a networked one. Computer networks consist of a collection of computers and devices that are connected to each other for the purposes of communication and resource sharing. Digital information can be transferred via physical networks, such as broadband cable networks and Integrated Switched Digital Networks (ISDN), as well as through satellites and wireless telephony. The Internet is the prime example of an interconnected global network. As a result of widespread access to the Internet in many parts of the world today, many people take it for granted that information can circle the globe almost instantaneously via electronic networks, which allow communication to transcend the traditional limitations of space and time. It can be easy to forget that this kind of connectedness is a relatively new phenomenon, and that computers themselves were not originally conceived of as communication tools. Rather, early computers were designed to function as isolated calculating devices that did not easily communicate with other computers. Information sharing among machines generally required the use of an additional physical storage medium, such as a punch card, that had to be physically transferred from computer to computer. Between the 1960s and 1980s, however, computers were transformed through the development of computer networks and data communication techniques.[55] Decades of work by the US military and other computer and network experts both in and outside the United States ultimately led to what we now know as the Internet.[56] As Janet Abbate puts it in her book *Inventing the Internet* (2000), "The history of the Internet is not . . . a story of a few heroic inventors; it is a tale of collaboration and conflict among a remarkable variety of players."[57]

A brief history of the Internet

The Internet's predecessor, ARPANET, was created by the US Department of Defense's Advanced Research Projects Agency (ARPA) as a way of allowing scientists to overcome the problems associated with running programs on remote computers.[58] On October 29, 1969, the first message was sent over ARPANET from UCLA to the Stanford Research Institution (SRI).[59] According to Leonard Kleinrock, head of the Network Measurement Center at UCLA, which was selected to be the first node on ARPANET, "the transmission itself was simply to 'login' to SRI from UCLA. We succeeded in transmitting the 'l' and the 'o' and then the system crashed! Hence, the first message on the Internet was 'lo!' "[60] By the end of 1969, four host computers connected approximately 1,000 researchers; just two years later, 23 host computers were linked into the network, and more continued to be added.[61] Although the original purpose of ARPANET was to share expensive resources, an electronic mail program was written in 1972, which would ultimately lead to a revolution in communication. In 1975, ARPANET was transferred to the Defense Communications Agency, which increased network security and limited access. Due to pressure for greater access, however, it split ARPANET into two networks in 1982. MILNET became a military network with tight security, while ARPANET reverted to connecting ARPA researchers.[62]

Although ARPANET was once again supporting researchers, it was only accessible to a few academic research institutions. In 1979, only 15 of the 120 academic computer science departments in the US were hooked up to ARPANET, and, as a result, scientists began building other networks.[63] For example, CSNET (Computer Science Network) was built in 1981 with support from the National Science Foundation (NSF). A network of IBM users called BITNET was also developed, linking thousands of computers around the world. By 1986, the NSF was developing a nationwide network designed to serve academia.[64] Outside the US, state-run networks were developed in a number of countries by the mid-1970s. European fears of US imperialism and ARPA managers' concern not to provoke the American public's ire by sharing tax-supported resources with "foreigners" prevented the US government-owned ARPANET from connecting to other state-run networks. The use of different protocols also prevented connections among networks around the world.[65]

As ARPANET aged, plans were made to decommission it. During 1988 and 1989, ARPANET host connections were transferred to NSFNET, and on February 28, 1990, ARPANET was formally decommissioned.[66] The transition from ARPA to the NSF was particularly significant because it "marked the end of military operation of the Internet."[67] In 1991, the NSF developed a privatization plan in which Internet service would be taken over by commercial Internet Service Providers (ISPs). On April 30, 1995, the US government's ownership of the Internet's infrastructure was formally terminated.[68] Although privatization played a role in opening up the Internet to a much larger segment of the public, so too did the development of the World Wide Web. Around the same time that ARPANET was being decommissioned, Tim Berners-Lee and his colleagues at CERN, a physics lab in Switzerland, developed the World Wide Web. The idea was "to connect hypertext with the Internet and personal computers, thereby having a single information network to help CERN physicists share all the computer-stored information at the laboratory."[69] The world's first website (info.cern.ch) was put online on August 6, 1991; it explained what the World Wide Web was and how to use it to find information.[70]

Internet   Consists of a worldwide collection of computers and sub-networks exchanging data using wires, cables, and radio links.

World Wide Web (WWW)   A huge web of interlinked documents, images, and multimedia accessible over the Internet by a system of hypertext links and URLs.

protocols (computing)   A set of rules controlling the transfer of data between computers. Common Internet protocols include HTTP, FTP, Telnet, POP3, and IMAP.

HyperText Transfer Protocol (HTTP)   A protocol for retrieving interlinked resources that led to the establishment of the World Wide Web.

web browser   A software application that enables users to display and interact with content located on the World Wide Web.

File Transfer Protocol (FTP) A network protocol that allows an FTP client to connect to an FTP server to exchange or manipulate files on that server.

search engine   A tool designed to search for information on the World Wide Web.

Although the terms *Internet* and *World Wide Web* are often used interchangeably in common parlance, the two are not synonymous. The Internet is actually the physical networking infrastructure, a massive network of networks that allows computers to communicate with other computers connected to the network. Technically speaking, the Internet consists of a matrix structure that connects all senders and receivers "through a sub-network of routing systems or servers, which distribute messages as a series of 'packets,' indifferent to the initial representational form encoded by the signal and decoded by the end-user."[71] Information travels over the Internet via a variety of languages called *protocols*. The World Wide Web uses one kind of protocol, the *HyperText Transfer Protocol (HTTP)*, to allow applications (e.g., *web browsers*) to find and access resources stored on other computers that are connected to the Internet. The web is only one mechanism through which information can be exchanged on the Internet. Other ways include instant messaging and *File Transfer Protocol (FTP)*. One way of thinking about the distinction between the Internet and the web is that the Internet can and did exist without the web, whereas the "Web requires the Internet as its transport mechanism."[72]

Prior to the development of the web, the Internet was most commonly used for file transfers and email. Its text-only interface and the difficulty of locating and retrieving information limited its popularity and use.[73] Berners-Lee's hypertext system made it possible to link information rather than having to present it linearly, which helped to improve access.[74] Although CERN had developed a web browser, a National Center for Supercomputing Applications (NCSA) team led by Marc Andreesen developed Mosaic, the first web browser that was designed to run on most personal computers. Distributed by the NCSA for free on the Internet, more than 40,000 copies of Mosaic were downloaded in the first month, and by the spring of 1994, more than a million copies were thought to be in use.[75] In 1994, Andreesen left the NCSA and developed a commercial version of Mosaic called Netscape.[76] Although the advent of web browsers like Mosaic and then Netscape led to dramatic increases in web usage, finding information on the web could still be difficult, since all users could do was type in an URL or follow links from page to page. The development of new programs called *search engines* made it possible to search for specific topics on the web, increasing the web's usefulness and, as a result, its use.

Researching to Learn   *Investigating the History of the Internet*

Sample Keyword Searches

Broad search: Internet AND history

Narrower searches:
- ARPANET AND "United States" AND "Department of Defense"
- Berners-Lee AND "World Wide Web"

Advanced searches:
- ("World Wide Web" OR Internet OR web) AND history
- (Berners-Lee OR CERN) AND "World Wide Web" AND history

Note:
- *Use quotation marks to search for terms as a phrase.*
- *Use AND to find documents with all terms listed.*
- *Use OR to find documents that contain at least one of the terms.*
- *Use parentheses to combine AND and OR statements in creative ways.*

Free Web Resources

Elon University/Pew Internet Project. "Imagining the Internet: A History and Forecast." www.imaginingtheinternet.org/

Internet Society (ISOC). "Histories of the Internet." www.isoc.org/internet/history/

Internet World Stats. "History and Growth of the Internet." www.internetworldstats.com/emarketing.htm

Kleinrock, Leonard. "The Day the Infant Internet Uttered its First Words." www.cs.ucla.edu/~lk/LK/Inet/1stmesg.html.

"The Website of the World's First-Ever Web Server." CERN. http://info.cern.ch/

World Wide Web Consortium. "A Little History of the World Wide Web." www.w3.org/History.html

Books: Find Them @ Your Library

Abbate, Janet. *Inventing the Internet.* Cambridge, MA: MIT Press, 2000.

Berners-Lee, Tim. *Weaving the Web: The Original Design and Ultimate Destiny of the World Wide Web.* New York: Collins Business, 2000.

Gillies, James and Robert Cailliau. *How the Web Was Born: The Story of the World Wide Web.* Oxford: Oxford University Press, 2000.

Hafner, Katie. *Where Wizards Stay Up Late: The Origins of the Internet.* New York: Simon & Schuster, 1998.

Moschovitis, Christos J. P. *History of the Internet.* Santa Barbara, CA: ABC-CLIO, 1999.

Articles: Find Them @ Your Library

Berners-Lee, Tim, et al. "The World-Wide Web." *Communications of the ACM* 37, no. 8 (1994): 76–82.

Hayes, Jerry. "Telecommunication Memories: 75, 50, and 25 Years Ago." *IEEE Communications Magazine* 46, no. 8 (2008): 26–9.

"Internet History From ARPANET to Broadband." *Congressional Digest* 86, no. 2 (February 2007): 35–64.

Kahn, Robert E. "The Role of Government in the Evolution of the Internet." *Communications of the ACM* 37, no. 8 (1994): 15–19.

Leiner, Barry M. et al. "The Past and Future History of the Internet." *Communications of the ACM* 40, no. 2 (1997): 102–8.

Table 9.1 History and Growth of the Internet[77]

Date	Number of Users	% World Population
December 1995	16 million	0.4%
December 1996	36 million	0.9%
December 1998	70 million	1.7%
December 1999	248 million	4.1%
December 2000	361 million	5.8%
August 2001	513 million	8.6%
September 2002	587 million	9.4%
December 2003	719 million	11.1%
December 2004	817 million	12.7%
December 2005	1,018 million	15.7%
December 2006	1,093 million	16.7%
December 2007	1,319 million	20.0%
December 2008	1,574 million	23.5%
March 2009	1,588 million	23.7%

Growth of the web

The web is now a globe-spanning system that has grown dramatically since Berners-Lee posted his first webpage in 1991. In December 1995, there were already 16 million Internet users around the world. The number more than doubled each year, to 36 million in 1996, 70 million in 1997, and 147 million in 1998. The annual doubling of total Internet users has since ceased, but we are still seeing dramatic increases. An important milestone in Internet history was reached sometime in 2005 when the one-billionth user went online. At that point, over 15 percent of the world's population was online, a dramatic increase from 0.4 percent just 10 years earlier (see table 9.1). Experts predict that the two billion mark will be reached by 2015, and that most of the new users will reside in Asia.[78]

The 2005 Pew Global Attitudes Survey found that Internet use is still increasing in both industrialized and developing countries, with the most dramatic rates of increase having occurred in Great Britain, Poland, and France (see table 9.2). The Netherlands had the highest percentage of Internet users, with 72 percent of its 2005 population reporting that they use the Internet to access the web or to send and receive email.[79] The survey also found that the majority of Internet users are on the young end of the adult spectrum, though growth rates of Internet users by age group had begun to shift by 2005 (see figure 9.1). In the United States, Canada, and Western Europe, for example, the growth rate for adults aged 50–64 outpaced that of young adults. Nevertheless, there were still more young adults online. In Canada and France, for example, over 90 percent of adults aged 18–29 report using the Internet, compared to 68 percent of Canadians and 52 percent of the French aged 50–64. Also, in countries with relatively low Internet usage, the most dramatic increases between 2002 and 2005 occurred among young adults. In China and India, Internet use rose by 15 percent for those under 30.[80]

Table 9.2 Internet Users, 2002–2005[81]

Country	2002 (%)	2005 (%)	Change (%)
Netherlands	–	72	–
Great Britain	47	71	24
Canada	68	71	3
United States	64	70	6
Germany	47	60	13
France	41	57	16
Spain	–	53	–
Morocco	–	41	–
Poland	20	38	18
Lebanon	36	37	1
China	24	33	9
Turkey	18	32	14
Jordan	25	20	–5
Russia	7	15	8
India	3	14	11
Indonesia	5	7	2
Pakistan	4	5	1

Question wording: "Do you ever go online to access the Internet or the World Wide Web or to send and receive email?"

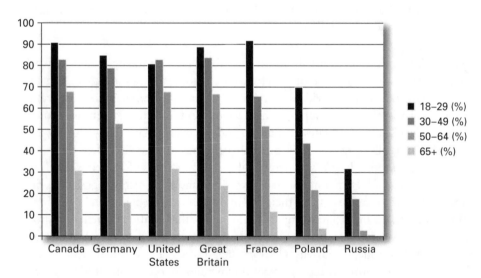

Figure 9.1 Internet Users by Age Group, 2005[82]

In the United States, over half the adult population using the Internet is between the ages of 18 and 44. The age group known alternatively as "Generation Y," the "Net Generation," or the "Millennials" (born between 1977 and 1990) makes up 26 percent of the adult population and 30 percent of the Internet-using population, and they are often considered the most net savvy.[83] However, a 2008 Pew Internet and American Life Project survey indicates that although Generation Y is the most likely group to use the Internet for entertainment and for communication with family and friends,[84] Generation X (born between 1965 and 1976) is the most likely to integrate the web into their daily life, using it for consumer, financial planning, and research tasks such as banking, shopping, and finding health information.[85]

Online participation and social networks in the network society

The web has also facilitated the development of a wide variety of social and political networks that differ in both form and function from their pre-digital counterparts. Clay Shirky, media writer and educator, observes that human beings have always been social creatures, but new technologies have provided simple ways of creating groups, which has led "to new groups, lots of new groups, and not just more groups but more kinds of groups."[86] He argues that our communication tools have now become "flexible enough to match our social capabilities," and, as a result:

> we are witnessing the rise of new ways of coordinating action that take advantage of that change. These communications tools have been given many names, all variations on a theme: "social software," "social media," "social computing," and so on. Though there are some distinctions between these labels, the core idea is the same: we are living in the middle of a remarkable increase in our ability to share, to cooperate with one another, and to take collective action, all outside the framework of traditional institutions and organizations.[87]

The sociologist Manuel Castells argues that these new technologies and networks have created a different type of society, which he refers to as the network society. In the network society, individuals and businesses benefit from new communication technologies because they support the development and dissemination of knowledge, which in turn facilitates adaptation and discovery.[88] Like many globalization theorists, Castells observes that the network society has disrupted traditional spatial and temporal barriers, which he talks about in terms of "timeless time" and "a space of flows."[89] He maintains that new communication technologies erase time and disconnect localities "from their cultural, historical, geographical meaning".[90] While this can mean, as Shirky argues, that many of the traditional barriers to group action have collapsed, freeing us "to explore new ways of gathering together and getting things done,"[91] Castells observes that there are also other, less positive effects of this collapse, including social fragmentation, obsession with image, and commercialization of communication spaces.[92]

Web 2.0
The term Web 2.0 was coined by Dale Dougherty in 2004 in response to a proliferation of new web applications that provided more opportunities for interaction, collaboration, participation, and content creation than traditional, static websites.[93] These new kinds of interactive sites, which include blogs, wikis, photo-

and video-sharing, and social network sites (like Facebook, MySpace, and Linkedin), have also been referred to collectively as the "participatory web." Rather than a primarily unidirectional medium characterized by the delivery of content from corporations and media outlets to individual consumers, the web has evolved into a platform that allows most users not only to consume content but also to respond to the content of others and to produce and publish their own. Because of the participatory aspects of Web 2.0, it has been heralded by some as the democratization of the web.

Wikis

Many are particularly excited by the way that Web 2.0 applications like wikis rely on collective intelligence. The motto that many participatory web enthusiasts espouse, "None of us is as smart as all of us," points to the exciting possibilities that are opened up when we tear down the silos that isolate us and instead pool our disparate knowledge, experiences, and strengths. As Henry Jenkins puts it, "None of us can know everything; each of us knows something; and we can put the pieces together if we pool our resources and combine our skills."[94] However, others are concerned about replacing the "authoritative heft of traditional institutions with the surging wisdom of crowds."[95] Many point out that there is value in attuning to experts, and that you cannot develop an informed perspective on a topic by giving equal weight to the claims of both experts and novices alike. They worry that the ideas of people who have earned advanced degrees, gained experience in the field, and spent much of their lives researching a topic are being treated the same as the opinions of people with no education or experience. They argue that when we fail to make distinctions among information sources, we increase our chances of getting inaccurate information. In some cases, such as when we are looking up biographical information about our favorite celebrity for our own amusement, the consequences of acquiring inaccurate information are slight. In other cases, they are far more dire. Do you want a person without a medical degree operating on your ailing parent? Do you want a contractor with no experience building your house? Do you want to take advice on climate change from someone who has no scientific education or experience? In short, critics fear that the "democratization" of information on the web has turned into a free-for-all, where any idea is considered as good as any other, and accuracy and authority are increasingly ignored.

Wikipedia, in particular, the most prominent example of wiki technology in action, has engendered a great deal of controversy. On a January 29, 2007 episode of the Colbert Report, Stephen Colbert distilled the essence of the controversy by describing Wikipedia as "[t]he encyclopedia where you can be an authority even if you don't know what the hell you're talking about."[96] Colbert's satire uses Wikipedia, the online encyclopedia that anyone can edit, to highlight the idea that what counts as truth and reality in society is changing, in part due to Web 2.0 technologies. He suggests that "truth" is frequently being determined by consensus (the majority wanting something to be true, regardless of evidence) rather than by things like facts, research, science, and the analysis of evidence by experts. The popularity of the site only fuels critics' concerns. According to Alexa's list of most visited sites, in spring 2009, Wikipedia was the most popular site in its Reference category and the seventh busiest site in the world. High use in addition to high-profile errors in Wikipedia have generated a great deal of media attention. Wikipedia scandals include the biographical entry for John Seigenthaler, Sr, a former official in the Kennedy administration, which incorrectly stated for a time that "he was thought to have been directly involved in the Kennedy assassinations of both John and his brother Bobby. Nothing was ever proven."[97] Additionally, a number of companies, including Microsoft, have attempted to hire outside services to write or edit Wikipedia entries on their companies, deleting negative content and adding positive material, in violation of the encyclopedia's mission.[98]

Despite these and other marks on its record, there have been studies that suggest that the quality of Wikipedia entries might be better than many had anticipated. A study conducted by the journal *Nature* showed that on scientific topics, Wikipedia articles had an average of about four inaccuracies (which included things like factual errors, omissions, and misleading claims), while articles in the *Encyclopedia Britannica* contained an average of three inaccuracies. Jimmy Wales, who cofounded Wikipedia in 2001, responded: "It showed people Wikipedia isn't as good as *Britannica*, but it's pretty good."[99] Indeed, many were surprised at how good. Others point out that in addition to its relatively high level of accuracy, Wikipedia has a distinct advantage over *Britannica*, in that it is more timely. Important (and not so important) events are posted almost immediately after they occur. Furthermore, the entries are often more in depth, since they are constantly being added to by people around the world who care about specific topics. An October 2006 Pew Internet Project report, for example, pointed out that the Wikipedia entry on Web 2.0 is "one of the richest sources of information on the term," while MSN's free online version of Encarta Encyclopedia didn't have a Web 2.0 entry.[100] Two and a half years later, it still didn't.

Social network sites

Social network sites, such as Facebook, MySpace, and LinkedIn, constitute another Web 2.0 technology that is changing the way people use the Internet, communicate with one another, share information, and form groups. Social network sites can be defined as:

> web-based services that allow individuals to (1) construct a public or semi-public profile within a bounded system, (2) articulate a list of other users with whom they share a connection, and (3) view and traverse their list of connections and those made by others within the system.[101]

blog Originally short for "web log," a blog is a type of website that is usually maintained by a person or corporation and that is written in the form of an online journal. Blogs contain regular entries that are usually posted in reverse chronological order. Today, most blogs are created using some sort of online software that facilitates the production of blog posts and the integration of interactive features, such as reader comments.

Most social network sites contain ways of sharing content, including images, media, and text, and many also bring together a variety of Web 2.0 applications in one place, including *blogs* and status updates (or *micro-blogging*). Although social network sites allow people to search for and meet strangers with similar interests and experiences, they are often used primarily to communicate with people who are already a part of their lives. Social networks sites are unique, however, in that they "enable users to articulate and make visible their social networks," which can in turn "result in connections between individuals that would not otherwise be made."[102]

> **micro-blogging** Form of blogging that allows users to send brief text updates (or photos or audio clips) and publish them, either to be viewed by anyone or by a restricted group that can be chosen by the user. Status updates on Facebook and "tweets" on Twitter are both forms of micro-blogging.

Young people are the most likely to use social network sites. In the United States, 75 percent of adults aged 18–24 use social networks, compared to just 7 percent of adults age 65 or older. However, a 2009 Pew Internet Project data memo reports that the share of adult Internet users in the United States who have a profile on an online social network site more than quadrupled from 8 percent in 2005 to 35 percent in December 2008. While 65 percent of teens who are online use social network sites and only 35 percent of online adults do, there are actually more adults on these sites because adults make up a larger portion of the US population than do teenagers.[103] Overall, men and women are equally as likely to use social network sites; users are more likely to be students; whites are less likely than African-Americans or Hispanics to have an online profile; and people with lower annual household incomes are more likely to have an online profile than those with higher incomes, although this is probably because more young people use social networks, and they generally make less money than older people (see table 9.3). Nevertheless, the large number (75 percent) of young adults aged 18–24 using online social networks provides some evidence that the digital divide might be narrowing in the US.

Online political networking

While the majority of Americans use social network sites for social purposes, such as staying in touch with friends, many also use them to organize with others for an event, issue, or cause.[104] During the 2008 American presidential campaign, for example, social network sites were popular venues for people to seek out political information, join organizations, and declare their affiliations.[105] While only 10 percent of Americans report using social network sites like Facebook to gather information or to become involved in political issues, half of Americans under 30 who have a social network profile use network sites to get or share information about politics and political campaigns. However, their online political activities are not limited to social network sites; they also use both older Internet technologies like email and newer ones like online videos. A Pew Internet and American Life national survey found that 46 percent of all Americans "used the internet, email, or cell phone text messaging to get news about the campaign, share their views and mobilize others."[106] The figure was calculated by adding the number of people who reported engaging in at least one of the following activities:

* 40 percent of all Americans accessed news and information about the 2008 presidential campaign from the Internet;

Table 9.3   Demographics of Social Network Users[107]

The percentage of online Americans in each demographic category who have a profile on a social network website.

All Adults	35
Sex	
Women	35
Men	35
Age	
18–24	75
25–34	57
35–44	30
45–54	19
55–64	10
65+	7
Race	
White, non-Hispanic	31
Black, non-Hispanic	43
Hispanic	48
Annual Household Income	
Less than $30,000	45
$30,000–$49,999	38
$50,000–$74,999	30
$75,000	31
Education	
Less than HS	43
HS grad	31
Some college	41
College grad	33
Locale	
Urban	34
Suburban	26
Rural	23

- 19 percent went online once a week or more to perform an activity related to the campaign, and 6 percent did so on a daily basis;
- 23 percent of Americans reported receiving emails soliciting a candidate's support or engaging them in a discussion about the campaign once a week or more;
- 10 percent used email to contribute to the political debate once a week or more;
- 4 percent exchanged political views using text messaging.[108]

Because many Americans reported that they engaged in several of the activities listed above, the figures add up to more than 46 percent. Additionally, 35 percent of Americans reported that they have watched online political videos, a figure which is three times higher than the 2004 race. The Internet also proved useful to 39 percent

Researching to Learn   *Investigating Social Networking Sites*

Sample Keyword Searches

Broad search:
- online social networks
- social network sites

Narrower searches:
- "online social networks" AND privacy
- "social network sites" AND "college students"

Advanced searches:
- (facebook OR myspace) AND ("high school students" OR teenagers OR teens) AND privacy

Note:
- *Use quotation marks to search for terms as a phrase.*
- *Use AND to find documents with all terms listed.*
- *Use OR to find documents that contain at least one of the terms.*
- *Use parentheses to combine AND and OR statements in creative ways.*

Free Web Resources

Dwyer, Catherine, et al., "Trust and Privacy Concern within Social Networking Sites: A Comparison of Facebook and MySpace." http://csis.pace.edu/~dwyer/research/DwyerAMCIS2007.pdf

Hodge, Matthew J. "The Fourth Amendment and Privacy Issues on the "New" Internet: Facebook. Com and MySpace.com." *Southern Illinois University Law Journal* (2006). www.law.siu.edu/research/31fallpdf/fourthamendment.pdf.

Journal of Computer-Mediated Communication 13, no. 1 (October 2007) of the focuses on social network sites. http://jcmc.indiana.edu/vol13/issue1/

Nussbaum, Emily. "Say Everything." *New York.* http://nymag.com/news/features/27341/

Ofcom. "Social Networking: A Quantitative and Qualitative Research Report into Attitudes, Behaviours and Use," April 2, 2008. www.ofcom.org.uk/advice/media_literacy/medlitpub/medlitpubrss/socialnetworking/report.pdf

Online Social Networks: Research Report (London, UK: Communities and Local Government, 2008). www.communities.gov.uk/documents/communities/pdf/1000435.pdf

Social Networking section on the Pew Internet and American Life Project site. www.pewinternet.org/topics/SocialNetworking.aspx

Articles: Find Them @ Your Library

Dalsgaard, Steffen. "Facework on Facebook: The Presentation of Self in Virtual Life and its Role in the US Elections." *Anthropology Today* 24, no. 6 (December 2008): 8–12.

Eberhardt, David M. "Facing Up to Facebook." *About Campus* 12, no. 4 (Sept 2007): 18–26.

Hinduja, Sameer and Justin W. Patchin, "Personal Information of Adolescents on the Internet: A Quantitative Content Analysis of MySpace." *Journal of Adolescence* 31, no. 1 (Feb 2008): 125–46,

Walther, Joseph B. et al. "The Role of Friends' Appearance and Behavior on Evaluations of Individuals on Facebook: Are We Known by the Company We Keep?" *Human Communication Research* 34, no. 1 (Jan 2008): 28–49.

Thelwall, Mike. "Social Networks, Gender, and Friending: An Analysis of Myspace Member Profiles." *Journal of the American Society for Information Science and Technology* 59, no. 8 (June 2008): 1321–30.

Gueorguieva, Vassia. "Voters, MySpace, and YouTube: The Impact of Alternative Communication Channels on the 2006 Election Cycle and Beyond." *Social Science Computer Review* 26, no. 3 (Fall 2008): 288–300.

of online Americans who used it to find unfiltered campaign materials, including videos of debates, speeches, position papers, and transcripts. Many voters are also using the Internet to bypass soundbite-driven traditional media. For example, 18 percent of Americans have watched an online video that was not produced by a traditional news organization or by a specific campaign. Young voters continue to be at the vanguard of Internet use, as 12 percent of 18–29 year olds have posted their own political commentary on an online newsgroup, website, or blog.[109]

The Digital Divide

Although Internet use has been on the rise in many developing countries, there remains a "stark divide between countries with high rates of Internet use and those with less access to this technology."[110] This gap between those with and without access to digital and information technology is often referred to as the *digital divide*. The term includes unequal access to physical ICT technologies, such as computers, mobile phones, and broadband Internet access, as well as to imbalances in the education and experience needed to develop information and technology skills. Digital divides can exist within countries, manifesting themselves in terms of demographic characteristics like age, income, race, language, and cultural background. Countries also sometimes excel in one ICT area, such as use of mobile phones, while lagging behind in others, such as high-speed Internet access. Digital divides also exist between developed and developing countries. The term *global digital divide* refers to disparities in technology access and use between countries or global regions. The 1999 Human Development Report pointed out that the World Wide Web not only connects but also excludes, providing the connected with ever greater advantages:

digital divide Refers to unequal access to physical ICTs, such as computers, mobile phones, and Internet access, as well as to imbalances in the education and experience needed to develop information and technology skills.

global digital divide Disparities in technology access and use between countries or global regions.

> The network society is creating parallel communications systems: one for those with income, education and – literally – connections, giving plentiful information at low cost and high speed; the other for those without connections, blocked by high barriers of time, cost and uncertainty and dependent on outdated information.[111]

For example, in 2005, fewer than 10 percent of the populations of Indonesia and Pakistan said that they use the Internet.[112] In all societies, education and income level are the primary factors determining Internet use. Those with higher education and income levels are more likely both to use computers and to access the Internet. In India, for example, 36 percent of people with at least some college education reported using the Internet in 2005, compared to fewer than 14 percent of those with less education.[113]

Although the US is on the information-rich side of the global digital divide, it nevertheless has an internal digital divide. A December 2008 Pew Internet and

American Life Project survey found that 57 percent of Americans earning less than $30,000 a year went online to use the web or email. In contrast, 95 percent of people earning $75,000 or more use the Internet. We see a similar trend for education levels in the US as well, with only 35 percent of those with less than a high school education using the Internet compared to 95 percent of those with a college degree.[114] (See table 9.4.) Data from a May 2008 survey found that "offline Americans are overwhelmingly over age 70, have less than a high school education, and speak a language other than English.[115] For example, while 57 percent of Latinos in the US use the Internet, 78% of those whose dominant language is English use the Internet compared with 32% of Latinos whose dominant language is Spanish.[116] Only 17 percent of Latinos age 71 and older use the Internet. As a result of these disparities, programs like Generations on Line Espanol have been launched to help elderly Latinos learn how to use the Internet.[117]

Table 9.4 Demographics of US Internet Users[118]

Adults	Use the Internet
Total adults	74%
Women	75%
Men	73%
Age	
18–29	87%
30–49	82%
50–64	72%
65+	41%
Race/ethnicity	
White, non-Hispanic	77%
Black, non-Hispanic	64%
Hispanic	58%
Geography	
Urban	71%
Suburban	74%
Rural	63%
Household Income	
Less than $30,000/yr	57%
$30,000–$49,999	77%
$50,000–$74,999	90%
$75,000+	94%
Educational attainment	
Less than high school	35%
High school	67%
Some college	85%
College+	95%

In-Focus: Internet Censorship

Government censorship of websites can also be considered a digital divide of sorts in that it keeps information out of the hands of its citizenry. Governments around the world block content for a variety of political, religious, and social reasons.[119] Some countries' censorship efforts are limited in scope, blocking access to a particular site or type of site without dramatically limiting its citizens' access to the universe of online information. Although Singapore's filtering program was highly publicized, for example, it blocks only a handful of pornographic sites.[120] Germany demanded that Nazi propaganda be eliminated from the search results of the German version of Google, but this move did little to prevent Germans from accessing such information, since users need only to use Google.com instead of Google.de to find it.[121] Additionally, in the United States, people encounter state-mandated Internet filtering in public libraries and schools, with the stated objective of protecting children from pornography and other age-inappropriate content. These government filters do not extend into people's homes, however, and in many cases, adult library users can request that the filtering software be disabled.

While any form of censorship might be considered objectionable to civil liberties advocates, many of these censoring activities do not pose a very substantial or extensive threat to people's access to information. However, this is not always the case. Some countries filter political content during elections or when they think control over information is critical to the preservation of their power. Others filter content more consistently and extensively. Saudi Arabia heavily censors social content, while Myanmar and Vietnam focus primarily on political issues. Iran stands out for its heavy filtration of both social and political topics. Countries that filter political opposition groups' websites include Bahrain, China, Ethiopia, Libya, Myanmar, Pakistan, Saudi Arabia, Syria, Thailand, Tunisia, Uzbekistan, and Vietnam.[122]

China is particularly worth noting as it has one of the most extensive Internet monitoring and censorship programs in the world, having spend "tens of millions of dollars building what has come to be known as the 'Great Firewall of China.' "[123]

Blocking occurs at various network levels and spans a range of topics. Every Internet service provider in China has a staff of "web police" who are required to monitor websites and chat-rooms for "dangerous content."[124] An analysis of filtered content tested by the Open Net Initiative shows that the Chinese filtering efforts focus heavily on keywords that fall under the following categories:

Tiananmen Square protests of 1989 A series of demonstrations held in and near Tiananmen Square in Beijing in the People's Republic of China that were led primarily by students and intellectuals. The protests began on April 14 and culminated in the Tiananmen Square Massacre, which is referred to in China as the June Fourth Incident to avoid confusion with two other Tiananmen Square protests.

1 National minority independence movements, the most well known being Tibet, but also including Xinjiang, Inner Mongolia, and some Taiwanese politicians supporting independence for Taiwan.

2 The *Tiananmen Square protests of 1989*.

3   Chinese communist leaders.
4   *Falun Gong.*
5   Any keywords relating to uprisings or suppression.[125]

The government is also constantly monitoring user-generated sites like Wikipedia and YouTube as well as popular blogging sites. In fact, when the state became concerned about bloggers espousing dissident ideas, it shut down blogging domains for weeks. The domains were brought back, but only after filters were installed that would reject posts containing designated keywords.[126] Individual YouTube videos have been blocked, as have the entire Wikipedia and YouTube sites for varying periods. Even the search engine Google was blocked in China for a time until it devised a way of eliminating the accessibility of "disfavored" content.[127] While Google admitted that removing search results is inconsistent with its mission, it argued that "providing no information (or a heavily degraded user experience that amounts to no information) is more inconsistent with our mission."[128] News sites like Voice of America and BBC are also blocked in China,[129] as are sites focusing on human rights, including Amnesty International, Human Rights Watch, and the Asian Human Rights Commission.[130]

> **Falun Gong**   An eclectic spiritual movement that began in China in the latter half of the 20th century that consists of an amalgam of religions and exercises. The Chinese Communist Party banned the organization in 1999.

ICTs and development

On September 8, 2000, the United Nations' General Assembly adopted the *Millennium Declaration*, committing rich and poor countries alike to a set of eight targets designed to end extreme poverty around the globe by 2015.[131] Rich and poor countries alike committed themselves – at the highest political level – to a set of eight time-bound targets that, when achieved, will end extreme poverty worldwide. Section III. 20 resolves: "To ensure that the benefits of new technologies, especially information and communication technologies, in conformity with recommendations contained in the ECOSOC 2000 Ministerial Declaration, are available to all."[132] In an effort to achieve this goal, the General Assembly endorsed a World Summit on the Information Society (WSIS), which took place in two phases. Phase one was held in Geneva in December of 2003, and led to the adoption of the Geneva Declaration of Principles and Geneva Plan of Action. The Declaration of Principles declared a commitment to harnessing the potential of information and communication technologies to promote Millennium Development Goals and to create an inclusive and development-oriented Information Society. It also highlighted some of the challenges to achieving this goal, such as establishing policies that attract investment in ICT infrastructure as well as establishing ubiquitous connectivity in order to

> **Millennium Declaration**   United Nations declaration signed in September 2000 consisting of eight goals and 21 targets that 192 United Nations member states and at least 23 international organizations have agreed to achieve by the year 2015. The 8 Millennium Development Goals (MDGs) are
>
> 1   eradicating extreme poverty and hunger
> 2   achieving universal primary education
> 3   promoting gender equality and empowering women
> 4   reducing child mortality
> 5   improving maternal health
> 6   combating HIV/AIDS, malaria, and other diseases
> 7   ensuring environmental sustainability
> 8   developing a global partnership for development

accelerate countries' social and economic progress.[133] The Plan of Action called on governments to work with the private sector and civil society to devise national e-strategies. Sample targets include connecting villages, universities, schools, libraries, health centers, and local governments with ICTs. Other targets include facilitating the presence and use of all the world's languages on the web and insuring that more than half the world's inhabitants have access to ICTs.[134]

Phase two of WSIS took place in Tunis in November of 2005 and was designed to put the Geneva Plan of Action into motion and to reach consensus about issues revolving around Internet governance.[135] Outcomes of the Tunis phase were the Tunis commitment and the Tunis Agenda for the Information Society. The Tunis Agenda called for the creation of the Internet Governance Forum, a multi-stakeholder body designed to discuss Internet policy issues, develop solutions to problems, advise stakeholders, and publish their proceedings. The Tunis Agenda also recommended providing affordable access to ICTs by reducing international Internet costs charged by *backbone* providers and supporting the creation and development of regional ICT backbones and Internet exchange points to broaden network access.[136]

> **backbone**   Used to describe the part of a network that connects other networks together. The Internet's backbone consists of high-capacity, high-speed lines that can extend over great distances.

In a 2007 report on the world's progress toward these goals, the UN Secretary-General Ban Ki-moon stated that by 2015, all the major regions of the world except for sub-Saharan Africa are on track to reduce the number of people living in extreme poverty to less than half the 1990 rate.[137] He also observed that progress had been made in introducing ICTs to the poor around the world.[138] He estimated that by the beginning of 2008, more than 3 billion people, or half the world's population, would have mobile phones. As a result, he speculated "it is likely that the goal established by the World Summit on the Information Society – that half the world's inhabitants should have access to information and communications technologies – will be met."[139] Reality exceeded his projections, as a 2009 International Telecommunication Union (ITU) report, produced to provide policy-makers with a tool for benchmarking and assessing progress toward the goals established during both phases of WSIS, indicated that the number of mobile phone subscribers worldwide reached 4 billion by the end of 2008. This translates into a global mobile phone penetration rate of 61 percent.[140] The developing world in particular has seen a telecommunications revolution. By the end of 2008, mobile phones had reached a nearly 50 percent penetration rate in the developing world, up from close to zero ten years earlier. Worldwide, developing countries made up 64 percent of mobile subscriptions by the end of 2007, up from 44 percent five years earlier (see figure 9.2). The mobile phone adoption rate has been faster than any other technology in the past and it has become the most widespread ICT today.[141]

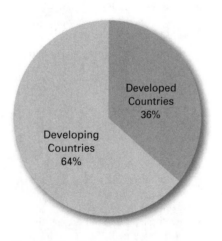

Figure 9.2   Mobile Cellular Subscriptions, 2007[142]

Africa in particular has the highest mobile phone growth rate, up 32 percent in 2006–7. Mobile penetration on the continent has risen sharply from 1 in 50 in the year 2000 to over a quarter of the population as of 2009.[143] Growth rates continue to be strongest in areas where penetration is relatively low.[144] For example, in Burundi in 2008, mobile phone use was up 78 percent to 480,000 users as a result of expanded network coverage, increased competition, and reduced costs. The government of the small coffee-growing nation of 8 million people lifted taxes on telecom equipment, which made phones more affordable. Mobile subscribers are expected rise to 700,000 by 2012.[145] The Democratic Republic of Congo is another market with a huge growth potential. In 2008, 15 percent of the population owned mobile phones, a figure that is expected to jump to 47 percent by 2013. The region's wireless penetration is also expected to increase from 48 percent to 88 percent during that same period.[146]

The number of Internet users has grown at a slower rate around the world, but particularly in developing countries. The ITU estimates that nearly a quarter of the world's 6.7 billion people are using the Internet, but only 13 out of every 100 people in the developing world were online by the end of 2007.[147] For example, in Africa in 2007, fewer than 5 percent of the population used the Internet; in Asia, fewer than 15 percent, in contrast to Europe and the Americas, where Internet use was at 43 and 44 percent respectively (see figure 9.3). While widespread use of mobile phones in developing countries is helping to bridge the digital divide, many of the most effective applications and services for fostering development, including e-commerce, e-government, and e-banking, are contingent upon high-speed Internet connections.[148] While more Internet users are switching from dial-up to broadband high-speed connections, broadband penetration in 2007 had reached fewer than 0.2 percent in Africa, 11 percent in the Americas, and 14 percent in Europe.[149] In the future, fixed networks are unlikely to make great inroads into the developing world, but mobile broadband does have the potential to expand high-speed Internet access. More and more countries are taking advantage of IMT-2000/3G networks to provide high-speed Internet connections.[150]

The ITU has also developed an ICT Development Index designed "to track progress in the development of ICTs in countries, and to monitor the global digital divide."[152] The index measures:

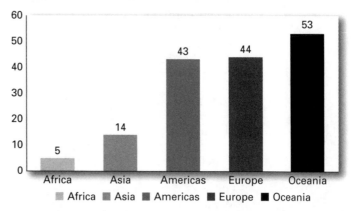

Figure 9.3   Internet Users Per 100 Inhabitants, 2007[151]

- the development of ICTs in countries relative to other countries, tracking ICT progress over time;
- the level of ICT advancement in all countries, charting global changes in developed and developing regions;

- differences among countries' ICT development;
- and the development potential of ICTs.[153]

Or put another way, the three stages in the evolution toward an information society include:

- ICT readiness, such as infrastructure and access;
- ICT use;
- ICT capability (i.e., the extent to which people have the skills to utilize the technology).[154]

According to the 2007 ICT Development Index results, Europe's Nordic countries are the most ICT advanced, with Sweden topping the list, followed by third ranked Denmark, fourth ranked Netherlands, sixth ranked Norway, eighth ranked Switzerland, and ninth ranked Finland. Korea, Iceland, Luxembourg, and the United Kingdom also were ranked among the top 10. The 10 lowest ranked countries are all from Africa (see tables 9.5 and 9.6).

Table 9.5   Top Ranked ICT Development Countries, 2007[155]

Country	Rank
Sweden	1
Korea	2
Denmark	3
Netherlands	4
Iceland	5
Norway	6
Luxembourg	7
Switzerland	8
Finland	9
United Kingdom	10

Table 9.6   Lowest Ranked ICT Development Countries, 2007[156]

Country	Rank
Tanzania	145
Mali	146
Ethiopia	147
Mozambique	148
Eritrea	149
Burkina Faso	150
D.R. Congo	151
Guinea-Bissau	152
Chad	153
Niger	154

The ICT Development Index's 2007 analysis of the digital divide between developing and developed countries indicates that the digital divide continues to persist, particularly between countries that scored high and those that scored low on the index. However, the divide between countries that scored high and those that scored in the "upper" and "medium" groups decreased slightly during the 2002–7 period. This is likely due to the increased penetration of mobile phones in developing countries.[157] Most developing countries also have access to high-speed Internet, but penetration rates remain low. Although we are still seeing mobile broadband penetration rates of less than 1 percent in the developing world, this technology has the potential to help bridge the digital divide in the coming years.[158]

New Media

Digital and networking technologies have also led to changes in media. Technically, any vehicle through which we receive information can be considered *media*. For example, one of the definitions of "medium" (the singular form of media) is "a means or channel of communication or expression."[159] This definition is quite broad though, so it can be useful to make a distinction between media and delivery technologies. Recorded sound, for example, is a medium, whereas CDs, MP3 files, and LP records are all delivery technologies. Delivery technologies come and go, whereas media forms tend to persist once they have taken hold.[160] When people use the term media today, however, they are usually referring to the *mass media*, which traditionally has included print journalism, radio, and television. The term "mass media" simply refers to the technological instruments through which communication flows from a sender of messages to a large number of receivers (i.e., the masses). The message senders, or mass media outlets, are companies that send messages using the media. Television and newspapers are examples of mass media, while CNN and the *New York Times* are mass media outlets. Typical mass media content includes entertainment, news, and educational programming.

The period that began with the widespread adoption of radio and television and that flourished throughout the rest of the twentieth century is sometimes referred to as the "broadcast era." For most of this period, there were limited channels, so people across a given nation listened to and watched much of the same content. As such, broadcast media really was a mass media, reaching the majority of the masses. It was also, for the most part, a one-way technology, in that communication flowed linearly from the broadcaster to the masses.

Since the advent of the Internet, the phrase *new media* has emerged to distinguish digital media from print and broadcast media. Like ICTs in general, new media is characterized by the

> **media**   Tools used to store and deliver information or data. The term is often used synonymously with mass media, but it can also refer to a single medium used to communicate any data for any purpose.
>
> **mass media**   Media that is designed to reach a mass audience, such as the population of a nation-state. The term has traditionally referred to nationwide television and radio networks and mass-circulation newspapers and magazines.

> **new media**   Refers to both digital forms of media that have emerged since the last part of the twentieth century as well as to the ways traditional media forms are evolving in the digital media environment.

convergence Describes the blurring of boundaries between, or the coming together of, media, information technology, and telecommunications sectors.

convergence of the computing, telecommunications, and media sectors. New media "encompasses forms of media content that combine and integrate data, text, sound, and images of all kinds,"[161] and it distributes that content through any one of a variety of networks, including broadband, satellite, and wireless systems. The "computer," whether it is a desktop, a laptop, or a handheld device, has evolved into a single media platform able to deal with multiple media forms.

We've also seen convergence at the level of industry in the form of mergers and alliances between computing, telecommunications, and media sectors. For example, 1989 saw the $14 billion merger of Time Inc. and Warner Communications to form Time-Warner, the world's largest media merger up to that point. In 1996, computer company Microsoft and television network NBC joined forces to establish MSNBC, an online site and cable channel. Time-Warner set another media merger record with its $350 billion merger with America On Line (AOL) in 2000.[162] Henry Jenkins argues that these "new patterns of cross-media ownership" made it "more desirable for companies to distribute content across those various channels rather than within a single media platform. Digitization set the conditions for convergence; corporate conglomerates created its imperative."[163]

At the same time that we've seen media convergence, we've also witnessed the proliferation of media outlets, television channels, and user-generated content. The widespread availability of devices for capturing and editing digital video and the growth of video sharing sites like YouTube have led to what some have referred to as the democratization of media. In the past, capturing and editing video required expensive equipment that only large companies could afford, as well as a great deal of technical expertise and training. Today, the technology has become inexpensive and easy to use, allowing people to become not only consumers but also producers of media. As a result, consumers have more choices about what they consume, as they are no longer limited to the content produced by major media outlets. As the popularity of YouTube indicates, people also enjoy watching content produced by other amateur videographers around the world. On many new media sites, users also have the ability to group, share, comment, and rate content. New media can thus also break down the one-way message flow of traditional mass media, accommodating and encouraging interactivity. Israel-based musician and producer Kutiman has even taken this a step further, remixing sounds and images from YouTube videos into his own unique songs and *video mashups*.[164] While media companies are busy attempting to "accelerate the flow of media content across delivery channels to expand revenue opportunities, broaden markets, and reinforce viewer commitments," consumers are also finding ways to use different media technologies "to bring the flow of media more fully under their control and to interact with other consumers."[165]

video mashup The combination of multiple sources of video into a derivative work.

demassification The process of breaking up something standardized or homogeneous into smaller elements that appeal to specific segments of the population. In the media world, it refers to a shift from attempting to reach the largest possible audiences (mass media) to going after narrower segments of the mass audience.

New media has also contributed to the *demassification* of media. Media delivered online is generally available 24/7, which marks a dramatic contrast with broadcast media. Internet users and TIVO subscribers can watch content when they feel like watching it, whereas with traditional broadcast media, people tuned in together en masse at a given time to listen to/watch specific programs. The proliferation of content produced by both media outlets and individuals, in addition to the time-shifting features of new media that allow for access to content on demand, has led to audience fragmentation. There are now fewer people watching any one show or reading any one news publication at any one time. New and old media may still, in some cases, reach many people, but they don't tend to reach the masses as traditional mass media had in the past.

The global village

One way of understanding the differences between new and older media is to look back at the work of media and communication scholar Marshall McLuhan and his metaphor of the "global village." In his book *The Gutenberg Galaxy* (1962), McLuhan claimed that "the new electronic interdependence recreates the world in the image of a global village."[166] The phrase struck a chord, making its way into popular culture and common parlance.[167] The metaphor evokes a time long since past when people lived in villages where they had relatively equal access to public information, since information was distributed by the town crier, whose voice reached everyone.[168] The advent of print expanded the reach of information beyond the voice of the crier and the expanse of a single village crowd. Print also shattered the experience of the simultaneous delivery of a single message to everyone in a community, since people tend not to read the same texts at the same time in the same place. McLuhan suggested, however, that radio and television ultimately reconstituted that original village experience, but at a much larger level. It was not uncommon for people in a given country, if not literally around the entire globe, to sit down and listen to/watch the same programs at the same time.[169] With the advent of global cable news stations, the village did appear to have become global in scope. However, the evolution of television from 3 or 4 channels to "a five-hundred-channel universe"[170] ultimately fragmented the audience, once again shattering the simultaneous delivery of a single message to the masses.

The metaphor of the global village also broke down at the level of communication exchanges. The original village allowed people to both receive and send information. There was the opportunity to ask questions, to engage in dialogue, both with the town crier and with other members of the village. With broadcast media, global villagers could listen and watch but they had fewer opportunities to talk back, to contribute, and, by participating, to shape the conversation. However, as Paul Levinson, author of *Digital McLuhan* points out, "the internet made an honest metaphor out of the global village."[171] The Internet provides various forums for people to express their ideas, to build consensus, to debate, and to vote. From blogs, to wikis, to chat forums, there is no shortage of places for people to post, comment, share, and debate. We can comment on news stories, rate videos, and respond to politicians on their blogs. However, the simultaneity and the shared message aspect of the village that mass media retained prior to the proliferation of television channels are also eliminated from the Internet version of the village, since there are too many sources of information and conversations occurring synchronously and asynchronously all the time to keep track of even a fraction of them.

Globalization and media

Those who view the relationship between ICTs and globalization in a positive light argue that ICTs promote "opportunities for shared information, borderless communication and global commerce."[172] Many also maintain that the global reach and proliferation of media encourages the spread of democracy and empowers citizens to challenge oppressive local governments. The idea is that the more people are exposed to various points of view by going online or by watching/listening to a variety of television and radio programs, the less susceptible they will be to nationalistic propaganda and oppressive governmental control.[173] Moreover, citizens' ability to easily capture images and videos on their mobile devices documenting abusive government actions and then to upload them to the web for the whole world to bear witness to also empowers citizens and helps keep governments accountable.

Critics of global media point to the "unequal distribution of international communications power and resources,"[174] arguing that "the processes of globalization involve the domination of certain cultures over others."[175] In this framework, the internationalization and commercialization of global communications is seen as critical to the dominance of developed nations in general and the United States in particular.[176] Such critics have argued that there is a one-way flow of information and cultural products from the developed to the developing world that undermines the cultural sovereignty of developing countries. Critics like Herbert Schiller and Noam Chomsky argue that because most media is owned by Western corporations, "cultural products and media outputs in lesser developed countries are forced to occupy a position of subordination, not only on the international scene but on the local one as well."[177] In other words, critics see a pattern of domination (which some refer to as *cultural imperialism*) that is characterized by unidirectional rather than reciprocal information exchanges and cultural flows. This unidirectional flow of information is viewed as compromising the local cultural integrity of recipient countries.[178] Some argue that this is in turn leading to the cultural *homogenization* of the world into a "global monoculture of consumption," as Western culture infiltrates, dominates, and ultimately eradicates other cultures.[179]

cultural imperialism A form of domination that involves privileging one culture (usually that of a large, powerful nation) over less powerful ones or imposing/injecting the cultural practices of a dominant culture into other cultures, often culminating in the adoption of the cultural practices of the imperial power.

homogenization The process of blending or erasing differences to make something uniform in composition.

Those who view globalization of media as leading to cultural imperialism have been widely criticized by a variety of scholars who argue that global media flows originating in developed countries don't necessarily overpower indigenous cultures or engender a monoculture. In fact, they see this argument as a condescending misrepresentation of indigenous peoples that positions them as passive, fragile, and incapable of resisting or negotiating cultural messages for their own purposes. Although most would agree that "western cultural forms have a ubiquitous presence in the world,"[180] they would also argue that cultural flows from the West to the developing world often lead to *cultural hybridity* and *heterogenization* rather than to the homogenization of cultures.[181] Consumers of Western media in the developing world don't simply absorb the ideologies inscribed in them. Rather they

> **cultural hybridity** Refers to cultural forms and practices that result from interactions between two or more different cultures.
>
> **heterogenization** The process of breaking up into different elements or dissimilar parts.

actively interpret, evaluate, reject, ignore, and transform elements of the texts they consume, creating their own meanings based on their own cultural codes.[182] The cultural imperialism argument is also undermined by television programming statistics in many countries around the world. These often indicate that though Western media is present around the globe, people still tend to prefer high quality local programming to imported content.[183] Other critics point out that it is inaccurate to describe the flow of cultural goods as a one-way phenomenon, from the developed to the developing world, or from the "West to the rest." Clearly, culture moves from the rest to the West as well, as seen in the growth of non-Western immigrant populations as well as non-Western restaurants, music, and religions in the developed countries.[184] The dispersal of peoples around the globe and the advent of satellite technology has made it possible for media flows to move in a variety of directions. For example, India is the largest film producer in the world. It not only dominates the film industry within India, but also exports its films around the globe.[185] However, the counter-argument here is that, with some exceptions, these flows are still not generally reciprocal. Although cultural exports from developing countries do make it to Western countries, they often don't make it into the mainstream Western media. As such, they are often viewed primarily by people who share the language and culture of those who produced the film, which does not constitute a true reciprocal flow.[186]

Conclusion

The umbrella term "information and communication technologies" (ICTs) encompasses the digital technologies and infrastructure that have facilitated globalization processes. They are the services, platforms, and devices that have eroded the barriers of time and space, making swift and efficient international communication flows possible. The development of digital technologies in the 1980s and the World Wide Web in the 1990s both dramatically accelerated the changes associated with the shift from the Industrial Age to an Information Age. However, despite ICT advances across the globe, digital divides continue to persist both within and between countries. Organizations like the UN recognize how important ICTs and information literacy are to development efforts and to ending poverty. Though the world has made strides toward greater ICT equity, particularly in the mobile phone arena, there is still much work to be done to provide people around the world with access to the information and communication tools that can enhance their chances of achieving their goals for themselves, their families, and their communities. This chapter also looked at global media in the context of ICTs, as media has been part of a larger process of convergence with computing and telecommunications technologies. Perhaps nowhere is this convergence more obvious than on many of today's mobile devices, which enable users to talk, text, email, web-surf, take pictures and video, as well as watch/listen to various media. Media forms are thus changing, but they are also more pervasive than ever, as professional and amateur media forms flow around the world in seconds. While some argue that global media flows are unidirectional, flowing from the "West to the rest," others point out that flows do actually go both ways, and that media flows from the developed world do not remake the developing world into its own image. Rather, they often lead to hybridity and heterogenization – that is, to new cultural forms.

Notes

1   Clay Shirky, *Here Comes Everybody: The Power of Organizing without Organizations* (New York: Penguin Press, 2008), 17.

2   Andrew Walker, "Ted Turner: Maverick Mogul," BBC News (January 30, 2003), http://news.bbc.co.uk/2/hi/americas/2709453.stm.

3   Bill Clinton, "Remarks by the President and the Vice President to the People of Knoxville," Knoxville Auditorium Coliseum, Knoxville, Tennessee (October 10, 1996), http://clinton6.nara.gov/1996/10/1996-10-10-president-and-vp-remarks-in-knoxville-tn.html.

4   Mike Pesca, "Racetracks Place Survival Odds on Casinos," *All Things Considered*, National Public Radio (April 9, 2008), www.npr.org/templates/player/mediaPlayer.html?action=1&t=1&islist=false&id=89507551&m=89508068.

5   *The New York Times Guide to Essential Knowledge* (New York: St Martin's Press, 2007), 448.

6   Terry Flew and Stephen McElhinney, "Globalization and the Structure of New Media Industries," in Leah A. Lievrouw, Sonai M. Livingstone (eds.), *Handbook of New Media* (Thousand Oaks, CA: SAGE, 2006), 287.

7   Organisation for Economic Co-operation and Development, *Information and Communication Technologies and Rural Development* (Paris, France: OECD, 2001), 11.

8   Manuel Castells, *The Rise of the Network Society* (Malden, MA: Blackwell Publishers, 2000), 101.

9   Ithiel de Sola Pool, *Technologies of Freedom* (Cambridge, MA: Belknap Press, 1983), 23.

10 Henry Jenkins, *Convergence Culture: Where Old and New Media Collide* (New York: New York University Press, 2006), 16.

11 John B. Thompson, *The Media and Modernity* (Stanford, CA: Stanford University Press, 1995), 81–2.

12 Ibid., 82.

13 "The Knowledge Industry," *Time* (December 21, 1962), www.time.com/time/magazine/article/0,9171,940171,00.html.

14 Christopher May, *The Information Society: A Sceptical View* (Malden, MA: Polity Press, 2002), 5.

15 Peter Drucker, *The Age of Discontinuity* (New Brunswick, NJ: Transaction Publishers, 1992), 287.

16 Ibid., 27.

17 May, *The Information Society: A Sceptical View*, 6.

18 Daniel Bell, *The Coming of Post-industrial Society* (New York: Basic Books 1973), 127.

19 Peter Golding, "Forthcoming Features: Information and Communications Technologies and the Sociology of the Future," *Sociology* 34, no. 1 (2000), 169.

20 May, *The Information Society: A Sceptical* View, 8.

21   Google, Corporate Information, Google Management, www.google.com/corporate/execs.html.

22   Alvin Toffler, *Future Shock* (New York: Bantam, 1970), 12.

23   Ibid., 11.

24   Ibid., 350.

25   Ibid., 353.

26   David Shenk, *Data Smog: Surviving the Information Glut* (San Francisco, CA: HarperEdge, 1997), 27.

27   Ibid., 28.

28   Orrin E. Klapp, *Overload and Boredom: Essays on the Quality of Life in the Information Society* (New York: Greenwood Press, 1986), 2.

29   Richard Saul Wurman, *Information Anxiety* (New York: Doubleday, 1989), 35.

30   Ibid., 32.

31   Ibid., 36.

32   Angela Edmunds and Anne Morris, "The Problem of Information Overload in Business Organisations: A Review of the Literature," *International Journal of Information Management* 20 (2000), 22.

33   Shenk, *Data Smog: Surviving the Information Glut*, 28.

34   Douglas Rushkoff, *Playing the Future: What We Can Learn from Digital Kids* (New York: Riverhead, 1996), 5.

35   Kevin A. Miller, *Surviving Information Overload* (Grand Rapids, MI: Zondervan, 2004), 198.

36   Jesse Alpert and Nissan Hajaj, "We Knew the Web was Big . . ." (July 25, 2008), http://googleblog.blogspot.com/2008/07/we-knew-web-was-big.html.

37   Anil Aggarwal *Web-based Education: Learning from Experience* (Hershey, PA: Information Science Publishers, 2003), 31.

38   Edmunds and Morris, "The Problem of Information Overload," 19.

39   Paul G. Zurkowski, *The Information Service Environment: Relationships and Priorities* (Washington, DC: National Commission on Libraries and Information Science, 1974).

40   "Presidential Committee on Information Literacy," *American Library Association* (July 24, 2006), www.ala.org/ala/mgrps/divs/acrl/publications/whitepapers/presidential.cfm.

41   Ibid.

42   Ibid.

43   "Information and Media Literacy," UNESCO, http://portal.unesco.org/ci/en/ev.php-URL_ID=15886&URL_DO=DO_TOPIC&URL_SECTION=201.html.

44   The National Forum on Information Literacy (NFIL), which is a US-based umbrella group of more than 90 organizations from education, business, government, and community service, plus international organizations. All are committed to the empowerment of individuals in today's information society. Combined membership in the Forum member organizations totals more than 5,000,000. For more information, go to www.infolit.org.

45   The International Federation of Library Associations and Institutions (IFLA), which is the leading international NGO body representing the interests of library and information services and their users. For more information, go to www.ifla.org.

46   "Beacons of the Information Society: The Alexandria Proclamation on Information Literacy and Lifelong Learning," adopted in Alexandria, Egypt at the Bibliotheca Alexandrina on November 9, 2005, National Forum on Information Literacy, www.infolit.org/International_Colloquium/index.htm.

47   "Training-the-Trainers in Information Literacy," UNESCO, http://portal.unesco.org/ci/en/ev.php-URL_ID=25623&URL_DO=DO_TOPIC&URL_SECTION=201.html.

48   Ibid.

49   Martin Lister et al., *New Media: A Critical Introduction* (New York: Routledge, 2003), 14.

50   Ibid.

51   Ibid.

52   Terry Flew, *New Media: An Introduction*, 2nd edn. (New York: Oxford University Press, 2005), 9.

53   Kevin Kawamoto, *Media and Society* (Boston, MA: Allyn and Bacon, 2003), 10.

54   Nicholas Negroponte, *Being Digital* (New York: Vintage), 4.

55   Janet Abbate, *Inventing the Internet* (Cambridge, MA: The MIT Press, 2000), 1.

56   Ibid., 2.

57   Ibid., 3.

58   Ibid., 2.

59   Leonard Kleinrock "The Day the Infant Internet Uttered its First Words," UCLA Computer Science Department, www.cs.ucla.edu/~lk/LK/Inet/1stmesg.html.

60   Ibid.

61   Elizabeth C. Hanson, *The Information Revolution and World Politics* (Lanham, MA: Rowman and Littlefield, 2008), 59.

62   Ibid., 59.

63   Ibid., 60.

64   Ibid., 60.

65   Ibid., 61.

66   Abbate, *Inventing the Internet*, 195.

67   Ibid.

68   Ibid., 199.

69   "The Website of the World's First-Ever Web Server," CERN, http://info.cern.ch/.

70   Ibid.

71   Flew, *New Media: An Introduction*, 15.

72   Erin Jansen, *NetLingo: The Internet Dictionary* (Ojai, CA: NetLingo Inc., 2002), 420.

73   Abbate, *Inventing the Internet*, 212–13.

74   Ibid., 215.

75   Ibid., 217.

76   Ibid.

77   Source: "History and Growth of the Internet," Internet World Stats, www.internetworldstats.com/emarketing.htm.

78   Jakob Nielsen, "One Billion Internet Users" (December 19, 2005), www.useit.com/alertbox/internet_growth.html.

79   Andrew Kohut, Richard Wike, and Nicole Speulda, "Truly a World Wide Web: Globe Going Digital," 2005 Pew Global Attitudes Survey (Washington DC: Pew Research Center, 2006), 2, http://pewglobal.org/reports/pdf/251.pdf.

80   Ibid., 3.

81   Source: Andrew Kohut, Richard Wike, and Nicole Speulda, "Truly a World Wide Web: Globe Going Digital," 2005 Pew Global Attitudes Survey (Washington DC: Pew Research Center, 2006), 2, http://pewglobal.org/reports/pdf/251.pdf. Reproduced by permission of the Pew Research Center.

82   Source: Andrew Kohut, Richard Wike, and Nicole Speulda, "Truly a World Wide Web: Globe Going Digital," 2005 Pew Global Attitudes Survey (Washington DC: Pew Research Center, 2006), 3, http://pewglobal.org/reports/pdf/251.pdf. Reproduced by permission of the Pew Research Center.

83   Sydney Jones and Susannah Fox, "Pew Internet Project Data Memo: Generations Online in 2009" (January 28, 2009), 1, www.pewinternet.org/~/media//Files/Reports/2009/PIP_Generations_2009.pdf.

84   Ibid., 3.

85   Ibid., 1.

86   Shirky, *Here Comes Everybody*, 20.

87   Ibid., 20–1.

88   May, *The Information Society: A Sceptical View*, 11.

89   Castells, *The Rise of the Network Society*, 406.

90   Ibid.

91   Shirky, *Here Comes Everybody*, 22.

92   May, *The Information Society: A Sceptical View*, 12.

93   Mary Madden and Susannah Fox, "Riding the Waves of 'Web 2.0,'" Pew Internet Project (October 5, 2006), 1, www.pewinternet.org/~/media//Files/Reports/2006/PIP_Web_2.0.pdf.pdf.

94   Jenkins, *Convergence Culture*, 4.

95   Madden and Fox, "Riding the Waves of 'Web 2.0,'" 2.

96   Stephen Colbert, "The Word – Wikilobbying," *Colbert Nation* (January 29, 2007), www.colbertnation.com/the-colbert-report-videos/81454/january-29-2007/the-word---wikilobbying.

97   Gregory M. Lamb, "Online Wikipedia is not Britannica – but It's Close," *Christian Science Monitor* (January 5, 2006), www.csmonitor.com/2006/0105/p13s02-stct.html.

98   Brian Bergstein, "Microsoft Offers Cash for Wikipedia Edit," *Washington Post* (January 24, 2007), www.washingtonpost.com/wp-dyn/content/article/2007/01/24/AR2007012401590.html.

99   Lamb, "Online Wikipedia is not Britannica," *Christian Science Monitor*.

100   Madden and Fox, "Riding the Waves of 'Web 2.0'," 3.

101   Danah M. Boyd and Nicole B. Ellison, "Social Network Sites: Definition, History, and Scholarship," *Journal of Computer-Mediated Communication* 13 (2008), 211.

102   Ibid.

103   Amanda Lenhard, "Adults and Social Network Websites," Pew Internet Project Data Memo,

Pew Internet and American Life Project (January 14, 2009), 1, www.pewinternet.org/~/media//Files/Reports/2009/PIP_Adult_social_networking_data_memo_FINAL.pdf.pdf.

104   Ibid., 6.

105   Ibid., 11.

106   "The Internet and the 2008 Election," Pew Internet and American Life Project (June 15, 2008), www.pewinternet.org/Press-Releases/2008/The-internet-and-the-2008-election.aspx.

107   Source: Amanda Lenhard, "Adults and Social Network Websites," Pew Internet Project Data Memo, Pew Internet and American Life Project (January 14, 2009), 5, www.pewinternet.org/~/media//Files/Reports/2009/PIP_Adult_social_networking_data_memo_FINAL.pdf.pdf.

108   Ibid.

109   Ibid.

110   Kohut, Wike, and Speulda, "Truly a World Wide Web: Globe Going Digital," 2.

111   United Nations Development Programme, "New Technologies and the Global Race for Knowledge," Human Development Report 1999: Globalization with a Human Face (New York: Oxford University Press, 1999), 63, http://hdr.undp.org/en/media/hdr_1999_ch21.pdf.

112   Kohut, Wike, and Speulda, "Truly a World Wide Web: Globe Going Digital," 2.

113   Ibid.

114   "Demographics of Internet Users," Pew Internet and American Life Project, November 19–December 20, 2008 Tracking Survey, www.pewinternet.org/Static-Pages/Data-Tools/Download-Data/~/media/Infographics/Trend%20Data/January%202009%20updates/Demographics%20of%20Internet%20Users%201%206%2009.jpg.

115   Susannah Fox and Jessica Vitak, "Degrees of Access (May 2008 data)" (July 9, 2008), www.pewinternet.org/Presentations/2008/Degrees-of-Access-(May-2008-data).aspx.

116   Susannah Fox and Gretchen Livingston, *Latinos Online: Hispanics with Lower Levels of Education and English Proficiency Remain Largely Disconnected from the Internet* (Washington DC: Pew Hispanic Center and Pew Internet Project, 2007), 4, www.pewinternet.org/~/media//Files/Reports/2007/Latinos_Online_March_14_2007.pdf.pdf.

117   Generations on Line, www.generationsonline.org/espanol/.

118   Source: Amanda Lenhard, "Adults and Social Network Websites," Pew Internet Project Data Memo, Pew Internet and American Life Project (January 14, 2009), 5, www.pewinternet.org/~/media//Files/Reports/2009/PIP_Adult_social_networking_data_memo_FINAL.pdf.pdf.

119   Jonathan Zittrain and John Palfrey, "Introduction," in Ronald Deibert et al. (eds.), *Access Denied: The Practice and Policy of Global Internet Filtering* (Cambridge, MA: MIT Press, 2008), 2.

120   Ibid., 3.

121   Zittrain and Palfrey, "Reluctant Gatekeepers: Corporate Ethics on a Filtered Internet," in *Access Denied*, 108.

122   Robert Faris and Nart Villeneuve, "Measuring Global Internet Filtering," in *Access Denied*, 9.

123   Rupert Wingfield-Hayes, "Web Censorship: Correspondent Reports," BBC News (May 29, 2006), http://news.bbc.co.uk/nolpda/ifs_news/hi/newsid_5024000/5024874.stm.

124   Ibid.

125   Ronald Deibert and Rafal Rohozinski, "Good for Liberty, Bad for Security? Global Civil Society and the Securitization of the Internet," in *Access Denied*, 141.

126   Zittrain and Palfrey, "Internet Filtering: The Politics and Mechanisms of Control," in *Access Denied*, 48.

127   Ibid.

128   "Google Censors Itself for China," BBC (January 25, 2006), http://news.bbc.co.uk/1/hi/technology/4645596.stm.

129   Zittrain and Palfrey, "Internet Filtering: The Politics and Mechanisms of Control," 49.

130   Deibert and Rohozinski, "Good for Liberty, Bad for Security?," 133.

131   "About the Millennium Development Goals," End Poverty 2015 Millennium Campaign, www.endpoverty2015.org/goals.

132   "United Nations Millennium Declaration," United Nations (September 8, 2000), www.un.org/millennium/declaration/ares552e.htm.

133   "Declaration of Principles. Building the Information Society: A Global Challenge in the New Millennium," World Summit on the Information

Society, Geneva (December 12, 2003). www.itu.int/wsis/docs/geneva/official/dop.html.

134 "Plan of Action," World Summit on the Information Society, Geneva (December 12, 2003), www.itu.int/wsis/docs/geneva/official/poa.html.

135 "Basic Information: About WSIS," World Summit on the Information Society, www.itu.int/wsis/basic/about.html.

136 "Tunis Agenda for the Information Society," World Summit on the Information Society, Tunis (November 18, 2005), www.itu.int/wsis/docs2/tunis/off/6rev1.html.

137 Ban Ki-moon, "Annex 1: Report of the Secretary-General," *Strengthening Efforts to Eradicate Poverty and Hunger: Dialogues at the Economic and Social Council* (New York: United Nations, 2007), 243, www.un.org/ecosoc/docs/pdfs/07-49285-ECOSOC-Book-2007.pdf.

138 Ibid., 263.

139 Ibid.

140 Measuring the Information Society – The ICT Development Index, 3, www.itu.int/ITU-D/ict/publications/idi/2009/index.html.

141 Ibid., 1.

142 Source: Measuring the Information Society – The ICT Development Index, www.itu.int/ITU-D/ict/publications/idi/2009/index.html, 4. Reproduced by permission of the International Telecommunication Union.

143 Ibid., 3.

144 Ibid., 4.

145 "Burundi Mobile Phone Users up 78 pct in 2008," Reuters (March 26, 2009), www.reuters.com/article/rbssTechMediaTelecomNews/idUSLQ55822720090326.

146 Franz Wild, Mark Lee, and Cathy Chan, "MTN May Buy ZTE's 51% Stake in Congo Phone Venture," Bloomberg.com (March 26, 2009), www.bloomberg.com/apps/news?pid=20601109&sid=aJhhlj8.5.9A&refer=home.

147 Measuring the Information Society – The ICT Development Index, 1.

148 Ibid.

149 Ibid.

150 Ibid., 6.

151 Source: Measuring the Information Society – The ICT Development Index, www.itu.int/ITU-D/ict/publications/idi/2009/index.html, 5.

Reproduced by permission of the International Telecommunication Union.

152 Ibid., 11.

153 Ibid., 12.

154 Ibid., 14.

155 Source: Measuring the Information Society – The ICT Development Index, www.itu.int/ITU-D/ict/publications/idi/2009/index.html, 22. Reproduced by permission of the International Telecommunication Union.

156 Source: Measuring the Information Society – The ICT Development Index, www.itu.int/ITU-D/ict/publications/idi/2009/index.html, 22. Reproduced by permission of the International Telecommunication Union.

157 Ibid., 48.

158 Ibid., 71.

159 "Medium, n. II. 4. A." *Oxford English Dictionary*, http://dictionary.oed.com.

160 Jenkins, *Convergence Culture*, 14.

161 Flew, *New Media: An Introduction*, 2.

162 Ibid., 11–12.

163 Jenkins, *Convergence Culture*, 11.

164 "Remixing YouTube, One Video at a Time," *All Things Considered*, National Public Radio (March 16, 2009), www.npr.org/templates/story/story.php?storyId=101959636.

165 Jenkins, *Convergence Culture*, 18.

166 Marshall McLuhan, *The Gutenberg Galaxy* (Toronto, Canada: University of Toronto Press, 1962), 31.

167 Paul Levinson, *Digital McLuhan: A Guide to the Information Millennium* (New York: Routledge, 1999), 65.

168 Ibid., 66.

169 Ibid.

170 Brian Fawcett "What McLuhan Got Wrong about the Global Village and Some Things He Didn't Foresee," in John George Moss and Linda M. Morra (eds.), *At the Speed of Light there is Only Illumination: A Reappraisal of Marshall McLuhan* (Ottawa, Canada: University of Ottawa Press, 2004), 217.

171 Levinson, *Digital McLuhan: A Guide to the Information Millennium*, 66.

172 Flew and McElhinney, "Globalization and the Structure of New Media Industries," 291.

173 Ibid.

174 Ibid., 292.
175 Jonathan Xavier Inda and Renato Rosaldo, "Introduction: A World in Motion," in Jonathan Xavier Inda and Renato Rosaldo (eds.), *The Anthropology of Globalization* (Malden, MA: Blackwell Publishers, 2002), 13.
176 Flew and McElhinney, "Globalization and the Structure of New Media Industries," 292.
177 Nickesia S. Gordon, *Media and the Politics of Culture: The Case of Television Privatization and Media Globalization in Jamaica (1990–2007)* (Sydney, Australia: Universal-Publishers, 2008), 61.

178 Ibid., 62.
179 Inda and Rosaldo, "Introduction: A World in Motion," 13–14.
180 Ibid., 15.
181 Gordon, *Media and the Politics of Culture*, 63.
182 Inda and Rosaldo, "Introduction: A World in Motion," 16.
183 Gordon, *Media and the Politics of Culture*, 64.
184 Inda and Rosaldo, "Introduction: A World in Motion," 18.
185 Gordon, *Media and the Politics of Culture*, 64.
186 Ibid., 65.

10

WAR AND VIOLENT CONFLICT

"*Mankind must put an end to war or war will put an end to mankind.*" (John F. Kennedy, Speech to UN General Assembly, New York, September 25, 1961)[1]

"*The inclination to aggression is an original, self-subsisting instinctual disposition in man, and I return to my view that it constitutes the greatest impediment to civilization.*" (Sigmund Freud, *Civilization and Its Discontents*, 1930)[2]

"*It is a fearful thing to lead this great peaceful people into war, into the most terrible and disastrous of all wars, civilization itself seeming to be in the balance. But the right is more precious than peace, and we shall fight for the things which we have always carried nearest our hearts – for democracy, for the right of those who submit to authority to have a voice in their own governments, for the rights and liberties of small nations, for a universal domination of right by such a concert of free peoples as shall bring peace and safety to all nations and make the world itself at last free.*" (Woodrow Wilson, Request for Declaration of War on Germany, Washington, DC, April 2, 1917)[3]

"*What difference does it make to the dead, the orphans, and the homeless, whether the mad destruction is wrought under the name of totalitarianism or the holy name of liberty or democracy? I assert in all humility, but with all the strength at my command, that liberty and democracy become unholy when their hands are dyed red with innocent blood.*" (Mahatma Gandhi, *Non-Violence in Peace and War*, 1942)[4]

Learning to Question, Questioning to Learn

- What distinguishes war from other types of violent conflict?
- What factors cause or contribute to war?
- Are we, as a species, genetically predisposed to engage in war?
- Is there such a thing as a just war?
- What are some of the ways that international law has attempted to restrict war?
- In addition to human casualties, what are some of the other major costs of war?

Introduction

This chapter begins with a discussion of different definitions of war, followed by an analysis of a variety of types of wars and violent conflicts. Next, the chapter looks at the prehistory and history of war, beginning with our early human ancestors and extending to the present day. It then addresses the question "What causes war?" from a variety of perspectives. Ethical and legal issues are then discussed, including an analysis of just war theory and international laws of war. The chapter ends with a discussion of the costs of war, including human and environmental casualties, damage to infrastructure and economies, and the diversion of enormous sums of money from social and economic development programs to the military.

When Does Violent Conflict Become War?

Although "war" is an all too familiar term, it would be a mistake to assume that it has only one definition that is shared by all. Definitions of war are in fact multiple and varied, influenced by historical, political, legal, social, and cultural contexts and ideologies. Conflicts described as "war" by some are labeled rebellions, struggles, riots, guerrilla uprisings, terrorism, gang violence, or genocide by others. Which of the conflicts/events listed below, for example, do you think should be categorized under the label "war"?

- continuous Palestinian rocket fire from Gaza into Israel;
- bombing of the Federal Building in Oklahoma City;
- US invasion of Panama in December 1989;
- drug wars in Columbia and Mexico;
- attack on World Trade Center and the Pentagon on September 11, 2001;
- the Cold War;
- the 1994 Hutu militia-led massacre of 800,000+ Tutsis in Rwanda;
- Korean War;
- urban gang wars;
- trade wars;
- assassination of terrorist leaders by state governments;
- terrorist bombing of Pam Am Flight 407 over Lockerbie, Scotland;
- a state-sponsored assassination of another state's leader;
- Israeli bombing of nuclear facilities in Iraq in 1988.

People's definitions of war, in addition to their relationship to specific conflicts, will inevitably lead to disagreements about which of the actions listed above constitute actual wars and which fall under some other label. Despite definitional ambiguities, however, there are a number of common themes that emerge in discussions of war that require further analysis. In his classic strategic text *On War* (1832), Prussian military theorist Karl von Clausewitz famously claimed, "war is a mere continuation of policy by other means."[5] He went on to describe war as a "real political instrument" and "a continuation of political commerce."[6] Underlying Clausewitz's political understanding of war is the implicit assumption that war involves states.[7] In *The Social Contract*, Rousseau makes this relationship between states and war explicit, defining war in terms of a relation "not between man and man, but between State and State."[8] Because, as Rousseau maintains, relations can only exist between similar entities, "each State can have for enemies only other States, and not men."[9] For Rousseau then, only states can be said to engage in war, and then only with each other rather than with "men" or with other entities that are "disparate in nature."[10] Violent conflicts between non-state actors or between a state and a non-state organization cannot accurately be described as war. The *Oxford English Dictionary*'s (*OED*) definition of war is broader still, defining it as "Hostile contention by means of armed forces, carried on between nations, states, or rulers, or between parties in the same nation or state."[11] This definition's explicit reference to parties in the same state thus indicates that civil wars, even though they involve a conflict between a state and a non-state group, can be categorized as "wars."

While statehood plays a major role in many definitions of war, some scholars argue that these definitions are problematic because of what they exclude. For example, many of today's violent conflicts involving non-state actors, such as terrorist organizations, are excluded from state-centered definitions of war. So too are the thousands of historical conflicts that occurred prior to the division of the world into states. As such, some scholars question whether it makes sense to exclude from discussions of war conflicts between displaced, non-state groups, nomadic societies, and pre-state peoples.[12] In *A History of Warfare* (1993), John Keegan observes that state-centered war theories do not allow for the possibility that "war antedates the state, diplomacy and strategy by many millennia," or that warfare might be nearly as old as humanity itself.[13] It is also worth noting that state-centered definitions of war tend to further the interests of the state, legitimizing the state's engagement in violent conflict and condemning similar actions by non-state actors who could potentially pose a threat to it. In other words, states contrast their own lawful and "legitimate" involvements in violent conflicts with the actions of "rebel," non-state actors, which they roundly condemn.[14]

However, some discussions of war do attempt to extend the definition to include non-state actors. For example, *The Stanford Encyclopedia of Philosophy* defines war as "an *actual, intentional* and *widespread* armed conflict between political communities."[15] In this framework, the term "political community" could include both states and those that intend to become states, such as a rebel organization fighting a civil war. This definition could also potentially include conflicts between states and terrorist groups, since some terrorist groups can be considered "political communities," particularly when their activities are designed to achieve or influence the development of statehood.[16] While this definition includes more entities than states, it nevertheless creates additional parameters that circumscribe the types of conflicts that can be described as "war." There are broader definitions still that attempt to account for many of the violent conflicts that traditional definitions of war exclude, including undeclared military actions, conflicts between non-state peoples, ongoing terrorist campaigns, guerrilla uprisings, wars without a central controlling body, and wars without a clear beginning or a clear end.[17] For example, the *miniAtlas of Human Security* defines war as any armed conflict with over 1,000 battle-deaths in a year."[18] While this definition of war is broader, in that it is not contingent upon the status of the combatants, it also applies yet another specific condition that had heretofore not been considered: the number of battle-deaths. While 1,000 deaths may well seem like an arbitrary number, it nevertheless poses the question "What is the relationship between war and casualties?" Can a conflict without or with very few casualties accurately be called a war?

Types of War and Violent Conflict

Inter-state and intra-state conflicts

If war is defined as an intentional and widespread conflict that occurs only between states, then war is always international in scope. International or *inter-state wars* are the first type of conflict that many people think of when they hear the term "war." Despite the important place it occupies in our conceptualization of war, the number of inter-state wars has actually remained relatively low since World War II.[19] From 1946 to 2003, two former colonial powers – the United Kingdom and France – and the two Cold War *superpowers* – the United States and Russia – topped the list of countries that fought the most inter-state wars (see table 10.1).

> **inter-state wars/conflicts** A sustained and intentional armed conflict between at least two states; an international conflict.
>
> **superpower** A state with the power to dominate and influence other countries around the world.

Table 10.1 Countries Involved in the Most Inter-state Conflicts, 1946–2003[20]

Number of Wars	Countries	Number of Wars	Countries
21	United Kingdom	5	Portugal
19	France	5	Canada
16	United States	4	Vietnam, Republic of
9	Russia	4	Chad
7	Australia	4	Libya
6	Israel	4	Spain
6	Egypt	4	Syria
6	China	4	New Zealand
6	Thailand	4	Italy
5	Vietnam, Democratic Republic of	4	Iran
5	Turkey	4	Ethiopia
5	Jordan	4	Iraq

intra-state wars/conflicts　Conflicts that occur between a government and a non-state group. Civil wars fall under this category.

low-intensity conflict　A protracted political and military confrontation between states or groups that is below conventional war and above routine, peaceful competition.

Today, *intra-state conflicts*, or civil wars, are far more common than inter-state ones. In 1946, 47 percent of conflicts were intra-state; by 2005, that figure had increased to 100 percent.[21] The majority of today's intra-state conflicts are *low-intensity conflicts (LIC)* taking place in the developing world. In contrast with conventional wars, which typically involve large armies, heavy weapons, major battles, and high death tolls, most LICs kill far fewer people and are fought by a relatively small number of lightly armed forces. Despite the lower death tolls, intra-state wars have increased in duration, with lengthy internal conflicts becoming "a distinctive feature of the post-World War II era."[22] From 1900 to 1944, the average length of civil wars was one and a half years; during the second half of the twentieth century, that increased to over four years.[23]

Internal wars are often anti-regime wars, waged in order to maintain or overthrow a government. Sometimes the aim is simply to gain or keep political power, while in other cases the goal is to change the social system, as was the case with the African National Congress (ANC) in South Africa. Other internal wars are fought not over the government or the social system but rather to establish or defend an ethnic or religious group or territory. Such wars include those led by national minorities or repressed national majorities seeking autonomy, secession, or the elimination of discrimination.[24] Some intra-state wars are sparked when governments are weak. Warlords and rebel groups challenge the government and other paramilitary groups for control of power, money, and resources, often wreaking chaos, death, and destruction.

State-based conflicts

state-based wars/conflicts　Conflicts that involve at least one national government.

non-state conflicts　Conflicts between militias, warlords, or ethnic groups without the involvement of national governments.

extra-state wars/conflicts　Conflicts between a state and an armed group outside the state's own territory. These are mostly colonial conflicts.

internationalized intra-state wars/conflicts　Conflicts that occur when the government, or an armed group opposing it, receives military support from one or more foreign states.

While the terms inter-state war and intra-state war are two primary ways of categorizing armed conflict, another categorization strategy is to distinguish between state-based conflicts and non-state conflicts. *State-based conflicts* involve at least one national government, while *non-state conflicts* occur between militias, warlords, or ethnic groups without the direct involvement of a state government.[25] Both inter-state and intra-state wars fall under the label "state-based conflict," but so too do *extra-state conflicts* and *internationalized intra-state conflicts*. Extra-state wars include conflicts between a state and an armed group outside the state's territory. This label most often applies to wars of independence from colonial rule, and, as such, they are often called decolonization wars. The majority of extra-state wars occurred in the 1950s and 1960s, disappearing by the mid-1970s.[26] However, the legacy of this period is with us still. Prior to the postcolonial period, which witnessed the proliferation of new states after the break-up of colonial empires, most states were strong enough to withstand both inter-state and intra-state war. States that failed to assert their sovereignty were likely to be subsumed, in whole or in part, within the boundaries of their more powerful neighbors. In contrast, former colonies achieved statehood not through a process of building and asserting their strength, but through support from the international community. Many of these states lacked resources and infrastructure, but the international system provided them with economic and military support to help them maintain their borders and sovereignty. However, many of these states remained internally weak, which in turn led to domestic instability. Cold War military interventions also exacerbated existing problems. These unstable conditions allowed for the emergence of rebel groups intent on challenging weak governments' tenuous control over power and resources. In other words, the international system "has encouraged and supported the proliferation of weak states that are susceptible to protracted civil wars."[27]

Internationalized intra-state conflicts are those in which a state, a non-state internal group, or both receive military support from other governments, and foreign troops participate in the conflict. The US-led invasion of Iraq in 2003 began as an inter-state conflict but soon became an internationalized intra-state conflict.[28] Studies show that international interventions in civil wars tend to increase levels of violence, exacerbate instability, and extend the duration of the conflict. In short, by providing resources necessary for maintaining the war, interventions can cause civil wars to continue for years, until the intervening state or states finally withdraw.[29]

Non-state conflicts and one-sided violence

In addition to state-based conflicts, there are two other major forms of political violence that are relevant to discussions of war: (1) non-state conflicts fought between militias, warlords, and ethnic and religious groups and (2) *one-sided violence*, which includes genocides and other mass killings of defenseless civilians. Non-state conflicts are those that do not include governments. They tend to occur in poor countries with weak governments that have neither the power nor the resources to stop them.[30] In 2002, five non-state conflicts raged in the Democratic Republic of Congo. And conflicts between Hindus and Muslims in Gujarat, a state in western India that shares a border with Pakistan, killed at least 1,500 people in 2002.[31] However, non-state conflicts tend to be much less deadly, with battle-deaths comprising only a quarter of those in state-based conflicts.[32]

one-sided violence The Uppsala Conflict Data Program developed the term in 2002 to refer to "the use of armed force by the government of a state or by a formally organized group against civilians which results in at least 25 deaths per year."

Another form of organized political violence is one-sided violence. The Uppsala Conflict Data Program developed the term in 2002 to refer to "the use of armed force by the government of a state or by a formally organized group against civilians which results in at least 25 deaths per year."[33] The definition's focus on the actions of governments or organized groups excludes both personal violence and fatalities caused by riots and other types of unorganized violence. Additionally, one-sided

genocide The intent to destroy, in whole or in part, a national, ethnic, racial, or religious group.

violence involves the intentional and the direct use of armed force. Its victims are civilians who are deliberately targeted by government or non-state groups.[34] Genocide, politicide, and terrorism are all forms of one-sided violence. According to international law, *genocide* is "the intent to destroy, in whole or in part, a national, ethnic, racial or religious group." Included under the definition are the following acts:

[K]illing members of the group; causing serious bodily or mental harm to members of the group; deliberately inflicting on the group conditions of life calculated to bring about its physical destruction in whole or in part; imposing measures intended to prevent births within the group, and forcibly transferring children of the group to another group.[35]

Genocide is most common during or immediately after a civil war. Given how difficult it can be to judge intent, controversy often emerges around whether given acts can accurately be labeled genocide.[36] Because the legal definition of genocide does not include the slaughter of people for their political beliefs, some experts use the term *politicide* to describe the deliberate destruction of a group based on their political beliefs or affiliations. Like genocide, politicides often take place during or after civil wars, as was the case in Cambodia in 1975–9, when the Khmer Rouge committed most of its mass killings after the fighting had stopped.[37] Some experts argue that despite the absence of political mass murder from the UN's "Convention on the Prevention and Punishment of the Crime of Genocide," genocide and politicide are really just two "aspects of the same phenomena and need no separate theoretical explanations."[38]

politicide The deliberate destruction of a group based on their political beliefs or affiliations. This definition has been used because such groups are not covered under the UN Convention on the Prevention and Punishment of the Crime of Genocide.

Terrorism can also be viewed as an act of one-sided violence. Like the term "war," definitions of terrorism are multiple and varied. However, most of them take into account three primary factors: the method, the target, and the purpose. The method of terrorism is violence, the target is civilians, government, and/or infrastructure (buildings, transportation, power, and service installations), and the purpose is to instill fear in order to force political or social change.[39] Today we tend to associate terrorism with small, ideologically driven, non-state groups that commit acts of violence against civilian noncombatants in order to achieve political goals; however, governments sometimes commit acts of terror against their own civilian populations to achieve desired political results, such as maintaining power or eradicating revolutionary movements. Some argue that such acts committed by governments should be labeled "oppression" rather than terrorism, which suggests that the term terrorism applies only to non-state actors. Others maintain that states are in fact the world's most deadly terrorists.[40] Defining state terrorism is complicated by the fact that states depend on violence to some degree to protect their sovereignty (via a military) and to protect their people (via a police force).

terrorism Strategy of using violence primarily against civilians usually for political gain.

However, in contrast to these forms of sanctioned state violence, state terrorism consists of violence that is generally carried out unpredictably and in secrecy. Moreover, it differs in purpose, as it is designed to strengthen government control by instilling fear in the population.[41]

Fear also contributes to the misconception that terrorism is rampant, with acts of terror increasing yearly. The terrorist attacks on New York and the Pentagon on September 11, 2001 catapulted terrorism to the forefront of American concerns. Due to the heightened focus on terrorism ever since, many Americans assume that international terrorist attacks are increasing and that they personally are constantly at risk. Evidence suggests, however, that these fears are overblown. As John Mueller, professor of political science and author of *Overblown: How Politicians and the Terrorism Industry Inflate National Security Threats, and Why We Believe Them*, puts it: "Americans worry intensely about 'another 9/11,' but if one of these were to occur every three months for the next five years, the chance of being killed in one of them is 0.02 percent."[42] Data also suggests that the number of international terrorist incidents has declined in recent years.[43] High-casualty attacks have increased, however. Nevertheless, international terrorism has killed fewer than 1,000 people a year on average over the past 30 years.[44]

Data from 1989–2004 suggests that death tolls from one-sided violence in general tend to be significantly lower than those resulting directly from armed conflicts.[45] That same period was characterized by random spikes of violence rather than by the consistently high levels of violence that many people believed to be the norm. Most of these spikes were the product of the actions of a small number of groups, including Serbian opposition forces, al-Qaeda, and the governments of Rwanda, the DRC, and Afghanistan.[46] The data also indicate that the violence was not distributed evenly around the globe. Rather, there were identifiable zones of violence, with the highest levels of one-sided violence occurring in Africa, followed by Asia, Europe, and the Americas (see table 10.2 and figure 10.1).[47]

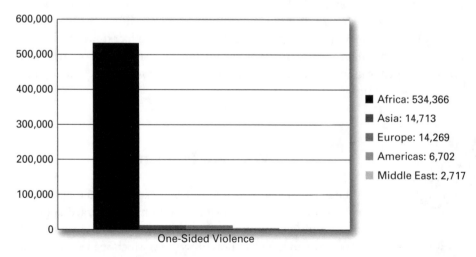

Figure 10.1   One-Sided Violence by Region, 1989–2004

Table 10.2   One-Sided Violence by Region, 1989–2004[48]

	Fatality Estimate	Number of Actors	Number of Countries
Europe	14,269	8	5
Middle East	2,717	7	4
Asia	14,713	27	10
Africa	534,366 (34,366)	31	18
Americas	6,702	5	4
World	572,767 (72,767)	78	41

Note: Estimates excluding the 1994 Rwanda genocide are included in parentheses. The lowest figure of the 500,000–800,000 Rwandan casualties estimate is used in this report.

In Focus: Geno/Politicide Risk Factors

Since World War II, nearly 50 episodes of genocide and political mass murder have taken place, claiming more lives than all of the victims of international and internal wars since 1945.[49] While the causes of these atrocities cannot be neatly identified, careful analysis of these tragedies has led to the delineation of a number of geno/politicide risk factors. The first is political upheaval. Conflict situations are more likely to lead to geno/politicide when they have been plagued by high magnitude internal wars over the preceding 15 years. The second risk factor is a history of prior genocides. In fact, the risk of a new geno/politicide is three times more likely when an internal conflict situation emerges in countries that had witnessed a prior case of genocide. The third risk factor involves elite ideology and regime type. Countries in which regimes adhered to an exclusionary ideology were two and a half times more likely to see internal conflicts lead to genocides than were those without exclusionary ideologies. The fourth risk factor focuses on ethnic and religious divisions. In countries in which the political elite consisted almost entirely of an ethnic minority, geno/politicide was two and a half times more likely. International interdependencies make up the final major risk factor. Countries with low trade openness are two and a half times more likely to see internal conflicts lead to geno/politicide.[50]

hominid   Any member of the biological family *Hominidae*, which includes extinct and extant humans, chimpanzees, gorillas, and orangutans.

Homo sapiens sapiens   Modern humans are members of the *Homo sapiens* species, of which the only extant subspecies is *Homo sapiens sapiens*.

War and Pre-history

Although our *hominid* ancestors date back at least 2.5 million years and *Homo sapiens sapiens* (modern humans) emerged approximately 200,000 years ago, human history only extends back 5,000 years to the invention of writing, which made a historical record possible.[51] The vast span of human existence prior to written records is called *pre-history*. Pre-historians rely upon archaeological evidence, evolutionary science, and research on extant hunter-gatherer societies to study the origins of humanity and human civilizations. Their research suggests that our

hunter-gatherer, pre-historic ancestors were rarely peaceful. Prior to the development of agriculture, permanent structures, writing, and metal tools, early humans were already gathering together to engage in organized warfare. These early wars were often the result of competition over resources,[52] but they were also waged for religious reasons, or to avenge a perceived wrong committed by another tribe.[53] Although tribes or clans would sometimes engage in face-to-face battles, raids were the most common form of warfare.[54]

The development of agriculture about 10,000 years ago slowly led to changes in warring practices. People who stayed in one place to farm became the targets of hunter-gatherers, who would conduct raids targeting domesticated animals and food stores.[55] Many farming communities in turn developed fortified settlements, including walls and moats, to protect themselves, their animals, and their produce.[56] As farming expanded and hunter-gatherer societies declined in number, violent conflicts emerged primarily between farming peoples.[57] As in former times, raids remained the most common form of warfare. The main objective was often the acquisition of livestock and produce, but women were frequently raped and kidnapped as well.[58] Warfare was conducted with spears, axes, clubs, knives, bows and arrows, shields, and occasionally forms of leather armor. However, many warriors often fought naked or partially naked, covering themselves with body paint.[59]

As populations increased and occupied larger territories, battles became more common and more deadly than they had in simpler tribal farming societies. Armed raids required more time, longer distances, and larger forces. When the land itself became the desired object of tribes that were on the move due to population pressures, land depletion, natural disasters, or invasions by other tribes, open battles would occur. Such battles could wreak great destruction, as both sides were more willing to risk their own lives over a place to settle and farm than over livestock or produce. Open battles remained, however, unorganized affairs. Combatants fought each other individually, rather than as an organized unit, and very few tactical or formational strategies were employed beyond the occasional use of ambushes.[60]

Within 5,000 years of the advent of agriculture, societies had grown increasingly complex. Food surpluses facilitated this complexity, freeing segments of the population from the daily task of farming. This allowed some people to experiment with tasks like metalworking or horse-raising, for example. Over time, labor became diversified, trading economies developed, society grew increasingly *stratified*, and hierarchies and complex political structures came into being. Authoritarian kings emerged, many claiming to be divine monarchs. To maintain power and to continue accumulating resources, they relied upon an emerging class of professional soldiers as well as upon an increasingly organized military.[61]

The History of War

Warfare and early civilizations

neolithic age A period beginning about 9500 BCE in the Middle East that is traditionally considered the last part of the Stone Age. It began with the rise of farming and ended when metal tools became widespread, ushering in the Copper Age, Bronze Age, or Iron Age, depending on the geographical region.

civilization Refers to a complex society that includes large concentrations of people in urban areas, agriculture, and hierarchical social and political structures that generally include states and priesthoods, the division of labor, and writing and formal record keeping.

By 3500 BCE, *neolithic* settlements were evolving into what are now commonly called *civilizations*. Civilizations are comprised of large concentrations of people in urban areas and hierarchical social and political structures that generally include states and priesthoods, the division of labor, and writing and formal record-keeping.[62] The first known civilizations developed in three river valley areas: the Tigris-Euphrates Valley (Mesopotamia), the Nile Valley (Egypt), and the Indus Valley (India and Pakistan). Sumer is thought to have been the first civilization, emerging in 3500 BCE in southern Mesopotamia as a series of independent, frequently warring city-states. Located at the center of the most significant trade routes in the ancient world, they vied with each other for supremacy and control of trade. However, these city-states were also faced with external pressures, as interloping tribes would attempt to wrest parts of the fertile valley from their control. In short, this area saw a great deal of military activity as various rivals attempted to control commerce.[63]

In contrast with the constant conflict taking place in Mesopotamia, Egypt emerged around 3100 BCE on the banks of the Nile River, where it flourished for 1,300 years in relative isolation from the rest of the world. The founder of Egypt was said to be Menes, a warrior ruler who established Egypt as a unified kingdom. Because of its isolation, the Egyptians did not maintain a standing army for centuries. Instead, temporary active armies were assembled when pharaohs called for them for protection or adventure. Between 2000 and 1600 BCE, however, pharaohs began keeping standing armies, though their military strategies were primarily defensive. Over time, this too changed, as pharaohs shifted from the defensive to the offensive, extending Egyptian rule into Nubia, Palestine, and Syria.[64]

Warfare in these early civilizations grew more sophisticated with the development of writing and the use of metals. In fact, these two advances occurred in most early civilizations around the same time. For example, around 3500 BCE, the Sumerians were the first to develop a written script called cuneiform. Shortly thereafter, in 3200 BCE, the Egyptians also developed a form of writing called hieroglyphics. Around that same period, people began mixing copper with tin to make bronze, a new metal that made stronger weapons and tools. Similar progressions occurred in the Indus Valley and China's Yellow River Valley sometime before 2500 BCE. Iron later replaced bronze in the Middle East around 1000 BCE, in Europe shortly thereafter, and in Indian and China a few hundred years later.[65] The use of metals led to some profound changes in weapons. The sword, for example, was probably introduced into warfare by the Assyrians sometime before 2000 BCE.[66]

Other developments occurring at the dawn of military history include the introduction and then the decline of the chariot, and the increasing presence of the horseman on the battlefield. Chariots, which were first introduced in Sumer about 2500 BCE, dominated warfare from 1700 to 1200 BCE.[67] They tended to be used by elite forces, nobles, and members of royal families. Cavalry did not appear until soon after 1000 BCE, and the Assyrians were the first to use them in large numbers. Cavalries were often made up of lesser nobles who were wealthy enough to own horses and to supply themselves with weapons and armor.[68] Despite these kinds of developments in warfare, organization and battle maneuvering were rare until after 1000 BCE when they were first used by the Egyptians and then later by the Assyrians.[69]

War in Ancient Greece

Although the Peloponnese Peninsula in Greece had been inhabited since around 4000 BCE, a powerful civilization did not emerge there until the Late Bronze Age. Mycenae, an ancient city-state, gained influence and strength in the period between 1350 and 1200 BCE. An expansionist civilization, Mycenaean culture was built upon warfare. The city-state broadened its military reach to secure raw materials and goods to support its population. Eventually, however, warrior chiefs evolved into conquerors and administrators, raiding shifted to trading, and Mycenae transitioned from a military center to a center of trade. Mycenae also spread the language, culture, and trade that would eventually develop into Hellenistic Greece, though it did not survive to see this come to pass. A series of fires from 1250 to 1100 BCE crippled the Mycenaean civilization, ushering in a period known as the Greek Dark Ages, from 1100 to 800 BCE.[70]

By the end of the Dark Ages, the population of Greece had shifted from a large empire to a series of smaller political units scattered throughout the country. These city-states usually included a fortress (called the acropolis) and a market, with the population residing in houses and farms surrounding the area. City-states had differing and sometimes shifting forms of government, including monarchies, *oligarchies*, *plutocracies*, *tyrannies*, and democracies, and it was not uncommon for city-states to establish colonies, sometimes in places as far away as France and Russia. Athens, a naval power, and Sparta, a land power, were among the larger of the city-states and serve as examples of the disparate ways city-states developed militarily.[71]

Sparta cultivated a warrior society, devoting much of its capital and human resources to the war machine. In Sparta, all male citizens, or "equals," were expected to devote their adult life to military training and service. Taken away from their parents at the age of 7, these boys and men lived their lives by a code of absolute obedience and austerity.[72] Only a tenth of the population of Sparta were full citizens, but their "sole skill and their major

oligarchy From the Greek words for "few" and "rule," the term refers to a form of government in which power resides with a small elite segment of society, distinguished by royalty, wealth, family, military influence, or religious authority.

plutocracies From the Greek words for "wealth" and "rule," the term refers to rule by the wealthy or power provided by wealth.

tyranny From the Greek word for "sovereign," it refers to a form of government in which a single ruler holds absolute power.

helots   Sparta's serf-like laborers who made up Sparta's agricultural workforce. Their servitude released every Spartan citizen from labor so that they could focus on war. Helots were bound to a plot of land and often considered expendable.

perioikoi   Category of people in Spartan society who were a social class above the helots but segregated from the Spartans. Free men but not citizens, they engaged in trade, fishing, crafts, and weapon-making.

preoccupation was warfare."[73] While this system supported a strong and efficient military force, it also demanded that those who were not citizens perform much of the work of the society. Sparta thus relied heavily upon a serf-like labor force known as *helots* to perform agricultural labor, while skilled labor was provided by the *perioikoi*, free men who were without citizen rights.[74] The helots, who made up the majority of the population, had to be watched carefully by Spartan soldiers to ensure that they did not rebel. Thus Sparta was constantly preoccupied not only with defeating its enemies from without but also with subduing its workforce within.

Athens, Sparta's neighbor in the Greek peninsula, also relied upon war to sustain its economy. Its societal structure was, however, quite different. It transformed itself from a monarchy into a democratic city-state in which all free Athenian male citizens could participate. It also became the center of intellectual and cultural life in Greece.[75] While it did not put all its resources into war the way Sparta did, it did develop into a major naval power. It led a defensive naval campaign against Persia, unifying and demanding payment from Greek states that wanted protection.

Maintaining the Athenian fleet had a major impact on the Athenian economy, which in turn influenced its decisions regarding warfare. A fleet of 100 ships required approximately 15,000 rowers, all of whom were paid for their services. The naval operation was also so extensive that it required a large administrative class. Because naval jobs were an integral part of many people's livelihoods, it was in the financial interest of many to maintain the military economy. In some cases, that meant voting to pursue rather than avoid war.[76] Democracy, in this case, did not contribute to making Athens less war-like than Sparta. Instead, Athens continued to demand funds for the navy from their reluctant allies even after the Persian invaders had been driven from the region. The significant economic benefits that a war economy provided simply made it difficult for Athens to disengage from war practices. It also contributed to the breakdown in Athenian–Spartan relations, as Sparta and its allies grew more concerned about the growth of Athenian power. Eventually, hostilities turned into war. The Peloponnesian War lasted from 431 to 404 BCE and was essentially a conflict between Athens and its empire and Sparta and its allies. The war reshaped the Ancient Greek world, transforming Athens from the strongest city-state in Greece to a state of complete devastation, never to regain its prewar prosperity. Sparta became the leading power in Greece, but the ideological conflict embodied by democratic Athens and oligarchic Sparta led to civil wars across the Greek world. By the end of the Peloponnesian War, the golden age of Greece had come to an end.

Warfare from 600 BCE to 1450 CE

From 600 BCE to 1450 CE, military technology throughout Eurasia did not change a great deal from earlier times. Iron and steel weapons remained the mainstay, though refinements in type and production were continually being made. For example, the crossbow was first manufactured in China in the fourth century BCE, and some larger empires, such as those of China and Persia, began large-scale mass production of weapons. China also revitalized the wall as a means of defense, rebuilding and reinforcing the Great Wall along its northern frontiers in the early fifteenth century. Significant inventions and advances in military technology during this period include gunpowder and "Greek fire," a petroleum-based incendiary substance that could be shot from tubes and could not be extinguished by water. Later, in the eleventh through thirteenth centuries, the Chinese invented rockets and a flame-thrower like device, the precursor to guns and cannons. By the mid-fifteenth century, the Chinese had developed cannons, which the Mongols and then others in the Middle East and Europe soon replicated.[77]

During the seventh and eighth centuries, Arabs conquered a large empire, which facilitated the expansion of Islam. While the militaries of most major empires during this era were primarily land forces, there were some that developed naval forces. The Vikings, for example, traded and fought along the coasts of Europe. The Mongols also developed a fleet. Kubilai Khan, the grandson of Genghis Khan, who established himself as emperor of China, twice invaded Japan in 1274 and 1281, but both invasions failed.[78]

Warfare from 1450 to 1750

Warfare changed profoundly during this period, particularly in Europe, leading to what scholars have described as the Military Revolution. Almost everything about warfare, from weapons and tactics to scale and organization, was transformed. Although gunpowder had been invented in China by the 900s and brought to Europe by the 1200s, it was not until the mid-1400s that it revolutionized warfare through its use in hand-held *ballistic* weapons. Prior to the development of the *arquebus*, the forerunner of small arms and rifles, the primary weapons of the infantry and cavalry were hand-held thrusting and cutting devices and projectiles, such as swords, spears, and bow and arrows. The 1600s saw the development of the *musket*, and by the mid-1700s, the musket had become the principal infantry weapon in Europe and North America. The gunpowder revolution also led to the development of more sophisticated cannons and bombs.[79]

> **ballistics** The science of the motion of projectiles, such as bullets, shells, or bombs.
>
> **arquebus** Muzzle-loaded firearm used in the fifteenth to seventeenth centuries that was a forerunner of the musket and later the rifle.
>
> **musket** A muzzle-loaded long gun, which is intended to be fired from the shoulder. It replaced the arquebus, and was in turn replaced by the rifle.

Tactical and strategic changes accompanied changes in weapons and technologies. On land, armies combined new technologies with older ones to create diversified forces. At sea, new ship-building technologies made ships more maneuverable. Navies employed speed, cannons, and new fleet formations to defeat their enemies. Warfare was almost continuous in Europe between 1450 and 1750, leading to dramatic increases in war spending and taxation as well as to the growth of government bureaucracies. Some scholars argue that the centuries of intensive European wars created the preconditions for republican forms of government, characterized by a contractual

Scientific Revolution A period occurring roughly during the later part of the Middle Ages and through the Renaissance in which scientific ideas in physics, astronomy, and biology evolved rapidly.

Industrial Revolution Refers to changes in economic and social organization that began around 1760 in England and later in other countries as the result of the replacement of hand tools with power-driven machines.

feudalism The social and economic system that characterized European societies during the Middle Ages (9th to 15th centuries). The king owned the land and gave it to his leading nobles in return for their loyalty and military service. The nobles in turn allowed peasants to farm their land for a portion of their produce.

capitalism An economic system in which wealth, and the means of producing wealth, are privately owned and controlled rather than publicly or state-owned and controlled.

imperialism The policy of extending a state's rule over foreign countries, or of acquiring and holding colonies and dependencies.

relationship between states and citizens. As more men were required to serve in their national armies and to pay higher taxes, they began to demand state-guaranteed rights. The Military Revolution is also inextricably linked to other historic changes, including the *Scientific Revolution*, the *Industrial Revolution*, and the transition from *feudalism* to *capitalism*.[80]

This was also the period when the burgeoning states of northwestern Europe embarked on a program of exploration and conquest that enabled them to forcibly implant their political economies in other parts of the world, a process referred to as *imperialism*. European imperialism began in the fourteenth century with Portugal, Castile, and Genoa's occupation of Madeira, the Canary Islands, and the Azores, respectively. The Portuguese conquest of the port of Ceuta in Northern Africa and the Strait of Gibraltar in 1415 were important early examples of European expansion. By the second half of the fifteenth century the Portuguese began working their way south along the coast of Africa, in search of a sea route to India. The Spanish too were after a new route to India, but instead wound up in the Americas, an accident that initiated Spanish imperialism in the so called "New World." Despite some earlier attempts, it was not until the seventeenth century that Britain, France, and the Netherlands successfully established overseas empires outside Europe.[81]

Technological advances made imperialism possible. Europeans developed larger, faster, and stronger ships that could accommodate not only sufficient provisions for long voyages but also cannons, guns, horses, and soldiers. Their ability to develop and then bring weapons with them to other parts of the world allowed them to dominate the indigenous inhabitants of these lands. While Europeans provided a range of justifications to support these conquests, most motives revolved around gaining control of resources and labor. The quest for new trade routes and the discovery of resources in the other lands went hand in hand with the use of their advanced weapons.

Warfare from 1750 to 1900

The Industrial Revolution brought improvements in weapons technology, making warfare increasingly deadly. Guns became ever more accurate, cannons were able to launch payloads further, and warships became stronger and faster. Innovations in steam power and mechanized transport made it possible to move armies to theaters of war faster than ever before. Eli Whitney's development of interchangeable parts made it easier for soldiers to set up, use, and repair guns and cannons. The first machine-gun was invented toward the end of this period by Sir Hiram Maxim, in 1884. Maxim guns, as they were called, were soon used with terrifying effect in various wars between invading colonizers and indigenous people. During the First Matabele War (1893–4), 50 British soldiers fought off 5,000 warriors with just four Maxim guns. British writer and politician Hilaire Belloc (1870–1953) summed up well the new imbalance of power between Europeans and indigenous people:

> Whatever happens we have got
> The Maxim gun, and they have not.[82]

Wars also expanded in size during this period, as military and political systems developed that made it easier to conscript huge numbers of soldiers. Use of the cavalry declined, while the infantry expanded. Women began playing a bigger role in supporting the military, providing medical attention, food, and laundry services. Drafts also became more popular during the nineteenth century.[83]

From 1754 to 1815, a series of wars were fought that shaped the future of North America. The US achieved its independence from Britain, France no longer played a significant role in North America, Canada remained aligned with Britain, Spain lost much of its empire in North and South America, and North American Native peoples found that their lands were increasingly being encroached upon. Europe was also reshaped by war, first by Napoleon, who conquered every major European power before he himself was defeated in 1815. Uprisings broke out in numerous European countries after Napoleon's defeat, leading to a series of civil wars between 1815 and 1870. In China, the Taiping Rebellion brought 14 years of civil war, and the US Civil War led to the deaths of 1 million Americans. By the 1880s, European competition for colonies in Africa and Asia was fierce. The colonial rivalries roiling during this period would later contribute to World War I, the largest and most devastating war the world had yet seen.[84]

Warfare from 1900 to 1950

The twentieth century was the most violent in recorded history; more than 100 million people were killed in wars.[85] The first half of the century saw the two largest wars in history: the Great War (1914–18), later named World War I, and World War II (1939–45). In the early 1900s, European states had become so entangled in political alliances and economic competition that the conditions were ripe for war. The ensuing world wars were indeed global conflicts, involving states and societies far beyond the conflicts' origins. They were also laboratories for the development and deployment of new technologies and strategies. The use of airplanes, tanks, rockets, submarines, and battleships significantly increased both the firepower and the reach of modern armies. As a result, casualty rates were high. Although figures vary widely, there were approximately eight million military battle deaths and more than six and half million civilian deaths during World War I (see table 10.3). During World War II, the casualty rate increased to approximately 15 million military deaths and 26–34 million civilian deaths (see table 10.4).[86] Germany's blitz of London with

Table 10.3 World War I Casualties and Costs[87]

Nations	Total Force Mobilized	Military Battle Deaths	Military Wounded	Civilian Dead	Economic and Financial Cost ($ million)
ALLIES					
France	8,410,000	1,357,800	4,266,000	40,000	49,877
British Empire	8,904,467	908,371	2,090,212	30,633	51,975
Russia	12,000,000	1,700,000	4,950,000	2,000,000	25,600
Italy	5,615,000	462,391	953,886	No reliable data	18,143
United States	4,355,000	50,585	205,690	No reliable data	32,320
Belgium	267,000	13,715	44,686	30,000	10,195
Serbia	707,343	45,000	133,148	650,000	2,400
Montenegro	50,000	3,000	10,000	No reliable data	No reliable data
Rumania	750,000	335,706	120,000	275,000	2,601
Greece	230,000	5,000	21,000	132,000	556
Portugal	100,000	7,222	13,751	No reliable data	No reliable data
Japan	800,000	300	907	No reliable data	No reliable data
Total	*42,188,810*	*4,889,090*	*12,809,280*	*3,157,633*	*193,667*
CENTRAL POWERS					
Germany	11,000,000	1,808,546	4,247,143	760,000	58,072
Austria-Hungary	7,800,000	922,500	3,620,000	300,000	23,706
Turkey	2,850,000	325,000	400,000	2,150,000	3,445
Bulgaria	1,200,000	75,844	152,390	275,000	1,015
Total	*22,850,000*	*3,131,890*	*8,419,533*	*3,485,000*	*86,238*

Table 10.4 World War II Casualties and Costs[88]

Nations	Total Forces Mobilized (million)	Military Dead	Military Wounded	Civilian Dead	Economic and Financial Costs ($ billion)
United States	14.9	292,100	571,822	Negligible	350
United Kingdom	6.2	397,762	475,000	65,000	150
France	6	210,671	400,000	108,000	100
Soviet Union	25	7,500,000	14,012,000	10–15,000,000	200
China	6–10	500,000	1,700,000	1,000,000	No estimate
Germany	12.5	2,850,000	7,250,000	500,000	300
Italy	4.5	77,500	120,000	40–100,000	50
Japan	7.4	1,506,000	500,000	300,000	100
All other participants	20	1,500,000	No estimate	14–17,000,000	350
Total	*102.5–106.5*	*14,834,033*	*No estimate*	*26–34,000,000*	*1,600*

unmanned medium-range rockets, Allied fire bombings of Dresden and Tokyo, and the US deployment of the atomic bomb all contributed to the dramatic increase in civilian casualties.

The Cold War

After World War II, global conflict was dominated by the *Cold War*, a time of rising political tensions and posturing between the two superpowers – the United States and the Soviet Union – and their respective allies. The two squared off against each other over political, ideological, and economic differences. Both believed that their political economies, democratic capitalism for the US and state-run communism for the Soviets, were diametrically opposed, and that each country was working to further its control over the world through conquest and the expansion of *spheres of influence*. Although the Cold War did not culminate in a direct violent clash between the US and the Soviets, it did contribute to many conflicts around the world. As nationalist movements in the developing world rose to throw off old colonial regimes, political instability and weak states emerged, especially in Africa and Asia. Before some of these emerging movements and states could consolidate control, the superpowers intervened in their affairs in pursuit of their own interests. The US and the Soviets also engaged in *proxy wars*, supporting opposing sides in selected intra-state conflicts in which they thought they could obtain important military and ideological advantages. Opposing factions were supplied with advisors, arms, money, and materials. The three major proxy wars that occurred during this period were the Korean War (1950–3), the Vietnam War (1954–75), and the Soviet invasion of Afghanistan (1979–89).[89]

Another major consequence of the Cold War was an escalating *arms race*, a competition to produce larger weapons arsenals, greater armies, and superior military technologies. The most significant weapon during this period was the nuclear bomb. After the US developed and deployed nuclear weapons at the end of World War II, the Soviets successfully exploded their own atomic bomb in 1949.[90] By 1951, the US developed an even more powerful nuclear weapon, the hydrogen bomb.[91] The US also developed nuclear-powered submarines, as did the Soviets four years later.[92] Both Cold War adversaries accumulated tremendous stockpiles of nuclear weapons and developed intercontinental ballistic missile systems (ICBMs) with a range that exceeded the distance between the "northeastern border of the continental United States and the northwestern border of the continental Soviet Union."[93] The build-up of nuclear arms on both sides led to the popularization of the doctrine of *mutually assured destruction* (MAD). According to this theory

Cold War Refers to the ideological stand-off between two superpowers, the United States and the Soviet Union, from 1945 to 1989. While not directly fighting one another, each side sought to expand its influence by keeping the other from spreading its form of government and political system, resulting in many proxy wars throughout the world.

sphere of influence An area or region over which an organization or state exercises cultural, economic, military or political domination.

proxy war A war that occurs when two powers use a third party as a substitute for fighting each other directly.

arms race A competition between two or more parties for military supremacy.

mutually assured destruction (MAD) The deterrence doctrine that maintains that full-scale use of nuclear weapons by two opposing sides would result in the destruction of both.

of deterrence, direct engagement in nuclear war would lead to the destruction of both regimes. Many consider MAD to be a critical factor that prevented the two powers from going to war with each other.[94]

Since the early 1970s, nuclear non-proliferation efforts have attempted to reduce the numbers of nuclear weapons in the world. Through various treaties, such as the 1972 Anti-Ballistic Missile Treaty and the Strategic Arms Reduction Treaties (START I–III), global nuclear arms totals have been reduced from a high of approximately 70,000 warheads in 1986 to fewer than 27,000 in 2006.[95] The US alone had produced more than 70,000 warheads since 1945, but by 2006, more than 60,000 of those had been disassembled.[96] Countries that have obtained nuclear weapons have also tried to prevent other states from developing them, with mixed results. For a time, the *nuclear club* included the US, the Soviet Union (now Russia), China, France, and the UK. Today it also includes Pakistan, India, Israel, and North Korea. South Africa developed nuclear weapons but later disassembled its arsenal.[97] Today, there are concerns not only about additional states developing nuclear weapons but also about non-state actors, for example terrorists, obtaining them. While this threat is often associated with radical Islamist groups, the reality is that any "super-empowered angry man" or organization might unleash a weapon of mass destruction.[98]

nuclear club Name given to countries that possess nuclear weapons: US, Britain, France, China, Russia, India, Pakistan, North Korea. Israel is also believed to have nuclear weapons.

War since the collapse of the Soviet Union

In 1989 the Berlin Wall came down, and in 1991 Mikhail Gorbachev, the Soviet Union's last premier, resigned. With these events, the Soviet Union came to an end, and with it, the Cold War. Many hoped that the end of the Cold War would diffuse the tensions that it had shaped and fueled around the world. Unfortunately, the opposite often occurred. As the global power structures shifted, many states that had been affected by US/Soviet interventions became increasingly unstable. In some places, the vacuum of Soviet power intensified ethnic, political, and religious rivalries, which later erupted into war. Ethnic cleansing occurred in Europe, for example, leading to the fragmentation of Yugoslavia into warring ethnic and religious factions.

Since the end of the Cold War, conflicts have continued to erupt around the world. India and Pakistan have continued to fight over the region of Kashmir, and conflicts between Israel and its Arab neighbors continue to threaten peace in the Middle East and the world.[99] Small, Islamist non-state groups increasingly have attracted the world's attention through terrorism, unsettling countries that are skilled in conventional warfare but less prepared to deal with terrorism. Russia, for example, continues to battle Chechen guerillas, while the United States pursues al-Qaeda, the Islamist group that brought down the World Trade Center in New York and damaged the Pentagon in Washington, DC. The US invaded Afghanistan and then Iraq, but terrorist strikes continued around the world, including attacks in Madrid and London.[100] However, while the violence that has continued to plague the world since the end of the Cold War is frightening, statistics suggest that the world is actually becoming less war-prone. Since the mid-1970s, the world has seen the most sustained decline in the number of international conflicts in two centuries. Moreover, from 1992 to 2005, the number of civil wars also declined by three-quarters.[101] But to better understand war and why it persists, we need to look at some of the factors that cause or create the conditions for war.

Causes of War

Savage brutes or peaceful primitives?

When people ponder the origins and causes of war, they often wonder whether war is an intrinsic part of human nature. Are we, as a species, genetically predisposed to engage in war? Or are the causes of war rooted in civilization, the state, the international system, politics, or ideology? Might we ever learn to avoid war, or is it more likely that, as long as humans exist, so too will war? Philosophers Thomas Hobbes and Jean-Jacques Rousseau both considered such questions, but they arrived at very different answers. Their two perspectives have since developed into two distinct schools of thought about human beings' relationship to war. For Hobbes, writing in the mid-1600s, humans were intrinsically violent and always likely to turn on one other, fighting over everything from greed to reputation. The creation of the state helped control humans' violent nature, forcing them to live peacefully with each other, if not always with other states. In stark contrast to Hobbes, Rousseau, writing approximately 100 years later, argued that human nature was intrinsically good, and that it was the state and civilization that were the problem. Aboriginal humans, he maintained, lived in harmony with nature and with each other. War only emerged with the agricultural revolution, which brought with it population growth, private property, the state, and war.[102]

During much of the twentieth century, Rousseau's perspective held sway in the field of anthropology. Many anthropologists believed that warfare was uncommon among hunter-gatherer societies, emerging only later in human history alongside the appearance of agriculture and the state.[103] The title of Margaret Mead's 1940 article on the subject, "Warfare Is Only an Invention – Not a Biological Necessity," epitomizes this view.[104] However, by the end of the twentieth century, researchers had accumulated extensive evidence that disproved the idea that the majority of pre-state hunter-gatherer societies were peaceful.[105] Cross-cultural research on warfare has established that, although there were some societies that did not engage in war, or that did so extremely rarely, 90–95 percent of known societies have actively participated in warfare.[106]

Evolutionary science has also undermined Rousseau's notion that man, in his original state prior to civilization, was peaceful. Instead, science indicates that humans have an innate, evolution-shaped potential for violence and aggression.[107] While this understanding of humans' relationship to violence might be viewed as closer to

Hobbes's theories than Rousseau's, it is important to note that science has not "proven" Hobbes's notion that the natural state of humanity is "solitary, poor, nasty, brutish, and short," and characterized by war, "continual fear, and danger of violent death."[108] Rather, science suggests that violence and aggression have proven to be useful tools in the evolutionary struggle to survive. While humans could be said to have a genetic predisposition toward violence and aggression, these behaviors are best viewed as options rather than as irresistible, hard-wired commands. Because conditions influence the tendency toward aggression, violence levels fluctuate and can at times decline dramatically.[109] Although most societies across cultures and history have engaged in war, there are a few exceptions that have not or that have remained peaceful. There has been a variety of studies of small peaceful societies living in remote environments, but there are also well-known examples of peaceful states, such as Switzerland and Sweden, neither of which have engaged in warfare for 200 years.[110]

Human evolution and war

When war is approached from an evolutionary perspective, the question "What causes war?" is reframed as "What are the evolutionary rewards that can make the highly dangerous activity of fighting worthwhile?"[111] In this framework, competition is the primary cause of conflict and fighting, both in humans and in all other animal species.[112] Specifically, competition over resources and the struggle for reproduction are the root causes of conflict.[113] People fight, in other words, "to gain the very same things that constitute the objects of human desire in general."[114] While this was true of our ancient ancestors who fought over hunting grounds and access to women, it is not difficult to see that many conflicts today are also resource conflicts (either in whole or in part), fought over access to things like water, land, food, oil, minerals, etc. Derivative, or "second-level causes" and motivations for violent conflict include dominance (rank, status, prestige, honor), revenge, security, worldviews (ideas and ideals), kinship (including ethnic and national identities), spiritual/religious factors, and fun or adventure.[115] In short, scholars who approach war from an evolutionary perspective argue that the main cause of fighting and wars is competition over scarce resources. The quest for power and dominance is but a secondary, related aim that facilitates the fulfillment of the former.[116] In other words, while power is something that is doggedly pursued, it is valuable precisely because it ensures that "somatic and reproductive resources can be defended or won."[117]

Power factors that cause war

While the evolutionary perspective provides a way of understanding why war has not been eliminated from human society through natural selection processes, it is not as useful when it comes to determining the specific conditions that make war likely or how those conditions might be altered to avert war. In other words, while it might be true that most wars are about competition over resources at some level, we can learn other things about war that might ultimately be more valuable in helping us prevent it. Another way of approaching the causes of war is to look at those power factors that influence the probability of war. In his book *Causes of War*, Stephen Van Evera explores five major causes of war that he argues can be prevented, reduced, or addressed in some way. The first cause he looks at is false optimism. War is more likely, he argues, "when states fall prey to false optimism about its outcome."[118] In other words, if the losers could foresee their defeat and both sides could foretell the costs, they would not pursue war. The future losers would settle the dispute rather than taking up arms, and all would avoid the costs. It is our inability to see into the future and the false hopes this allows that lead states to war.[119] The second cause of war that Van Evera examines revolves around the first-strike advantage, a situation in which the first to use force gains an advantage over the adversary. He argues, "War is more likely when the advantage lies with the first side to mobilize or attack."[120] In short, by improving the attacker's prospects of victory, the first-strike advantage creates the temptation to start war.[121] The third cause of war involves power shifts and vulnerability. He maintains: "War is more likely when the relative power of states fluctuates sharply – that is, when windows of opportunity and vulnerability are large."[122] Another way of putting this idea is that "War is more likely when states expect better results from a war begun now than a war begun later."[123] A declining state, for example, might decide to launch a war now in order to prevent a future conflict under less attractive circumstances. The fourth cause revolves around cumulative resources, which Van Evera defines as a possession that "helps its possessor to protect or acquire other resources."[124] He argues: "War is more likely when resources are cumulative – that is, when the control of resources enables a state to protect or acquire other resources."[125] For example, industrial capacity is a cumulative resource since states cannot be military powers without a large industrial base. Wars are fought for control of the world's strongest industrial regions, and the winners of these conflicts significantly increase their profits and power.[126] Finally, Van Evera argues that "war is more likely when conquest is easy."[127] If a state feels it has nothing to lose and something to gain, it is more likely to go to war.

Causes of civil wars

Other scholars point out that different types of wars have very different causes. The causes of civil wars, for example, are generally quite different from the causes of international ones. Analyses of civil wars suggest that the poorest countries tend to have the highest risk of civil war. Or more specifically still: "Countries with low, stagnant, and unequally distributed per capita incomes that have remained dependent on primary commodities for their exports face dangerously high risks of prolonged conflict."[128] Good political institutions and ethnic and religious homogeneity or tolerance, which some argue can avert civil war, are ineffective in the face of failed economic development. Moreover, substantial ethnic and religious diversity within a society actually decreases the risk of civil war, while more limited ethnic differentiation can be a risk factor for civil war. Rebel leaders generally gain support for their campaigns against the existing government by focusing on a real or perceived political grievance, such as a minority group's exclusion from the political process. However, while grievances can lead to civil wars, statistics indicate that "secessionist rebellions are considerably more likely if the country has valuable natural resources, with oil being particularly potent."[129] In other words, some insurgencies that have an ethnic or religious component to them are nevertheless fueled more by the desire for resources than by an ethnic or religious-based political objective. In some cases, rebel groups are driven solely by greed and the power to control resources. Some economists, for example, view rebellion simply as "the use of resources to exploit others for an economic gain."[130]

autocracy A form of government in which one person has uncontrolled or unlimited authority over others.

Finally, some argue that democracy itself decreases the risk of civil war, while political repression increases it. However, statistics suggest that *autocracies* are about as stable as full democracies. Instead, changes in political institutions are linked to civil war, while stable political institutions are correlated with safety. In poor countries, political institutions are actually less stable in democracies than in autocracies, leading to an increased risk of civil war. Only half of democracies in developing countries last beyond their first elections, and the average duration of democracies in developing countries is only nine years. Democracies do, however, tend to become more stable as incomes rise. Ultimately, at high income levels, democracies do reduce the risk of civil war.[131]

Ethical and Legal Dimensions of War

Just war theory

Humans have a long history not only of engaging in war but also of finding ways to both justify and restrict it. Just war theory is one important intellectual tradition through which the ethics of war has been explored. Based largely on medieval and post-medieval Christian teachings, including the writings of St Augustine and Thomas Aquinas,[132] this tradition is the "intellectual progenitor" of international law[133] and it represents a collective ongoing intellectual and moral project to understand and delineate the parameters of war.[134] Just war theory restricts war by constructing an ethical framework for (1) resorting to war, (2) conducting war, and (3) terminating war and negotiating peace.[135]

Resorting to war

jus ad bellum Latin phrase referring to the justice of a war. It delineates the requirements that must be met in order for a war to be justifiable.

The right to fight a war, known by its Latin phrase, *jus ad bellum*, or the justice of war, has gradually been restricted over time. In order for a war to be considered just, political communities must adhere to six requirements:

1 *Just Cause:* The first requirement is that the cause for going to war should be just. Examples of frequently cited just causes include self-defense, the defense

of others, and punishment for wrongdoing. However, some see resisting aggression as the only real just cause.

2 *Legitimate Authority:* The second requirement says that states can go to war only if the proper authorities have been consulted (these authorities are usually specified in the state's constitution) and a public declaration has been made of its intent, usually to its citizenry and the enemy.

3 *Last Resort:* The third requirement is that a state can resort to war only if it has exhausted all other alternatives for a peaceful resolution.

4 *Right Motivation:* The fourth requirement is that states must have the right motivation, pursuing war only for the sake of the just cause rather than for any ulterior motives. Because of the difficulty in determining intent, however, this rule did not later appear in international law.

5 *Chance of Success:* The fifth requirement is that a state should not go to war if there is no probability of success. If resorting to war will not bring about any measurable effects, then war should be avoided. This provision did not make its way into international law, since it has been viewed as biased against small and weak states.

6 *Goal of Peace:* Finally, the sixth requirement is that a state must weigh the costs and benefits of war, pursuing warfare only if the vision of postwar peace is preferable to the state of affairs that would continue if the war were not fought.[136]

Requirements four through six are sometimes collectively referred to as the *principle of proportionality*, which states that a war can only be just if its moral benefits are greater than its costs. This principle positions war as an evil that can only be justified if it culminates in an overall greater good.[137]

> **principle of proportionality**   A war can only be just if its moral benefits are greater than its costs.

The right to wage an aggressive war was abolished in international law by the 1928 Briand-Kellogg Pact and by the United Nations Charter. The only just reason for fighting a war that remains in international law is the right to self-defense, although this right is often expanded to include the right to fight to defend the sovereignty of other states. However, some political movements claim that liberation wars are just wars, while others argue that attacks to limit genocide, such as the NATO attack on Yugoslavia in 1999, also constitute just war.[138]

Conducting war

Just war theory distinguishes between the right to wage war, the *jus ad bellum*, and the rights and duties that must be adhered to once the war has started, the *jus in bello*, or justice in war.[139] The

> ***jus in bello***   Latin phrase referring to justice in a war.

first rule for conducting war is to obey all international weapons prohibition laws. For example, chemical and biological weapons are forbidden by many treaties, and states are thus expected to abide by these rules if their campaigns are to be considered just. Secondly, soldiers are prohibited from using weapons against civilians. They are expected to discriminate between the civilian population and legitimate military targets, with only minor collateral civilian casualties. The third provision is one of proportionality. It requires soldiers to use only as much force as they need to in order to achieve the desired end. In this framework, weapons of mass destruction are considered out of proportion with legitimate military objectives. The fourth rule demands benevolent treatment of war prisoners. Prisoners of war should not be threatened with death, starvation, or torture. Rather, they should be quarantined from the battle zone until the war ends, at which point they should be exchanged for one's own prisoners of war. The fifth principle is that soldiers should not use weapons that are "evil in themselves," including genocide, rape, ethnic cleansing, etc. Finally, just war rules on conducting war require that there be no reprisals, which prevents retaliations that are not based on just causes for war.[140]

Terminating war

jus post bellum Latin phrase referring to justice after war.

Finally, rules for terminating war, referred to as *jus post bellum*, or justice after war, regulate the ending of wars. Although rules for easing the transition from war to peace can help ensure that the peace is fair, stable, and lasting, little international law has been devised to address it. One proposed rule is that the peace settlement should be reasonable and publicly proclaimed. The settlement should also secure the basic rights that had been violated and that had led to the justified war. Additionally, the victor needs to discriminate between leaders, soldiers, and civilians, avoiding sweeping sanctions that punish civilians. Also, fair and public trials should be held for war crimes committed by leaders in particular, but also by soldiers. Appropriate and proportionate punishment should be delivered, and any financial restitution mandates must be proportional and discriminate. Finally, rehabilitation of aggressive states is permissible and may involve disarmament, human rights education, police and judicial retraining, and structural transformations leading to a just society.[141]

Over time, international law gradually replaced just war doctrine in providing guidelines for the permissible use of force. However, it absorbed much of the basic just war parameters, bridging medieval Europe's religious tradition and the modern state's emerging secular system. For example, the Nuremberg Trials, famous for the prosecution of Nazi leaders after World War II, tried defendants for both crimes of war and crimes against humanity, paralleling the just war distinction between *jus ad bellum* and *jus in bello*.[142] Additionally, many of the rules that emerged within the just war tradition have been codified into specific international agreements and laws, including The United Nations Charter and The Hague and Geneva Conventions.

International law and rules for war

Following a just war theoretical framework, which suggests that while war is reprehensible, it may be necessary in certain contexts, states have sought to formalize rules delineating when war is justifiable and what wartime actions are impermissible. Using international law, nation-states have established rules for war. International law refers to a system of agreements between nation-states that signify their adherence to specified values, standards, and regulations. It differs from other legal systems in that it focuses primarily on states rather than on private citizens. When a state's representative signs on to a treaty or convention, the country is agreeing to the document, thereby making it law. Thus, by signing onto dozens of treaties dealing with various aspects of war, nation-states have created international laws for their own conduct as it pertains to war.

The most significant early efforts to legally restrict war occurred at the two Hague Conferences. Convened in The Hague, The Netherlands, by Czar Nicholas II of Russia, the first Hague Conference (1899) sought to limit the total number of armaments and to establish rules for the conduct of warfare. Some progress was made, as laws dealing with the conduct of war on land were agreed to. There was even an agreement to limit the use of projectiles from balloons. The second Hague Conference was convened in 1907 with similar goals in mind, and it produced more rules covering issues of neutrality during conflict as well as rules for war-time maritime and naval conduct. Additionally, specific types of weapons, including poisonous gas, were outlawed. The Permanent Court of Arbitration was also established at the second Hague Conference; it was designed to settle disputes between nation-states.[143] Dozens of representatives from nation-states attended these conferences, and while the rules established were quickly ignored during the subsequent world wars, a precedent had been set and international rules for war had become a permanent part of international relations. Ironically, there was to be a third Hague Convention in 1916 to celebrate 100 years of unbroken peace in Europe, but World War I rendered the idea moot.[144]

Following World War I, efforts to craft international laws to restrict and control war have been driven by international organizations, such as the League of Nations and the United Nations, as well as by nation-states and non-governmental organizations. The Charters of both the League and the UN specify that states should not resort to war except in self-defense. The following articles from the UN Charter detail the expectations of member states:

Article 2.3: All nations shall settle their international disputes by peaceful means in such a manner that international peace and security, and justice, are not endangered.

Article 2.4: All Members shall refrain in their international relations from the threat or use of force against the territorial integrity or political independence of any state, or in any other manner inconsistent with the Purposes of the United Nations.

Article 51: Nothing in the present Charter shall impair the inherent right of individual or collective self-defense if an armed attack occurs against a Member of the United Nations, until the Security Council has taken measures necessary to maintain international peace and security. Measures taken by Members in the exercise of this right of self-defense shall be immediately reported to the Security Council and shall not in any way affect the authority and responsibility of the Security Council under the present Charter to take at any time such action as it deems necessary in order to maintain or restore international peace and security.[145]

In addition to the establishment of the UN's Charter, which sought to restrict war, the international community also created specific laws for war. In 1949, four Geneva Conventions were signed that laid out the proper conduct of war as well as the proper treatment of combatants, prisoners, civilians, and the sick and injured. Additionally, the Nuremberg Trials (1945–6) and the Tokyo Tribunals (1946–8) established the precedent that international law regarding war was to be taken seriously and that leaders of nation-states might be held accountable for violating them. At these trials, thousands of defendants were tried for acts of aggression that had been outlawed under international law.

Since the Geneva Conventions, the international community has sought to limit various types of instruments of warfare as well as weapons proliferation. See table 10.5 for a selected list of treaties dealing with the laws of war.

Global conflict issues and international law

Landmines

Landmines, or anti-personnel mines, are explosive devices "designed to be exploded by the presence, proximity or contact of a person and that will incapacitate, injure or kill one or more persons."[146] Although they are dangerous weapons of war, they

Table 10.5   Selected Treaties Relating to the Laws of War

Year	Agreement	Purpose
1856	Paris Declaration Respecting Maritime Law	Abolished privateering and established other rules regarding naval blockades and the use of flags on ships.
1864	First Geneva Convention for the Amelioration of the Condition of the Wounded and Sick in Armed Forces in the Field	Established rules for the extraction of the wounded from the battle field and led to the formation of the International Committee of the Red Cross.
1899	Hague Conventions I. Pacific Settlement of International Disputes II. Laws and Customs of War on Land III. Adaptation to Maritime Warfare of Principles of Geneva Convention of 1864 IV. Prohibiting Launching of Projectiles and Explosives from Balloons Hague Declarations I. On the Launching of Projectiles and Explosives from Balloons II. On the Use of Projectiles the Object of Which is the Diffusion of Asphyxiating or Deleterious Gases III. On the Use of Bullets Which Expand or Flatten Easily in the Human Body	Established rules for settling disputes and restricted conduct during war.

Table 10.5   *(cont'd)*

Year	Agreement	Purpose

1907	Hague Conventions
	   I. The Pacific Settlement of International Disputes
	   II. The Limitation of Employment of Force for
	        Recovery of Contract Debts
	   III. The Opening of Hostilities
	   IV. The Laws and Customs of War on Land
	   V. The Rights and Duties of Neutral Powers and
	        Persons in Case of War on Land
	   VI. The Status of Enemy Merchant Ships at the
	        Outbreak of Hostilities
	   VII. The Conversion of Merchant Ships into War-Ships
	   VIII. The Laying of Automatic Submarine Contact Mines
	   IX. Bombardment by Naval Forces in Time of War
	   X. Adaptation to Maritime War of the Principles
	        of the Geneva Convention
	   XI. Certain Restrictions with Regard to the Exercise of
	        the Right of Capture in Naval War
	   XII. The Creation of an International Prize Court
	   XIII. The Rights and Duties of Neutral Powers in Naval War
		Established rules for settling disputes and restricted conduct during war.

1922	The Washington Naval Treaty – also known as the Five-Power Treaty	Limited naval armaments among the signature nations.
1923	Hague Draft Rules of Aerial Warfare	Established rules on how to conduct air warfare.
1925	Geneva protocol for the Prohibition of the Use in War of Asphyxiating, Poisonous or Other Gases, and of Bacteriological Methods of Warfare	Limited use of chemical and biological weapons.
1928	Kellogg-Briand Pact – also known as the Pact of Paris	Outlawed war as a means of settling disputes.
1929	Geneva Convention, Relative to the treatment of prisoners of war	Established rules for the treatment of prisoners of war.
1930	Treaty for the Limitation and Reduction of Naval Armament – also known as London Naval Treaty	Limited submarine warfare and naval shipbuilding.
1938	Amsterdam Draft Convention for the Protection of Civilian Populations Against New Engines of War	Sought to protect civilians from armed attack, bombardment, chemical and biological weapons.
1945	United Nations Charter	Allows war only in self-defense.
1946	Judgment of the International Military Tribunal at Nuremberg	Established the legal precedent of holding individuals liable for violating laws against aggression.
1947	Nuremberg Principles	Principles delineating what constituted war crimes.
1948	United Nations Convention on the Prevention and Punishment of the Crime of Genocide	Defined genocide and required nations act to stop genocide.

Table 10.5 *(cont'd)*

Year	Agreement	Purpose
1949	Geneva Convention I for the Amelioration of the Condition of the Wounded and Sick in Armed Forces in the Field	Established laws for the treatment of the wounded and the sick in armed forces on land.
1949	Geneva Convention II for the Amelioration of the Condition of Wounded, Sick and Shipwrecked Members of Armed Forces at Sea	Established laws for the treatment of the wounded and the sick in armed forces at sea.
1949	Geneva Convention III Relative to the Treatment of Prisoners of War	Established laws regarding prisoners of war.
1949	Geneva Convention IV Relative to the Protection of Civilian Persons in Time of War	Established rules for the protection of civilians during wartime.
1954	Hague Convention for the Protection of Cultural Property in the Event of Armed Conflict	Established rules for protecting cultural property during war.
1971	Zagreb Resolution of the Institute of International Law on Conditions of Application of Humanitarian Rules of Armed Conflict to Hostilities in which the United Nations Forces May be Engaged	Dealt specifically with the use of United Nations forces in conflict.
1972	Bacteriological Warfare Convention	Banned entire categories of toxin weapons.
1977	Geneva Protocol I	Addition to the Geneva Conventions of 1949: Relating to the Protection of Victims of International Armed Conflicts.
1977	Geneva Protocol II	Addition to the Geneva Conventions 1949: Relating to the Protection of Victims of Non-International Armed Conflicts.
1978	Red Cross Fundamental Rules of International Humanitarian Law Applicable in Armed Conflicts	Required contracting parties to distinguish between combatants and civilians and to endeavor to protect civilians.
1980	Convention on Certain Conventional Weapons (CCW)	Limited weapons that have an indiscriminate impact.
1992	Chemical Weapons Convention	Prohibited the development and use of chemical weapons.
1997	Convention on the Prohibition of the Use, Stockpiling, Production and Transfer of Anti-Personnel Mines and on their Destruction – also known as the Ottawa Treaty	Banned the use of landmines.
1998	Rome Statute of the International Criminal Court	Established the International Criminal Court.
2000	Optional Protocol to the Convention on the Rights of the Child on the Involvement of Children in Armed Conflict	Banned the use of child soldiers.

are particularly insidious because they are indiscriminate killers that continue to threaten civilians long after the wars that prompted their deployment have ended. More than 90 percent of the victims of landmines are civilians, and many of these are women and children.[147] Landmines also have a variety of other negative effects on societies. For example, fear of landmines inhibits travel, prevents farmers from using arable land, undermines the resettlement of refugees, and limits the reconstruction of entire regions of former war zones. In 1999, it was estimated that landmines killed or maimed between 15,000 and 20,000 people annually. Recently, however, casualties have started to fall, with 5,751 identified in 2006.[148]

In 1997, the International Campaign to Ban Landmines successfully pushed for the ratification of the Mine Ban Treaty.[149] The Convention, which emerged from the work of NGOs that pushed nation-states to promulgate a treaty, came into force on March 1, 1999. It provides that contracting parties will ban the use, transfer, and stockpiling of anti-personnel mines. They will also destroy existing stockpiles by 2003 and clear minefields by 2009.[150] Although many members of the international community have made banning and removing landmines a priority, their efforts have sometimes been attenuated by a variety of factors, including cost. While landmines are cheap to produce, costing only $3–$30 apiece, they are much more expensive to remove and deactivate, with estimates ranging from $300 to $1,000 a mine, depending upon the design.[151] Another obstacle is the sheer number of landmines out there. Although no one knows how many landmines remain in the ground, estimates range from 60 to 100 million in more than 75 countries around world, with more being deployed in new theaters of conflict every day.[152] Finally, a number of countries, including the US, have refused to sign the Mine Ban Treaty, limiting its efficacy.

Small arms sales

The five permanent members of the UN Security Council – the US, Britain, France, China, and Russia – together account for 85 percent of all the arms shipped around the world.[153] The manufacture and sale of arms is a lucrative business for these countries, but it has also played a role in fueling violent conflict, particularly in the developing world, where over two-thirds of the legal exports of small arms are sent.[154] Small arms are particularly popular in the developing world because they are inexpensive to manufacture, they are easy to smuggle, they require little training or organizational support to use, they are easily repaired, and they are light and manageable enough for children as young as 10 years old to handle. However, widespread poverty, social inequities, and the availability of large numbers of small arms often make for an explosive combination.[155] What we've seen is that post-Cold War conflicts in the developing world tend to be fought using these small arms and light weapons, and somewhere between 60 and 90 percent of direct conflict deaths result from them.[156]

Despite how lucrative arms trading is, in 1991, the five permanent members of the UN Security Council began attempting to limit the amount of arms they were trading. By 1992, they had established the UN Conventional Arms Register, a body to which all arms sales were to be reported. Its success, however, was limited. Although the 1990s saw the overall aggregate spending on arms decrease, arms shipments to certain areas in the developing world exploded. In 2006, the efforts of NGOs and nation-states to limit arms proliferation paid off in a vote at the UN to begin crafting a treaty to control the legal international arms trade. Should the Arms Trade Treaty (ATT) emerge, the illegal arms trade will nevertheless remain a problem that will demand the world's attention.[157]

Resource-based conflicts

Funds to purchase arms come from a variety of places, but attention is increasingly being paid to the role of natural resources in driving violent conflict, particularly in the developing world. As previously discussed, one risk factor for the eruption of violent conflict in a developing country is a heavy reliance upon the export of some type of natural resource, such as oil, timber, diamonds, and precious metals. Wars not only are waged over control of such resources but also are often funded by the extraction of them. In some cases, there are complex links among the private sector activities of large multinational corporations (MNCs) engaged in primary resource extraction, the global arms trade, and the states and rebel groups engaging in and often profiting from war. For example, in Angola, where Cold War tensions had manifested themselves in a long-term civil war, oil MNCs provided huge drilling bonuses and payments to the government. Oil profits were in turn used to purchase arms rather than to fund development projects that would benefit the people of Angola. The government justified its actions by saying that they needed to use the oil money to fight Unita, the opposition movement. However, the government had other motivations for prolonging the war; arms dealers paid them millions of dollars in commissions to negotiate arms deals. If the war ended, so would the profitable arms deals. In short, the Angolan government found that war itself can be a lucrative business.[158]

Diamonds have also funded and fueled many conflicts. While the government of Angola funded the civil war through oil profits, the rebel group Unita funded its activities through diamonds. Trade in rough diamonds also helped fuel conflicts in Sierra Leone and the Democratic Republic of the Congo. Due to the prevalence of this problem, diamonds extracted from conflict zones came to be called *blood diamonds* or *conflict diamonds*. In May 2000, members of the international community and the diamond industry met in Kimberley, South Africa to discuss ways of stemming the flow of diamonds that were fueling violent conflict. In December of that year, the United Nations adopted a resolution supporting the creation of an international certification scheme for rough diamonds. By November 2002, the *Kimberley Process Certification Scheme (KPCS)* was developed, documenting the requirements for the production and trade of rough diamonds. The KPCS requires members to certify shipments of rough diamonds as "conflict-free." The KPCS entered into force in 2003, and by November

blood diamonds or conflict diamonds Rough diamonds used by rebel movements to finance wars against legitimate governments.

Kimberley Process Certification Scheme (KPCS) A joint initiative involving governments, industry, and civil society to stem the flow of conflict diamonds.

2008, 49 members from 75 countries had signed up to it (the members of the European Community together counted as one). Experts estimate that international trade in conflict diamonds has declined from estimates of up to 15 percent during the 1990s to less than 1 percent today.[159] The Kimberley Process can therefore be viewed as an important step toward eliminating the financing of wars in these regions.

In Focus: Private Military Companies

One contemporary trend in warfare is the increased use of private military companies (PMCs) in theaters of conflict around the world. Although PMCs have existed for hundreds of years,[160] they have become more prominent since the end of the Cold War. PMCs are hired by state and non-state actors alike to engage in conflict-related activities, including providing security, intelligence, training, supplies of weapons and vehicles, combat support, and post-combat reconstruction. These companies, then, take on many of the responsibilities that have come to be associated primarily with government. By the 1990s, PMCs had become global in scope and activity, impacting the processes and outcomes of conflicts. PMCs have been particularly active in Africa. For example, more than 80 firms participated in the war in Angola.[161]

The now defunct South African firm Executive Outcomes was one of the most well-known and controversial PMCs as well as one of the first firms hired in Angola. In 1993, it retrained Angolan army forces and led them into battle.[162] Later, Sierra Leone paid Executive Outcomes $35 million to defeat rebel RUF forces and to reestablish the government's control over the economically productive parts of the country.[163] Executive Outcomes successfully retook the diamond fields in the eastern part of the country and drove the RUF back to the border areas, fulfilling its mission. However, the stability engendered by the victories did not last long. Fewer than 100 days after Executive Outcomes left the country, a coup toppled the government, and rebel fighters once again terrorized the populace. Approximately 10,000 civilians were later killed by the same rebel group that Executive Outcomes had once easily defeated.[164] This highlights one of the issues revolving around the use of PMCs. Without their continued presence, which is secured by enormous amounts of money, the instability that the PMCs have been brought in to quell often re-emerges in their absence.

Executive Outcomes was arguably the most important innovator in the contemporary military contracting business, providing a model that many have since attempted to follow. Despite its fiscal and military successes, the company disbanded on January 1, 1999 for a variety of reasons, including its historical links to apartheid that continued negatively to affect its reputation.[165] Years later, Blackwater, later renamed Xe, took Executive Outcomes's place as the world's most well-known active PMC. During the Second Gulf War, Blackwater incited an international outcry when its guards shot and killed 17 Iraqi civilians in Nisour Square, Baghdad. FBI reports indicated that Blackwater guards recklessly violated American rules for the use of lethal force; military investigators called the deaths unjustified and potentially criminal; and Iraqi officials characterized the events as murder.[166] As a result, the episode increased public scrutiny of the potential problems revolving around the use of PMCs.

Critics of PMCs argue that one of their most troubling features is that they operate beyond the reach of international scrutiny and responsible representative governments. They point out that traditional soldiers are more accountable than PMC employees, since soldiers who break military rules are subject to military justice. In contrast, PMC employees are free from the restraints of military rules and ethics. Although they can be fired, they are not immediately accountable to a larger military or governmental organization. As a result, critics conclude, "opportunistic behavior of PMC employees is more likely to occur than among soldiers."[167] Others maintain that the threat of losing lucrative employment is an effective way of ensuring a PMC employee's good behavior. In other words, if PMC employees are paid enough, they will be unlikely to risk their positions by engaging in improper conduct. However, many argue that we should not depend on market forces to ensure that PMC employees conduct themselves properly; instead, governments employing PMCs must enact legislation to ensure accountability. In the US, a December 2006 Government Accountability Office report found that the military did not have an effective means of overseeing PMCs and that "officials were unable to determine how many contractors were deployed to bases in Iraq."[168] Although a one-line amendment was included into the US Congress's 2007 defense-spending bill indicating that PMCs in war zones could be subject to the court martial system, doubts remained about the military's ability effectively to monitor the more than 100,000 private contractors working on its behalf.[169]

Researching to Learn   *Investigating Private Military Companies*

Sample Keyword Searches

Broad search:

- "Private Military Companies" OR "Private Military Firms"

Narrower searches:

- Blackwater OR "Executive Outcomes"
- Blackwater AND Iraq

Advanced searches:

- ("Private Military Companies" OR "Private Military Firms") AND (oversight OR regulation)
- (Blackwater OR "Executive Outcomes") AND "developing countries"
- "Executive Outcomes" AND (Angola OR "Sierra Leone")

Note:

- *Use quotation marks to search for terms as a phrase.*
- *Use AND to find documents with all terms listed.*
- *Use OR to find documents that contain at least one of the terms.*
- *Use parentheses to combine AND and OR statements in creative ways.*

Free Web Resources

"Blackwater Sheds Name, Shifts Focus." *Washington Post.* February 14, 2009.
   www.washingtonpost.com/wp-dyn/content/article/2009/02/13/AR2009021303149.html

"International Convention against the Recruitment, Use, Financing and Training of Mercenaries."

www2.ohchr.org/english/issues/mercenaries/docs/1989UNConvention_English.pdf

Isenberg, David. "Slippery Slope: Contractors' Impact on Military Culture." *United Press International.* January 23, 2009.
www.cato.org/pub_display.php?pub_id=9907

Lindemann, Marc. "Civilian Contractors under Military Law." *Parameters* (Autumn, 2007): 83–94.
www.carlisle.army.mil/usawc/Parameters/07autumn/lindeman.pdf

Singer, P. W. "Outsourcing War." *Foreign Affairs* (March/April 2005).
www.foreignaffairs.org/20050301faessay84211-p0/p-w-singer/outsourcing-war.html

United Nations. "The Working Group on the Use of Mercenaries as a Means of Violating Human Rights and Impeding the Exercise of the Right of Peoples to Self-Determination." Office of the United Nations High Commissioner for Human Rights.
www2.ohchr.org/english/issues/mercenaries/

United States House of Representatives. "Hearing on Private Security Contracting in Iraq and Afghanistan." October 2, 2007. United States House of Representatives Committee on Oversight and Government Reform.
http://oversight.house.gov/story.asp?ID=1509

Wallwork, Major Richard D. "Operational Implications of Private Military Companies in the Global War on Terror." British Army, School of Advanced Military Studies MMAS Monograph, 2005.
http://cgsc.cdmhost.com/cgi-bin/showfile.exe?CISOROOT=/p4013coll3&CISOPTR=383&filename=384.pdf

Books: Find Them @ Your Library

Avant, Deborah D. *The Market for Force: The Consequences of Privatizing Security.* New York: Cambridge University Press, 2005.

Chesterman, Simon and Chia Lehnardt, eds. *From Mercenaries to Market: The Rise and Regulation of Private Military Companies.* New York: Oxford University Press, 2007.

Lanning, Michael Lee. *Mercenaries: Soldiers of Fortune, from Ancient Greece to Today's Private Military Companies.* New York: Ballantine Books, 2005.

Mandel, Robert. *Armies without States: The Privatization of Security.* Boulder, CO: L. Rienner, 2002.

Musah, Abdel-Fatau and Kayode Fayemi. *Mercenaries: An African Security Dilemma.* Sterling, VA: Pluto Press, 2000.

Scahill, Jeremy. *Blackwater: The Rise of the World's Most Powerful Mercenary Army.* New York: Nation Books, 2008.

Singer, Peter Warren. *Corporate Warriors: The Rise of the Privatized Military Industry.* Ithaca, NY: Cornell University Press, 2003.

Articles: Find Them @ Your Library

Howe, Herbert M. "Private Security Forces and African Stability: The Case of Executive Outcomes." *Journal of Modern African Studies* 36.2 (June 1998): 307–61.

Leander, Anna. "The Market for Force and Public Security: The Destabilizing Consequences of Private Military Companies." *Journal of Peace Research* 42.5 (2005): 605–22.

Leander, Anna. "The Power to Construct International Security: On the Significance of Private Military Companies." *Millennium: Journal of International Studies* 33 (June 2005): 803–25.

Mandel, Robert. "The Privatization of Security." *Armed Forces & Society* 28 (Oct 2001): 129–51.

Renou, Xavier. "Private Military Companies Against Development." *Oxford Development Studies* 33.1 (Mar 2005): 107–15.

Walker, Clive and Dave Whyte. "Contracting Out War?: Private Military Companies, Law and Regulation in the United Kingdom." *International and Comparative Law Quarterly* 54 (2005): 651–89.

Zabci, Filiz. "Private Military Companies: 'Shadow Soldiers' of Neo-colonialism." *Capital & Class* 92 (Summer 2007): 1–10.

The Costs of War

War deaths

War, whether civil or international, just or unwarranted, always has severe costs. Among them are costs to peoples' lives, including death, disfigurement, and psychological damage; societal costs, including infrastructure and economic destruction; and environmental damage. Although it is not possible to quantify the full impact of war, attempts to calculate the effects of war often focus on the most immediate and horrific impacts: the number of deaths and casualties. But whose deaths get counted? Do we count only the number of combatants killed in battle, or should soldiers who died from war-related causes like disease and malnutrition be included as well? Should we also count civilian deaths, and, if so, should we count all those who were directly killed by combatants, accidentally killed in the crossfire, and indirectly killed by war-related health problems? Then there are the combatants and civilians who survived the conflict itself. Should we attempt to account for how many years have been trimmed from their natural lifespan as a consequence of disease, injury, and other harmful war-related conditions?

One study focusing on direct violent deaths from war from 1955 to 2002 found that 5.4 million people died from war injuries in the 13 countries studied. Figures ranged from 7,000 in the Democratic Republic of Congo to 3.8 million in Vietnam. On the basis of World Health Survey Programme data and passive reports, the study estimated that between 1985 and 1994, 378,000 people died annually from war injuries. These findings suggest that war has killed more people since the mid-twentieth century than previously estimated (see table 10.6). One of the limitations of this study, however, is that it only estimates direct violent deaths from war. Studies suggest that in some countries, direct war deaths represent only a small fraction of the total deaths caused by the war.

Table 10.6   Violent War Deaths from 1955 to 2002[170]

Countries	Deaths
Vietnam	3,812,000
Ethiopia	579,000
Bangladesh	269,000
Sri Lanka	215,000
Bosnia	176,000
Zimbabwe	141,000
Laos	62,000
Georgia	35,000
Burma	31,000
Philippines	30,000
Guatemala	20,000
Namibia	16,000
Republic of Congo	7,000
Total	5,393,000

In their study of deaths due to armed conflict, Bethany Lacina and Nils Petter Gleditsch distinguish between combatant deaths, battle deaths, and war deaths. Combatant deaths include the "number of battle-connected fatalities among military personnel."[171] The term "battle deaths" is used to describe "all people, soldiers and civilians, killed in combat" (excluding one-sided violence), whereas the term "war deaths" includes "all people killed in battle as well as all those whose deaths were the result of the changed social conditions caused by the war,"[172] such as displacement and disease. According to Lacina and Gleditsch's datasets, the five conflicts that generated the largest number of battle deaths from 1946 to 2002 were the Vietnam War (1955–75), the Korean War (1950–3), the Chinese Civil War (1946–9), the Iran–Iraq War (1980–8) and the Afghan Civil War (1978–2002) (see figure 10.2). By comparing estimates of battle deaths with total war deaths in nine major African conflicts since the end of World War II, Lacina and Gleditsch also revealed that battle deaths make up a small percentage of total deaths in many conflicts (see table 10.7 and figure 10.3). Although these figures should be viewed as estimates,

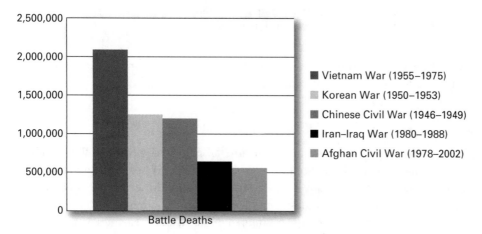

Figure 10.2 Conflicts with the Largest Battle Death Totals[173]

Table 10.7 Battle and Total War Deaths in Selected African Conflicts[174]

Country	Years	Total War Deaths Estimates	Battle Deaths	Percentage Battle Dead
Sudan	1963–73	250,000–750,000	20,000	3–8%
Nigeria	1967–70	500,000–2 million	75,000	4–15%
Angola	1975–2002	1.5 million	160,475	11%
Ethiopia (not including Eritrean insurgency)	1976–91	1–2 million	16,000	2%
Mozambique	1976–92	500,000–1 million	145,400	15–29%
Somalia	1981–1996	250,000–350,000	66,750	19–27%
Sudan	1983–2002	2 million	55,500	3%
Liberia	1989–96	150,000–200,000	23,500	12–16%
Democratic Republic of Congo	1998–2001	2.5 million	145,000	6%

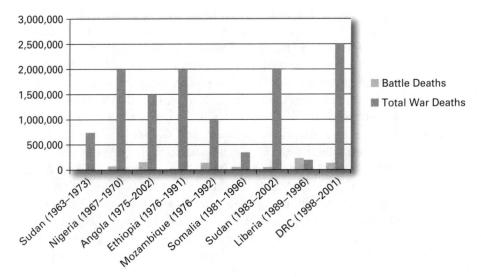

Figure 10.3 Battle and Total War Deaths in Selected African Conflicts[175]
Note: High total war deaths estimates used from table 10.7.

it is nevertheless startling to note that direct battle deaths only make up approximately 2 to 3 percent of the total war deaths in some conflicts.

Psychological casualties

In addition to physical casualties, war also takes a psychological toll, wounding soldiers and civilians alike. Soldiers engaged in combat operations are subject to many stressors that can negatively affect their mental health. Seeing destroyed homes, ravaged towns, and dead bodies; coming under attack; engaging in hand to hand combat; witnessing someone close get injured or killed; killing enemies or accidentally killing civilians; getting wounded oneself: all common combat stressors faced by active soldiers. Inactive soldiers face stressors as well, including anxiety around redeployment, length of deployment, and the loss of personal space and freedom.

post-traumatic stress disorder (PTSD) An anxiety disorder that can develop after exposure to one or more traumatic events that threatened or caused physical or psychological harm.

The US Army's Mental Health Advisory Team found correlations between exposure to these kinds of stressors and a variety of mental health problems. Specifically, depression, anxiety, and *post-traumatic stress disorder (PTSD)* were conditions associated with combat and deployment stressors.[176] Combat stress sometimes manifests itself in psychological breakdown during or shortly after battle. In other cases, symptoms like fatigue, sleep disturbances, headaches, memory problems, or concentration issues don't become evident until after soldiers have returned home.[177] Psychological distress can have real physical effects as well. One study estimated that the number of US Vietnam veterans dying prematurely after returning home was two times the number of those who were killed in the war.[178]

Lost childhoods

War can be particularly brutal on children physically, emotionally, and development-ally. During the 1990s, an estimated 1.5 million children were killed, 4 million were injured, and 12 million were displaced by warfare. Others were recruited into the military and trained to fight. Some estimate that children under the age of 15 are participants in conflicts in more than 30 countries, recruited by both opposition forces and governments. At the end of the twentieth century, there were an estimated 300,000 children engaged in combat.[179] The effects on children serving in combat operations can be devastating. Deformities, skin diseases, infections, malnutrition, drug addiction, and sexually transmitted diseases are among the physical costs,[180] but children are also negatively affected psychologically and morally. Instead of going to school and finding their place in their communities and the world, child soldiers are ripped from their homes and families and forced to fight alongside adults. Indoctrinated by brutal adults before their own values have fully formed, they can become thoughtless killers, carrying out horrific atrocities. Other children are turned into slave-like workers constantly threatened with instant death should they choose to rebel. Although these situations produce a variety of severe psychological problems, with rehabilitation and counseling, many child soldiers do recover and are able to return to normal life.[181]

Damage to physical and socioeconomic capital

While loss of life is the most horrific cost of war, armed conflicts also lead to the loss of "things," or physical capital, that communities rely upon to function. Infrastructure, in particular, is often targeted in war. Roads, bridges, railways, buildings, energy supplies, and communication systems are all frequently attacked in an effort to weaken the enemy. Schools, hospitals, and water supplies are also often damaged, and agricultural and industrial production can be hampered if not halted. Even after the war, fear of landmines can interfere with agriculture, leading to reduction of food output, increases in food prices, and, ultimately, people's inability to feed themselves. In some cases, landmines lead to the abandonment of rural areas altogether.[182]

In addition to the direct costs of wars, which include damage to infrastructure, crops, and trading networks, there are also indirect costs, which sometimes exceed the direct ones. Indirect costs include inflation, indebtedness, diversion of labor from production to the military, and declining investments.[183] The fear of continued violence frightens off investors and discourages redevelopment projects. The destruction of private and public infrastructure lowers the standard of living and increases unemployment. When people have trouble finding a way to earn a living, quality of life deteriorates and the general population sinks into poverty. In short, war weakens social, political, and economic institutions. This in turn leads to a series of problems, including:

Researching to Learn *Investigating Child Soldiers*

Sample Keyword Searches

Broad search:
- "child soldiers"

Narrower searches:
- "child soldiers" AND psychological aspects
- "child soldiers" AND "Sierra Leone"

Advanced searches:
- "child soldiers" AND ("Sierra Leone" OR "Democratic Republic of Congo") AND (reintegration OR rehabilitation)
- "child soldiers" AND ("psychological effects" OR "mental health" OR PTSD)

Note:
- *Use quotation marks to search for terms as a phrase.*
- *Use AND to find documents with all terms listed.*
- *Use OR to find documents that contain at least one of the terms.*
- *Use parentheses to combine AND and OR statements in creative ways.*

Free Web Resources

Coalition to Stop the Use of Child Soldiers
   www.child-soldiers.org/home
Coalition to Stop the Use of Child Soldiers. "Child Soldiers: Global Report 2008."
   www.childsoldiersglobalreport.org/files/country_pdfs/FINAL_2008_Global_Report.pdf
Human Rights Watch. "Children in Sudan: Slaves, Street Children and Child Soldiers." September 1, 1995. 1-56432-157-6. Online. UNHCR Refworld.
   www.unhcr.org/refworld/docid/3ae6a8264.html
Human Rights Watch. "Easy Prey: Child Soldiers in Liberia." September 1, 1994.
   www.hrw.org/en/node/78677
Human Rights Watch. "'My Gun Was as Tall as Me': Child Soldiers in Burma." October 2002.
   www.hrw.org/legacy/reports/2002/burma/
Red Hand Day: A Worldwide Initiative to Stop the Use of Child Soldiers
   www.redhandday.org/

United Nations. Office of the Special Representative of the Secretary-General for Children and Armed Conflict, United Nations
   www.un.org/children/conflict/english/index.html

Books: Find Them @ Your Library

Beah, Ishmael. *A Long Way Gone: Memoirs of a Boy Soldier.* New York: Frarrar, Straus, and Giroux, 2007.

Briggs, Jimmie. *Innocents Lost: When Child Soldiers Go to War.* New York: Basic Books, 2005.

Kuper, Jenny. *Military Training and Children in Armed Conflict: Law, Policy, and Practice.* New York: Nijhoff, 2005.

Rosen, David. *Armies of the Young: Child Soldiers in War and Terrorism.* New Brunswick, NJ: Rutgers University Press, 2005.

Singer, Peter Warren. *Children at War.* New York: Pantheon Books, 2005.

Wessells, Michael G. *Child Soldiers: From Violence to Protection.* Cambridge, MA: Harvard University Press, 2006.

Articles: Find Them @ Your Library

de Silva, Harendra, Chris Hobbs and Helga Hanks. "Conscription of Children in Armed Conflict – A Form of Child Abuse. A Study of 19 Former Child Soldiers." *Child Abuse Review* 10, 2 (Mar/Apr 2001): 125–34.

Francis, David J. "'Paper Protection' Mechanisms: Child Soldiers and the International Protection of Children in Africa's Conflict Zones." *Journal of Modern African Studies* 45, 2 (Jun 2007): 207–31.

Kimmel, Carrie and Jini L. Roby. "Institutionalized Child Abuse: The Use of Child Soldiers." *International Social Work* 50, 6 (Nov 2007): 74054.

Shepler, Susan. "The Rites of the Child: Global Discourses of Youth and Reintegrating Child Soldiers in Sierra Leone." *Journal of Human Rights* 4, 2 (Apr–Jun 2005): 197211.

Somasundaram, Daya. "Child soldiers: Understanding the Context." *BMJ: British Medical Journal* 324, 7348 (May 5, 2002): 1268–71.

- an inadequate supply of food and water;
- an increase in the number of people without work and shelter;
- a decrease in the availability of health care and other social services;
- disruptions in power and communication;
- increases in the number of vulnerable people requiring support and care, including refugees, displaced, people, widows, orphans, and the disabled.[184]

Damage to the environment

People have long recognized the negative impact that war can have on the environment as well as the devastating and prolonged effects wartime environmental damage can have on civilians. For example, the Bible commands:

> When thou shalt besiege a city a long time, in making war against it to take it, thou shalt not destroy the trees thereof by forcing an axe against them: for thou mayest eat of them, and thou shalt not cut them down (for the tree of the field *is* man's *life*) to employ *them* in the siege."[185]

Similarly the Qur'an prohibits Muslims from harming trees during Muslim holy wars, and the Buddhist and Hindu principle of *ahimsa* mandates respect for the environment in times of both peace and war.[186] There is a long tradition, then, of protecting the lives, health, and livelihoods of civilians through rules prohibiting the destruction of crops and vegetation as a wartime military tactic. However, it wasn't until the Vietnam War that an organized movement demanding environmental protection in times of war got underway. Specifically, the effects of *napalm* and *Agent Orange* on Vietnam's citizens and environment spurred protests and calls for change. Napalm, a gasoline jelly that ignites spontaneously when dropped from aircrafts, was routinely sprayed from US airplanes over vast areas of vegetation where enemy fighters were thought to be hiding. Agent Orange, a powerful herbicide and *defoliant* that has since been found to cause birth defects, cancer, and death was also used in Vietnam, causing human suffering as well as environmental contamination and loss of forest wildlife. Some estimates suggest that the US sprayed approximately 55 thousand tons of chemical defoliants over Vietnam. About 86 percent of the spraying missions were directed against forests and 14 percent against crops.[187]

ahimsa   A Sanskrit term meaning to do no harm, and an important tenet of the religions that originated in ancient India, including Hinduism, Buddhism, and Jainism.

napalm   A gasoline jelly that ignites spontaneously when dropped from aircrafts and that was routinely sprayed from US airplanes during the Vietnam War.

Agent Orange   Code name for a powerful herbicide and defoliant used by the US military in its herbicidal warfare program during the Vietnam War.

defoliant   Any chemical sprayed or dusted on plants to cause its leaves to fall off.

As a result of international outrage regarding the use of chemical defoliants in Vietnam, the UN General Assembly issued a resolution expanding the existing prohibition on chemical weapons to include those directed at plants and animals.[188] In 1977, two additional protocols to the 1949 Geneva Conventions were adopted and ultimately ratified or acceded to by 161 states; the US was not among them, however. Protocol I contains environmental protection provisions during armed conflict. Article 35(3) reads: "It is prohibited to employ methods or means for warfare which are intended, or may be expected, to cause widespread, long-term and severe damage to the natural environment."[189] Article 55 specifies:

1   Care shall be taken in warfare to protect the natural environment against widespread, long-term and severe damage. This protection includes a prohibition of the use of methods or means of warfare, which are intended or may be expected to cause such damage to the natural environment and thereby to prejudice the health or survival of the population.
2   Attacks against the natural environment by way of reprisal are prohibited.[190]

In 1991, the Iraqi invasion and occupation of Kuwait and the subsequent Gulf War brought renewed attention to wartime treatment of the environment. The international community was outraged by Iraq's concerted attempts to destroy Kuwait's environment and resources, blowing up more than 700 Kuwaiti oil wells, igniting more than 600 of them, and dumping an estimated 6–11 million barrels of oil directly into the Persian Gulf.[191] The purposeful discharge of oil into the Gulf devastated the marine environment and harmed migratory bird populations.[192] Many of the damaged oil wells that were not aflame leaked oil profusely, forming large pools that killed birds when they mistook them for water. In other places, the oil seeped into the fragile desert soil, destroying plant life and potentially contaminating aquifers.[193] However, the oil well fires were perhaps the most striking and horrific of the environmental assaults, causing intense atmospheric pollution that was predicted to increase rainfall and flooding in places as far away as China and India.[194] Experts estimated that the burning crude oil pumped 50,000 tons of sulfur dioxide (the primary chemical causing acid rain), 100,000 tons of carbon (in the form of soot), and 800,000 tons of carbon dioxide (one of the leading causes of global climate change) into the atmosphere.[195] A total of seven fire-fighting teams battled the blazes for 10–14 hours a day, every day, successfully extinguishing the fires in approximately eight months, much sooner than previous estimates of two to three years.[196] While much of the anticipated severe weather and flooding did not come to pass, clouds of toxic smoke did stretch from Romania to Pakistan, black snow fell in the Himalayas,[197] and black rain fell in Iran and Turkey.[198] The severity and scope of the environmental devastation vividly illustrated that environmental damage often cannot be confined to one locale. Because each part of the environment is interconnected with other parts, linked, for example, by the global climatic system, those who would protect the global environment must protect local environments as well, including environments plagued by wars.[199] Reflecting the growing consensus that wanton environmental destruction cannot be tolerated as a war tactic, the UN Security Council declared Iraq liable for all damages arising from its illegal occupation of Kuwait, including environmental damages and destruction of natural resources.[200]

Environmental concerns were raised once again in the context of the 1999 Kosovo conflict, in which Serbian forces poisoned wells and destroyed the landscape in order to incite Kosovar Albanians to leave their homes. NATO's subsequent bombing campaign, which was designed to bring an immediate halt to violence and repression, also caused environmental damage. However, the conflict also marked one of the world's largest efforts to assess and report upon wartime environmental destruction. NGOs and concerned citizens monitored environmental effects within both Yugoslavia and neighboring countries, providing up-to-the-minute reports online and in the media. When the conflict ended, the UN Environment Program developed a taskforce to assess damage, just as it had during the Gulf War.[201]

Reports focusing on the environmental damage caused by NATO's bombing campaign indicate that NATO deliberately attacked environmentally sensitive targets that posed pollution threats to the Danube River, the Black Sea, and the Balkan region in general, bombing, for example, oil refineries, petrochemical plants, chemical and fertilizer factories, and pharmaceutical plants.[202] Despite the damage caused, there was little international support for holding NATO countries legally responsible. This was also true, but to an even greater extent, of the 1990–1 Gulf War, where the US and its allies destroyed factories and refineries, littered the country with more than one million unexploded bomblets, and left an estimated 320 tons of depleted uranium lying about in the desert.[203] Some argue that these examples illustrate that international environmental law during wartime is inadequate, failing both to prohibit environmentally damaging tactics and to impose legal accountability when tactics are deemed violations of international law.[204]

Military spending

Finally, maintaining a military and engaging in war both cost enormous sums of money. For example, as seen in table 10.8, NATO countries spent $862,863 million on defense in 2007. The US alone spent 65 percent of that figure (see figure 10.4). Additionally, the US spent a higher percentage of its GDP, 4 percent, on the military than did other NATO countries. Globally, military spending in 2007 reached an estimated $1,339 billion, which amounted to a 6 percent increase over 2006 and a 45 percent increase over 1998. Or, put another way, the world spent 2.5 percent of its total domestic product on defense. US military spending amounted to 45 percent of the 2007 global total, followed by the UK, China, France, and Japan, each of which accounted for 4–5 percent. US military expenditures increased a dramatic 59 percent after 2001, climbing higher than at any time since World War II, due to its operations in both Afghanistan and Iraq. Many other countries increased their military spending in 2007 as well. Some of the factors that drive increases in world military spending are foreign policy objectives, real or perceived threats, war and violent conflict, contributions to peacekeeping operations, and the availability of economic resources.[205]

Table 10.8   Defense Expenditures of NATO Countries, 2007[206]

Country	US Dollars (millions)	% of GDP
United States	556,961	4.0
United Kingdom	68,903	2.5
France	61,784	2.4
Germany	42,552	1.3
Italy	28,648	1.4
Canada	17,926	1.3
Spain	16,724	1.2
Turkey	11,810	1.8
Netherlands	11,480	1.5
Greece	8,208	2.6
Poland	7,833	1.8
Norway	5,875	1.5
Belgium	5,164	1.1
Denmark	4,175	1.3
Portugal	3,309	1.5
Romania	2,608	1.5
Czech Republic	2,527	1.4
Hungary	1,776	1.3
Bulgaria	1,198	3.0
Slovak Republic	1,139	1.5
Slovenia	693	1.5
Lithuania	453	1.2
Latvia	443	1.6
Estonia	387	1.9
Luxembourg	286	.6
NATO Total	*862,863*	*2.7*

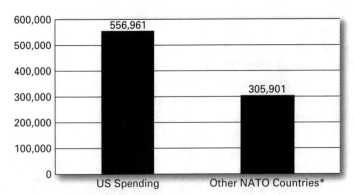

Figure 10.4   Defense Expenditures of NATO Countries, 2007[207]
* Other NATO countries included: United Kingdom, France, Germany, Italy, Canada, Spain, Turkey, Netherlands, Greece, Poland, Norway, Belgium, Denmark, Portugal Romania, Czech Republic, Romania, Bulgaria, Slovak Republic, Slovenia, Lithuania, Latvia, Estonia, Luxembourg.

Military expenditures not only cost societies enormous amounts of money, they also have a variety of social costs. Investments in the military divert money away from economic and social projects and programs, such as education, health care, and infrastructure development. They also divert people with professional skills, such as scientists and engineers, away from jobs that would enhance the civilian economy. In developing countries, the tension between spending money on the military and spending it on social and economic services is often exacerbated. On the one hand, military spending can improve security, which is a necessary condition for development. On the other, however, developing countries do not have a great deal of money to begin with, so they often have to commit huge proportions of their small national budgets to military expenditures. In some developing countries, governments spend more on the military than on health, communications, infrastructure, and other social development projects. For example, in 2003, Oman, Syria, Burma, Sudan, Pakistan, Eritrea, and Burundi all spent more on the military than on health and education combined. In sub-Saharan Africa, the number of people living in poverty is anticipated to grow from 316 million in 1999 to 404 million by 2015. HIV/AIDS is the leading cause of death in this region, though other health problems, including malaria and tuberculosis also threaten the population. Clearly, these are serious problems that will take a tremendous amount of resources to address. And yet between 1995 and 2001, this region saw a 47 percent increase in military expenditures. Although poverty is caused by a variety of complex factors, government spending on the military simply means that there is less money out of an already inadequate supply for health, education, development, and other poverty reduction projects.[208]

Conclusion

Definitions of war vary, ranging from state-centered definitions that view war as a violent conflict between states to broader definitions that include the actions of non-state actors, such as rebel groups and terrorists. The work of anthropologists, pre-historians, historians, and evolutionary biologists all suggest that war and violent conflict have been constants in most human societies, dating back to our earliest human ancestors. Answers to the question "What causes war?" are multiple and varied, influenced heavily by the academic and theoretical framework used to approach the question. While competition over resources may be at the root of many, if not most, conflicts, it is also important to recognize that different types of wars (e.g., civil wars as opposed to international wars) are often caused by different factors. To understand why such wars begin and how they might be prevented, these types of differences must be examined. When war cannot be prevented, international law delineates proper conduct during war. However, even when wars are considered just – undertaken, for example, in self-defense – they nevertheless exact a variety of costs, including human and environmental casualties, damage to infrastructure and economies, and the diversion of enormous sums of money from social and economic development programs to the military.

Notes

1   Fred R. Shapiro, *The Yale Book of Quotations* (New Haven, CT: Yale University Press, 2006), 421.

2   Sigmund Freud, *Civilization and Its Discontents* (New York: Norton, 2005), 118.

3   Woodrow Wilson, "Request for Declaration of War on Germany, Washington, DC, April 2, 1917," *My Fellow Americans: The Most Important Speeches of America's Presidents, From George Washington to George W. Bush* (Naperville, IL: Sourcebooks MediaFusion, 2003), 86.

4   Mahatma Gandhi, *Non-Violence in Peace and War* (Ahmedabad, India: Navajivan Publishing House, 1942), 357.

5   Carl Philipp G. von Clausewitz, *On War*, trans. James John Graham (London: N. Trubner & Co., 1873), 12. This line is frequently misquoted as a "continuation of politics" rather than policy. See Ralph Keyes, *The Quote Verifier: Who Said What, Where, and When* (New York: St Martin's Press, 2006), 241.

6   Clausewitz, *On War*, 12.

7   Alexander Moseley, "The Philosophy of War," *The Internet Encyclopedia of Philosophy*, www.iep.utm.edu/w/war.htm.

8   Jean-Jacques Rousseau, *The Social Contract* (1762; repr., New York: Cosimo Classics, 2008), 19.

9   Ibid., 20.

10 Ibid.

11 "War, n.1" *The Oxford English Dictionary Online*, http://dictionary.oed.com/cgi/entry/00181778.

12 Moseley, "The Philosophy of War."

13 John Keegan, *A History of Warfare* (New York: Vintage, 1994), 3.

14 Ibid., 5.

15 Brian Orend, "War," in Edward N. Zalta (ed.), *Stanford Encyclopedia of Philosophy* (Fall 2008 edn.), http://plato.stanford.edu/archives/fall2008/entries/war/.

16 Ibid.

17 Moseley, "The Philosophy of War."

18 Human Security Report Project, "Part 1: When States Go to War," in *miniAtlas of Human Security* (Myriad Editions Limited), 10, www.miniatlasofhumansecurity.info/en/access.html.

19 Human Security Report Project, "Part I: The Changing Face of Global Violence," in *The Human Security Report 2005: War and Peace in the 21st Century* (New York: Oxford University Press, 2005), 23, www.humansecurityreport.info/HSR2005_PDF/Part1.pdf.

20 Source: Human Security Report Project, "Part I: The Changing Face of Global Violence," in *The Human Security Report 2005: War and Peace in the 21st Century* (New York: Oxford University Press, 2005), 26, http://www.humansecurityreport.info/HSR2005_PDF/Part1.pdf.

21 Human Security Report Project, "Part 1: When States Go to War," 10.

22 Ann Hironaka, *Neverending Wars* (Cambridge, MA: Harvard University Press, 2005), 1.

23 Ibid.

24 Klaus Jurgen Gantzel and Torsten Schwinghammer, *Warfare Since the Second World War*, trans. Jonathan P. G. Bach (New Brunswick, NJ: Transaction Publishers, 2000), 20.

25 Human Security Report Project, "Part 1: When States Go to War," 10.

26 Human Security Report Project, "Part I: The Changing Face of Global Violence," 23.

27 Hironaka, *Neverending Wars*, 6–7.

28 Human Security Report Project, "Part 1: When States Go to War," 9.

29 Hironaka, *Neverending Wars*, 145.

30 Human Security Report Project, "Part 2: Warlords and Killing Fields," in *miniAtlas of Human Security* (Myriad Editions Limited), 19, www.miniatlasofhumansecurity.info/en/files/miniAtlas_part2.pdf.

31 Ibid., 23.

32 Ibid., 19.

33 Kristine Eck, Margareta Sollenberg, and Peter Wallensteen, "One-Sided Violence and Non-State Conflict," in Lotta Harbom (ed.), *States in Armed Conflict 2003* (Uppsala, Sweden: Universitetstryckeriet, 2004), 136.

34 Kristine Eck and Lisa Hultman, "One-Sided Violence Against Civilians in War: Insights from New Fatality Data," *Journal of Peace Research* 44, no. 2 (2007), 235.

35 "Convention on the Prevention and Punishment of the Crime of Genocide," New York (December 9, 1948); Entry Into Force (January 12, 1951), www.un.org/millennium/law/iv-1.htm.

36 Human Security Report Project, "Part 2: Warlords and Killing Fields," 20.

37 Human Security Centre, "Part 1: The Changing Face of Global Violence," 41.

38 Barbara Harff, "Genocide," Commissioned by the Human Security Centre (July 17, 2003), 3, www.humansecurityreport.info/background/Harff_Genocide.pdf.

39 Harvey W. Kushner, "Introduction," in Encyclopedia of Terrorism (Thousand Oaks, CA: Sage Publications, 2003), xxiii.

40 Ibid., 345.

41 Ibid., xxiii.

42 John Mueller, "The Threat of Terrorism is Exaggerated," Terrorism: Opposing Viewpoints (New York: Greenhaven Press, 2009), 32.

43 Human Security Centre, "Part 1: The Changing Face of Global Violence," 40.

44 "Overview: War and Peace in the 21st Century," Human Security Report 2005 (New York: Oxford University Press, 2005), 6, www.humansecurityreport.info/HSR2005_HTML/Overview/.

45 Human Security Report Project, "Part 2: Warlords and Killing Fields," 24.

46 Eck and Hultman, "One-Sided Violence Against Civilians in War," 238.

47 Ibid.

48 Source: Kristine Eck and Lisa Hultman, "One-Sided Violence Against Civilians in War: Insights from New Fatality Data," Journal of Peace Research 44, no. 2 (2007), 239.

49 Ibid., 2.

50 Ibid., 6–7.

51 Peter N. Stearns et al., The Encyclopedia of World History, 6th edn. (Boston, MA: Houghton Mifflin Company, 2001), 1.

52 Azar Gat, War in Human Civilization (New York: Oxford University Press, 2006), 137.

53 Michael S. Neiberg, Warfare in World History (New York: Routledge, 2001), 7.

54 Gat, War in Human Civilization, 117.

55 Ibid., 167.

56 Ibid.

57 Ibid., 172.

58 Ibid., 184.

59 Ibid., 185–6.

60 Ibid., 187.

61 Neiberg, Warfare in World History, 7.

62 Encyclopedia of World History, 21.

63 R. Ernest Dupuy and Trevor N. Dupuy, The Harper Encyclopedia of Military History (New York: Harper Collins, 1993), 8.

64 Ibid., 4–5.

65 Ibid., 1.

66 Ibid., 3.

67 Ibid.

68 Ibid.

69 Ibid., 4.

70 George Derr, "Mycenae," in Marsha E. Ackermann et al. (eds.), Encyclopedia of World History: The Ancient World, Prehistoric Eras to 600 CE (New York: Facts on File, 2008), 289–90.

71 Marc Schwarz, "Greek City-States," in Ackermann et al. (eds.), Encyclopedia of World History, 167.

72 Stearns, The Encyclopedia of World History, 60.

73 Ben Kiernan, Blood and Soil (New Haven, CT: Yale University Press, 2007), 47.

74 Ibid., 45, 47.

75 Schwarz, "Greek City-States," 167.

76 Robin Osborne, Greek History (New York: Routledge, 2004), 82.

77 Marsha E. Ackermann et al., Encyclopedia of World History: The Expanding World, 600 CE–1450 (New York: Facts on File, 2008), xxviii–xxxix.

78 Ibid., xl.

79 Ibid., xxxv.

80 Ibid., xxxv–xxxvii.

81 Erwin Fahlbusch et al., The Encyclopedia of Christianity (Grand Rapids, MI: Eerdmans, 1999), 609.

82 Alan Stephens and Nicola Baker, Making Sense of War (Cambridge: Cambridge University Press, 2006), 135.

83 Ackermann, Encyclopedia of World History, xxxvi.

84 Ibid., xxxvii–xxxviii.

85 Charles Hauss, International Conflict Resolution (New York: Continuum 2001), 4.

86 Ibid., 1309.

87 Source: R. Ernest Dupuy and Trevor N. Dupuy, The Harper Encyclopedia of Military History (New York: Harper Collins, 1993), 1083.

88   Source: R. Ernest Dupuy and Trevor N. Dupuy, *The Harper Encyclopedia of Military History* (New York: Harper Collins, 1993), 1309.

89   Ackermann, *Encyclopedia of World History*, xlii.

90   Klaus Larres and Ann Lane, *The Cold War: The Essential Readings* (Oxford: Blackwell Publishers, 2001), 66.

91   Richard C. S. Trahair, *Encyclopedia of Cold War Espionage, Spies, and Secret Operations* (Westport, CO: Greenwood Press, 2004), 408.

92   Paul E. Fontenoy, *Submarines: An Illustrated History of Their Impact* (Santa Barbara, CA: ABC-CLIO, 2007), 41.

93   Thomas Graham, *Disarmament Sketches: Three Decades of Arms Control and International Law* (Seattle, WA: University of Washington Press, 2002), 36.

94   Ackermann, *Encyclopedia of World History*, xlii.

95   Robert S. Norris and Hans M. Kristensen, "Global Nuclear Stockpiles, 1945–2006," *Bulletin of the Atomic Scientists* (July/August 2006), 66.

96   Ibid., 64.

97   US Department of State, "Nuclear Non-Proliferation Treaty (NPT), Accomplishments and Challenges" (October 19, 2001), www.state.gov/t/isn/rls/fs/2001/5485.htm.

98   Gat, *War in Human Civilization*, 660.

99   Ackermann, *Encyclopedia of World History*, xli–xlii.

100 Ibid., xlii.

101 Human Security Report Project, "Part 1: When States Go to War," 9.

102 Gat, *War in Human Civilization*, 5.

103 Ibid., 12.

104 Ibid., 11.

105 Ibid., 13.

106 Lawrence Keeley, *War Before Civilization: The Myth of the Peaceful Savage* (New York: Oxford University Press, 2001), 28.

107 Gat, *War in Human Civilization*, 41.

108 Thomas Hobbes, *Leviathan* (Indianapolis, IN: Hackett Publishing Company, 1994), 76.

109 Gat, *War in Human Civilization*, 40.

110 Ibid., 40.

111 Ibid., 56.

112 Ibid., 137.

113 Ibid., 56–76.

114 Ibid., 137.

115 Ibid., 87–113.

116 Ibid., 668.

117 Ibid., 668–9.

118 Stephen Van Evera, *Causes of War* (Ithaca, NY: Cornell University Press, 1999), 4.

119 Ibid.,14.

120 Ibid., 4.

121 Ibid., 39.

122 Ibid., 4.

123 Ibid., 73.

124 Ibid., 105.

125 Ibid., 4.

126 Ibid., 110.

127 Ibid., 4.

128 Paul Collier, et al., *Breaking the Conflict Trap: Civil War and Development Policy* (Washington, DC: World Bank and Oxford University Press, 2003), 53.

129 Ibid., 60.

130 Ibid., 63.

131 Ibid., 64–5.

132 Frederick H. Russell, *The Just War in the Middle Ages* (New York: Cambridge University Press, 1977).

133 David Rodin, *War and Self-defense* (Oxford: Clarendon Press, 2002), 2.

134 Daniel S. Zupan, *War, Morality, and Autonomy* (Burlington, VT: Ashgate, 2004), 1.

135 Orend, "War."

136 Ibid.

137 David P. Barash and Charles P. Webel, *Peace and Conflict Studies* (Thousand Oaks, CA: Sage, 2002), 416–17.

138 Ingrid Detter, *The Law of War* (Cambridge: Cambridge University Press, 2005), 157.

139 Ibid., 156.

140 Orend, "War."

141 Ibid.

142 Richard A. Falk, *The Costs of War: International Law, the UN, and World Order After Iraq* (New York: Routledge, 2008), 27.

143 William R. Slomanson, *Fundamental Perspectives on International Law*, 3rd edn. (Belmont, CA: Wadsworth/Thomson Learning, 2000), 458–9.

144 Arthur Eyffinger, "A Highly Critical Moment: Role and Record of the 1907 Hague Peace Conference," *Netherlands International Law Review* 54 (August 2007), 224–6.

145 United Nations Charter, "UN Charter Index," www.un.org/aboutun/charter/.

146 Edmund Jan Ozmanczyk, "Landmines Convention," in *Encyclopedia of the United Nations and International Agreements* (New York: Routledge, 2003), 1253.

147 Detter, *The Law of War*, 227.

148 "What's the Problem?" International Campaign to Ban Landmines, www.icbl.org/problem/what.

149 See the International Campaign to Ban Landmines (ICBL), www.icbll.org.

150 Detter, *The Law of War*, 228.

151 Susan Willett, *Costs of Disarmament* (Geneva, Switzerland: UNIDIR, 2002), 12.

152 "What's the Problem?" International Campaign to Ban Landmines.

153 Slomanson, *Fundamental Perspectives on International Law*, 482.

154 Vicky Randall, *Politics in the Developing World* (New York: Oxford University Press, 2008), 384.

155 Michael Renner, *Small Arms, Big Impact: The Next Challenge of Disarmament*, Worldwatch Paper 137 (Darby, PA: Diane Publishing, 1997), 8.

156 Randall, *Politics in the Developing World*, 384.

157 Jackie Dent, "Britain Welcomes UN Arms Control Vote," *Guardian* (October 17, 2006), www.guardian.co.uk/world/2006/oct/27/armstrade.politics.

158 Anna Richardson, "Angola's Oil Boom Fuels Civil War," *Independent* (February 27, 2000), http://findarticles.com/p/articles/mi_qn4158/is_20000227/ai_n14292892.

159 "Background," Kimberly Process, http://www.kimberleyprocess.com/background/index_en.html

160 For example, from the Middle Ages to the mid-16th century, Italian city-states employed military contractors called condottieri to protect them. See Jurgen Brauer and Hurbert van Tuyll, "The Renaissance, 1300–1600, The Case of the Condottieri and the Military Labor Market," in Jurgen Brauer and Hubert van Tuyll (eds.), *Castles, Battles, and Bombs* (Chicago, IL: University of Chicago Press, 2008), 80–118.

161 Peter Warren Singer, *Corporate Warriors* (Ithaca, NY: Cornell University Press, 2003), 9.

162 Ibid., 9.

163 Ibid., 112.

164 Ibid., 115.

165 Ibid., 117–18.

166 Ginger Thompson and James Risen, "5 Guards Face US Charges in Iraq Deaths," *New York Times* (December 5, 2008), www.nytimes.com/2008/12/06/washington/06blackwater.html?_r=1.

167 Brauer and Tuyll, "The Renaissance, 1300–1600," 316.

168 Jeremy Scahill, *Blackwater* (New York: Nation Books, 2008), 58.

169 Ibid., 57–8.

170 Source: Ziad Obermeyer, Christopher J. L. Murray, and Emmanuela Gakidou, "Fifty Years of Violent War Deaths from Vietnam to Bosnia: Analysis of Data from the World Health Survey Programme," *BMJ* 336, no. 7659 (June 28, 2008), 1482–6.

171 Meredith Reid Sarkees, "The Correlates of War Data on War: An Update to 1997," *Conflict Management and Peace Science* 18, no. 1 (2000), 128.

172 Bethany Lacina and Nils Petter Gleditsch, "Monitoring Trends in Global Combat: A New Dataset of Battle Deaths," *European Journal of Population* 21 (2005), 148.

173 Source: Bethany Lacina and Nils Petter Gleditsch, "Monitoring Trends in Global Combat: A New Dataset of Battle Deaths," *European Journal of Population* 21 (2005), 154.

174 Source: Bethany Lacina and Nils Petter Gleditsch, "Monitoring Trends in Global Combat: A New Dataset of Battle Deaths," *European Journal of Population* 21 (2005), 159.

175 Source: Bethany Lacina and Nils Petter Gleditsch, "Monitoring Trends in Global Combat: A New Dataset of Battle Deaths," *European Journal of Population* 21 (2005), 159.

176 Thomas W. Britt, Amy B. Adler, and Carl Andrew Castro, *Military Life: The Psychology of Serving in Peace and Combat* (Westport, CO: Praeger Security International, 2006), 17.

177 Ibid., 18.

178 Theodore Nadelson, *Trained to Kill: Soldiers at War* (Baltimore, MD: Johns Hopkins University Press, 2005), 90.

179 James Alan Marten, *Children and War: A Historical Anthology* (New York: New York University Press, 2002), 2.

180   Ibid., 3.
181   Marten, *Children and War: A Historical Antho-logy*, 4.
182   Eugenia Date-Bah, *Jobs After War: A Critical Challenge In The Peace And Reconstruction Puzzle* (Geneva, Switzerland: In Focus Programme on Crisis Response and Reconstruction, International Labour Office, 2003), 9–11.
183   Ibid., 10.
184   Ibid., 11.
185   Deuteronomy 20:19, *Holy Bible*, King James Version (New York: World Publishing, 1989), 139.
186   Carl E. Bruch, "Introduction," in Jay Austin and Carl Bruch (eds.), *The Environmental Consequences of War: Legal, Economic, and Scientific Perspectives* (New York: Cambridge University Press, 2000), 14.
187   Karen Hulme, *War Torn Environment: Interpreting The Legal Threshold* (Boston, MA: Martinus Nijhoff Publishers, 2004), 5.
188   Ibid., 5–6.
189   Ibid., 10.
190   Ibid., 11.
191   Bruch, "Introduction," 2.
192   Ibid., 2–3.
193   Hulme, *War Torn Environment*, 165.
194   Ibid., 13.
195   Ibid., 165.
196   Samira A. S. Omar, Ernest Briskey, Raafat Misak, and Adel A. S. O. Asem, "The Gulf War Impact on the Terrestrial Environment of Kuwait: An Overview," in Austin and Bruch (eds.), *The Environmental Consequences of War*, 333.
197   Steven A. Yetiv, *The Persian Gulf Crisis* (Westport, CO: Greenwood Press, 1997), 119.
198   Bruch, "Introduction," 2.
199   Hulme, *War Torn Environment*, 13.
200   Bruch, "Introduction," 3.
201   Ibid., 4.
202   Richard Falk, "The Inadequacy of the Existing Legal Approach to Environmental Protection in Wartime," in Austin and Bruch (eds.), *The Environmental Consequences of War*, 149.
203   Austin and Bruch, *The Environmental Consequences of War*, 655.
204   Falk, "The Inadequacy of the Existing Legal Approach to Environmental Protection in Wartime," 150.
205   Petter Stalenheim, Catalina Perdomo, and Elisabeth Skons, "Summary: Chapter 5. Military Expenditure," in *SIPRI Yearbook 2008: Armaments, Disarmament and International Security*, http://yearbook2008.sipri.org/05.
206   Source: "Financial and Economic Data Relating to NATO Defence: Defence Expenditure of NATO Countries (1985–2008)," North Atlantic Treaty Organization, www.nato.int/docu/pr/2009/p09-009.pdf.
207   Source: Adapted from "Financial and Economic Data Relating to NATO Defence: Defence Expenditure of NATO Countries (1985–2008)," North Atlantic Treaty Organization, www.nato.int/docu/pr/2009/p09-009.pdf.
208   Jane Chanaa, *Guns or Growth? Assessing the Impact of Arms Sales on Sustainable Development* (Oxford: Oxfam, 2004), 8–14.

11

PEACE

"*You cannot simultaneously prevent and prepare for war. The very prevention of war requires more faith, courage and resolution than are needed to prepare for war. We must all do our share, that we may be equal to the task of peace.*" (Albert Einstein, in *Einstein on Peace*)[1]

"*'Deterrence' means simply this: making sure any adversary who thinks about attacking the United States, or our allies, or our vital interests, concludes that the risks to him outweigh any potential gains. Once he understands that, he won't attack. We maintain the peace through our strength; weakness only invites aggression.*" (US President Ronald Reagan. Address to the Nation, March 23, 1983)[2]

"*The arms race can kill, though the weapons themselves may never be used . . . by their cost alone, armaments kill the poor by causing them to starve.*" (Vatican statement to the UN, 1976)[3]

"*Man is the only animal that deals in that atrocity of atrocities, War. He is the only one that gathers his brethren about him and goes forth in cold blood and calm pulse to exterminate his kind. He is the only animal that for sordid wages will march out . . . and help to slaughter strangers of his own species who have done him no harm and with whom he has no quarrel, . . . And in the intervals between campaigns he washes the blood off his hands and works for 'the universal brotherhood of man.'*" (Mark Twain, *What is Man?*)[4]

Learning to Question, Questioning to Learn

- What is the relationship between war and peace?
- Is peace more than simply the absence of war? If so, then how do we define it?
- What forms of violence beyond armed conflict pose the biggest threats to peace in the global context?
- What conditions foster peace?
- Can preparing for war ensure peace?
- Might nonviolent resistance be a successful strategy for overcoming violent injustice?
- What kinds of organizations promote and enforce peace, and historically, how successful have they been?

Introduction

Although peace is often defined as the absence of war, peace need not always be understood in relation to armed conflict, since war is not the only form of violence that disrupts peace. Slavery, starvation, and rape, for example, are all incompatible with peace. This chapter begins with a discussion of various definitions of peace, followed by an overview of the history of peace movements and their objectives and strategies. The final sections focus on peaceful conflict resolution and organizations that work to eradicate violent social conditions that are antithetical to peace.

What Constitutes Peace? Defining Our Terms

The term "peace" is most commonly understood in relation to war. As war's opposite, peace is the absence or cessation of fighting between nations. This definition, however, is more accurately captured by the term *negative peace*. Negative peace refers to the absence of armed conflict and military operations between nations, but it does not mean that various forms of violence within a given nation are also absent. For example, a nation that is not at war with another nation may nevertheless support discriminatory institutions that deny certain individuals access to things like education, employment, or health care. By supporting and perpetuating unjust institutions and practices, such states cause their citizens psychological, social, and economic harm, regardless of whether or not they are at war with another nation. In other words, unjust social arrangements constitute non-conflict forms of violence, or *structural violence*. Structural violence includes social conditions that trap people in poverty, disease, discrimination, degradation, enslavement, and abuse. Although structural violence does not involve active, organized military violence, the suffering of those afflicted by exploitation and abuse is no less acute than that of those who are the victims of the direct violence of war. For example, slavery is a particularly insidious form of structural violence. An enslaved person may live in a nation that is not at war, but both the enslavers and the enslaved are certainly not at peace.

negative peace The absence of direct violence or armed conflict.

structural violence Unjust economic, social, and political conditions and institutions that harm people by preventing them from meeting their basic needs.

The struggle to eradicate structural violence is sometimes referred to as the quest for *positive peace*. In contrast with negative peace, positive peace focuses on global justice and human rights for all people.[5] Instead of an absence, positive peace can be defined as the presence of "life affirming and life-enhancing values," such as "cooperation, harmony, friendship, and love."[6] Advocates for positive peace argue that lack of adequate resources to meet basic human needs is a particularly insidious form of violence. They point out, for example, that in countries where there is not enough food, or where there is inadequate access to clean water or to medical care, people endure particularly

positive peace The presence of social justice, including equal opportunity, access to the basic necessities of life, and the eradication of structural violence.

brutal forms of violence, such as starvation and watching loved ones die of treatable diseases.

The *Holocaust* in Europe during World War II can serve as an example of one way in which structural violence can operate. In several concentration camps, more people died of "natural causes" than in gas chambers or ovens. The victims in these camps

> **Holocaust** The genocide of minority groups, particularly Jews, in Europe by Nazis and their collaborators.

were starved, overworked, denied medical care, experimented upon, and generally kept in conditions designed to bring about misery. Because of these conditions, peoples' immune systems failed and their bodies shut down. Though these victims did not perish from a gunshot or in a gas chamber, the violence inflicted upon them was no less severe. While the Nazi regime can be clearly identified as the source of the structural violence suffered by the victims in these camps, the causes of structural violence in societies today are often difficult to discern. When considering the forms of structural violence that disrupt peace within a country, it is useful to consider questions such as "How does a country's economic system contribute to the violence its citizens endure?" "How might the personal decisions and everyday behaviors of individual citizens contribute to the structural violence endured by others?" Looking at the history of the modern peace movement can provide some context for addressing these kinds of questions.

Origins of the Modern Peace Movement

Peace movements have both secular and religious foundations. For example, the first Olympic Games were designed as a month-long period of peace when competition took the form of athletics rather then warfare. The early Christian Church set itself in opposition to serving in the Roman legions, and other religions incorporate elements of peaceful existence within their belief systems. The secular peace movement, however, is a relatively new phenomenon, emerging as recently as two centuries ago.[7] One of the religious groups that has been at the forefront of the peace movement has been the Quakers. Because the Quakers have been forceful in advocating an end to armed conflict as well as calling for the promotion of positive peace, their activities have often overlapped with those of secular peace groups.

The 1800s

The Quakers
A variety of secular and religious-based peace movements existed in the 1800s. Foremost among the religious groups advocating for peace were the Religious Society of Friends, commonly known as the Quakers, for whom opposition to violence was a central religious tenet. The Friends began in England in the seventeenth century and one of their most well-known statements of belief became the *Peace Testimony*, which expresses their commitment

> **Peace Testimony** Once a pledge taken by Quakers to refuse to take part in wars or to serve in combat positions; now also an obligation to protest against wars.

to refrain from participation in war. Their early passive resistance to war (refusing to fight) broadened over the years, as many actively engaged in protests against specific wars and the governments sponsoring them.

In the 1800s, the Quaker commitment to peace was also evident in their struggles against structural violence. In the United States, Quakers influenced and participated in the *abolition* and *suffrage* movements, both of which were struggles against forms of structural violence that enslaved many and denied both women and slaves the right to vote. Many non-Quakers in these movements were influenced by their Quaker counterparts' commitment to nonviolence, using peaceful protests and petitions to achieve their movement's goals. For example, Elizabeth Cady Stanton (1815–1902), an American social activist and leading figure in the early women's rights movement, was a great friend and admirer of the Quaker abolitionist, social reformer, women's rights advocate, and fellow American Lucretia Coffin Mott (1793–1880), whom Stanton first heard speak in 1840 at the International Anti-Slavery Convention in London. Mott was among that segment of the Quaker population, the Hicksite Quakers (followers of Elias Hicks), who recognized early the web of interconnectedness that joins us all and the concomitant responsibilities that such a web entails. For example, their belief that slavery was evil and should be opposed led to their refusal to use cotton cloth, cane sugar, and other goods that were produced through slave labor. The older Mott mentored Stanton, and the two went on to work together, including organizing the 1848 *Women's Rights Convention in Seneca Falls*, New York.

abolition   The eradication of slavery.

suffrage/suffragette   The struggle for voting rights for women; a person engaged in the struggle for women's civil right to vote.

Women's Rights Convention in Seneca Falls   The 1848 convention held to discuss the social, civil, and religious condition and rights of woman.

Secular peace movements

Secular peace movements that began to attract wider participation emerged in Europe and the US around the same time. Working together, US and European peace activists held a series of conferences in Europe between 1840 and 1850. The Quaker-driven Peace Society, which sought to make war extinct, joined forces with other pacifists to hold conferences in London in 1842 and again in 1843. The short-lived Peace of Nations Society (founded 1847) working with the Peace Society held conferences in Brussels (1848), Paris (1848), Frankfurt (1850), and London (1851).[8] The goal of these meetings was to encourage nations to seek peaceful ways of resolving their disputes. While these meetings were largely dismissed by European powers, they may have helped motivate several European nations to draft the *Paris Declaration of 1856*, which was a "collection of principles on the methods for employing and conserving the use of force in armed conflicts."[9]

Paris Declaration of 1856   An international document abolishing privateering and codifying international norms for state maritime practice.

The peace movement was broadened when Czar Nicholas II of Russia joined in the call for an international conference on peace. At the Czar's urging, two international conferences were held at The Hague (1899 and 1907). The focus of the delegates was not on eliminating war, but rather on constructing rules for the acceptable conduct of wars. From these conferences, a series of declarations emerged that attempted to prohibit the use of certain types of weapons and methods of delivery. For example, draft treaties were written that prohibited the launching of projectiles and explosives from balloons and the use of both expanding bullets and projectiles diffusing suffocating gas. Rather than establishing an international *peacekeeping* force, participating nations set up an arbitration system to settle disputes – the *Permanent Court of Arbitration* (PCA). The PCA was intended to provide nations with a peaceful dispute resolution forum, though nations were not required to try arbitration prior to engaging in military conduct. The principles that were established at the Hague Convention had a lasting effect. They served as the foundation for the *1925 Geneva Protocols*, which prohibited the use of poisonous gas in warfare. In 1971 and 1989, the UN used both the Hague principles and the Geneva Protocols to move toward prohibiting the "development, production, and stockpiling of biological and toxic weapons."[10]

While the *Hague Conventions* focused attention on European peace efforts, peace movements in the US were also actively trying to influence US policies. One of the first peace campaigns in the United States that was successful in ending a war occurred in the 1840s. Peace activists who were opposed to the *US–Mexican War* protested US actions. A small but influential group of intellectuals, religious leaders, pacifists, and politicians denounced the war from its beginning as a war of aggression. In 1846, Henry David Thoreau, a young essayist and poet, staged the most well-known act of protest against the Mexican war. On July 23, Thoreau was jailed in Concord, Massachusetts because he refused to pay taxes that would support what he believed to be an unjust war. Although Thoreau only spent a night in jail because a relative paid his tax without his consent, the experience contributed to his penning of the still influential essay "Civil Disobedience," which would latter serve as a source of inspiration for nonviolent activists such as Mahatma Gandhi and Martin Luther King, Jr. In his essay, Thoreau argued that the government would be forced to end the Mexican War if all who opposed it went to jail for their beliefs:

peacekeeping The use of military forces to keep the various sides of a conflict from engaging in direct combat usually while peace negotiations are underway. This often allows humanitarian and other aid to reach the civilians caught in the conflict.

Permanent Court of Arbitration Designed to provide a forum for dispute resolution between various combinations of states, private parties, intergovernmental organizations, and commercial agents.

Geneva Protocols, 1925 More than a dozen nations came together to construct a treaty to prohibit the use of chemical and biological weapons, though manufacturing and storing of such weapons was allowed. Since then, dozens of other nations have signed up to the treaty.

Hague Conventions The first Hague Convention (1899) required nations to settle disputes peacefully, established laws of warfare, and prohibited certain types of weapons, including projectiles from balloons and certain types of bullets; the Second Hague Convention (1907) more specifically addressed state conduct during war.

US–Mexican War This war (1846–8) divided the US as many felt manifest destiny required the country to take control of all the land between the two oceans, while others felt it was a war of aggression against Mexico. When the war was over, the US was much larger, having gained control over Texas, California, Nevada, and Utah, and parts of Colorado, Arizona, New Mexico, and Wyoming.

Cast your whole vote, not a strip of paper merely, but your whole influence. A minority is powerless while it conforms to the majority; it is not even a minority then; but it is irresistible when it clogs by its whole weight. If the alternative is to keep all just men in prison, or give up war and slavery, the State will not hesitate which to choose.

Researching to Learn *Investigating the Life and Work of Henry David Thoreau*

Sample Keyword Searches

Broad search:
- Henry David Thoreau

Narrower searches:
- Thoreau AND "civil disobedience"
- Thoreau AND transcendentalism

Complex search: "Henry David Thoreau" AND (biography OR criticism)

Note:
- *Use quotations to search for terms as a phrase*
- *Use AND to find documents with all terms listed,*
- *Use OR to find documents with either one term or the other,*
- *Use parentheses to combine AND and OR statements in creative ways*

Free Web Resources

The Writings of Henry D. Thoreau.
This website for a project that publishes Thoreau's complete works features a biography, a quotation search engine, recommended editions of Thoreau's works, portions of his journals, and annotated links to related sites.
www.library.ucsb.edu/thoreau/

The Thoreau Society.
Website of the Thoreau Society, the oldest and largest organization devoted to an American author.
www.thoreausociety.org/
"Transcendentalism." *Stanford Encyclopedia of Philosophy.* February 6, 2003. http://plato.stanford.edu/entries/transcendentalism/

Primary Sources: Find @ Your Library

Selected Books by Thoreau:
Excursions. Boston, MA: Ticknor & Fields, 1863.
The Maine Woods. Boston, MA: Ticknor & Fields, 1864.
Torrey, Bradford and Francis H. Allen, eds. *The Writings of Henry David Thoreau.* MS edn. 20 vols. Boston, MA & New York: Houghton, Mifflin, 1906.
A Yankee in Canada, with Anti-Slavery and Reform Papers. Boston, MA: Ticknor & Fields, 1866.
Walden; or, Life in the Woods. Boston, MA: Ticknor & Fields, 1854; republished as *Walden.* Boston, MA: Ticknor & Fields, 1862; Edinburgh: David Douglas, 1884.
Week on the Concord and Merrimack Rivers. Boston & Cambridge, MA: Munroe, 1849; London, UK: Walter Scott, 1849.

Journals and Notebooks:
Broderick, John C. et al., eds. *The Journal of Henry David Thoreau,* 2 volumes. Princeton, NJ: Princeton University Press, 1981.

Cameron, Kenneth Walter, ed. *Thoreau's Literary Notebooks in the Library of Congress,* Hartford, CT: Transcendental Books, 1964.

Secondary Sources: Find @ Your Library

Biographies: Texts about Thoreau's life
Channing, William Ellery. *Thoreau: The Poet-Naturalist. with Memorial Verses.* Boston: Roberts, 1873; enlarged edition, ed. Franklin Benjamin Sanborn. Boston, MA: Charles E. Goodspeed, 1902.
Emerson, Ralph Waldo. "Thoreau." *Atlantic Monthly* 10 (August 1862): 239–249.
Atkinson, Brooks. *Henry Thoreau: The Cosmic Yankee.* New York: Knopf, 1927.
Borst, Raymond R. *The Thoreau Log: A Documentary Life of Henry David Thoreau, 1817–1862.* New York: Macmillan, 1992.
Emerson, Edward. *Henry Thoreau as Remembered by a Young Friend.* Boston, MA: Houghton Mifflin, 1917.
Harding, Walter. *The Days of Henry David Thoreau,* New York: Knopf, 1965.
Lebeaux, Richard. *Young Man Thoreau.* Amherst, MA: University of Massachusetts Press, 1977.
Lebeaux, Richard. *Thoreau's Seasons.* Amherst, MA: University of Massachusetts Press, 1984.
Richardson, Robert D. Jr. *Henry Thoreau: A Life of the Mind,* Berkeley. CA: University of California Press, 1986.

Criticism: Texts about Thoreau's Writings:
Buell, Lawrence. *The Environmental Imagination: Thoreau, Nature Writing, and the Formation of American Culture.* Cambridge, MA: Harvard University Press, 1995.
Burbick, John. *Thoreau's Alternative History: Changing Perspectives on Nature, Culture, and Language.* Philadelphia, PA: University of Pennsylvania Press, 1987.
Cain, William E. *A Historical Guide to Henry David Thoreau.* Oxford/New York: Oxford University Press, 2000.
Cain, William E., ed. *The Oxford Guide to Henry David Thoreau.* Oxford: Oxford University Press, 2000.
Dolis, John. *Tracking Thoreau: Double-Crossing Nature and Technology.* Madison, WI: Dickinson University Press, 2005.
Harold, Bloom. *Henry David Thoreau.* Philadelphia, PA: Chelsea House Publishers, 2003.
Myerson, Joel. *The Cambridge Companion to Henry David Thoreau.* Cambridge: Cambridge University Press, 1995.
Myerson, Joel. *Emerson and Thoreau: The Contemporary Reviews.* Cambridge: Cambridge University Press, 1992.
Porte, Joel. *Consciousness and Culture: Emerson and Thoreau Reviewed.* New Haven, CT: Yale University Press, 2004.

If a thousand men were not to pay their tax-bills this year, that would not be a violent and bloody measure, as it would be to pay them, and enable the State to commit violence and shed innocent blood.[11]

For Thoreau, every individual was responsible for protesting unjust government policies. "Any man more right than his neighbor," he maintained, "constitutes a majority of one."[12]

Antiwar and peace activists became a force again in US politics in the late 1800s. The Anti-Imperialist League emerged at the end of the 1800s in reaction to the *Spanish–American War* (1898) and grew to more then 30,000 members. The goal of the organization was to fight American conquest overseas, including the annexation of Hawaii, but particularly US actions in the Philippines. One of the most noteworthy members of the organization was Mark Twain. Twain became the organization's vice-president and he remained in that position until his death in 1910. His infamous essay, "To the Person Sitting in Darkness," was critical of the US for suppressing the Filipino people's right to self-governance. He suggested that the US was hypocritical for espousing liberty at home while denying it to others abroad.[13] (For a better sense of his view on war, see Twain's "War Prayer".) To many members of the League, including Andrew Carnegie and former President Cleveland, the fact that many Filipinos took up arms against the US suggested that US presence there was unwelcome. According to the League, US actions in the Philippines constituted blatant American imperialism, which undermined the very ideals upon which the nation was founded. Many Americans, however, believed that US expansion into Asia was simply a continuation of *manifest destiny*. The League and its leaders were labeled as traitors by various politicians and military leaders because of the organization's defense of the Filipinos.[14] When President William McKinley, a supporter of US imperialism, was re-elected in 1900, much of the momentum of the Anti-Imperialist League evaporated, and while the organization continued to exist for a few more years after the 1900 election, it never again played a significant role in US politics.

Spanish–American War The 1898 war between the US and Spain that ended in the Treaty of Paris whereby the US took control over Cuba, Guam, Puerto Rico, and the Philippines. While this marked the end of the Spanish empire, it also marked the emergence of the US as a colonial power.

manifest destiny The belief that the US was preordained to stretch from the Atlantic to the Pacific. This belief provided justification for territorial expansion and to the near extermination of Native Americans.

The early 1900s

World War I

Despite the demise of the Anti-Imperialist League, peace activists in America again organized as it became clear the US would become embroiled in World War I. This involvement prompted some of them to form the People's Council of America for Democracy and Peace (1917–19). The goals of the organization were to secure global peace by prohibiting forcible annexations of territories, prohibiting conscription by governments, promoting self-determination for all peoples, and extending liberty to all Americans. The organization also sought to establish an

"The War Prayer," by Mark Twain

It was a time of great and exalting excitement. The country was up in arms, the war was on, in every breast burned the holy fire of patriotism; the drums were beating, the bands playing, the toy pistols popping, the bunched firecrackers hissing and spluttering; on every hand and far down the receding and fading spread of roofs and balconies a fluttering wilderness of flags flashed in the sun; daily the young volunteers marched down the wide avenue gay and fine in their new uniforms, the proud fathers and mothers and sisters and sweethearts cheering them with voices choked with happy emotion as they swung by; nightly the packed mass meetings listened, panting, to patriot oratory which stirred the deepest deeps of their hearts and which they interrupted at briefest intervals with cyclones of applause, the tears running down their cheeks the while; in the churches the pastors preached devotion to flag and country and invoked the God of Battles, beseeching His aid in our good cause in outpouring of fervid eloquence which moved every listener. It was indeed a glad and gracious time, and the half-dozen rash spirits that ventured to disapprove of the war and cast a doubt upon its righteousness straightway got such a stern and angry warning that for their personal safety's sack they quickly shrank out of sight and offended no more in that way.

Sunday morning came – next day the battalions would leave for the front; the church was filled; the volunteers were there, their young faces alight with martial dreams visions of the stern advance, the gathering momentum, the rushing charge, the flashing sabers, the flight of the foe, the tumult, the enveloping smoke, the fierce pursuit, the surrender! – then home from the war, bronzed heroes, welcomed, adored submerged in golden seas of glory! With the volunteers sat their dear ones, proud, happy, and envied by the neighbors and friends who had no sons and brothers to send forth to the field of honor, there to win for the flag or, failing, die the noblest of noble deaths. The service proceeded; a war chapter from the Old Testament was read; the first prayer was said; it was followed by an organ burst that shook the building, and with one impulse the house rose, with glowing eyes and beating hearts, and poured out that tremendous invocation –

"God the all-terrible! Thou who ordainest,
Thunder they clarion and lightning thy sword!"

Then came the "long" prayer. None could remember the like of it for passionate pleading and moving and beautiful language. The burden of its supplication was that an ever-merciful and benignant Father of us all would watch over our noble young soldiers and aid, comfort, and encourage them in their patriotic work; bless them, shield them in the day of battle and the hour of peril, bear them in His mighty hand, make them strong and confident, invincible in the bloody onset; help them to crush the foe, grant to them and to their flag and country imperishable honor and glory.

An aged stranger entered and moved with slow and noiseless step up the main aisle, his eyes fixed upon the minister, his long body clothed in a robe that reached his feet, his head bare, his white hair descending in a frothy cataract to his shoulders, his seamy face unnaturally pale, pale even to ghastliness. With all eyes following him and wondering, he made his silent way; without pausing, he ascended to the preacher's side and stood there, waiting. With shut lids the preacher, unconscious of his presence, continued his moving prayer, and at last finished it with the words, uttered in fervent appeal, "Bless our arms, grant us the victory, O Lord our God, Father and Protector of our land and flag!"

The stranger touched his arm, motioned him to step aside – which the startled minister did – and took his place. During some moments he surveyed the spellbound audience with solemn eyes in which burned an uncanny light; then in a deep voice he said:

"I come from the Throne – bearing a message from Almighty God!" The words smote the house with a shock; if the stranger perceived it he gave no attention. "He has heard the prayer of His servant your shepherd and will grant it if such shall be your desire after I, His messenger, shall have explained to you its import – that is to say, its full import. For it is like unto many of prayers of men, in that it asks for more than he who utters it is aware of – except he pause and think.

"God's servant and yours has prayed his prayer. Has he paused and taken thought? Is it one prayer? No, it is two – one uttered, the other not. Both have reached the ear of Him Who heareth all supplications, the spoken and the unspoken. Ponder this – keep it in mind. If you would beseech a blessing upon yourself, beware! Lest without intent you invoke a curse upon a neighbor at the same time. If you pray for the blessing of rain upon your crop which needs it, by that act, you are possibly praying for a curse upon some neighbor's crops which may not need rain and can be injured by it.

"You have heard your servant's prayer – the uttered part of it. I am commissioned of God to put into words the other part of it – that part which the pastor, and also you in your hearts, fervently prayed silently. And ignorantly and unthinkingly? God grant that it was so! You heard these words: 'Grant us the victory, O Lord our God! That is sufficient. The *whole* of the uttered prayer is compact into those pregnant

words. Elaborations were not necessary. When you have prayed for victory you have prayed for many unmentioned results which follow victory – *must* follow it, cannot help but follow it. Upon the listening spirit of God the Father fell also the unspoken part of the prayer. He commandeth me to put it into words. Listen!

"O Lord our Father, our young patriots, idols of our hearts, go forth to battle – be Thou near them! With them, in spirit, we also go forth from the sweet peace of our beloved firesides to smite the foe. O Lord our God, help us to tear their soldiers to bloody shreds with our shells; help us to cover their smiling fields with the pale forms of their patriot dead; help us to drown the thunder of the guns with the shrieks of their wounded, writhing in pain; help us to lay waste their humble homes with a hurricane of fire; help us wring the hearts of their unoffending widows with unavailing grief; help us to turn them out roofless with their little children to wander unfriended the wastes of their desolated land in rags and hunger and thirst, sports of the sun flames of summer and the icy winds of winter, broken in spirit, worn with travail, imploring Thee for the refuge of the grave and denied it – for our sakes who adore Thee, Lord, blast their hopes, blight their lives, protract their bitter pilgrimage, make heavy their steps, water their way with their tears, stain the white snow with the blood of their wounded feet! We ask it, in the spirit of love, of Him Who is the Source of Love, and Who is the ever-faithful refuge and friend of all that are sore beset and seek His aid with humble and contrite hearts. Amen.

(*After a Pause*) "Ye have prayed it; if ye still desire it, speak! The messenger of the Most High waits."

It was believed afterward that the man was a lunatic, because there was no sense in what he said.[15]

international organization to promote peace internationally.[16] Because of their commitment to peace, the Council opposed US military involvement in the war in Europe.

Bolshevik Revolution   This was the first Marxist inspired revolution of the twentieth century and led to the creation of the Soviet Union. Many in Europe and the US were afraid that the revolutionary sentiment would spread.

red scare   Occurred in two phases from 1917 to 1920, and from the late 1940s through the late 1950s. These periods were characterized by a fear that communism was spreading and that communists had infiltrated the US and the US government.

Dissent and "radical" ideas, however, were becoming increasingly suspect in the US, due in part to the *Bolshevik Revolution* (1917) in Russia. The US's *"red scare"* of 1917 led to a crackdown on the Council and other "radical" groups as well as to the passage of a series of troubling laws, including the Espionage Act (1917) and the Sedition Act (1918). The Espionage Act allowed the government to arrest and fine anyone who attempted to obstruct enlistment in the armed forces, while the Sedition Act made speaking out against the government during wartime a crime punishable by a $10,000 fine, 20 years in prison, or both.[17] This meant that peace activists were particularly vulnerable, as criticism of US involvement in the war constituted "sedition." In 1918, Eugene Debs, a member of the Council, gave an antiwar speech in Ohio, where he called for draft resistance to World War I. He was arrested and sentenced to 10 years in prison. In 1920, while still in prison, he ran for President on the socialist ticket. Although he lost the election to Warren G. Harding, the new President commuted Debs's sentence to time served and he was released in 1921.

In addition to laws that jeopardized the liberties of peace activists, a special congressional committee, the Overman Committee, was established to look into the "radical activities" of peace, labor, women's, and other "left"-leaning organizations. While the Overman Committee was holding its investigations, federal law-enforcement officer J. Edgar Hoover and US Attorney General Alexander Palmer launched a series of raids, known as the "Palmer Raids" (1918–21), arresting, imprisoning, and/or deporting more than 10,000 "radicals." Crackdowns on peace and feminist activists during World War I were brutal. They were beaten, jailed, tortured, and exiled from the country. One of the most recognized names of the deported was Emma Goldman. A US citizen who had been born in Lithuania, she was deported to Russia because the US government was frightened by her anarchist ideas. She gave speeches and wrote essays against conscription and in favor of workers' and women's rights. Prior to her deportation, she had been imprisoned in 1916 for distributing birth control literature and in 1917 for obstructing the draft.[18] These kinds of pressures contributed to the demise of the People's Council of America for Democracy and Peace after World War I, but other organizations weathered the crackdowns.

One such organization was the Women's International League for Peace and Freedom (WILPF). Founded in 1915 in opposition to the war, the WILPF is the oldest women's peace organization in the world. Its early platform maintained that government policy and spending should be directed toward international arbitration, the promotion of world peace, and full rights for women. Its internationalist perspective, which became increasingly unpopular in the US in the postwar era, became the grounds on which nationalist groups denounced the peace movement as an un-American conspiracy of communists, radicals, and socialists. Jane Addams, founder of Hull House, an innovative social reform institution that assisted the poor through education, outreach, and social services, was the WILPF's first president. In 1931, she won the Nobel Peace Prize for her work with the organization. Yet, for this same work, J. Edgar Hoover called her the "most dangerous woman in America."[19]

By 1918, many people were tired of war, and President Wilson's rhetoric declaring World War I to be the "war to end all wars" had mass appeal. As the war was ending, President Wilson addressed the US Congress and laid out his *Fourteen Points* for sustaining global peace. The fourteenth point expressed the need for an international organization responsible for promoting peace. Later, he spent six months in Paris at the 1919 Paris Peace Conference working to integrate the development of this international organization into the *Treaty of Versailles*. Wilson was successful in getting the establishment of the League of Nations (LoN) included as one of the treaty's provisions, but he was unable to get the US Senate to ratify the Treaty. As a result, the US never joined the LoN, although Wilson was awarded the Nobel Peace Prize in 1919 for his peacemaking efforts.[20]

> **Fourteen Points** A speech given by US President Woodrow Wilson to the US Congress on January 8, 1918. Given 10 months before the end of World War I, it became the framework for the peace treaty that ended the war. Included in it was a call for an association of nations that would protect nation-state sovereignty and keep the peace.
>
> **Treaty of Versailles** Ended World War I and demanded that Germany take full responsibility for the war and make reparations to the states it had injured.

The League's purpose was to provide a forum where nations could discuss and debate issues. Specifically, the organization tried to promote disarmament, diplomacy, and the use of collective security to prevent conflicts. (For an overview of the League of Nations, see chapter 3.) The LoN had some success in fostering cooperation among nations. For example, disputes between Sweden and Finland over a group of islands and between Yugoslavia and Albania over border demarcation were brought before the organization and successfully handled without armed conflict erupting. The LoN also fought, albeit with limited success, against drug trafficking and sexual slavery, and on behalf of refugees. Despite its successes, the organization was relatively weak. Not all nations had joined it and many began to question whether it could really prevent conflict. Many pacifists and some European leaders, including French Foreign Minister Aristide Briand, began to call for a treaty that would outlaw war once and for all. In 1928, Briand and his American counterpart Frank B. Kellogg collaborated on the Pact of Paris, also known as the Kellogg-Briand Pact. The US and France both signed this treaty and 62 nations eventually followed suit. Two key sections read:

> The contracting parties solemnly declare in the names of their respective peoples that they condemn recourse to war for the solution of international controversies, and renounce it as an instrument of national policy.

> The parties agree that the settlement or solution of all disputes or conflicts of whatever natures or of whatever origin they may be, which may arise among them, shall never be sought except by pacific means.[21]

Despite these efforts, neither the Kellogg-Briand Pact nor the League of Nations was able to prevent war. A key problem of them both was that they lacked the ability to carry out enforcement of their decisions. The Kellogg-Briand Pact, for example, did not contain any provisions for what should be done when a nation violated the treaty. Without any kind of punishment for an offending nation, many countries did not take either the treaty or the LoN seriously. World War II soon proved that more than aspirational treaties grounded in good intentions were needed if armed conflict was to be prevented.

World War II

Peace movements were not very active in the US between the two world wars. However, as political tension increased in Europe in the 1930s, peace organizations again formed. In September 1933, a new organization emerged: the American League against War and Fascism. The driving force behind this group was fear of fascism. Among the organization's goals was an end to the manufacture and transport of munitions, support for the rights of oppressed people, including women and colonial peoples, and support for workers of the world.[22] Other antiwar groups also emerged during this time, including the Socialist League for Industrial Democracy, the National Student League, and the National Student Federation of America. These three joined forces at the end of 1933 to initiate an annual student strike against war. The following year, a new organization, the American Youth Congress, made up primarily of students, joined the three groups, and together they sponsored a series of strikes. By 1936, more than half a million people participated in these strikes. The students pledged not to support the US in any war efforts.[23]

The spread of fascism in Europe splintered peace groups, and they eventually fell apart altogether as a result of the Spanish Civil War (1936–9). German and Italian involvement in the Spanish conflict led many peace advocates to abandon their ideals and to call instead for a military response to the fascist governments' involvement in Spain. In the United States, meanwhile, the attack on Pearl Harbor in 1941 caused many peace advocates to abandon all hope of US non-involvement in the world war. There were, however, more than 700,000 US conscientious objectors during the war, many of whom were imprisoned for their refusal to fight:

Over six thousand COs who refused to serve in the Army and in Civilian Public Service camps, or whose drafts boards deemed them insincere, went to Federal prison. In fact, one out of every six men in US prisons during World War II was a draft resister. Among them were Elijah Muhammad, the leader of the Nation of Islam, and legendary jazz musician Sun Ra. War resisters found themselves behind bars for up to six years. Some were even held up to two years after the war ended.[24]

The Cold War

After Hitler's defeat, the Soviet Union began to dominate Eastern Europe, while the US asserted its influence over Western Europe, ushering in the Cold War. The

Cold War (1945–89) was a difficult period for peace activists. US fear of the spread of *communism* and *totalitarianism*, and Soviet fear of US global domination rose to paranoid levels in both countries. In the US, this fear manifested itself in the form of *McCarthyism*, a period of intense anti-communist suspicion in the United States spanning the late 1940s to the mid- to late 1950s. The term derives from Joseph McCarthy, a US Republican Senator from Wisconsin. Senator McCarthy led the charge to expose the communists who had allegedly infiltrated American institutions and the government, spying on citizens and subverting American values. Many people, both prominent figures and average Americans, were forced to appear before any one of a number of anti-communist committees and panels in federal, state, and local government, where they were accused of being communists or communist sympathizers and pressured into producing lists of names of other communists.

One of the most notable of these anti-communist bodies was the House Un-American Activities Committee. In 1947, the committee held nine days of hearings in order to determine whether Hollywood was implanting communist messages and values into the movies. Ten movie industry professionals refused to answer questions (the most famous of which was "Are you now or have you ever been a member of the Communist Party?"), citing their First Amendment rights to freedom of speech and assembly. Although being a member of the Communist Party was not, and had ever been, illegal, the "*Hollywood Ten*," as they came to be known, were convicted on contempt of Congress charges. The Motion Picture Association of America, eager to show that it did not support communism, issued a statement declaring that it would fire or suspend without pay the Hollywood Ten, putting into place Hollywood's first *blacklist*. The studios went on to blacklist more than 300 Hollywood professionals, including directors, radio commentators, actors, and screenwriters. Even world famous actors, including Charlie Chaplin, were not immune. Chaplin had to leave the US to find work, while some writers attempted to revive their careers by producing works under pseudonyms. Only about 10 percent of the entertainment industry's blacklisted professionals succeeded in rebuilding careers within the industry.[25]

communism   A form of government where all property and industry is collectively owned and run through the state.

totalitarianism   A form of government where political control lies with the state and the state tolerates no criticism.

McCarthyism   During the late 1940s–50s, Senator Joseph McCarthy, a Republican from Wisconsin, led the US government's investigation of thousands of Americans who were falsely charged with being communist or communist sympathizers. Lives were destroyed and careers ruined.

Hollywood Ten   A group of Hollywood screenwriters, producers, and directors who, in 1948, refused to testify before the House Un-American Activities committee (HUAC). The committee was investigating alleged communist ties to Hollywood. The ten who refused to testify were fined and imprisoned for one year. They were also blacklisted from working in Hollywood, a ban that was only lifted in the 1960s. The ten were Herbert Biberman, Alvah Bessie, Lester Cole, Edward Dmytryk, Ring Lardner Jr., John Howard Lawson, Albert Maltz, Samuel Ornitz, Adrian Scott, and Dalton Trumbo.

blacklist   Actors, directors, musicians, and other US entertainment professionals were prohibited from working because of false charges that they were communists or communist sympathizers. The ban lasted from 1947 until the late 1950s.

Actor and singer Paul Robeson was even more profoundly affected, as his passport was rescinded because of his outspoken praise of the Soviet Union and his criticism of American racism and segregation. From 1950 to 1958, Robeson was banned from traveling outside the US because he was unwilling to sign a statement saying he was not a communist and that he would not criticize the US while abroad.

The travel ban ended in 1958 when the US Supreme Court ruled, in *Kent vs. Dulles*, that the Secretary of State could not deny passports to American citizens nor require citizens to sign affidavits about their political beliefs.[26]

The fear of nuclear war and annihilation that characterized the Cold War climate contributed to the emergence of these kinds of oppressive practices, and also led many to claim that peace activists were simply naive. Peace through strength was a more popular position during this period. As a result, peace activists struggled against the perception that their calls for peace would lead to America's defeat in the Cold War. Despite this new obstacle, advocates for peace and progressive social change continued their fight. Civil rights activist and leader W. E. B. DuBois joined with thousands of other Americans to form the Progressive Citizens of America (PCA), an organization that supported many progressive causes, such as ending racism, colonialism, and economic injustice. The PCA, led by former Vice-President Henry A. Wallace, also argued that the US would be better served by having a less antagonistic relationship with the Soviet Union. Instead of arming those countries that stand in opposition to the Soviet Union, a decision Wallace argued would only incite radicals on both the far right and the far left of the political spectrum, US foreign policy objectives would be better served by making peace with the Soviet Union. Wallace argued that, "we must explore with the Russians the need of the peoples of the world and prepare jointly to meet them."[27] The US did not pursue this foreign policy route, however. Instead, peace movements were deflated as a result of both the Korean War (1950–3) and the Soviet Union's and the US's competition to secure their areas of interest in Europe.

The Vietnam era

Peace movements re-emerged with unprecedented strength in the United States as American involvement in Vietnam escalated. While many Americans were early supporters of the Vietnam War (1965–73), their attitudes began to change as the war continued and thousands of US soldiers were killed. Various antiwar groups staged protests, sit-ins, and resistance campaigns against the draft. This period also corresponded with the civil rights struggle in the US, and many peace activists were members of the civil rights movement as well. For these activists, protesting the war and fighting for civil rights were both social justice causes with the goal of ending violence – both the violence of war and the structural violence endured daily by millions of Americans.

Jim Crow State laws that enforced "separate but equal" race segregation in the US South. From 1876 until 1965, forced racial segregation resulted in inferior accommodations and discriminatory treatment of African-Americans.

Entrenched forms of structural violence were prevalent throughout American society, but they were particularly visible in the southern states, in part because of the discriminatory *Jim Crow* laws enacted there after the Civil War. These laws enforced segregation in all public facilities, from classrooms to restrooms. Proponents of the laws argued that the state had a compelling interest in keeping the races separated. Segregation, they maintained, did not violate the US Constitution as long as the facilities afforded both races were equal. The US Supreme Court had upheld the idea of separate facilities in the *Plessey v. Ferguson* (1896) case. The doctrine of *separate but equal* resulted in forced segregation and unfair and unequal facilities and laws. For black Americans, Jim Crow meant not only legalized discrimination but also enforced poverty and a life of constant fear. Violence against African-Americans was often tolerated by the white majority and ignored by authorities. Lynching was used to terrorize black Americans. For many white southerners, however, "separate but equal" meant power and privilege.

Jim Crow laws became a major focus of the struggle for civil rights, and activists used the Gandhian philosophy of non-violent resistance to overcome oppression. In 1960, for example, in Nashville, Tennessee, Rev. *James Lawson* and other civil rights leaders organized weekly sit-ins at segregated lunch counters. Both the police and some white citizens viciously attacked the protesters, who refused to fight back. Many protesters were arrested, and rather than pay what they argued was an unjust fine, dozens chose to remain in jail. Their tormentors were forced to accept that violence was not going to achieve the end they desired. Instead, the city was forced to accept the demands of the students and lunch counters became desegregated.[28] In this way, the civil rights struggle was often successful in challenging both direct violence and structural violence.

In some cases, however, groups calling themselves peace activists turned to violence, arguing that a violent revolution was the only way by which peace could be achieved. The logic of this argument is quite similar to the "peace through military strength" argument that dominated much of American political thought during the Cold War, particularly during the Reagan era. The philosophical underpinning of this argument is that a nation must possess enormous military might and weapons in order to deter other nations from attacking or harming its interests, a philosophy that is summed up in the Latin phrase *vis pacem, para bellum* – if you wish peace, prepare for war. The activists of the 1960s and 1970s who abandoned peaceful protest similarly claimed that the American government only understood violence. Thus, groups such as the *Weatherman* and the *Black Panthers* argued that they had to demonstrate a willingness to use force. Only then, they argued, would the American government take their demands seriously. For these activists, as for many political leaders, violence, and being prepared to use it, was an acceptable means for achieving peace. Many antiwar activists distanced themselves from such rhetoric, however, and some paid a high price for their nonviolence. In several cases, nonviolent demonstrators were attacked by the police and the National Guard, and some protesters, along with innocent bystanders, were killed. The most infamous case was the killing

Plessey v. Ferguson The US Supreme Court case (1896) that upheld the policy of "separate but equal." The court found racial segregation was constitutional.

separate but equal The phrase used to describe a system of segregation that purported to provide the same access to services, accommodations, and rights, but in a racially divided context.

James Lawson A civil rights activist and minister who led the Nashville lunch counter sit-ins and participated in the civil rights struggle along with Dr Martin Luther King. After studying the principles of nonviolence in India, he became a conscientious objector. He was imprisoned for his refusal to be drafted.

Weatherman A group of revolutionary activists whose goal was the overthrow of the US government. Before disbanding in 1975, the organization engaged in riots, bombings, and other violent anti-government campaigns.

Black Panthers An African-American civil rights and revolutionary organization that supported armed resistance to state repression. Active in the 1960s–70s.

of four students and the wounding of nine at Kent State University. On May 4, 1970, National Guard troops opened fire on unarmed students, some of whom had been protesting the illegal invasion of Cambodia by the US and some of whom were simply walking to class.

A significant feature of the civil rights and antiwar movements of this period was the diversity of their members. Unlike previous peace organizations that often draw their members from specific groups, such as white students, for example, these movements drew members whose backgrounds cut across race, class, gender, and religion. For many, these movements provided them with their first exposure to people from different backgrounds. Middle-class whites who participated in civil rights programs, such as voter registration drives in rural, predominantly black areas of Mississippi, were exposed to forms of racism and poverty that they had never seen before. They were also exposed to forms of police brutality that their privileged existence had heretofore spared them.

Post-Vietnam

After the Vietnam War, many peace activists continued their work by campaigning against the proliferation of nuclear weapons. The US and Soviet nuclear build-up and the vitriolic rhetoric that accompanied it prompted many to believe that a nuclear war was inevitable. Various groups coalesced in opposition to the spread of nuclear weapons. The anti-nuclear movement employed a variety of strategies. One remarkable protest took place at Greenham Common in Britain. Begun in 1981, this 19-year, non-stop protest was led by women who set up an encampment outside a military installation where US nuclear warheads had been deployed. These women believed that the spread of nuclear weapons would endanger world peace by provoking a response from the Soviet Union. Specifically, they wanted the nuclear weapons that had been placed in Greenham to be removed. Women of all backgrounds coalesced at Greenham, where they set up tents and temporary shelters. They also engaged in a variety of protest actions, including chaining themselves to the fence of the military base that housed the weapons, blocking trucks from entering the base by lying down on the road, and cutting through the fence with bolt cutters to gain access to the military installation. The fact that a highly secure military base could be violated by unarmed, nonviolent women became highly symbolic to the anti-nuclear movement of the 1980s.[29] The British government tried a variety of tactics to remove the women, everything from talking to them, to bulldozing their shelters, to spreading wild rumors about the reason the women were protesting. Despite arrests and harassment, the women persevered. Nuclear weapons were removed from the site in 1991 and the US Air Force left the following year. The protest continued until 2000, however, as a statement against nuclear weapons in general.

As had happened before, the peace movement in the 1980s joined forces with other movements, including the anti-apartheid movement. College campuses across the US became staging grounds for protests against the *apartheid* government of South Africa. In many cases, students built *shanty towns* to try to drive home the point to their college and university administrators that university funds (mainly endowment and investment funds) were invested in companies that did business with and helped support the racist government of South Africa. Joining in the struggle to end structural violence were professional organizations that saw as their professional and personal responsibility the alleviation of the suffering of impoverished people around the world. Examples include Doctors Without Borders (formed in 1971),[30] an organization that sends medical personnel into the most dangerous of places in order to provide medical care to those who would otherwise not have access to it, and International Physicians for the Prevention of Nuclear War (IPPNW),[31] which won the Nobel Peace Prize for its work in 1995. This organization focuses on "creating a more peaceful and secure world, free from the threat of nuclear annihilation."[32]

Peace movements also intersected with *feminist* movements that sought not only to empower women but also to end war. For the feminist movement, focusing on war was a logical shift, as civilians, primarily women, were increasingly war's victims. The wars that dominated the second half of the twentieth century were characterized less by organized militaries fighting one another and more by guerrilla and militia struggles where civilians bore the brunt of the casualties. Feminists correctly argued that women and girls often suffer disproportionately not only during wars, but also during the postwar period. In the wake of war's destruction, women struggle to provide for themselves and their families while suffering traumas, such as abandonment and rape.

apartheid A system of racial segregation in South Africa. From 1948 to 1994, citizens were divided into the following groups: Blacks, Coloureds, Whites, and Indians. This distinction determined access to all services and accommodations. All groups except Whites were denied their civil and political rights. Whites who questioned the system also had their rights violated.

shanty towns Informal settlements on the outskirts of cities where people construct dwellings from various "found" materials, such as cardboard, plastic, and corrugated metal. These settlements usually are illegal and lack basic infrastructure such as water, sanitation, electricity, etc.

feminism/feminist A philosophy that all humans should be treated equally regardless of gender/a person who believes in equality.

Taliban The ruling party/group in Afghanistan from 1996 to 2001. Their Sunni Islamic fundamentalist interpretation of the Koran resulted in a repressive state that violated its citizens' human rights, and particularly those of women's. Resurgent again in 2004, but operating out of Pakistan and parts of Afghanistan.

Feminists also argued that while women suffer from wars and their aftermaths, they are rarely given any voice in conflict resolution. In a telling example of this, as leaders of Afghanistan gathered to structure a post-*Taliban* society in 2002, women were virtually absent from the talks about the country's future. What makes this case stand out is the focus that outside supporters of overthrowing the Taliban regime had placed on the gender-based human rights violations endemic throughout Afghan society. US First Lady Laura Bush gave a series of speeches decrying the treatment of women under the Taliban, and President George W. Bush suggested that US intervention in Afghanistan was necessary to end the abuse of the women in that country. But in the aftermath of the Taliban rule, women were once again politically silenced.

Feminists dating back to the suffragette movement have long argued that for women, positive and negative peace are intertwined. Specifically, the absence of war does not mean that women are living in peace. Because of oppression, women in Afghanistan did not have peace even when the country was not "at war." For those women, the terror of being vulnerable to life-threatening violence was the norm. Thus, feminists argue, empowering women must accompany efforts to promote peace.

Another example of the overlap of various movements is the emergence of the Green Party in various countries in the 1980s. The four pillars of the movement are ecology, justice, democracy, and peace. The Green Party in the US is an anti-war, pro-union, environmentalist, feminist, anti-racist, anti-nuclear party that emphasizes the link between the overlapping and re-enforcing nature of negative and positive peace. Ralph Nader, the US Green Party's presidential nominee in 1996 and 2000, argued, for example, that excessive military spending prevented the funding of health care and other programs designed to address structural violence. While not very successful in the US, the Green Party has been much more so in Europe, particularly in Germany.

The shift from envisioning peace as simply the absence of war to promoting positive peace is most evident in the aforementioned link between professional organizations and the struggle for a decent quality of life. Whether they are made up of physicians, scientists, lawyers, or teachers, these organizations consist of people who are willing to use their talents and to give of their time to try to make the world more peaceful. This type of grassroots activism is at the heart of the non-governmental organization movement. Many NGOs are antiwar, others work for improved social conditions, and still others work to secure positive and negative peace.

Where are we now?

nuclear club Name given to countries that possess nuclear weapons: US, Britain, France, China, Russia, India, Pakistan, North Korea. Israel is also believed to have nuclear weapons.

Doomsday Clock According to the Bulletin of the Atomic Scientists, the Bulletin's founders created the Doomsday Clock in 1947 to convey how "close humanity is to catastrophic destruction – the figurative midnight" – and to monitor "the means humankind could use to obliterate itself. First and foremost, these include nuclear weapons, but they also encompass climate-changing technologies and new developments in the life sciences and nanotechnology that could inflict irrevocable harm."

The post-World War II era has proven to be a time of great hope for the spread of peace, but it has also been a time of great fear. On the one hand, war, with its increasing brutality, continues unabated. There have been roughly 30 wars or ongoing armed conflicts each year since the end of World War II. Arms sales and transfers continue at a dizzying pace. The easy availability of weapons has increased both the number of conflicts and the intensity of those conflicts. While nuclear threats appeared to have receded at the end of the Cold War, 2006 saw the number of nations clamoring to get into the *nuclear club* increase, as both North Korea and Iran stepped up their efforts to expand their nuclear programs. The threat of unstable nations or terrorist groups obtaining nuclear, chemical, or biological weapons has also increased. In a graphic illustration of this continued nuclear threat, in January of 2007, the Bulletin of the Atomic Scientists (BAS) moved the minute hand of the *Doomsday Clock*, a universally recognized indicator of the world's vulnerability to nuclear weapons, two minutes ahead to sit at five minutes until "midnight," or the apocalypse. Created in 1947, the Doomsday Clock has been adjusted by the Bulletin's Board of Directors and Board of Sponsors (which includes 18 Nobel Laureates) only 17 times prior to January 2007. The BAS statement explained:

> We stand at the brink of a Second Nuclear Age. Not since the first atomic bombs were dropped on Hiroshima and Nagasaki has the world faced such perilous choices. North Korea's recent test of a nuclear weapon, Iran's nuclear ambitions, a renewed emphasis on the military utility of nuclear weapons, the failure to adequately secure nuclear materials, and the continued presence of some 26,000 nuclear weapons in the United States and Russia are symptomatic of a failure to solve the problems posed by the most destructive technology on Earth.[33]

In addition to nuclear threats and armed conflicts, the world has witnessed several *genocides*. They have occurred despite the global community's pledge in the aftermath of the European Holocaust never to allow another genocide to occur. Moreover, people around the world are still struggling to provide the necessities for themselves and their families, as the gap between the world's rich and poor continues to widen. According to the Worldwatch Institute:

genocide The intent to destroy, in whole or in part, a national, ethnic, racial, or religious group.

> The global economy has grown sevenfold since 1950. Meanwhile, the disparity in per capita gross domestic product between the 20 richest and 20 poorest nations more than doubled between 1960 and 1995. Of all high-income nations, the United States has the most unequal distribution of income, with over 30 percent of income in the hands of the richest 10 percent and only 1.8 percent going to the poorest 10 percent.[34]

The amount of wealth being concentrated in the hands of the few is exemplified by the fact that in 2003 "three families – Bill Gates, the Sultan of Brunei and the Walton family (Wal-Mart) – had a combined wealth of some $135 billion. This equals the annual income of 600 million people living in the world's poorest countries."[35]

But despite all these threats to both positive and negative peace, it is also important to note that in the postwar era, the human rights movement has thrived. The term "human rights" refers to the innate rights and freedoms that humans are entitled to regardless of where they live (see chapter 4). Increased transportation and communication have broken down barriers to human understanding of the fate of others. These developments have led to increased consciousness among many about the impact of their actions on others thousands of miles away. Likewise, access to information about the violations of peoples' human rights around the world makes it possible for the average individual to take action and to demand that governments protect the human rights of their citizens. Groups such as Amnesty International[36] and Human Rights Watch[37] work to protect people everywhere by monitoring countries' human rights records, publicizing human rights abuses, and providing a structure through which individuals around the world can work together to send letters and communiqués to offending governments demanding that they respect and protect their citizens' human rights. The importance of human rights today is illustrated in the willingness of some nations to sever relations with others over violations of rights.

In addition to the progress made by the human rights movement, peace initiatives, once the domain of the nation-state, are increasingly coming from international organizations, regional organizations, individuals, and NGOs. The United Nations,[38] successor to the League of Nations, has had some success at preventing conflicts and at bringing conflicts to a speedy end. UN peacekeeping missions receive strong worldwide support, but regional organizations, such as the Economic Community of West African States (ECOWAS), have also worked toward peaceful solutions to crises in their regions. Prominent individuals are also playing a key role in the advancement of peace. One such example is Nelson Mandela, who has worked diligently to bring about an end to the hostilities in Central Africa.

The easy access to information via the Internet and other advancements in communications has made possible global populist demands for peace. Technology is playing an increasing role as a conduit of information and a way for individuals and groups to both inform others and to be informed about various threats to peace. For example, US and British plans to invade Iraq in early 2003 brought about the world's largest demonstrations for peace. The BBC estimated that "between six and 10 million people are thought to have marched in up to 60 countries" in one weekend during February 2003.[39] These internationally coordinated protests were made possible by the ease with which the various social organizations, groups, and individuals around the world could communicate. What forms peace movements will take in the future are unclear, but the Internet will likely remain an important forum for peace and human rights groups to communicate, share information, and promote their agendas.

Waging Peace

Pacifism

Although peace activists often subscribe to a *pacifist* philosophy, not all pacifists are alike. In fact, pacifists can be divided into three categories: universal, private, and antiwar. Universal pacifists believe that violence is wrong in all its forms. They argue that the line between offensive and defensive uses of violence is too often blurry, and that therefore violence should not be used at all, even in self-defense. For example, disagreements emerged over what constitutes self-defense when the *contras*, who were sponsored by the US, laid naval mines in Nicaragua's harbors. The Reagan administration described this as a self-defense operation designed to protect the US from the spread of Marxist-Leninism. However, the Nicaraguans and many other countries around the world saw the move as an offensive act of war. Nicaragua took the US to

pacifist Someone who believes that violence is not an appropriate response to conflict.

contras Name given to armed guerrillas whose goal was to overthrow the Nicaraguan government. Operating from border states, and with US government support, contras raided Nicaragua, killing many government officials and civilians.

the International Court of Justice and the Court found in favor of Nicaragua, thus supporting their claim that the US had violated international law by supporting the contras. Universal pacifists would view this as an example of how the category of self-defense can be manipulated to justify aggression and violence, and, as a result, all such actions should be eschewed.

Private pacifists oppose personal violence and therefore do not condone the use of violence by unauthorized individuals; but they would support, as a last resort, the use of police or military force to counter criminals or aggressors. Private pacifists believe that the use of violence must be avoided as much as possible; however, because there are people who commit heinous acts, violence must remain an option, albeit a rarely used one. A private pacifist would argue that the use of violence to stop someone from inflicting violence on another, for example, would be acceptable. For private pacifists, there are clear situations where violence is a regrettable necessity.

Antiwar pacifists oppose political violence but they might use violence as a last resort for personal self-defense. Antiwar pacifists are probably the most commonly known type of pacifists. They oppose the organized use of military violence, arguing that citizens often do not have all the information necessary to asses their government's use of military force. Citizens are often asked to trust their governments' motives, but government leaders can be corrupt. Allowing them unrestricted use of violence over their own or another country's citizens is dangerous. Antiwar pacifists argue that when governments and their leaders have the authority and ability to use violence, they will be more likely to use it as a tool to settle disputes. The victor of such disputes may not be the one who was "morally right" but rather the one with the most might. As the Athenian spokesperson to the Melians succinctly stated: "You know as well as we do that right, as the world goes, is only in question between equals in power, while the strong do what they can and the weak suffer what they must."[40] Additionally, antiwar pacifists argue that countries that use violence to handle external threats are more likely to use violence against their own citizens who question the use of that violence. As an example, antiwar pacifists point to conscription or military drafts. Governments enforce drafts by arresting or threatening to arrest those who refuse to comply. Fear of imprisonment in the US, for example, led thousands of American men to flee to Canada rather than be forcibly conscripted into the military during the Vietnam War. Had the men stayed, they would have been arrested and their liberties taken away.

Nonviolent resistance

One method of operationalizing one's belief in pacifism is through nonviolent resistance. No other figure in history is so inextricably linked with the concept of nonviolence as is Mohandas Gandhi. While in South Africa, Gandhi began his practice of nonviolent resistance against the racist government of South Africa. He arrived in South Africa in 1893 to work as a lawyer. Gandhi was appalled at the discriminatory treatment of Indians, many of whom had been recruited by the South African government to work on the sugar plantations. He led several civil disobedience campaigns, including strikes by plantation workers and protest marches against the anti-Asian laws. He was arrested and imprisoned several times. His experiences led him to develop his philosophy of the satyagraha ("devotion to truth") which required nonviolent resistance to oppression. After achieving several of his goals in South Africa, including the ending of poll taxes on Indians and the recognition of their marriages, he returned to his native India in 1914 and began a resistance campaign against British colonial rule there.[41] He argued that colonialism was only possible if native peoples cooperated with their colonial masters. By choosing to resist colonialism nonviolently, Gandhi exposed the true nature of the enterprise. Colonial powers had based their rationale for colonialism on the *white man's burden*." This suggested that the "civilized" world had a responsibility to export their "advanced" forms of social organizations, including religious, economic, and political systems, to the "uncivilized" corners of the world. This became a justification for colonialism. When Gandhi's nonviolent movement to resist British rule began in earnest, the British responded with vicious violence. This violence, Gandhi argued, exposed the reality of colonialism, which was a system of oppression designed to subjugate and humiliate the local population while stealing their resources. As British violence against nonviolent protesters who were demanding freedom and dignity increased, it became increasingly difficult for Britain to argue that their actions represented the "civilized" world. Gandhi believed that nonviolent resistance works because it rips away the façade of the oppressors and leaves them holding the moral low ground. The British eventually left India, but Gandhi did not have much time to enjoy his freedom: he was assassinated in 1948. His legacy, however, lived on and his philosophy of nonviolent resistance has become the foundation of most modern peace movements.

> **white man's burden**   Based on a poem that Rudyard Kipling wrote about US military involvement in the Philippines, the phrase refers to the "noble enterprise" of bringing Christianity and "civilization" to developing countries. This provided many with a justification for colonialism.

The twentieth century was humanity's most violent, but it was also the century of the maturation of the strategy of nonviolent protest as a response to government violence. In addition to Gandhi's anti-colonial protests, there are many other examples of successful nonviolent resistance. American suffragettes, in 1918, marched in Washington, DC and chained themselves to the gates of the White House, only to be arrested and tortured in prison. In South Africa in 1984, a group of citizens led by Mkhuseli Jack boycotted white-owned stores in Port Elizabeth in a nonviolent protest against the racist policies of the apartheid regime. Protesting against Argentina's brutal military dictatorships and its "Dirty War" (a term used to describe the years 1976–83, when more than 10,000 people disappeared at the hands of the government), Argentinean women organized the Madres de Plaza de Mayo (Mothers of the May Square, or Mothers of the Disappeared). Beginning in 1977, these women silently paraded in front of government offices holding the pictures of their disappeared loved ones, demanding accountability of the government. Three of the founding members of the organization disappeared, but the women persevered and only stopped their protests in January 2006. In Poland, a workers' union movement known as *solidarność* successfully took on the communist government by using work stoppages. The solidarity movement, as it became known in the US, was led by Lech Walesa. He and his colleagues in a Gdansk shipyard organized to protest against food price increases and for the right to have labor unions that were independent of the communist government. The government initially gave into their demands, but later drove the movement underground. However, in June 1989, Walesa and Solidarity won the first post-communist democratic election in Poland.

Critics of nonviolent resistance argue that it is not always effective and that it is not an adequate response to overwhelming state violence. For those who support this position, responding to violence with violence is the only acceptable reaction because all individuals are entitled to a right to defend themselves. Supporters of nonviolence counter this argument using Denmark during World War II as an example. In 1940, Hitler's Germany invaded Denmark. Through a series of negotiations, the Danish government was able to broker a deal with the Germans that gave Germany official control of the country, but gave the Danish government control of the day-to-day administrative duties of the state. Danish factories were retooled in order to make war related-materials for the German military. Danish citizens felt that their government officials had sold out to the Germans and began a series of civil disobedience actions to disrupt production of German war materials. The work slowdowns, the street protests, and the leafleting infuriated the Germans, who, in response, put more pressure on the Danish officials to end the resistance. But because those officials had lost legitimacy in the eyes of the Danes, there was little they could do to stop the resistance. The Germans responded with increasingly harsh measures. When the Germans issued an order to arrest all Danish Jews who would then be deported to concentration camps outside Denmark, the Danes worked together to hide Jews and to provide them safe passage out of the country. Many hid Jews in their homes, while others helped ferry them to the safety of Sweden. By the time the Nazi regime began initiating the round-up of Jews in Denmark, there were very few left in country. The Germans were outraged and began a series of crackdowns designed to crush the Danish resistance. Deprivation of water, electricity, and food were used as weapons; the Danes responded by walking away from the factories, bringing production of German war materials to a stop. The Germans had to scramble to find ways to produce all the materials needed for their multi-front war, and were ultimately forced to relent and give in to Danish demands for access to food, water, and electricity. In their resistance against the Nazis, the Danes demonstrated that nonviolence can succeed even in the face of overwhelming violence. What if many others had resisted Hitler by not working in the camps, or by refusing to be conscripted into the German military, or by refusing to work toward the war effort?[42]

Nation-states and international organizations

States and IOs often engage in peace-building exercises, sometime enthusiastically and sometimes reluctantly. One inherent problem in the nation-state system concerns the competing views of self-interest. Nation-states rely on the concept of

sovereign/sovereignty The principle that emerged from the Peace of Westphalia (1648) which suggests that a political entity has the sole authority to make decisions about policy, procedure, and institutions within a given geographic territory.

sovereignty, the ability of states to control their territories and for governments to operate in the best interest of the citizens of that territory. However, states often have overlapping "interests." Since the founding of the UN in 1945, the number of member nations had increased by 2006 from 51 to 192. This means that three times as many nations are trying to secure and protect their interests in the international arena, and this often leads to conflict. Peace in the world of multiple competing interests has proven difficult to realize. Although the UN has had some success in both preventing conflict and operating as peacekeepers, the UN can only do what its members authorize, and, as a result, it will always be dependent upon its members to work toward peace. Much discussion and debate at the UN revolves around avoiding war and developing effective policies to end existing conflicts. Despite their best efforts, UN antiwar strategists are having very little success, as is evident every time we turn on the news or pick up a newspaper. Why is initiating and sustaining peace so difficult and what tools do the peace-seeking governments and organizations have at their disposal?

Several mechanisms can be employed by nation-states to try to resolve conflicts peacefully before they become violent. One of the most effective and frequently used ways to settle disputes peacefully is through diplomatic negotiations. Professional diplomats, who often work through a country's diplomatic offices (the US Department of State, for example), endeavor to find durable, peaceful solutions to disputes. Each nation has a foreign office that is responsible for carrying out foreign policy as determined by that nation's leaders. A whole host of diplomats, analysts, ambassadors, political figures, and interest groups play key roles in designing a country's foreign policy.

Second, in addition to diplomacy, a country can offer its "good offices" (influence) to intercede in a conflict. Here the disputant parties agree to have a third party intercede in the conflict. The third country does this by offering to bring the parties together, though not usually in the same room. The representative whose "good offices" are being used then shuttles back and forth, acting as a conduit of information. This is particularly helpful when foreign relations between two nations have been halted or when it would be unwise because of domestic concerns for a leader to announce a willingness to sit down and meet with the "enemy" state.

Third, mediation can be used. Rather than acting as a go-between for two conflicting states, the mediator participates in the process by offering proposals to help settle the dispute. Designing and offering a peace plan is integral to mediation. For example, in 1978, the US concluded mediation between the Israelis and the Egyptians in what was known as the Camp David Accords. The Accords marked the beginning of the end of the formal state of hostilities that had existed between the two nations since the founding of the state of Israel in 1948. With this agreement, the groundwork was laid for a peace treaty between Israel and Egypt, which was concluded in 1979.

Fourth, because disputant states sometimes cannot agree on the facts leading up to a dispute, a commission of inquiry can be used to help settle the facts. The commission is an ad hoc (as needed) group that comes together at the behest and approval of the disputant states. The make-up of the commission is mutually agreed upon by the disputing parties. For example, in 1904 both Britain and Russia agreed to a Commission of Inquiry to resolve a dispute over which country was at fault in the North Sea incident in which a Russian gunboat fired on a British fleet, causing deaths and damage to the British ships. The Commission of what became known as the Dogger Bank Case reviewed the facts, found that the Russian ships were at fault, and ordered Russia to pay a penalty to the British.

Fifth, arbitration, is one of the oldest dispute mechanisms, and it involves submitting claims to pre-approved arbitrators whose decision is final. The arbitrators hear all the evidence and make their decision. The parties are allowed to pick the arbitrators and therefore often feel more comfortable accepting the decisions handed down. Two of the textbook cases of arbitration are the *Jay Treaty* and the *Alabama case*. The Jay Treaty provided that arbitration be used to settle resultant claims of both the British and the Americans after the Revolutionary War. The arbitration body set up after the war heard more than 500 claims. In 1872, the US sought arbitration over claims that Britain had supplied ships to the US South during the Civil War, thus inflicting damages on the US. The Alabama case was won by the US, and Britain was ordered to pay $15.5 million in damages. Many peace organizations saw the success of the Jay Treaty and the later

> **Jay Treaty**   A treaty between the US and Britain after the revolutionary war to resolve left-over issues, such as the dispensation of property. It averted another war between the two states and was hailed by many as the new peaceful way to resolve conflicts.

> **Alabama case**   Resolved a dispute between Britain and the US over British support to the American South during the US Civil War. Britain was found liable for damages to US warships by Confederate ships built or outfitted by Britain.

Alabama case and believed that arbitration would be the future method for preventing war. US President Grant expressed his belief that a day would come when arbitration, rather than war, would settle disputes between nations, while President Taft suggested that arbitration could have been employed to prevent the War of 1812, the Mexican–American War (1948), and the Spanish–American War (1898). Taft believed that arbitration could make war less possible and peace more permanent.[43] Use of arbitration as a tool to prevent war was also one of the founding principles of the Hague peace conferences.[44]

Sixth, adjudication requires both sides in a dispute to submit their claim to a court. The court is empowered to hear and compel testimony. Claimants are not allowed to choose the judges and decisions handed down carry a great deal of weight in the international community. The first large-scale attempt to create a permanent court, the *Permanent Court of International Justice* (PICJ), was done in conjunction with the League of Nations. The PICJ was disbanded with the League and was replaced by the International Court of Justice (ICJ). The ICJ is one of the principal organs of the UN and was established

> **Permanent Court of International Justice**   The court of the League of Nations, which existed from 1920 to 1940 and heard 29 cases. Replaced in 1940 by the ICJ or World Court.

alongside the UN in 1945. States join the ICJ when they join the UN. The ICJ is made up of 15 judges hailing from different countries. The ICJ is often listed in treaties as the forum where disputes over those treaties will be adjudicated. One of the more difficult aspects of the ICJ as a dispute mechanism is that it lacks enforcement powers and therefore must rely on the disputant states, or, in extreme situations, the UN Security Council, to carry out its rulings.

Seventh, the International Criminal Court (ICC) is fairly new in the international arena. While the ICJ is an adjudicatory body to which nation-states can take their cases, the purpose of the ICC is to bring to justice the leaders of countries that engage in gross violations of human rights. The ICC came into existence on July 1, 2002 when the requisite number of states signed the statute that established it. Unlike the ad hoc tribunals set up after the war to punish Germany and Japan – the *Nuremberg Trials* and the *Tokyo Tribunals* – the ICC is designed to be permanent. In addition to punishing those guilty of violating people's rights, it is hoped that the Court will act as a deterrent to human rights abuses because leaders will realize that they may have to pay for their crimes.

Nuremberg Trials Post-World War II (1945–9) trials of dozens of officials of Nazi Germany who were charged with war crimes, more specifically with the crime of waging an aggressive war.

Tokyo Tribunals War crimes trials for 25 Japanese defendants, seven of whom were sentenced to death. Thousands of other Japanese were charged with lesser crimes.

Finally, international and regional organizations can play a role in the promotion of peaceful settlements of disputes. As noted earlier, the former League of Nations was an international organization that had some success in helping nations avoid conflict. Central to the LoN's goal of maintaining peace was the use of arbitration as a dispute mechanism. Article 13 of the LoN's founding Charter even spelled out what types of conflicts would be suitable for arbitration. The UN has followed this lead, but with its own variations. It too is designed to be the forum where debate occurs and disputes are resolved. According to the UN, there are two kinds of war, offensive and defensive. All nations that join the UN pledge to forgo offensive military actions, unless approved or organized by the UN, and instead agree to use their militaries for defensive purposes only.

While the UN provides a forum for nations to resolve their disputes peacefully, not all nations choose to do so. Since the founding of the UN, there have been, on average, 30 armed conflicts per year. Not all of these are between nation-states – some are civil wars – but many are between member nations of the UN. Many nations simply ignore the prohibition against the use of force, while others try to argue that their military action is in self-defense. Some countries also argue that their actions are anticipatory self-defense. The US argued this in the case of Iraq in 2003. In this case, the Bush administration argued that the US and its allies had to invade Iraq to overthrow its leader because they feared that if they didn't, *Saddam Hussein* would be a threat in the future. Not all nations agree with this use of anticipatory self-defense, however.

Saddam Hussein Dictator of Iraq from 1979 until the US-led invasion in 2003. In 2006 he was found guilty of crimes against humanity by a special court and hanged in December 2006.

Should a dispute arise, the UN can make recommendations for a peaceful settlement as well as make use of peacekeepers and observer missions in order to provide a buffer between warring sides while they negotiate a more permanent settlement. The bulk of the peace role of the UN falls on the *Security Council* and not the *General Assembly*. Of the six principal organs of the UN (see chapter 3), the Security Council is responsible for making the key decisions regarding UN actions. For example, it has the power to authorize the use of force and the use of peacekeepers. However, the General Assembly also makes recommendations to the Security Council. The *Secretary-General* of the UN also acts as a negotiator. Because the Secretary-General is seen as neutral by many states, the power of mediation is available to him or her.

Ideally, the UN would like to see disputes go first to a relevant regional organization, the African Union or the Organization of American States, for example (for more about these organizations, see chapter 3), but this happens very rarely. Regional organizations approach conflict resolution in a manner similar to the UN, with the one exception being the European Union. Because the EU has a court – the *European Court of Justice* – set up to deal with conflicts, disputes can be adjudicated more easily in the European context. The EU is also experimenting with fielding its own peacekeeping operations. The African Union established a peacekeeping force for *Darfur, Sudan* in 2005 and has plans to have a more permanent peacekeeping force ready to be deployed anywhere on the continent by 2010. Peacekeeping as part of other regional organizations, the *Conference on Security and Cooperation in Europe* (CSCE), for example, has met with little enthusiasm. The preferred method of peacekeeping is still through the UN, as the organization, despite its limitations, is seen as non-partisan.

Ending structural violence

Positive peace, or the ending of structural violence, is more complicated than either preventing or stopping a war. Ending structural violence involves ending the abject poverty that daily puts so many lives at risk. The UN, nation-states, and a multitude of NGOs work at finding solutions to structural violence. The UN not only compiles the socioeconomic indicators that track the condition of humanity, but also works through its various agencies to promote and develop programs that target structural violence. Table 11.1 provides examples of these agencies, while table 11.2 ranks countries according to their overall human development. The United Nations' Human Development Index[45] compares countries' basic quality-of-life indicators, including life expectancy, literacy rates, poverty levels, and overall well-being.

In addition to various agencies designed to promote better conditions for humanity, the UN has also used its influence to try to promote global peace

United Nations Security Council (UNSC) The 15-member organ of the UN that is responsible for maintaining peace and security. There are 10 rotating members who serve two-year terms and five permanent members who have veto power: US, Britain, China, Russia, and France.

General Assembly (UN) The organ of the UN that acts as its legislative branch. All member nations can send delegates to the General Assembly. It is also a forum for international dialogue.

Secretary-General (UN) The official spokesperson for the UN. In charge of the administrative machinery of the organization. Ban Ki-moon from South Korea became the Secretary-General in 2007.

European Court of Justice This is the supreme court of the EU whose purpose is to provide a forum for dispute resolution between member states.

Darfur, Sudan A region of the country of Sudan that has been the scene of widespread violence, including genocide. More than 400,000 people died between the start of the violence in 2003 and 2008.

Conference on Security and Cooperation in Europe Created during the Cold War as a military alliance in Europe, its purpose is to ensure peace and good governance in the region.

Table 11.1 Agencies of the UN[46]

International Labour Organization (ILO)	Founded in 1919, the ILO seeks to promote justice and internationally recognized human and labor rights.
Food and Agriculture Organization (FAO)	Attempts to eradicate hunger by promoting sustainable agriculture via collecting data, providing expert policy analysis, and providing a forum for nations to share and discuss agricultural policy.
United Nations Educational, Scientific and Cultural Organization (UNESCO)	Promotes cooperation in the fields of education, science, culture, and communication. Goals are to reduce the number of people living in poverty, to increase the number of children, boys and girls, who have access to education, and to promote sustainable development.
World Health Organization (WHO)	The goal is to work to secure health as a state of complete physical, mental and social well-being and not merely the absence of disease or infirmity.
United Nations Conference on Trade and Development (UNCTAD)	Promotes the integration of developing countries into the global economy in a sustainable way.
United Nations Environment Programme (UNEP)	Promotes the sustainable use of the environment.
United Nations Children's Fund (UNICEF)	Focuses on the following areas: child development, education and gender equity, child protection and advocacy, HIV/AIDS and general health-related issues for children.
United Nations Development Programme (UNDP)	A global development network that provides a forum for countries to explore development related issues.
United Nations Development Fund for Women (UNIFEM)	Works to improve the lives of women around the world.
United Nations Population Fund (UNFPA)	Collects data on population-related issues, supports the rights of women and girls over their reproductive choices, and promotes healthy births and HIV prevention.
Office of the United Nations High Commissioner for Refugees (UNHCR)	Provides basic necessities for millions of the world's refugees.
United Nations Human Settlements Programme (UN-HABITAT)	Promotes the development of environmentally and socially sustainable human settlements.
United Nations Relief and Works Agency for Palestine Refugees in the Near East (UNRWA)	Provides refugee assistance for Palestinians displaced after the establishment of the state of Israel.
World Food Programme (WFP)	Works to end world hunger.
Office of the United Nations High Commissioner for Human Rights (OHCHR)	Works to promote human rights and collects data on human rights protection and violations.
Joint United Nations Programme on HIV/AIDS (UNAIDS)	Collects information about AIDS and works toward the eradication of the disease.

Table 11.2 Human Development Index (HDI) Ranking, 2006[47]

1. Norway	2. Iceland	3. Australia	4. Ireland
5. Sweden	6. Canada	7. Japan	8. United States
9. Switzerland	10. Netherlands	11. Finland	12. Luxembourg
13. Belgium	14. Austria	15. Denmark	16. France
17. Italy	18. United Kingdom	19. Spain	20. New Zealand
21. Germany	22. Hong Kong, China (SAR)	23. Israel	24. Greece
25. Singapore	26. Korea, Rep. of	27. Slovenia	28. Portugal
29. Cyprus	30. Czech Republic	31. Barbados	32. Malta
33. Kuwait	34. Brunei Darussalam	35. Hungary	36. Argentina
37. Poland	38. Chile	39. Bahrain	40. Estonia
41. Lithuania	42. Slovakia	43. Uruguay	44. Croatia
45. Latvia	46. Qatar	47. Seychelles	48. Costa Rica
49. United Arab Emirates	50. Cuba	51. Saint Kitts and Nevis	52. Bahamas
53. Mexico	54. Bulgaria	55. Tonga	56. Oman
57. Trinidad and Tobago	58. Panama	59. Antigua and Barbuda	60. Romania
61. Malaysia	62. Bosnia and Herzegovina	63. Mauritius	64. Libyan Arab Jamahiriya
65. Russian Federation	66. Macedonia, TFYR	67. Belarus	68. Dominica
69. Brazil	70. Colombia	71. Saint Lucia	72. Venezuela, RB
73. Albania	74. Thailand	75. Samoa (Western)	76. Saudi Arabia
77. Ukraine	78. Lebanon	79. Kazakhstan	80. Armenia
81. China	82. Peru	83. Ecuador	84. Philippines
85. Grenada	86. Jordan	87. Tunisia	88. Saint Vincent and the Grenadines
89. Suriname	90. Fiji	91. Paraguay	92. Turkey
93. Sri Lanka	94. Dominican Republic	95. Belize	96. Iran, Islamic Rep. of
97. Georgia	98. Maldives	99. Azerbaijan	100. Occupied Palestinian Territories
101. El Salvador	102. Algeria	103. Guyana	104. Jamaica
105. Turkmenistan	106. Cape Verde	107. Syrian Arab Republic	108. Indonesia
109. Viet Nam	110. Kyrgyzstan	111. Egypt	112. Nicaragua
113. Uzbekistan	114. Moldova, Rep. of	115. Bolivia	116. Mongolia
117. Honduras	118. Guatemala	119. Vanuatu	120. Equatorial Guinea
121. South Africa	122. Tajikistan	123. Morocco	124. Gabon
125. Namibia	126. India	127. São Tomé and Principe	128. Solomon Islands
129. Cambodia	130. Myanmar	131. Botswana	132. Comoros
133. Lao People's Dem. Rep.	134. Pakistan	135. Bhutan	136. Ghana
137. Bangladesh	138. Nepal	139. Papua New Guinea	140. Congo
141. Sudan	142. Timor-Leste	143. Madagascar	144. Cameroon
145. Uganda	146. Swaziland	147. Togo	148. Djibouti
149. Lesotho	150. Yemen	151. Zimbabwe	152. Kenya
153. Mauritania	154. Haiti	155. Gambia	156. Senegal
157. Eritrea	158. Rwanda	159. Nigeria	160. Guinea
161. Angola	162. Tanzania, U. Rep. of	163. Benin	164. Côte d'Ivoire
165. Zambia	166. Malawi	167. Congo, Dem. Rep. of the	168. Mozambique
169. Burundi	170. Ethiopia	171. Chad	172. Central African Republic
173. Guinea-Bissau	174. Burkina Faso	175. Mali	176. Sierra Leone
177. Niger			

initiatives. For example, the UN International Year for the Culture of Peace in 2000 was followed by the International Decade for a Culture of Peace and Nonviolence for the Children of the World (2001–10). The goal of these initiatives is to create a culture of peace, defined as promoting respect for life through education, equality of opportunity for all peoples, the protection of human rights, and the ending of violence.[48] Building a culture of peace requires taking into consideration both the positive and negative components of peace. In addition to the work done by the UN to eradicate structural violence (as exemplified by the agencies listed in table 11.1), many NGOs and IOs also work to promote positive peace. (See chapter 3 for a more detailed discussion of the type of work NGOs carry out in their capacity as positive peace activists.)

Peace work, both negative and positive, is done also at the personal level. Many people take on the cause of peace as a mission. Some citizens risk their lives to go to places at war in order to try to end the violence. For example, dozens of US citizens went to Nicaragua and placed themselves along the border where US backed guerillas (contras) were making raids into Nicaragua. A grassroots organization, Witness for Peace, emerged out of these activists' outrage over US policy in Latin America, particularly toward Nicaragua. They believed that if American citizens were killed by the US-backed contras, then people in the US would pay more attention to what was going on and demand an end to US support of the contras. They also hoped that the contras too would realize this and therefore not attack areas where American citizens had stationed themselves. Another goal of Witness for Peace was to document the atrocities committed against the Nicaraguan civilians by the contras. By distributing this information in the US, the organization was successful at challenging American assumptions about the effects of US Latin American policy.[49] Similarly, in the months leading up to the US war on Iraq in 2003, dozens of US citizens, including actor Sean Penn, went to Baghdad, Iraq's capital, as a sort of human shield.[50] Their goal was not to prop up Saddam Hussein's government, but rather to force the US to consider nonviolent alternatives for resolving the dispute. These individuals' personal commitment to peace caused them to risk their lives in regions fraught with conflict in an effort to foster peace.

Global Connections: The Personal Dimension of Peace

What can you do to help make the world a more peaceful place? Is this even a responsibility you are willing to take on? If not, do you have an obligation not to contribute to making the world a more violent place? These kinds of questions illustrate that the struggle for peace can also be an internal, conscience-examining exercise characterized by individuals examining their lives, priorities, and choices in order to evaluate who they are, what they desire, and where they are headed. More specifically, we can talk about peace as the inner struggle to accept ourselves, to work toward goals that elevate our minds and spirits, or to make responsible

Researching to Learn   *Peace Studies and Conflict Resolution*

Academic Programs

The European University Center for Peace Studies (EPU)
Located in Stadtschlaining/Austria.
   www.aspr.ac.at/epu/index.htm

Global Directory of Peace Studies and Conflict Resolution Programs
A comprehensive, annotated guide to peace studies and conflict resolution programs at colleges and universities worldwide.
   www.peacejusticestudies.org/globaldirectory/

The University for Peace
Established by the UN on December 5, 1980, the University for Peace's mission is "to provide humanity with an international institution of higher education for peace and with the aim of promoting among all human beings the spirit of understanding, tolerance and peaceful coexistence, to stimulate cooperation among peoples and to help lessen obstacles and threats to world peace and progress, in keeping with the noble aspirations proclaimed in the Charter of the United Nations."
   www.upeace.org/

Organizations

Association for Conflict Resolution (ACR)
ACR is a professional organization dedicated to enhancing the practice and public understanding of conflict resolution. ACR represents and serves a diverse national and international audience that includes more than 6,000 mediators, arbitrators, facilitators, educators, and others involved in the field of conflict resolution and collaborative decision-making.
   www.acrnet.org/

International Peace Research Association (IPRA)
Founded in 1964, IPRA promotes peace research and peace education. With more than 1,300 members from some 90 countries, IPRA is one of the most respected scholarly association in the field. IPRA has links with more than 200 research institutions and is a member of the International Social Science Council.
   http://soc.kuleuven.be/pol/ipra/

The Peace and Justice Studies Association (PJSA)
PJSA is a non-profit organization that was formed in 2001 due to a merger of the Consortium on Peace research, Education, and Development (COPRED) and the Peace Studies Association (PSA). The organization is dedicated to bringing together academics, K-12 teachers and grassroots activists to explore alternatives to violence and share visions and strategies for peacebuilding, social justice, and social change. PJSA also serves as a professional association for scholars in the field of peace and conflict resolution studies.
   www.peacejusticestudies.org/index.php

The Peace History Society
Founded in 1964 to encourage and coordinate national and international scholarly work exploring and articulating the conditions and causes of peace and war and communicating the findings of scholarly work to the public.
   www.peacehistorysociety.org/

United States Institute of Peace
The United States Institute of Peace is an independent, nonpartisan, national institution established and funded by Congress. Its goals are to help prevent and resolve violent international conflicts, promote post-conflict stability and democratic transformations, and increase peace-building capacity, tools, and intellectual capital worldwide.
   www.usip.org/index.html

Scholarly Journals: Find Them @ Your Library

Harvard Human Rights Journal
This journal is published by students in the Harvard Law school. It publishes cutting-edge human rights analysis by students, scholars and practitioners.
   www.law.harvard.edu/students/orgs/hrj/

Human Rights Quarterly

For 25 years, this quarterly journal has been publishing scholarly articles on various aspects of human rights including current research and policy analysis. It tracks human rights related developments at the United Nations, regional organizations, and NGOs. It also provides reviews of books dealing with human rights. http://muse.jhu.edu/journals/human_rights_quarterly

International Journal of Peace Studies

Dedicated to enhancing alternative discourse on a wide range of theoretical issues in peace research and improving our knowledge in the quest for peace. www.gmu.edu/academic/ijps/

Journal of International Human Rights

Published at Northwestern University, this journal focuses on human rights and international human rights law by publishing the research of academics and practitioners. www.law.northwestern.edu/jihr/

Peace and Change: A Journal of Peace Research

This scholarly journal is co-published by the PJSA and the Peace History Society. The journal features articles related to the creation of a peaceful, just, and humane society. www.blackwellpublishing.com/journal.asp?ref=0149-0508

The Peace Chronicle

A 32-page newsletter published by PJSA three times a year, featuring new scholarship and literature, the latest developments in peace research, peace studies and peace education, central issues in the peace and justice movement, book and film reviews, and other selected resources for educators and activists. www.peacejusticestudies.org/publications.php

Research Portals

Conscientious Objection in America: Primary Sources for Research

www.swarthmore.edu/Library/peace/conscientiousobjection/co%20website/default1.html

H-Peace

H-Peace is an international electronic network affiliated with the Peace History Society that seeks to broaden understanding about historical and contemporary peace, justice, and disarmament concerns. www.h-net.org/~peace/

Peace Agreements Digital Collection

The Peace Agreements Digital Collection, part of the Margarita S. Studemeister Digital Library in International Conflict Management, strives to contain the full text of agreements signed by the major contending parties ending inter- and intra-state conflicts worldwide since 1989. It is a collection constantly under development by the Jeannette Rankin Library Program as a means to strengthen worldwide access to information on peaceful means to end international conflict. www.usip.org/library/pa.html

Swarthmore College Peace Collection

www.swarthmore.edu/Library/peace/conscientiousobjection/co%20website/default1.html

United Nations: Peace and Security

www.un.org/peace/

United Nations Treaty Collection

http://untreaty.un.org/English/treaty.asp

---

global citizens People who see their local actions as having global consequences and who have accepted that they have a responsibility to work to better the conditions of the world and its people.

decisions that at best help others and at the very least do no harm. Being at peace with oneself and the world could translate into seeing oneself as a *global citizen* and thinking about everyday "personal" decisions in new and deeper ways.

Consider the following examples: many smart consumers seek out the lowest priced items to purchase. However, while these items may be low-cost for the consumer, their production often exacts a costly toll on the workers who produce them. For example, textile factories in developing countries often provide unsafe working conditions for their employees. As you make what you might view as a personal choice over whether or not to buy something like a piece of clothing, do you consider whether the item was made in a sweatshop where workers, including children, are forced to work 10 or more hours a day in unsafe conditions, making barely enough money to feed themselves? In the grocery store, do you wonder whether the fruit you're thinking of purchasing was produced on a plantation where workers are exposed to harmful pesticides? Do you know whether the burger you ate for lunch came from cattle grazed on former Amazonian rainforest land that had been cleared for that purpose? We may believe the choice to stop and purchase a burger is one of convenience or preference, but decisions such as these have consequences, some of which include the perpetuation of structural violence in other countries.

In Focus: United Fruit

Although even the most "personal" of choices can often have far-reaching implications, consumers rarely think about how the products they purchase arrived at the store or how their decision to buy specific products might contribute to the structural violence endured by others. Take, for example, the historical relationship between bananas, a powerful US fruit company, and the indigenous people of Guatemala. US consumer demand for bananas helped build one of the most powerful companies in the world – United Fruit Company (UFCO). From 1920 to 1944, UFCO dominated Guatemala. Guatemala was a poor country where 90 percent of the population owned only 10 percent of the land. The Native American population made up the majority of the country's impoverished people. UFCO helped create a landless class of peasants who had few options but to work on the banana plantations, where they were exposed to extremely harmful pesticides and chemicals. Any attempt at unionizing labor was crushed. Higher-paying jobs were given to non-indigenous workers, and women were brought to the plantations to work as prostitutes.

Guatemala had its first democratic election in 1944 and when Jacobo Arbenz was elected President, he attempted to redistribute land to the country's poor and he nationalized 234,000 acres of UFCO land. The company refused payment for the land and asked the US government for help in getting its land back. In 1954, CIA-trained mercenaries, assisted by US fighter planes and pilots, overthrew Arbenz and replaced him with Carols Castillo Armas. Armas returned the land to UFCO, abolished taxes on interests and dividends to foreign investors, eliminated the secret ballot, and jailed critics. Over the next 40 years, thousands of Native Americans were killed by the Guatemalan government because they were seen as obstacles to the accumulation of wealth by the landed elite. Interestingly, Allen Dulles, head of the CIA during the Armas coup, had previously served on the board of trustees for UFCO.

The term "banana republic," coined by American writer O. Henry, is relevant to this discussion, as it was first used to describe not a chain of "casual luxury" clothing stores owned by Gap Inc.,[51] but rather a Latin American country that was dependent upon agriculture and run by a small group of elites working in the service of US business interests, primarily the United Fruit Company.[52] The term emerged in the early 1900s, particularly in reference to Honduras, where UFCO, with the aid of US government forces, put in place a government that would allow the company to pursue trade and other practices that would be beneficial to the company but not necessarily to the country or its people.[53] Today, the term typically is used to refer to dictatorial governments that are heavily influenced, economically or politically, by outside forces. These governments are usually unstable, non-democratic, and corrupt, and their countries are typically poor and heavily dependent upon agriculture. The decisions of individual consumers then, in this case consumers purchasing fruit produced in banana republics, can have real economic and political consequences, contributing to the perpetuation of structural violence in affected countries.

Conclusion

The complex definition of peace includes not only the absence of war but also the elimination of the conditions that bring about human suffering, misery, and death. While some argue that war and structural violence are "natural" or inevitable facts of life, others maintain that humans have the capacity for compassion and for the development of alternative forms of dispute resolution. The twenty-first century, while excessively violent, was also hopeful as nonviolent resistance successfully challenged some of the most entrenched and dangerously violent regimes. The success of Gandhi, the US civil rights movement, and other nonviolent movements all demonstrate not only that might does not make right, but also that might does not always win. While various individuals and local groups fight for peace, numerous IOs also work for positive and negative peace in the global arena. Although the UN is the most well known, nation-states, NGOs, and IOs are increasingly playing a more active role in building peace. Because there are few choices facing us daily that do not have consequences for others, the struggle to come to peace with ourselves and our actions is one way that we contribute to either building or undermining positive peace. Those who see themselves as global citizens understand that individual choices often have far-reaching consequences in our ever-shrinking, interdependent world. Global citizens also recognize that the internal struggle for peace is manifested in their daily decision making processes, processes that include the larger decision to attempt to avoid contributing to structural violence.

Notes

1 Albert Einstein, *Einstein on Peace*, ed. Otto Nathan and Heinz Norden (New York: Avenel Books, 1960; 1981 edn.), 397.

2 Ronald Reagan, Address to the Nation, White House, Washington, DC (1983), http://edition.cnn.com/SPECIALS/2004/reagan/stories/speech.archive/defense.htmlhttp://edition.cnn.com/SPECIALS/2004/reagan/stories/speech.archive/defense.html.

3 Vatican Statement to the UN, 1976, www.daytonpeacemuseum.org/PEACE%20QUOTES111505.pdf.

4 Mark Twain, *What is Man?* (London: Green Integer, 1999).

5 Betty A. Reardon, *Comprehensive Peace Education* (New York: Teachers College Press, 1988).

6 Patrick Hayden, "A Defense of Peace as a Human Right," *South African Journal of Philosophy* 21 (2002), 147.

7 David P. Barash and Charles P. Webel, *Peace and Conflict Studies* (Thousand Oaks, CA: Sage Publications, 2002), 34.

8 For more information on these peace conferences, see Sir Adolphus William Ward, *Securities of Peace: A Retrospect 1848–1914* (New York: The Macmillan company, 1919).

9 William R. Slomanson, *Fundamental Perspectives on International Law*, 3rd edn. (Belmont, CA: Wadsorth, 2000), 457.

10 Ibid., 458–9.

11 Henry David Thoreau, *Walden and Other Writings by Henry David Thoreau* (New York: Bantam, 1962), 85.

12 Ibid.

13 Mark Twain, *To the Person Sitting in Darkness* (New York: Anti-Imperialist League of New York, 1901).

14 "1899 Platform of the American Anti-lmperialist League," *Modern History Sourcebook: American Anti-Imperialist League*, www.fordham.edu/halsall/mod/1899antiimp.html.

15 Mark Twain, *From Europe and Elsewhere* (New York: Harper & Bros, 1923).

16 Swarthmore College Peace Collection, "People's Council of America for Democracy & Peace Records, 1917–1919," www.swarthmore.edu/Library/peace/CDGA.M-R/pcadp.htm.

17 The Supreme Court Historical Society, "History of the Court, the White Court 1910–21" www.supremecourthistory.org/02_history/subs_history/02_c09.html.

18 Berkley Digital Library, "The Emma Goldman Papers Project" http://sunsite.berkeley.edu/Goldman.

19 Eileen Murphy, "Pax Populi: World's Largest Women's Peace Group Gathers at Goucher," www.citypaper.com/news/story.asp?id=4981.

20 For a list of all recipients of the Nobel Peace Prize go to http://nobelpeaceprize.org/eng_lau_list.html.

21 Slomanson, *Fundamental Perspectives on International Law*, 486.

22 *The Daily Worker* [New York], "Manifesto and Program of the American League Against War and Fascism," *Daily Worker* 11, no. 156 (June 30, 1934), www.marxisthistory.org/history/usa/groups/alawf/1933/1001-alawf-manifestoprogram.pdf.

23 David Adams, *The American Peace Movements* (New Haven, CT: Advocate Press, 1985), www.culture-of-peace.info/apm/chapter3-10.html.

24 Corporation for Public Broadcasting, "The Good War and Those Who Refused to Fight It," www.pbs.org/itvs/thegoodwar/bars.html.

25 Dan Georgakas, "Hollywood Blacklist," *Encyclopedia of the American Left* (Urbana and Chicago, IL: University of Illinois Press, 1992), www.writing.upenn.edu/~afilreis/50s/blacklist.html.

26 For more on the history of Robeson, see, Martin Duberman, *Paul Robeson: A Biography* (New York: Alfred A. Knopf, 1988).

27 "Wallace Sees Focus of Reaction," *New York Times* (June 10, 1947), sec. 1A, 1, 7.

28 For more on this, see Corporation for Public Broadcasting, "American Experience – Eyes on the Prize (Nonviolent Protests)," www.pbs.org/wgbh/amex/eyesontheprize/story/04_nonviolence.html.

29 For more on this, see Cynthia Enloe, *Bananas Beaches and Bases: Making Feminist Sense of International Politics* (Berkeley, CA: University of California Press, 2001).

30 For more on Doctors without Borders, go to www.doctorswithoutborders.org.

31 For more on International Physicians for the Prevention of Nuclear War, go to www.ippnw.org.

32 International Physicians for the Prevention for Nuclear War, "About IPPNW," www.ippnw.org/IPPNWBackground.html.

33 "'Doomsday Clock' Moves Two Minutes Closer To Midnight," *The Bulletin Online* (January 18, 2007), www.thebulletin.org/media-center/announcements/20070117.html.

34 Worldwatch Institute, *Vital Signs 2003* (New York: W.W. Norton, 2003), 88–9. For more on the Worldwatch Institute, go to www.worldwatch.org/.

35 Jeremy Seabrook, *The No-Nonsense Guide to World Poverty* (London, UK: Verso, 2004), 27.

36 For more information on Amnesty International, go to www.amnesty.org.

37 For more information on Human Rights Watch, go to www.hrw.org.

38 For more on the United Nations, go to www.un.org.

39 "Millions Join Global Anti-war Protests," BBC (February 17, 2003), http://news.bbc.co.uk/1/hi/world/europe/2765215.stm.

40 Thucydides, "The Melian Dialogue (Book 5, Chapter 17)," *The Peloponnesian War*, translated into English by Richard Crawley (Boston, MA: E. P. Dutton & Co, 1914).

41 The M. K. Gandhi Institute for Nonviolence, "About Gandhi" (1998–2005), www.gandhiinstitute.org/AboutGandhi/index.cfm.

42 For more on this topic, see: John Danstrup, *A History of Denmark* (Copenhagen, Denmark: Wivel, 1947); Joren Haestrup, *Secret Alliance* (Odense, Denmark: Odense University Press, 1976); Richard Petrow, *The Bitter Years; The Invasion and Occupation of Denmark and Norway* (New York: Morrow, 1974); Jacques Semelin, *Unarmed Against Hitler: Civilian Resistance in Europe, 1939–1943* (Westport, CT: Praeger, 1993); and John Orem Thomas, *The Giant Killers: The Story of the Danish Resistance Movement* (New York: Taplinger, 1975).

43 "President Taft on International Peace," *American Journal of International Law 5* (July 1911), 718–25.

44 "The Hague Conference process thus produced the Permanent Court of Arbitration (PCA) in 1907, which still functions a century later." William R. Slomanson, *Fundamental Perspectives on International Law*, 5th edn. (Belmont, CA: Thomason Wadsworth, 2007), 390.

45 For more information on the UN Index, go to http://hdr.undp.org/hdr2006/report.cfm.

46 Source: All information from the UN website, www.un.org.

47 Source: Data taken from: UN Development Programme, "Statistics of the Human Development Report," http://hdr.undp.org/hdr2006/statistics/.

48 UNESCO, www3.unesco.org/iycp/uk/uk_sum_cp.htm.

49 Rory McCarthy, "We'll have blood on our hands," *Guardian* (December 17, 2002), http://film.guardian.co.uk/interview/interviewpages/0,6737,861540,00.html.

50 For more on Witness for Peace, go to www.witnessforpeace.org/sites/nicaragua.html.

51 "What Does Business Casual Mean Anyway? Job Seekers and Employees Perplexed When it Comes to Workplace Fashion, According to Yahoo! HotJobs and Banana Republic Survey," *Gap Inc.* (September 20, 2006), www.gapinc.com/public/Media/Press_Releases/med_pr_BananaRepublicSurvey092006.shtml.

52 O. Henry, *Cabbages and Kings* (Whitefish, MT: Kessinger Publishing, 2004).

53 For more on banana republics and US involvement in Guatemala, see Alison Acker, *Honduras and the Making of a Banana Republic* (Cambridge, MA: South End Press, 1989); Lester D. Langley and Thomas David Schoonover, *The Banana Men: American Mercenaries and Entrepreneurs in Central America, 1880–1930* (Lexington, KY: University Press of Kentucky, 1996); Richard H. Immerman, *The CIA in Guatemala: The Foreign Policy of Intervention* (Austin, TX: University of Texas Press, 1982); and Juan Carlos Zarate, *Forging Democracy: A Comparative Study of the Effects of US Foreign Policy on Central American Democratization* (Lanham, MD: University Press of America, 1994).

GLOSSARY

acid rain Process through which sulfur dioxide (SO_2) and nitrogen oxides (NOx) that are emitted into the air mix with atmospheric water and oxygen and then fall back to the land in the form of acid.

abolition The eradication of slavery.

abolitionist Someone seeking the eradication of slavery.

absolute poverty Poverty as defined in the same terms across cultures and countries (cf. relative poverty).

adjudication Settling a dispute through a formal structure such as a court room.

African Charter of Human and Peoples' Rights Adopted by African nations in 1982, this international human rights document covers a wide range of human rights including the right to develop, the right to peace, the right to a clean environment, and the right to the common heritage of humankind.

African Union An organization of African states that is designed to promote peace, human rights, democracy, and inter-continental cooperation.

Age of Exploration Sometimes also called the "Age of Discovery" this refers to the period in the fifteenth to seventeenth centuries when European explorers and traders began extending Europe's influence around the world.

Agent Orange Code name for a powerful herbicide and defoliant used by the US military in its herbicidal warfare program during the Vietnam War.

agricultural revolution A period of rapid change in agricultural production, including improved methods of farming and higher yields.

ahimsa A Sanskrit term meaning to do no harm, and an important tenet of the religions that originated in ancient India, including Hinduism, Buddhism, and Jainism.

Alabama case Resolved a dispute between Britain and the US over British support to the American South during the US Civil War. Britain was found liable for damages to US warships by Confederate ships built or outfitted by Britain.

Amnesty International An NGO dedicated to the protection of political and civil human rights.

amphibians Cold-blooded vertebrates, such as frogs or salamanders, that can live in the water and on land.

analog Analog systems translate a signal into continuously variable, measurable, physical quantities, such as length, width, voltage, or pressure.

animist A belief system that is rooted in the doctrine that souls and spirits inhabit all living things.

anthropogenic Effects, processes, or materials that are the result of human activities.

antigenic drift The process through which viruses change slightly from year to year.

antigenic shift Sudden and substantial change, seen only with influenza A viruses, resulting from the recombination of the genomes of two viral strains.

apartheid A system of racial segregation in South Africa. From 1948 to 1994, citizens were divided into the following groups: Blacks, Coloureds, Whites, and Indians. This distinction determined access to all services and accommodations. All groups except Whites were denied their civil and political rights. Whites who questioned the system also had their rights violated.

appease To be pacific, or to concede in order to avert or ameliorate conflict.

arms race A competition between two or more parties for military supremacy.

arquebus Muzzle-loaded firearm used in the fifteenth to seventeenth centuries that was a forerunner of the musket and later the rifle.

arrears The portion of a state's assessment that remains unpaid after it is due.

Asian values A political phrase used in the 1990s that suggested Asian institutions and political ideologies reflected the culture and history of the region. For human rights discourse, this referred to the primacy of group rights over individual rights.

assessment The amount of money each country is asked to contribute to the UN's regular budget.

asylum Protection granted to individuals who have fled their home country typically due to political reasons. The protection is usually granted by a foreign sovereign authority.

autarky Complete economic independence.

autocracy A form of government in which one person has uncontrolled or unlimited authority over others.

baby boom Refers to a period of increased birth rates within a certain timeframe, and typically within a specific geographic region.

backbone Used to describe the part of a network that connects other networks together. The Internet's backbone consists of high-capacity, high-speed lines that can extend over great distances.

balance-of-payment Refers to the total exports and imports of a given country in a given time period.

Balkans Geographic and historic term for a peninsula in Southeastern Europe. Countries most commonly included in the Balkan region are Albania, Bosnia and Herzegovina, Bulgaria, Croatia, Greece, Kosovo, Montenegro, Macedonia, and Serbia.

ballistics The science of the motion of projectiles, such as bullets, shells, or bombs.

barons A nobility title, referring to one who owes his position to a monarch, but who exercises control over a specified territory.

Battle in Seattle Refers to the clash between anti-globalization, pro-democracy, human rights, environmental, and other groups with police at the WTO meeting in Seattle, Washington, in 1999.

BCE Before the Common Era. BCE is an alternative notation for BC (Before Christ), and CE is an alternative for AD (Anno Domini, "In the year of Our Lord.") The Common Era is the period of measured time beginning with the year 1 on the Gregorian calendar. The CE/BCE system of notation is chronologically equivalent to dates in the AD/BC system, but it is preferred by many because of the absence of religious references.

Bill of Rights The first 10 changes, or amendments, to the US Constitution, laying out the rights of US citizens.

bioaccumulate To accumulate in a biological or ecological system over time. Usually refers to the accumulation of toxins.

biodiversity The number and variety of different living organisms within an ecosystem as well as the genetic variation within each species.

biofuels A fuel made from recently dead biological materials.

biogas Gas produced when bacteria digest organic material.

biotechnologies Use of microorganisms for industrial and commercial enterprise.

Black Panthers An African-American civil rights and revolutionary organization that supported armed resistance to state repression. Active in the 1960s–70s.

blacklist Actors, directors, musicians, and other US entertainment professionals were prohibited from working because of false charges that they were communists or communist sympathizers. The ban lasted from 1947 until the late 1950s.

blog   Originally short for "web log," a blog is a type of website that is usually maintained by a person or corporation and that is written in the form of an online journal. Blogs contain regular entries that are usually posted in reverse chronological order. Today, most blogs are created using some sort of online software that facilitates the production of blog posts and the integration of interactive features, such as reader comments.

blood diamonds or conflict diamonds   Rough diamonds used by rebel movements to finance wars against legitimate governments.

Bolshevik Revolution   This was the first Marxist inspired revolution of the twentieth century and led to the creation of the Soviet Union. Many in Europe and the US were afraid that the revolutionary sentiment would spread.

bourgeois class   Marx's term for the merchant class in a capitalist society.

Bretton Woods Conference   An attempt to establish common rules for financial and commercial global transactions. By regulating the international monetary system, the industrial powers that met in 1944 in Bretton Woods sought to prevent the economic policies that led to the global depression of the 1920s–30s.

bubonic plague/Black Death   A pandemic caused by a bacterium that swept through Central Asia and Europe around the 1340s, killing millions.

bureaucrats   Also known was civil servants or public servants, these folks administer the day-to-day running of a government.

bush meat   Meat from wild animals. It is also often used to refer to the unsustainable and sometimes illegal killing of wildlife, particularly in tropical areas.

capitalism   An economic system in which wealth, and the means of producing wealth, are privately owned and controlled rather than publicly or state-owned and controlled.

carrying capacity   The ability of the natural environment to sustain the human population.

Centers for Disease Control and Prevention   US government agency that conducts research and disseminates information on health and safety issues.

charter   A document incorporating an institution and outlining its rights and duties.

Christendom   A Christian idea that social and political life should be united under the rule of the Catholic Church.

chytrid fungus   Transferred through water, this fungus attaches itself to amphibians' skin making it hard for them to breath. It also affects their nervous system and eventually leads to their death.

city states   Cities that have sovereign control over a territory. Modern examples include Singapore, the Vatican, and Monaco.

civil libertarians   Refers to people who place individual human rights over state authority.

civil rights   Rights that individuals possess by virtue of their citizenship – for example, the right to free speech.

civilization   Refers to a complex society that includes large concentrations of people in urban areas, agriculture, and hierarchical social and political structures that generally include states and priesthoods, the division of labor, and writing and formal record keeping.

Cold War   Refers to the ideological stand-off between two superpowers, the United States and the Soviet Union, from 1945 to 1989. While not directly fighting one another, each side sought to expand its influence by keeping the other from spreading its form of government and political system, resulting in many proxy wars throughout the world.

colonialism   One territorial sovereign exerting control and sovereignty over another land by usurping control from local leaders, thereby destroying indigenous culture, economies, and political structures.

Commercial Revolution   Lasting from roughly the sixteenth to the eighteenth century, this was a period of European economic expansionism.

Committee on Human Rights   The 18-member Committee monitors the compliance of participating states with the tenets of the Covenant on Civil and Political Rights.

communism   A form of government where all property and industry is collectively owned and run through the state.

Communist Revolution   A Marxist-inspired overthrow of a government in order to install a communist type of political and economic system.

compulsory jurisdiction   Occurs when states accept the International Court of Justice's authority to review cases involving them.

Conference on Security and Cooperation in Europe Created during the Cold War as a military alliance in Europe, its purpose is to ensure peace and good governance in the region.

constitutional government   A government that is ruled by a constitution which lays out the duties and functions of the government.

contras   Name given to armed guerrillas whose goal was to overthrow the Nicaraguan government. Operating from border states, and with US government support, contras raided Nicaragua, killing many government officials and civilians.

Convention Against Torture and Other Cruel, Inhuman, or Degrading Treatment or Punishment   This international human rights instrument is designed to end torture. It came into force in 1987.

convergence   Describes the blurring of boundaries between, or the coming together of, media, information technology, and telecommunications sectors.

coral bleaching   The whitening of corals resulting from the stress-induced expulsion of the algae zooxanthellae.

coral reefs   Large marine formations created from the calcium carbonate skeletons of coral animals that support living corals and various forms of plant and animal life.

cosmopolitanism   Belief that all humans are connected and belong to one humanity.

country   A term used interchangeably with state or nation-state to describe a geographical entity with a sovereign ruler.

coup d'état   The overthrow, usually violent, of an existing government.

crime against humanity   Widespread, systematic, gross violations of human rights by governments, their agents, or other ruling authorities.

Crime Statute of the International Criminal Court Establishes the International Criminal Court (ICC) and outlines the structure, types of crimes which can come before the court, and the rules under which the court will operate.

Crimean War   War fought from October 1853 to February 1856 mainly on the Crimean Peninsula between the Russians and the British, French, and Ottoman Turkish, with support, from January 1855, from the army of Sardinia-Piedmont.

crowd diseases   Diseases, such as typhus, tuberculosis, and smallpox, that tend to develop in situations of overcrowding and poor sanitation.

cultural hybridity   Refers to cultural forms and practices that result from interactions between two or more different cultures.

cultural imperialism   A form of domination that involves privileging one culture (usually that of a large, powerful nation) over less powerful ones or imposing/injecting the cultural practices of a dominant culture into other cultures, often culminating in the adoption of the cultural practices of the imperial power.

cultural relativist   In the human rights context, this refers to those who argue that human rights must take into account the cultural values of a society.

culture   Refers to the beliefs, values, norms, ideals, symbols, and lifestyles of a specified entity.

curie   A unit of measurement that describes the amount of radioactivity in a sample. It measures the amount of atoms that decay each second. One curie equals 37 billion decays per second.

Darfur, Sudan   A region of the country of Sudan that has been the scene of widespread violence, including genocide. More than 400,000 people died between the start of the violence in 2003 and 2008.

Declaration of the Rights of Man and of the Citizen Emerging in the aftermath of the French Revolution, this document espouses a series of both individual and collective rights to which all French men were entitled.

defoliant   Any chemical sprayed or dusted on plants to cause its leaves to fall off.

deforestation   The clearing of forests, usually by logging or burning, which not only releases carbon into the atmosphere but also often results in soil erosion, desertification, and the loss of habitats and biodiversity.

demassification   The process of breaking up something standardized or homogeneous into smaller elements that appeal to specific segments of the population. In the media world, it refers to a shift from attempting to reach the largest possible audiences (mass media) to going after narrower segments of the mass audience.

demographers   Scholars and practitioners who study population and its impacts on society.

demographic transition   Theory/model that links industrial development with declining fertility.

deoxyribonucleic acid (DNA)   The building block of all living organisms. It contains the genetic blueprint for the cell.

desertification   The gradual transformation of habitable land into desert.

deterritorialization   Geographical territory, or place, becomes less of a constraint on social interactions.

developed countries   Countries with high levels of economic development, protection of political rights, and high scores on the UN human development index. Developed countries typically have either industrial or post-industrial-based economies.

developing countries   Usually refers to low-income countries with little industrialization compared to developed nations. These countries are also sometimes referred to as the "Third World," the "Global South," and the "less developed countries."

development   Efforts to improve the material well-being of a country.

digital   Process whereby real-world information is converted into binary numeric form (0s and 1s).

digital divide   Refers to unequal access to physical ICTs, such as computers, mobile phones, and Internet access, as well as to imbalances in the education and experience needed to develop information and technology skills.

disciplines   Most often used to refer to the division of fields of knowledge at the university or college level.

disease   A state in which a function or part of the body is no longer in a healthy condition.

domestication   The controlled selection and protected development of naturally occurring plant and animal species. Through the domestication process, wild animals become accustomed to living in the company of and/or laboring for human beings. As a result of human control for multiple generations, the behavior, life cycle, and/or physiology of domesticated animals are altered from their wild state.

Doomsday Clock   According to the Bulletin of the Atomic Scientists, the Bulletin's founders created the Doomsday Clock in 1947 to convey how "close humanity is to catastrophic destruction – the figurative midnight" – and to monitor "the means humankind could use to obliterate itself. First and foremost, these include nuclear weapons, but they also encompass climate-changing technologies and new developments in the life sciences and nanotechnology that could inflict irrevocable harm."

ecological footprint   A measurement of human impact on the earth that compares human consumption of resources with the earth's capacity to renew them and to absorb waste.

economic liberalism   Attributed to Adam Smith, this economic system has a very limited scope of government involvement in economic matters.

economic modernization   The transformation of an economy from one that focused on outmoded means of production to one that is able to keep pace with rapid technological and industrial changes.

ecosystems   A community of plants, animals, and smaller organisms that live, feed, reproduce and interact in the same area or environment.

ECOWAS   A region organization for nations in West Africa. Its purpose is to promote trade and political cooperation in the region. The organization also has a military arm that has intervened in West African states.

El Niño and La Niña   El Niño refers to a warming of Pacific water that creates changes in climatic weather patterns, such as increased rain in some areas. La Niña refers to unusually cold water in the Pacific that likewise causes weather disruptions.

empire   A political entity with control over a vast territory wherein culturally distinct and diverse populations live.

encomienda system   A forced labor system introduced by the Spanish during the conquest of the Americas that effectively transferred indigenous land to the Conquistadors and made the local populations landless slaves.

enculturation   Process through which one becomes a member of a culture demonstrating an understanding of its rules, norms, and expectations.

endemic disease   Diseases that persist in a specific place for a given population year-round at fairly constant rates.

enteric fermentation   Fermentation that takes place in the digestive systems of ruminant animals, mammals that digest plant-based food by regurgitating semidigested food and chewing it again.

environmental technologies   Technologies that cause limited to no harm to the environment or that use the environment in a sustainable way – solar power, for example.

enzootic disease   Disease affecting or peculiar to animals of a specific geographic area.

epidemic   A disease outbreak affecting many individuals in a community or a population simultaneously.

ethnocentric   Viewing the world primarily from the perspective of one's own culture.

ethno-nationalism   Characterized by an extreme attachment to ethnicity, a belief that only ancestry gives one the right to belong to a particular group, and a desire to establish independent nation-states based solely on ethnicity.

European Convention on Human Rights   Adopted in 1950, this Convention is designed to protect and promote human rights in the European context. It established the European Court of Human Rights.

European Court of Human Rights   Hears human rights-related cases for parties to the EU.

European Court of Justice   This is the supreme court of the EU whose purpose is to provide a forum for dispute resolution between member states.

European Social Charter   Adopted in 1961 by EU, it establishes the social and economic rights of the member nations.

European Union (EU)   A regional organization for European states that seeks to create unified social, political, and economic policies.

e-waste   Surplus electronics that are not recycled – old computers, for example.

export subsidies   A form of subsidy provided by a government to help companies or manufacturing sectors lower their export costs.

extra-state wars/conflicts   Conflicts between a state and an armed group outside the state's own territory. These are mostly colonial conflicts.

ex-urban   Areas beyond suburbs that serve as commuter towns to nearby urban areas.

Falun Gong   An eclectic spiritual movement that began in China in the latter half of the 20th century that consists of an amalgam of religions and exercises. The Chinese Communist Party banned the organization in 1999.

fauna   Refers to animal life.

femininity   Socially constructed roles, behaviors, attitudes, and attributes that a given culture associates with women.

feminism/feminist   A philosophy that all humans should be treated equally regardless of gender/a person who believes in equality.

feminist scholars   Scholars who explore the nature of gendered politics, power relations, and sexuality by examining existing societal constructs.

feminist theorists   Scholars who explore the nature of gendered politics, power relations, and sexuality by examining existing societal constructs.

fertility   Measure of reproduction; the number of children born per couple, person, or population.

feudal   A term that came into use in the 17th century to describe Europe's political and military arrangement of territories.

feudalism The social and economic system that characterized European societies during the Middle Ages (9th to 15th centuries). The king owned the land and gave it to his leading nobles in return for their loyalty and military service. The nobles in turn allowed peasants to farm their land for a portion of their produce.

fiefdoms Generally referred to as inherited lands over which a baron or lord ruled with limited or no outside interference.

File Transfer Protocol (FTP) A network protocol that allows an FTP client to connect to an FTP server to exchange or manipulate files on that server.

flora Refers to plant life.

food security State of affairs where all people at all times have access to safe and nutritious food to maintain a healthy and active life.

fossil fuels Non-renewable sources of energy such as oil, gas, and coal.

Fourteen Points A speech given by US President Woodrow Wilson to the US Congress on January 8, 1918. Given 10 months before the end of World War I, it became the framework for the peace treaty that ended the war. Included in it was a call for an association of nations that would protect nation-state sovereignty and keep the peace.

free trade The promotion of trade in goods and services by reducing tariffs and other trade barriers.

French Revolution Violent political upheaval in France beginning in 1789, which replaced the monarchy system of government.

GATT The General Agreement on Tariffs and Trade was a treaty whose functions were taken over by the WTO.

General Assembly (UN) The organ of the UN that acts as its legislative branch. All member nations can send delegates to the General Assembly. It is also a forum for international dialogue.

Geneva Protocols, 1925 More than a dozen nations came together to construct a treaty to prohibit the use of chemical and biological weapons, though manufacturing and storing of such weapons was allowed. Since then, dozens of other nations have signed up to the treaty.

genocide The intent to destroy, in whole or in part, a national, ethnic, racial, or religious group.

geothermal energy A renewable energy source that uses heat from the Earth for energy – hot springs, for example.

germ theory The theory that certain diseases are caused by the invasion of the body by microorganisms. The French chemist and microbiologist Louis Pasteur, the English surgeon Joseph Lister, and the German physician Robert Koch are given much of the credit for the development and acceptance of the theory.

global citizens People who see their local actions as having global consequences and who have accepted that they have a responsibility to work to better the conditions of the world and its people.

global digital divide Disparities in technology access and use between countries or global regions.

globalization A complex web of social processes that intensify and expand worldwide economic, cultural, political, and technological exchanges and connections.

gold standard A monetary system that issues currency that is backed up by gold whereby the holder of the currency can redeem that note for an equivalent amount of gold.

Great Leap Forward A political and social plan in China from 1958 to 1960 that was designed to transform China from an agrarian to an industrial society. Instead, it triggered a famine that left between 14 and 43 million dead.

Green Revolution An effort by scientists (1940s–60s) to engineer fewer improved strains of wheat and corn in order to increase food supplies in developing countries.

greenhouse gases Gases, such as carbon dioxide, methane, ozone, and nitrous oxide, that warm the earth's atmosphere by absorbing infrared radiation.

gross domestic product (GDP) A measure of a country's total output and national income in a year.

gross national product (GNP) A measure of the goods and services produced by a country in a given year, including gains on overseas investments.

habeas corpus This Latin phrase refers to a legal action which provides relief from arbitrary detention and allows those held in detention to be informed of the charges against them.

Hague Conventions   The first Hague Convention (1899) required nations to settle disputes peacefully, established laws of warfare, and prohibited certain types of weapons, including projectiles from balloons and certain types of bullets; the Second Hague Convention (1907) more specifically addressed state conduct during war.

helots   Sparta's serf-like laborers who made up Sparta's agricultural workforce. Their servitude released every Spartan citizen from labor so that they could focus on war. Helots were bound to a plot of land and often considered expendable.

hemorrhagic fever   Any of a group of viral infections, such as Ebola and yellow fever, that occur primarily in tropical climates, are usually transmitted to humans by insects or rodents, and are characterized by high fever, small purple spots, internal bleeding, low blood pressure, and shock.

heterogenization   The process of breaking up into different elements or dissimilar parts.

Hollywood Ten   A group of Hollywood screenwriters, producers, and directors who, in 1948, refused to testify before the House Un-American Activities committee (HUAC). The committee was investigating alleged communist ties to Hollywood. The ten who refused to testify were fined and imprisoned for one year. They were also blacklisted from working in Hollywood, a ban that was only lifted in the 1960s. The ten were Herbert Biberman, Alvah Bessie, Lester Cole, Edward Dmytryk, Ring Lardner Jr., John Howard Lawson, Albert Maltz, Samuel Ornitz, Adrian Scott, and Dalton Trumbo.

Holocaust   The genocide of minority groups, particularly Jews, in Europe by Nazis and their collaborators.

hominid   Any member of the biological family *Hominidae*, which includes extinct and extant humans, chimpanzees, gorillas, and orangutans.

Homo sapiens sapiens   Modern humans are members of the *Homo sapiens* species, of which the only extant subspecies is *Homo sapiens sapiens*.

homogeneity   Sameness, or lacking difference.

homogenization   The process of blending or erasing differences to make something uniform in composition.

human immunodeficiency viruses   Types of viruses that break down the body's ability to fight opportunistic infections.

human rights   The basic standards of living to which all humans are entitled.

Human Rights Council   A body within the UN that is charged with protecting and promoting human rights worldwide.

human security   Rather than viewing security from a state-centered approach, human security is a people-, or person-, centered understanding of security that takes into account the multitude of variables that impinge upon a person's or community's ability to be safe and/or secure.

humanitarian intervention   Military intervention by one sovereign state into another using the pretext of removing an abusive regime.

HyperText Transfer Protocol (HTTP)   A protocol for retrieving interlinked resources that led to the establishment of the World Wide Web.

immunize/immunization   The process/procedure of rendering a subject immune or resistant to a specific disease. Although the term is sometimes used interchangeably with vaccination and inoculation, the act of inoculation may not always successfully render a subject immune.

imperialism   The policy of extending a state's rule over foreign countries, or of acquiring and holding colonies and dependencies.

indigenous peoples   A particular group of inhabitants of a geographic space whose connections to that space are the earliest known human connections to that land.

indulgence   In the Catholic faith, after a sinner has confessed and received absolution, the guilt of sin is removed but temporal punishment is still required by Divine Justice, either in this life or in Purgatory. An indulgence removes the temporal punishment that the penitent had incurred in the sight of God.

Industrial Revolution   Refers to changes in economic and social organization that began around 1760 in

England and later in other countries as the result of the replacement of hand tools with power-driven machines.

infection A state in which disease-causing microbes have invaded or multiplied in body tissues.

informal employment Economic activity that takes place outside the formal, measureable market of an economy.

information literacy The ability to define an information need and to effectively and efficiently find, evaluate, and use information ethically and responsibly.

interdisciplinary Integrating the theories, methodologies, and insights of various disciplines and exploring the connections and blurring the boundaries among them.

intergovernmental organizations (IOs) Organizations made up of nation-states.

International Conference on Human Rights Held in Austria in 1993, this global conference was designed to move forward a global human rights agenda.

International Court of Justice (ICJ) The judicial organ of the United Nations that has the power to hear cases involving nation-states.

International Covenant on Civil and Political Rights This international human rights instrument codifies the rights found in the first section of the Universal Declaration of Human Rights. It came into force in 1976.

International Covenant on Economic, Social and Cultural Rights This international human rights instrument codifies the rights found in the second part of the Universal Declaration of Human Rights. It came into force in 1976.

International Criminal Court (ICC) Coming into force in 2002, this permanent international court is designed to hear cases of gross violations of human rights, genocide, crimes against humanity, and war crimes. It is a court of last resort and will only act when nation-states cannot or will not.

International Declaration on Human Genetic Data Adopted unanimously in 2003 by the United Nations Education, Scientific, and Cultural Organization (UNESCO), this document sought to establish guidelines for the collection, use, and distribution of human genetic data.

international financial institutions Financial institutions that are established in more than one state. The most notable are those established in Bretton Woods after World War II – the World Bank and the IMF.

international governmental organization (IGO) International organizations that nation-states join for specific purposes, such as promoting peace, enhancing trade, and encouraging cooperation.

International Labour Organization (ILO) Founded in 1919, this specialized UN agency works to promote decent working conditions across the globe.

International Monetary Fund (IMF) One of the Bretton Woods international financial institutions that sets global economic policy. It was designed to help countries with short-term development goals.

internationalized intra-state wars/conflicts Conflicts that occur when the government, or an armed group opposing it, receives military support from one or more foreign states.

Internet Consists of a worldwide collection of computers and sub-networks exchanging data using wires, cables, and radio links.

inter-state wars/conflicts A sustained and intentional armed conflict between at least two states; an international conflict.

intra-state wars/conflicts Conflicts that occur between a government and a non-state group. Civil wars fall under this category.

James Lawson A civil rights activist and minister who led the Nashville lunch counter sit-ins and participated in the civil rights struggle along with Dr Martin Luther King. After studying the principles of nonviolence in India, he became a conscientious objector. He was imprisoned for his refusal to be drafted.

Jay Treaty A treaty between the US and Britain after the revolutionary war to resolve left-over issues, such as the dispensation of property. It averted another war between the two states and was hailed by many as the new peaceful way to resolve conflicts.

Jim Crow   State laws that enforced "separate but equal" race segregation in the US South. From 1876 until 1965, forced racial segregation resulted in inferior accommodations and discriminatory treatment of African-Americans.

jus ad bellum   Latin phrase referring to the justice of a war. It delineates the requirements that must be met in order for a war to be justifiable.

jus in bello   Latin phrase referring to justice in a war.

jus post bellum   Latin phrase referring to justice after war.

Kimberley Process Certification Scheme (KPCS)   A joint initiative involving governments, industry, and civil society to stem the flow of conflict diamonds.

Kyoto Protocol   A UN Convention designed to lower greenhouse gas emissions that contribute to climate change.

lagoons   Places where factory farms store animal waste.

laissez-faire   An economic philosophy that suggests economies work best with limited government involvement.

League of Arab States   A regional international organization of Arab states designed to promote cooperation among, and safeguard the sovereignty of, member states.

League of Nations   Established by the Treaty of Versailles, which ended World War I, this organization was designed to provide a forum for conflict dispute resolution, thereby preventing war.

liberal model of citizenship   Sees citizenship as a legal status, while stressing political liberty and freedom from interference by other citizens and political authority.

liberalize   To reduce restrictions on trade.

locavore   The practice of eating only those foods produced within a short distance of where you live.

low-intensity conflict   A protracted political and military confrontation between states or groups that is below conventional war and above routine, peaceful competition.

Maastricht Treaty   Signed in 1992, it formally created the EU.

Magna Carta   Signed by King John of England iin 1215, this document proclaimed certain rights inherent in individuals and declared the King himself was the subject of state laws.

malaria   A vector-born disease that is carried by mosquitoes and kills millions each year.

malnutrition   A medical condition in which the body receives too few of the nutrients it needs.

Malthusian Catastrophe   A society's return to a subsistence level of existence as a result of overtaxing its available agricultural resources.

manifest destiny   The belief that the US was preordained to stretch from the Atlantic to the Pacific. This belief provided justification for territorial expansion and to the near extermination of Native Americans.

Marxists   Followers of the economic and political theories of Karl Marx and Friedrich Engels who believe that capitalism exploits workers, that class struggle creates historical change, and that capitalism will ultimately be superseded by a classless society.

masculinity   Socially constructed roles, behaviors, attitudes, and attributes that a given culture associates with men.

mass media   Media that is designed to reach a mass audience, such as the population of a nation-state. The term has traditionally referred to nationwide television and radio networks and mass-circulation newspapers and magazines.

McCarthyism   During the late 1940s–50s, Senator Joseph McCarthy, a Republican from Wisconsin, led the US government's investigation of thousands of Americans who were falsely charged with being communist or communist sympathizers. Lives were destroyed and careers ruined.

media   Tools used to store and deliver information or data. The term is often used synonymously with mass media, but it can also refer to a single medium used to communicate any data for any purpose.

Médecins Sans Frontières   An NGO that delivers medical and humanitarian assistance to underserved areas of the world.

megacities   Rapidly growing urban areas that have more than 10 million inhabitants.

mercantilism   An economic system that is predicated on protectionist policies where a political entity tries to maximize exports while minimizes imports in order to gain economic advantage.

mercenary   A private citizen who is paid by a political entity to provide armed support.

metacities   Agglomerations of several cities, towns, and suburbs that have expanded so that they coalesce into a single, sprawling urban mass of more than 20 million people.

microbes   Microscopic organisms, including viruses, bacteria, parasites, and fungi.

micro-blogging   Form of blogging that allows users to send brief text updates (or photos or audio clips) and publish them, either to be viewed by anyone or by a restricted group that can be chosen by the user. Status updates on Facebook and "tweets" on Twitter are both forms of micro-blogging.

microcredit   The extension of small loans to poor people who are typically ineligible for traditional lines of credit, facilitating their pursuit of income generating self-employment projects with the potential to help them escape from poverty.

migrants   People who have left their homes in order to settle in another country or city.

migration   Human movement from one location to another.

Millennium Declaration   United Nations declaration signed in September 2000 consisting of eight goals and 21 targets that 192 United Nations member states and at least 23 international organizations have agreed to achieve by the year 2015. The 8 Millennium Development Goals (MDGs) are

1   eradicating extreme poverty and hunger
2   achieving universal primary education
3   promoting gender equality and empowering women
4   reducing child mortality
5   improving maternal health
6   combating HIV/AIDS, malaria, and other diseases
7   ensuring environmental sustainability
8   developing a global partnership for development

Moore's Law   Observation made by Gordon E. Moore, co-founder of Intel, that the number of transistors that can be placed on a circuit will double approximately every two years. It is also used more generally to refer to the rapid pace of technological change in the late 20th century.

morbidity   The incidence or prevalence rate of a disease. Morbidity rates refer to the number of people who have a disease, whereas mortality rates refer to the number of people who have died from it.

mortality   The relative frequency of deaths in a defined population during a specified interval of time.

most-favored-nation (MFN) status   Although most-favored-nation sounds like certain countries are granted special treatment, in the WTO the MFN principle means non-discrimination. Each member nation treats virtually every other member equally. So if a country improves the benefits it extends to one member nation, it must do so for all other WTO members so that they all remain "most-favored."

multiculturalism   Belief that different cultures can coexist peacefully within a given territory.

multidisciplinary   Drawing upon different disciplinary perspectives without necessarily exploring the connections or blurring the boundaries among them.

multinational corporation   A corporation or enterprise that manages production or delivers services in more than one country.

multinational corporations (MNCs)   A corporation or enterprise that manages production or delivers services in more than one country.

musket   A muzzle-loaded long gun, which is intended to be fired from the shoulder. It replaced the arquebus, and was in turn replaced by the rifle.

mutually assured destruction (MAD)   The deterrence doctrine that maintains that full-scale use of nuclear weapons by two opposing sides would result in the destruction of both.

NAFTA   A free trade agreement between the US, Canada, and Mexico that sought to encourage trade between the three countries.

napalm   A gasoline jelly that ignites spontaneously when dropped from aircrafts and that was routinely sprayed from US airplanes during the Vietnam War.

Napoleonic Wars   A series of global conflicts fought during Napoleon Bonaparte's rule over France from 1799 to 1815.

nation   Refers to a shared cultural or ethnic identity rather than to a legally recognized geographic territory.

nationalism   A political ideology of attachment to a political entity.

nation-state   A type of state that provides sovereign territory for a particular culture or ethnic group. However, it is also frequently used interchangeably with the terms "state" and "country."

nation-state system   Refers to the division of the world into sovereign territories over which local rulers maintain the power to govern. Also known as the Westphalian model.

natural increase   The yearly difference in number of births and deaths in a population (birth rate minus death rate).

natural law   A set of universal and immutable moral laws that are inscribed in nature.

negative growth rate   Indicates that population figures are declining.

negative peace   The absence of direct violence or armed conflict.

neoliberalism   A rejection of Keynesian economic theory, which posited that the state must play an active role in a capitalist economy in order to level out the inevitable boom and bust cycles. Neoliberals argue that deregulation and privatization of state-owned enterprises and limited government involvement in the economy are the best ways for countries' economies to grow and individual freedoms to flourish.

neolithic age   A period beginning about 9500 BCE in the Middle East that is traditionally considered the last part of the Stone Age. It began with the rise of farming and ended when metal tools became widespread, ushering in the Copper Age, Bronze Age, or Iron Age, depending on the geographical region.

new media   Refers to both digital forms of media that have emerged since the last part of the twentieth century as well as to the ways traditional media forms are evolving in the digital media environment.

Nobel Peace Prize   Prize named after Alfred Nobel, a Swedish industrialist who wanted it awarded to groups and individuals who promoted peace.

non-governmental organizations (NGOs)   A legally constructed organization made up of individuals. These have a limited, if any, role for nation-states.

non-state conflicts   Conflicts between militias, warlords, or ethnic groups without the involvement of national governments.

North Atlantic Treaty Organization (NATO)   A regional collective self-defense organization.

nuclear club   Name given to countries that possess nuclear weapons: US, Britain, France, China, Russia, India, Pakistan, North Korea. Israel is also believed to have nuclear weapons.

Nuremberg Trials   Post-World War II (1945–9) trials of dozens of officials of Nazi Germany who were charged with war crimes, more specifically with the crime of waging an aggressive war.

Oceania   Refers to a group of islands located in the Pacific Ocean.

Office of the United Nations High Commissioner for Human Rights (UNHCHR)   The principle office for human rights at the UN.

oligarchy   From the Greek words for "few" and "rule," the term refers to a form of government in which power resides with a small elite segment of society, distinguished by royalty, wealth, family, military influence, or religious authority.

one-sided violence   The Uppsala Conflict Data Program developed the term in 2002 to refer to "the use of armed force by the government of a state or by a formally organized group against civilians which results in at least 25 deaths per year."

Organization of American States (OAS)   A regional organization for the states of the Americas, whose purpose is to promote social and economic development in the Western hemisphere.

Organization of Petroleum Exporting Countries (OPEC) Made up of oil-producing countries, this organization tries to stabilize the oil market by regulating the supply of the commodity.

organs Agencies within an organizations that perform specific functions.

oversalinization The accumulation of too much salt in water or soil.

ozone depletion Refers to the deterioration of the ozone layer, which serves to protect the earth from the dangerous ultraviolet light of the sun.

pacifist Someone who believes that violence is not an appropriate response to conflict.

pandemic A disease outbreak affecting many people in many different regions around the world.

Paris Declaration of 1856 An international document abolishing privateering and codifying international norms for state maritime practice.

pathogen A disease-causing organism, such as a bacteria, virus, parasite, or fungus.

Peace of Westphalia Common term for two treaties signed in 1648 to end Europe's Thirty Years War.

Peace Testimony Once a pledge taken by Quakers to refuse to take part in wars or to serve in combat positions; now also an obligation to protest against wars.

peacekeeping The use of military forces to keep the various sides of a conflict from engaging in direct combat usually while peace negotiations are underway. This often allows humanitarian and other aid to reach the civilians caught in the conflict.

perioikoi Category of people in Spartan society who were a social class above the helots but segregated from the Spartans. Free men but not citizens, they engaged in trade, fishing, crafts, and weapon-making.

Permanent Court of Arbitration Designed to provide a forum for dispute resolution between various combinations of states, private parties, intergovernmental organizations, and commercial agents.

Permanent Court of International Justice The court of the League of Nations, which existed from 1920 to 1940 and heard 29 cases. Replaced in 1940 by the ICJ or World Court.

permanent members Refers to the five members of the UN Security Council who wield veto power: the US, France, Britain, China, and Russia.

persistent organic pollutants Chemical substances that do not break down in the environment.

pH balance The measure of a solution's acidity.

photosynthesis Process by which plants, and some other species, use the energy of sunlight to create the sugars necessary for respiration.

plague Infectious fever caused by the bacillus *Yersinia pestis*, a bacterium transmitted from rodents to humans by the bite of infected fleas. Plague was responsible for some of the most devastating epidemics in history, including the Black Death in the fourteenth century, which killed as many as one-third of Europe's population.

plastic soup Refers to the floating pile of garbage in the Pacific Ocean that is generally trapped in a fixed location due to wind and water patterns.

Platform for Action An agenda for women's empowerment that emerged from the Fourth World Conference on Women in Beijing in 1995.

Plessey v. Ferguson The US Supreme Court case (1896) that upheld the policy of "separate but equal." The court found racial segregation was constitutional.

plutocracies From the Greek words for "wealth" and "rule," the term refers to rule by the wealthy or power provided by wealth.

politicide The deliberate destruction of a group based on their political beliefs or affiliations. This definition has been used because such groups are not covered under the UN Convention on the Prevention and Punishment of the Crime of Genocide.

positive peace The presence of social justice, including equal opportunity, access to the basic necessities of life, and the eradication of structural violence.

positivism In the context of human rights, this philosophy argues that consent is a fundamental precondition to the establishment of human rights norms.

post-traumatic stress disorder (PTSD)   An anxiety disorder that can develop after exposure to one or more traumatic events that threatened or caused or psychological harm.

pre-Columbian   Refers to North and South America before Columbus landed.

pre-history   The entire space of human existence prior to the advent of written records.

preventive diplomacy   Diplomatic efforts designed to reduce chances of impending conflict, or to prevent an imminent conflict.

principle of proportionality   A war can only be just if its moral benefits are greater than its costs.

privateering   The practice of states using private vessels to attack enemies during wartime.

Protestant Reformation   Martin Luther's attempt to reform the Catholic Church that led to a schism within the church and the development of the Protestant sect.

protocols (computing)   A set of rules controlling the transfer of data between computers. Common Internet protocols include HTTP, FTP, Telnet, POP3, and IMAP.

protocols (international relations)   This refers to legal agreements that are designed to complement existing treaties.

protozoa   Single-celled organisms. The word means "little animal," a name they were given because many species behave like tiny animals, hunting and gathering other microbes as food.

proxy war   A war that occurs when two powers use a third party as a substitute for fighting each other directly.

push–pull factors   Forces that drive people away from a place (push) and pull them to a new one.

quarantine   Isolation imposed in order to prevent the spread of a disease.

quotas   Limits on the amount of a product a country will allow into its market in an effort to protect domestic manufacturers.

red scare   Occurred in two phases from 1917 to 1920, and from the late 1940s through the late 1950s. These periods were characterized by a fear that communism

was spreading and that communists had infiltrated the US and the US government.

refugees   People who have fled their home from persecution, crossed an international border, and cannot avail themselves of the protection of their home government.

relative poverty   Poverty as defined by measuring poverty relative to a country's overall economic position.

remit/remittances   Money sent home by workers employed in another country.

Renaissance   Term referring to the rebirth that occurred in Europe between the fourteenth and seventeenth centuries.

replacement levels   The level that needs to be sustained over the long run to ensure that a population replaces itself. For most countries having low or moderate mortality levels, replacement level is close to 2.1 children per woman.

republican model of citizenship   A model of rule that places the individual at the center suggesting he or she is capable of being ruled and of ruling. This view of citizenship focuses on the person as a political agent.

responsibility to protect   Responsibility of the international community to protect people from gross human rights violations when individual nation-states cannot or will not.

Saddam Hussein   Dictator of Iraq from 1979 until the US-led invasion in 2003. In 2006 he was found guilty of crimes against humanity by a special court and hanged in December 2006.

sanctions   Typically refers to economic restrictions, or embargos, placed on a nation-state.

schistosomiasis   An infection caused by small, parasitic flatworms and characterized by inflammation of the intestines, bladder, liver, and other organs. Annually affecting approximately 200 million people a year in Africa, Asia, South America, and the Caribbean, it is one of the world's most serious parasitic infections.

schools of thought   A group of theorists who share common ideas.

Scientific Revolution   A period occurring roughly during the later part of the Middle Ages and through the Renaissance in which scientific ideas in physics, astronomy, and biology evolved rapidly.

search engine A tool designed to search for information on the World Wide Web.

Secretariat The administrative organ of the UN led by the Secretary-General.

Secretary-General (UN) The official spokesperson for the UN. In charge of the administrative machinery of the organization. Ban Ki-moon from South Korea became the Secretary-General in 2007.

secular Not religious.

sentinel species A species whose presence, absence, or condition in an area indicates certain environmental conditions. They are often among the most sensitive species living in an area and can thus provide advanced warning of environmental degradation to monitoring biologists.

separate but equal The phrase used to describe a system of segregation that purported to provide the same access to services, accommodations, and rights, but in a racially divided context.

shanty towns Informal settlements on the outskirts of cities where people construct dwellings from various "found" materials, such as cardboard, plastic, and corrugated metal. These settlements usually are illegal and lack basic infrastructure such as water, sanitation, electricity, etc.

Silk Road Ancient trade route linking Rome and China. The 4,000-mile route started at Sian, followed the Great Wall of China to the northwest, bypassed the Takla Makan Desert, climbed the Pamirs, crossed Afghanistan, and went on to the Levant, where merchandise was then shipped across the Mediter-ranean Sea.

slash and burn farming A process whereby existing organic material is cut down and burned to clear land for farming.

social Refers to the way humans interact and organize.

social animals Animals that live in close physical contact with other animals in large groups.

social contract A political philosophy that suggests rulers and those they rule over have a contract whereby the ruled allow the rulers to reign as long as they act in the interests of the ruled. When a ruler no longer is seen to do so, the ruled reserve the right to replace the ruler.

social network sites Websites that facilitate the building of online social networks of members with similar interests and the sharing of information using technologies like chat, blogs, discussions, and mailing tools.

socialization The process through which one learns the accepted rules of behavior for a culture or society.

South African War Also called the Boer War, or the Anglo-Boer War (October 11, 1899–May 31, 1902). The war was fought between Great Britain and the two Boer (Afrikaner) republics: the South African Republic (Transvaal) and the Orange Free State.

sovereign/sovereignty The principle that emerged from the Peace of Westphalia (1648) which suggests that a political entity has the sole authority to make decisions about policy, procedure, and institutions within a given geographic territory.

Soviet bloc During the Cold War, this referred to the Soviet Union and its allies (East Germany, Bulgaria, Czechoslovakia, Hungary, Poland, and Romania). It is sometimes also referred to as the Eastern bloc.

Spanish–American War The 1898 war between the US and Spain that ended in the Treaty of Paris whereby the US took control over Cuba, Guam, Puerto Rico, and the Philippines. While this marked the end of the Spanish empire, it also marked the emergence of the US as a colonial power.

sphere of influence An area or region over which an organization or state exercises cultural, economic, military or political domination.

state Refers to a sovereign, internationally recognized, and geographically defined territory with a population and a government.

state-based wars/conflicts Conflicts that involve at least one national government.

steppe The belt of grassland extending over 5,000 miles, from Hungary in the west through Ukraine and Central Asia to Manchuria in the east.

stoicism A philosophy, prevalent in ancient Greece and Rome, that maintains that freedom and universal understanding can be obtained by self-control and freeing oneself from mundane desires.

stratified   Social classes arranged in hierarchical order, with different status levels.

structural adjustment programs (SAPs)   World Bank and IMF programs that imposed neoliberal economic policies on countries seeking to borrow from these organizations or seeking to restructure their existing debt.

structural violence   Unjust economic, social, and political conditions and institutions that harm people by preventing them from meeting their basic needs.

subjects   Historically, a term used in monarchical societies to refer to those whose lives were controlled by the king or queen. Modern usage refers to citizens of a monarchical society.

Suez Crisis   A military attack on Egypt by Britain, France, and Israel after Egypt nationalized the Suez Canal.

suffrage/suffragette   The struggle for voting rights for women; a person engaged in the struggle for women's civil right to vote.

suffragists   Those who struggle for voting rights for women.

superpower   A state with the power to dominate and influence other countries around the world.

supranational   A supranational organization is one that has been given the authority by its member nations to make decisions that take precedence over individual member nations' policies. The supranational organization relies on nations to carry out its decisions because it usually lacks any enforcement powers of its own.

survival sex   Engaging in sex in order to survive a threat or to secure money for food or shelter.

sustainable development   The use of resources in such a way that human needs are met while environmental damage is minimized.

symbiotic   Refers to a relationship in which two dissimilar organisms rely upon each other for mutual gain.

tailings   Waste materials produced from the process of extracting minerals from ore. Tailings often contain toxic chemicals that can harm both humans and wildlife.

Taliban   The ruling party/group in Afghanistan from 1996 to 2001. Their Sunni Islamic fundamentalist interpretation of the Koran resulted in a repressive state that violated its citizens' human rights, and particularly those of women. Resurgent again in 2004, but operating out of Pakistan and parts of Afghanistan.

tariffs   Taxes placed on imported goods.

technology   The development and use of tools, crafts, and techniques to solve problems and to control/adapt to specific environments.

temporal affairs   Refers to secular, rather than sacred, matters.

terrorism   Strategy of using violence primarily against civilians usually for political gain.

Tiananmen Square protests of 1989   A series of demonstrations held in and near Tiananmen Square in Beijing in the People's Republic of China that were led primarily by students and intellectuals. The protests began on April 14 and culminated in the Tiananmen Square Massacre, which is referred to in China as the June Fourth Incident to avoid confusion with two other Tiananmen Square protests.

Thirty Years War   Beginning as a religious conflict, it spread across Europe and devastated the continent, lasting from 1618 to 1648.

Tokyo Tribunals   War crimes trials for 25 Japanese defendants, seven of whom were sentenced to death. Thousands of other Japanese were charged with lesser crimes.

totalitarianism   A form of government where political control lies with the state and the state tolerates no criticism.

treaty   A legally binding agreement between two or more states, sovereigns, or international organizations.

Treaty of Versailles   Ended World War I and demanded that Germany take full responsibility for the war and make reparations to the states it had injured.

Trusteeship Council   The organ of the UN that was responsible for assisting with the transition of former colonies to independent countries. It went out of commission in 1994.

tsunamis   A series of huge waves.

tyranny   From the Greek word for "sovereign," it refers to a form of government in which a single ruler holds absolute power.

United Nations   International organization founded to prevent war and to promote peace and international cooperation. Total membership in 2009: 192 nation-states.

United Nations Commission on Human Rights Made up of 18 delegates chosen to begin work on the first international human rights document. The number was later expanded to 53.

United Nations Division for the Advancement of Women   Advocates for gender equality and the empowerment of women and girls around the world. It does through research and information dissemination.

United Nations Economic and Social Council   The organ of the UN that promotes international co-operation and development. It performs the majority of the United Nations' work.

United Nations Educational, Scientific and Cultural Organization (UNESCO)   Serves as a clearinghouse of information and promotes international cooperation in the areas of education, science, and culture.

ungendered   Lacking any recognition or acknowledgement of gender.

United Nations General Assembly   The organ of the UN that acts as its legislative branch. All member nations can send delegates to the General Assembly. It is also a forum for international dialogue.

United Nations Security Council (UNSC)   The 15-member organ of the UN that is responsible for maintaining peace and security. There are 10 rotating members who serve two-year terms and five permanent members who have veto power: US, Britain, China, Russia, and France.

United Nations Statistical Yearbook   Published each year by the UN, it catalogues a wide range of economic, social, and environmental data.

Universal Declaration of Human Rights   Adopted by the United Nations in 1948, the declaration describes the rights to which all human beings are entitled.

universalist   Someone who argues that human rights are universal and not dictated by culture. Thus, they argue that human rights are inherent in the individual – the same for everyone, everywhere.

United Nations World Tourism Organization (UNWTO)   The UNWTO promotes sustainable and responsible global tourism.

urbanization   The increase in the urban portion of the total population.

US–Mexican War   This war (1846–8) divided the US as many felt manifest destiny required the country to take control of all the land between the two oceans, while others felt it was a war of aggression against Mexico. When the war was over, the US was much larger, having gained control of Texas, California, Nevada, and Utah, and parts of Colorado, Arizona, New Mexico, and Wyoming.

vaccination   The introduction of a mild or "killed" form of a bacterium or virus, or pieces of the pathogen, into a person's body in order to train the immune system to resist infection by the agent.

vector   An organism, often an insect that transmits an infectious agent to a host. For example, mosquitoes are the vectors for the malaria parasite. Mosquitoes transmit malaria to humans, who act as the carriers or hosts.

vector-borne diseases   Pathogenic microorganisms that are transferred from host to host by blood-sucking arthropods like mosquitoes and ticks.

video mashup   The combination of multiple sources of video into a derivative work.

virus   A strand of DNA or RNA in a protein coat that must get inside a living cell in order to grow and reproduce. Viruses cause a variety of human illnesses, including chickenpox and AIDS.

Warsaw Pact   A collective self-defense organization made up of the Soviet Union and its allies. It was disbanded in 1991.

water scarcity   Lacking enough water to meet basic daily needs.

water stress   When demand for water outstrips availability.

water wars   Conflicts with controlling water as a central feature.

Weatherman   A group of revolutionary activists whose goal was the overthrow of the US government. Before disbanding in 1975, the organization engaged in riots, bombings, and other violent anti-government campaigns.

Web 2.0   Web applications that provide more opportunities for interaction, collaboration, participation, and content creation than traditional, static websites. The term typically includes blogs, wikis, photo and video sharing, and social network sites.

web browser   A software application that enables users to display and interact with content located on the World Wide Web.

West Bank   Refers to land on the West Bank of the Jordan river that has been central to the conflicts in the Middle East. Although made up primarily of Palestinians, much of the area has been controlled by Israel since 1967.

Westernization   Process whereby non-Western countries and societies adopt social, legal, dietetic, religious, technological, linguistic, political, and economic ideals and norms of countries in the Western world – Western Europe and the US.

Westphalian system   The current political structure of the sovereignty of the nation-state.

wetlands   Land areas, such as swamps and marshes, in which the soil is either permanently or seasonally saturated with moisture.

white man's burden   Based on a poem that Rudyard Kipling wrote about US military involvement in the Philippines, the phrase refers to the "noble enterprise" of bringing Christianity and "civilization" to developing countries. This provided many with a justification for colonialism.

Women's Rights Convention in Seneca Falls   The 1848 convention held to discuss the social, civil, and religious condition and rights of woman.

World Bank   One of the international financial institutions created at Bretton Woods that sets global economic policy. It was designed to help countries with long-term development goals.

World Health Organization (WHO)   The UN agency that monitors health-related issues around the world.

World Trade Organization (WTO)   An international organization designed to promote free and uniform trade and banking and finance rules and regulations.

World Wide Web (WWW)   A huge web of interlinked documents, images, and multimedia accessible over the Internet by a system of hypertext links and URLs.

zero population growth rate   Population neither grows nor declines.

zoonotic/zoonosis   An animal disease that can be transmitted to humans.

zooxanthellae   Single-celled algae that live symbiotically with corals.

INDEX